Christianity

Also by Alister E. McGrath from Wiley Blackwell

Emil Brunner: A Reappraisal (2014)

The World of C.S. Lewis (2013)

Christian History: An Introduction (2013)

Historical Theology: An Introduction to the History of Christian Thought, Second Edition (2012)

Reformation Thought: An Introduction, Fourth Edition (2012)

Theology: The Basic Readings, Second Edition (edited, 2012)

Theology: The Basics, Third Edition (2012)

Luther's Theology of the Cross: Martin Luther's Theological Breakthrough, Second Edition (2011)

Darwinism and the Divine: Evolutionary Thought and Natural Theology (2011)

The Christian Theology Reader, Fourth Edition (edited, 2011)

Christian Theology: An Introduction, Fifth Edition (2011)

Science and Religion: A New Introduction, Second Edition (2009)

The Open Secret: A New Vision for Natural Theology (2008)

The Order of Things: Explorations in Scientific Theology (2006)

Christianity: An Introduction, Second Edition (2006)

Dawkins' God: Genes, Memes, and the Meaning of Life (2004)

The Intellectual Origins of the European Reformation, Second Edition (2003)

Christian Literature: An Anthology (edited, 2003)*

A Brief History of Heaven (2003)

The Blackwell Companion to Protestantism (edited with Darren C. Marks, 2003)

The Future of Christianity (2002)

Reformation Thought: An Introduction, Third Edition (2000)

Christian Spirituality: An Introduction (1999)

Historical Theology: An Introduction (1998)

The Foundations of Dialogue in Science and Religion (1998)

The Blackwell Encyclopedia of Modern Christian Thought (edited, 1995)

A Life of John Calvin (1990)

* out of print

Christianity

An Introduction

THIRD EDITION

Alister E. McGrath

WILEY Blackwell

This edition first published 2015
© 2015 John Wiley & Sons, Ltd.

Registered Office
John Wiley & Sons, Ltd., The Atrium, Southern Gate, Chichester, West Sussex, PO19 8SQ, UK

Editorial Offices
350 Main Street, Malden, MA 02148-5020, USA
9600 Garsington Road, Oxford, OX4 2DQ, UK
The Atrium, Southern Gate, Chichester, West Sussex, PO19 8SQ, UK

For details of our global editorial offices, for customer services, and for information about how to apply for permission to reuse the copyright material in this book please see our website at www.wiley.com/wiley-blackwell.

The right of Alister E. McGrath to be identified as the author of this work has been asserted in accordance with the UK Copyright, Designs and Patents Act 1988.

Library of Congress Cataloging-in-Publication Data

McGrath, Alister E., 1953–
   Christianity : an introduction / Alister E. McGrath. – Third Edition.
      pages   cm
   Includes bibliographical references and index.
   ISBN 978-1-118-46565-3 (pbk.)   1. Christianity.   I. Title.
   BR121.3.M33 2015
   230–dc23

                                        2014030311

A catalogue record for this book is available from the British Library.

Cover image: Interior of the church La Sagrada Familia, Barcelona. Photo © Jose Fuste Raga/Corbis

Set in 10/13pt Minion by SPi Publisher Services, Pondicherry, India
Printed in Singapore by C.O.S. Printers Pte Ltd

3   2016

Brief Contents

Contents

Preface

The study of Christianity is one of the most fascinating, stimulating, and intellectually and spiritually rewarding undertakings available to anyone. This book aims to lay the foundations for such a study, opening doors to discovering more about the world's leading religion. It can only hope to whet its readers' appetites and lead them to explore Christianity in much greater detail.

Anyone trying to sense the modern world or the process by which it came into existence needs to understand something about the Christian faith. Christianity is by far the largest religion in the world, with somewhere between 2,500 and 1,750 million followers, depending on the criteria employed. To understand the modern world, it is important to understand why Christianity continues to be such an important presence in, for example, the United States and is a growing presence in China.

This book sets out to provide an entry-level introduction to Christianity, understood both as a system of beliefs and as a social reality. It is an introduction in the proper sense of the term, in that it has been written on the basis of the assumption that its readers know little or nothing about the history of Christianity, its practices and beliefs. Every effort has been made to keep the language and style of this book as simple as possible.

Alister McGrath
Oxford University

List of Illustrations and Maps

Introduction

At some point around AD 60, the Roman authorities woke up to the fact that there seemed to be a new secret society in the heart of their city, which was rapidly gaining recruits. They had not the slightest idea what it was all about, but it seemed to involve some mysterious and dark figure called Chrestus or Christus (Latinized form of the ancient Greek word Christos, "anointed") as the cause of all the trouble. His origins lay in one of the more obscure and backward parts of the Roman empire. But who was he? And what was this new religion all about? Was it something they should be worried about, or could they safely ignore it?

It soon became clear that this new religion might have the potential to cause real trouble. The great fire that swept through Rome at the time of the Emperor Nero in AD 64 was conveniently blamed on this new religious group. Nobody liked them much, and they were an obvious scapegoat for the failings of the Roman authorities to deal with the fire and its aftermath. The Roman historian Tacitus (c. 56–c. 117) gave a full account of this event some fifty years after the fire. He identified this new religious group as "the Christians," a group that took its name from someone called "Christus," who had been executed by Pontius Pilate back in the reign of Tiberius. This "pernicious superstition" had found its way to Rome, where it had gained a huge following. It is clear that Tacitus understands the word "Christian" to be a term of abuse.

Yet, muddled and confused though the official Roman accounts of this movement may be, they were clear that the movement centered in some way on that figure called Christus. It was not regarded as being of any permanent significance, being seen as something of a minor irritation. At worst, it was a threat to the cult of the emperor (or emperor worship). Yet, three hundred years later, this new religion had become the official religion of the Roman empire.

Christianity: An Introduction, Third Edition. Alister E. McGrath.
© 2015 John Wiley & Sons, Ltd. Published 2015 by John Wiley & Sons, Ltd.

So what was this new religion? What did it teach? Where did it come from? Why was it so attractive? How did it come to be so influential in its first few centuries? What happened after it had achieved such success at Rome? And how has it shaped the lives of individuals and the history of the human race? It is these questions that the present book will begin to answer.

So where do we start? What is the most helpful entry point to a study of Christianity? Looking at Christian beliefs? Exploring the history of the church? Surveying Christian art? In the end, the best place to begin is the historical event that got all of these under way. It is impossible to think or talk about any aspect of the Christian faith without talking about Jesus of Nazareth. He is the center from which every aspect of the Christian faith radiates outward. We therefore turn immediately to Jesus and his significance for Christianity, to begin our exploration there.

1

Jesus of Nazareth and the Origins of Christianity

Christianity is rooted in the historical figure of Jesus of Nazareth, often also referred to as "Jesus Christ." Christianity is not simply the body of teachings that derive from Jesus of Nazareth – ideas that could be dissociated from the person and history of their originator. Marxism, for example, is essentially a system of ideas grounded in the writings of Karl Marx (1818–1883). But Marx himself is not part of Marxism. At a very early stage, however, the identity of Jesus became part of the Christian proclamation. The Christian faith is thus not merely about emulating or adopting the faith of Jesus of Nazareth; it is also about placing faith in Jesus of Nazareth.

The Significance of Jesus of Nazareth for Christianity

As we have already noted, the figure of Jesus of Nazareth is central to Christianity. Christianity is not a set of self-contained and freestanding ideas; it represents a sustained response to the questions raised by the life, death, and resurrection of Jesus of Nazareth.

Before we begin to explore the historical background to Jesus and the way in which the Christian tradition understands his identity, we need to consider his place within Christianity. To begin with, we shall consider the ways in which Christians refer to the central figure of their faith. We have already used the name "Jesus of Nazareth"; but what of the related name, "Jesus Christ"? Let's look at the latter in more detail.

The name "Jesus Christ" is deeply rooted in the history and aspirations of the people of Israel. The word "Jesus" (Hebrew *Yeshua*) literally means "God saves" – or, to be more precise, "the God of Israel saves." The word "Christ" is really a title, so that the name "Jesus Christ" is better understood as "Jesus who is the Christ." As a derivative of the verb "to anoint" (*chriō*), the word "Christ" is the Greek version of the Hebrew term "Messiah," which

Christianity: An Introduction, Third Edition. Alister E. McGrath.
© 2015 John Wiley & Sons, Ltd. Published 2015 by John Wiley & Sons, Ltd.

refers to an individual singled out or raised up by God for some special purpose (p. 23). As we shall see, this captured the early Christian belief that Jesus of Nazareth was the culmination and fulfillment of the hopes and expectations of Israel.

Initially, since so many of the first Christians were Jews, the question of Christianity's relationship with Israel was seen as being of major significance. What was the relation of their old religion to their new faith? Yet, as time passed, this matter became less important. Within a generation, the Christian church came to be dominated by "Gentiles" – that is, people who were not Jews – to whom the term "Messiah" meant little – if anything. The name "Jesus Christ" seems to have been understood simply as a name. As a result, even in the New Testament itself, the word "Christ" came to be used as an alternative way of referring to Jesus of Nazareth.

This habit of speaking persists today. In contemporary Christianity, "Jesus" is often seen as a familiar, intimate form of address, often used in personal devotion and prayer, whereas "Christ" is more formal, often being used in public worship.

As we have noted, Christianity is an historical religion, which came into being in response to a specific set of events, which center upon Jesus of Nazareth and to which Christian theology is obliged to return in the course of its speculation and reflection. Yet the importance of Jesus far exceeds his historical significance. For Christians, Jesus is more than the founder of their faith or the originator of Christianity: he is the one who makes God known, who makes salvation possible, and who models the new life with God that results from faith. To set this out more formally:

1   Jesus tells and shows what God is like;
2   Jesus makes a new relationship with God possible;
3   Jesus himself lives out a God-focused life, acting as a model of the life of faith.

In what follows we shall explore each of these ideas briefly; then we shall consider them further later in this volume.

First, Christianity holds that Jesus of Nazareth reveals both the will and the face of God. The New Testament sets out the idea that God, who is invisible, is in some way made known or made visible through Jesus. Jesus does not simply reveal what God is like, or what God expects of believers. Rather he enables us to see God. This point is made repeatedly in the New Testament – for example in statements like this: "Anyone who has seen me has seen the Father" (John 14: 9). God the Father is here understood to speak and act in the Son. God is revealed through, in, and by Jesus. To have seen Jesus is to have seen the Father.

This point is developed further in the doctrine of the incarnation – the characteristically Christian idea that God entered into the world of time and space in the person of Jesus of Nazareth. The doctrine of the incarnation provides a basis for the distinctively Christian belief that Jesus opens a "window into God." It also underlies the practice, especially associated with the Orthodox church, of using icons in worship and personal devotion. The doctrine of the incarnation affirms that Jesus "fleshes out" what God is like.

In the second place, Jesus is understood to be the ground of salvation. One of the more significant titles used in the New Testament to refer to Jesus is "Savior." Jesus is the "Savior, who is Christ the Lord" (Luke 2: 11). According to the New Testament, Jesus saves his people from their sins (Matthew 1: 21); in his name alone is there salvation (Acts 4: 12); and he is the "author of their salvation" (Hebrews 2: 10). One of the earliest symbols of faith used by Christians was a fish. The use of this symbol may reflect the fact that the first disciples were fishermen. Yet this is not the main reason for adopting the symbol. The five Greek letters spelling out the word "fish" in Greek (I-CH-TH-U-S) are an acronym of the Christian creedal slogan "Jesus Christ, Son of God, Savior" (see p. 258).

Third, Jesus is understood to disclose the contours of the redeemed life. Jesus of Nazareth shows us both what God is like and what God wants from us. Jesus is not simply the basis of the life of faith; he is also the model for that life. Traditionally, this was interpreted ethically in terms of exercising self-denial and showing self-giving love. Yet this feature is also important spiritually – for example, in the Christian use of the "Lord's Prayer," a prayer also used by Jesus of Nazareth. The way in which Jesus prayed is seen as an example for the way in which Christians ought to pray, in much the same way as the moral example of Jesus is seen as normative for Christian ethics.

The Sources of Our Knowledge about Jesus of Nazareth

Christianity is an historical religion, which came into being in response to a specific set of events – above all, the history of Jesus of Nazareth. The fact that Jesus of Nazareth is an historical figure raises two fundamental questions, which remain integral to Christian reflection. First, how does the story of Jesus of Nazareth fit into his historical context – namely that of first-century Judaism? And, second, what documentary sources do we possess for our knowledge of Jesus and its perceived significance?

We shall consider both these questions in the present chapter.

Christianity began as a reform movement within the context of Judaism, which gradually clarified its identity as it grew and began to take definite shape in the world of the first-century Roman Empire. There are no historical grounds for believing that the term "Christian" originated from Jesus of Nazareth himself. Early Christians tended to refer to each other as "disciples" or "saints," as the letters of the New Testament make clear. Yet others used alternative names to refer to this new movement. The New Testament suggests that the term "Christians" (Greek *Christianoi*) was first used by outsiders, to refer to the followers of Jesus of Nazareth. "It was in Antioch that the disciples were first called 'Christians'" (Acts 17: 26). It was a term imposed upon them, not chosen by them. Yet it seems to have caught on.

However, we must be careful not to assume that the use of the single term "Christian" implies that this new religious movement was uniform and well organized. As we shall see, the early history of Christianity suggests that it was quite diverse, without well-defined authority structures or carefully formulated sets of beliefs. These began to crystallize during the first centuries of Christian history and became increasingly important in the fourth, when Christianity became a legal religion within the Roman empire.

Traditionally, the birth of Jesus of Nazareth is dated to the opening of the Christian era, his death being dated to some point around AD 30–33. Yet virtually nothing is known of Jesus of Nazareth from sources outside the New Testament. The New Testament itself provides two groups of quite distinct sources of information about Jesus: the four gospels and the letters. Although parallels are not exact, there are clear similarities between the gospels and the classical "lives" written by leading Roman historians of the age – such as Suetonius' *Lives of the Caesars* (written in AD 121).

The gospels mingle historical recollection with theological thought, reflecting both on the identity and on the significance of Jesus of Nazareth. The four gospels have their own distinct identities and concerns. For example, the gospel of Matthew seems especially concerned with establishing the significance of Jesus for a Jewish readership, whereas the gospel of Luke seems more concerned with explaining his importance to a Greek-speaking community. Establishing the identity of Jesus is just as important as recording what he said and did. The gospel writers can be thought of as trying to locate Jesus of Nazareth on a map, so that his relationship with humanity, history, and God may be understood and appreciated. This leads them to focus on three particular themes:

- What Jesus taught, particularly the celebrated "parables of the Kingdom." The teaching of Jesus was seen as important in helping believers to live out an authentic Christian life, which was a central theme of Christian discipleship – most notably in relation to cultivating attitudes of humility toward others and obedience toward God.
- What Jesus did – especially his ministry of healing, which was seen as important in establishing his identity, but also in shaping the values of the Christian community itself. For example, most medieval monasteries founded hospitals as a means of continuing Christ's ministry in this respect.
- What was said about Jesus by those who witnessed his teaching and actions. The gospel of Luke, for example, records Simeon's declaration that the infant Jesus was the "consolation of Israel," as well as the Roman centurion's assertion that Jesus was innocent of the charges brought against him. These can be seen as constituting public recognition of the identity of Jesus.

The letters of the New Testament – sometimes still referred to as "epistles" (Greek *epistolē*, plural *epistolai*) – are addressed to individuals and churches and often focus on issues of conduct and belief. These letters are important in helping us grasp the emerging understandings of the significance of Jesus of Nazareth within the Christian community. The example of Jesus is regularly invoked to emphasize the importance of imitating his attitudes – for example, treating others better than yourself (Philippians 2). Although the letters make virtually no direct reference to the teachings of Jesus, certain patterns of behavior are clearly regarded as being grounded in those teachings – such as humility, or a willingness to accept suffering.

The letters also emphasize the importance of certain patterns of behavior – for example repeating the actions of the Last Supper, using bread and wine as a way of recalling and celebrating the death and resurrection of Christ (pp. 112–117). The sacraments of both baptism and the eucharist are clearly anticipated in the New Testament and are traced back to the ministry of Jesus himself.

Yet, perhaps more importantly, the letters also reveal understandings of the identity and significance of Jesus of Nazareth that were becoming characteristic of early Christian communities. The most important of the themes associated to such understandings are the following:

- Jesus of Nazareth is understood to be the means by which the invisible God can be known and seen. Jesus is the "image" (Greek *eikōn*) "of the invisible God" (Colossians 1: 15), or the "exact representation" (Greek *charaktēr*) of God (Hebrews 1: 3).
- Jesus is the one who makes salvation possible and whose life reflects the themes characteristic of redeemed human existence. The use of the term "savior" (Greek *sōtēr*) is highly significant in this respect.
- The core Christian belief in the resurrection of Jesus of Nazareth is seen as a vindication of his innocence, a confirmation of his divine identity, and the grounds of hope for believers. Through faith, believers are understood to be united with Christ and sharing in his sufferings at present, while also sharing in the hope of his resurrection.

Each of these themes would be further developed as the Christian community reflected on their significance and on their relevance for the life and thought of believers. We shall explore some of these more developed ideas about Jesus in a later chapter, setting out the shape of Christian beliefs.

Jesus of Nazareth in His Jewish Context

From the outset, Christianity saw itself as continuous with Judaism. Christians were clear that the God whom they followed and worshipped was the same God worshipped by the Israelite Patriarchs Abraham, Isaac, and Jacob. The New Testament sees the great hope of the coming of a "Messiah" to the people of Israel as having been fulfilled in Jesus of Nazareth. As we saw earlier (p. 3), the New Testament use of the title "Christ" (the Greek translation of the Hebrew word "Messiah") reflects this belief.

There seems to have been a general consensus within Judaism that the Messiah would be like a new king David, opening up a new era in Israel's history. While Israel looked forward to the coming of a messianic age, different groups understood this in diverging ways. The Jewish desert community at Qumran thought of the Messiah primarily in priestly terms, whereas others had more political expectations. Yet, despite these differences, the hope of the coming of a "messianic age" seems to have been widespread in early first-century Judaism and is echoed at points in the gospel's accounts of the ministry of Jesus.

During the first phase of its development, Christianity existed alongside (or even within) Judaism. Christians insisted that the God who was known and encountered by the great heroes of faith of Israel – such as Abraham, Isaac, Jacob, and Moses – was the same God who was more fully and clearly revealed in Jesus. It was therefore of importance to the early Christians to demonstrate that Jesus of Nazareth, the central figure of the Christian faith, brought the great messianic hopes of Judaism to fulfillment.

The continuity between Judaism and Christianity is obvious at many points. Judaism placed particular emphasis on the Law (Hebrew *Torah*), through which the will of God was made known in the form of commands, and on the Prophets, who made known the will of

God in certain definite historical situations. The New Testament gospels report that Jesus of Nazareth emphasized that he had "not come to abolish the Law or the Prophets, but to fulfill them" (Matthew 5: 17).

The same point is made by Paul in his New Testament letters. Jesus is "the goal of the Law" (Romans 10: 4, using the Greek word *telos*, which means "end," "goal," or "objective"). Paul also stresses the continuity between the faith of Abraham and that of Christians (Romans 4: 1–25). The letter to the Hebrews points out the continuity of relationship both between Moses and Jesus (Hebrews 3: 1–6) and between Christians and the great figures of faith of ancient Israel (Hebrews 11: 1–12: 2).

The New Testament makes it clear that Christianity is to be seen as being continuous with Judaism and as bringing to completion what Judaism was pointing toward. This has several major consequences, of which the following are the most important. First, both Christians and Jews regard more or less the same collection of writings – known by Jews as "Law, Prophets, and Writings" and by Christians as "the Old Testament" – as having religious authority. Although some more radical thinkers within Christianity – such as the second-century writer Marcion of Sinope – argued for the breaking of any historical or theological link with Judaism, the main line within the Christian movement both affirmed and valued the link between the Christian church and Israel. A body of writings that Jews regard as complete in itself is seen by Christians as pointing forward to something that will bring it to completion. Although Christians and Jews both regard the same set of texts as important, they use different names to refer to them and interpret them in different ways. We shall consider this point further when we look at the Christian Bible.

Second, New Testament writers often laid emphasis on the manner in which Old Testament prophecies were understood to be fulfilled or realized in the life and death of Jesus Christ. By doing this, they drew attention to two important beliefs: that Christianity is continuous with Judaism; and that Christianity brings Judaism to its true fulfillment. This is particularly important for some early Christian writings – such as Paul's letters and the gospel of Matthew – which often seem to be particularly concerned with exploring the importance of Christianity for Jews. For example, the gospel of Matthew notes at twelve points how events in the life of Jesus can be seen as fulfilling Old Testament prophecies.

This continuity between Christianity and Judaism helps us understand some aspects of early Christian history. The New Testament suggests that at least some Christians initially continued to worship in Jewish synagogues, before controversy made this problematic. The letters of Paul help us understand at least some of the issues lying behind those controversies. Two questions were of particular importance and were keenly debated in the first century.

First, there was a debate about whether Christian converts should be required to be circumcised. Those who emphasized the continuity between Christianity and Judaism believed they should be. Yet the view that ultimately prevailed was that Christians were no longer subject to the cultic laws of Judaism – such as the requirement to be circumcised or to observe strict dietary laws.

Second, there was the question of whether non-Jewish converts to Christianity were to be treated as Jews. Those who emphasized the continuity between Judaism and Christianity argued that Gentile believers should be treated as if they had become Jews – and hence they would be subject to Jewish religious observances and rituals, such as the requirement for males to be circumcised. For this reason, a group within early Christianity demanded the circumcision of male Gentile converts.

Yet the majority, including Paul, took a very different position. To be a Christian was not about reinforcing a Jewish ethnic or cultural identity, but about entering a new way of living and thinking, which was open to everyone. By the late first century Christians largely saw themselves as a new religious movement, originating within Judaism but not limited by its cultic and ethnic traditions.

The Gospels and Jesus of Nazareth

Our primary sources for the life of Jesus of Nazareth are the four gospels of the New Testament – Matthew, Mark, Luke, and John. The first three of these gospels are often referred to as "the Synoptic Gospels," in that each lays out a summary (Greek *sunopsis*) of the activities and teachings of Jesus. There is little historical information about Jesus available from any other source. Thus the great Roman historians of this age provide little on this score, although they are important sources for our understanding of the way in which Jesus was received within early Christianity.

It is easy to understand this lack of interest in Jesus in the writings of Roman historians. They had relatively little time for events that took place in the backwaters of their empire, such as the distant and unimportant province of Judaea. Their histories focused on Rome itself and on the leading figures and events that shaped its destiny.

Three Roman historians make reference to Jesus in their writings: Pliny the Younger, writing around AD 111 to the Emperor Trajan about the rapid spread of Christianity in Asia Minor; Tacitus, who wrote around AD 115 concerning the events of AD 64, when Nero made the Christians scapegoats for the burning of Rome; and Suetonius, writing around AD 120 about certain events during the reign of Emperor Claudius. Suetonius refers to a certain "Chrestus" who was behind riotings at Rome. "Christus" was still an unfamiliar name to Romans at this stage, whereas "Chrestus" was a common name for slaves at this time (the Greek adjective *chrēstos* meant "useful").

Four points emerge from the brief comments of these three historians:

1 Jesus had been condemned to death by Pontius Pilate, procurator of Judaea, during the reign of the Roman Emperor Tiberius (Tacitus). Pilate was procurator (governor) of Judaea from AD 26 to AD 36, while Tiberius reigned from AD 14 to AD 37. The traditional date for the crucifixion is some time around AD 30–33.
2 By the time of Nero's reign, Jesus had attracted sufficient followers in Rome for Nero to make them a suitable scapegoat for the burning of Rome. These followers were named "Christians" (Tacitus).
3 "Chrestus" was the founder of a distinctive group within Judaism (Suetonius).
4 By AD 112, Christians were worshipping Jesus of Nazareth "as if he were a god," abandoning the worship of the Roman emperor to do so (Pliny).

The main sources for the life of Jesus of Nazareth are thus the four gospels. Each of these texts presents related, though distinct, accounts of the ministry of Jesus. Matthew's gospel, for example, brings out the importance of Jesus for the Jewish people and is particularly concerned to explore the way in which Jesus brings the expectations of Israel to their proper fulfillment. Mark's gospel takes the form of a rapidly paced narrative, often leaving readers breathless as they are led from one event to another. Luke's gospel has a particular interest in bringing out the importance of Jesus for non-Jewish readers. John's gospel is more reflective in its approach, characterized by a distinctive emphasis on the way in which the coming of Jesus brings eternal life to those who believe in him.

The gospels cannot really be thought of as biographies of Jesus in the modern sense of the term, although they unquestionably provide much helpful biographical information. They do not present us with a full account of the life of Jesus. Mark's gospel, for example, focuses on a few years of Jesus' life, which are characterized by his intensive public ministry and end in his crucifixion and resurrection. Matthew and Luke both give brief accounts of the birth and childhood of Jesus before resuming their narratives of his public ministry.

It is clear that the gospels weave together several sources to build up their overall portrayal of the identity and significance of Jesus. Thus Mark's gospel draws on material that is traditionally attributed to Peter, Jesus' leading disciple. Furthermore, the gospels are more concerned with bringing out the significance of the life of Jesus than with documenting it in full detail. Nevertheless, they present us with a portrait of Jesus that mingles history and theology to tell us who Jesus is – not simply in terms of his historical identity, but in terms of his continuing importance for the world.

We will follow the account of the birth and early ministry of Jesus of Nazareth as laid out in the Synoptic Gospels. Space does not allow a detailed interaction with the historical, theological, and cultural issues raised by these accounts. In what follows we shall set out the basic narratives and reflect on their general significance.

The Birth of Jesus of Nazareth

Mark's account of the ministry of Jesus begins with Jesus' appearance as an adult in Galilee; it makes no reference to his birth or childhood. Matthew and Luke provide different yet complementary accounts, which narrate the birth of Jesus and have had a major impact on Christian art (and subsequently on traditional Christmas cards and carols). Matthew's account is related from the standpoint of Joseph, and Luke's from that of Mary. Neither the day nor the year of Jesus' birth are known for certain. Non-Christians often assume that Christians believe that Jesus was born on December 25. In fact Christians have chosen to celebrate the birth of Jesus on Christmas Day. December 25 is the date fixed for the celebration of the birth of Jesus, not the date of his birth itself.

Early Christian writers suggested a variety of dates for the celebration of Jesus' birth – for example, Clement of Alexandria (c. 150–c. 215) advocated May 20. By the fourth century the date of December 25 had been chosen, possibly to take advantage of a traditional Roman holiday associated with this date. For Christians, the precise date of the birth of Jesus is actually something of a non-issue. What really matters is that he was born as a human being and entered into human history.

The traditional Christmas story has become somewhat stylized over the years. For example, most traditional versions of the story tell of the "three wise men" and of Jesus "being born in a stable." In fact the New Testament relates that the wise men brought three gifts to Jesus; many have simply assumed that, as there were three gifts, there must have been three wise men. Similarly, we are told that Jesus was born in a manger; many have assumed that, since mangers are kept in stables, Jesus must have been born in a stable.

The birthplace of Jesus is identified as Bethlehem, a minor town in the region of Judaea, not far from Jerusalem. Its significance lies in its associations with King David, given particular emphasis by the Prophet Micah. Writing in the eighth century before Christ, Micah declared that a future ruler of Israel would emerge from Bethlehem (Micah 5: 2). This expectation is noted in Matthew's gospel (Matthew 2: 5–6), where it is presented as one of many indications that the circumstances of the birth and early ministry of Jesus represent a fulfillment of Israelite prophecies and hopes.

Luke stresses the humility and lowliness of the circumstances of the birth of Jesus. For example, he notes that Jesus was placed in a manger (normally used for feeding animals), and that the first people to visit him were shepherds. Although the force of the point is easily lost, it needs to be remembered that shepherds were widely regarded as socially and religiously inferior people in Jewish society, on account of their nomadic lifestyle.

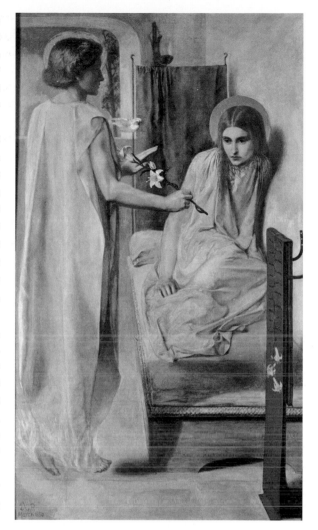

Figure 1.1   The angel Gabriel declaring to Mary that she is to bear the savior of the world, by Dante Gabriel Rossetti; this incident is related early in Luke's gospel. Dante Gabriel Rossetti (1828–1882), *Ecce Ancilla Domini* (*The Annunciation*), 1850. Oil on canvas, mounted on wood, 72 × 42 cm. Source: Erich Lessing/AKG Images.

Both Matthew and Luke stress the importance of Mary, the mother of Jesus. In later Christian thought, Mary would become a focus for personal devotion, on account of her obedience and humility. She often had a particular appeal to women, who felt marginalized by the strongly masculine ethos of Christianity, for example during the Middle

Figure 1.2   The birth of Christ, as depicted by Fra Angelico in a mural in the monastery of San Marco, Florence, between 1437 and 1445. Fra Giovanni da Fiesole (1387–1455) and workshop, *Birth of Christ, with the Saints Catherine of Alexandria and Peter the Martyr* (1437–1445). Fresco, 193 × 164 cm. Florence, S. Marco, upper storey, dormitory, cell No.5 (east corridor). Source: Rabatti-Domingie/AKG Images.

Ages. The hymn "Stabat mater" (a Latin title that means "The Mother Stood [by the Cross]"), which was written in the thirteenth century, describes the deep feeling of sorrow experienced by Mary at the death of her son on the cross. This hymn, which was subsequently set to music by several major composers, had a deep impact on the spirituality of the Middle Ages and beyond. At the time of the Reformation, devotion to Mary was often criticized. It was suggested that this devotion could threaten the central place of Jesus Christ in Christian prayer and worship. Nevertheless, most Christians regard Mary as an excellent example of several cardinal Christian virtues, especially obedience to and trust in God.

The place of Joseph in the gospels' accounts of Jesus should also be noted. At no point is he described as the "father of Jesus," despite the numerous references, here and elsewhere, to Mary as the "mother of Jesus." Matthew shows how Joseph was legally related to David (Matthew 1: 1–17), so that Jesus possessed the legal status of being descended from David. Yet Joseph is not understood to be Jesus' physical father. For Matthew and Luke, it is understood that the conception of Jesus is due to God, although the theme of the virginity of Mary – seen as immensely important by some Christian writers – is given less weight than might be expected.

The Early Ministry of Jesus of Nazareth

The gospels all locate the beginning of the public ministry of Jesus in the countryside of Judaea, by the Jordan River. It is specifically linked with the activity of John the Baptist, who attracted widespread attention with his calls to repentance. It is clear that John's ministry takes place at a moment of some significance in the history of Israel. Perhaps there were those who felt that God had abandoned Israel; perhaps there were those who felt that the great acts of divine deliverance and encouragement in the past would never be repeated. Israel was under Roman occupation and seemed to have lost its identity as the people of God.

The New Testament picks up two themes that may help us understand why John the Baptist attracted such enormous interest at the time. The final work of Jewish prophecy – the book of Malachi, probably dating from the fifth century before Christ – spoke of God sending a messenger, to prepare the way for the coming of God (Malachi 3: 1–2). It also hinted at the return of Elijah, one of the great figures of faith in Israel, before this event. When John the Baptist appeared, he wore the same simple clothes of camel's hair as Elijah had before him. Malachi spoke of the need for corporate repentance. The whole people of God needed to repent of its sins before national restoration to divine favor was possible. John the Baptist spoke of this same need for repentance and offered baptism as a symbol of an individual's willingness to repent. (The word "baptism" comes from a Greek word meaning "to wash" or "to bathe.")

The implications of these developments would have been clear to anyone with a knowledge of the Jewish prophets and alert to the signs of the times. The coming of John the Baptist could be seen as a pointer to the coming of God. John himself made this point, declaring that someone greater than him would follow him – someone whose sandals he was not worthy to untie (Mark 1: 8). And at that moment Jesus appeared. Mark's vivid and racy account of this encounter makes it clear that John was referring to Jesus, even though he did not specifically name him. John is thus seen as the forerunner of Jesus, pointing the way to his coming – a bridging figure between the Old and New covenants.

After Jesus was baptized by John, he slipped away into a solitary place for 40 days and nights. This period of Jesus' ministry – usually referred to as "the temptation of Christ" – involved his being confronted with all the temptations he would encounter during his ministry. Although Mark only hints at this (Mark 1: 12), Matthew and Luke provide fuller details (e.g., Luke 4: 1–13), allowing us to see how Jesus was confronted with the temptation to personal power and glory. The New Testament writers subsequently stress the importance of Jesus' obedience to the will of God. The period of Lent, immediately before Easter (pp. 240–241), marks the time of year when Christians are encouraged to examine themselves in this way, following the example of Christ.

A theme that now emerges is that of the rejection of Jesus by his own people. This theme culminates in the crucifixion, in which Jesus is publicly repudiated by a crowd in Jerusalem and taken off to be crucified by the Roman authorities. The theme also appears at earlier points in the ministry of Jesus and is particularly linked with the severely hostile criticism of Jesus by the Pharisees and the teachers of Jewish law. For the New Testament writers, the paradox is that those who were most deeply committed to and familiar with the Jewish law failed to recognize its fulfillment when this took place.

Nevertheless, the theme of "rejection" can be found much earlier than this. One incident in particular illustrates this point: the rejection of Jesus in his home town of Nazareth. Luke's gospel relates how Jesus attended synagogue regularly on the sabbath. On one occasion he was asked to read a section from the prophecy of Isaiah, which included the following words:

> The Spirit of the Lord is on me, because he has anointed me to preach good news to the poor. He has sent me to proclaim freedom for the prisoners and recovery of sight for the blind, to release the oppressed, to proclaim the year of the Lord's favour. (Luke 4: 18–19)

After reading these words, Jesus solemnly declared that he they had been fulfilled – implying that he himself was their fulfillment. The synagogue congregation was outraged by what it clearly saw as a self-serving publicity stunt, probably amounting to blasphemy. Its members threw him out of their town, even trying to push him over the edge of a nearby hill. After this, Jesus moved to minister in the region of Capernaum, on the northwestern shore of Lake Galilee.

Jesus then gathered around himself a small group of disciples, who would accompany him as he traveled and would subsequently form the core of the early church. The group of twelve apostles (often referred to simply as "the twelve") was drawn from a variety of backgrounds, mostly from jobs in the rural economy of the region. Two pairs of brothers – Peter and Andrew, James and John – were called to leave behind them their fishing business on Lake Galilee and follow Jesus. At a late stage, possibly a year or so into his ministry, Jesus

Figure 1.3   Jesus of Nazareth calling Peter and Andrew by the Sea of Galilee (1481), by Domenico Ghirlandaio. Domenico Ghirlandaio (Domenico Bigordi) (1449–1494), *The Calling of SS. Peter and Andrew*, 1481. Fresco. Source: Vatican Museums and Galleries/Bridgeman Art Library.

divided the twelve into two groups of six, sending them out into the countryside to preach the kingdom of God.

Jesus began his ministry of teaching and healing in the region around Galilee and subsequently expanded it into Judaea. On the basis of the accounts provided in the gospels, it may be estimated that this period lasted roughly three years. Important though both the teaching and healing are in their own rights, their true importance lies partly in what they demonstrate about Jesus. This becomes clear from a question posed later by John the Baptist. By this stage, John had been imprisoned by Herod Antipas, ruler (or, more precisely, "tetrarch") in the region of Galilee. Still uncertain as to the true identity of Jesus, John asked him this question: "Are you the one who was to come, or should we expect someone else?" The implications of the question are enormous. Is Jesus the Messiah? Has the messianic age finally dawned?

Jesus answers this question indirectly, by pointing to what has happened in his ministry: "The blind receive sight, the lame walk, those who have leprosy are cured, the deaf hear, the dead are raised, and the good news is preached to the poor" (Matthew 11: 6). In other words, the expected signs of the messianic age were present in his ministry. Jesus does not directly answer the question of whether he is the Messiah. The implication, however, is that the healing miracles are to be seen as signs, pointing to a right understanding of the identity and significance of Jesus as the long-awaited Messiah.

The Teaching of Jesus of Nazareth: The Parables of the Kingdom

The theme of the "kingdom of God" (or, in the case of Matthew's gospel, "the kingdom of heaven") is widely agreed to be central to the preaching of Jesus. The public ministry of Jesus begins with his declaration that the kingdom of God has "drawn near" and that "the time is fulfilled" (Mark 1: 15). The Greek word *basileia*, traditionally translated as "kingdom," does not so much express the idea of a definite political region over which a king rules as the action of "ruling" itself. In other words, the Greek word refers to the idea of "kingship" rather than of a "kingdom."

The "Sermon on the Mount" (the block of teaching contained in Matthew 5: 1–7: 29) is often referred to as setting out the "ethics of the kingdom of God." The acknowledgement of the rule of God is expected to lead to a certain pattern of behavior, which is embodied in the life and ministry of Jesus of Nazareth himself and echoed in his teaching. The basic theme of Jesus' preaching can thus be thought of in terms of the coming of the kingly rule of God. This theme is expressed in the prayer that Jesus instructed his followers to imitate, which is widely known as "the Lord's Prayer."

Jesus' preaching about the kingdom is best understood in terms of "inauguration." Something has happened that sets in motion a series of events that has yet to reach its fulfillment. A series of parables express the idea that the kingdom is something that progresses from a seemingly insignificant starting point to something much greater. The Parable of the Mustard Seed (Matthew 13: 31–32) illustrates this idea of growth and development. The Parable of the Vineyard (Matthew 21: 33–41) makes the point that those who are entitled to be tenants of the vineyard are those who produce its fruit, a clear indication of the

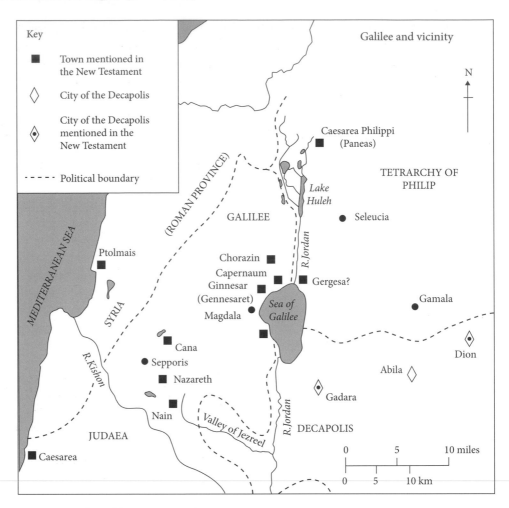

Figure 1.4 The Galilean ministry of Jesus.

need, for those who claim to be within the kingdom, to conform to its ethics. The kingly rule of God carries obligations.

Jesus' teaching about the kingdom is largely expressed using "parables," which can be thought of as earthly stories with heavenly meanings. The word "parable" conveys a number of ideas, including "illustration" and "mystery" or "riddle." A parable conveys a spiritual truth – but the meaning may not be clear, and may therefore require illustration. Some of the parables are based on shrewd observation of everyday life in rural Palestine. Just as a pearl of great value is worth one's selling lesser possessions in order to own it, so the kingdom of God is worth one's giving up everything for it (Matthew 13: 45–46). Just as a small amount of yeast can raise a large amount of dough, so the kingdom of God can exercise a wide influence throughout the world, despite its small beginnings (Matthew 13: 33). Just as a shepherd will go out and look for a sheep that has got lost, so God will seek out those who have wandered away (Luke 15: 4–6).

Sometimes the parables are more complex. The Parable of the Prodigal Son (Luke 15: 11–32) tells of a son who decides to leave his father's home and to seek his fortune in a distant land. Yet life away from his father turns out not to be as rosy as the prodigal son had expected. He falls on hard times. The prodigal son comes to long to return home to his father. However, he is convinced that his father will have disowned him and will no longer wish to acknowledge him as his son. The remarkable feature of the parable is the picture of God it gives us. The father sees the returning son long before the son notices him; he rushes out to meet him and to celebrate the return of the son he had given up for lost. The message of the parable is that, just as the father was overjoyed at the return of his son, so God will be overjoyed at the return of sinners.

The teaching of Jesus concerning the kingdom of God is an important element in the Christian faith. However, Christianity is not only about what Jesus taught. It is also about the person of Jesus himself. Who is he? And what is his importance? For the New Testament, the death and resurrection of Jesus are of central importance to any full understanding of his identity and significance. We shall consider these themes in what follows.

The Crucifixion of Jesus of Nazareth

Christianity is the only major faith to focus attention on the death of its founder and to see this episode as being of pivotal importance to its ideas and ethos. This emphasis is not a later development; it can be seen from the outset. One of the earliest literary witnesses to the central importance of the crucifixion is Paul's first letter to the Christian church at Corinth, which probably dates from the early months of AD 55. In the first chapter of this letter, Paul lays considerable emphasis upon the fact that Jesus of Nazareth was crucified. The subject of his preaching was "Christ crucified" (1: 23); the power lying behind the gospel proclamation is "the cross of Christ" (1: 17); the entire Christian gospel can even be summarized as "the message of the cross" (1: 18).

Yet crucifixion was seen as a scandalous form of death within Roman imperial culture. It was reserved for traitors, rebels, and the lower classes. Crucifixion was a widespread form of execution in the Roman empire, and we possess many accounts of the process from classical writers. The Latin word "crucifixion" literally means "being placed on a cross." The victim was generally flogged or tortured beforehand, and then might be tied or nailed to the cross in practically any position. This form of punishment appears to have been employed ruthlessly in order to suppress rebellions in the provinces of the Roman empire – such as the revolt of the Cantabrians in northern Spain, as well as those of the Jews. Probably the most famous example of crucifixion being used as a deterrent was in 71 BC, when the Romans crucified 6,000 slaves who had joined Spartacus' rebellion. The crosses were erected along the Appian Way, one of the busiest commercial transport routes in Italy.

Josephus' accounts of the crucifixion of the many Jewish fugitives who attempted to escape from besieged Jerusalem at the time of its final destruction by the Roman armies in AD 70 make deeply disturbing reading. In the view of most Roman legal writers, notorious criminals were to be crucified on the exact location of their crime, so that "the sight may deter others from such crimes." Perhaps for this reason, the Roman Emperor Quintillian crucified criminals on the busiest thoroughfares, in order that the maximum deterrent effect might be achieved.

Crucifixion was a punishment reserved for the lowest criminals, which clearly implied that Jesus belonged to this category of people in Roman eyes. For a Jew, anyone hanged upon a tree was cursed by God (Deuteronomy 21: 23), which would hardly commend the Christian claim that Jesus was indeed the long-awaited Messiah. Indeed, one of the Dead Sea scrolls suggests that crucifixion was regarded as the proper form of execution for a Jew suspected of high treason.

The New Testament makes two statements about the crucifixion of Jesus of Nazareth, which are integral to its understanding of his identity and significance. First, the crucifixion really happened – specifically, during the time when Pontius Pilate was the Roman governor of Judaea. And, second, this event needed to be interpreted correctly. It did not signify shame, guilt, or rejection by God. When rightly understood, it was about the forgiveness of sins and the dawn of new hope.

Before we reflect further on the interpretation of the crucifixion, we need to outline the basic structure of the gospel narratives of this event. The background to the crucifixion is the triumphal entry of Jesus into Jerusalem, mounted on a donkey, in fulfillment of a great messianic prophecy of the Old Testament (Zechariah 9: 9). Jesus enters Jerusalem as its king, an event recalled and celebrated by Christians on Palm Sunday. Yet this final week in the life of Jesus is marked by increasing controversy, culminating in his betrayal, arrest, and execution. Luke relates how Jesus and his disciples gather together "in an upper room" to celebrate Passover (Luke 22: 14–23).

The Jewish feast of Passover commemorates the events leading up to the exodus and the establishment of the people of Israel. The Passover lamb, slaughtered shortly before and eaten at the feast, symbolizes this great act of divine redemption. It is thus very significant that the Last Supper and the crucifixion of Jesus took place at the feast of Passover. The Synoptic Gospels clearly treat the Last Supper as a Passover meal where Jesus initiates a new version of the meal. While Jews celebrated their deliverance by God from Egypt by eating a lamb, Christians would henceforth celebrate their deliverance by God from sin by eating bread and drinking wine.

John's gospel suggests that Jesus is crucified at exactly the same moment as the slaughter of the Passover lambs, so that Jesus is to be seen as the true Passover lamb, who died for the sins of the world. In the light of this, the full meaning of the words of John the Baptist, as presented in John's gospel, becomes clearer: "Behold the Lamb of God, who takes away the sin of the world" (John 1: 29). The point being made is that the death of Christ is understood to take away sin and to cleanse believers from its guilt and stain.

The coincidence of the Last Supper and of the crucifixion with the Passover feast makes it clear that there is a connection between the exodus and the death of Christ. Both are to be seen as acts of divine deliverance from oppression. However, while Moses led Israel from a specific captivity in Egypt, Jesus of Nazareth is seen as delivering his people from a universal bondage to sin and death. While there are parallels between the exodus and the cross, there are also differences. Perhaps the most important difference relates to the New Testament's affirmation of the universality of the redemption accomplished by Christ. For the New Testament, the work of Christ benefits all who put their trust in him, irrespective of their ethnic identity or their historical or geographical location.

The Last Supper – famously depicted by Michelangelo in 1498 – is of particular importance to Christians, in that it is remembered in Christian worship. The use of bread and wine as a remembrance of Jesus – which focuses on the sacrament usually referred to as "Holy Communion," "the Lord's Supper," "the eucharist," or "the mass" – has its origins here. We shall return to consider this "remembrance" in greater detail later (pp. 116–117). The Last Supper is followed by the betrayal of Jesus to the Jewish authorities for 30 pieces of silver (Matthew 27: 1–10).

After a theological interrogation, Jesus is handed over to the Roman authorities. He is brought before Pontius Pilate, who was the Roman governor of Judaea from AD 26 to AD 36. Pilate's inclination would probably have been to order some token punishment, but to take things no further. However, the crowd demands that Jesus be crucified. Washing his hands of the whole affair, Pilate sends Jesus off to be flogged and crucified. Jesus is then humiliated by the Roman soldiers, who dress him up in a caricature of royal costume, including a crown of thorns.

The floggings administered by the Romans were vicious; they had been known to cause the death of victims before they were crucified. Under Jewish law, victims were only allowed to be flogged with 40 strokes; this was invariably reduced to 39, as an act of leniency. But under Roman law there were no limits to the extent of the suffering to be inflicted. The whips used for this purpose generally consisted of several strands of leather with small pieces of metal or broken bones at the end; these tore apart the skin of those being whipped, with the result that many did not survive the ordeal.

Clearly Jesus was severely weakened by his beating and proved unable to carry his own cross. Simon of Cyrene was forced to carry it for him. Finally they reached Golgotha, the place of execution (Matthew 27: 32–43). This place is also often referred to as "Calvary," from the Latin word *calvaria*, which means "skullcap, top of the skull" – the literal meaning of the Aramaic word of "Golgotha." As Jesus hangs on the cross, he is mocked by those watching him die, while the Roman soldiers cast lots for his clothes. After being taken down from the cross, Jesus is buried in a borrowed tomb (Matthew 27: 57–61). That is not, however, the end of the story, according to the New Testament.

The Resurrection of Jesus of Nazareth

The gospels now turn to narrate a series of events traditionally referred to as "the resurrection." This phrase is used to refer to both an historical event – the "empty tomb" – and a specific interpretation of the significance of this event. The discovery of the empty tomb was not in itself the resurrection; other interpretations were possible, such as the body's having been stolen. The idea of "resurrection" is a specific interpretation of the discovery of the empty tomb.

The gospels' resurrection narratives have three main elements:

1   The tomb in which the corpse of Jesus was laid late on the Friday afternoon was discovered to be empty on the Sunday morning. Those who discovered the empty tomb were frightened by what they found; their reports were not taken seriously by many of those in Jesus' close circle of friends.

2   The disciples reported experiencing personal encounters with Jesus, in which he appeared to them as a living human.

3   The disciples began to preach Jesus as the living Lord rather than as a dead teacher from the past.

The "empty tomb" tradition is of considerable importance here (Matthew 28: 1–10; Mark 16: 1–8; Luke 24: 1–11; John 20: 1–10). The story is told from different angles in each of the gospels and includes divergence on minor points of detail, which is so characteristic of eye witness reports. Interestingly, all four gospels attribute the discovery of the empty tomb to women. The only Easter event to be explicitly related in detail by all four of the gospel writers is the visit of the women to the tomb of Jesus. Yet Judaism dismissed the value of the testimony or witness of women, regarding only men as having significant legal status in this respect. Mark's gospel even names each of the women three times: Mary Magdalene, Mary the mother of James, and Salome (Mark 15: 40, 47; 16: 1). It is interesting that Mark does not mention the names of any male disciples who were around at the time.

The resurrection of Jesus of Nazareth appears to have come as a surprise to the disciples. There was, in Jewish thought, no real precedent for a resurrection of this kind. Far from fitting into popular Jewish expectations of the resurrection of the dead, what happened to

Figure 1.5   Piero della Francesca's depiction of the resurrection of Christ, c. 1460–1464. Piero della Francesca (c.1410/20–1492), *The Resurrection of Christ* (c. 1460–1464). Fresco (removed), 225 × 200 cm. Sansepolcro, Pinacoteca Comunale. Source: Rabatti-Domingie/AKG Images.

Jesus actually contradicted them. Most Jews at the time seem to have believed in the resurrection of the dead at the end of time itself. The Pharisees, for example, believed in a future resurrection, and held that men and women would be rewarded or punished after death according to their actions. The Sadducees, however, insisted that there was no resurrection of any kind. No future existence awaited men and women after death. (Paul was able to exploit the differences between Pharisees and Sadducees on this point: see Acts 26: 6–8.)

Thus the Christian claim about the resurrection of Christ in history – rather than at the end of history – does not fit any known Jewish pattern at all. The resurrection of Jesus is not declared to be a future event, but something that had already happened in the world of time and space, in front of witnesses.

In addition to reporting the basic events that underlie the Christian gospel, the New Testament includes extensive reflection on the identity and significance of Jesus. The present chapter provides an analysis of the main lines of reflection we find in the New Testament, as well as exploring how Jesus has been understood as a result of the church's long reflections on how best to represent and describe him. This process of reflection and development is often likened to the growth of a plant.

But, before we can begin to explore Christian understandings of the meaning of Jesus, we need to consider the all-important distinction between events and meanings. In what way can something that happened in history be said to possess a meaning over and above the event itself?

Events and Meanings: The Interpretation of the History of Jesus

In thinking about the significance of Jesus, we need to explore the relation between the events of his life and their deeper meaning. Christianity does not merely recite the history of Jesus; it affirms a specific way of making sense of that history, particularly his death on the cross and resurrection. The Christian faith certainly presupposes that Jesus existed as a real historical figure, and that he was crucified. Christianity is not, however, simply about the mere facts that Jesus existed and was crucified. Some words of the Apostle Paul, probably written 15 years after the resurrection, will help make this point clear.

> Now, brothers, I want to remind you of the gospel I preached to you, which you received and on which you have taken your stand. By this gospel you are saved … For what I received I passed on to you as of first importance: that Christ died for our sins according to the Scriptures, that he was buried, that he was raised on the third day according to the Scriptures, and that he appeared to Peter, and then to the Twelve [Apostles]. (1 Corinthians 15: 1–5)

Paul here seems to be using (and passing on to his readers) an accepted formula or form of words, which was in general use in the early church and which he transmits to Corinthian Christians. This formula makes a clear distinction between the *event* of the death of Christ and the *significance* of this event. That Christ died is a simple matter of history; that Christ died *for our sins* is an insight that lies right at the heart of the Christian faith itself.

This important distinction between an *event* and its *meaning* can be illustrated with the help of an event that took place in 49 BC, when the great Roman commander Julius Caesar crossed a small river with a legion of soldiers. The name of the river was Rubicon, and it marked an important frontier within the Roman empire. It was the boundary between Italy and Cisalpine Gaul, a colonized region to the northwest of Italy, in modern-day France.

Considered simply as an event, Caesar's crossing was not especially important. The Rubicon was not a major river, and there was no particular difficulty about crossing it. People had crossed wider and deeper rivers before and since. As a simple event, it was not remarkable. But that is not why the crossing of that river was important. It is the meaning of the event that guarantees its place in history books, in that its political significance was enormous. Crossing this national frontier with an army was a deliberate act of rebellion against Rome. It marked a declaration of war on the part of Caesar against Pompey and the Roman senate. The *event* was the crossing of a river; the *meaning* of that event was a declaration of war.

In many ways, the death of Christ may be said to parallel Caesar's crossing of the Rubicon. The event itself appears unexceptional, except to those who know its significance. On the basis of contemporary records, we know that an incalculable number of people died like that at the time. Jesus would not have been alone in being executed in this way. Indeed the gospels' accounts of the crucifixion make it absolutely clear that two other criminals were crucified with Jesus on that day, one on either side of him. As an event, the crucifixion hardly seems important or noteworthy. It is one more witness to the cruel and repressive measures used by the Romans to enforce conformity throughout their empire.

Yet the New Testament makes it clear that behind the external event of the crucifixion of Jesus of Nazareth lay what this event *signified*; and this is the reason why it was *important*. Pompey and the Roman senate were not especially interested in the mechanics of how Julius Caesar crossed the Rubicon: for them, the bottom line was crystal clear – it meant war. Similarly, Paul was not particularly interested in the historical details of the crucifixion of Jesus. The historicity of the crucifixion is assumed; what really matters is its theological significance as the ground of salvation, forgiveness, and victory over death. The Christian proclamation was about far more than the simple historical fact that Jesus was crucified. It was about the significance of this event for humanity: Jesus was numbered among sinners, so that sinners might be forgiven.

Thus far we have focused on the distinction between "event" and "meaning." Once the importance of this distinction has been appreciated, we are in a position to move on and look at some of the interpretations of Jesus that we find in the New Testament.

The New Testament Understandings of the Significance of Jesus

Who is Jesus of Nazareth? What does he *mean*? One of the easiest ways to begin to reflect on these questions is to look at the terms used to refer to Jesus in the New Testament, especially in the gospels. These terms are often referred to as the "Christological titles" of the New Testament. Each of them must be considered as the outcome of a process of reflection on what Jesus said and did and on the impact that he had upon people. In what follows we shall explore three of these titles – "Messiah," "Lord," and "Son of God" – which have found their way into the creeds of the churches, and we shall consider their implications for the Christian understanding of the identity of Jesus.

1   *Messiah*   It is very easy for a modern western reader to assume that "Christ" was Jesus' surname and to fail to appreciate that it is actually a title – "Jesus the Christ," or "Jesus the Messiah." The Hebrew word "Messiah" means "the anointed one" – someone who has been ritually anointed with oil, as a mark of having been singled out by God as having special powers and functions. Some of Israel's greatest kings were referred to as "the Lord's anointed" (1 Samuel 24: 6). As time passed, the term gradually came to refer to a deliverer, himself a descendant of David, who would restore Israel to the golden age it enjoyed under the rule of David.

During the period of Jesus' ministry, Palestine was occupied and administered by Rome. There was fierce nationalist feeling at the time, fueled by intense resentment at the presence of a foreign occupying power, and this appears to have given a new force to the traditional expectation of the coming of the Messiah. For many, the Messiah would be the deliverer who expelled the Romans from Israel and restored the line of the greatest king of Israel, David.

Jesus does not appear to have been prepared to accept the title "Messiah" in the course of his ministry. For example, when Peter acclaims him as Messiah – "You are the Christ!" – Jesus immediately tells Peter to keep quiet about it (Mark 8: 29–30). It is not clear what the full significance of the "Messianic secret" is. Why should Mark emphasize that Jesus did not make an explicit claim to be the Messiah, when he was so clearly regarded as such by so many?

Perhaps the answer may be found later, in Mark's gospel, when Mark recounts the only point at which Jesus explicitly acknowledges his identity as the Messiah. When Jesus is led, as a prisoner, before the High Priest, he admits to being the Messiah (Mark 14: 61–62). Once violent or political action of any sort is no longer possible, Jesus reveals his identity. He was indeed the deliverer of the people of God – but not, it would seem, in any political sense of the term. The misunderstandings associated with the title "Messiah," particularly in Zealot circles, appear to have caused Jesus to play down the messianic side of his mission.

2   *Lord*   A second title used to refer to Jesus of Nazareth in the New Testament is "Lord" (Greek *kurios*). The word is used in two main senses in the New Testament. It is used as a polite title of respect, particularly when addressing someone. When Martha addresses Jesus as "Lord" (John 11: 21), she is probably, although not necessarily, merely treating him with proper respect. However, the word is also used in another sense.

The confession that "Jesus is Lord" (Romans 10: 9; 1 Corinthians 12: 3) was clearly regarded by Paul as a statement at the heart of the Christian gospel. Christians are described as those who "call upon the name of the Lord" (Romans 10: 13; 1 Corinthians 1: 2). But what does this imply? It is clear that there was a tendency in first-century Palestinianism to use the word "Lord" (Greek *kurios*; Aramaic *mare*) to designate a divine being, or at the very least a figure who is decidedly more than just human – in addition to this word's function as a polite or honorific title. But of particular importance is the use of this Greek word *kurios* to translate the special cypher of four letters used to refer to God in the Old Testament.

This cipher was often referred to as the "Tetragrammaton" (a Greek word meaning "the four letters"), and written as "Yahweh."

When the Old Testament was translated from Hebrew into Greek, the word *kurios* ("Lord") was generally used to render this special sacred name of God. Of the 6,823 instances in which the sacred name is used in the Hebrew, the Greek word *kurios* is used to translate it on 6,156 occasions. This Greek word thus came to be an accepted way of referring, directly and specifically, to the God who had revealed himself to Israel at Sinai and had entered into a covenant with his people on that occasion. Jews would not use this term to refer to anyone or anything else. To do so would be to imply that this person or thing was of divine status. The historian Josephus tells us that the Jews refused to call the Roman emperor *kurios*, because they regarded this name as reserved for God alone.

The writers of the New Testament had no hesitation in using this sacred name to refer to Jesus, with all that this implied. A name that was used exclusively to refer to God was regarded as referring equally to Jesus. In fact, on several occasions the New Testament takes an Old Testament text that refers to "the Lord" – in other words, to "the Lord God of Israel" – and deliberately applies or transfers the reference to "the Lord Jesus." Perhaps the most striking example of this tendency may be found by comparing Joel 2: 32 with Acts 2: 21. The passage in Joel refers to a coming period in the history of the people of God, in which the Spirit of God will be poured out upon all people (Joel 2: 28). On this "great and dreadful day of the Lord" (that is, God) "everyone who calls upon the name of the Lord will be saved" (Joel 2: 31–32) – in other words, all who call upon the name of *God* will be saved.

This prophecy is alluded to in Peter's great sermon on the Day of Pentecost (Acts 2: 17–21), which ends with the declaration that "everyone who calls upon the name of the Lord shall be saved" (Acts 2: 21). Yet the "Lord" in question here is none other than "Jesus of Nazareth," whom, Peter declares, God has made "both Lord and Christ" (Acts 2: 36).

3   *Son of God*   A third title used by the New Testament to refer to Jesus is "Son of God." In the Old Testament the term is occasionally used to refer to angelic or supernatural persons (see Job 38: 7; Daniel 3: 25). Messianic texts in the Old Testament refer to the coming Messiah as a "Son of God" (2 Samuel 7: 12–14; Psalm 2: 7). The New Testament use of the term seems to mark an intensification of its Old Testament meaning, with an increased emphasis upon its exclusiveness.

The belief that Jesus was the "son of God" arose partly from reflection on the resurrection. Paul opens his letter to the Christians at Rome by stating that Jesus "was descended from David at the human level, and was designated as the Son of God … by his resurrection from the dead" (Romans 1: 3–4). This brief statement picks out two reasons why Jesus was understood to be the Son of God. First, on the physical level, he was a descendant of David, the great king of Israel to whom God had promised a future successor as king. A similar point is made by Matthew as he opens his gospel (Matthew 1: 1). Second, Jesus' resurrection established his identity as the Son of God. We see here how an appeal to the resurrection clinches the argument as to the true identity of Jesus as the "son of God."

The New Testament uses other terms to refer to Jesus of Nazareth – for example, "Son of Man" (traditionally understood to emphasize the humanity and humility of Jesus), and "Savior" (a theme we shall explore in more detail in Chapter 3, when we consider the Christian understanding of the nature and grounds of salvation).

Later in this work we shall be exploring some classic approaches to the identity of Jesus, along with other basic ideas of the Christian faith, when we reflect on the creeds.

Jesus of Nazareth and Women

Much recent discussion within Christian churches in the West has focused on the place of women within the church, particularly in professional ministries. Should women be ordained? The gospels' accounts of the ministry of Jesus are important to such discussions. They show that women were an integral part of the group of people who gathered round him. They were affirmed by him, often to the dismay of the Pharisees and other Jewish religious traditionalists. Not only were women witnesses to the crucifixion; they were also the first witnesses to the resurrection. The only Easter event to be explicitly related in detail by all four of the gospel writers is the visit of the women to the tomb of Jesus. Yet, as stated above, first-century Judaism disparaged women's testimonials and their credibility.

It is interesting to note that the gospels occasionally portray women as being much more spiritually perceptive than men. For example, Mark portrays the male disciples as having little faith (Mark 4: 40, 6: 52), while he commends women: a woman is praised for her faith (Mark 5: 25–34), a foreign woman, for responding to Jesus (Mark 7: 24–30), and a widow is singled out as an example to follow (Mark 12: 41–44). Further, Jesus treated women as human subjects rather than simply as objects or possessions. Throughout his ministry, Jesus can be seen engaging with and affirming women – often women who were treated as outcasts by contemporary Jewish society on account of their origins (e.g., Syro-Phoenicia or Samaria) or their lifestyle (e.g., prostitutes).

Jesus refused to make women scapegoats in sexual matters – for example in adultery. The patriarchal assumption that men are corrupted by fallen women is conspicuously absent from his teaching and attitudes, most notably toward prostitutes and the woman taken in adultery. The Talmud – an important source of Jewish law and teaching – recommended that its readers (who are assumed to be men) should "not converse much with women, as this will eventually lead you to unchastity." Such advice was studiously ignored by Jesus, who made a point of talking to women (the conversation with the Samaritan woman, related in John 4, being an especially celebrated instance). In much the same way, the traditional view that a woman was "unclean" during her period of menstruation was dismissed by Jesus, who taught that it is moral impurity that defiles a person (Mark 7: 1–23).

Luke's gospel is of particular interest in relation to understanding Jesus' attitude to women. Luke brings out clearly how women are among the "oppressed" liberated by the coming of Jesus. Luke also sets out his gospel in a way that emphasizes that both men and women are involved in, and benefit from, the ministry of Jesus of Nazareth. The following passages demonstrate this parallelism especially clearly:

Luke 1: 11–20, 26–38	Zacharias and Mary rejoice at God's faithfulness
Luke 2: 25–38	Simeon and Anna praise the infant Jesus
Luke 7: 1–17	A centurion and a widow
Luke 13: 18–21	A man with mustard seed and a woman with yeast
Luke 15: 4–10	A man finds a lost sheep and a woman finds a lost coin

By this arrangement of material, Luke expresses that men and women stand together side by side before God. They are equal in honor and grace; they have the same gifts bestowed upon them and have the same responsibilities.

Luke also draws our attention to the significant role of women in the spreading of the gospel. For example, Luke indicates that "many women" (Luke 8: 2–3) were involved in spreading the news of the coming of the Kingdom of God. Indeed, Luke specifically names some of these women: "Mary (called Magdalene) from whom seven demons had come out; Joanna the wife of Cuza, the manager of Herod's household; Susanna; and many others." Granting women such a significant role would have seemed incomprehensible to the male-dominated society of contemporary Palestine.

It is probably difficult for modern western readers, who are used to thinking of women as having the same rights and status as men, to appreciate how novel and radical these attitudes were at the time. Possibly the most radical aspect of Jesus' approach to women is that he associated freely with them and treated them as responsible human beings, indulging in theological conversation with them, encouraging and expecting a response. It is hardly surprising that early Christianity proved to have a deep appeal for women.

It is entirely possible that Jesus' teachings attracted women partly on account of the new roles and status they were granted in the Christian community. There were many cults in Greece and Rome that limited their membership to men or allowed women to participate only in very limited ways. We shall explore developments in Christian attitudes toward women during the Roman empire in a later section of this work (pp. 127–129).

The Reception of Jesus of Nazareth outside Judaism

Although its historical origins lay in Palestine, Christianity rapidly gained a following in the Greek-speaking world, especially within the cities of the Roman empire. The missionary journeys of Paul of Tarsus, described in the New Testament, played an important role in spreading Christianity in Europe and Asia Minor. Paul was a Jewish religious leader who converted to Christianity, changing his name from "Saul" to "Paul." His missionary expeditions took him to many cities and regions throughout the northeastern Mediterranean area – including Europe. As Christianity began to gain a foothold on the European mainland, the question of how it was to be preached in a non-Jewish context began to be of increasing importance.

Early Christian preaching to Jewish audiences, especially in Palestine, tended to focus on demonstrating that Jesus of Nazareth represented the fulfillment of the hopes of Israel. Peter's sermon to Jews in Jerusalem (Acts 2) follows this pattern. Peter argues there that Jesus represents the culmination of Israel's destiny. God has declared him to be both "Lord and Christ" – highly significant terms (pp. 23–24), which Peter's Jewish audience would have understood and appreciated. But what were Christians to do when preaching to Greek audiences, who knew nothing of the Old Testament and had no connection with the history of Israel?

An approach that came to be particularly significant in the early Christian world can be found in Paul's sermon; it was preached on the Areopagus, the famous hill in the Greek city of Athens, possibly around AD 55. Since his audience included no Jews, Paul made no reference there to the ideas and hopes of Judaism. Instead he presented Jesus of Nazareth as someone who revealed a god whom the Athenians knew about but had yet to encounter definitively. "What therefore you worship as unknown, this I proclaim to you" (Acts 17: 23). Paul declared that the god who was made known through Jesus of Nazareth was the same god who had created the world and humanity – the god in whom, as the Athenian poet Aratus declared, "we live and move and have our being" (Acts 17: 28).

Where early Christian preaching to Jewish audiences presented Jesus as the fulfillment of the hopes of Israel, Paul's preaching to Greek audiences presented the Christian faith as the fulfillment of the deepest longings of the human heart and of the most profound intuitions of human reason. This view was easily adapted so as to incorporate some of the core themes of classic Greek philosophy, such as the idea of the "word" (Greek *logos*) – the fundamental rational principle of the universe, according to popular Platonic philosophy in the first century. This theme is developed in the opening chapter of the gospel of John, which presents Jesus of Nazareth as the "word" by which the universe was originally created and that entered into the world to illuminate and redeem it. "And the Word became flesh and lived among us, and we have seen his glory" (John 1: 14).

This was not necessarily seen as dismantling or displacing Christianity's historical and theological roots in Judaism. Rather it was seen as a way of affirming Christianity's cultural origins, while at the same time setting out the universal appeal of the Christian faith, which was held to transcend all ethnic, racial, and cultural barriers. The universal validity of the Christian gospel meant that it could be proclaimed in ways that would resonate with every human culture. As we shall see, this approach to the appeal of Christianity would be of immense significance throughout its history, especially in missionary contexts.

The material presented in this chapter clearly leads us into other areas of the Christian faith. One is that of its ideas, particularly those concerning the identity and significance of Jesus of Nazareth. We shall consider these further in Chapter 3. Yet our reflections in the present chapter also lead us to think further about the Christian Bible, the source of our understanding of the context against which Jesus of Nazareth is to be set, of our knowledge of his teaching and deeds, and of our information about how Jesus was understood within the first Christian communities. In the next chapter we shall consider the Christian Bible in more detail.

2

The Christian Bible

Anyone beginning to study Christianity soon realizes that the Bible plays a very important role in Christian life and thought. If you attend a Christian service of worship, you will hear the Bible read publicly as an integral part of that worship. You will probably hear a sermon preached, based on one of the biblical passages read during the service. If you join a small group of Christians who meet for study and prayer, you may well find that their meetings include "Bible study" – that is, reflection on the meaning and relevance of a short passage from the Bible.

So what is this Bible? And why is it so important? In this chapter we shall explore the structure and contents of the Christian Bible and the role it plays for Christians.

The term "the Bible" is used by Christians to refer to the collection of writings that they regard as authoritative. Other ways of referring to this collection of texts are also used in Christian writings, such as the descriptions "Sacred Scripture" or "Holy Scripture." However, the term "Bible" is the most widely used.

The unusual word "Bible" needs explanation. Like many words in modern English, it is the almost direct transliteration of a Greek original. The Greek word that has been taken into English is *biblia* – literally meaning "books." The whole Greek phrase is in the plural (*ta biblia*, "the books"; singular *biblion*) and refers to the collection of books, or writings, brought together in the Bible.

So what sorts of books are gathered together in this way? And how are they arranged? In the next two sections of this chapter we shall explore the two groups of writings known as the "Old Testament" and "New Testament."

Christianity: An Introduction, Third Edition. Alister E. McGrath.
© 2015 John Wiley & Sons, Ltd. Published 2015 by John Wiley & Sons, Ltd.

Box 2.1   The books of the Old Testament

TITLE	ABBREVIATION
Genesis	Gen
Exodus	Ex
Leviticus	Lev
Numbers	Num
Deuteronomy	Dt
Joshua	Jos
Judges	Jdg
Ruth	Ru
1 Samuel	1Sa
2 Samuel	2Sa
1 Kings	1Ki
2 Kings	2Ki
1 Chronicles	1Ch
2 Chronicles	2Ch
Ezra	Ezr
Nehemiah	Neh
Esther	Est
Job	Job
Psalms	Ps
Proverbs	Pr
Ecclesiastes	Ecc
Song of Songs	SoS
Isaiah	Is
Jeremiah	Jer
Lamentations	Lam
Ezekiel	Ez
Daniel	Dan
Hosea	Hos
Joel	Joel
Amos	Am
Obadiah	Ob
Jonah	Jon
Micah	Mic
Nahum	Nah
Habakkuk	Hab
Zephaniah	Zep
Haggai	Hag
Zechariah	Zec
Malachi	Mal

The Old Testament

The Christian Bible is divided into two major sections, traditionally referred to as the Old Testament and the New Testament. The Old Testament consists of 39 books, beginning with Genesis and ending with Malachi. It is almost entirely written in Hebrew, the language of Israel; however, some short sections are written in Aramaic, an international language widely used in the diplomacy of the ancient Near East. The Old Testament itself includes a number of different kinds of writings, of which the most important are the following:

1   THE FIVE BOOKS OF THE LAW These are sometimes also referred to as the Five Books of Moses, reflecting a traditional belief that they were largely written by Moses. In more scholarly works, they are sometimes referred to as the Pentateuch (from the Greek words for "five" and "bookcase"; *teuchos*). They are: Genesis, Exodus, Leviticus, Numbers, and Deuteronomy. These books deal with the creation of the world, the calling of Israel as a people, and its early history, including the exodus from Egypt. The story they tell ends with the people of Israel being about to cross over the Jordan and enter the promised land. One of the most important themes of these books is the giving of the Law to Moses and the implications of this act for the life of Israel.

2   THE HISTORICAL BOOKS Joshua, Judges, Ruth, 1 and 2 Samuel, 1 and 2 Kings, 1 and 2 Chronicles, Ezra, Nehemiah, and Esther are "historical" books in that they deal with various aspects of the history of the people of God, from their entry into the promised land of Canaan to the return of the people of Jerusalem from exile in the city of Babylon. They include detailed accounts of the conquest of Canaan, the establishment of a monarchy in Israel, the great reigns of Kings David and Solomon, the breakup of the single nation of Israel into two parts (the northern kingdom of Israel and the southern kingdom of Judah), the destruction of Israel by the Assyrians, the defeat of Judah and the exile of its people, both caused by the Babylonians, and the final return from exile and rebuilding of the temple. The books are arranged in historical order.

3   THE PROPHETS This major section of the Old Testament contains the writings of a group of individuals understood to be inspired by the Holy Spirit who sought to make the will of God known to their people over a period of time. There are 16 prophetic writings in the Old Testament, which are usually divided into two categories. First, there are the four *major prophets*: Isaiah, Jeremiah, Ezekiel, and Daniel. These are followed by the twelve *minor prophets*: Hosea, Joel, Amos, Obadiah, Jonah, Micah, Nahum, Habakkuk, Zephaniah, Haggai, Zechariah, and Malachi. The use of the words "major" and "minor" does not imply any judgment about the relative importance of the prophets. It refers simply to the length of the books in question. The prophetic writings are arranged roughly in historical order.

Other types of book can be noted, for instance the "wisdom" writings: Job, Proverbs, Ecclesiastes. These works deal with the question of how true wisdom may be found, and they often provide some practical examples of wisdom.

From what has been said, it will be clear that the phrase "Old Testament" is used by Christian writers to refer to those books of the Christian Bible that were (and still are) regarded as sacred by Judaism. For Christians, the Old Testament is seen as setting the scene for the coming of Jesus, who brings its leading themes and institutions to fulfillment. The same texts, of course, continue to be held as sacred by Jews to this day. This means that the same collection of texts is referred to in different ways by different groups. This has stimulated a few proposals for alternative ways of referring to this collection of texts, none of which has gained general acceptance. Three main alternative names for the Old Testament may be noted.

1 THE HEBREW BIBLE This way of referring to the Old Testament stresses the fact that it was written in Hebrew and is sacred to the Hebrew people. However, it fails to do justice to the way in which Christianity sees an essential continuity between the Old and the New Testament. A minor difficulty is also caused by the fact that parts of the Old Testament are written in Aramaic rather than Hebrew.

2 THE FIRST TESTAMENT This way of referring to the collection of texts avoids using the word "old," which is held by some to be pejorative. "Old," it is argued, means "outdated" or "invalid." Referring to the Old Testament as the "First Testament" and the New as the "Second Testament" is held by some to emphasize the continuity between the two collections of texts.

3 TANAKH This is an acronym of the Hebrew words for "law, prophets, and writings" (*torah, nevi'im, ketuvim*), which is the standard Jewish description of the works that Christians call the "Old Testament." Tanakh is perfectly acceptable for Jewish use but does not reflect the specifically Christian understanding of the nature of the continuity between Israel and the church.

There is presently no generally accepted substitute within Christianity for the traditional phrase "Old Testament," which will therefore be used throughout this study. Nevertheless, readers should be aware of the alternatives and of the issues that led to their being proposed.

There are some disagreements within Christianity over exactly what is included in the Bible, which primarily focus on the Old Testament. The most important of these disagreements concerns a group of works usually referred to as "the Apocrypha" (from the Greek word for "covered, hidden") or as "the Deuterocanonical works." This category includes books such as the Wisdom of Solomon and the book of Judith. These books, although dating from the period of the Old Testament, were not originally written in the Hebrew language and are thus not included in the Hebrew Bible.

Protestants tend to regard these "apocryphal" books as interesting and informative, but not as being of doctrinal importance. Catholics and Orthodox Christians, on the other hand, regard them as an integral part of the text of the Bible. This difference is probably best reflected in the way in which Protestant and Catholic Bibles are laid out. Many Protestant Bibles do not include the Apocrypha at all. Those that do – such as the famous King James's Bible of 1611 – include these texts as a third section of the Bible. Catholic Bibles – such as the Jerusalem Bible – include them within the Old Testament section of the Bible.

Major Themes of the Old Testament

The Old Testament is a remarkably complex work, which merits much fuller study than is possible in this overview. If you have the time to take the study of the Old Testament further, you are strongly recommended to make use of one of the excellent introductions currently available (which are noted in the Further Reading section for this chapter). What follows is a very basic and brief introduction to some of the themes of the Old Testament.

The creation

The Old Testament opens with an affirmation that God created the world. The fundamental theme asserted in the opening chapters of the book of Genesis is that God is the originator of all there is in the world. No created thing can compare with God. This point is of particular importance, given the importance of worship of, for example, the sun or the stars among other religions of the ancient Near East. In the Old Testament, God is superior to everything in creation. The height of God's creation is declared to be humanity, which alone is created in the image and likeness of God. Humanity is understood to be the steward (not the possessor!) of God's creation and is entrusted with its care.

The account of the creation is followed by an account of the nature and origins of sin. One of the fundamental points made in Genesis 3 is that sin enters the world against God's intentions. Sin disrupts the close relationship between God and the creation; it leads to humanity rebelling against God and asserting its autonomy. This theme recurs throughout the Bible. For example, the story of the Tower of Babel (Genesis 11: 1–9) is basically about human attempts at self-assertion in the face of God. God's hostility to sin is depicted in a number of ways; the expulsion of Adam and Eve from the Garden of Eden and Noah's flood are two of them.

So how important is the theme of creation to the Old Testament? In the twentieth century, the great Old Testament scholar Gerhard von Rad (1901–1971) argued that the most characteristic insight of the Old Testament was that its God was sovereign over history, especially the history of Israel. In the Old Testament, faith in God is primarily faith in a God who acts within, and is sovereign over, cosmic and human history. While von Rad is careful to stress that the faith of Israel included reference to creation, he believed that the primary emphasis lay on God bringing Israel out of Egypt and into Canaan. The doctrine of creation takes its place as a secondary doctrine, providing a certain context for the affirmation of divine lordship over history.

Abraham: Calling and covenant

The calling of Abraham is seen as being of foundational importance to the emergence of Israel, both as a nation and as the people of God. The central theme of God's calling of Abraham (Genesis 12: 1–4) carries the idea that God has chosen an individual whose descendants will possess the land of Canaan and will become a great nation. The theme of the fulfillment of this promise is of major importance throughout the Pentateuch. It is also of importance in the New Testament – to Paul, who sees Abraham's willingness to trust in the promises of God as a prototype of Christian faith.

The idea of a "covenant" between God and Abraham and his descendants is introduced at this point. The ritual of circumcision is seen as the external sign of belonging to the covenant of the people of God. For Paul, it is of particular importance that God's promise to Abraham precedes the external sign of this covenant; this, according to Paul, implies that the promise takes precedence over the sign. As a result, Gentiles (that is, those who are not ethnic Jews) do not require to be circumcised when they convert to Christianity.

The book of Genesis traces the fortunes of Abraham and his descendants, showing the manner in which the covenant between God and Abraham is realized. The book ends with an account of the way in which Abraham's descendants settle in the land of Egypt, thus setting the scene for the next major theme of the Old Testament.

The exodus and the giving of the Law

The story of the exodus (a word of Greek origin that literally means "exit" or "way out") is well known. A new ruler arises in Egypt (he is referred to as "Pharaoh"), who regards the descendants of Abraham as a potential threat. The identity of this Pharaoh is unknown, although there are good reasons for suggesting that he may have been Ramesses II (who ruled during the period 1279–1213 BC). He subjected the Hebrews to a series of oppressive measures designed to limit their numbers and influence. The book of Exodus describes God's call to Moses to be the liberator of Israel from its bondage in Egypt.

One of the most important Old Testament festivals is closely linked with the exodus from Egypt. The Passover festival began in the period before the exodus. The origins and purpose of the festival are described at Exodus 11: 1–12: 30. It marks an act of divine judgment against Egypt. The regulations for the marking of the festival are laid down with some precision. Each household or group of households in Israel is to sacrifice a perfect lamb or goat and to daub its blood across the sides and tops of the doorframes. This will mark off its inhabitants as God's own people and will distinguish them from their Egyptian oppressors. These people are then to eat a meal, in order to recall their time in Egypt. Part of the meal consists of "bitter herbs," which symbolize the bitterness of their bondage. Another major part of the meal is unleavened bread. This "bread made without yeast" points to the haste in which the people were asked to prepare to leave Egypt. There was not even enough time for dough to rise through the action of the yeast. The festival is named "the Lord's Passover," which refers to the fact that God will "pass over" the houses of his own people as he brings vengeance on the firstborn sons of the Egyptians. In commemoration of this act of deliverance, the Passover is to be celebrated every year as a "lasting ordinance." Further regulations concerning its celebration are mentioned later (Exodus 12: 43–49).

The theme of the covenant between God and Israel is developed further in the book of Exodus. Two particular points should be noted. First, a specific name is now used to refer to God. This is the term "Lord," which is the English word designed to translate a cypher of four letters that is used to name God specifically. This group of four letters, often referred to as the "Tetragrammaton" (from the Greek words for "four" and "letters"), is sometimes represented as "Yahweh" or "Jehovah" in English versions of the Bible. Other Hebrew words may be used to refer to gods in general; but the specific name "Lord" is used only to refer to the "God of Abraham, Isaac, and Jacob." Unlike other Hebrew words for "god," it is never used for any other divine or angelic being. These other Hebrew words act as common nouns, designating "god" or "gods" in general, and can be used with reference to Israel's own God or to other gods (such as the pagan gods of other nations). But the Tetragrammaton is used only in naming the specific God whom Israel knew and worshipped.

Second, the obligations that being the covenant people of God impose on Israel are made clear. This is a series of specific and unconditional demands, which are now usually referred to as the "Ten Commandments," and which Moses received at Mount Sinai. These commandments continue to be of major importance within Judaism and Christianity alike, especially as Israel enters the promised land of Canaan and attempts to establish a society that is based on this covenant between God and the people.

After leaving Egypt, the people of Israel spend a period of 40 years wandering in the wilderness of Sinai, before finally crossing the Jordan River to enter the promised land of Canaan. The occupation of Canaan was seen as consolidating the distinctive identity of

---

Box 2.2   The Ten Commandments

1   I am the LORD your God, who brought you out of the land of Egypt, out of the house of slavery. You shall have no other gods before me.

2   You shall not make for yourself an idol, whether in the form of anything that is in heaven above, or that is on the earth beneath, or that is in the water under the earth. You shall not bow down to them or worship them; for I the LORD your God am a jealous God, punishing children for the iniquity of parents, to the third and the fourth generation of those who reject me, but showing steadfast love to the thousandth generation of those who love me and keep my commandments.

3   You shall not make wrongful use of the name of the LORD your God, for the LORD will not acquit anyone who misuses his name.

4   Remember the sabbath day, and keep it holy. Six days you shall labour and do all your work. But the seventh day is a sabbath to the LORD your God; you shall not do any work – you, your son or your daughter, your male or female slave, your livestock, or the alien resident in your towns. For in six days the LORD made heaven and earth, the sea, and all that is in them, but rested the seventh day; therefore the LORD blessed the sabbath day and consecrated it.

5   Honor your father and your mother, so that your days may be long in the land that the LORD your God is giving you.

6   You shall not murder.

7   You shall not commit adultery.

8   You shall not steal.

9   You shall not bear false witness against your neighbor.

10   You shall not covet your neighbor's house; you shall not covet your neighbor's wife, or male or female slave, or ox, or donkey, or anything that belongs to your neighbor. (Exodus 20: 2–17)

Israel. In particular, it established that the worship of the Lord and obedience to the covenant between the Lord and Israel were of central importance to the identity and wellbeing
of people. The book of Joshua describes elaborate measures being taken to ensure that the

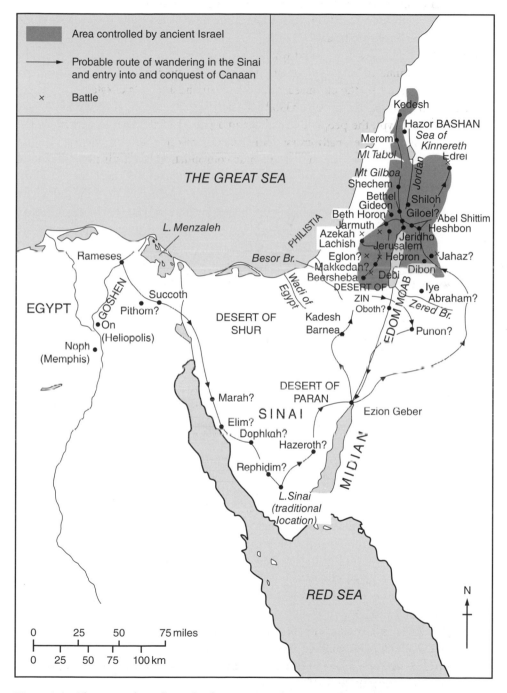

Figure 2.1 The route of Israel's exodus from Egypt and conquest of Canaan.

worship of the Lord was not in any way compromised by indigenous Canaanite religions. Canaanite religion was strongly oriented toward fertility issues – such as the fertility of the land, animals, and humans. Its major deities – including Baal and Ashtaroth – feature regularly in biblical accounts of the history of Israel over the next centuries. Canaanite religion continued to exercise a fascination on Israel for some time to come and is a regular subject of condemnation in the prophetic literature.

The establishment of the monarchy

In its early period Israel had no king. During the period following the conquest of Canaan, the region was ruled by a series of charismatic religious and political leaders known as "judges." The book of Judges documents the serious threats (partly from internal disunity, partly from external forces) that arose at this time to the unity of Israel and notes the role of judges such as Gideon, Samson, and Samuel in this regard. Under Samuel, the last of the "judges," a series of moves were made that resulted in the establishment of the monarchy. The first king was Saul, who probably reigned during the period 1020–1000 BC. Saul's reign is portrayed as divisive and tragic. One of his most significant internal opponents was David. Following Saul's death in a battle against the Philistines, David launched a military campaign that eventually led to the restoration of the unity of Israel and the expansion of its territory. Although opposition to David continued throughout his reign, particularly from the supporters of Saul, David was able to maintain his hold on the nation until the final years of his reign.

The reign of David (c. 1000–961 BC) saw significant developments taking place in Israel's religion. David's conquest of the city of Jerusalem led to its becoming the center of Israel's religious life, a development that would be consolidated during the reign of Solomon. The role of the king became important religiously, as he was seen to be a son of God. The theme of a future successor to David, who would rule over a renewed people of God, became a significant element of messianic hopes within Israel and explains the importance of the "David" theme within parts of the New Testament. For New Testament writers (especially Matthew and Paul), Jesus of Nazareth is to be seen as the successor to David as king of Israel. Many Old Testament writings, particularly within the Psalter, extol the greatness of the king, the temple, and the city of Jerusalem (often referred to as "Zion"). All three are seen as tokens of God's favor toward Israel.

David was succeeded as king by Solomon, who reigned during the period 961–922 BC. During his reign the temple was constructed as a permanent place of worship for the Lord. A strongly centralized administrative system was set in place and extensive trading agreements were negotiated with neighboring countries. Solomon's extensive harem caused disquiet to some, on account of the pagan religious beliefs of some of his wives. Solomon was famed for his wisdom, and some collections of proverbs in the Old Testament are attributed to him.

After the death of Solomon, the nation of Israel proved unstable. Eventually the nation split into two sections, each with its own king. The northern kingdom, which would now be known as "Israel," would eventually cease to exist under the Assyrian invasions of the eighth century. The southern kingdom of Judah, which retained Jerusalem as its capital city, continued to exist until the Babylonian invasions of the sixth century. At this point the monarchy ended. Jewish hopes increasingly came to focus on the restoration of the monarchy and the rise of a new figure like David. From a Christian perspective, these expectations could be directly related to the coming of Jesus of Nazareth.

The priesthood

The centrality of religion to the identity of Israel gave the guardians of its religious traditions a particularly significant role. The emergence of the priesthood is a major theme in its own right. One of the most significant functions of the priesthood related to the cultic purity of Israel. This purity could be defiled (or "made unclean," as this type of occurrence is often described) by various forms of pollution. The priesthood was responsible for ensuring the cleanliness of the people, which was seen as being vital for the proper worship of the Lord.

More importantly, the priesthood was responsible for the maintenance of the sacrificial system, and particularly for the Day of Atonement ritual, in which sacrifices were offered for the sins of the people. A distinction is to be drawn between "uncleanliness" (which arises from natural bodily functions) and "sin" (which has strongly ethical overtones). Sin was seen as something that created a barrier between Israel and God. It is significant that most of the Old Testament images or analogies for sin take the form of images of separation. In order to safeguard the continuing relationship between the Lord and Israel, the priesthood was responsible for ensuring that the proper sacrifices were offered for sin.

A related theme is that of the temple. During the first period of its history, Israel used a movable tent or tabernacle for its religious rites. However, when David captured the Jebusite city of Jerusalem and made it his capital, he declared his intention to build a permanent place of worship for the Lord. This was actually carried out under the direction of his successor, Solomon. The splendor of the building is a frequent theme in Old Testament writings dating from around this period. The temple was destroyed by the Babylonians in 586 BC and rebuilt after the return from exile, half a century later. The Second Temple (as the building erected by the returned exiles is known) appears to have been rather less magnificent. However, with the end of the monarchy, the temple came to have increased civil significance, in that temple authorities were responsible for both religious and civil matters.

A more splendid temple was constructed under Herod. Although work on this project appears to have begun in the decades immediately prior to the birth of Christ, the work was only completed in AD 64. The temple was destroyed, never to be rebuilt, during the suppression of a Jewish revolt against the Romans in the city in AD 70. The western wall of the temple largely survived; it is now widely referred to as "the wailing wall" and constitutes an important place of prayer for Jews to this day.

Prophecy

The English word "prophet" is generally used to translate the Hebrew word *nabi*, which is probably best understood as meaning "someone who speaks for another," or perhaps "a representative." The phenomenon of prophecy was widespread in the ancient Near East, not restricted to the "prophets of the Lord." The Old Testament refers to a number of "prophets of Baal" – charismatic individuals who claimed to act or speak on behalf of the Canaanite deity Baal. Early prophets of importance include Elijah and Elisha, both of whom were active during the ninth century BC. However, the most important period of prophetic activity focuses on the eighth to the sixth centuries BC and deals with the will of the Lord for Israel during a period of enormous political turbulence, which arose from the increasing power of Assyria and Babylonia. Prophets such as Jeremiah proclaimed a coming period of exile, which would be both a punishment for the past sins of the people and an opportunity for them to renew their religious practices and beliefs. After the period of exile in Babylon, post-exilic prophets such as Haggai and Malachi address some of the issues that came to be of importance as the returning exiles attempted to restore Jerusalem and its temple.

The prophets of Israel were seen as affirming the Lord's continued commitment to and presence within Israel. Yet, with the ending of the classic period of prophecy, the Holy Spirit seemed to have ceased to operate. God came to be viewed in distant and remote terms. No longer was the "voice of God" heard within Israel. Even the most senior rabbis (or "teachers") could expect to catch nothing more than an echo of the voice of God – an idea that was expressed in the technical phrase *bath qol* (literally, "the daughter of the voice"). The enormous interest in both John the Baptist and Jesus of Nazareth partly reflects this concern. Might the coming of these two figures signal the renewal of prophecy and the restoration of Israel? The account of the baptism of Jesus (see Mark 1: 10–11) clearly indicates that the coming of Jesus marks the inauguration of a period of renewed divine activity and presence.

Exile and restoration

One of the most important events recounted in the Old Testament is the exile of Jerusalem to Babylon in 586 BC. In 605 BC the Babylonian Emperor Nebuchadnezzar defeated the massed Egyptian armies at Carchemish, establishing Babylon as the leading military and political power in the region. Along with many other territories in this region, the land of Judah became subject to Babylonian rule, possibly in 604 BC.

Jehoiakim rebelled against Babylon. He may have been encouraged in this move by a successful Egyptian counterattack against Babylon in 601, which may have seemed to suggest that Babylon's power was on the wane. It was a serious misjudgment. Judah was invaded by Babylonian forces, and Jerusalem was besieged. The king, the royal family, and the circle of royal advisors gave themselves up to the besieging forces early in 597 BC. They were deported to Babylon, along with several thousands of captives. A failed rebellion a few years later led to the deportation of most of the population of Jerusalem to Babylon. Jerusalem was left unpopulated and vulnerable, its temple desecrated.

The prophets of Israel interpreted this period of exile in the first place as a judgment against Judah, on account of its lapse into pagan religious beliefs and practices; and, in the second, as a period of national repentance and renewal that would lead to the restoration of a resurgent people of God. Following the conquest of Babylon in 539 BC by Cyrus, king of Persia (559–530 BC), the exiled inhabitants of Judaea were allowed to return to their homeland.

The return of the deported inhabitants of Jerusalem to their home city after decades of exile was seen by Old Testament writers as a demonstration of the faithfulness of the Lord and as an

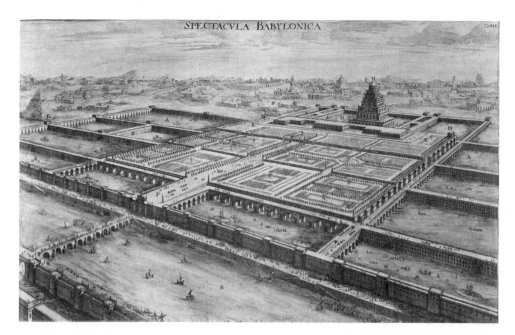

Figure 2.2 The Hanging Gardens of Babylon, one of the greatest wonders of the Ancient World, after Johann Bernhard Fischer von Erlach, c. 1700. Source: AKG Images.

Box 2.3 How to refer to passages in the Bible

How do you identify the biblical passage you want to study or talk about? To make this as easy as possible, a kind of shorthand way of referring to biblical passages has evolved over the centuries. To locate a verse in the Bible, you need to identify three things: the *book* of the Bible; the *chapter* of that book; and the *verse* of that chapter. To make sure you understand this, turn to the Acts of the Apostles, chapter 27, verse 1. What is the name of the centurion mentioned in this verse? If your answer is not "Julius," check your reference again. Now try turning to Paul's letter to the Romans, chapter 16, verse 5. Who was the first convert to Christ in Asia? If you answer is not "Epenetus," check it again.

The above system is potentially cumbersome. Writing out everything – as in "Paul's letter to the Romans, chapter 16, verse 5" – takes up too much space. So this entire formula is abbreviated as follows: Rom 16: 5. This is the standard form of reference, and it has the following features:

1   an abbreviation of the name of book of the Bible being referred to, usually two or three letters in length (such as 1Ki for "1 Kings," Mt for "Matthew," or 1Co for "1 Corinthians");
2   the number of the chapter of that book, usually followed by a colon (:) or a full stop (.);
3   the number of the verse in that chapter.

There is no need to identify the writer of the book (such as Paul) or to state whether it is found in the Old or New Testament. All that is needed is these three parameters.

Having got used to referring to individual verses, we now need to explore how to refer to a passage of more than one verse. This is very simple. The reference "Mt 3: 13–17" points to the passage that begins at Mt 3: 13 and ends at Mt 3: 17. To indicate a passage within a single chapter of a biblical book, you need only include in the span the opening and the closing verse; the chapter itself is mentioned just once. But sometimes the passage will contain material from two or more chapters. In that case the numbers of the straddled chapters will feature on both sides of the dash. Here is an example of this kind: 1Th 4: 13–5: 11. This is a reference to a passage that begins at 1Th 4: 13 and ends at 1Th 5: 11.

Now that you are familiar with the basic aspects of this system, there are some minor points that need qualifying. First, some biblical books are so brief that they consist only of one chapter (Obadiah; Philemon; 2 John; 3 John; Jude). In this case, only the verse number is cited. Thus Phm 2 is a reference to the second verse of Philemon. Second, individual Psalms are treated as chapters of the Psalter. Thus a reference to Ps 23: 1 is a reference to the first verse of the twenty-third Psalm.

Finally, you will find that this system is not always followed in older books. Roman numerals, superscript numbers, and all kinds of punctuation may be used. To give you an idea of the variety, here are several such stylistic variants in the way of referring to Paul's second letter to the Corinthians, chapter 13, verse 14:

2Co 13: 14	II Cor. xiii.14	2 Cor 13.14	*II Cor* 13.14

affirmation of the repentance of the people of God. The temple was rebuilt and the religious cult re-established. The post-exilic writings of the Old Testament are notable for their emphasis on the need to maintain racial and religious purity and for the importance they attach to religious festivals as national events. Jerusalem had no king; the temple and its priests gradually came to assume most of the roles of the monarchy, including responsibility for civil matters.

The term "Jews" now began to be used to refer to the returned exiles (see, for example, Ezra 4: 23, 5: 1). Up until this time, the people of God had been referred to as "Israelites" or "Judahites." The term "Jew" comes to be used in the post-exilic period to designate the people of God, and will be used regularly in later writings for this purpose.

The New Testament

The New Testament consists of 27 books, which can be classified into a number of different categories – such as "gospels" and "letters." Their common theme is the identity and significance of Jesus, and this includes the practical and ethical implications of following him. Christians were proclaiming the words and actions of Jesus almost immediately after his death. Christian churches were being established in the eastern Mediterranean within a matter of years. The earliest written documents in the New Testament take the form of letters sent by prominent Christians to these churches. Yet the preaching of the words and deeds of Jesus went on in the background. It was only at a later stage, probably in the early AD sixties, that the words and deeds of Jesus were committed to writing, in the form that we now know as "the gospels." We shall begin our study of the New Testament by examining these works.

The gospels

The English word "gospel" comes from an Old English word *godspel* meaning "good news," which was used to translate the Greek word *euangelion*. The word "gospel" is used in two different senses within Christianity. First, it refers to events that center on Jesus of Nazareth, which are seen as being good news for the world. The gospel is primarily the "good news" of the coming of Jesus of Nazareth, with all that this has to offer humanity.

Box 2.4   The books of the New Testament

BOOK	ABBREVIATION
Matthew	Mt
Mark	Mk
Luke	Lk
John	Jn
Acts	Ac
Romans	Rom
1 Corinthians	1Co
2 Corinthians	2Co
Galatians	Gal
Ephesians	Eph
Colossians	Col
1 Thessalonians	1Th
2 Thessalonians	2Th
1 Timothy	1Ti
2 Timothy	2Ti
Titus	Tit
Philemon	Phm
Hebrews	Heb
James	Jas
1 Peter	1Pe
2 Peter	2Pe
1 John	1Jn
2 John	2Jn
3 John	3Jn
Jude	Jud
Revelation	Rev

The term is also used in a secondary and derivative sense, to refer, en bloc, to the four writings that open the New Testament – Matthew, Mark, Luke, and John – and focus on the life, death, and resurrection of Jesus of Nazareth ("the gospel"). Strictly speaking, these books should be referred to as "the gospel according to Matthew," "the gospel according to Luke," and so on – as they sometimes are. This mode of reference makes it clear that it is always the same "gospel" or "good news" that is being described, despite the different styles and approaches of the compilers of each of these four works.

The four "gospels" are best understood as four distinct yet complementary portraits of Jesus, seen from different angles and drawing on various sources. The first three share many features and are widely regarded as drawing on common sources in circulation within early Christian circles.

The gospel writers were not biographers – or even historians – by our standards, nor were they interested in providing a comprehensive account of everything that Jesus said and did. The gospel's accounts of Jesus clearly contain a solid base of historical information. Nevertheless, this is linked with an *interpretation* of this information. Biography and theology are interwoven to such an extent that they can no longer be separated. The early Christians were convinced that Jesus was the Messiah, the Son of God, and their savior; and they believed that these conclusions should be passed on to their readers along with any

Figure 2.3   The gospel of Mark: a manuscript illumination from the Lindisfarne Gospels, c. 698–700. Manuscript illumination, Irish–Northumbrian, c. 698/700. Mark the Evangelist. From the Lindisfarne Gospels, written and illuminated by Bishop Eadfrith in Lindisfarne monastery. Source: British Library/AKG Images.

biographical details that helped cast light on them. For this reason, fact and interpretation are thoroughly intermingled in the gospels. To tell the story of Jesus involved explaining who he was and why he was so important. Interpretation of the significance of Jesus is therefore found alongside the historical material that is the basis of these theological conclusions.

The gospels were not written by Jesus himself, nor do they date from his lifetime. It is generally thought that Jesus was crucified around AD 30–33, and that the earliest gospel (probably Mark) dates from about AD 65. There is probably a gap of about thirty years between the time at which the events described in the gospels took place and the time at which they were first written down in the form of a gospel. By classical standards, this was a relatively short time. The Buddha, for example, had one thing in common with Jesus: he wrote nothing. Yet the definitive collection of his sayings (the Tripitaka) is thought to date from around four centuries after his death – more than ten times the interval between the death of Jesus and the appearance of the first gospel.

Even before Mark's gospel was written, Christians were committed to writing down their understanding of the importance of Jesus of Nazareth. The New Testament letters date mainly from the period AD 49–69 and provide confirmation of the importance of Jesus – as well as of interpretative work around him – in this formative period.

Some may find this gap of about thirty years puzzling. Why were these things not written down immediately? Might people not forget what Jesus said and did, or what happened at the crucifixion and resurrection? It is difficult for twentieth-century readers, who are so used to information being recorded in written or other visual form, to appreciate that the classical world – and this extends also to the archaic, Hellenistic, and late antique periods – communicated a lot more than us by means of the spoken word. The great Homeric epics, almost one thousand years before Jesus, are good examples of the way in which stories were passed on with remarkable accuracy from one generation to another. If there is one ability that modern westerners have probably lost, it is the ability to remember a story or narrative as it is told, and then to pass it on to others.

Studies of traditional cultures, including the period of the New Testament, have shown how the passing down of stories from one generation to another was characteristic of the entire premodern era. Indeed there are excellent grounds for arguing that early educational systems were based upon learning by rote. The fact that most people in the West today find it difficult to commit even one narrative to memory naturally tends to prejudice them against believing that anyone could ever do it. Yet the recitation of narratives that were held to be important to a community's history or understanding of its own identity appears to have been routine in more traditional cultures.

The period between the death of Jesus of Nazareth and the writing of the first gospel is usually referred to as the "period of oral tradition," meaning the period in which accounts of Jesus' birth, life, and death, as well as his teaching, were passed down with remarkable accuracy from one generation to another. In this period it seems that certain of Jesus' sayings and certain aspects of his life, especially those connected to his death and resurrection, were singled out as being of particular importance and were passed down from the first Christians to those who followed them. Other things were not passed down and have been lost forever. The early Christians seem to have identified what was essential and what was not in Jesus' words, deeds, and fate and transmitted to us only what pertained to the former class.

The period of oral tradition may thus be regarded as a period of sifting, in which the first Christians assessed the data and decided what needed to be set down for those who followed them. In this process of transmission, some of Jesus' sayings may have become detached from their original context and perhaps on occasion even acquired a new one, as a result of the uses to which the first Christians put them – which were, in the main, to proclaim the gospel to those outside the early community of faith and to deepen and inform the faith of those inside it.

The gospel of John – sometimes referred to as the "Fourth Gospel," in order to emphasize its distinct literary character – differs from the three synoptic gospels in several respects. Probably written in Asia Minor around AD 90, this gospel does not include much of the teaching of Jesus of Nazareth found in the synoptic gospels – such as the parables of the kingdom, or the Lord's Prayer. Some scholars suggest that the work is structured around seven "signs," pointing to the true identity and significance of Jesus.

Some other works purporting to be gospels were in circulation in the early church. These are generally regarded as originating from groups with particular agendas. The gospel of Judas, for example, is a relatively late document, almost certainly originating from a marginalized sect within Christianity that was convinced that everyone else had got Jesus of Nazareth seriously wrong. No documentary evidence within the body of literature accepted by Christians as authoritative at the time (and that body included some works that never made it into the New Testament canon) supported the case that this particular group wished to make. Its members remedied this situation by writing their own gospel. Only Judas *really* understood Jesus, we are told; the other disciples got him wrong and passed on hopelessly muddled accounts of his significance.

The gospel of Judas portrays Jesus of Nazareth as a spiritual guru similar to the gnostic teachers of the second and third centuries; this portrait bears little relation to the one found in the synoptic gospels. Christianity becomes a kind of mystery cult, in which Jesus of Nazareth has been reinvented as a gnostic teacher with gnostic ideas. The gospel of Judas has indeed the potential to illuminate our understanding of gnosticism in the mid-second century and beyond, especially its often noted parasitic relationship with existing worldviews. But it seems to have nothing historically credible to tell us of the origins of Christianity or of the identity of Jesus of Nazareth.

The New Testament letters

The New Testament includes a series of letters written to individuals or churches by leading figures of the early church. These letters often clarify points of Christian doctrine and practice and offer encouragement to Christians in the face of hostility from other religious groupings or from the secular authorities. It is clear, for example, that Christianity was subject to various forms of harassment from Jews in the first decades of its existence. It must be remembered that, for much of the first century, Christianity was numerically very weak and was often forced to hold its meetings in secret, for fear of persecution from the local Roman authorities. In particular, the reigns of Nero and Domitian witnessed concerted efforts to eliminate the growing Christian church; some documents in the New Testament are written in the face of this kind of situation.

By far the largest collection of letters in the New Testament is attributed to Apostle Paul. According to the New Testament, Paul (initially known as "Saul") was a Jew and a native of Tarsus, the capital city of the Roman province of Cilicia, who had been hostile toward Christianity to begin with and had approved of Jewish attempts to suppress it. Then Paul underwent a dramatic conversion while on the road to Damascus (Acts 9: 1–31), and this led to his becoming one of the early Christian movement's most important advocates. His Jewish origins are reflected in the seriousness with which he engaged the question of Christianity's relation to Judaism.

Some scholars ask whether all the letters attributed to Paul in the New Testament were actually written by him. The letters to the Ephesians and Colossians show stylistic differences from Paul's earlier writings, which, some suggest, would point to a different author. Others suggest that Paul's style may have changed over time, or that these letters were written on behalf of Paul – or perhaps dictated by him – with occasional interpolations.

During the course of his three missionary journeys in Southeastern Europe, Paul established a number of small Christian groups in Asia Minor, Macedonia, and Greece. He subsequently remained in touch with some of them, by letter. Not all of these letters have survived; Paul himself makes reference to other letters to the church at Corinth and to a letter to the church at Laodicea. The use of the term "church" here is potentially misleading; early Christians did not meet in buildings designated as "churches," they gathered in secret in small groups. The word "church" is probably better translated as "congregation" or "gathering" in this context. Paul's early letters are often concerned with matters of doctrine, particularly the second coming of Christ and the relation between Jews and Gentiles. The later letters reflect the increasing importance of church order and structure, as Christianity was growing into a permanent presence in the eastern Mediterranean region.

The fixing of the New Testament canon

The Christian Bible is a collection of 66 books, of which 39 are found in the Old Testament and 27 in the New Testament. But how were the contents of the Bible decided upon? By what process were the 66 books of the Bible selected? At a fairly early stage in its history, the Christian church had to make some important decisions as to what "Scripture" actually designated. The patristic period witnessed a process of decision making in which limits to the New Testament were laid down – a process usually known as "the fixing of the canon."

The technical term "canon" derives from the Greek word *kanōn*, meaning "rule," "standard," or "fixed reference point." The phrase "the canon of Scripture" thus refers to a limited and defined group of writings that are accepted as authoritative within the Christian church. The term "canonical" is used to refer to scriptural writings accepted to be within the canon. Thus the Gospel of Luke is considered "canonical," whereas the Gospel of Thomas is considered "extra-canonical" (that is, lying outside the canon of Scripture).

However, within a short period, early Christian writers (such as Justin Martyr) were referring to "the New Testament" (to be contrasted with the "Old Testament") and insisting that both were to be treated with equal authority. By the late second century, when Irenaeus was writing, it was generally accepted that there were four canonical gospels, and there was a widespread consensus that these four gospels, together with Acts and various letters, had the status of inspired Scripture. Thus Clement of Alexandria recognized four gospels, Acts, 14 letters of Paul (the letter to the Hebrews being regarded as Pauline), and Revelation; and Tertullian in the early third century declared that alongside the "law and the prophets" were the "evangelical and apostolic writings," which were both to be regarded as authoritative within the church.

Gradually agreement was reached on the list of books that were recognized as inspired Scripture and on the order in which they were to be arranged. This process of reception did not involve the arbitrary authoritarian imposition of the views of influential bishops or churches. It was a gradual process of reflection and consultation, in which a consensus as to which writings were to be regarded as authentic and helpful gradually emerged within Christian communities. In AD 367 the influential Greek Christian writer Athanasius circulated a letter that summed up this consensus by identifying the 27 books of the New Testament (as we now know it) as being canonical. Athanasius was not imposing his own views at this point but reporting the views of the church as a whole – views that he clearly expected his readers to take very seriously. Christianity has always stressed the importance of the *consensus fidelium* ("agreement of the faithful"), and the formation of the canon is an excellent example of this gradual movement toward the emergence of such a consensus within the Christian movement throughout the Mediterranean area.

A number of criteria played a role in deciding whether a given writing was to be accepted as "canonical" or not. Three of the most important considerations in evaluating claims to canonicity of writings were:

1 *Their apostolic origins or connections* Were they to be attributed to, or based upon, the preaching and teaching of the first generation of apostles or those in their immediate circle? Some were clearly works of the apostles – for instance the letters of Peter and Paul. In other cases, such as the letter to the Hebrews, things were not quite so straightforward. This criterion was of major importance in the second century, when the church had to defend itself in the face of attacks from various groups, each claiming to have an "authoritative" revelation of its own.

2 *The extent to which they had secured general acceptance within Christian communities throughout the region* Individual churches were moving toward agreement as to which texts were to be regarded as authoritative. While there were inevitably disagreements over certain texts, the process of fixing the canon can be seen as "crystallizing" this consensus. Eusebius of Caesarea, who wrote in the early part of the fourth century, no longer used the criterion of apostolic authority, which had been so important to writers of the second century. For Eusebius, the issue was the reception of a book. In other words, was the book quoted by early and "orthodox" church fathers? The debate had clearly moved on – namely from apostolic credentials to reception within the global Christian community.

3 *The extent to which they were used in the liturgy* One of the main uses of the Bible was in Christian worship. An important criterion for canonicity was thus the extent to which a book was used liturgically – that is, read publicly when early Christian communities gathered for worship. This practice is already referred to in the New Testament: "And when this letter has been read among you, have it read also in the church of the Laodiceans; and see that you read also the letter from Laodicea" (Colossians 4: 16).

This process of determining the canonical works of the New Testament was not always an easy or straightforward one. There was debate, especially around a number of books. The western church had hesitations about including the letter to the Hebrews, because it was not specifically attributed to an apostle; the eastern church had reservations about the book of Revelation (sometimes also referred to as "the Apocalypse"). Four of the smaller books (2 Peter, 2 and 3 John, and Jude) were often omitted from early lists of New Testament writings. Some writings, which are now outside the canon, were regarded favorably within some sections of the church, although they ultimately failed to gain universal acceptance as canonical. Examples include the first letter of Clement, an early bishop of Rome who wrote around AD 96, and the *Didache*, a short early Christian manual on morals and church practices probably dating from the first quarter of the second century.

The arrangement of the material was also subject to considerable variation. Agreement was reached at an early stage that the gospels should have the place of honor within the canon, being followed by the Acts of the Apostles. The eastern church tended to place the seven "catholic epistles" or "general letters" (that is, James, 1 and 2; Peter, 1, 2 and 3; John; and Jude) before the 14 Pauline letters (Hebrews being accepted as Pauline), whereas the western church placed Paul's letters immediately after Acts and made the catholic letters follow them.

The Christian Understanding of the Relation of the Old and New Testaments

Texts are open to multiple interpretations. Christianity offers a specific reading of the Old Testament, which differs from that offered by Jewish readers and scholars. This is reflected in many ways, including in the understanding of the phrase "Old Testament" itself. As we noted in an earlier section, early Christians used this phrase to express the theological framework within which these texts were to be read. History was divided into the periods of the "Old Covenant" between God and Israel and the "New Covenant" between God and all of humanity. The Christian notions of an "Old Testament" and a "New Testament" are strongly theological in nature, in that they express the belief that the contents of the Old Testament belong to a period of God's dealings with the world that has been fulfilled through the coming of Christ in the New Testament.

From a Christian perspective, the collection of writings described as the "Old Testament" refers to the history of God's actions in the world – actions undertaken in preparation for the coming of Jesus Christ. Christians regard the New Testament as an extension of the same pattern of divine activity and presence as that declared in the Old, so that the New Testament both *continues* and *extends* the witness to the words and deeds of the God of Israel.

This way of thinking is reflected in the New Testament. New Testament writers clearly saw themselves as continuing the history of salvation narrated in the Old Testament. Matthew's gospel, for example, brings out the continuity between Jesus and Moses, the gospel and the Law, and the church and Israel. Paul's letters often focus on the continuity between the faith of Christians and that of Abraham. The letter to the Hebrews provides what is virtually a point by point comparison between Christianity and Judaism, stressing both the continuity between them and the way in which Christianity brings to perfection the themes of the Old Testament.

The coming of Jesus of Nazareth is thus seen as fulfilling the hopes of the people of Israel. Jesus did not come to abolish the Law or the Prophets but to fulfill it (Matthew 5: 17). This helps us understand the extraordinary amount of engagement with the Old Testament that we find in the New Testament. On a conservative reading of the New Testament, there are at least 300 specific references to texts from the Old Testament, and more than 2,000 allusions to Old Testament texts or themes.

Yet, despite this emphasis on continuity with the old covenant, the New Testament understands the coming of Jesus of Nazareth as inaugurating something *new*. For example, full membership of the people of God is no longer considered to be determined by a person's ethnic origins but by his or her faith. Race no longer determines religious identity; Jews and Gentiles have equal status within the people of God, on the basis of their faith and common possession of the Holy Spirit. Similarly, the food laws and cultic observances of the Old Testament are no longer regarded as binding on Christians, because Christ has fulfilled the demands of the law and has declared all foods to be clean.

New Testament writers did not see these developments as a distortion of the meaning or intention of the Old Testament; rather they saw them as its intended outcome. Paul's letters are of particular importance in developing this theme. For example, Paul argues that the Old Testament understands Abraham as the father of all those who believe, not just as a patriarch of Israel (Romans 4: 9–17; Galatians 3: 6–9). Fulfillment of the proper intention of the Old Testament required cultic, theological, and spiritual redirection. Christianity thus provided a framework for the rereading of the Old Testament, allowing its proper meaning to be discerned and implemented.

Not all Christians were happy with this close relationship between the Christian faith and Judaism. The second-century writer Marcion of Sinope, who was excommunicated in the year 144, argued that the Old Testament concerned a religion that had nothing to do with Christianity. According to Marcion, Christianity was a religion of love that had no place whatsoever for law. The Old Testament relates to a different god than the New; the Old Testament's god, who merely created the world, was obsessed with the idea of law and seemed predisposed to use violence excessively. The New Testament's god, however, redeemed the world and was concerned with love. Marcion argued that Jesus of Nazareth came in order to depose the Old Testament's god and usher in the worship of the true God of grace. A similar teaching was associated with the Manicheans, who had a significant influence on the leading Christian writer Augustine of Hippo (354–430) during his younger period.

In refuting the Manichean view of the Old Testament as an embarrassment or irrelevance, Augustine argued that it was necessary to see the Old Testament in the light of the New in order to appreciate its full significance and importance for Christians. Augustine's views are set out succinctly in his famous dictum: "The New Testament lies hidden in the Old, and the Old Testament is unveiled in the New." Gregory the Great took this a stage further, remarking that "the Old Testament is a prophecy of the New Testament; and the best commentary on the Old Testament is the New Testament."

The majority position within Christian theology has followed Augustine and Gregory. On the one hand, it emphasizes the *continuity* between the two testaments; on the other, it notes the *distinction* between them. The *Catechism of the Catholic Church* (1992) provides a particularly clear statement of this approach, drawing as it does on the idea of a "typological" reading of the Old Testament. A "type" (Greek *tupos*) is a person, thing, or action that precedes and prefigures a greater person, thing, or action – such as the coming of Jesus Christ.

> The Church, as early as apostolic times, and then constantly in her Tradition, has illuminated the unity of the divine plan in the two Testaments through typology, which discerns in God's works of the Old Covenant prefigurations of what he accomplished in the fullness of time in the person of his incarnate Son. Christians therefore read the Old Testament in the light of Christ crucified and risen. Such typological reading discloses the inexhaustible content of the Old Testament; but it must not make us forget that the Old Testament retains its own intrinsic value as revelation reaffirmed by our Lord himself.

The Translation of the Bible

The Bible is written in the classical languages of the ancient world – Hebrew, Greek, and, to very limited extent, Aramaic. So what is a modern western reader of the Bible, unable to read any of these languages, meant to do? Unlike the Muslim Qu'ran, which, as tradition insists, should be read in the original classical Arabic language, the Bible, as most Christians accept, can be published and read in the language that ordinary people can understand. In the twenty-first century most Christian denominations have produced vernacular translations of the Bible for their members, aiming to render the original biblical texts in accessible and engaging ways.

This process can be illustrated from most modern European languages and is especially important in the case of English. Although demands for the Bible to be translated into the vernacular became particularly significant in the sixteenth century, they can be traced back much further. One of those who pressed most vigorously for an English version of the Bible in the fourteenth century was John Wycliffe (c. 1330–1384), widely hailed as a champion of biblical translation. Wycliffe argued that the English people had a right to read the Bible in their own language rather than be forced to listen to what their clergy wished them to hear in Latin – the language of the church, which ordinary people did not understand. As Wycliffe pointed out, the ecclesiastical establishment had considerable vested interests in not allowing the laity access to the Bible. Its members might even discover that there was a massive discrepancy between the lifestyles of bishops and clergy and those commended – and practiced! – by Jesus of Nazareth and the apostles.

In practice, one of the most influential biblical translations of the Middle Ages was the "Vulgate" – a Latin translation of both the Old and New Testaments, which was finalized in the twelfth century. Latin was at the time the language used by the church and scholars throughout Western Europe. As a result, this translation achieved considerable influence, even though it is now known to be inaccurate at several points.

As it happens, the translations that Wycliffe inspired – we are not sure how much translation work he himself actually carried out – were not based on the original Greek and Hebrew texts of the Bible, but on this standard medieval "Vulgate." In other words Wycliffe was translating into English a Latin translation. But what if the Vulgate translation was inaccurate?

This question came to be of considerable importance during the sixteenth century, when the famous scholar Erasmus of Rotterdam criticized the inaccuracy of the Vulgate. Erasmus pointed out that this version translated the opening words of Jesus' ministry (Matthew 4: 17) as "do penance, for the Kingdom of heaven is at hand." The translation suggested that the coming of the kingdom of heaven had a direct connection with the sacrament of penance. Erasmus pointed out that the Greek text should be translated as "repent, for the Kingdom of heaven is at hand." Where the Vulgate seemed to refer to an outward practice (the sacrament of penance), Erasmus insisted that the text spoke of an inward psychological attitude – that of "being repentant."

These demands were taken up again by Martin Luther in the 1520s. Luther insisted that lay people should have the right to read and interpret the Bible for themselves. Why did the Bible have to be locked away from the people, imprisoned in the fetters of a dead language that only a charmed circle could read? Why could not educated lay people be allowed to read the Bible for themselves, in their own languages? Having realized the need for such a translation, Luther decided that the task was too important to leave to anyone else. He would do it himself – and he translated the New Testament directly from the original Greek into everyday German.

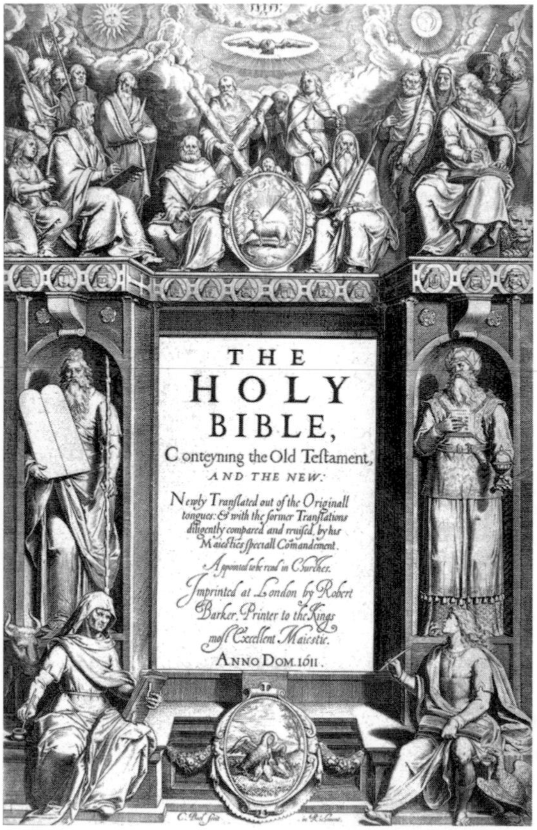

William Tyndale followed Luther's lead and published the first English translation of the New Testament directly from the original Greek text; he did so anonymously, in 1526. Although Tyndale had hopes to translate the entire Bible into English, he managed only a few Old Testament books – from Hebrew. In the event, the first English translation of the complete Bible to be printed – the Coverdale Bible – appeared in 1535. It was followed by the more accurate Matthews Bible of 1537 and by the Great Bible of 1539. In 1560, a group of English émigrés based in Calvin's city of Geneva produced a particularly good translation, accompanied by illustrations and marginal notes. This rapidly became the favorite Bible of English-speaking Protestants.

However, the world's best-known English translation of the Bible dates from the early seventeenth century. In 1604 James I commissioned a new translation. More than fifty scholars were assembled for the task, working at Westminster, Oxford, and Cambridge. In 1611 the fruit of their labors was finally published. This new translation – generally known as the "Authorized Version" or the "King James Version" of the Bible – would achieve the status of a classic, becoming the standard and most widely used English translation of the Bible until the end of World War I in 1918.

Figure 2.4 The frontispiece to the King James Bible of 1611, widely regarded as the most influential English translation of the Bible. *The Holy Bible*, published by Robert Barker, 1611. Source: Alamy.

The King James Version of the Bible was an outstanding translation by the standards of 1611 and beyond. Yet translations eventually require revision – not necessarily because they are defective, but because the language itself into which they are made changes over time. Translation involves aiming at a moving target, which has accelerated over the centuries. English is developing more quickly today than at any time in its previous history. Some words have ceased to be used; others have changed their meanings. Many words used by King James's translators have now changed their meaning. Their version can be misleading, simply because the English of 1611 is not the English of the twenty-first century. For example, consider the sentence: "For this we say unto you by the word of the Lord, that we which are alive and remain unto the coming of the Lord shall not prevent them which are asleep" (1 Thessalonians 4: 15). A modern reader would find this puzzling, mostly because the 1611 meaning of the word "prevent" does not correspond to its modern sense. For King James's translators, "prevent" meant what we now understand by "precede" or "go before" – not "hinder," which is the modern sense of "prevent." Given the fact that linguistic change such as this means that the King James Bible has the potential to mislead and confuse, there is a clear case for revising the translation. The extent of that revision is a matter for discussion; the need is beyond doubt. When a translation requires explanation, it has ceased to function as a working translation.

There is no difficulty here. All living languages, including English, change over the years. Linguistic development is simply a sign of life – it means that a language is being used and adapted to new situations. The task of translating is ongoing, not completed once and for all. Any modern translation of the Bible – whether into English, Swahili, or Mandarin – must be seen as provisional, requiring amendment as the language undergoes change and development. Translation is a never-ending task.

Debates over the correct translation of the Bible continue to this day. Yet there are other debates within Christianity over how to use the Bible. One of the most important of these discussions concerns whether the Bible stands on its own or needs to be read in the light of "tradition." In what follows we shall consider this matter further.

The Bible and Tradition

A series of controversies in the early church brought home the importance of the concept of tradition. The word "tradition" comes from the Latin term *traditio*, which means "handing over," "handing down," or "handing on." It is a thoroughly biblical idea; we find St. Paul reminding his readers that he was handing on to them core teachings of the Christian faith that he himself had received from other people (1 Corinthians 15: 1–4).

The term "tradition" can refer both to the action of passing teachings on to others – something that, Paul insists, must be done within the church – and to the body of teachings that are passed on in this manner. Tradition can thus be understood as a process as well as as a body of teaching. In particular, the Pastoral Epistles – three later New Testament letters that are particularly concerned with questions of church structure and with the transmission of Christian teaching (1 Timothy, 2 Timothy, and Titus) – stress the importance of "guarding the good deposit which was entrusted to you" (2 Timothy 1: 14). The New Testament also uses the notion of "tradition" in a negative sense, meaning something like "human ideas and practices that are not divinely authorized." Thus Jesus of Nazareth was openly critical of certain human traditions within Judaism (e.g., see Matthew 15: 1–6; Mark 7: 13).

The importance of the idea of tradition first became obvious in a gnostic controversy that broke out during the second century. The controversy centered on a number of questions, including how salvation was to be achieved. (The word "gnostic" derives from the Greek noun *gnōsis*, "knowledge," and refers to belief in certain secret ideas that had to be known in order for individuals to secure salvation.) Christian writers found themselves having to deal with some highly unusual and creative interpretations of the Bible. How were they to deal with these? If the Bible was to be regarded as authoritative, was every interpretation of it to be treated as of equal value with any other?

Irenaeus of Lyons (c. 130–c. 200), one of the church's greatest early theologians, did not think so. The question of how the Bible was to be interpreted was of the greatest importance. Heretics, he argued, interpreted the Bible after their own taste. Orthodox believers, in contrast, interpreted the Bible in ways that their apostolic authors would have approved. The apostles passed on to their successors both the biblical texts and a certain way of reading and understanding them.

> Everyone who wishes to perceive the truth should consider the apostolic tradition, which has been made known in every church in the entire world. We are able to number those who are bishops appointed by the apostles, and their successors in the churches to the present day, who taught and knew nothing of such things as these people imagine.

Irenaeus' point is that a continuous stream of Christian teaching, life, and interpretation can be traced from the time of the apostles to his own period. The church is able to point to those who have maintained the teaching of the church, and to standard public creeds that set out the main lines of Christian belief. Tradition is thus the guarantor of faithfulness to the original apostolic teaching and a safeguard against innovations and misrepresentations of biblical texts such as the gnostics would introduce.

This development is of major importance, as it underlies the emergence of "creeds" – public, authoritative statements of the basic points of the Christian faith, which are based upon the Bible but avoid maverick interpretations of biblical material. The creeds thus provide a framework – a "rule of faith" (*regula fidei* in Latin) – setting out the right interpretation of the Bible. Their emergence was stimulated by two important factors:

1 the need for public statements of faith that represented the church's interpretation of the Bible and could be used in teaching and in defending the Christian faith against misrepresentations;
2 the need for personal "confessions of faith" at the time of baptism.

We have already touched on the first point; the second needs further exploration. It is known that the early church attached special importance to the baptism of new members. In the third and fourth centuries, a definite pattern of instruction and baptism developed: new members of the church were instructed in the basics of the Christian faith during the period of Lent and baptized on Easter Day. These new members of the church were asked to confirm their faith by assenting to key statements of Christian belief.

According to the *Apostolic Tradition*, a work written by Hippolytus of Rome (died c. 236) in the early years of the third century, three questions were put to each baptismal candidate: "Do you believe in God, the Father Almighty? Do you believe in Jesus Christ, our Savior? Do you believe in the Holy Spirit, the holy church, and the forgiveness of sins?" As time went on, these questions were gradually changed into a statement of faith, which each candidate was asked to make.

The most important creed to emerge from these "baptismal creeds" is the Apostles' Creed, which is widely used in Christian worship today. Traditionally this creed is set out as twelve statements, each of which is attributed to one of the twelve apostles. Although it is now widely agreed that this creed was not actually written by the apostles themselves, it is nevertheless "apostolic" in the sense that it contains the main ideas of the Christian faith that the church received from the apostles. The Apostles' Creed offers a very convenient summary of some of the main topics of the Christian faith, and we shall use it as a basis for our discussion of the leading beliefs of Christianity in the following chapter.

3

Christian Creeds and Beliefs

Christianity is not simply about religious and devotional practices, or about the cultivation of ethical behavior. It is also about a "big picture" of reality – an understanding of God, the world, and human identity and purpose. While individual Christians generally understand this "big picture" in different ways, there is a clear family resemblance between their outlooks. This way of understanding the world is usually framed in terms of "beliefs" or "doctrines" (from the Latin word *doctrina*, meaning "teaching," "body of beliefs/views"). In the present chapter we shall look at some of these Christian beliefs, including disagreements within Christianity on some matters of importance – for example, the nature of baptism or the identity of the church.

Some writers present Christian beliefs as if they were isolated ideas, disconnected from others. It is easy to see how this approach arises. Textbooks and lecture courses on Christian doctrines tend to deal with beliefs in separate chapters, creating the impression that each doctrine is like a hermetically sealed compartment. Yet it is important to realize that Christian doctrines are interconnected. Doctrines are not self-contained, watertight compartments, each one of which may be mastered without reference to anything else. They are more like a web with intersecting nodes.

For example, in thinking about the doctrine of creation, it is important to appreciate its interconnectedness with other leading themes of faith. To consider the Christian doctrine of creation leads into reflection on the nature of God, the identity of Jesus Christ, the role of the Holy Spirit, the nature of salvation, or sacramental theology – to mention just the more obvious themes; others can easily be added to these. There is a sense in which to study any single doctrinal theme is actually to study the whole web of faith, the grand narrative of the gospel or the big picture of faith, as it intersects at this node, or as it focuses on this theme.

Christianity: An Introduction, Third Edition. Alister E. McGrath.
© 2015 John Wiley & Sons, Ltd. Published 2015 by John Wiley & Sons, Ltd.

Faith is a principled conviction that a certain way of thinking is trustworthy, reliable, and relevant. It is a way of seeing things that cannot be proved to be right, yet proves to be reliable. Faith is about entering into this way of thinking and allowing it to become a way of living. It is about embracing a "big picture" of reality, which is capable of catching the imagination, illuminating the reason, and creating an ethical vision for how we should live in the world. What draws some people to Christianity is this "big picture," rather than the individual arguments that lead to it. While science takes things apart so that we can see how they work, faith puts them back together again, so that we can see what they mean.

This "big picture" of faith sketched in the creeds, amplified in theology textbooks, and applied in and through sermons helps to shape the Christian view of the world. Faith leads to the consequence that the Christian community of faith sees the world in its own distinct manner. The philosopher and social scientist Charles Taylor terms this kind of consequence a "social imaginary," understood as

> the ways people imagine their social existence, how they fit together with others, how things go on between them and their fellows, the expectations that are normally met, and the deeper normative notions and images that underlie these expectations.

In this chapter we shall present an overview of basic Christian beliefs. So where should we start? Perhaps the most obvious question to consider is why Christianity, in marked contrast with other major world religions, has creeds. So how did Christianity come to develop them? And why?

The Emergence of Creeds

Early Christian statements of faith were often very short – for example, the simple confession that "Jesus is Lord!" (Romans 10: 9; 1 Corinthians 12: 3). Yet the New Testament also contains a number of slightly longer creed-like statements, such as the following:

> There is one God, the Father, from whom are all things and for whom we exist, and one Lord, Jesus Christ, through whom are all things and through whom we exist. (1 Corinthians 8: 6)

> I handed on to you as of first importance what I in turn had received: that Christ died for our sins in accordance with the scriptures, and that he was buried, and that he was raised on the third day in accordance with the scriptures. (1 Corinthians 15: 3–4)

> [Jesus Christ] was revealed in flesh, vindicated in spirit, seen by angels, proclaimed among Gentiles, believed in throughout the world, taken up in glory. (1 Timothy 3: 16)

Yet these and other similar statements are scattered throughout the biblical texts and are not integrated into a greater whole. The creeds gather these threads together and express them in more systematic forms. These statements of faith were easily memorized through constant repetition in public worship or private instruction, allowing new Christians to confess and summarize their faith. They are an expression, not the cause, of faith. The early Christians regarded the creeds as being like ancient aqueducts – channels through which water is directed and flows, but not the life-giving water itself.

For the first three centuries Christians had to manage without any formal creeds. At that point Christianity was still an illegal religion within the Roman empire; believers were thus forced to meet in secret to worship. There was no way in which Christian leaders could meet together to discuss developing a common set of beliefs. The risk of arrest by the Roman authorities was simply too great. As a result, there were no agreed universal public norms of faith throughout the Christian world.

Yet a remarkable degree of consensus appears to have emerged within and across the Christian world of the late second century. For reasons that are not fully understood, Christians throughout the Roman empire were beginning to converge on a specific group of texts that they read aloud in public worship and regarded as authoritative in matters of life and thought, and on a set of basic shared beliefs. While there were local variations, collections of texts very similar to the modern New Testament and "confessions of faith" very similar to the modern Apostles' Creed (quoted in Box 3.1) were taking shape by about 190.

These collections of texts and "confessions of faith" were used by individual congregations and seem to have been spread primarily through the movement of Christians across imperial frontiers. The leaders of Christian communities in the metropolitan cities – such as Alexandria, Antioch, Jerusalem, and Rome – developed their own distinct ways of teaching the faith, and this gave rise to prototypes of the creeds. Those used in Rome were especially significant on account of the status of Rome as the Eternal City, the capital of the empire.

Given imperial hostility toward Christianity, admission to Christian worship was a serious and solemn matter in the first three centuries. New Christians were only admitted

---

Box 3.1   The Apostles' Creed

I believe in God, the Father Almighty,
creator of heaven and earth.

I believe in Jesus Christ, God's only Son, our Lord,
who was conceived by the Holy Spirit,
born of the Virgin Mary,
suffered under Pontius Pilate,
was crucified, died, and was buried;
he descended to the dead.
On the third day he rose again;
he ascended into heaven,
he is seated at the right hand of the Father,
and he will come to judge the living and the dead.

I believe in the Holy Spirit,
the holy catholic Church,
the communion of saints,
the forgiveness of sins,
the resurrection of the body,
and the life everlasting. Amen.

once they had been carefully vetted (they might, after all, be Roman spies) and thoroughly instructed in the basics of their faith. At their baptism, which marked formal admission into the Christian community, believers were asked to confirm their faith by responding to three questions:

1   Do you believe in God the Father Almighty?
2   Do you believe in Jesus Christ, the Son of God?
3   Do you believe in the Holy Spirit?

These questions were sometimes asked in more extended and elaborate forms; the basic threefold pattern, however, was widely used in both western and eastern churches. The answers given to these three questions were not seen as representing full accounts of the Christian faith, but simply as summaries of its most important themes. By answering "I believe" to each of these questions, the person who was about to be baptized was affirming her commitment to the overall Christian way of thinking rather than to three of its components.

From the end of the second century, documents that are clearly recognizable as having the form of creeds began to be used by leading churches and Christian leaders as convenient summaries of their personal and corporate faith. Although slightly different forms of words were used across the Christian world, their shared features are more obvious than their minor divergences. The Latin phrase *regula fidei* ("rule of faith") came to be widely used to refer to these statements. Tertullian (c. 160–c. 225), a Latin-speaking theologian writing in the late second and early third century, provided his own statement of this "rule of faith." Christians, Tertullian declared, believed

that there is one only God, the Creator of the world, who produced all things out of nothing through his own Word, who was sent forth first of all; that this Word is called his Son, and, under the name of God, was seen "in diverse manners" by the patriarchs, heard at all times in the prophets, was brought down by the Spirit and power of the Father into the Virgin Mary, was made flesh in her womb, and, being born of her, went forth as Jesus Christ; he then preached the new law and the new promise of the kingdom of heaven, and worked miracles; having been crucified, he rose again on the third day; having ascended into the heavens, he sat at the right hand of the Father; sent in his place the power of the Holy Spirit to guide those who believe; will come with glory to take the saints to the enjoyment of everlasting life and of the heavenly promises.

Although there are some obvious differences with what is later found in the Apostles' Creed, there are remarkable similarities between Tertullian's personal "rule of faith" and this later creed.

These "rules of faith" were adopted by individual churches and Christian leaders; they were not imposed upon them by any centralized authority. They commanded respect on account of their merits and were adopted and adapted over a period of several generations, until a degree of consensus emerged. The Apostles' Creed was the final outcome of a long process of reflection and refinement across the Christian world, a process leading to a "rule of faith" that commanded assent not on account of any external authority, but because of its internal qualities.

But why is this document known as the Apostles' Creed? What role did the apostles have in drawing it up? In the Middle Ages it was widely believed that this creed was written by the twelve apostles, each apostle contributing one of its short statements. This suggestion, which is found as early as the fourth century, is best regarded as a pious legend. Around AD 390, the Council of Milan referred to a "Symbolum apostolorum" ("Creed of the Apostles"), urging believers to recognize its importance and to use it as a summary of faith. There is no doubt that the material included in this creed is authentically apostolic, in that it is deeply rooted in the New Testament. Perhaps it might be referred to as the "Apostolic Creed" rather than "Apostles' Creed." Indeed, many earlier Christian writers used the Latin formula *symbolum apostolicum* to make this point.

So what of the Nicene Creed? To understand the development of this document, we need to appreciate Christianity's radical change in status in the early fourth century, as a result of the conversion of the Roman Emperor Constantine. We shall consider this matter in more detail in our discussion of early Christian history (pp. 129–131). Christianity was now a legal religion. Its laity and its leaders were no longer subject to any form of state harassment, victimization, or persecution. Christian worship no longer had to take place in secret. Christian leaders were free to meet and travel.

As Christianity moved toward becoming the state religion of the Roman empire, Constantine made it clear that he expected it to fulfill the functions of classical Roman religion – above all, by acting as a unifying force within the empire. Divisions within Christianity had to be sorted out, so that the church could offer the world a model of the unity that Constantine wished to see prevailing across his realm.

There were several debates within Christianity at this time, and one of them concerned the status of the great metropolitan bishops – in other words, the bishops of Rome, Alexandria, Antioch, Constantinople, and Jerusalem. Which of these bishops took priority within the empire? Who was the most senior bishop? And there were other divisions too, most notably over the best way of expressing the identity and significance of Jesus Christ.

Constantine wanted these issues sorted out, and he summoned a council of Christian bishops to express a consensual theological framework that would bring religious harmony to his empire. They met in AD 325 at the town of Nicaea, not far from the great new imperial city of Constantinople. Agreement was reached, and a new creed was developed on that basis. What we now know as the "Nicene Creed" is actually a later development of the creed of 325, agreed upon at the Council of Chalcedon in 451. This creed was longer than the Apostles' Creed and included additional material clarifying how Christians should think about the divinity and the humanity of Jesus of Nazareth.

Yet there is another difference between the two creeds presented so far (Box 3.1 and Box 3.2). The Apostles' Creed was a product of Christian communities, which took shape over many generations and commanded wide assent and support. The Nicene Creed was developed by a committee of bishops, in response to the Roman emperor's demand for religious consensus. There has always been a sense in which the Apostles' Creed is a "people's creed," whereas the Nicene Creed is a "bishop's creed."

Having reflected on how the creeds arose, we may now turn to consider their contents – beginning with the notion of "faith" itself.

Box 3.2   The Nicene Creed

We believe in one God,
the Father, the Almighty,
maker of heaven and earth,
of all that is, seen and unseen.

We believe in one Lord, Jesus Christ,
the only Son of God,
eternally begotten of the Father,
God from God, Light from Light,
true God from true God,
begotten, not made,
of one Being with the Father;
through him all things were made.
For us and for our salvation
he came down from heaven,
was incarnate of the Holy Spirit and the Virgin Mary
and became truly human.
For our sake he was crucified under Pontius Pilate;
he suffered death and was buried.
On the third day he rose again
in accordance with the Scriptures;
he ascended into heaven
and is seated at the right hand of the Father.
He will come again in glory to judge the living and the dead,
and his kingdom will have no end.

We believe in the Holy Spirit, the Lord, the giver of life,
who proceeds from the Father and the Son,
who with the Father and the Son is worshipped and glorified,
who has spoken through the prophets.
We believe in one holy catholic and apostolic Church.
We acknowledge one baptism for the forgiveness of sins.
We look for the resurrection of the dead,
and the life of the world to come. Amen.

What Is Faith?

The Christian creeds open in the language of faith: "I believe in God …." Before we begin to reflect on what it is that Christians believe in, we need to ask what it means to "believe." What is faith? Christian writers down the ages have distinguished two senses of the word "faith." First, it designates a "faith by which we believe" – that is to say, the act of trust and assent that says "yes" to God and reaches out to hold fast to God as the secure ground of life and thought. Second, it designates a "faith that we believe" – that is to say, a set of beliefs. In this second sense of the word, "faith" refers to the content of what Christians believe rather than to the act of believing and trusting. Although these two senses of the word "faith" are inseparable – they are like two sides of the same coin – it is nevertheless helpful to distinguish between them. Creeds relate mainly to faith in the second sense of the word – that is, they are a publicly agreed summary of the main points of Christian belief.

It is helpful here to make a distinction between "faith" (which is generally understood relationally) and "belief" (which is generally understood cognitively or conceptually). Faith primarily describes a personal act of trust, a relationship with God that is characterized by trust, commitment, and love. For Christians, to have faith in God is to place one's trust in God, believing him to be worthy of such trust.

Beliefs represent an attempt to put into words the substance of that faith. One has to admit that words are often not up to the task of representing what they describe, yet one has also to recognize the need to try to entrust to words what they ultimately could not contain. Words, after all, are of critical importance in communication, argument, and reflection. It is simply unthinkable for Christians not to try to express in words what they believe. The eleventh-century theologian Anselm of Canterbury made this point succinctly through the Latin phrase *fides quaerens intellectum* ("faith seeking understanding"). Yet these creedal formulations are, in a sense, secondary to the primary act of trust and commitment.

The Christian faith is not a checklist of beliefs. In a sense, Christianity is a profoundly relational faith, which rests on the believer's trusting acceptance of a God who has been proved worthy of such trust in the first place. As the poet Samuel Taylor Coleridge (1772–1834) once remarked, "faith is not an accuracy of logic, but a rectitude of heart." Yet, despite this relational emphasis within Christianity, there remains a cognitive dimension to faith. Christians do more than simply trust in God or in Christ. They also believe certain quite definite things about them. We shall be looking at some of those beliefs later in this chapter. For the moment, however, we focus on the idea of faith.

So, when the creeds declare that Christians "believe in God," what do they mean? A useful starting point is this: to believe in God is to trust in God. This is not an adequate definition of faith, but it is an excellent starting point for further exploration. God is the one who may be trusted in the midst of life's turbulence, confusion, and ambiguities. Trusting someone leads to commitment. As William Temple (1881–1944), a former archbishop of Canterbury, put it in his opening speech at the Second World Conference on Faith and Order at Edinburgh in 1937, "faith is not only the assent of our minds to doctrinal propositions: it is the commitment of our whole selves into the hands of a faithful Creator and merciful Redeemer."

This pattern recurs throughout the narratives of calling and response that we find in the Christian Bible. One of the great examples of faith is Patriarch Abraham. Abraham trusted God and left behind his family home in order to go to a distant land (Genesis 15; 17). To believe in God is to believe that God may be trusted, which leads us to entrust ourselves to God. To believe in God goes far beyond the mere factual acceptance of God's existence; it is to declare that this God may be trusted. It is a familiar theme, and it has been explored by just about every major Christian writer down the ages.

Similarly, to believe in Jesus of Nazareth goes far beyond accepting his historical existence. In its full-blooded sense, faith in Jesus is about recognizing Jesus as one who may be trusted.

When Jesus of Nazareth asked a man whom he had just healed whether he "believes" in the Son of Man (John 9: 35), the healed man was quite clear that he was not being asked whether he believed that Jesus existed. He knew that he was being asked whether he was ready to trust Jesus and to commit himself to him.

It is therefore no accident that the gospels of the New Testament go to such length to illustrate why Jesus of Nazareth may be trusted and what shape this trust would take. The calling of the first disciples is of especial importance here. In Mark's account of this dramatic event (Mark 1: 16–20), Jesus spoke these simple words: "Come, follow me." No explanation or elaboration is offered. Yet the fishermen left everything immediately and followed Jesus. No reason is given for their decision to follow this stranger who has so dramatically entered into their lives. Mark leaves us with the impression of an utterly compelling figure, who commands assent by his very presence. They abandon their nets – the basis of their meager existence as fishermen – and follow Jesus into the unknown. He does not even tell them his name. Yet they choose to entrust themselves to him.

This is where their faith in Jesus Christ began; it is not where it ended. For the gospels enable us to see the disciples growing in their faith, as they gradually come to understand more about the identity and significance of Christ. To begin with, they trusted him; as time passed, they also came to understand something of who he was and why he mattered. Even in the New Testament, this leads to supplementing personal trust in God and Christ with beliefs concerning their identity – in other words, with doctrinal or creedal statements. For example, John's gospel provides an account of the things that Jesus said and did; and it does this in order to bring its readers to the point at which they can commit themselves to him, both personally and intellectually. The narrative of the words and deeds of Jesus has been written so that "you may believe that Jesus is the Christ, the Son of God, and that by believing you may have life in his name" (John 20: 31).

Faith and reason

The rise of an Age of Reason in western culture, which most historians suggest is to be dated roughly to the two hundred years between 1750 and 1950, saw religious faith regarded with suspicion. Thinkers of the Enlightenment regarded faith as little more than belief unsupported by evidence – lacking any real warrant or logical basis. The Age of Reason led to a new confidence in the capacity of unaided human reason to explain and master the world. Reason, it was argued, was capable of deducing anything that needed to be known about God. There was no need to propose divine revelation. We could rely totally upon reason instead.

This position is generally known as "rationalism" and is still encountered today in some quarters. However, its credibility has been severely shaken by the growing realization that different cultures have different understandings of rationality. Reason, it turned out, was not the universal quality that many rationalists believed it to be. As the noted French philosopher Blaise Pascal (1623–1662) put it: "Reason's final step is to realize that there are an infinite number of things which lie beyond it. It is simply feeble if it does not get as far as realizing that."

The worldview of the Enlightenment is increasingly regarded with suspicion by post-modern writers, who see it as highly limiting and restrictive, in effect as confining humanity to the very narrow world of what can be proved by reason. Strictly speaking, it limits human knowledge to the realms of logic and mathematics. For the literary critic Terry Eagleton, this view shuts down serious discussion of all major religious, moral, social, and cultural issues. "We hold many beliefs that have no unimpeachably rational justification, but are nonetheless reasonable to entertain."

The mainstream Christian tradition takes a critical yet positive attitude toward human reason. Faith goes beyond what is logically demonstrable, yet it is nevertheless capable of having a rational motivation and a foundation. The truths of Christianity may lie beyond reason's ability to discover them. Yet, when they are disclosed, their rationality is grasped. Thus faith is to be seen as a form of motivated or warranted belief. It is not a blind leap into the dark, but a discovery of a bigger picture of things. Faith is not irrational; it simply transcends the limits of reason.

One of the most important recent discussions of the relation of faith and reason is contained in Pope John Paul II's 1998 encyclical letter *Fides et ratio* (*Faith and Reason*). In the opening to that letter John Paul II (Karol Josef Wojtyla, 1920–2005) sets out the classic Christian approach to this question as follows:

> Faith and reason are like two wings on which the human spirit rises to the contemplation of truth; and God has placed in the human heart a desire to know the truth – in a word, to know himself – so that, by knowing and loving God, men and women may also come to the fullness of truth about themselves.

This rich statement deserves close attention. The basic idea is that human beings long to know the truth and are constantly searching for it. "In the far reaches of the human heart there is a seed of desire and nostalgia for God."

So: Can reason alone lead humanity to this truth? John Paul II pays a handsome tribute to philosophy as the legitimate object in the human quest for truth. Philosophy is "one of noblest of human tasks" and is "driven by the desire to discover the ultimate truth of existence." Yet unaided human reason cannot fully penetrate to the mystery of life. It cannot answer questions such as "Why are we here?" For this reason, John Paul II argues, God graciously chose to disclose through revelation those things that would otherwise remain unknown. "The truth made known to us by Revelation is neither the product nor the consummation of an argument devised by human reason."

The letter stresses that faith is not blind trust opposed to the evidence presented by the world. Rather it points out that the world – which Christians see as God's creation – is studded with hints about God's existence and nature. John Paul II appeals to Paul's sermon preached on the Areopagus in Athens (Acts 17), arguing that it is entirely reasonable to infer the existence of God from the wonders of nature and from a human sense of divinity within us. These do not count as "proofs"; they are, however, confirmation or corroboration of the basic themes of faith.

But what about "proofs" of God's existence? What role do they play in any account of the Christian faith? And is God's existence something that can be proved in the first place? We shall consider these questions in the next section.

Can God's existence be proved?

The mainstream Christian attitude to proofs for the existence of God can be set out as follows:

1   The existence of God is something that reason cannot prove conclusively. Yet the fact that the existence of God lies beyond reason does not mean that the existence of God is contrary to reason. Faith in God transcends reason but does not contradict it.
2   Good reasons may be put forward for suggesting that God exists; these do not, however, count as "proofs" in the sense of "rigorous logical demonstrations." In this strict sense of the word, proof is limited to logic and mathematics.

In what follows we shall explore the question of proofs of God's existence in a little more detail, focusing on Thomas Aquinas (1225–1274) – probably the most famous and influential theologian of the Middle Ages. Born in Italy, he achieved fame through his teaching and writing, at the university of Paris and in other northern universities. His name is chiefly associated with the *Summa theologiae*, a treatise composed toward the end of his life and not totally finished at the time of his death. However, he also wrote many other significant works, particularly the *Summa contra Gentiles*, which represents a major statement of the rationality of the Christian faith and of the existence of God.

Aquinas believed that it was entirely proper to identify pointers toward the existence of God – pointers drawn from general human experience of the world. His "five ways" represent five lines of argument in support of the existence of God, each of which draws on some aspect of the world that "points" to the existence of its creator.

So then, what kind of pointers does Aquinas identify? His basic line of thought is that the world, being created by God, mirrors God as its creator – an idea that is given more formal expression in Aquinas' doctrine of the "analogy of being." Just as an artist might sign a painting to identify it as her handiwork, so God has stamped a divine "signature" upon the creation. What we observe in the world – for example, the signs of its ordering – can be explained if God was its creator. If God both brought the world into existence and impressed a divine image and likeness upon it, then something of God's nature can be known from the creation.

So where in creation might we look to find evidence for the existence of God? Aquinas argues that the ordering of the world is the most convincing evidence of God's existence and wisdom. This basic assumption underlies each of his five ways, although it is of particular importance in the case of the argument often referred to as the "argument from design" or the "teleological argument." We shall consider the first and the last of these ways to illustrate the issues.

The first way begins from the observation that things in the world are in motion or change. The world is not static but dynamic. Examples are easy to list. Rain falls from the sky. Stones roll down valleys. The earth revolves around the sun (incidentally, this fact was unknown to Aquinas). This kind of argument is usually referred to as the "argument from motion"; however, it is clear that the "movement" in question (*motus* in Aquinas' Latin) should be understood in very general or basic terms, so that the word "change" would be more appropriate as a translation of *motus* at many points.

So how did nature come to be in motion? Why is it changing? Why isn't it static? Aquinas argues that everything that moves is moved by something else. For every motion, there is a cause. Things don't just move; they are moved by something else. Hence each cause of motion must itself have a cause. And that cause must have a cause as well. And so Aquinas argues that there is a whole series of causes of motion lying behind the world as we know it. Now, unless there is an infinite number of these causes, there must be a single one right at the origin of the series. All motion is ultimately derived from this original cause of motion. This is the starting point of the great chain of causation, which we see reflected in the way the world behaves. Thus, from the fact that things are in motion, Aquinas argues for the existence of a single original cause of all motion. And this cause, he insists, is none other than God.

In more recent times, this argument has been restated in terms of God's being the one who brought the universe into existence – which is why it is often referred to as the "cosmological argument" (the Greek word *kosmos* meant "universe," but also "order," hence the world as an ordered system). The most commonly encountered statement of the cosmological argument runs along the following lines:

1   Everything in the universe depends on something else for its existence.
2   What is true of the individual parts of the universe is also true of the universe itself.
3   The universe thus depends on something other than itself for its existence – for as long as it has existed or will exist.
4   Hence the universe depends on God for its existence.

The argument basically assumes that the existence of the universe is something that requires explanation. It will be clear that this type of argument relates directly to modern cosmological research, particularly to the "big bang" theory of the origins of the cosmos.

Aquinas' fifth and final way is known as the teleological argument, which takes its name from the Greek word *telos*, meaning "purpose" or "goal." Aquinas notes that the world shows obvious traces of intelligent design. Natural processes and objects seem to be adapted to life with certain definite objectives in mind. They seem to have a purpose; they seem to have been designed. But things don't design themselves: they are designed by someone or something else. Arguing from this observation, Aquinas concludes that it must be conceded that the source of the natural ordering of processes and objects is God.

How useful are these arguments? The great French mathematician and philosopher Blaise Pascal had two major concerns about the kind of approach adopted by Aquinas. First, he found it difficult to accept that the rather abstract philosophical "god" who resulted from such arguments was anything like the living God of the Old and New Testaments. It is a point with which many would agree. As Pascal put it, "the metaphysical proofs for the existence of God are so remote from human reasoning, and so complex, that they have little impact."

But, second, Pascal argued that these "proofs" assumed that God was known primarily through reason. For Pascal, the human heart also had its reasons for believing (or not believing!) in God. "We know the truth, not only through our reason, but also through our heart." God's appeal for the human condition extended far beyond any resonance between the world as we know it and the ideas of the Christian faith. It went right to the deep-seated longing for God that Pascal held to be the culmination of the human quest for meaning and significance.

In more recent years, new interest has developed in "inductive" arguments for the existence of God – arguments that are based on the capacity of the Christian faith to make sense of things. Here the criterion of assessment is how well a system can make theory and observation fit in with each other. Although this approach is developed by many philosophers, for instance Richard Swinburne, its most accessible statements are found in more popular writings, particularly those of C. S. Lewis (1898–1963) and G. K. Chesterton (1874–1936).

After losing faith in his early agnosticism, Chesterton published a newspaper article explaining why he and many others now regarded Christianity with intense intellectual seriousness. "We have returned to it because it is an intelligible picture of the world." Chesterton realized that testing a theory meant checking it out against observation. "The best way to see if a coat fits a man is not to measure both of them, but to try it on." Let Chesterton himself explain what he has in mind.

> Numbers of us have returned to this belief; and we have returned to it, not because of this argument or that argument, but because the theory, when it is adopted, works out everywhere; because the coat, when it is tried on, fits in every crease … We put on the theory, like a magic hat, and history becomes translucent like a house of glass.

Chesterton's argument is that it is the Christian vision of reality as a whole – rather than any of its individual components – that proves so compelling. Individual observations of nature do not "prove" Christianity to be true; rather Christianity validates itself through its ability to make sense of those observations. "The phenomenon does not prove religion, but religion explains the phenomenon."

For Chesterton, a good theory – whether scientific or religious – is to be judged by the amount of illumination it offers and by its capacity to accommodate what we see in the world around us and experience within us. "With this idea once inside our heads, a million things become transparent as if a lamp were lit behind them." The same idea is also expressed in Lewis's famous statement: "I believe in Christianity as I believe that the sun has risen, not only because I see it, but because by it I see everything else."

Thus far we have briefly explored some of the issues relating to faith and the creeds, looking especially at the rationality of faith. We now need to begin to engage with some specific items of belief. Let's begin by looking at the opening statement of the creeds: "I believe in God."

The Christian Understanding of God

God lies at the heart of the Christian faith. But which God? Is it the same God as that of Judaism or Islam? And what is this God like? It is clear that the little word "God" needs considerable expansion, if we are to understand what it means. Israel's reflections on the identity of its God – which it styled by using phrases such as "the Lord God of Israel" – took place against a background of polytheism. Each nation in the region had its own god; many had highly developed pantheons, recognizing many different gods, each with its own distinctive function or sphere of influence. Simply talking about "God" was thus not particularly informative. It invited the question: Which of these gods do you mean? Part of the task of Christian theology is to identify the God in which Christians believe.

This process of clarifying the identity of God can be followed in both the Old and New Testaments. For the Old Testament prophets, Israel knew and worshipped the God who had brought them out of Egypt and led them into the promised land. In the New Testament, we find this idea picked up and developed further. Christians believe in the same God as Abraham; this God is, however, finally and fully disclosed in Jesus of Nazareth (pp. 87–89). Thus Paul speaks of "the God and Father of our Lord Jesus Christ" (2 Corinthians 1: 3). By this, Paul means both the God in whom Jesus of Nazareth believed, and the God who is revealed in Jesus' words and deeds.

The New Testament teaches that Christians worship and know the same God as Israel. Nevertheless, they hold that this God is supremely and finally revealed in Jesus of Nazareth. Thus the letter to the Hebrews opens by declaring that the same God who spoke to Israel "in many times and in various ways" through the prophets has now "spoken to us through a Son," who is to be recognized as the "exact representation" of God (Hebrews 1: 1–3). This point is of great importance, as it demonstrates how the Christian understanding of God is linked with the person of Christ. As a second-century Christian writer put it, "we must learn to think of Jesus as of God" (1 Clement 1: 1).

So what do Christians believe about this God? The opening words of the Apostles' Creed state that Christians believe in a God who is "the Father Almighty, Creator of heaven and earth." We shall turn to explore the very rich and powerful theme of creation in the following section. To begin with, we shall look at the idea of God as "Father Almighty." We can break this down into two segments, each of which really deserves a chapter to itself. However, limits on space mean that we will have to consider them both briefly, beginning with the question of what it means to speak of God as "Father." How are we to understand this analogy?

Perhaps the best starting point is to reflect on the way in which Christian theology uses analogies as a way of grasping God in manageable and imaginatively engaging forms.

Christian analogies for God

One of the most noticeable and interesting things about the biblical representation of God is that extensive use is made of images. We may begin by considering one of the most familiar of these analogies and images: "The Lord is my shepherd' (Psalm 23: 1). This image of God as a shepherd is encountered frequently in the Old Testament (e.g., Isaiah 40: 11; Ezekiel 34: 12) and is taken up in the New Testament to refer to Jesus, who is declared to be the "good shepherd" (John 10: 11).

To speak of "God as a shepherd" is to affirm that "God is *like* a shepherd." In other words, the image of a shepherd is analogical, helping us to think about the nature of God. It does not mean that God is identical with a human shepherd. Rather it means that some aspects of a human shepherd help us think about God more effectively, engaging both the reason and the imagination.

So then, is every aspect of this human analogy to be carried over to God? After all, every analogy breaks down at some point, if it is taken too far. How far can we press this analogy before it ceases to be reliable? To explore the issue, we could draw up a brief list of things that are true about shepherds.

1   Shepherds look after sheep.
2   Shepherds protect their sheep against danger.
3   Shepherds lead their sheep to food and water.
4   Shepherds are human beings.

The first three aspects of the analogy can clearly be carried over to thinking about God. God cares, protects, and leads. In all these respects the analogy of the shepherd works well and illuminates the character of God.

Yet shepherds are ultimately human beings. So is this aspect of the analogy also to be carried over? It is quite clear that we are not meant to think of God as a human being. Christians do not think that God is a human being. This, it would seem, is one aspect of the analogy that we are not meant to press too far.

With these points in mind, let us return to think about the analogy of "God as Father." What does it convey about God? And what are the limits of this analogy?

God as Father

The Christian tradition is saturated with language about God as Father – for example, the Lord's Prayer opens with the words "Our Father." If Jesus of Nazareth referred to God in this way, this element is clearly of major importance to Christian faith. But how are we to interpret this image? What does it mean to speak of God in this way? In particular, do Christians think that God is male? Does speaking of God as "father" mean that Christianity believes in a male deity?

Box 3.3   The Lord's Prayer

> Our Father in heaven,
> hallowed be your name.
> Your kingdom come.
> Your will be done, on earth as it is in heaven.
> Give us this day our daily bread.
> And forgive us our debts, as we also have forgiven our debtors.
> And do not bring us to the time of trial, but rescue us from the evil one.
> (Matthew 6: 9–13; see also Luke 11: 2–4)

What does the analogy of God as Father convey? The following ideas might come to mind, and we shall explore each of them briefly.

1 Fathers are human beings.
2 Fathers bring their children into existence.
3 Fathers care for their children.
4 Fathers are male.

The first of these characteristics is clearly not meant to be transferred to our thinking about God. As we saw in the case of the shepherd analogy, this is the inevitable consequence of using language drawn from the created order when we refer to the creator.

The second is clearly important. Christians believe that God is our originator. Without God we would not be here. Both the Old and the New Testament stress the complete dependence of humanity upon God, from beginning to end. We shall explore the theme of God as creator in more detail later in this chapter (pp. 78–82).

The third aspect of the analogy is also clearly applicable to God. There can be no doubt that the analogy of God as father conveys – and is intended to convey – the idea of care. The Old Testament in particular often compares God's relation with his people to a father's relationship with his young son. When the son is very young, he is totally dependent upon his father for everything, and their relationship is very close. But, as the son grows older, he gradually comes to exercise his independence and to break away from his father, so that the relationship becomes more distant.

The Prophet Hosea used this illustration to help his readers grasp how Israel has become a virtual stranger to the God who called it into existence:

> When Israel was a child, I loved him, and out of Egypt I called my son. But the more I called Israel, the further they went away from me. They sacrificed to the Baals, and they burned incense to images. It was I who taught Ephraim to walk, taking them by the arms, but they did not realize it was I who healed them. I led them with the cords of human kindness, with ties of love. (Hosea 11: 1–4)

This aspect of the analogy is also picked up by Jesus of Nazareth in the Sermon on the Mount (Matthew 7: 9–11). Human fathers want to give their children good things. So how much more will God, as a heavenly father, want to give good things to those who ask for them in prayer?

Yet it is the fourth aspect of this analogy that has generated most interest and needs further discussion. Both the Old and the New Testament use male language about God. The Greek word for "god" (*theos*) is unquestionably masculine, as are most of the analogies used for God throughout Scripture – such as father, king, and shepherd. Does this mean that God *is* male?

This question needs to be answered in the negative. To begin with, we need to note that the Bible also uses female imagery to refer to the love of God for humanity. Just as a mother can never forget or turn against her child, so God will not forget or turn against his people (Isaiah 49: 15). There is a natural bond of affection and sympathy between God and his children, simply because he has brought them into being. Thus God loved us long before we loved God (1 John 4: 10, 19). Psalm 51: 1 refers to God's "great compassion." Interestingly, the Hebrew word for "compassion" (*rachmin*) is derived from the word for "womb" (*rechmen*). God's compassion toward his people is that of a mother toward her child (cf. Isaiah 66: 12–13). Compassion, so to speak, stems from the womb.

The statement that a "father" is a good analogy for God in ancient Israelite society is not equivalent to saying that God is male. To speak of God as father is to say that the role of the father in ancient Israel allows us insights into the nature of God. It is not to say that God is "male" in human herms. As we have noted, the Old Testament also uses mothers in analogies for aspects of God's love for Israel. Although the cultural context of the ancient world means that there are many more references to paternal role models than to maternal, there is no doubt that both fathers and mothers function as analogies for God in the Bible.

The *Catechism of the Catholic Church* thus stresses the manner in which parental imagery – both of fatherhood and of motherhood – brings out some central themes of the Christian faith:

> By calling God "Father," the language of faith indicates two main things: that God is the first origin of everything and transcendent authority; and that he is at the same time goodness and loving care for all his children. God's parental tenderness can also be expressed by the image of motherhood, which emphasizes God's immanence, the intimacy between Creator and creature. The language of faith thus draws on the human experience of parents, who are in a way the first representatives of God for man.

Yet there is a more important point here, grounded in the doctrine of creation. Neither male nor female sexuality is to be attributed to God. For Christians, God *creates* both male and female. Yet this does not mean that God *is* either male or female. Sexuality is seen as an attribute of the created order; it does not correspond to any such polarity within the creator God.

In fact the Old Testament completely avoids attributing sexual functions to God, on account of the strongly pagan overtones of such associations. Thus Canaanite fertility cults emphasized the sexual functions of both gods and goddesses, whereas the Old Testament refuses to endorse the idea that God's gender and sex(uality) are a significant matter, or to think of the act of creation in sexual terms – for example, as the mating of a god and goddess.

This leads us to another important theme in Christian thinking about God: the concept of a personal God, to which we now turn.

A personal God

Down the ages, theologians and ordinary Christian believers alike have spoken and thought about God in strongly personal terms. Christianity thinks and speaks of God in terms of divine love, trustworthiness, and purpose, which have strongly personal associations. Many spiritual writers have pointed out that the Christian practice of prayer is partly modeled on the relationship between a child and a parent. Prayer expresses a gracious relationship of trust and dependency.

Similarly, one of Paul's most important ways of thinking about salvation – reconciliation – is modeled on the dynamics of human personal relationships. The transformation, through faith, of the relationship between God and sinful human beings is like the reconciliation of two persons – say, an alienated husband and his wife.

For early Christian writers, the word "person" expressed the individuality of a human being as seen in his or her words and actions, especially in social relationships. A person is someone who plays a role in a social network. "Individuality" does not imply social relationships, whereas "personality" relates to the part played by an individual in a web of relationships – a part by virtue of which that person is perceived by others to be distinctive. Our identity is expressed partly through our relationships. The basic Christian idea of "a personal God" is that of a God with whom believers can be in a relationship analogous to any relationship with a human person.

It is helpful to consider the overtones of the phrase "an impersonal God." There are strongly negative overtones to the idea of "impersonal," and they have passed into Christian thinking about the nature of God. "Impersonal" suggests a God who is distant or aloof, who deals with humanity in general terms, who pays no heed to human individuality. On the contrary, having a personal relationship with God, such as love, suggests a reciprocal dimension to God's dealings with believers. This idea is incorporated into the notion of a personal God, but not into impersonal conceptions of the nature of God.

Personal relationships establish the framework within which such key biblical themes as "love," "trust," and "faithfulness" have meaning. Both the Old and the New Testament make frequent reference to the "love of God," the "trustworthiness of God," and the "faithfulness of God." "Love" is a word used primarily to refer to personal relationships. Furthermore, the core biblical themes of promise and fulfillment are given their proper context within personal relationships. This can be seen in the covenant between God and Israel: "I will be their God, and they will be my people" (Jeremiah 31: 33). The basic underlying idea is that of God's personal commitment to God's people and of God's people's commitment to their God.

A twentieth-century philosophical analysis of what it means to speak of a "person" is also helpful in clarifying what it means to speak of a personal God. In his major work *I and Thou* (1927), the Jewish writer Martin Buber (1878–1965) drew a fundamental distinction between two categories of relations: "I–Thou relations," which are understood to be "personal," and "I–It relations," which are impersonal.

1 *I–It relations* Buber uses this category to refer to the relation between subjects and objects – for example, between a human being and a pencil. The human being is active, whereas the pencil is passive. This type of relation is often referred to in more philosophical language as a subject–object relation, in which an active subject (in this case, the human being) relates to an inactive object (in this case, the pencil). According to Buber, the subject acts as an "I," and the object as an "it." The relation between the human being and the pencil could thus be described as an "I–It relation."

2 *I–Thou relations* At the heart of Buber's philosophy is the notion of an "I–Thou relation," which exists between two active subjects. It is something that is mutual (or reciprocal) and links two persons.

How does Buber's philosophy help us understand and explore the idea of God as a person? First, his approach affirms that God cannot be reduced to a concept – or to some neat conceptual formulation. According to Buber, only an "It" can be treated in this way. For

Buber, God is the "Thou" who can, by its nature, never become an It. That is, God is a being who escapes all attempts at objectification and transcends all description. Theology must learn to acknowledge and wrestle with the presence of God, realizing that this presence cannot be reduced to a neat package of contents.

Second, the approach allows valuable insights into the Christian idea of revelation. For Christian theology, God's revelation is not simply a making known of facts about God, but a self-revelation of God. Revelation of ideas about God is to be supplemented by the revelation of God as a person. Revelation includes knowledge of God as an "it" and as a "Thou." We come to know things about God; yet we also come to know God. Similarly, "knowledge of God" includes knowledge of God as both "it" and "Thou." To "know God" is not to have access to data *about* God, but to have a personal relationship *with* God.

Buber's approach helps us encompass the spectrum of understandings of God encountered within Christianity. The idea of God as an "I" lies at the heart of Christian prayer and worship, which are often taken in terms of a personal relationship with God. Yet some forms of Christian mysticism prefer to think of God more impersonally, believing that the use of personal language about God fails to do justice to divine immensity or to the complexity of the human experience of God.

God as almighty

The Apostles' Creed goes on to speak of God as "almighty." What do Christians mean when they say that God is "almighty"? At first sight, this might seem to be a rather pointless question. The meaning of the word "almighty" is perfectly obvious in everyday language: "capable of doing anything." So to say that "God is almighty" is to say that "God can do anything." What more is there to say?

Yet it is not quite as simple as this. We have to consider whether the word "almighty" might take on a somewhat different meaning when applied to God. To explore this, let's consider the statement in greater detail: "To say that God is almighty means that God can do anything."

On the face of it, this definition seems fairly straightforward. Yet it runs into some difficulties at an early stage. Consider the following question: "Can God draw a triangle with four sides?" It does not take much thought to see that this question has to be answered in the negative. Triangles have three sides; to draw something with four sides is to draw a quadrilateral, not a triangle.

However, on further reflection, it is not clear that this question causes problems for the Christian understanding of God. Four-sided triangles do not and cannot exist. The fact that God cannot make such a triangle is not a serious issue. It just forces us to restate our simple statement in a more complicated way. "To say that God is almighty means that God can do anything that does not involve logical contradiction." Or we could follow Thomas Aquinas, who remarked that it was not that God could not do such things; it was simply that such things cannot be done.

Yet the real issue concerns the Christian understanding of the nature of God. We can begin to engage with this important matter by considering this question: "Can God break promises?" There is no logical contradiction involved in people breaking promises.

It happens all the time. It may be regrettable, but there is no intellectual difficulty here. If God can do anything that does not involve a logical contradiction, God can certainly break a promise.

Yet, for Christians, this suggestion is unacceptable. The idea of a "covenant" between God and Israel is grounded on God's faithfulness and commitment. Christians hold that God remains faithful to what has been promised. If God cannot be trusted, whom can anyone trust? The suggestion that God might break a promise contradicts a vital aspect of the Christian understanding of God's character – namely God's faithfulness and truthfulness. One of the great themes of both the Old Testament and the New is the total trustworthiness and reliability of God. Humans may fail; God remains faithful.

The point here is that there is a tension between power and trust. An all-powerful cheater could easily make promises – but those promises cannot be trusted. Yet the Christian faith focuses on a God who could do anything – but who chose to act in certain ways. God did not need to enter into a covenant with Israel – but God chose to do so, and having done so, remained faithful to this promise. God does not act arbitrarily or whimsically; God acts reliably and faithfully.

God as spirit

The Christian tradition makes extensive appeal to the Holy Spirit. Christian baptism invokes the name of the "Father, Son, and Holy Spirit" (Matthew 28: 17–20). The recent rise of Pentecostal and charismatic movements (pp. 212–213) throughout the Christian world has seen a new emphasis given to the role of the Holy Spirit, particularly in worship and personal experience. So what is meant by the "Holy Spirit"?

The English language uses at least three words – "wind," "breath," and "spirit" – to translate a single Hebrew term regularly used to refer to the Holy Spirit: *ruach*. This important Hebrew word has a depth of meaning that makes it is virtually impossible to reproduce in English. *Ruach*, traditionally translated simply as "spirit," has a range of associations, each of which casts some light on the Christian notion of the Holy Spirit.

1   *Spirit as wind*   The Old Testament writers are careful not to identify God with the wind and thus reduce God to the level of a natural force. Nevertheless, a parallel is drawn between the power of the wind and that of God. To speak of God as spirit is to call to mind the surging energy of the "Lord of Hosts" and to remind Israel of the power and dynamism of the God who had called Israel out of Egypt. This image of the spirit as redemptive power is perhaps stated in its most significant form in the account of the exodus from Egypt in which a powerful wind divides the Red Sea (Exodus 14: 21). Here the idea of *ruach* conveys both the power and the redemptive purpose of God.

The image of the wind also allowed for the complexity of believers' experiences of God to be accounted for and visualized in a genuinely helpful manner. The Old Testament writers were conscious of experiencing the presence and activity of God in two quite distinct manners. Sometimes God was experienced as a judge, one who condemned Israel for its waywardness; yet at other times God was experienced as one who refreshed the chosen people like water in a dry land. The image of the wind conveyed both these ideas in a powerful manner.

2   *Spirit as breath*   The idea of spirit is associated with the idea of life. When God created Adam, God breathed into him the breath of life, as a result of which Adam became a "living being" (Genesis 2: 7). The basic difference between a living and a dead human being is that the former breathes, the latter does not. In ancient cultures, this led to the widespread thought that life was dependent upon breath. God is the one who breathes the breath of life into empty shells and brings them to life. God brought Adam to life by breathing into him. The famous vision of the Valley of the Dry Bones (Ezekiel 37: 1–14) also illustrates this point. Can these dry bones live? The bones only come to life when breath enters into them (Ezekiel 37: 9–10).

The model of God as spirit thus conveys the fundamental insight that God is the one who gives life, even the one who is able to bring the dead back to life. It is important to note that *ruach* is often linked with God's work of creation (e.g., Genesis 1: 2; Psalm 104: 27–31), even if the precise role of the spirit is left unspecified. There is clearly an association between "spirit" and the giving of life through creation.

3   *Spirit as charism*   The technical term "charism" (from the ancient Greek *charisma*, meaning "grace") denotes a state in which one is filled with the spirit of God to the point where one can perform tasks that would otherwise be impossible. The gift of wisdom is often portrayed as a consequence of being thus endowed by the spirit (Genesis 41: 38–39; Exodus 28: 3; 35: 31; Deuteronomy 34: 9). At times, the Old Testament attributes leadership or military prowess to the influence of the spirit, regarding them as gifts (Judges 14: 6, 19; 15: 14, 15). However, the most pervasive aspect of this feature of the spirit relates to the question of prophecy. One of the statements of the creeds identifies the Holy Spirit as the ultimate source and inspiration of prophecy.

Yet the Old Testament does not offer much in the way of clarification concerning the manner in which the prophets were inspired, guided, or motivated by the Holy Spirit. In the period before the Israelites were exiled to Babylon, prophecy was often associated with ecstatic experiences of God and linked with wild behavior (1 Samuel 10: 6; 19: 24). Nevertheless, this kind of activity gradually became associated with the message rather than the behavior of the prophet. The prophet's credentials rest upon being endowed with and by the spirit (Isaiah 61: 1; Ezekiel 2: 1–2; Micah 3: 8; Zechariah 7: 12); such endowment authenticates the prophet's message – a message that is usually described as "the word [*dabhar*] of the Lord."

But is the Holy Spirit divine? This question was discussed extensively in early Christianity. Leading writers such as Athanasius of Alexandria (c. 296–373) and Basil of Caesarea (c. 330–379) argued that the formula that had become universally accepted for baptism implied the full divinity of the spirit. Since the time of the New Testament (see Matthew 28: 18–20), Christians were baptized in the name of "the Father, Son, and Holy Spirit." Athanasius argued that the baptismal formula clearly pointed to the Spirit sharing the same divinity as that of the Father and the Son. This argument eventually prevailed.

However, early Christian writers were hesitant to speak openly of the Holy Spirit as "God," on the grounds that this practice was not explicitly endorsed by the Christian Bible – a point discussed at some length by Basil of Caesarea in his treatise on the Holy Spirit (written in AD 374–375). Even as late as AD 380, Gregory of Nazianzus conceded that many

Orthodox Christian theologians were uncertain as to whether to treat the Holy Spirit as a creator, as an activity, or as God.

This cautiousness can be seen in the final statement of the doctrine of the Holy Spirit formulated by a council meeting at Constantinople in AD 381. The Holy Spirit was there described not as "God," but as "the Lord and giver of life, who proceeds from the Father, and is worshipped and glorified with the Father and Son." This indicates that the Holy Spirit is to be treated as having the same dignity and rank as the Father and the Son, even if the term "God" is not used explicitly. This language is reflected in the Nicene Creed.

With the full recognition of the divinity of the Holy Spirit in the fourth century, the scene was set for the final development of the Christian doctrine of the Trinity. Yet the place of the spirit within the Trinity would become the subject of controversy between the eastern and western churches. The issue concerned how the spirit related to the Son. While the theologians of the Greek-speaking church were struggling to express the nature of the Son's relationship with the Holy Spirit, the theologians of the Latin West quickly came to the conclusion that the Holy Spirit proceeds from the Father and from the Son. This debate is often referred to as the *filioque* controversy (meaning "from the Son" in the Latin sequence *ex patre filioque*, "from the Father and from the Son"). Tensions simmered over this matter, especially when western versions of the Nicene Creed were developed that included this phrase.

Theologians remain divided as to how important this distinction is and how best the point at issue might be expressed. Historically, however, this disagreement contributed to the growing tensions between the eastern and the western churches, eventually leading to the Great Schism of 1054 (pp. 138–139).

The doctrine of the Trinity

For many, the doctrine of the Trinity is one of the most baffling areas of Christian theology. How can one God be "three persons"? Thomas Jefferson (1743–1826), the third president of the United States of America, was severely critical of what he termed the "incomprehensible jargon of the Trinitarian arithmetic." Why should Christians speak about God in this convoluted and puzzling way? Surely this compromised the simplicity of faith?

The best way of understanding this core Christian doctrine is to suggest that it is the inevitable and legitimate way of thinking about God that emerges from a sustained engagement with the biblical witness to the words and works of God. The doctrine of the Trinity can be regarded as the outcome of a process of critical reflection on the pattern of divine activity revealed in the Bible and continued in Christian experience. This is not to say that the Bible explicitly sets out a doctrine of the Trinity; rather it is to say that the Bible bears witness to a God who is to be understood in a trinitarian manner.

At first sight, there are only two biblical verses that are open to a trinitarian interpretation: Matthew 28: 19 and 2 Corinthians 13: 14. The first commands the first disciples to baptize people "in the name of the Father, Son, and Holy Spirit"; the second speaks of the Father, the Son, and the Holy Spirit in the familiar words of "the grace." Both these verses have become deeply rooted in the Christian consciousness, the former on account of its baptismal associations, the latter through the common use of the formula in Christian prayer and devotion. Yet these two verses, taken together or in isolation, cannot be considered to state a formal doctrine of the Trinity.

The ultimate grounds of the doctrine of the Trinity are not to be sought in these two verses, but in the pattern of divine activity to which the New Testament bears witness. The Father is revealed in Christ through the spirit. There is the closest of connections between the Father, the Son, and the Holy Spirit in the New Testament writings. Time after time, New Testament passages link together these three elements as part of a greater whole. The totality of God's saving presence and power are expressed by involving all three elements (for example, see 1 Corinthians 12: 4–6; 2 Corinthians 1: 21–22; Galatians 4: 6; Ephesians 2: 20–22; 2 Thessalonians 2: 13–14; Titus 3: 4–6; 1 Peter 1: 2).

The starting point for Christian reflection on the Trinity is the New Testament's witness to the presence and activity of God in Christ and through the spirit. For Irenaeus of Lyons, who wrote in the second century, the whole process of salvation, from its beginning to its end, bore witness to the action of the Father, the Son, and the Holy Spirit. Irenaeus made use of a phrase that would feature prominently in future discussions of the Trinity: "the economy of salvation." The use of the term "economy" here needs a little explanation. The Greek word *oikonomia* basically means "the way in which one's affairs are ordered" (the relation to the modern sense of the word "economy" will thus be clear). For Irenaeus, the "economy of salvation" meant the way in which God has ordered the salvation of humanity in history.

At the time, Irenaeus was under considerable pressure from gnostic critics, who argued that God the creator was quite distinct from (and inferior to) God the redeemer. As we noted earlier (p. 48), the second-century writer Marcion of Sinope had argued that the Old Testament God was merely a creator God, totally different from the redeemer God of the New Testament. As a result, the Old Testament should be shunned by Christians, who should concentrate their attention upon the New Testament. Irenaeus vigorously rejected this idea. He insisted that the entire process of salvation, from the first moment of creation to the last moment of history, was the work of one and the same God. There was a single economy of salvation, in which the one God – who was both creator and redeemer – was at work to redeem the creation.

In his *Demonstration of the Apostolic Preaching*, Irenaeus insisted upon the distinct yet related roles of Father, Son, and Holy Spirit within the economy of salvation. He thus affirmed his faith in

> God the Father uncreated, who is uncontained, invisible, one God, creator of the universe; this is the first article of our faith … And the Word of God, the Son of God, our Lord Jesus Christ … who, in the fullness of time, in order to gather all things to himself, he became a human being amongst human beings, capable of being seen and touched, to destroy death, bring life, and restore fellowship between God and humanity. And the Holy Spirit … who, in the fullness of time, was poured out in a new way on our human nature in order to renew humanity throughout the entire world in the sight of God.

This passage brings out clearly the idea of the Godhead, according to which each person is responsible for an aspect in the economy of salvation. Far from being a rather pointless piece of theological speculation, the doctrine of the Trinity is grounded directly in

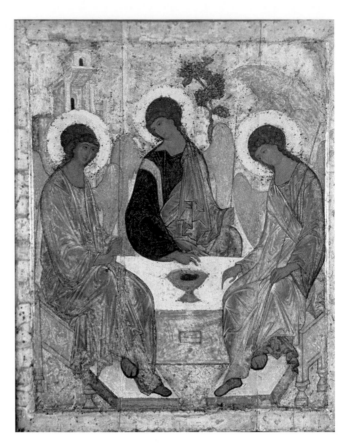

Figure 3.1   One of the most famous attempts to represent the Trinity: Andrei Rubljov's icon of 1411, depicting the three angels with Abraham, widely interpreted as an analogue of the Trinity.
Illustration: Rubljov, Andrei c. 1360/70–1427/30, *The Holy Trinity* (*The Three Angels with Abraham*) (1411). Icon painting. Moscow, Tretjakov Gallery.
Source: AKG Images.

the complex human experience of redemption in Christ and is concerned with the explanation of this experience.

The real difficulty for most Christians lies in the visualization of the Trinity. How can anyone make sense of such a complex and abstract idea? St. Patrick, the patron saint of Ireland, is rumored to have used the leaf of a shamrock to illustrate how a single leaf could have three different elements. The fourth-century writer Gregory of Nyssa used a series of analogies in his letters to help his readers grasp the reality of the Trinity, for example:

1   *The analogy of a spring, fount, and stream of water* The one flows from the other and they share the same substance – water. Although different aspects of the stream of water may be distinguished, they cannot be separated.
2   *The analogy of a chain* There are many links in a chain; yet to be connected to one is to be connected to all of them. In the same way, Gregory argues, someone who encounters the Holy Spirit also encounters the Father and the Son.
3   *The analogy of a rainbow* Drawing on the Council of Nicaea's statement – later incorporated into the Nicene Creed – that Christ is "light from light," Gregory argues that the rainbow allows us to distinguish and appreciate the different colors of a sunbeam. There is only one beam of light, yet the colors blend seamlessly into one another.

More recently, the American theologian Robert Jenson (born 1930) has argued that the trinitarian formula "Father, Son, and Holy Spirit" can be thought of as a proper name – a shorthand way of identifying exactly what God Christians are talking about. The doctrine of the Trinity is a summary of the story of God's dealings with Israel and the church. It narrates how God created and redeemed humanity, affirming that it is the story of the one and the same God throughout. Jenson develops this approach in a fresh and helpful direction, offering a creative restatement of the traditional doctrine of the Trinity.

Jenson thus argues that "Father, Son, and Holy Spirit" is the proper name for the God whom Christians know in and through Jesus Christ. It is imperative, he argues, that God should have a proper name – a name that Christians can use in prayer and in worship. "Father, Son, and Holy Spirit" is a proper name, which we are asked to use in naming and addressing God. As Jenson put it: "Linguistic means of identification – proper names, identifying descriptions, or both – are a necessity of religion. Prayers, like other requests and praises, must be addressed."

Jenson also points out that ancient Israel was set in a polytheistic context, in which the term "god" conveyed relatively little information. It was necessary to name the god in question. A similar situation was confronted by the writers of the New Testament, who were obliged to identify the god at the heart of their faith and to distinguish this god from the many other gods worshipped and acknowledged in the region, especially in Asia Minor.

The doctrine of the Trinity thus identifies and names the Christian God – but identifies and names this God in a manner consistent with the biblical testimonial. It is not a name that we have chosen; it is a name that has been chosen for us and that we are authorized to use. The Trinity is thus an instrument of theological precision, which forces us to be explicit about the God under discussion. Christians do not believe in a generic god, but in a very specific God who is known in and through a series of actions in history.

The doctrine of the Trinity plays a major role in contemporary Christian worship, spirituality, and theology. It explains the trajectory of revelation and salvation: God is revealed through Jesus Christ, and that revelation is interpreted by the Holy Spirit. God redeems humanity through Jesus Christ, and that salvation is applied to humanity through the agency of the Holy Spirit. It is an explanation of the pathway to knowledge of God and to fellowship with God. Christians believe in a saving encounter with God through Christ in the power of the Holy Spirit.

At one level, the Christian doctrine of the Trinity emphasizes the sheer immensity of God. The fallen and finite human mind is unable to comprehend the fullness of God. At another, it provides a framework both for making sense of, and deepening the quality of, Christian worship. Christians pray to the Father through the Son in the Holy Spirit. This trinitarian trajectory identifies the goal of Christian prayer and worship as God; the medium or means through which this goal is achieved as the risen Christ; and the power that inspires and elicits these actions as the Holy Spirit.

In the past, Christian theologians were primarily concerned with rebutting rationalist criticisms of the doctrine of the Trinity that held it to be incomprehensible nonsense. The influence of rationalism is now on the wane and the twentieth century has seen a massive recovery of confidence in the doctrine, largely through the pioneering theological work of Karl Barth and Karl Rahner. Yet the fading of rationalism must be set against the increasing importance of a new critic of Christian theology, especially at this point. In recent years, increasing attention has been paid to Islamic criticism of the doctrine of the Trinity. The three great monotheistic faiths of the world – Christianity, Judaism, and Islam – share a belief that there is only one supreme being: the Lord and creator of the universe. "Hear, O Israel, the Lord your God is one Lord" (Deuteronomy 6: 4). Islamic critics of Christianity regularly criticize Christians, however, for deviating from this emphasis upon the unity of God (to which they often refer through the Arabic word *tawhid*) in the doctrine of the Trinity. Muslim writers argue that this doctrine is a late invention that distorts the idea of the unity of God and ends up teaching that there are three gods.

The teaching of the Qu'ran on what Christians believe is not quite as clear as might be hoped for and has led some Christian interpreters of Islam to suggest that, according to the Qur'an, Christians worship a Trinity consisting of God, Jesus, and Mary (see Qu'ran 5.116). Although there are reasons for suspecting that Muhammad may have encountered heterodox forms of Christian belief in Arabia, including unorthodox statements concerning the Trinity, it seems more likely that the doctrine has simply been misunderstood as implying that Christians worship either three gods or a single God with three component parts. Christian responses to this Islamic criticism of the doctrine of the Trinity argue that it fails to appreciate the Christian emphasis upon the unity of God, or the Christian experience of the complexity of God's engagement with the world – which leads Christians to formulate the doctrine of God in this particular way. Clarification of this point will unquestionably help the relationship between Christianity and Islam in the contemporary world.

God as the creator

The creeds depict God as the creator of the world. How is this to be understood? What models or analogies illuminate this belief? Before we consider this question, we need to note that Christian writers quickly came to the conclusion not simply that God created the world, but that the world was created from nothing (*ex nihilo* in Latin). Various forms of gnosticism, developing an idea found in Plato's dialogue *Timaeus*, held that creation was merely the assembly of preexisting matter. Christian theologians held that God brought the world into being from nothing, and gave it shape and form.

The manner in which God acts as creator has been the subject of intense discussion within the Christian faith. Three models of, or ways of picturing, the manner in which God is to be thought of as creating the world have been particularly influential. Each one casts some light on the complex and rich Christian understanding of the notion of "creation."

1 *Emanation*   This term was widely used by early Christian writers to clarify the relation between God and the world. Its roots lie in Middle Platonism (e.g., Philo of Alexandria) and especially in the Neoplatonism of Proclus and Plotinus, and many early Christian writers sympathetic to this influential philosophical trend saw the image of "emanation" as a convenient and appropriate way of articulating Platonic insights. Emanation is typically thought of in terms of light or heat radiating from a natural source such as the sun, or from a human-generated source such as fire. This image of creation (hinted at in the Nicene Creed's phrase "light from light") suggests that the creation of the world can be regarded as an overflowing

of the creative energy of God. Just as light derives from the sun and reflects its nature, so the created order derives from God and expresses divine nature. There is, on the basis of this model, a natural or organic connection between God and the creation.

However, the model has three weaknesses. First, it reflects a Platonic way of thinking that was part of the intellectual furniture of the world of late classical antiquity but is not well known today. As a result, this model seems strange and implausible to many contemporary western Christians.

Second, the image of a sun radiating light or a fire radiating heat suggests that creation is an involuntary emanation from God (or results from him involuntarily) rather than reflecting a conscious and willful decision on God's part to create. The Christian tradition has consistently emphasized that the act of creation rests upon God's prior decision to create, which this model cannot adequately express.

This naturally leads us to the third weakness, which relates to the impersonal nature of the emanationist model. The idea of a personal God, expressing a personality both in the very act of creation and in the subsequent result – the creation itself – is difficult to convey through this image. Nevertheless, the model clearly articulates a close connection between creator and creation, leading us to expect that something of the identity and nature of the creator is to be found in the creation.

2 *Construction*   Some biblical passages portray God as a master builder constructing a designed and ordered world (for example, Psalm 127: 1). The imagery is powerful, conveying ideas of purpose, planning, and deliberate intention to create. The image is important in that it brings out both the skill of the creator and the beauty and ordering of the resulting creation.

However, the image has a deficiency. Like the idea of creation found in Plato's dialogue *Timaeus*, this approach portrays creation as the assembly or organization of preexisting matter. To "create" is here understood to mean to give shape and form to *something that is already there*. The image of God as a builder suggests the assembling of the world from material already to hand. But, as we noted earlier (p. 78), Christians soon came to regard creation "from nothing" as the best way of describing God's creative action.

Nevertheless, despite this difficulty, it can be seen that the model conveys the insight that the character of the creator is, in some manner, expressed in the natural world, just as the character of an artist is communicated or embodied in her work. In particular, the notion of "ordering" – that is, the imparting or imposing of coherence or structure on the material in question – is clearly affirmed by this model. Whatever else the complex notion of "creation" may mean within a Christian context, it certainly includes the fundamental theme of ordering – a notion that is especially significant in the creation narratives of the Old Testament.

3 *Artistic expression*   Many Christian writers from various periods in the history of the church speak of creation as the handiwork of God, comparing it to a work of art that both is beautiful in itself and expresses the personality of its creator. This model of creation as the "artistic expression" of God as creator is particularly well expressed in the writings of the eighteenth-century North American theologian Jonathan Edwards and of the twentieth-century lay theologian Dorothy L. Sayers (1893–1957), especially in her remarkable book *The Mind of the Maker* (1941).

Figure 3.2   William Blake's watercolor "The Ancient of Days" (c. 1821), depicting God in the act of creating the world. Blake, William (1757–1827), "The Ancient of Days," frontispiece of *Europe: A Prophecy* (c. 1821). Relief etching, pen, and watercolor. Fitzwilliam Museum, University of Cambridge, UK. Source: Fitzwilliam Museum, University of Cambridge/Bridgeman Art Library.

Sayers, one of England's finest novelists of the period between the two World Wars, used the analogy between God creating the world and an author writing a novel in order to make two important points. First, the act of creation is a work of *love*. Sayers here sums up the wisdom of the Christian tradition down the ages. Love is the motivation for God's creation of the world. The creation is the expression of God's fundamental character. It is about bringing into being something that is valuable, something that really matters. Yes, it expresses the mind of its creator; but it is also something that is important in its own right. It matters partly because it is not identical with its creator, possessing instead its own distinct God-given identity.

Second, the creation has its own distinct integrity. It originates from God and reflects God's nature and character, but it is different from God. Sayers explores this point by asking us to imagine how an author creates and develops a character in a novel. Unless she respects the integrity of a character, he is likely to remain a two-dimensional and unreal fictional invention that readers will find difficult to take seriously.

The image of creation as "artistic expression" is helpful in that it supplements a deficiency of both models noted earlier – namely their impersonal character. The image of God as artist conveys the idea of personal expression in the creation of something beautiful, which reflects something of the creator. Once more, potential weaknesses need to be noted: for example, the model could easily lead to the idea of creation from preexisting matter, as in the case of a sculptor carving a statue from an already existing block of stone. However, the model offers us at least the possibility of thinking about creation from nothing, as in examples like the author who writes a novel or the composer who creates a melody and harmony. It also encourages us to seek for God's self-expression in the creation and adds theological credibility to a natural theology. There is also a natural link between the concept of creation as "artistic expression" and the highly significant concept of "beauty."

Now what are the implications of the belief in God as creator, as set out in the Christian creeds? Three implications may be noted.

First, a distinction must be drawn between God and the creation. A major theme of Christian theology, from the earliest of times, has been that of resisting the temptation to merge the creator and the creation. The theme is clearly stated in Paul's letter to the Romans, the opening chapter of which criticizes the tendency to reduce God to the level of the world. According to Paul, there is a natural human tendency, as a result of sin, to serve "created things rather than the creator" (Romans 1: 25). A central task of a Christian theology of creation is to distinguish God from the creation, while at the same time to affirm that it is God's creation. Many scholars believe that this distinction was of importance in shaping an intellectual framework within which the natural sciences could emerge.

In the second place, creation implies God's authority over the world. There is a characteristic biblical emphasis on the notion that the creator has authority over the creation. Humans are thus regarded as part of that creation; they have special functions within it. The doctrine of creation leads to the idea of human stewardship, which is to be contrasted with a secular notion of human ownership of the world. The creation is not ours; we hold it in trust for God. We are meant to be the stewards of God's creation, and we are responsible for the manner in which we exercise that stewardship. This insight is of major importance in relation to ecological and environmental concerns, in that it provides a theoretical foundation for the exercise of human responsibility toward the planet.

In the third place, the doctrine of God as creator implies the goodness of creation. This point is made in several places throughout the creation accounts of the Old Testament: "And God saw that it was good" (Genesis 1: 10, 18, 21, 25, 31). (Incidentally, the only thing that is "not good" about creation is that Adam was alone. Humanity is created as a social being, and humans are meant to exist in relation with one another.)

There is no place in Christian theology for the gnostic or dualist idea of the world as an inherently evil place. Christians holds that the world remains God's good creation and is capable of being redeemed and renewed. Affirming the goodness of creation also avoids the suggestion, unacceptable to most theologians, that God is responsible for evil. The constant biblical emphasis upon the goodness of creation is a reminder that the destructive force of sin is not present in the world by God's design or permission.

This is not to say that the creation is presently perfect. An essential component of the Christian doctrine of sin is the recognition that the world has departed from the trajectory upon which God placed it in the work of creation. It has become deflected from its intended course. It has fallen from the glory in which it was created. The world as we see it is not the world as it was intended to be. The existence of human sin, evil, and death are themselves tokens of the extent of the departure of the created order from its intended pattern. For this reason, most Christian reflections on redemption include the idea of some kind of restoration of creation to its original integrity, in order that God's intentions for it might find fulfillment. The Christian doctrine of salvation sets out some aspects of this theme, and we shall return to discuss it further later on (pp. 92–101).

The Christian Understanding of Humanity

"What are human beings, that you are mindful of them?" (Psalm 8: 4). From the beginning of history, people have wondered about their place in the greater scheme of things. Why are we here? What is our destiny? What is the meaning of human existence? The doctrine of creation offers the beginnings of an answer. It helps us to deepen our understanding and appreciation of the world in which we find ourselves placed.

The Christian understanding of God's creation is that humanity is part of it. Yet, although humanity is part of the created order, this does not mean that people are indistinguishable from the remainder of creation. Human beings have been set a little lower than the angels and have been "crowned with glory and honor" (Psalm 8: 5). Men and women are created "in the image of God" (Genesis 1: 27). In what follows we shall explore this idea further.

Figure 3.3   Michelangelo's fresco *The Creation of Adam* (1511–1512) from the Sistine Chapel, Rome. Michelangelo Buonarroti (1475–1564). Fresco, 280 × 570 cm. Rome, Vatican, Cappella Sistina (Sistine Chapel), 4th image. Source: Erich Lessing/AKG Images.

Humanity and the "image of God"

The brief yet deeply significant phrase "image of God" opens the way to a right understanding of human nature and of the overall place of humanity within the created order. Although humanity is not divine, it possesses a relationship with God that is different from that of other creatures. Humanity bears the image of God. For some, this is a statement of the privileged position of humanity within creation. Yet, for most Christian thinkers, it is above all an affirmation of responsibility and accountability toward the world in which we live.

So how are we to understand this relationship with God? How can we visualize it? What does it mean to speak of "being made in the image of God"? A number of models have been developed within Christian theology, of which we may note three.

First, the "image of God" can be seen as expressing the authority of God over humanity. In the ancient Near East monarchs would often display images of themselves as an assertion of their power in a region (see, for example, the golden statue of Nebuchadnezzar, described in Daniel 3: 1–7). To be created in the "image of God" could be understood there as being owned by God or as being accountable to God.

This idea seems to be reflected in an incident in the ministry of Jesus Christ (Luke 20: 22–25). Challenged as to whether it was right for Jews to pay taxes to the Roman authorities, Jesus requested that a coin be brought to him. He asked: "Whose image and title does it bear?" Those standing around replied that it was Caesar's. Christ then tells the crowd to give to Caesar what is Caesar's, and to God what is God's. While some might take this to be an evasion of the question, it is actually a challenge to those who bear God's image – that is, to humanity – to dedicate themselves to God.

Second, the idea of the "image of God" can be taken to refer to some kind of correspondence between human reason and the rationality of God as creator. On this understanding of things, there is an intrinsic resonance between the structures of the world and human thought. This approach is set out with particular clarity in Augustine of Hippo's major theological writing *On the Trinity*:

> The image of the creator is to be found in the rational or intellectual soul of humanity … [The human soul] has been created according to the image of God in order that it may use reason and intellect in order to apprehend and behold God.

For Augustine, humanity is created with the intellectual resources that allow people to find God by reflecting on the creation.

A third approach suggests that being made in the "image of God" affirms a human capacity to relate to God. On this understanding, to be created in the "image of God" is to possess the potential to enter into a relationship with God. The term "image" here expresses the idea that God has created humanity with a specific goal – namely in order for it to relate to God. Humanity is thus meant to exist in a relationship with its creator and redeemer. Augustine expressed this idea in a famous prayer: "You have made us for yourself, and our heart is restless until it finds its rest in you."

Blaise Pascal argued that the human experience of emptiness and yearning is both a reflection of the absence of such a relationship and a pointer to the true destiny of humanity. It illuminates human nature and discloses its ultimate goal – which, for Pascal, is God.

> What else does this longing and helplessness show us, other than that there was once in each person a true happiness, of which all that now remains is the empty print and trace?

Nothing and no one other than God is able to fill this "abyss" – a profound, God-shaped gap within human nature, implanted by God as a means of drawing people back to him.

This approach was developed further in the twentieth century by C. S. Lewis. Following Pascal, Lewis argues that there is a God-shaped gap within humanity that only God can fill. And in the absence of God people experience a deep sense of longing – a longing that is really for God, but is misunderstood as a longing for things within the world. And these things can never satisfy. If humanity is made for God, and God alone, then there is nothing else that will ultimately satisfy it. And, as Lewis argued, this God-given sense of longing provided a key to answering the great questions of life with which humanity has wrestled.

Yet the Christian understanding of human nature is not totally determined by the idea of being made in the image of God. Important though this idea may be, it needs to be supplemented with the idea of sin.

Humanity, the fall, and sin

For Christianity, humanity is sinful – that is, alienated from God; and, as a result of this fundamental disruption of its identity, it is alienated from society, from itself, and from the environment. What is sin? Although in everyday language the word "sin" means something like a "moral failing" or an "immoral act," the term has a more precise theological meaning. The fundamental sense of "sin" is something that separates humanity from God. Salvation is the breaking down of the barrier of separation between humanity and God on account of Christ.

Sin is thus the antithesis of salvation. It is quite simple to develop a list of fundamental New Testament concepts related to salvation and to link them to corresponding concepts related to sin. Some examples will help make this point.

Sin	Salvation
Alienation	Reconciliation
Captivity	Liberation
Guilt	Forgiveness
Condemnation	Vindication
Illness	Healing
Being lost	Being found

We shall explore some of these themes further, when we come to look at the Christian understanding of salvation later in this chapter (pp. 92–101).

Two narratives from the book of Genesis are often cited as illustrating some Christian insights into the profound contradictions within human nature – namely eating the fruit of the "tree of the knowledge of good and evil" and the construction of the Tower of Babel. The first of these Genesis narratives relates how Adam and Eve were placed in the garden of paradise and given complete freedom to eat of all its trees – except one (Genesis 2: 15–17). This limitation on their freedom proves too much for them. If they were to eat the fruit of the tree of the knowledge of good and evil, they would become like God himself, determining what is good and what is evil (Genesis 3: 1–5). We long for autonomy; we do not want to be accountable to anyone. As the great Russian novelist Fyodor Dostoyevsky pointed out in his novel *The Devils* (1871–1872), if there is no God, people are able to do as they please. This was one of the great themes of the golden age of atheism, which began with the French Revolution in 1789.

Much the same theme is found in the second Genesis narrative – the Tower of Babel (Genesis 11: 1–9). Karl Barth (1886–1968), one of the twentieth century's greatest Christian writers, saw in this narrative an illustration of one aspect of sinful human nature: the desire to assert human authority and power in the face of God. Barth suggested that the Tower of Babel could be interpreted as a symbol of our human longing to be able to have knowledge of God on our own terms. Yet this desire for human control contained within itself the seeds of its own negation. Like many, Barth was traumatized by the catastrophe of World War I, which discredited the optimistic progressivism of the Age of Reason. When humans take charge, Barth noted, they seem to mess things up.

Figure 3.4 Karl Barth (1886–1968). Source: Ullstein Bild/AKG Images.

Over the years, Christian thinkers have developed two fundamental images to help make sense of this puzzling human predicament: defection and deflection. The first is more characteristic of the Latin-speaking western church; the second, of the Greek-speaking eastern church.

The western view is found in the writings of Augustine of Hippo. For Augustine, humanity has defected from its true calling. Instead of using their God-given freedom to love God, human beings used it to advance their own self-centered agendas. As a result, they are now caught in a trap of their own making. Augustine argues that they are unable to break free from their entanglement with sin. Held captive by in-dwelling sin, human beings prove unable to do the good that they would like to do; instead they do the bad things they do not want to do (see Romans 7: 17–25). For Augustine, the freedom to love that ought to have led to fellowship with God – as Adam and Eve walked with God in the garden of Eden – led instead to self-love and to a desertion of God for the lesser good.

Augustine uses a series of images to illuminate how humanity has become trapped by sin in this way. It is like becoming ill and being unable to find a cure. It is like having fallen into a deep pit and being unable to get out. The essential point he wants to make is that, once sin – which he conceives of as an active force in human lives – has taken hold of people, they are unable to break free from its grasp. To use a modern analogy, it is like being addicted to heroin and unable to break the habit. Only God is able to heal this illness and to break the bonds that imprison humanity.

The eastern view can be found in the second-century writer Irenaeus of Lyons, who argued that humanity has been deflected from its true path by sin. Humanity has lost its way and needs to be helped back onto the right road. Irenaeus tends to see humanity as weak and easily misled. Humans were created as mere infants, not as mature beings, and they must learn and grow. Asked why God did not create humanity already endowed with perfection, Irenaeus replied that they were simply not ready to cope with it. "A mother is able to offer food to an infant, but the infant is not yet able to receive food unsuited to its age."

This way of thinking remains characteristic of churches that trace their roots back to the eastern, Greek-speaking part of the Mediterranean. Eastern and Russian Orthodoxy, for example, do not follow the western church in speaking of a "fall" but tend to think more in terms of a "wrong turn" or failure, which can be corrected through God's grace.

Yet, despite their differences, much the same insight lies beneath these two different ways of thinking about the human situation. On the Christian understanding of things, both eastern and western, human nature was intended to be the height of God's creation, but is now in need of radical remodeling and internal renewal. Like a once great palace fit for a king, it has fallen into disrepair and decay. Yet the situation can be redeemed. God's living presence within human nature could bring about the renewal, restoration, and repristination of what is now languishing in sin and death. If God were to enter into the human situation, the latter could be transformed from within. We can see here the prefiguring of a doctrine of the incarnation – the idea that God entered into our world and our history as one of us, in order to take us to heaven.

And this brings us to what many see as the central theme of Christian belief: the identity and significance of Jesus of Nazareth as the savior and redeemer of fallen humanity.

Jesus of Nazareth

Jesus of Nazareth is the central figure of the Christian faith. Christians have always insisted that there was something special, something qualitatively different about Jesus, which sets him apart from other religious teachers or thinkers. But what exactly is it that is special about him? This question is addressed in the area of Christian theology traditionally known as Christology. If theology can be understood as trying to make sense of God, then Christology is about trying to make sense of Jesus Christ.

The creeds insist that Jesus of Nazareth was a real historical person, who lived and died. Jesus was a first-century Jew who lived in Palestine in the reign of Tiberius Caesar and was executed by crucifixion under Pontius Pilate, the prefect of the Roman province of Judaea from AD 26 to 36. As we saw earlier (p. 1), the Roman historian Tacitus refers to Christians deriving their name from "Christ, who was executed at the hands of the procurator Pontius Pilate in the reign of Tiberius." The Christian faith certainly holds that Jesus existed as a real historical figure and that he was crucified.

Yet the Christian faith is not limited to the mere facts that Jesus lived in the Roman province of Judaea and was crucified by the Roman authorities. The interpretation of his life and death is of critical importance. The creeds weave together the leading themes of the New Testament's interpretation of the identity and significance of Jesus of Nazareth. Christian doctrine can be seen as the outcome of an extended and ongoing process of reflection on these biblical ideas and themes, including:

1   the terms that the New Testament uses to refer to Jesus;
2   the impact that Jesus made upon people during his ministry – for example, through his healing;
3   the resurrection, which New Testament writers interpret as an endorsement and validation of Jesus' exalted status in regard to God. Thus, for Paul, the resurrection demonstrates that Jesus is the Son of God (Romans 1: 3–4);
4   what Jesus is understood to have achieved, which is taken to be directly related to his identity. There is a close link between the Christian understanding of the person of Christ and the work of Christ. In other words, discussion of the identity of Jesus of Nazareth is interlocked with discussion of his achievement, and hence with his wider significance. We shall explore this issue further when reflecting on salvation in the following section.

In the present section we shall consider how Christian theology wove these various insights into a coherent understanding of the person of Christ, culminating in the concept of incarnation. As background to the definitive statement of this idea at the Council of Chalcedon (AD 451), we shall explore some aspects of the process of reflection on the New Testament within the earlier Christian tradition.

Early Christian approaches to the identity of Jesus of Nazareth

As we have seen from our analysis of the view of Jesus found in the New Testament (pp. 21–25), the first Christians believed that they were confronted with something so novel in the life, death, and resurrection of Jesus that they were obliged to employ a whole range of images, terms, and ideas to describe it. There was simply no single term or concept available that could capture the richness and profundity of their impressions and experience of Jesus. They were forced to use a whole variety of terms – many borrowed from Judaism – to illuminate the different aspects of their understanding of him. Taken together, these terms combined to build up an overall picture of Jesus.

At times, early Christian writers drew on ideas or concepts whose origins lay outside Judaism to try and build up this picture. For example, it is often thought that the opening section of John's gospel (John 1: 1–18), with its distinctive emphasis on the "Word" (Greek *logos*), is trying to explain how Jesus occupies the same place in the Christian understanding of the world as the idea of the Logos in secular Greek philosophy.

Yet this does not mean that Christians invented their understanding of Jesus' significance just because they happened to read a few textbooks of Stoic philosophy. Rather, they noticed an analogy or a parallel and saw the obvious advantages in using it to express something they already knew about. This use also went some way to make Christianity more understandable to an educated Greek audience. Even at this early stage in the Christian tradition, we can identify a principled determination to make the gospel both intelligible and accessible to those outside the church. The gospel was thus expressed using ideas and concepts that helped to bring out its central themes and to make them understandable to non-believers.

Two early viewpoints were quickly rejected as heretical. Ebionitism, a primarily Jewish sect that flourished in the early centuries of the Christian era, regarded Jesus as an ordinary human being, the human son of Mary and Joseph. This weak Christology soon came to be regarded as totally inadequate and passed into oblivion. More significant was the diametrically opposed view, which came to be known as docetism, from the Greek verb *dokein* (to "seem" or "appear"). This approach – which is probably best regarded as a tendency within theology rather than a definite theological position – argued that Christ was totally divine, and that his humanity was merely an appearance. The sufferings of Christ are thus treated as apparent rather than real. Docetism held a particular attraction for the gnostic writers of the second century, during which period it reached its zenith. By this time, however, other viewpoints were in the process of emerging, and they would eventually eclipse the docetic tendency.

The first period in the development of Christology centered on confirming and clarifying the best way of understanding the divinity of Jesus. That Jesus was human appeared to be something of a truism to most early patristic writers. What required explanation about Jesus concerned the manner in which he differed from other human beings rather than the ways in which he was similar to them. What was different about him? What was additionally true about him, that was true of no other person?

One debate proved to be of decisive importance in catalyzing the growing consensus within the Christian community about the best manner of conceptualizing the identity of Jesus of Nazareth: the Arian controversy of the fourth century.

The Arian controversy and the incarnation

One of the greatest challenges faced by the early church was the weaving together of the threads of the New Testament's testimonial to the identity of Jesus of Nazareth into a coherent theological tapestry. Christians gradually came to realize that no existing analogy or model was good enough to meet their needs in expressing the significance of Jesus of Nazareth. The concept of the incarnation began to emerge as one of central importance to the church's understanding of Jesus Christ.

While the idea was developed in slightly different ways by different writers, their core theme was that of God entering into history and taking on human nature in Jesus of Nazareth. This idea caused considerable philosophical difficulties for the prevailing schools of Hellenistic philosophy. How, many asked, could an immutable God enter into history?

Arius (c. 270–336), a priest in one of the larger churches of the great Egyptian city of Alexandria, argued that the best way of making Christianity's ideas about the identity of Jesus of Nazareth more attractive and credible to Hellenistic culture was to declare that he was not divine in any meaningful sense of the term. He was "first among the creatures" – that is, preeminent in rank, yet unquestionably a creature rather than a divine being. Now, Arius was careful to emphasize that the Son is not identical with other creatures; he argued that there is a clear distinction of rank between the Son and other human beings. Yet the basic idea was as clear as it was simple: Jesus of Nazareth was a human being and could not be regarded as divine in any meaningful way.

Arius' most important critic was Athanasius of Alexandria (c. 293–373). To Athanasius it seemed that Arius had destroyed the internal coherence of the Christian faith, rupturing the close connection between Christian belief and worship. Athanasius insisted that only

God can save. God, and God alone, can break the power of sin and bring humanity to eternal life. The fundamental characteristic of human nature is that it requires to be redeemed. No creature can save another creature. If Christ is not God, he is part of the problem, not its solution. The New Testament and the Christian liturgical tradition alike regarded Jesus Christ as the savior. Yet, as Athanasius emphasized, only God can save. So how are we to make sense of this? How can Jesus of Nazareth be our savior, if he is not divine? How can he save, if he is understood in a way that declares he is *not* able to save?

The only possible solution, Athanasius argued, was to accept that Jesus of Nazareth is none other than God incarnate. Salvation, for Athanasius, involves divine intervention, which he saw affirmed in a critically important biblical text: "the Word became flesh" (John 1: 14). God entered into the human situation, in order to change it.

In the end, the approach advocated by Athanasius triumphed, although it was some time before it achieved full acceptance in the Chalcedonian definition of the incarnation –called so because it received definitive formulation at the Council of Chalcedon in AD 451. In what follows we shall consider this landmark in more detail.

The incarnation: The Chalcedonian definition

The Christian doctrine of the person of Jesus Christ is often discussed in terms of "incarnation." "Incarnation" is a difficult yet important word, deriving from the Latin term for "flesh" and setting out the basic Christian belief that Jesus Christ is both divine and human. The doctrine of the incarnation declares that Jesus of Nazareth acts as God and for God in human history. Jesus is understood to be enabled and authorized to disclose God and to make promises in God's name.

The doctrine of the incarnation makes explicit what is implicit in the biblical affirmation that the "word became flesh and lived among us" (John 1: 14). The Greek word translated here as "lived" more accurately means "pitched his tent." As Christians travel on the journey of faith, they find a new tent pitched in their midst. God himself has come to dwell among them. The doctrine of the incarnation thus solidifies one of the great themes of the Christian faith: that God truly cares for humanity – not as a passive distant observer, but as an active fellow traveler on the road of human life.

The classic Christian understanding of the identity of Jesus of Nazareth is often summarized in the "doctrine of the two natures" – that is, the view that Jesus is perfectly divine and perfectly human – which was definitively stated by the Council of Chalcedon in AD 451. This doctrine laid down a controlling principle for classical Christology that has been accepted as definitive within orthodox Christian theology ever since. Chalcedon simply stated definitively what the first five centuries of Christian reflection on the New Testament had already established by using a variety of ways of speaking and thinking. The section of the Nicene Creed dealing with the identity of Jesus – which was modified and authorized by the Council of Chalcedon – reads like this:

> We believe in one Lord, Jesus Christ, the only Son of God, eternally begotten of the Father, God from God, Light from Light, true God from true God, begotten, not made, of one Being with the Father.

Figure 3.5   Mosaic depicting Jesus Christ, in the Byzantine church of Hagia Sophia, Istanbul, c. 1260. Istanbul/Constantinople (Turkey), Hagia Sophia, North Gallery. *Deesis* (*Christ with Mary and John the Baptist*). Mosaic, Byzantine, c. 1260. Source: Erich Lessing/AKG Images.

The point being made here is that Jesus of Nazareth is to be understood as both God and a human being. To make this point absolutely clear, the Council of Chalcedon used a technical term, already well established by this time. This is the Greek term *homoousios*, which is usually translated into English as "of one substance" or "of one being." Although this term was not itself biblical, it was widely regarded as expressing a thoroughly biblical insight. Jesus is "of one substance" with God, just as he is "of one substance" with humanity. In other words, Jesus is the same as God; it really is God who is encountered in Jesus, and not some messenger sent from God.

An important minority viewpoint must, however, be noted. The Council of Chalcedon did not succeed in establishing a consensus throughout the entire Christian world. A minority viewpoint emerged during the sixth century and is now generally known as monophysitism – literally, the view that there is "only one nature" (Greek *monos*, "one, single" and *phusis*, "nature") in Christ. The nature in question is understood to be divine rather than human. The intricacies of this viewpoint lie beyond the scope of this volume; the reader should note that the view itself remains normative within most Christian churches of the eastern Mediterranean world, including the Coptic, Armenian, Syrian, and Abyssinian churches.

Jesus of Nazareth as mediator between God and humanity

As we noted earlier, the doctrine of the incarnation established that Jesus Christ was to be thought of as perfectly human and perfectly divine. Important though this idea may be, it is not easy to visualize. So what models or analogies may be helpful as we try to visualize the place of Jesus of Nazareth on the Christian map of divine and human possibilities? In this section we shall explore one New Testament title for Christ that has been explored in some detail by Christian theologians – namely that of mediator: the idea that Jesus of Nazareth is a mediator between God and humanity at several points (Hebrews 9: 15; 1 Timothy 2: 5).

First, Jesus of Nazareth is able to mediate by transmitting knowledge of God to humanity. As someone who is both divine and human, Jesus can be thought of as a bridge or channel between God and humanity's knowledge of God. Second, Jesus is able to mediate between God and humanity, to re-establish the relationship between them. What was broken by sin can be repaired by grace.

This point is developed by many Christian theologians. A good example is found in John Calvin's *Institutes of the Christian Religion* (1559). Jesus Christ mediates between God and humanity. In order to act as a mediator, Calvin argues, Jesus Christ must be both divine and human. Since it was impossible for humans to ascend to God on account of their sin, God chose to descend to humanity instead. "The Son of God became the Son of Man, and received what is ours in such a way that he transferred to us what is his, making that which is his by nature to become ours through grace."

So what is mediated? Two complementary answers are given by the New Testament and by the long tradition of Christian theological engagement with Scripture: revelation and salvation. Christ mediates both knowledge of God and fellowship with God. This theme is expressed by many Christian writers, including Dorothy L. Sayers. She is perhaps best known for her crime novels, which featured Lord Peter Wimsey as an amateur aristocratic sleuth. However, she also developed a considerable interest in Christian theology, which is evident in works such as *The Mind of the Maker* and *Creed or Chaos?* In this second work Sayers argues that it is not good enough to agree that Jesus was a good teacher with some useful ideas, unless we have good reasons for asserting that there is something distinctive about Jesus that requires us to take those ideas with compelling seriousness. Hence, Sayers argues, the great questions of Christology are inevitable and must be addressed.

Having made this point, she then turns to consider the issue of mediation. Under what conditions is mediation between God and humanity possible? And in what way is Jesus capable of acting in his capacity as mediator? Her answer is that the "two natures" – in other words, the doctrine that Jesus is both truly human and truly divine – safeguard this idea.

> The central dogma of the Incarnation is that by which relevance stands or falls. If Christ was only man, then He is entirely irrelevant to any thought about God; if He is only God, then He is entirely irrelevant to any experience of human life.

We now turn to consider an especially significant response to Jesus, which has a particularly important place in today's world: that of Islam.

Islamic criticisms of the Christian understanding of Jesus of Nazareth

The growing global importance of Islam makes the question of how Muslims view Jesus of increasing significance to Christianity. Islam acknowledges that Jesus was a prophet and a messenger of God. The name "Jesus" (Arabic *isa*) is used 25 times. In most cases, this name is linked with the title "Son of Mary" (*ibn Mariam*); it is less frequently linked with that of Moses. Although the New Testament makes it clear that the name "Jesus" means "God saves" (Matthew 1.21), the Qu'ran offers no explanation of the name *isa*. The related term "Messiah" (*al masih*) is also used in the Qu'ran. Again, the rich Old Testament associations of this term as "God's anointed" do not seem to be understood. It is not clear why the Qu'ran should refer to Jesus as the "son of Mary." This title is used very rarely in the New Testament (Mark 6: 3). It is also unusual (but not unknown) in the Semitic world for any major figure to be named after his mother rather than father. The Qu'ran also refers to Jesus using quite elevated language. Thus he is described as the "word of God" and the "spirit of God," formulae that give him a place of honor within the Islamic understanding of the progression of revelation. This progression is held to reach its definitive climax in the revelation to Muhammad, which is committed to writing in the Qu'ran.

The Islamic view of the significance of the death and resurrection of Jesus is somewhat complex. Although there are points where the Qu'ran refers to the death of Christ, indicating that it was in accord with the will of God, the precise manner and significance of his death remains unclear. One passage seems to teach that Jesus was neither killed by the Jews nor crucified by his enemies, "although it seemed so to them." Rather Jesus was translated to heaven, some other unnamed person taking his place on the cross. The phrase "it seemed so to them" would thus bear the sense of either "the Jews thought that Jesus died on the cross" or "the Jews thought that the person on the cross was Jesus."

Perhaps most significantly, the idea of the incarnation is completely unacceptable to Islam. The Christian belief that Christ is the Son of God is seen by Islamic writers as a reversion to some form of paganism, characterized by the idea of God having physical children. The distinctively Christian notion of what the phrase "son of God" entails appears not to have been fully grasped at the time of the composition of the Qu'ran. It therefore must be stressed, in this context too, that the orthodox Christian doctrine of Jesus as the "Son of God" in no way means that God physically fathered Jesus. Muslims generally regard this description as an instance of the heresy of *ittakhadha*, by which Jesus is acknowledged to be the physical Son of God. This is not a correct perception. The point of using the title "Son" is fundamentally relational: it is an affirmation of the unique status of Jesus in relation to God, and hence of the unique role of Jesus within the Christian tradition as a bearer of divine revelation and as the agent of divine salvation.

The Christian Understanding of Salvation

A central theme of the Christian message is that the human situation has in some way been transformed by the death and resurrection of Jesus Christ. This change is often described as "salvation." Although the word "salvation" has a very specific meaning, it is often used in a more general sense. To begin with, let us reflect on some of the analogies or images of salvation that are found in Paul's letters in the New Testament. These have proved deeply influential on Christian reflection on what some theologians call "the benefits of Christ" – in other words, on the difference that Jesus of Nazareth made to humanity through his life, death, and resurrection.

New Testament images of salvation

The term "salvation" does not necessarily have any specifically Christian reference. It can be used in a thoroughly secular manner. For example, it was common for Soviet writers, especially during the late 1920s, to speak of Lenin as the "savior" of the Russian people. Military coups in African states during the 1980s frequently resulted in the setting up of "councils of salvation," which would try to restore political and economic stability. Salvation can thus be a purely secular notion, concerned with political emancipation or the general human quest for liberation.

Even in the realm of religion, salvation is not a specifically Christian idea. Many – but, it must be stressed, not all – of the world's religions have concepts of salvation. They differ enormously, both in their understanding of how salvation is achieved and in the shape or form that salvation is supposed to take.

In turning to explore the Christian notion of salvation in more detail, we need to engage with two questions. First, there is the question of how "salvation" itself is to be construed. In what way is the Christian understanding of the nature of salvation distinctive? We shall consider some ways of thinking about salvation in the present section.

Second, there is the question of how salvation is possible, and in particular how it is grounded in the history of Jesus Christ. Or, to put this another way: What is the basis of salvation, according to Christian doctrine? Both these questions have been the subject of intense discussion throughout history, and in the next section we shall consider some themes that emerge from this discussion.

We begin by considering how salvation is to be understood. Throughout his letters in the New Testament, Paul uses a rich range of images to illuminate and clarify what benefits Christ secures for believers. He clearly assumes that his readers will be able to grasp what these analogies are meant to convey. In what follows we shall explore some of these images and try to appreciate their importance.

The first image is that of salvation itself. The term has a number of meanings, including release from danger, captivity, or some form of fatal illness. Notions such as "healing" and "liberation" can be seen as being encompassed into the sphere of this important Pauline term. Augustine of Hippo suggested that the church was like a hospital, in that it was full of people who were in the process of being healed. Paul sees salvation as having past (e.g., Romans 8: 24), present (e.g., 1 Corinthians 1: 18), and future (e.g., Romans 13: 11) dimensions. Thus the word "salvation" can refer to something that has already happened in the past, to something that is happening in the present, and to something that will happen in the future.

Many Christian preachers use narratives to make this point. One favorite is the response of a Salvation Army officer to a child who asked whether the officer was saved. The reply makes the point perfectly: "I have been saved from the guilt of sin. I am being saved from the power of sin. And I shall finally be saved from the presence of sin."

A second image of importance is that of adoption. At several points, Paul speaks of Christians as having been "adopted" into the family of God (Romans 8: 15, 23; Galatians 4: 5). It is widely thought that Paul is here drawing on a legal practice, common in Greco-Roman culture (yet, interestingly, not recognized in traditional Jewish law). According to many interpreters of Paul, to speak of "believers" having been adopted into the family of

God is to make the point that believers share the same inheritance rights as Jesus Christ, and hence will receive the glory that Christ achieved (although only after first sharing in his sufferings).

A third image is that of "justification." At the time of the Reformation in the sixteenth century (pp. 151–154), many Protestant writers came to place particular importance on the image of justification. Especially in those letters dealing with the relation of Christianity to Judaism (such as Galatians and Romans), Paul affirms that believers have been "justified through faith" (e.g., Romans 5: 1–2). This is widely held to involve a change in a believer's legal status in the sight of God and in his or her ultimate assurance of acquittal before God, despite his or her sinfulness. The noun "justification" and the verb "to justify" thus came to signify entering into a right relationship with God, or perhaps being made righteous in the sight of God.

A fourth image is that of redemption. This term primarily bears the sense of "securing someone's release through a payment." In the ancient world, which acted as the backdrop to Paul's thought, "redemption" could be used to refer to the liberation of prisoners of war or to securing liberty for those who had sold themselves into slavery, often to pay off a family debt. Paul's basic idea appears to be that the death of Christ secures for believers freedom from slavery to the law or to death, in order that they might become slaves of God instead (1 Corinthians 6: 20; 7: 23).

A fifth image is that of reconciliation – the restoration of a broken relationship. Paul speaks of God having "reconciled us to himself through Christ," and he declares that "in Christ God was reconciling the world to himself" (2 Corinthians 5: 18–19). Paul uses the same word elsewhere in his writings to refer to the restoration of a fractured human relationship, asking husbands to be reconciled to their alienated wives. This strongly relational way of thinking about salvation is particularly accessible in modern western culture.

In more recent times, theologians and preachers have tried to translate these ideas into concepts that connect up easily with present cultural concerns. For example, some speak of salvation in terms of political liberation; others in terms of securing personal fulfillment. The basic theme, however, remains essentially the same: salvation is about God enabling humanity to become what it was really meant to be, despite its deflection and defection through sin (pp. 84–85).

We must now turn to the second of our questions about salvation. How are we to understand the manner in which the crucifixion and resurrection of Jesus of Nazareth fit into God's transformation of the human situation? This field of Christian thought is often referred to as "theories of the atonement." In what follows we shall look at a number of ways in which Christians understand how Jesus is the ground for salvation. These are best seen as complementary perspectives on a complex subject, or multiple layers of a stratified reality. We begin by reflecting on the theme of the victory of Jesus of Nazareth over death and sin.

Christ the victor: The defeat of death and sin

"Thanks be to God, who gives us the victory through our Lord Jesus Christ" (1 Corinthians 15: 57). The early church gloried in the triumph of Jesus of Nazareth upon the cross, and in the victory he won over sin, death, and Satan. The gates of heaven had been thrown wide open through the conquest of Calvary. The powerful imagery of the triumphant Jesus rising from the dead and being installed as "ruler of all" (Greek *pantokrator*) seized the imagination of the Christian East. The cross was seen as the focal point of a famous battle, comparable to the great Homeric epics, in which the forces of good and evil engaged, the good emerging victorious.

The early church seems to have been rather more concerned to proclaim Christ's victory over the enemies of humanity than to speculate over precisely how it came about. Jesus' resurrection and his triumphant opening of the gates of heaven to believers was something to be proclaimed and celebrated rather than subjected to theological analysis.

The Roman cultural context of early Christianity suggested one way of thinking about such a triumph. The victory of Jesus over his enemies was depicted as being like the great triumphant processions of ancient Rome, marking the achievement of Rome's military leaders. In its classical form, the triumphal parade proceeded from the Campus Martius through the streets of Rome, finally ending up at the temple of Jupiter on the Capitoline

Figure 3.6   A triumphal procession in Rome celebrating Titus' victory over the Jews in AD 70; carved on the Arch of Titus, triumphal arch in the Forum Romanum erected in AD 81. The New Testament portrays Jesus of Nazareth as a triumphant victor over sin and death. Rome (Italy), the Arch of Titus, section of the left internal relief: Triumphal procession with the seven-armed candlestick from the Temple of Solomon. Source: Erich Lessing/AKG Images.

Hill. The parade was led by the triumphant general's soldiers, who often carried placards with slogans that described the general and his achievements, or showed maps of the territories he had conquered. Other soldiers led carts containing booty that would be turned over to Rome's treasury. A section of the parade included prisoners, often the leaders of the defeated cities or countries, bound in chains.

It was a small step for Christian writers to use this imagery as a way of portraying Jesus of Nazareth's triumph over his enemies – such as sin and death. This powerful symbolism was firmly grounded in the New Testament, which spoke of the victorious Jesus as "making captivity a captive" (Ephesians 4: 8). While this theme can be found in some Christian art of this early period, its most dramatic impact was upon the hymns of the period. One of them portrays Christ's triumphant procession and celebrates his defeat of his foes.

> The royal banners forward go,
> The cross shines forth in mystic glow;
> Where he in flesh, our flesh Who made,
> Our sentence bore, our ransom paid.

Christ the harrower of hell: Atonement as restoration

A further development of this theme of victory over death depicts Jesus of Nazareth as extending the triumph of the cross and resurrection to the netherworld. The dramatic and colorful medieval idea of "the harrowing of hell" holds that, after dying upon the cross, Jesus descended to hell and broke down its gates in order that the imprisoned souls might go free. The idea rests (rather tenuously, it has to be said) upon a biblical text (1 Peter 3: 18–22) that speaks of Jesus "preaching to the spirits in prison."

The hymn "You Choirs of New Jerusalem," written by Fulbert of Chartres (c. 970–1028), expresses this theme in two of its verses, picking up the theme of Christ as the "lion of Judah" (Revelation 5: 5) defeating Satan, the serpent (Genesis 3: 15):

> For Judah's lion bursts his chains
> Crushing the serpent's head;
> And cries aloud through death's domain
> To wake the imprisoned dead.
>
> Devouring depths of hell their prey
> At his command restore;
> His ransomed hosts pursue their way
> Where Jesus goes before.

The idea rapidly became established in popular English literature of the Middle Ages. One of the most important pieces of Christian literature of this period is *Piers the Plowman*, traditionally attributed to William Langland. In this poem the narrator tells of how he falls asleep and dreams of Jesus of Nazareth throwing open the gates of hell and addressing the following words to Satan:

> Here is my soul as a ransom for all these sinful souls, to redeem those that are worthy. They are mine; they came from me, and therefore I have the better claim on them. ... You, by falsehood and crime and against all justice, took away what was mine, in my own domain; I, in fairness, recover them by paying the ransom, and by no other means. What you got by guile is won back by grace. ... And as a tree caused Adam and all mankind to die, so my gallows-tree shall bring them back to life.

It is clear that this highly dramatic understanding of the way in which Christ threw open the gates of death and hell, allowing their imprisoned masses to escape and enter into the joys of heaven, made a potent appeal on the imagination of the readers of Piers Plowman.

Such is the power of this image that it lingers, often unrecognized, in later writings. A particularly striking example can be found in C. S. Lewis's children's tale *The Lion, the Witch and the Wardrobe*. The book tells the story of Narnia, a land discovered by accident by four children as they rummage around in an old wardrobe. In this work we encounter the White Witch, who keeps the land of Narnia covered in a perpetual wintry snow. As we read on, we realize that she rules Narnia not as a matter of right, but by stealth. The true ruler of the land is absent; in his absence, the witch subjects the land to oppression. In the midst of this land of winter stands the witch's castle, within which many of the original inhabitants have been imprisoned as stone statues.

As the narrative moves on, we discover that the rightful ruler of the land is Aslan, a lion. As Aslan advances into Narnia, winter gives way to spring and the snow begins to melt. The witch realizes that her power is starting to fade and moves to eliminate the threat posed to her by Aslan. Aslan surrenders himself to the forces of evil and allows them to do their worst with him – yet by so doing he disarms them. Lewis's description of the resurrection of Aslan is one of his more tender moments, evoking as it does the deep sense of sorrow so evident in the New Testament accounts of the burial of Christ and the joy of recognition of the reality of the resurrection. Lewis then describes how Aslan – the lion of Judah, who has burst his chains – breaks into the castle, breathes upon the statues, and restores them to life before leading the liberated army through the shattered gates of the once great fortress – to freedom. Hell has been harrowed, and its inhabitants liberated from its dreary shades.

Figure 3.7 The Harrowing of Hell, as depicted in Jean de Berry's *Petites Heures* (14th century). Harrowing of Hell, folio 166 from Jean de Berry's *Petites Heures*. Source: Bibliothèque nationale de France, Paris, BNF Lat 18104.

Christ the redeemer: Atonement as satisfaction

A third approach to the meaning of the death of Christ integrates a series of biblical passages that deal with notions of judgment and forgiveness. The understanding of the work of Christ outlined in the previous sections has enormous attractions, not least on account of its highly dramatic character. However, it also has some serious weaknesses. For the eleventh-century writer Anselm of Canterbury, two were of particular importance. In the first place, it failed to explain why God should wish to redeem us. And, in the second, it was of little value in making us understand how Jesus of Nazareth was involved in the process of redemption. Anselm felt that more explanation was required.

To meet this need, he developed an approach to the achievement of Jesus of Nazareth that stressed the fact that God redeemed humanity in a way that is consistent with the moral ordering of the creation, which reflects God's own nature. God cannot create the universe as an expression of his own will and nature and then violate its moral order by acting in a completely different way in the redemption of humanity. God must redeem humanity in a way that is consistent with his own nature and purposes. Redemption must in the first place be moral, and in the second place be seen to be moral. God cannot employ one standard of morality at one point and another later on. God is therefore under a self-imposed obligation to respect the moral order of the creation.

Having established this point, Anselm considers how redemption is possible. The basic dilemma can be summarized as follows. God cannot restore humanity to fellowship without first dealing with human sin. Sin is a disruption of the moral ordering of the universe. It represents the rebellion of the creation against its creator. It represents an insult and an offense to God. The situation must be "made right" before the fellowship between God and humanity can be restored. God must therefore "make good" the situation in a way that is consistent with both divine mercy and divine righteousness. Anselm thus introduces the concept of "satisfaction" – a payment or some other action that compensates for the offense of human sin. Once this satisfaction has been brought, the situation can revert to normal. But this satisfaction must first be achieved.

Yet human beings do not have the ability to bring this kind of satisfaction. It lies beyond their resources. They need to do it – but they cannot. Humanity ought to render satisfaction for its sins, but it is unable to. God is under no obligation to bring satisfaction – but God could do it, if that were appropriate. Therefore, Anselm argues, if God were to become a human being, the resulting God-person would have both the obligation (as a human being) and the ability (as God) to render the necessary satisfaction. Thus the incarnation brings a just solution of this dilemma, leading to the transformation of the human situation. The death of Jesus of Nazareth upon the cross demonstrates God's total opposition to sin, while at the same time providing the means by which sin could be really and truly forgiven and the way opened to a renewed fellowship between humanity and God.

The basic idea is that the value of the satisfaction thus offered had to be equivalent to the weight of human sin. Anselm argued that the Son of God became incarnate in order that he, as God incarnate, should both take on the human obligation to bring satisfaction and possess the divine ability to pay a satisfaction of the magnitude required for redemption.

This idea is faithfully reproduced by Mrs Cecil F. Alexander (1818–1895) in her famous nineteenth-century hymn "There Is a Green Hill Far Away":

> There was no other good enough
> To pay the price of sin;
> He only could unlock the gate
> Of heaven, and let us in.

But how does the death of Jesus of Nazareth upon the cross affect us? In what way do we share in the benefits of his death and resurrection? Anselm felt that this point did not require discussion, and so he gave no guidance on the matter. Later Christian writers, however, felt that it needed to be addressed. Three main ways of understanding how believers relate to Christ in this respect may be noted.

1   *Participation* Through faith, believers participate in Jesus Christ. They are "in Christ," to use Paul's famous phrase. They are caught up in him and share in his risen life. As a result, they share in all the benefits won by Christ through his obedience upon the cross.
2   *Representation* Christ is the covenant representative of humanity. Through faith, we come to be within the covenant between God and humanity. All that Christ has won for us is available to us, on account of the covenant between God and his church. Christ, through his obedience upon the cross, represents God's covenant people and wins benefits for them as their representative. By coming to faith, individuals come to be within the covenant and thus participate in all its benefits won by Christ.
3   *Substitution* Jesus is here understood to be a substitute for believers. They ought to have been crucified on account of their sins; Jesus is crucified in their place. God thus allows Jesus to take human guilt upon himself, in order that his righteousness, won through obedience upon the cross, might become the believers' through faith.

The death of Christ as a perfect sacrifice

The New Testament draws on Old Testament imagery and expectations, in presenting the death of Jesus of Nazareth upon the cross as a sacrifice. This approach, which is especially associated with the letter to the Hebrews, interprets Christ's sacrificial offering as an effective and perfect sacrifice, which was able to accomplish what the sacrifices of the Old Testament were only able to intimate. Paul's use of the Greek term *hilastērion*, often translated as "mercy seat" (Romans 3: 25), is important here, as it is drawn from Old Testament sacrificial rituals related to the purging of sin.

This idea is developed subsequently within the Christian tradition. In order for humanity to be restored to God, the mediator must sacrifice himself; without this sacrifice, such restoration is simply impossible. Writing in the fourth century, Athanasius of Alexandria argues that Christ's sacrifice was superior in several respects to those required under the Old Covenant:

> Christ offers a sacrifice which is trustworthy, of permanent effect, and which is unfailing in its nature. The sacrifices which were offered according to the Law were not trustworthy, since they

had to be offered every day, and were again in need of purification. In contrast, the Saviour's sacrifice was offered once only, and was accomplished in its entirety, and can thus be relied upon permanently.

This point was developed further in Athanasius' *Festal Letters*, written annually to celebrate the feast of Easter. In these letters Athanasius develops the New Testament idea that there is an important analogy between the death of Christ on the cross and the sacrifice of a lamb during the Jewish festival of the Passover, which commemorates Israel's deliverance from Egypt:

> [Christ], being truly of God the Father, became incarnate for our sakes, so that he might offer himself to the Father in our place, and redeem us through his offering and sacrifice. … This is he who, in former times, was sacrificed as a lamb, having been foreshadowed in that lamb. But afterwards, he was slain for us. "For Christ, our passover, is sacrificed".
>
> (1 Corinthians 5: 7)

Augustine of Hippo brought a new clarity to the whole discussion of the nature of Christ's sacrifice through his crisp and highly influential definition of a sacrifice, set out in *City of God*: "A true sacrifice is offered in every action which is designed to unite us to God in a holy fellowship." On the basis of this definition, Augustine has no difficulties in speaking of Christ's death as a sacrifice: "By his death, which is indeed the one and most true sacrifice offered for us, he purged, abolished, and extinguished whatever guilt there was by which the principalities and powers lawfully detained us to pay the penalty." In this sacrifice Christ was both victim and priest; he offered himself up as a sacrifice: "He offered sacrifice for our sins. And where did he find that offering, the pure victim that he would offer? He offered himself, in that he could find no other."

These themes remain important to Christians, as can be seen from the *Catechism of the Catholic Church* (1992), which sets them out as follows:

> After agreeing to baptize [Jesus of Nazareth] along with the sinners, John the Baptist looked at Jesus and pointed him out as the "Lamb of God, who takes away the sin of the world." By doing so, he reveals that Jesus is at the same time the suffering Servant who silently allows himself to be led to the slaughter and who bears the sin of the multitudes, and also the Paschal Lamb, the symbol of Israel's redemption at the first Passover. Christ's whole life expresses his mission: "to serve, and to give his life as a ransom for many."

Christ the lover: Atonement and the enkindling of love

A leading theme of the New Testament's understanding of the death of Christ is that this act demonstrates the love of God for humanity and elicits a matching love in response. This theme is developed in Christian theology in terms of God stooping down to enter the created world and becoming incarnate in Christ. Augustine of Hippo was one of many patristic writers to stress that one of the motivations underlying the mission of Christ was to demonstrate God's love for us. The love of God for a wounded humanity is thus focused on an act of divine humility: the act of God's leaving the glory of heaven to enter the poverty and suffering of the created order and finally to suffer death upon the cross.

The recognition of the fact that Christ's death can be seen as a demonstration of divine love surfaces at the earliest stages of Christian thinking. The third-century writer Clement of Alexandria pointed out how the incarnation of Christ, and especially his death, represents a powerful affirmation of the love of God for humanity and a demand that humanity demonstrate a comparable love for God.

> For [Christ] came down, for this he assumed human nature, for this he willingly endured the sufferings of humanity, that by being reduced to the measure of our weakness, he might raise us to the measure of his power. And just before he poured out his offering, when he gave himself as a ransom, he left us a new testament: "I give you my love" (John 13: 34). What is the nature and extent of this love? For each of us he laid down his life, the life which was worth the whole universe, and he requires in return that we should do the same for each other.

Such thoughts have proved a powerful stimulus to the Christian imagination. This theme is developed in an imaginatively powerful way in one of the most reflective Spanish spiritual writers of the Renaissance. Juana de la Cruz (1481–1534) is remembered particularly for her *Book of Consolation*, which was widely admired during the Spanish Golden Age. Her discussion of the passion of Christ is notable in several respects, particularly her explicit use of feminine images to unlock its theological significance. The crucifixion of Jesus of Nazareth is here compared to a woman giving birth. For Juana, reflecting on the pain and sorrow that Jesus suffered in order to give life to the children of God is a powerful affirmation of the love of God for humanity – a love that is here expressed using strongly maternal imagery.

> Christ gave birth to us all with very great pains and torments at the time of his cruel and bitter passion. And since we cost him so dearly and the labor through which he gave birth to us was so grueling that it made him sweat drops of blood, he can do nothing but pray and plead for us before the Father, like a very compassionate mother, desiring that we should be saved and that our souls should be enlightened, so that he might not have suffered his pain and torment in vain.

Salvation and the "threefold office of Christ"

At the season of Epiphany (p. 239), the Christian churches recall the visit of the Magi (usually translated as "wise men") – the rulers from the East, who came to visit the infant Jesus at Bethlehem (Matthew 2: 1–12). These mysterious visitors brought three gifts with them: gold, frankincense, and myrrh. So might these three gifts tell us anything about how they understood the significance of this infant?

Early church writers believed that they did. Each of these gifts was appropriate for a certain kind of person. They were valuable items, appropriate as gifts for a king in the ancient world: gold was a precious metal, frankincense was a perfume or incense, and myrrh was anointing oil. Indeed, these same three items were apparently among the gifts that King Seleucus Callinicus offered to the god Apollo at the temple in Miletus in 243 BC.

Yet early Christian writers regarded these gifts as more than honorific. Each one disclosed something of the true significance of Jesus of Nazareth. Gold was appropriate for a king, expressing his authority; frankincense was appropriate for a priest, who would make sacrifice in the temple; and myrrh was a sign of his forthcoming death, in that he would be wrapped in clothes soaked in this oil.

This way of thinking eventually developed into what is usually called "the threefold office of Christ," which became particularly influential in reformed theology during the sixteenth and seventeenth centuries (although its ideas can be traced back much earlier than this). Christ, it is argued, brought to fulfillment the three great "offices" or "roles" of the Old Testament – the prophet, the priest, and the king.

These three categories were seen as a convenient summary of all that Jesus of Nazareth had achieved in order to redeem his people. Jesus is a prophet (Matthew 21: 11; Luke 7: 16), a priest (Hebrews 2: 17; 3: 1) and a king (Matthew 21: 5; 27: 11), bringing together in his one person the three great offices of the Old Testament. Jesus is the prophet who, like Moses, will see God face to face (Deuteronomy 17: 15); he is the king who, like David, will establish a new people of God and reign over it in justice and compassion (2 Samuel 7: 12–16); he is the priest who will cleanse his people of its sins. Thus the three gifts brought to Jesus by the Magi were to be seen as reflecting or prefiguring these three functions. The great nineteenth-century Princeton theologian Charles Hodge declared that fallen humanity needed "a Savior who is a prophet to instruct us; a priest to atone and to make intercession for us; and a king to rule over and protect us."

Grace

A central theme in the Bible is that God's choice of a people or of individuals is not determined by their merits but by God's love and that it comes about through God's will. This can be seen particularly in God's decision to choose Israel as his people. The Old Testament regularly affirms that Israel was chosen not because of anything it had to offer, but solely through the grace of God (Deuteronomy 7: 7; Isaiah 41: 8–9; Ezekiel 20: 5). This, of course, was not understood to abrogate Israel's responsibility to live up to its responsibilities as God's people. Many of the Old Testament prophets stressed the conditionality of Israel's election. Unless Israel behaved in ways appropriate to its identity and calling as God's chosen people, that status would be revoked.

Our attention in this section focuses on the idea of God's being gracious and generous. Salvation is not understood to be the consequence of human merit or achievement. This idea is often expressed through the concept of "grace." For Paul, Christians are saved through grace, not through works (Ephesians 2: 1–10). In other words, their salvation does not depend upon their achievements but upon the generosity and graciousness of God. Through grace, salvation is made possible for those who have neither the merit nor the intrinsic capacity to secure it for themselves. Hence grace affirms God's sheer generosity and goodness.

Such ideas were developed and clarified in the long process of wrestling with the Bible within the Christian church. Initially this process of reflection focused on the person of Christ and on the doctrine of the Trinity. The question of what it means to speak of a "gracious God" did not receive detailed attention until the late fourth and early fifth centuries. One especially important debate helped crystallize Christian perceptions of how best to systematize the New Testament's teaching on grace: the Pelagian controversy of the early fifth century.

The Pelagian controversy of the fifth century

The central figure in the controversy was Augustine of Hippo. Augustine had been converted to Christianity after a long struggle with a series of questions concerning the meaning of life – such as the origin of evil and how the good life may be lived out in practice. In Augustine's view, humanity was totally dependent upon God for its salvation. Human nature is frail, weak, and prone to becoming lost; it needs divine assistance and care if it is to be restored and renewed. Grace, according to Augustine, is God's generous and quite unmerited care for humanity, through which this process of healing may begin. Human nature requires transformation through the grace of God, so generously given. An integral aspect of Augustine's thinking at this point is the idea of "original sin" – that is, the idea that humanity was contaminated by sin from the moment of its first appearance.

For Augustine, humanity is universally affected by sin as a consequence of the fall. The human mind has been darkened and weakened by sin. The human will has been weakened (but not eliminated) by sin. Using the gospel's analogy of Christ as the physician, Augustine argues that Jesus of Nazareth both diagnoses the human situation (sin) and offers humanity a cure that it cannot secure by itself (grace). It is through the grace of God alone that this illness is recognized for what it is and that a cure is made available.

So what are the implications for our understanding of human nature? For Augustine, humanity is now imperfect: it is wounded and has been robbed of grace. God may have made humanity perfect; as a consequence of sin, humanity is now diseased and needs to be healed. One of the symptoms of sin that Augustine discusses in detail is the captivity of the human free will. For him, human freedom has been compromised by sin. Our desires and longings, which should have been directed toward God, are misdirected toward things of the world. "We look for happiness not in you," Augustine wrote in a prayer, "but in what you have created." The human free will has been weakened and incapacitated – but, to repeat, not eliminated or destroyed – through sin. In order for that free will to be restored and healed, the operation of divine grace is required.

In order to explain this point, Augustine uses the analogy of a pair of scales with two balance pans. One balance pan represents good, and the other evil. If the pans were properly balanced, the arguments in favor of doing good or doing evil could be weighed and a proper conclusion drawn. But, asks Augustine, what if the balance pans are loaded? What happens if someone puts several heavyweights in the balance pan on the side of evil? The scales will still work, but they are seriously biased toward making an evil decision. Augustine argues that this is exactly what has happened to humanity through sin. The human free will is biased toward evil. It really exists, and it really can make decisions – just as the loaded scales still work. But, instead of giving a balanced judgment, it is seriously biased toward evil. Using this and related analogies, Augustine argues that the human free will really exists in sinners but is compromised by sin.

Augustine's essential point is that humanity ultimately does not have control over its own behavior and abilities. He understands humanity to be born with a sinful disposition; an inherent bias toward acts of sinning is part of human nature. Augustine develops this point with the help of three important analogies: original sin as a "disease," as a "power," and as "guilt."

The first analogy treats sin as a hereditary disease, which is passed down from one generation to another. As we saw above, this disease weakens humanity and cannot be cured by human agency. Christ is thus the divine physician by whose "wounds we are healed" (Isaiah 53: 5), and salvation is understood in essentially sanative or medical terms.

The second analogy treats sin as a power that holds humanity captive and from whose grip people are unable to break free by themselves. The human free will is captivated by the power of sin and may only be liberated by grace. Christ is thus seen as the liberator, the source of the grace that breaks the power of sin.

The third analogy treats sin as an essentially judicial or forensic concept – guilt – which is passed down from one generation to the next. In a society that placed a high value on law – such as the late Roman empire, in which Augustine lived and worked – this was regarded as a particularly helpful way of understanding sin. Jesus of Nazareth thus comes to bring forgiveness and pardon.

But some were deeply uneasy about Augustine's ideas, feeling that they downplayed, or possibly even denied, human freedom and responsibility. The Pelagian debate centered on these themes. Augustine's opponent in this debate was Pelagius, a British Christian who had settled in Rome in the late fourth century. Pelagius was disturbed by the moral laxity of Roman Christians and argued vociferously against Augustine's doctrine of grace, which, he argued, failed to acknowledge the need for Christians to actively seek perfection. For Pelagius, there was nothing wrong with human nature. If God told people to be perfect, they were capable of being perfect. Where Augustine argued that sinfulness frustrated the human desire to be good and to do good, Pelagius argued that real problem was a lack of commitment.

In AD 413 Pelagius wrote a lengthy letter to a Roman woman of high birth named Demetrias, who had recently decided to turn her back on wealth in order to become a nun. In this letter Pelagius made clear the consequences of his views on human nature and free will. God has created humanity and knows precisely what it is capable of doing. Hence all the commands given to us can be obeyed, and are meant to be obeyed. It is no excuse to argue that human frailty prevents these commands from being fulfilled. God has made human nature, and only asks of it what it can manage.

Pelagius went on to make the somewhat uncompromising assertion that, since perfection is possible for humanity, it is obligatory. As things turned out, the moral rigor of this position and its unrealistic view of human nature served only to strengthen Augustine's hand, as he developed the rival understanding of a tender and kindly God attempting to heal and restore a wounded human nature.

Perhaps the sharpest contrast between Augustine and Pelagius is the one concerning the basis of salvation. What do people need to do to in order be saved? The two writers offer very different answers. To summarize them briefly: Augustine emphasizes trusting God's promises and receiving what fruit; Pelagius emphasizes living a good life and securing salvation through moral integrity and good works.

For Augustine, humanity is saved through an act of grace: even human good works are to be seen as the result of God's working within fallen human nature. Everything leading up to salvation is the free and unmerited gift of God, given out of love for sinners. Through the death and resurrection of Jesus of Nazareth, God is enabled to deal with fallen humanity in this remarkable and generous manner, giving us what we do not deserve (salvation), and withholding from us what we do deserve (condemnation).

For Pelagius, on the contrary, humanity is justified on the basis of its merits: human good works are the result of the exercise of the totally autonomous human free will, in fulfillment of an obligation laid down by God. A failure to meet this obligation opens the individual to the threat of eternal punishment. Jesus of Nazareth reveals, by his actions and teaching, exactly what God requires of the individual if that individual is to be saved. Salvation is thus the result of following the moral example of Jesus.

The Reformation debates of the sixteenth century

In the end, the western church opted for Augustine's approach. Many historians suggest that the basic issues of the Pelagian controversy are regularly replayed throughout the history of the church. The Reformation of the sixteenth century is widely regarded as taking up the basic issues of the Pelagian debate; but this time the language of "justification by faith" rather than that of "salvation by grace" is being used.

Earlier Christian theologians – such as Augustine – had given priority to those New Testament texts that use the language of "salvation by grace" (e.g., Ephesians 2: 5). However, Martin Luther's wrestling with the issue of how God was able to accept sinners led him to focus on those passages in which Paul spoke primarily of "justification by faith" (e.g., Romans 5: 1–2). Although it can be argued that the same fundamental point is being made in both contexts, the language used to express that point is different.

Martin Luther's program of reform for the church was based largely on his belief that the church had lost sight of any meaningful notion of grace. For Luther, the great question of life was, fundamentally, "How can I find a gracious God?" As a younger man, being terrified of hell and convinced of his own sinfulness, Luther gave an answer that was widespread in the popular Christian culture of his day: if you want to get right with God, make yourself into a good person. Humanity has the capacity to make itself righteous; when this happens, God endorses this transformation and accepts the transformed person into a relationship with him. This only happens through the institution of the church, which provides the God-given structures that lead securely and inevitably to salvation.

Yet Luther changed his mind and moved away from these early views. He developed a doctrine of justification through faith alone, which offered a radical alternative to the popular idea of making yourself good in order to secure divine acceptance. Luther came to the view that, when Paul speaks of the "righteousness of God" being revealed in the gospel, he does not mean that humanity is told what standards of righteousness it must achieve in order to be saved. Rather God provides the righteousness required for salvation as a free, unmerited gift. God's love is not conditional upon human transformation; it is rather the other way round – personal transformation follows divine acceptance and affirmation.

More radically still, Luther insisted that the believer was "at one and the same time a righteous person and a sinner" (*simul iustus et peccator*). While Luther admired Augustine for his emphasis on the unconditional love of God, he suggested that Augustine had become muddled when it came to the location of the gift of righteousness. Augustine considered this gift to be located within humanity, as a transforming reality; Luther argued that it was located outside us, being "reckoned" or "imputed" to humanity – not imparted. Humanity is like a patient under the care of a wise physician and on the way to recovery.

This approach was developed by other Protestant reformers of the sixteenth century, particularly by Philip Melanchthon and John Calvin. Two themes became characteristic of Protestant understandings of justification in the sixteenth century:

1   Justification is "by faith alone" (*sola fide*). It is not based on any human achievement, but on the graciousness of God.
2   Justification is an event in which the believer is declared to be righteous; this is followed by a process of renewal, generally referred to as "sanctification."

This understanding of justification differed at important points from that offered by Catholic writers; in consequence the doctrine of justification became a major source of disagreement between Protestant and Catholic writers. It is often seen as the great issue that divides these two major branches of Christianity, although this is probably a simplification of a complex situation.

Yet both sides in this debate affirmed that salvation is based on divine grace, not on human achievement. The divergence between them concerned what they meant by "justification" and how they thought it best to think about "justifying righteousness." The *Catechism of the Catholic Church* makes a statement about grace that most Christians would have little difficulty in accepting: "Our justification comes from the grace of God. Grace is *favour*, the *free and undeserved help* that God gives us to respond to his call to become children of God, adoptive sons, partakers of the divine nature and of eternal life."

The Church

The Apostles' Creed includes a clause that declares that Christians believe in the church. What is meant by this? How is the church to be defined, and what is its purpose? This area of Christian belief is traditionally designated "ecclesiology" (from the Greek word for "church," *ekklēsia*, which originally meant "gathering" or "assembly"). Although Christianity appeals to individuals, it is important to note the strongly communitarian aspects of the Christian faith. Christians prefer to gather together for worship rather than worshipping God individually at home.

So what do Christians understand by this word, "church"? The best way of exploring this theme is to pick up a statement of the Nicene Creed: "I believe in one holy catholic and apostolic church." These four adjectives – "one," "holy," "catholic" (or universal), and "apostolic" – are often referred to as the "four notes" or "four marks" of the church. What do they tell us about Christian thinking on the nature of the church? In what follows we shall explore this matter.

The unity of the church

The New Testament actually uses the word "church" in two somewhat different senses. At many points it designates individual Christian congregations – local visible gatherings of believers. For example, Paul wrote letters to churches in the cities of Corinth and Philippi. The book of Revelation makes reference to the "seven churches of Asia," probably meaning seven local Christian communities in the region of Asia Minor (modern-day Turkey). These would almost certainly have been "house churches" – clusters of believers who met in a home, being unable to meet in public for fear of arrest.

Yet at other points in the New Testament, especially in the letters to the Ephesians and Colossians, we find the term "church" being used in a wider, more general sense, meaning something like "the total body of Christian believers." The distinction between the local and the universal senses of "church" is of considerable importance and needs careful examination. How could both aspects be maintained?

Traditionally, this tension is resolved by arguing that there is one universal church, which is embodied or disclosed in local communities. On the basis of this approach it is possible to argue that there is one universal church, which consists of all Christian believers but takes the form of individual local churches in any given region.

One influential way of conceiving this distinction is due to the sixteenth-century writer John Calvin (1509–1564), who drew a distinction between the "visible" and the "invisible" church. At one level, the church is the community of Christian believers – a visible group. It is also, however, the fellowship of saints and the company of the elect – an invisible entity. In its invisible aspect, the church is the invisible assembly of the elect, known only to God; in its visible aspect, it is the community of believers on earth. The former consists only of the elect; the latter includes both good and evil, elect and reprobate.

The importance of this way of thinking (and of others like it) is best appreciated by considering the following question. How can anyone talk about "one" Christian church, when there are so many different Christian denominations? Faced with an apparent tension between a theoretical belief in "one church" and the observable reality of a plurality of churches, Christian writers have developed a number of approaches designed to allow the later to be incorporated in the framework of the former.

Some have adopted a basically Platonic approach, which draws a fundamental distinction between the empirical church (that is, the church as a visible historical reality) and the ideal church. Others have favored an eschatological approach. On this understanding, the present disunity of the church will be abolished on the last day. The present situation is temporary and will be resolved on the day of judgment. This viewpoint lies behind Calvin's distinction between the "visible" and "invisible" churches, which we considered above.

Some have found a biological approach helpful: they compared the historical evolution of the church to the development of the branches of a tree. This image, proposed by the eighteenth-century German Pietist writer Nicolas von Zinzendorf and taken up with enthusiasm by Anglican writers of the following century, allows the different empirical churches – for example the Roman Catholic, the Orthodox, and the Anglican – to be seen as possessing an organic unity, despite their institutional differences. The various churches are thus seen as branches on the same root – that is, as having a fundamental unity despite their diversity.

The holiness of the church

One of the most interesting debates over the doctrine of the church concerns whether its members are required to be holy. The debate is seen to be at its most intense during the Donatist controversy of the fourth century, which focused on the question of whether church leaders were required to be morally pure. Under the Roman Emperor Diocletian (284–313), the Christian church was subject to various degrees of persecution. The origins of the persecution date from 303; it finally ended with the conversion of Constantine and the issuing of the Edict of Milan in 313. Under an edict of February 303, Christian books were ordered to be burned and churches demolished. Those Christian leaders who handed over their books to be burned came to be known as *traditores* – "those who handed over [their books]." One such *traditor* was Felix of Aptunga, who later consecrated Caecilian as Bishop of the great North African city of Carthage in 311.

Many local Christians were outraged that such a person should have been allowed to be involved in a consecration, and they declared that they could not accept the authority of Caecilian. The new bishop's authority was compromised, it was argued, on account of the fact that the bishop who had consecrated him had lapsed under the pressure of persecution. The hierarchy of the Catholic church was tainted as a result of this development. The church ought to be pure; it should not be permitted to include such people. By 388, when Augustine of Hippo – destined to be a central figure in the controversy – returned from Rome to North Africa, a breakaway faction had established itself as the leading Christian body in the region, with strong support from the local African population.

The Donatists believed that the entire sacramental system of the Catholic church had become corrupted on account of the lapse of its leaders. How could the sacraments be validly administered by people who were tainted in this way? It was therefore necessary to replace these people with more acceptable leaders, who had remained firm in their faith under persecution. It was also necessary to rebaptize and re-ordain all those who had been baptized and ordained by the lapsed leaders. The faction that Augustine found on his return was larger than the church from which it had originally broken away.

Augustine responded by putting forward a theory of the church that he believed was more firmly grounded in the New Testament than the Donatist teaching. In particular, Augustine emphasized the sinfulness of Christians. The church is not meant to be a "pure body," a society of saints, but a "mixed body" (*corpus permixtum*) of saints and sinners. Augustine finds this image in two biblical parables: the parable of the net that catches many fishes; and the parable of the wheat and the weeds (or "tares," to use an older English word familiar to readers of the King James Bible). It is this latter parable (Matthew 13: 24–31) that is of especial importance and requires further discussion.

The parable tells of a farmer who sowed seed and discovered that the resulting crop contained both wheat and weeds. What could be done about it? It would be foolish to attempt to separate the wheat and the weeds while both were still growing, as the farmer would probably damage the wheat while trying to get rid of the weeds. But at harvest all the plants – whether wheat or weeds – could be cut down and sorted out, thus avoiding any damage to the wheat. The parable suggests that the separation of the good from the evil takes place at the end of time, not in history.

For Augustine, however, this parable refers to the church rather than the world. The church must expect to find itself comprising both saints and sinners. To attempt a separation in this world is premature and improper. That separation will take place in God's own time, at the end of history. No human can make that judgment or separation in God's place.

So then, in what sense is the church holy? For Augustine, the holiness of the church is not that of its members, but that of Christ. In this world the church cannot be a congregation of saints, because its members are contaminated by original sin. However, the church is sanctified and made holy by Christ – a holiness that will be perfected and finally realized at the last judgment. In addition to this theological analysis, Augustine makes the practical observation that the Donatists failed to live up to their own high standards of morality. Donatists, Augustine suggests, were just as capable as Catholics of getting drunk or beating people up.

Yet the Donatist vision of a "pure body" remains attractive to many. As so often happens in theological debates, the evidence is never entirely on one side of the argument. A strong case continues to be made for the idea of the church as a "pure body," especially in denominations that trace their identity back to the more radical wing of the Protestant Reformation, often known as "anabaptist." The radical Reformation conceived of the church as an "alternative society" within the mainstream of sixteenth-century European culture. For Menno Simmons, the church was an assembly of the righteous, at odds with the world, and not a "mixed body," as Augustine argued.

It will be clear that there are strong parallels with the Donatist view of the church as a holy and pure body, isolated from the corrupting influences of the world and prepared to maintain its purity and distinctiveness by whatever disciplinary means prove to be necessary.

Other writers have pointed out how "holiness" is often equated with "morality," "sanctity," or "purity," which often seem to bear little relation to the behavior of fallen human beings. Yet the Hebrew term *kadad*, which underlies the New Testament concept of "holiness," has a rather different meaning, bearing the sense of "being cut off" or "being separated." There are strong dedicatory overtones: to be "holy" is to be set apart for, and dedicated to, the service of God.

A fundamental element – indeed, perhaps *the* fundamental element – in the Old Testament's idea of holiness is that of "something or someone whom God has set apart." The New Testament restricts the sphere of holiness almost entirely to personal holiness; it applies "holy" to individuals, declining to pick up the idea of "holy places" or "holy things." People are "holy" in that they are dedicated to God; and they are distinguished from the world on account of their calling by God. A number of theologians have suggested a correlation between the idea of "the church" (the Greek word for which can bear the meaning of "those who are called out"), and "holy" (that is, those who have been separated from the world on account of their having been called by God).

To speak of the "holiness of the church" is thus primarily to speak of the holiness of the one who called that church and its members. The church has been separated from the world in order to bear witness to the grace and salvation of God. Therefore the term "holy," taken in this sense, affirms both the calling of the church and of its members and the hope that the church will one day share in the life and glory of God.

The catholicity of the church

The Christian creeds refer to the church as "universal" or "catholic." The term "catholic" derives from the Greek phrase *kath' holou* ("wholly, in its entirety"). The Greek words subsequently found their way into the Latin adjective *catholicus*, which came to have the meaning "universal" or "general." (The word "universal" is now often used as an alternative to "catholic," particularly within Protestant denominations.) This sense of the word is retained in the English phrase "catholic taste," which means "wide-ranging taste" rather than "taste for things that are Roman Catholic." Older versions of the English Bible often refer to some of the New Testament letters (such as those of James and John) as "catholic epistles," meaning that they are directed to all Christians (unlike those of Paul, which are generally directed to the needs and situations of individually identified churches, such as those at Rome or Corinth).

The developed sense of the word is perhaps best seen in the fourth-century catechetical writings of Cyril of Jerusalem. In his eighteenth catechetical lecture, Cyril teases out a number of senses of the word "catholic":

> The church is thus called "catholic" because it is spread throughout the entire inhabited world, from one end to the other, and because it teaches in its totality [*katholikōs*] and without leaving anything out every doctrine which people need to know relating to things visible and invisible, whether in heaven and earth. It is also called "catholic" because it brings to obedience every sort of person – whether rulers or their subjects, the educated and the unlearned. It also makes available a universal [*katholikōs*] remedy and cure to every kind of sin.

It will be clear that Cyril is using the term "catholic" in four ways, each of which deserves comment a little further:

1   Catholic is to be understood as "spread throughout the entire inhabited world." Here Cyril notes the geographical sense of the word. The notion of "wholeness" or "universality" is thus understood as a mandate for the church to spread into every region of the world.
2   Catholic means "without leaving anything out." With this phrase, Cyril stresses that the "catholicity" of the church involves the complete proclamation and explanation of the Christian faith. It is an invitation to ensure that the totality of the gospel is preached and taught, not just the sections of the creed that a catechist or a preacher happens to prefer.
3   Catholic means that the church extends its mission and ministry to "every sort of person." Cyril here makes the essentially sociological point that the Christian gospel and church are intended for all kinds of human beings, irrespective of their race, gender, or social status. We can see here a clear echo of St. Paul's famous declaration that "there is neither Jew nor Greek, there is neither slave nor free, there is neither male nor female; for you are all one in Christ Jesus" (Galatians 3: 28).
4   Catholic means that the church offers and proclaims "a universal remedy and cure to every kind of sin." Here Cyril makes a soteriological statement: the gospel, and the church that proclaims that gospel, can meet every human need and distress. Whatever sins there may be, the church is able to offer an antidote.

The apostolicity of the church

Fourth and finally, the church is declared to be "apostolic." What does this mean? The fundamental sense of the term is "originating with the Apostles" or "having a direct link with the Apostles." This epithet is a reminder that the church is founded on the apostolic witness and testimony. In the New Testament, the word "apostle" has two related meanings:

1   someone who has been commissioned by Christ and charged with the task of preaching the good news of the kingdom;
2   someone who was a witness to the risen Christ, or someone to whom Christ revealed himself as risen.

In declaring the church to be "apostolic," the creeds emphasize the historical roots of the gospel, the continuity between the church and Christ through the Apostles whom he appointed, and the continuing evangelistic and missionary tasks of the church.

The church can therefore be thought of as being "apostolic" in three ways, each laying emphasis on a different aspect of the church's history, calling, and function.

1   Historically, the origins of the church are to be traced back to the apostles. The New Testament tells something of this historical development, especially in the Acts of the Apostles, and brings out the critical role played by the apostles, as Christ's appointed representatives, in the expansion of the church.
2   Theologically, the church is "apostolic" in that it maintains and transmits the teaching of the apostles. Earlier we noted how the first Christians, when agreeing on the contents of the New Testament, regarded apostolic authorship as being of major importance. The New Testament can be thought of as a repository of apostolic teaching. In declaring that the church is "apostolic," the creeds are insisting that faithfulness to the apostolic tradition is an integral part of the church's task and an essential precondition for its right to call itself "Christian." This theme can be seen in some of the later writings of the New Testament, which are especially concerned with maintaining Christian faithfulness in the post-apostolic period. Thus Paul asks his successor Timothy to remain faithful to what he has been taught and to pass it down to those who will succeed him:

> Hold to the standard of sound teaching that you have heard from me, in the faith and love that are in Christ Jesus. Guard the good treasure entrusted to you, with the help of the Holy Spirit living in us.
>
> (2 Timothy 1: 13–14)

3   The church is apostolic, in that it is charged with the responsibility of carrying on the succession of apostolic ministry. The patterns of ministry found in the New Testament, although in an emerging form – for example, deacons, presbyters or "elders," and bishops – are to remain normative for Christianity. More importantly, the tasks entrusted by Christ to the apostles – such as pastoral care for the poor and the needy, teaching, and the preaching of the gospel to the world – are passed down within the church to their successors within the church.

Among the tasks passed down to the apostles' successors is Christ's command to do certain specific things, both as a reminder of his life, death, and resurrection and as a celebration and proclamation of his ongoing presence in the church. In view of the importance of these "sacraments" to the life of the church, we may consider them in some detail.

The Sacraments

The word "sacrament" is widely used to refer to certain acts of worship that are understood to possess special importance in maintaining and developing the Christian life. The term derives from the Latin word *sacramentum*, which originally meant "sacred oath," such as the oath of obedience that a Roman soldier might swear to the people and Senate of Rome. The third-century theologian Tertullian used this parallel as a means of bringing out the importance of sacraments in relation to Christian commitment and loyalty within the church. Baptism, for example, can be seen as a sign both of allegiance to Jesus of Nazareth and of commitment to the Christian community.

There has been considerable debate within the Christian community over the identity and function of sacraments, as well as over what to call them. The fundamental Christian practice of using bread and wine to recall the Last Supper is referred to in different ways by different Christian groups. The most commonly encountered descriptions are the mass, the eucharist, the Lord's Supper, and the Holy Communion. Generally speaking, Protestantism tends to accept only two sacraments – baptism and the eucharist – where Roman Catholicism and Greek Orthodoxy recognize seven. The seven sacraments of the Roman Catholic Church are generally grouped together in three categories: the sacraments of initiation (baptism, confirmation, and the eucharist), the sacraments of healing (reconciliation or penance, and the anointing or "unction" of the sick), and sacraments of vocation (marriage and ordination). The Greek Orthodox church also recognizes these seven sacraments, while using the term "chrismation" in place of confirmation.

What is a sacrament?

Although earlier Christian writers often refer to the sacraments, we find relatively little reflection on what determines whether something is a sacrament or not. The word was used somewhat uncritically, without any attempt to achieve theological precision on what the concept entailed. Augustine of Hippo is generally regarded as having laid down the general principles relating to the definition of sacraments. These principles can be set out as follows:

1   In the first place, a sacrament is fundamentally a sign. When applied to divine things, signs are called sacraments.
2   In the second place, this sign must bear some relation to the thing that is signified. If sacraments did not resemble the things of which they are the sacraments, they would not be sacraments at all.

These definitions, though useful, are still imprecise and inadequate. For example, does it follow that every "sign of a sacred thing" is to be regarded as a sacrament? Augustine himself understood by "sacraments" a number of things that are no longer regarded as sacramental in character – for example, the creeds and the Lord's Prayer. As time passed, it became increasingly clear that the definition of a sacrament simply as "a sign of a sacred thing" was inadequate. It was during the theological renaissance of the earlier Middle Ages that further clarification took place.

In the late twelfth century, the Parisian theologian Peter Lombard developed Augustine's definition, giving it a new clarity and precision. Peter's definition in his widely used and authoritative theological textbook *The Four Books of the Sentences* takes the following form:

> A sacrament bears a likeness to the thing of which it is a sign. … Something can properly be called a sacrament if it is a sign of the grace of God and a form of invisible grace, so that it bears its image and exists as its cause. Sacraments were therefore instituted for the sake of sanctifying, as well as of signifying.

This definition embraces each of the seven traditional sacraments noted above and excludes such things as the creed.

The rise of Protestantism ended this consensus within the western church. Martin Luther challenged this way of thinking about the sacraments, insisting that there were three basic elements that were essential to the definition of a sacrament: a physical sign; a divine promise; and an explicit command from Jesus of Nazareth that this physical sign should be used in this way. Luther's more radical definition limited the list of sacraments to two: baptism and the eucharist.

The function of sacraments

What do sacraments do? From what has already been said it can be seen that, in Christian theology, sacraments have universally been understood as signs. Sacraments thus signify divine grace. But this is only a partial answer. Do sacraments do more than simply signify the grace of God? Are the sacraments merely signs, or are they a special kind of sign – such as an effective sign, which causes what is being signified?

Traces of this view may be found in the second century. Ignatius of Antioch declared that the eucharist was "the medicine of immortality and the antidote that we should not die, but live for ever in Jesus Christ." The idea is, clearly, that the eucharist does not merely signify eternal life, but is somehow instrumental in effecting it. This approach was developed subsequently by many writers, and especially by Ambrose of Milan in the fourth century (c. 340–397). Ambrose argued that, in baptism, the Holy Spirit "coming upon the font or upon those who are to be baptized, effects the reality of regeneration."

In medieval theology a distinction was carefully drawn between the "sacraments of the Old Covenant" (such as circumcision) and the "sacraments of the New Covenant" (such as baptism). Early medieval theologians held that the sacraments of the Old Covenant merely signified spiritual realities, whereas the sacraments of the New Covenant actualized or caused what they signified. The thirteenth-century Franciscan writer known as St. Bonaventure (Giovanni di Fidanza, 1221–1274) made this point as follows, using a medical analogy:

> In the Old Law, there were ointments of a kind, but they were figurative and did not heal. The disease was lethal, but the anointings were superficial. … Genuinely healing ointments must

bring both spiritual anointing and a life-giving power; it was only Christ our Lord who did this, since through his death, the sacraments have the power to bring to life.

These views remain characteristic of modern Catholicism. Sacraments are understood to convey or enact the grace that they represent. However, many theologians add a qualifier here, noting that it is possible for an individual to resist this grace by placing an obstacle in its path. Thus the Second Vatican Council, while continuing to emphasize the effective causality of sacraments, noted the importance of believers' responding appropriately to them:

> Because [sacraments] are signs, they also instruct. They not only presuppose faith, but by words and objects they also nourish, strengthen and express it. That is why they are called "sacraments of faith." They do indeed confer grace, but in addition the very act of celebrating them most effectively disposes the faithful to receive this grace to their profit, to worship God duly, and to practise charity.

Protestantism found itself divided over the question of what the sacraments achieved. Luther was prepared to allow that sacraments caused what they signified. In his *Shorter Catechism* (1529) he made it clear that baptism brought about both the signification and the causation of divine forgiveness:

QUESTION	What gifts or benefits does Baptism bring?
ANSWER	It brings about the forgiveness of sins, saves us from death and the devil, and grants eternal blessedness to all who believe, as the Word and promise of God declare.

These views remain generally characteristic of Lutheranism to this day.

Other Protestant writers, however, were suspicious of such an approach, which they regarded as coming close to a magical view of sacraments. The Swiss reformer Huldrych Zwingli insisted that sacraments were signs, and nothing more:

> Sacraments are simply the signs of holy things. Baptism is a sign which pledges us to the Lord Jesus Christ. The Remembrance shows us that Christ suffered death for our sake. They are the signs and pledges of these holy things.

Zwingli therefore argues that both baptism and the eucharist (which he here refers to as "the Remembrance") are external signs of spiritual realities, which have no power in themselves to bring about what they signify. Baptism is thus a sign, but not a cause, of God's forgiveness of sins. This viewpoint remains influential within parts of modern Protestantism, and is especially found in modern evangelicalism.

Yet a third Protestant approach was set out by John Calvin and his successors in the reformed tradition. Calvin's approach can be seen as a mediating approach, roughly halfway between Luther's causative view and Zwingli's representationalist view of the sacraments. Calvin defines a sacrament as "an external symbol by which the Lord seals on our consciences his promises of good will towards us, in order to sustain the weakness of our faith." Yet, although the sacraments are external signs, he argues that there is such a close connection between the symbol and the gift it symbolizes that we can easily pass from one to the other. The sign is visible and physical, whereas the thing signified is invisible and spiritual – yet the connection between the sign and the thing signified is so intimate that it is permissible to apply the one to the other. Calvin was thus able to maintain the difference between sign and thing signified, while insisting that the sign really points to the gift it signifies.

In what follows we shall explore some questions linked to each of these sacraments that continue to be debated and discussed within Christian circles.

Debates about baptism

Should children be baptized? Matthew's gospel records Jesus Christ as commanding his disciples to go and make disciples and to baptize them (Matthew 28: 17–20). But what about children? Does this command extend only to adults, or does it include infants? The New Testament makes no specific references to the baptism of infants. However, it does not explicitly forbid the practice either, and there are also a number of passages that could be interpreted as condoning it – for example, references to the baptizing of entire households, which would probably have included infants (Acts 16: 15, 33; 1 Corinthians 1: 16). Paul treats baptism as a spiritual counterpart to circumcision (Colossians 2: 11–12). So if Jews were able to mark their male children as belonging to the household of faith in this way, why should not Christians also mark their children – male and female – by baptism?

Most mainline Christian churches accept that the baptism of infants is a valid practice, with roots in the apostolic period. Martin Luther and John Calvin, though severely critical of the Catholic church over many points of doctrine and practice, held that infant baptism was an authentic biblical practice. The reasons given for infant baptism vary. Augustine of Hippo argued that, since Christ is the savior of all people, all people require salvation. As baptism is a recognition both of the need for human salvation and of God's gracious willingness to provide it, all should be baptized. After all, he argued, little children were as much in need of salvation as adults.

Another line of defense of the baptism of infants can be found in the Old Testament, which stipulated that male infants born within the bounds of Israel should have an outward sign of their membership of the people of God. The outward sign in question was circumcision – that is, the removal of the foreskin. Infant baptism was thus to be seen as analogous to circumcision. It was a sign of belonging to a covenant community.

Writers such as Huldrych Zwingli argued that infant baptism affirmed publicly the more inclusive and gentle character of Christianity. The more inclusive character of Christianity was publicly demonstrated by the baptism of both male and female infants; Judaism, in contrast, recognized only the marking of male infants. The more gentle character of the gospel was publicly demonstrated by the absence of pain or blood shedding in the sacrament. Christ suffered – in being circumcised himself, in addition to his death on the cross – in order that his people need not suffer in this manner.

But not all are persuaded by the case for infant baptism. Many Baptist writers reject the traditional practice of baptizing infants. Baptism was to be administered only when an individual showed signs of grace, repentance, or faith. The practice of baptizing infants is held to be without biblical foundation. It may have become the norm in the post-apostolic period, but not in the period of the New Testament itself. It is also argued that the practice of infant baptism leads to the potentially confusing idea that individuals are Christians as a result of their baptism, thus weakening the link between baptism and Christian discipleship.

Debates about the eucharist

At the Last Supper Jesus commanded his disciples to remember him through bread and wine. It is clear that this was done from the earliest of times. The New Testament itself makes reference to the first Christians obeying Jesus Christ's command to remember him in this way (1 Corinthians 11: 20–27). This act of celebration and remembrance is referred to in different ways in the Christian churches: the mass, the Holy Communion, the Lord's Supper, and the eucharist (this last term derives from the Greek word for "thanksgiving").

An important debate within Christianity concerns whether, and if so in what manner, Christ may be said to be present at the Lord's Supper. This issue is often linked with the words spoken by Christ at the Last Supper. Taking the bread, he told his disciples: "this is my body" (Matthew 26: 26). What does this mean? The majority opinion within global Christianity is that Christ's words can only mean that, in some sense, Christ's body is present in the bread of the Lord's Supper.

One way of understanding this idea is the doctrine of "transubstantiation," which was formalized in 1215. This doctrine holds that the outward appearance of the bread remains unchanged, whereas its inward identity is transformed. In other words, the bread continues to look, taste, smell, and feel as if it were bread; at its most fundamental level, however, it has been changed. By a similar argument, the wine is held to have become the blood of Christ. This position is often stated using the Aristotelian distinction between "substance" (that which gives something its inward identity) and "accidents" (mere external appearances). On this view, the substance of the bread and wine is changed, but their accidents remain unaltered. Although this position is especially associated with the Catholic church, related viewpoints can be found in eastern Orthodoxy.

Martin Luther developed a somewhat different idea, often known as "consubstantiation," which holds that the bread remains bread but is additionally the body of Christ. Luther illustrated this notion by pointing to how a piece of iron, when placed in a hot fire, becomes red-hot. Although remaining iron, it has heat added to it. In the same way, the bread of the Lord's Supper remains bread, but additionally contains or conveys the body of Christ.

Not all Christians take this position. Some, following John Calvin, argue that the bread is an "efficacious sign." In other words, although the bread is not the body of Christ, it represents it in such a way that what is signified is effectively conveyed. Others follow the Swiss reformer Huldrych Zwingli, who argued that the bread symbolized Christ's body. The bread and the wine of the Lord's Supper are there to help believers recall the events of Calvary and to encourage them to recommit themselves to the church, to God, and to each other. Others still adopt another approach of Zwingli's, sometimes known as "memorialism," which holds that there is no objective change in either the bread or the wine. Any change that occurs is subjective, taking place in the mind of the beholder, who now "sees" the bread as a sign of Christ's body and as a reminder of his sacrifice upon the cross.

These, of course, represent only a few positions that Christians have defended. Nevertheless, they illustrate the ongoing debates within Christianity over how best to interpret both the biblical witness to the Last Supper and the long Christian history of repeating the actions Christ commanded, as a "reminder" (Greek *anamnēsis*) of him.

The Christian Hope

Finally, we come to the theme of the Christian hope – an idea often expressed through the phrase "the last things" (Greek *ta eschata*, from which derives the word "eschatology," meaning "understanding of the last things"). Christianity is a religion of hope, which focuses on the resurrection of Jesus as the ground for believing and trusting in a God who is able to triumph over death and to give hope to all those who suffer and die. Cyprian of Carthage (died 258), a martyr bishop of the third century, tried to encourage his fellow Christians in the face of suffering and death at times of persecution by holding before them a vision of heaven in which they would see the martyrs and the apostles face to face. More than that; they would be reunited with those whom they loved and cherished.

Cyprian here conceives of heaven as the "native land" of Christians, from which they have been exiled during their time on earth. The hope of return to their native land, there to be reunited with those whom they knew and loved, was held out as a powerful consolation in times of trial and suffering.

> We regard paradise as our native land ... Many of our dear ones await us there, and a dense crowd of parents, brothers, children, is longing for us, already assured of their own safety, and still longing for our salvation. What gladness there will be for them and for us when we enter their presence and share their embrace!

Cyprian himself was martyred for his faith in 258, presumably being consoled by precisely the ideas with which he sought to console others.

The word "heaven" is traditionally used to refer to the hope of dwelling in the presence of God forever. It is not understood geographically or spatially, as if it referred to a country or a region of the world. Its dominant sense is relational that is, the word is used to designate the state of dwelling with God, without any particular understanding of precisely where this dwelling is located.

The Christian vision of heaven is shaped by a number of controlling images or themes, of which two are particularly important: the New Jerusalem, and the restoration of creation. A radical transformation of all things will bring about a new order, reversing the devastating effects of sin upon humanity and upon the world. The image of resurrection conveys the ideas of both radical change and continuity: the new order of things, though utterly different from what we currently know and experience, nevertheless demonstrates continuity with the present order. The present age will be transformed and renewed, just as a seed is completely transformed in becoming a living plant.

In this closing section we shall focus on Christian beliefs concerning heaven, the most important of these "last things."

The New Testament and Christian hope

The eschatology of the New Testament is complex. However, one of its leading themes is that something that happened in the past has inaugurated something new, which will reach its final consummation in the future. The Christian believer is thus caught up in this tension between the "now" and the "not yet." In one sense, heaven has not yet happened; in another, its powerful lure already impacts upon life in a dramatic and complex fashion, as Christians are at one and the same time excited at its prospect and rendered dejected by knowing that they are not yet there.

The term "heaven" is used frequently in the Pauline writings of the New Testament to refer to Christian hope. Although it is natural to represent heaven as a future entity, Paul's thinking appears to embrace both a future reality and a spiritual sphere or realm, which coexists with the material world of space and time. Thus "heaven" is referred to both as the future home of the believer (2 Corinthians 5: 1–2; Philippians 3: 20) and as the present dwelling-place of Jesus Christ, from which he will come in final judgment (Romans 10: 6; 1 Thessalonians 1: 10; 4: 16).

As we shall see, one of Paul's most significant statements concerning heaven focuses on the notion of believers being "citizens of heaven" (Philippians 3: 20) and in some way sharing in the life of heaven in the present. The tension between the "now" and the "not yet" is evident in Paul's statements concerning heaven, which make it very difficult to sustain the simple idea of heaven as something that will not come into being until the future or cannot be experienced at all in the present. For Paul, the hope of heaven impacts upon life in the here and now, even though heaven, in all its fullness, remains to be consummated in the future.

The image of the "New Jerusalem" has exercised a decisively important influence over Christian reflection on heaven down the centuries. The origins of this image lie primarily in the book of Revelation, the closing book of the Christian Bible. Its powerful imagery has saturated Christian hymnody and theological reflection on how heaven is to be visualized. The consolation of heaven is here contrasted with the suffering, tragedy, and pain of life on earth. "Death will be no more; mourning and crying and pain will be no more, for the first things have passed away" (Revelation 21: 1–5).

The theme of the New Jerusalem is here integrated with motifs drawn from the creation account – such as the presence of the "tree of life" (Revelation 22: 2) – suggesting that heaven can be seen as the restoration of the bliss of the garden of Eden (Genesis 2), when God dwelt with humanity in harmony. The pain, sorrow, and evil of a fallen world have finally passed away, and the creation is restored to its original intention.

Probably the most helpful way of construing the New Testament's affirmations concerning heaven is to see the latter as a consummation of the Christian doctrine of salvation, in which the presence, penalty, and power of sin have all been finally eliminated and the total presence of God in individuals and in the community of faith has been achieved. This idea is clearly expressed in the vision of heaven set out in the *Catechism of the Catholic Church*: "Heaven is the ultimate end and fulfilment of the deepest human longings, the state of supreme, definitive happiness."

The New Testament parables of heaven are strongly communal in nature. Heaven is here portrayed as a banquet, a wedding feast, or a city – the new Jerusalem. Eternal life is thus not a projection of an individual human existence, but is rather to be seen as sharing, with the redeemed community as a whole, in the community of a loving God.

The nature of the resurrection body

What do resurrected individuals look like? To put this is somewhat simplistic terms, what sort of people will walk the streets of the New Jerusalem? Many early Christian writers argued that the "citizens of heaven" would be naked, re-creating the situation of human innocence in paradise. This time, however, nakedness would give rise neither to shame nor to sexual lust, but would simply be accepted as the natural and innocent state of humanity. Others, however, argued that the inhabitants of the New Jerusalem would be clothed in finery, which would reflect their status as citizens of God's chosen city.

It was clear to many writers that the final state of deceased believers was not of material importance to their appearance in heaven. The issue emerged as theologically significant during a persecution of Christians in Lyons around the years 175–177. Aware that Christians believed in the resurrection of the body, their pagan oppressors burned the bodies of those they had just martyred and threw their ashes in the River Rhône. This, they believed, would prevent the resurrection of these martyrs, in that there was now no body to be raised. Christian theologians responded by arguing that God was able to restore or reconstitute the bodies of believers, especially those who died violently or whose corpses have been destroyed by burning.

Methodius of Olympus (died c. 311) offered an analogy for this process of reconstitution that would prove highly influential in discussing the question. The resurrection could, he argued, be thought of as a kind of "rearrangement" of the constituent elements of humanity. It is as if a statue were melted down and reforged from the same material – yet in such a manner that any defects or damage are eliminated.

A similar argument is found in the *Four Books of the Sentences*, the masterpiece of the great twelfth-century theologian Peter Lombard. This book, which served as a core text-book for just about every medieval theologian, took the view that the resurrected body was basically a reconstituted humanity from which all defects had been purged.

A final question that has caused considerable debate among Christian theologians concerns the age of those who are resurrected. If someone dies at the age of 60, will she appear in the streets of the New Jerusalem as an old person? And if someone dies at the age of 10, will he appear as a child? This issue caused the spilling of much ink, especially during the Middle Ages. By the end of the thirteenth century an emerging consensus can be discerned. As each person reaches his or her peak or perfection around the age of 30, each person would be resurrected as (s)he would have appeared at that time – even if (s)he never lived to reach that age or died long afterwards. Peter Lombard's discussion of the matter is typical of his age: "A boy who dies immediately after being born will be resurrected in that form which he would have had if he had lived to the age of thirty." The New Jerusalem will thus be populated by men and women as they would appear at the age of 30 (the age, of course, at which Jesus of Nazareth was crucified) – and with every blemish removed.

Christian burial or cremation?

A further issue concerning the form of the resurrection body became especially important during the twentieth century, when the practice of cremation was increasingly common among Christian nations, partly on account of the prohibitive cost of burial. Was cremation inconsistent with belief in the resurrection? Was our resurrection to eternal life dependent on being buried intact? The question, as we have already noted (p. 119), had been debated in earlier periods. Christian theologians argued that God would not be troubled by this inconvenience. God would still be able to reconstitute the bodies of those whose bodies have been dismembered or destroyed.

For centuries cremation was expressly forbidden by the Catholic church. Two reasons were often invoked. In the first place, cremation was seen as a pagan practice that denied the doctrine of the resurrection. Second, the body was believed to be the temple of the Holy Spirit. However, some significant changes in the Catholic practice took place in the twentieth century. In 1963, the Vatican lifted the ban on cremation for Catholics. Still, no allowance was made for any prayer or rituals to be used with the cremated remains. This meant that all funeral services were to occur in the presence of the body, while cremation was to take place afterwards. In 1997 the Vatican granted permission for the cremated remains of a body to be brought into church for the liturgical rites of burial. It is still, however, the official church's preference for the funeral rites to take place in the presence of the body and for cremation to follow afterwards.

In Protestant circles perhaps the most influential answer to this question was offered by the famous American evangelist Billy Graham in a nationally syndicated newspaper column:

> In Corinthians 5, Paul makes the contrast between living in a tent, a temporary home that can be pulled down and put away, and living in a permanent home that will last forever. Our bodies are our temporary tents. Our resurrected bodies will be our permanent homes. They are similar in appearance but different in substance. Cremation is therefore no hindrance to the resurrection.

Graham's point was clear: the Christian hope of resurrection is grounded in the trustworthiness of the divine promises, not in the precise circumstances of a person's funeral arrangements. These ideas are important in a number of respects, not least in relation to Christian funeral services. We shall consider these services in a later chapter.

Conclusion

This brief overview of Christian beliefs is little more than a sketchy map of a complex and fascinating landscape, which deserves much more extensive exploration and discussion. Happily there are many guides available to you, if you wish to explore this field further. Some suitable starting points are noted in the Further Reading section, which will help you take things further.

We now turn to provide an overview of Christian history. The next chapter surveys some of the major themes in the history of Christianity, from the apostolic age to the present day.

4

Christian History
An Overview

It is impossible to understand the present state and forms of Christianity without a knowledge of its history. To study Christian history is not about retreating from the present into the past, but about providing a lens that brings the present into sharper focus. The long shadows of past debates, discussions, and personalities figure large in contemporary Christianity. Given the importance of this history, we shall accord it careful attention. This large chapter considers the history of Christianity under five broad sections, as follows:

1 the period of the early church, sometimes referred to as the "patristic period," during which the Christian faith began to gain a significant following throughout the Mediterranean world;
2 the Middle Ages, a period of Christian history in Western Europe that witnessed significant cultural and intellectual developments: the complex cultural phenomenon known as the Renaissance is included in this period;
3 the age of reformation in Western Europe, which witnessed the birth of Protestantism in certain parts of Europe and the consolidation of Catholicism in others, eventually leading to the Wars of Religion;
4 the modern age: this section looks at the development of Christianity in the eighteenth and nineteenth centuries, with particular reference to developments in Western Europe and North America that culminated in the outbreak of the Great War (later known as the "First World War") of 1914–1918;
5 the twentieth century: this final section considers the dramatic changes in the shape of global Christianity in the century following the end of the Great War; it includes discussion of important developments in Africa, South America, and Asia.

Christianity: An Introduction, Third Edition. Alister E. McGrath.
© 2015 John Wiley & Sons, Ltd. Published 2015 by John Wiley & Sons, Ltd.

The Early Church, c. 100–c. 500

The first major era of Christian history (c. 100–451), during which Christianity began to expand rapidly throughout the Mediterranean world and beyond, is sometimes called the "patristic period." The unusual and to many unfamiliar term "patristic" comes from the Greek word *patēr* ("father"), which was applied to a group of Christian leaders such as Athanasius of Alexandria or Augustine of Hippo; these are often referred to as "fathers of the church."

It is difficult to make sense of the historical development of Christianity without a good grasp of this formative period, particularly its great theological debates, and the important implications of the unexpected acceptance of Christianity as the legitimate religion of the Roman empire. We shall therefore begin our discussion of early Christianity by reflecting on its emergence within Judaism and on its rapid transformation into a faith that refused to recognize ethnic or social boundaries.

The apostolic age

The first major period in Christian history is generally known as the "apostolic age." The term "apostle" derives from the Greek verb *apostelein*, "to send," and is often used to designate those commissioned by Jesus of Nazareth to continue and extend his ministry. Traditionally, this is understood as the period when the apostles were still alive, providing historical continuity between the church and the original community of faith that gathered around Jesus of Nazareth. We know frustratingly little about this period, even though it is clearly of immense historical importance. However, we can begin to sketch some of its aspects, providing an important transition to the better understood history of the early church.

As we noted earlier, at the heart of the Christian movement lay a series of reports and interpretations of the words and deeds of Jesus of Nazareth (pp. 3–5). His significance was presented in terms of both his identity and his function, using a rich range of Christological titles and images of salvation, often drawn from the Jewish roots of Christianity. Initially Christian groups appear to have been established in leading urban centers such as Jerusalem, by individuals who had personally known Jesus of Nazareth or were familiar with members of his immediate circle.

Other Christian communities were established by figures with more complex associations with the Jerusalem church, most notably Paul of Tarsus (pp. 26, 45). According to the New Testament itself, Paul was responsible for establishing Christian churches in many parts of the Mediterranean world. At first Christianity would almost certainly have been seen simply as one more sect or group within a Judaism that was already accustomed to considerable diversity in religious expression. As recent historical studies of this period have made clear, Judaism was far from being monolithic at the time.

These Christian communities were scattered throughout the Roman empire, each facing its own distinctive local challenges and opportunities. This raises two significant historical questions, neither of which can be answered with any degree of certainty. First, how did these individual Christian communities maintain their religious identity within their local cultural context? It is clear, for example, that early Christian worship served to emphasize the distinctiveness of Christian communities, helping to forge a sense of shared identity over and against society in general.

Second, how did these individual communities understand themselves as relating to a larger universal community, increasingly referred to as "the church" in the later writings of the New Testament? There is evidence that these small communities maintained contact with each other through correspondence, through traveling teachers who visited clusters of churches, and especially through the sharing of foundational documents, some of which (though not all) were later incorporated into the canon of the New Testament (pp. 45–47).

Women played an important role in Christianity during the apostolic or patristic age. As we have noted, Christianity emerged from Palestinian Judaism, which often adopted strongly negative attitudes toward women. For this reason, the gospels note that Jesus of Nazareth's encounters with women occasionally provoked hostility and criticism from the official representatives of Judaism. The gospel's accounts of the ministry of Jesus confirm that women were an integral part of the group of people who gathered around him. They were affirmed by him, often to the dismay of the Pharisees and other religious traditionalists. The gospel of Luke emphasizes the significant role of "many women" (Luke 8: 2–3) in the spreading of the gospel.

Our most important source for the history of apostolic Christianity is the Acts of the Apostles, generally agreed to have been written by the same Luke who compiled the third of the four gospels. Acts emphasizes the important role of women in providing hospitality for early Christian missionaries to Europe: women converts such as Lydia made their homes available as house churches and staging posts for missionaries. Luke appears to be concerned to bring out clearly the important historical fact that the early church attracted significant numbers of prominent women from cultures that gave them a much higher social role than they had in Judaism and offered them a significant role in its overall evangelistic and pastoral ministry.

In particular, Luke singles out Priscilla and Aquila as a husband and wife team that was engaged in an evangelistic and teaching ministry (Acts 18: 1–3, 24–26). Paul commends to the Roman church "our sister Phoebe, a servant of the church at Cenchrea" (Romans 16: 1), commenting on how helpful she had been to him. Other passages in the New Testament letters (such as 1 Timothy 3: 11 and 5: 9–10) point to women exercising a recognized and authorized ministry of some form within the church. Amid the large number of folks whom Paul lists as sending greetings in his Epistle to the Romans are Prisca, a "fellow-worker"; and Tryphaena and Tryphosa, "workers in the Lord" – descriptions that Paul also applies to men in the same passage.

Paul's extended list of greetings in his letter to the Romans also includes Junia, who is named, along with Andronicus, as "prominent among the apostles" (Romans 16: 7). Andronicus is a male name; Junia, a female name. (One early manuscript reads "Julia" rather than "Junia.")

Early Christianity and the Roman empire

It is impossible to make much sense of the development of early Christianity without a good understanding of the Roman empire. Many historians regard this empire as having reached its zenith during the reign of Emperor Trajan, who ruled from 98 to 117. Christianity had its origins in the Roman province of Judaea, a relatively obscure and politically insignificant region, and would expand rapidly throughout the empire, eventually becoming its official religion. In view of the importance of the Roman imperial context to the rise and shaping of Christianity, we shall look at this context in more detail.

The expansion of Roman influence began during the period when Rome was a republic. However, political weaknesses led to power being centralized in a single figure of authority – the emperor (originally *imperator* meant "general" – "one who gives orders," from *imperare*, "to command" and *imperium*, "power"). For political reasons, this supreme ruler was not referred to as "king," as this term was always regarded as unacceptable by Romans, presumably on account of the kings' abuses of power in the archaic period, before they were expelled. As dedicated republicans, Romans were anxious not think of themselves as having fallen back into odious monarchy – the power of one. The term translated by us as "emperor" – *imperator* – was used as a title for Rome's supreme ruler mainly because it avoided language that could have linked his function to the discredited institution of kingship. It was during the reign of the first emperor, Augustus, that the gospel of Luke places the birth of Jesus of Nazareth.

A significant degree of Roman territorial expansion took place during the reign of Augustus, especially in Egypt and in Northern Europe. The imperial province of Egypt became particularly important, providing substantial grain imports that fed the Roman population. Augustus' successor Tiberius, who reigned from AD 14 to AD 37, proved an ineffective emperor, who preferred to live in seclusion on the island of Capri. Much later, under Trajan, the stability of the empire was initially restored, and a period of further expansion followed. A major program of public building in Rome enriched the city, emphasizing its status as the center of the greatest empire the world had then known.

Even in the New Testament there are clear signs of awareness of the Roman authorities' antagonism toward Christianity. The Roman historian Tacitus (AD 56–117) provides some evidence of popular resentment in the aftermath of the Great Fire of Rome (AD 64) when he speaks of Christians as "a class hated for their abominations." The Revelation of St. John, the final work in the New Testament canon, is widely regarded as reflecting active hostility toward Christian groups in the late first century AD. It is thought to reflect the situation during the final years of the reign of the Roman Emperor Domitian, particularly around 95. Yet, although Domitian was a strong supporter of traditional Roman religion, there are no historical records of any official persecution of Christians during his reign.

A form of Roman "civil religion" began to emerge at this time; it was linked with worship of the emperor as an expression of allegiance to the Roman state and empire. A dead emperor who was held worthy of the honor could be voted the status of *divus* (state divinity) and incorporated into the Roman pantheon. Refusal to take part in this imperial cult was regarded as an act of treason. First-century Roman religion tended to draw a distinction between state cult, which gave Roman society stability and cohesion, and the private views of individuals. (The Latin noun *religio* derives from a verb meaning "to bind together.") The role of the state cult was to give the city and the empire a stable and sacred foundation. Religion was primarily understood in terms of "devotion" (*pietas*) – a social activity and an attitude that promoted unity and loyalty to the state.

Roman citizens were free to adopt, in private, other religious practices and beliefs, so long as they did not conflict with this "official" civil religion. These private religions would take place in the household, the head of the family (*paterfamilias*) taking charge of domestic prayers and ceremonial rites in much the same way as the public representatives of the people performed the state ceremonial rites. During the first century AD these private religions often took the form of mystery cults, which originated in Greece or Asia and were brought back to Rome by soldiers and merchants. The best known was the cult of Mithras, which is thought to have originated in Persia.

At that time Christianity would have fitted easily into this pattern of Roman religious diversity. Yet Christians found it difficult to accept the distinction between public and private religious beliefs, holding that their allegiance to their one God prevented them from taking part in the official Roman cult. This became increasingly problematic in the face of the rise of the imperial cult in the late first century. Especially in the eastern regions of the empire, worshipping the emperor came to be seen as a mark of loyalty to Rome. Christians, who refused to worship any God other than their own, were perceived as potentially seditious on the grounds that they did not display this form of loyalty.

The imperial cult was so deeply rooted in the major cities of the eastern Roman empire that it was inevitable that some form of confrontation between Christianity and the state authorities would take place. One of the most frequently cited pieces of evidence here is the famous letter of Pliny the Younger to the Emperor Trajan, which dates from about 112. In this letter Pliny asked advice as to how to deal with the growing number of Christians who refused to worship the image of the Roman emperor. It is quite clear from Pliny's letter that Christianity had fallen under suspicion as a result of the refusal to worship the emperor, which suggested that Christians were bent on overthrowing the existing social order.

The negative attitude of Christians toward the imperial cult helps us understand one of the more puzzling developments of this age: the tendency of Roman critics to ridicule Christianity as a form of "atheism." This makes no sense if "atheism" is understood in the modern sense of the term – namely as rejection of the belief in God. Yet the term "atheism" was widely used in classical culture to refer to a rejection of the official state religion. The classical Greek philosopher Socrates was condemned to death in 399 BC, four centuries before the apostolic age, for his "atheism" – that is, on the grounds that he rejected the "official" religion of the city of Athens. Socrates, of course, was no atheist in the modern sense of the word.

Early Christian worship and organization

Lacking any official religious recognition and protection, early Christianity could not be a public religion in the Roman empire. There were no buildings dedicated to public Christian worship. It is easy to see why the secrecy surrounding Christian gatherings and worship roused suspicions about this new faith within Roman society. Rumors rapidly developed that Christians indulged in orgies and cannibalism. And we can understand how this took place. There is much evidence that early Christian gatherings included a "love feast" (*agapē*, meaning "love" in Greek), which could easily be misunderstood as involving sexual behaviors. Equally, it is not difficult to see how the practice of consuming bread and wine as symbols of the body and blood of Christ could be misinterpreted by outsiders as some kind of cannibalism.

We possess several important witnesses to early Christian worship. One is a manual of church order and Christian living that dates from the late first or early second century and is known as the *Didache* (*The Teaching*: *didachē* is a Greek word meaning "teaching"). This work describes how Christians gathered together on the Lord's Day – in other words, on Sunday – "to break bread and give thanks." The service is clearly understood to take place in a private home, not in a public place.

Justin Martyr composed his *First Apology* in Rome, around AD 155. In this work he describes two early Christian worship services. First, he provides an account of the baptism of new converts. Following their baptism, the new recruits are led into the assembly of Christian believers. After prayers for the community and for the new converts, the worshippers greet one another with a kiss. Bread, wine, and water are then brought to the president, who offers a eucharistic prayer, ascribing glory to the Father in the name of the Son and Spirit, and expresses gratitude that the gathered worshippers have been counted as worthy of receiving the bread and wine. Justin does not use the term "priest" to refer to the president of this "thanksgiving" ceremony (*eucharistia*), presumably because the term had associations with Roman civil religion, which was then strongly hostile to Christianity.

The second event that Justin describes is a regular Sunday gathering of the community of faith. Why meet on a Sunday, rather than on the Jewish sabbath? Justin explains that the community gathers on Sunday – the first day of the week – both because it was the first day of creation and because this was the day on which Jesus rose from the dead. Only those who have been baptized are permitted to attend this service. The service begins with some readings from the "memoirs of the apostles" (almost certainly a reference to the gospels) or from the writings of the prophets, followed by a sermon based on these texts. This is in turn followed by prayers and the celebration of the eucharist along the lines just described. At the end of the service, those with sufficient means are invited to bring gifts to the president, who will distribute them to those in need.

Funeral rites were also important for early Christians. Romans tended to cremate their dead and to place their ashes in carved urns. Christians insisted on burial, seeing this as resting on the precedent of the burial of Christ. From the beginning of the second century, Christians constructed vast underground burial sites by digging into the soft porous pumice rock underneath the city of Rome and the neighboring area. This network – known as "the catacombs" – consisted of passages and tunnels with niches carved into the walls in which bodies could be placed, to await the resurrection. With the legalization of Christianity in the fourth century the catacombs gradually fell into disuse, as Christians were able to provide funeral rites for their dead openly, without fear of persecution.

Even in Rome, early Christianity was not well organized, partly on account of difficulties in coordinating while the Christian movement remained illegal. Although the movement had leaders, they were unable to offer any kind of centralized control. The terms *episcopos* (bishop), *diakonos* (deacon) and *presbuteros* (elder) were all used to refer to leaders of the Christian community. It is significant that all three of these words were widely used in secular culture too, to refer to administrative positions within large households of the day. An *episcopos* was a domestic supervisor, a *diakonos* a servant, and a *presbuteros* a senior member of the household. Christianity appears to have taken over familiar secular words here and to have invested them with specifically Christian meanings, in effect transferring these terms to the "household of faith."

At this early stage there is no suggestion that a bishop had oversight of a group of churches or an ecclesiastical region. This development took place later, when Christianity became the official religion of the Roman empire, even if there are some early anticipations of it. At the early stage, a "bishop" was often simply the leader of a single Christian community. The Roman churches of the second century are perhaps best compared to secular Roman clubs or societies (*collegium*, plural *collegia*), or to Jewish synagogues – essentially independent associations with no centralized control.

Women and early Christianity

As we noted earlier, women played an important role in the apostolic church (pp. 25–26). Yet, for reasons that are not fully understood, the churches tended to adopt more traditional, culturally accommodated approaches to headship and hierarchy. In the Greco-Roman world, the ideal woman was portrayed as self-effacing, industrious, and loyal to her family. Funerary monuments provide some of the clearest expressions of these cultural norms, celebrating a deceased woman's conformity to what was expected of her. This inscription on a first-century Roman tombstone illustrates how these virtues were embodied and commended.

> Here lies Amymone, wife of Marcus, best and most beautiful of women. She made wool, she was devoted to the gods and her family. She was modest, careful with money, and chaste. She stayed at home.

Inevitably, the assimilation of such cultural norms led to the exclusion of women from positions of communal and liturgical leadership, even if women may have exercised considerable social and political influence behind the scenes. There were three orders of ministry within the early church: bishops, priests, and deacons. Although women rapidly found themselves excluded from the former two roles, they remained active as deaconesses. This ministry is recorded from the second century on and played a significant role in the pastoral life of the churches.

The "Didascalia of the Apostles," which seems to date from the first half of the third century, suggests that male deacons should be compared to Christ and deaconesses to the Holy Spirit. In practical terms, it seems that deacons undertook pastoral ministry to men and deaconesses to women. The Council of Chalcedon ruled that women should not be allowed to be ordained as deaconesses until they were 40; this suggests a need to regularize this ministerial order, which was already well established within the Christian world.

Martyrdom remained one of the most significant areas in which women played a leading role. Two of the most celebrated women martyrs were Perpetua and Felicitas, who were martyred together in Carthage in the first decade of the third century. The traditional account of their martyrdom offers some insights into the social dynamics of the churches at this time. Perpetua, a Roman noblewoman, was a nursing mother; Felicitas was her pregnant slave. Perpetua had been baptized against the explicit wishes of her father, indicating that she was prepared to break with familial traditions and loyalties on account of her faith. The fact that both a noblewoman and her slave were martyred together reflects a growing tendency for martyrdom to become a means of self-empowerment for women at this period, when imperial hostility to Christianity often led to sporadic harassment and occasionally to systematic persecution.

One of the most remarkable witnesses to the aspirations of women in the early church is found in the cult of Thecla of Iconium. This cult is thought to have originated in the second half of the second century and is described in a document of this period known as *The Acts of Paul and Thecla*. The document presents a noblewoman, Thecla, who is described as a traditional "stay at home" aristocrat. One day she overhears the preaching of Apostle Paul through an open window. Enthralled by what she hears, she leaves behind her fiancé and her home to follow Paul, and eventually to travel and proclaim the gospel herself.

One of the core themes of this intriguing work is the rejection of the social role assigned to women of noble birth at this time in imperial Roman culture – especially the traditional bonds of familial loyalty, the expectation that they will marry, and their dedication to their home – as an effect of the countercultural values and beliefs of the Christian faith. At one point Thecla is condemned to death by the Roman authorities at the instigation of her mother, who is outraged by her rejection of traditional cultural norms. Yet Thecla eventually wins out.

The story is important, because it affirms the role of women in carrying out church responsibilities that were then being increasingly allotted to males – such as public leadership and evangelism. Thecla is prepared to dress as a man in order to be able to carry out such a role. As early as 190, the Roman theologian Tertullian from Carthage expressed concern that some were using the story of Thecla to justify the public ministry of women in churches, especially in baptizing and preaching – something to which Tertullian was opposed.

Yet Christian women were now playing a significant role outside the mainstream of church life. The Montanist movement of the mid-second century, for example, centered on three charismatic individuals in the province of Phrygia: Montanus himself and two women colleagues, Prisca (sometimes called Priscilla) and Maximilla. Montanism is perhaps best understood as a religious renewal movement, similar in some ways to modern Pentecostalism (p. 212). Contemporary sources suggest that, among the movement's followers, Prisca and Maximilla achieved greater status than Montanus himself. Although Montanism had considerable influence within the churches, especially in Africa, it is best seen as a movement operating outside the administrative and power structures of the church, thus allowing women to assume leadership roles that were becoming problematic within church structures, which were increasingly conforming to Roman social norms.

The same is true of the monastic movement, which often arose as a response to concerns about the morality and spirituality of mainline Christian communities, especially in the cities. The *amma* (meaning "mother" in Aramaic) became a recognized female figure of spiritual wisdom and discernment in the monastic spirituality of the deserts of Egypt, Palestine, and Syria, especially during the fourth and fifth centuries. Syncletica of Alexandria (died c. 350) is one of a number of female spiritual writers whose sayings are included in the collection traditionally known as *The Sayings of the Desert Fathers*.

If space permitted, other women of importance in early Christianity could be noted – such as Monica, the mother of Augustine of Hippo. Despite the increasing limitations placed on women within the churches, many found ways to subvert them and to exercise a significant public ministry.

The conversion of the Emperor Constantine

One of the most severe outbursts of persecution came about in February 303, during the reign of the Emperor Diocletian (284–313). An edict was issued ordering the destruction of all Christian places of worship, the surrender and destruction of all their books, and the cessation of all acts of Christian worship. Christian civil servants were to lose all privileges of rank or status and to be reduced to the status of slaves. Prominent Christians were forced to offer sacrifice according to traditional Roman practices. It is an indication of how influential Christianity had become that Diocletian forced both his own wife and his own daughter, who were known to be Christians, to comply with this order. The persecution continued under successive emperors, including Galerius, who ruled the eastern region of the empire.

In 311 Galerius ordered the cessation of the persecution. It had been a failure and had merely hardened Christians in their resolve to resist the re-imposition of classical Roman pagan religion. Galerius issued an edict that permitted Christians to live normally again and to "hold their religious assemblies, provided that they do nothing which would disturb public order." The edict explicitly identified Christianity as a religion and offered it the full protection of the law. The legal status of Christianity, which had been ambiguous up to this point, was now resolved. The church no longer existed under a siege mentality.

Flavius Valerius Aurelius Constantinus Augustus (272–337) – better known simply as "Constantine" – became emperor during a complex and difficult period in Roman imperial history, which is regarded by many historians as marking the transition between classical antiquity (taken as a whole) and late antiquity. A series of crises in the late third century (235–284) came close to bringing the Roman empire to collapse under the threat of invasion, a damaging civil war, outbreaks of the plague, and serious economic depression. In the end Constantine defeated his opponents and was proclaimed emperor in 313.

Constantine showed no particular attraction for Christianity in his early period. He declared himself to be a Christian shortly after his decisive victory at the Milvian Bridge, to the north of Rome, on October 28, 312, after which he was proclaimed emperor. This point is affirmed by both Christian and pagan writers. What is not clear is precisely why or when this conversion took place.

Some Christian writers suggested that this conversion may have taken place before the decisive battle, as Constantine saw a heavenly vision ordering him to place the sign of the cross on his soldiers' shields. "In this sign you shall conquer" (*in hoc signo vinces*). Whatever the reasons for the conversion and no matter whether it dates from before or after the battle of the Milvian Bridge, the reality and consequences of this conversion are not in doubt.

The first change in imperial attitudes toward Christianity took place in 313, when Constantine and Licinus issued the Edict of Milan, proclaiming freedom of religion in both the western and the eastern parts of the Roman empire. This did not give Christianity any

Figure 4.1   Constantine, the first Christian Roman emperor. Source: Nimatallah/AKG Images.

privileges; nevertheless, it opened the way to its playing a significant role in Roman society, allowing Christians to emerge from the shadows and the margins and to assume major social roles. In the years that followed Rome gradually became Christianized.

Yet Constantine proceeded cautiously. Initially he retained traditional Roman pagan symbolism, anxious not to create popular discontent against his program of religious reform. The triumphal arch constructed in 315 to mark Constantine's victory in the Battle of the Milvian Bidge makes use of no Christian symbolism, but shows sacrifices being made to gods such as Apollo, Diana, and Hercules. In the late 310s Constantine often made moves that could be interpreted as a reaffirmation of traditional paganism as much as of Christianity.

An important turning point took place in 321, when Constantine decreed that Christians and non-Christians should worship on the "day of the Sun." While this clearly reflected the Christian practice of meeting and worshipping on Sunday, it could also be presented as a reaffirmation of the sun cult favored by earlier emperors such as Aurelian. The Roman mints continued for some time to produce coins showing figures of traditional Roman deities, reassuring the population that traditional Roman paganism was still being taken seriously. Constantine proved to be an able diplomat, moving Rome toward Christianity while publicly retaining traditional religious symbols.

Yet alongside these traditional pagan images Christian symbols now began to appear on Roman coins. Furthermore, Constantine stipulated that his statue erected in the Forum should depict him bearing a cross – "the sign of suffering that brought salvation," according to the inscription provided by the emperor himself. Christianity was now more than just legitimate; it was on its way to becoming the established religion of the empire.

A critical step in this process took place in 324–325, when Constantine led an army against the eastern Emperor Licinus. Licinus' defeat made Constantine sole emperor over the entire Roman empire. Christianity would now be tolerated throughout the empire. The city of Constantinople (from the Greek *Kōnstantinou polis*, meaning "the city of Constantine") was established as a "new Rome" and would become the administrative center of the empire.

Christian theology now emerged from the hidden world of secret church meetings, to become a matter of public interest and concern throughout the Roman empire. Increasingly, doctrinal debates assumed both political and theological importance. Constantine wished to have a united church; he was thus concerned that doctrinal differences should be debated and settled as a matter of priority. This led to his calling of the Council of Nicaea in 325, which was to settle doctrinal disputes within the church and to allow Christianity to function in a way that Constantine believed was appropriate for the religion of an empire like his.

The conversion of Constantine and his victory over Licinus in 324 removed any remaining barriers to Christians openly practicing their faith throughout the Roman empire. Christianity was offered the same legal protection as other religions, and Christians were granted freedom to worship as and where they pleased. The most immediate result was that Christians felt confident enough to worship in public, no longer needing to meet secretly in private houses. The way was now clear for them to construct and own their own purpose-built churches.

Within a generation, Christianity had moved from being a persecuted movement on the fringes of imperial culture to being adopted by the establishment. The Christian church was simply not prepared for this radical transition. Its bishops were once merely leaders of congregations; they now became pillars of Roman society, with power and influence. Its churches were once private homes; they were now massive dedicated buildings, publicly affirming the important place of Christianity in imperial culture. The simple forms of early worship were replaced by ceremonies and processions of increased complexity, adapted to the splendor of the great basilicas that now sprang up in imperial cities.

There were setbacks – most notably, the curious reign of Julian the Apostate from 361 to 363, memorable mainly for its unsuccessful attempts to re-establish a fading and tarnished paganism as the official imperial religion. A later source reports that Julian's final words were "You have won, O Galilean" (*Vicisti, Galilaee*). Yet Julian's abortive attempt to restore the fortunes of paganism merely proved to be an interlude in the inexorable rise of the political, social, and intellectual influence of Christianity. His successor, Jovian, rescinded Julian's legal measures directed against Christianity. Theodosius the Great, who reigned as emperor from 379 to 395, finally issued a series of measures that made Christianity the official religion of the Roman empire, bringing to a conclusion the slow process of Christianization initiated by Constantine.

The cities and the rise of monasticism

Early Christianity established itself primarily in cities – such as the Greek-speaking port cities on the eastern Mediterranean coastline, including Ephesus and Pergamon – rather than in remote rural areas. Cities, especially ports, were centers of commerce and trade, hence one of the classical means by which new religious and philosophical ideas were spread in the ancient world. They also offered a greater degree of anonymity than was possible in the countryside, allowing Christians to conceal themselves during an age that was generally hostile to their beliefs and practices. Christian communities were able to meet in secret, celebrate their beliefs, and begin to share their vision with outsiders.

The link between Christianity and the cities of the Roman empire became so significant that later on, at a time when the empire had adopted Christianity as its official religion, the Latin term for a "country-dweller" (Latin *paganus*) began to be used in western Christian circles to characterize someone who retained older Roman religious beliefs. A Latin term that originally lacked religious associations of any kind thus came to refer primarily to someone who practiced traditional forms of religion.

As Christianity grew more deeply embedded in the imperial cities, a number of significant institutional developments began to take place. One was the rise of the "metropolitan bishop" – that is, a bishop who was seen to be the titular leader of all the churches in a city rather than of one specific Christian community. The most important of these were the bishops of Alexandria, Antioch, Constantinople, Jerusalem, and Rome. After the legalization of Christianity, these metropolitan bishops began to wield considerable political power – especially the bishop of Rome, who was considered to have a symbolic authority linked with the imperial authority of the city of Rome itself.

The growing presence of Christianity in the cities of the Roman empire was seen by many Christians as a positive development. Not only was it an important witness to the increasing influence of the Christian faith; it was a means by which Christianity could begin to work for the transformation of urban culture and society. Christianity, some argued, was like yeast in bread dough – a small presence, which would gradually grow and eventually change things for the better.

Other Christians, however, were not so sure that this development was quite such a positive thing. While they did not rule out the possibility that urban expansion of the Christian faith might bring about a moral and spiritual transformation of the degeneracy of the imperial cities, it was quite possible that the reverse might happen. Might the immorality and debauchery of the cities – a frequent topic of concern in early Christian sermons – end up contaminating and corrupting the church?

One of the most important developments to take place within early Christianity was the rise of monasticism. (The terms "monk" and "monasticism" both come from the Greek word *monachos*, meaning "solitary" or "alone.") The origins of the monastic movement are generally thought to lie in remote hilly areas of Egypt and in parts of eastern Syria. Significant numbers of Christians began to make their homes in these regions, in order to get away from the population centers and all the distractions these offered. Anthony of Egypt, who left his parents' home in 273 to seek out a life of discipline and solitude in the desert, is an excellent representative of this growing trend.

The theme of withdrawal from a sinful and distracting world acquired central importance for these communities. Yet it soon became clear that there were two quite different ways of withdrawing from the world. Some saw monasticism as a solitary and ascetic life; others as a form of communal religious life. The more communal approach began to gain the upper hand in the fifth century.

One important early monastery was established by Pachomius (c. 292–348) – who is generally recognized as the founder of this communal form of monasticism – during the years 320–325. This monastery developed an ethos that would become normative in later monasticism. Members of the community agreed to submit themselves to a common life that was regulated by a rule, under the direction of a superior. The physical structure of the monastery played an important role in reinforcing its spiritual values. The monastery complex was surrounded by a wall, a feature that highlighted the idea of separation and withdrawal from the world.

The monastic ideal proved to have a deep attraction for many people. By the fourth century, monasteries had been established in many locations in the Christian East, especially in the regions of Syria and Asia Minor. It was not long before the movement was taken up in the western church. By the fifth century monastic communities had come into existence in Italy (especially along the western coastline), Spain, and Gaul.

Figure 4.2   The Abbey of Montecassino. Source: Pirozzi/AKG Images.

This development was consolidated after the fall of the western Roman empire. During the sixth century the number of monasteries in the region grew considerably. It was during this period that one of the most comprehensive monastic "rules" – the Rule of Benedict – made its appearance. Benedict of Nursia (c. 480–c. 550) established his monastery at Monte Cassino (also known as "Montecassino") at some point around 525. The Benedictine community followed a rule that was dominated by the notion of an unconditional following of Christ, which was sustained through regular corporate and private prayer and the reading of scripture. These monasteries acted as agents in the transmission of Christian theology and spirituality after the collapse of the Roman empire, preparing the way for the theological and spiritual renaissance of the Middle Ages.

The fall of the Roman empire

By the end of the fourth century Roman power was in decline in the West. In 387 a Gallic tribal army overwhelmed Rome's defenses and briefly took control of the city. Yet the tipping point in the decline of Rome was 408, when a Visigoth army led by Alaric laid siege to the city. In August 410 Alaric invaded Rome and pillaged it. This invasion was only a temporary development, lasting a few days. Yet, before it withdrew, Alaric's army burned many parts of Rome, shaking the confidence of an entire civilization. The Eternal City was in danger of being overthrown, if not completely destroyed.

But this sack of Rome did not mark the end of the Roman empire. The administration of the empire was increasingly located in the East, at the new imperial city of Constantinople. As a result of earlier decisions made with this possibility in mind, Rome was no longer even the capital city of the western empire. The government of the western empire continued without interruption for another generation. Most historians regard the western Roman empire as coming to an end sometime around the year 476; the eastern empire, whose capital was the great city of Constantinople, continued to exist for the best part of another thousand years. Yet the symbolic importance of the sack of Rome was massive. The era of the Eternal City seemed to be coming to an end.

The traditional date of the fall of the Roman empire in the West – 476 – is the year when Romulus Augustus, the last western emperor, was overthrown by the German military ruler Odoacer (433–493), who then declared himself king of Italy. The administrative changes Odoacer put in place in Italy effectively ended any idea of a "Roman empire." A nominal imperial center was maintained at the city of Ravenna for some time, but it never had the symbolic (let alone the actual) power of Rome.

The real importance of the decline of imperial power for the Christian church is best appreciated from the standpoint of the emergence of the Middle Ages. Looking back at the period of the breakup of the Roman empire, it is clear that many of the characteristic features of the church in the Middle Ages were a result of this imperial decline. Three developments are of particular interest.

First, the erosion of Roman political and military power created a vacuum that was never really satisfactorily filled by the successors to the emperors. These rulers tended to see themselves as exercising local rather than international authority. Furthermore, such rulers often did not survive long enough to establish the traditions and institutions that would secure social and political stability. Gradually the institution of the church began to emerge as a focus of constancy and continuity. Gregory the Great, who was pope from 590 until his death in 604, brought about reform and renewal of the church and set in place missionary undertakings in Northern Europe that led to the further expansion of Christian influence within the territories of the former Roman empire.

Second, the rise of the monasteries created centers of learning, local administration, and leadership that were independent of national or international agencies. Although clearly affected to some extent by political and economic developments, the monasteries were able to offer intellectual and spiritual continuity in times of uncertainty and turbulence.

Third, the church continued to use Latin in its liturgy, preaching, administration, and works of theology. The language of the Roman empire had a long history of use in political, philosophical, and theological contexts and proved highly adapted to the needs of the western church. The emergence of Latin as an international language helped hold the western church together, enhancing its sense of being a coherent community. As academic communities gradually emerged from religious contexts – such as the great monastic cathedral schools – it was inevitable that Latin should function as the language of the academy in the Middle Ages.

These developments are all of major importance for an understanding of the history of Christianity in the West during the Middle Ages, which we shall consider in the next section.

The Middle Ages and the Renaissance, c. 500–c. 1500

With the collapse and gradual disintegration of the western Roman empire in the fifth century, the face of Europe began to change. A patchwork of regions and city-states began to emerge, each competing for territory and influence. Yet during this period of fragmentation the Christian church gradually began to develop a political and temporal role that placed it at the heart of western culture. As some degree of political and economic stability developed around the year 1100, the church was poised to exercise a major role in shaping the culture of the Middle Ages.

By the year 600 Christianity had established itself throughout much of the region of what we now know as the Middle East, including the coastal areas of western North Africa. To the north, Christianity extended up to the Danube and the Rhine. Christian expansion had also taken place to the east of the Roman Empire, in Persia, where a form of Christianity that came to be known as Nestorianism had gained influence. Christianity is also thought to have become established in India by the end of the third century.

The situation of Christianity in the Mediterranean region changed significantly through the rise of Islam – the religious belief system based on the teachings of Muhammad (570–632). After Muhammad's death, Islam spread through military conquest throughout much of the Middle East, including the Roman colonies of North Africa. Islam established itself in Spain through invasions from Morocco and began to expand into France in the eighth century, until military defeat checked this development.

Christians were called by Muslims "the People of the Book" and allowed a degree of religious freedom in territories controlled by them. Yet, while Christians living under Islamic rule were not forced to convert, they were obliged to pay special taxes and to wear clothing that distinguished them from Muslims. While Muslim men were permitted to marry Christian women, Christian men were not permitted to marry Muslim women.

Fear of further Islamic expansion into Europe, whether from Spain in the southwest or from Turkey in the southeast, was a constant concern throughout the Middle Ages and extended well into the early modern period. The fall of the great Byzantine city of Constantinople to Islamic armies in 1453 caused concern throughout Europe, as some believed that it represented a tipping point, marking the possible end of a Christian Europe.

The emergence of the Middle Ages is a complex and fascinating story, involving the political and social renewal of Western Europe, the slow decline and fall of the great Byzantine empire in the East, the rediscovery of the philosophical and scientific writings of the ancient world preserved by Arabic scholars, and the great renewal of letters and arts that we know as the Renaissance. All of these shaped the narrative of Christian history, as we shall see in what follows.

The development of Celtic Christianity

The rise of Christianity in the Celtic regions of Europe – more specifically in Ireland, Scotland, Cornwall, Brittany, and Wales – is of considerable interest, not least because this version of Christianity found itself in opposition to the more romanized forms that rapidly gained ascendancy in England. Although the origins of Celtic Christianity seem to lie in

Wales, it is Ireland that established itself as a major missionary center during the fifth and sixth centuries. Other centers of missionary activity in the Celtic sphere of influence are known from this period, most notably Candida Casa (modern-day Whithorn, in the Galloway region of Scotland), which was established by bishop Ninian in the fifth century. The significance of this missionary station was that it lay outside the borders of Roman Britain and was thus able to operate without the restrictions then associated with Roman forms of Christianity.

The person who is traditionally held to be responsible for the evangelization of Ireland was a romanized Briton by the name of Magonus Sucatus Patricius, more usually known by his Celtic name, Patrick (c. 390–c. 460). There are some difficulties in clarifying the details of Patrick's career. Many scholars argue that the confusion arises through some traditions that claim that Palladius (sent by Pope Celestine I as the first bishop to Irish Christians in 431) became attached to Patrick. According to the traditional account of his life, Patrick was taken captive in Wales by a raiding party at the age of 16 and sold into slavery in Ireland, probably in the region of Connaught. Here he appears to have discovered the basics of the Christian faith. After six years in captivity, he was able to escape and make his way back to his family.

It is not clear precisely what happened between Patrick's escape from captivity and his subsequent return to Ireland as a missionary. A tradition dating back to the seventh or eighth century refers to Patrick spending time in Gaul before his return to Ireland. It is possible that some of Patrick's views on church organization and structures may reflect first-hand acquaintance with the monasticism of certain regions of southern France. There is excellent historical evidence for trading links between Ireland and the Loire Valley around this time.

Patrick returned to Ireland and established Christianity in the region. It is clear that some form of Christianity already existed; not only does Patrick's conversion account presuppose that others in the region knew about the gospel; contemporary records dating from as early as 429 speak of the "Palladius" noted earlier as the bishop of Ireland, indicating that at least some form of rudimentary ecclesiastical structures existed in the region. Irish representatives are also known to have been present at the Synod of Arles (314). Patrick's achievement is perhaps best understood in terms of the consolidation and advancement of Christianity, rather than related to its establishment in the first place.

The monastic idea took hold very quickly in Ireland. Historical sources indicate that Ireland was largely a nomadic and tribal society at this time, without permanent settlements of any importance. The monastic quest for solitude and isolation was ideally suited to the Irish way of life and allowed local noble families to be integrated into monastic structures. Whereas in Western Europe as a whole monasticism tended to lie on the margins of the authority structures of the church, in Ireland it rapidly became its dominant form. The Irish church was monastic in its outlook, the abbot rather than the bishop being seen as the figure of spiritual authority.

The authority structures that emerged within Celtic Christianity thus differed significantly from those that dominated the Roman–British church around this time. The Irish monastic model came to be seen as a threat to the Roman model of the episcopate, in which the government of the church resided firmly in the hands of the bishops. None of the abbots of Iona ever allowed bishops to formally ordain them, rejecting the need for any such official recognition.

In Ireland, some of the older bishoprics (including Armagh) were reorganized on a monastic basis, while others were absorbed by monasteries. Abbeys were responsible for the pastoral care of the churches that grew up in their vicinity. The Roman episcopal system was thus marginalized. The Celtic church leaders were openly critical of worldly wealth and status, including the use of horses as a mode of transport and any form of luxury.

Theologically, Celtic Christianity also stressed the importance of the world of nature as a means of knowing God. This is especially clear from the ancient Irish hymn traditionally ascribed to Patrick and known as "St. Patrick's Breastplate." The theme of a "breastplate" was common in Celtic Christian spirituality. It is based upon Paul's references to the "armor of God" (Ephesians 6: 10–18) and develops the theme of the believer being protected by the presence of God and a whole range of associated powers. Although strongly trinitarian in its structure, it shows a fascination with the natural world as a means of knowing God. The God who made the world is the same God who will protect Christians from all dangers.

The Irish monasteries acted as centers for missionary activity, often using sea lanes as channels for the transmission of Christianity. Brendan (died c. 580) and Columba (died c. 597) are excellent examples of this type of missionary. In a poem entitled "The Navigation of St. Brendan" (c. 1050), Brendan is praised for his journeys to the "northern and western isles" (usually assumed to be Orkney, Shetland, and the Hebrides, off the coast of Scotland).

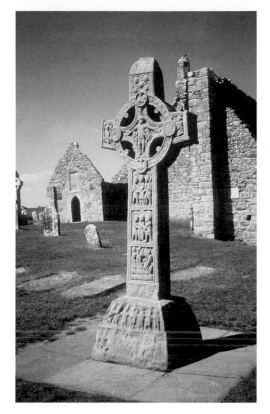

Figure 4.3 A Celtic Cross from Ireland, widely regarded as a symbol of the distinctive forms of Christianity that emerged in this region. Source: Juergen Sorges/AKG Images.

Columba brought Christianity from the north of Ireland to the western Isles of Scotland and established the abbey of Iona as a missionary outpost. From there, Christianity spread southward and eastward. Aidan (died 651) is an excellent example of a monk from Iona who acted as a missionary in this way. At the invitation of the king of the region of Northumbria, he established a missionary monastery on the island of Lindisfarne, off the east coast of northern England. Celtic Christianity began to penetrate into France and became increasingly influential in the region.

The rise of the monastic and cathedral schools

For modern readers, the universities stand at the center of the world's intellectual reflection and scholarly research. Yet the idea of the university had yet to develop in the ninth century; as we shall see, this new institution would not emerge until the late eleventh century. During the period 800–1100, it was schools attached to monasteries and cathedrals that began to achieve distinction as centers of scholarship. These were the precursors of the great universities of Europe.

The development of cathedral schools was often due to the educational vision of the bishop of the diocese. As the traditional educational structures of the Roman empire were getting eroded in the late fifth century, bishops made arrangements to ensure that their clergy would continue to be well educated. In part this was a pragmatic decision, reflecting the need to have a literate clergy, capable of writing and possessing basic administrative skills. Yet it was often a decision that was also based on a love of learning and a desire to keep scholarship alive in a time when there were limited opportunities for study and research.

Although the earliest cathedral schools developed in Spain during the sixth and early seventh centuries, some of the most important schools of this kind developed in England. The conversion of England to Christianity as a result of Gregory the Great's decision to send missionaries to the region created an urgent need for theological education. Provision had to be made for the education of clergy in a region with little recent history of Christian scholarship. Cathedral schools initially developed at Canterbury (597) and Rochester (604) in Kent, in the south of England, soon to be followed by a major school at York Minster in the north of England (627).

The next wave of cathedral schools were established in France, especially at the cathedrals of Chartres, Laôn, Liège, Orléans, Paris, Rheims, and Rouen. The cathedral school of Paris would eventually become the University of Paris in the twelfth century. These schools were under the control of the local bishop and generally focused on educating the local clergy.

Yet cathedral schools were not the only centers of learning. Some of Europe's great monasteries, most of which followed the Order of St. Benedict, emerged as centers of excellence in scholarship, building up large libraries. Indeed many monasteries considered scholarship to be essential to their calling. Three elements were of particular importance in Benedictine spirituality: liturgical prayer, manual labor, and *lectio divina*, which meant "divine reading" in Latin – a quiet, meditative reading of the Bible. Although many monks were able to commit biblical texts to memory, the important place given to *lectio divina* inevitably created a demand for texts of the Bible, which had to be copied out by hand.

Many monasteries established a *scriptorium* – a special room or section of the library dedicated to the copying of manuscripts – and built up libraries, which often contained classical works of history and literature alongside biblical texts and works of Christian theology. Monastic libraries of the Carolingian era were filled with Christian and pagan works, which were copied carefully for purposes of transmission. Many of the classical works widely consulted today have survived as a result of this copying process in the Carolingian period. For example, two of the earliest surviving manuscripts of Julius Caesar's *Gallic Wars* were created in France in the ninth century. By copying manuscripts, monasteries kept alive some of the key sources of classical culture centuries before the dawn of the Renaissance saw them being rediscovered by the humanists and given new life.

The "Great Schism" between East and West (1054)

Relations between western and eastern Christianity were generally problematic throughout the history of early Christianity, often reflecting deep political rivalry between the pope at Rome and the emperor at Constantinople. Although clear and genuine theological differences were in the process of emerging between the two Christian churches – the eastern and western – from about 700 on, these were often not the primary cause of the tensions that culminated in the formal break between them in 1054.

Tensions had arisen between East and West during the Photian Schism (863–867), partly as a result of the western church's introduction of the phrase *ex patre filioque* ("from the Father and from the Son") into its versions of the creed (pp. 73–74), without consulting or securing approval from the eastern church. The western churches now spoke of the Holy Spirit as "proceeding from the Father and the Son"; the eastern churches retained the older form of words, which spoke of the Holy Spirit as simply "proceeding from the Father."

The schism of 1054 was, however, a more serious matter. Tensions had risen over other differences between East and West. Should unleavened or leavened bread be used at the eucharist? Eastern Christians retained the traditional practice of using leavened bread (that is, bread made from flour to which yeast has been added, causing it to rise); the West increasingly used bread made without any yeast. The East resented the increasingly strident claims to universal authority on the part of popes and felt that Constantinople's claims to spiritual and political authority were not being given due weight in the West.

Yet many scholars argue that the final breaking point was the intransigence of two leading Christians of the eleventh century: Leo IX, pope from 1049 to 1054, and Michael Cerularius, Patriarch of Constantinople from 1043 to 1059. Leo's enforcement of western norms in southern Italian churches (which up until then had generally followed Byzantine liturgical and devotional practices) was seen as tantamount to a claim to papal sovereignty over the entire church. Cerularius seems to have come to the conclusion that the only way of safeguarding the identity of the Byzantine church was to break any remaining relations with Rome and to eliminate any papal influence at Constantinople.

Although various attempts were made during the Middle Ages to mitigate this breach of communion, none of them really achieved very much. In part, this reflected the bitter aftermath of the Fourth Crusade (1202–1204; see 140). Although intent on neutralizing Islamic military expansion in the eastern Mediterranean, the western armies ended up besieging and finally occupying Constantinople in 1204. Whether this was an intended goal of the crusades remains disputed among historians. But, accidental or deliberate, the sacking of Constantinople solidified the alienation between East and West. Reconciliation between the eastern and western churches now became virtually impossible. As a result, the western church developed along more or less independent lines during the Middle Ages, without feeling under obligation to take Constantinople's views into account.

The crusades: Spain and the Middle East

Although by 1100 the church in western Europe had established its own identity and concerns, it could not ignore developments elsewhere in the region. It was clear that the military expansion of Islam posed a major threat to the church throughout the southern flank of Europe. The origins of the crusades lie in eleventh-century requests for military assistance in stemming – or even reversing – Islamic territorial gains.

The term "crusade" is often used specifically, to designate a series of military campaigns carried over an extended period of time in the Balkans and the Middle East. The immediate cause of the First Crusade was the defeat of Byzantine armies by the Turks at the Battle of

Manzikert in 1071, which led to the loss of the interior of Asia Minor. Constantinople was now vulnerable, no longer having any buffer zone to protect itself against Turkish armies. Alexius I, the Byzantine emperor, appealed to Pope Gregory VII, asking for military assistance in the face of this critical threat. It was not the best time to make such an appeal. Relations between the eastern and western churches had plunged to new depths in 1054 on account of the Great Schism. Gregory turned down Alexius' request.

Nevertheless, his successor Urban II responded positively. In 1095 Urban launched a passionate appeal for Christian princes across Europe to take up arms in a holy war in the Middle East. The First Crusade (1096–1099) was fueled by a religious passion that prompted armies made up of both knights and peasants to journey to the Middle East. Jerusalem was captured in 1099.

The historical roots of the First Crusade remain contested. Historians have offered various explanations – such as Urban II's desire to extend his religious and political influence eastward, or rising concerns about Islamic encroachment in Europe. Some have suggested that the outcome of the crusade was a further destabilization of the Byzantine rulers, in that it showed them to be militarily and diplomatically incompetent.

Yet most historians agree that the crusade achieved a relatively small and short-lived victory. It would only be a matter of time before the four "crusader states" that resulted from this incursion – the principality of Antioch, the county of Edessa, the kingdom of Jerusalem, and the county of Tripoli (secured during a later campaign in 1101) – would fall back into Islamic hands. There is also widespread agreement that the religious fervor that made so many civilians volunteer for military service in the First Crusade diminished significantly in subsequent campaigns, which were generally conducted by military professionals and mercenaries and had little popular support.

The fall of Edessa in 1144 triggered the Second Crusade (1145–1149). This crusade was followed by a series of campaigns. Some historians hold that there were altogether nine crusades; we here follow those who suggest that there were eight:

the Third Crusade (1188–1192);
the Fourth Crusade (1202–1204);
the Fifth Crusade (1217);
the Sixth Crusade (1228–1229);
the Seventh Crusade (1249–1252);
the Eighth Crusade (1270).

Although the crusades were presented primarily as an attempt to secure the holy sites of Christianity and prevent further Islamic expansion into Europe, it is clear that other agendas were being pursued as well. One of the most significant of these secondary agendas concerns the tensions between Rome and Constantinople. Simmering tensions exploded during the Fourth Crusade, when, as we have seen, an army that had been raised to capture Jerusalem ended up laying siege to Constantinople in July 1203, by accident or by design (see p. 139). The city fell in April 1204 and was sacked by the crusaders, with great loss of life – an action subsequently condemned by Pope Innocent III. The crusader armies, diverted by their attack on Constantinople, never continued their intended journey to Jerusalem.

The crusades can be seen as representing a period in history when the power and influence of the papacy was at its height. By the fourteenth century, a degree of decentralization was taking place across Europe, power being increasingly concentrated in nation-states, which were anxious to preserve their own identity and interests.

Academic theology: The rise of scholasticism

Scholastic theology is widely regarded as an intellectual landmark of the Middle Ages. It offered a systematic approach to Christian theology: one that was based on a rigorous rational foundation and made full use of the disciplines of rhetoric, dialectic, and logic (these were taught in the West in most academic contexts). The intricacy and comprehensiveness of leading works of scholastic theology led the great medieval scholar Etienne Gilson (1884–1978) to describe them as "cathedrals of the mind."

In the late eleventh century Anselm of Canterbury produced a rational defense of the incarnation, demonstrating that this distinctively Christian doctrine was a proper and necessary consequence of basic beliefs concerning the nature of God and the human predicament. Anselm's positive and orthodox approach to the relation of faith and reason – summarized in his motto *fides quaerens intellectum* ("faith seeking understanding"; see pp. 60–61) – created a new awareness of the possibility of a rational approach to theology.

This was taken a step further through the use of dialectical reasoning to resolve theological contradictions – for example, in the interpretation of biblical passages. Anselm of Laôn (died 1117) explored some disputed questions of biblical interpretation, noting how patristic commentators often offered quite different understandings of biblical passages. Having noted these divergences, Anselm of Laôn then offered means of resolving them – in effect producing a synthesis out of a dialectic.

This approach was continued by Peter Abelard (1079–1142) in his *Sic et Non* (*Yes and No*), in which he considered 150 debated theological points and set out the contested ones for resolution by his readers. A similar approach lay behind Peter Lombard's twelfth-century textbook *The Four Books of the Sentences*, which presented a variety of patristic statements on various issues and left it to readers to resolve them. As a result, commentaries on the *Sentences* became one of the most widely used genres of academic theological literature in the Middle Ages.

By the beginning of the thirteenth century, there was a new theological appetite for the systematic articulation of theological positions, justified in terms of their rational and biblical basis, and the views of patristic writers. The most famous work of scholastic theology is Thomas Aquinas' *Summa theologiae* (*The Totality of Theology*, 1265–1274). Aquinas here wove together the reconciliation of competing biblical and patristic statements, within a rational framework that was intended to ensure that the Christian faith could be defended against its rational critics – such as Jews and Muslims, both of whom were present at Paris in the thirteenth century.

One of the most influential misrepresentations of scholastic theology is the assertion that it debated how many angels might dance on the head of a pin. This suggestion dates from the seventeenth century and is not found in any medieval writings. This is not to deny that medieval writers did discuss a number of questions relating to angels. For example,

Figure 4.4   Thomas Aquinas, from the series of portraits of famous men in the Palazzo Ducale in Urbino (c. 1476), by Justus van Gent (active between 1460 and 1480). Source: Erich Lessing/ AKG Images.

Aquinas sets out a detailed theology of angels, distinguishing nine quite distinct types of angels and arranging them hierarchically.

One of the most distinctive features of scholastic theologies of the thirteenth century is its growing awareness of additional cultural and intellectual resources made available for Christian theology through increased contact with the Islamic world. One of these resources was the rediscovery of Aristotle, now rightly recognized as one of the most significant intellectual developments of the Middle Ages.

Secular and religious power in the Middle Ages

By the thirteenth century, the church in Europe had become a major influence in international politics and in the internal affairs of regions by fostering a sense of identity at the level of local communities and by giving individuals a sense of location and purpose within a greater scheme of things. The church has always played an important international role in European society. Medieval Europe bore little relation to its modern counterpart, composed as the latter is of individual well-defined nation-states. In the Middle Ages Europe consisted of an aggregate of generally small principalities, city-states, and regions, often defined and given a shared sense of identity more by language and historical factors than by any sense of common political identity.

The church was the only international agency to possess any significant transnational credibility or influence throughout the Middle Ages. It played a decisive role in the settling of international disputes. Under Innocent III (pope from 1198 to 1216), the medieval papacy reached a level of political authority without precedent in Western Europe. Although the church had vigorously asserted its independence from kings and emperors in previous decades, secular rulers regularly attempted to encroach on its claims to political influence. Innocent regarded the defense of the *libertas ecclesiae* ("freedom of the church") as central to his program for the revitalization of the church.

This policy was given theological justification in a decree issued in October 1198, in which Innocent III set out the principle of the subordination of the state to the church. Just as God established "greater" and "lesser" lights in the heavens to rule the day and the night – a reference to the sun and the moon – so God ordained that the power of the pope exceeds that of any monarch. Just as the moon takes its light from the sun, to which it is inferior in size and quality, so the power of the king derives from the authority of the pope. The authority of the church was often recognized with great reluctance by secular rulers; there was, however, no other institution in Western Europe with anything remotely approaching its influence.

Innocent's reforming agendas were given additional substance at the Fourth Lateran Council of 1215. Aware of difficulties in securing the attendance of bishops from across

Europe, in April 1213 Innocent III issued a summons to bishops and other senior church figures, calling them to a council to be held in Rome in November 1215. As a result, the council was unusually well attended and its decisions were seen as a landmark in the consolidation of the internal organization and external influence of the church.

Further reforms of papal elections were introduced in the thirteenth century. Alarmed by how long it took cardinals to choose a new pope, Gregory X, pope from 1271 to 1276, introduced rules designed to discourage delays. Cardinals were to gather and remain in a closed area (the "conclave") until they had made a decision. Food was to be supplied through a window, in order to avoid contact with the outside world. After three days of conclave, the cardinals were to receive only one meal a day; after another five days, they were to receive just bread and water.

Yet there were many within the church at the time who were troubled by the soaring power and influence of the papacy and tried to prevent its getting out of control. The conciliarist movement argued that ecclesiastical power should be decentralized. Instead of being concentrated in the hands of a single individual, it should be dispersed within the body of the church as a whole and entrusted to a more representative and accountable group – namely "general councils." This movement reached the height of its influence in the fourteenth and fifteenth centuries.

Popular religion: The cult of the saints

To make sense of how Christianity developed during the Middle Ages, it is important to appreciate how it impacted on different groups of people. So how did Christianity relate to the everyday world outside the universities, monasteries, and royal courts? In recent years scholarship has paid increased attention to the phenomenon of "popular religion" or "folk religion," in which Christian ideas and practices were implemented in rural life and adapted to it.

The phenomenon of "folk religion" often bore a tangential relation to the more precise yet abstract statements of Christian doctrine that the church preferred – but that many lay people found unintelligible or unattractive. In parts of Europe, something close to "fertility cults" emerged, which were connected and enmeshed with the patterns and concerns of everyday life. The agrarian needs of rural communities – such as haymaking and harvesting – were firmly associated with popular religion.

For example, in the early sixteenth century the saints were regularly invoked and asked to ward off animal and infant diseases, the plague, and eye trouble or to ensure that young women find appropriate husbands. The direct connection between religion and everyday life was taken for granted. The spiritual and the material were interconnected at every level.

The medieval Catholic church was encountered by ordinary people through its practices and images rather than through its abstract theological ideas. The liturgy of the church, especially the mass, enacted dramatically a visual "grand narrative" of human history and experience. Its ritual observance and symbolic gestures shaped the congregation's perception of the world and of their own location within it. It offered spectacle and instruction, theater and dogma, in a form that reaffirmed the medieval worldview and the necessary place of the institutional church as an instrument and vehicle of salvation. Outside that church there was no salvation.

The drama of the liturgy was supplemented by images – often gospel scenes painted on church walls for the benefit of those who could not read; or images of saints, especially Mary, whose intercessory powers were affirmed and proclaimed by the church. Saints were mediators of divine grace who would hear and mitigate the prayers of ordinary people. In all churches throughout Western Europe the cult of the saints was represented iconically: through paintings, altarpieces, and statues.

But what was this cult of the saints, which had such a huge impact at the time? The recognition of the importance of the saints (Latin *sancti*, "holy ones") dated back to early Christianity, where vigils were often held at the tombs of prominent Christian leaders, especially those who had been martyred for their faith. Gradually a cultic form of veneration of the saints developed, with three distinct elements.

1 *Commemoration* A specific day would be set aside in the church's calendar to recall the life and teachings of a saint. Some saints were recognized as having universal significance; others were seen as being of local importance.
2 *The cult of relics* Relics (Latin *reliquiae*, "remains, things that are left behind") were material objects associated with the saints that were seen as "pledges" or "tokens" of the saint's intercessory power. Such relics included bodily parts as well as objects that had belonged to or had been used by the saint, such as clothes or books.
3 *Pilgrimages to shrines associated with saints* In the Middle Ages there were many sacred sites – such as Santiago de Compostela in northern Spain, linked with Apostle James, or the tomb of the martyred Archbishop Thomas à Becket at Canterbury.

The cult of the saints played a major role in medieval Christianity, especially at the popular level. One way of understanding this phenomenon is to consider the idea of a heavenly court. For many in the Middle Ages, God was to be compared to a monarch surrounded by a glittering company of courtiers – namely the saints. One of the key themes in the cult of the saints is the notion of a saint's intercessory power – in other words, his or her ability to get heard at the court of heaven. The idea of saints as advocates gained a huge following in the Middle Ages.

This idea is perhaps best represented by the concept of a "patron saint" – that is, a heavenly intercessor or advocate on behalf of a nation, place, or profession. Some examples of this development may be noted.

1 *A place* During the Middle Ages, it was common for a city that grew to prominence to acquire the remains of a famous saint who had lived and was buried elsewhere and to transfer them to its own cathedral. This possession was seen as conferring considerable prestige on the city. The best known example is offered by the city of Venice, which is traditionally held to have secured the remains of Saint Mark from Egypt in the ninth century. The iconic basilica of St. Mark was built to house these relics. The patron saint of Venice had originally been the martyr Theodore of Amasea; once the relics of Mark arrived, however, the city decided to upgrade its patron saint.
2 *A profession* Luke – the author of both the gospel bearing his name and the Acts of the Apostles – was a physician, which often led to his being spoken of as a "physician of the

soul" in Christian spiritual and devotional writings. It was natural that he would be adopted as the patron saint of the medical profession. Hospital chapels were often dedicated to Luke for this reason.

The rise of the Ottoman empire: The fall of Constantinople (1453)

By the beginning of the fifteenth century, many had concluded that Constantinople was unable to survive as an independent city. The city had already fallen to crusaders in 1204 and was no longer regarded as invincible, despite its formidable system of defenses. By the late fifteenth century, Islamic leadership was in the process of passing from the Abbasid caliphate to the Ottomans, who regarded the conquest of Christendom's greatest city as a *jihad* – a holy war. The expansionist policies of the Ottoman Turks led to the city's being surrounded and deprived of any economic or political hinterland. The Second Rome was isolated. It had earlier been fatally weakened through a natural disaster. Between 1348 and 1350 the Black Death spread within the city, killing as much as a half of its population. It was just a matter of time before the city fell.

In 1452 the Ottoman Sultan Mehmed II (1432–1481) constructed a fortress on Ottoman territory, just north of Constantinople, which served the dual purpose of cutting off the city's links with Black Sea ports and of acting as the launching point for the siege of Constantinople a year later. Mehmed II laid siege to Constantinople in April and May 1453. After 57 days the city fell. Strained relations between the Christian West and East led to a marked absence of support, political or military, for the besieged city. Having secured the city, Mehmed continued to expand Ottoman influence in the region now known as the Balkans. Bosnia was conquered in 1463; Albania in 1478; Herzegovina in 1482; and Montenegro in 1498.

Although western rulers had relatively little sympathy for the ailing Byzantine empire, which many regarded as religiously heterodox and politically degenerate, the advance of Ottoman forces into the western sphere of influence caused alarm. In 1521 Belgrade was captured. In 1539 Vienna was under siege. A surprise Ottoman naval victory at the Battle of Preveza in 1538 gave the Ottomans control over much of the Mediterranean Sea. It seemed to some that the advance of the Ottoman empire was unstoppable. An Islamic Europe seemed a real possibility.

Yet all was not well for the Ottoman empire. The siege of Vienna fizzled out inconclusively. An attempt to capture the island of Malta in 1565 pitted a large Ottoman force of around 50,000 with a much smaller Maltese army of around 6,000, including the crusader order of the Knights of St. John. The siege failed. The turning point was the Battle of Lepanto (1571), when a naval force put together by Southern European nations inflicted a decisive defeat on the Ottoman navy off the coast of southern Greece. This defeat is widely regarded as checking Ottoman expansion in the region.

Yet land-based expansion continued. Ottoman armies invaded the southern Ukraine and mounted a second siege of Vienna in the late summer of 1683. After two months, the large besieging army was attacked by a substantial army mustered by Emperor Leopold I (1640–1705). In 1699, following the Ottoman defeat at the Battle of Senta (1697), a peace treaty was signed between the Ottomans and the Habsburgs that ended the Ottoman control of large parts of Central Europe.

The Ottoman empire left a complex legacy in Eastern Europe. Many small nations in the Balkans developed complex religious demographies, Islamic, Orthodox Christian, and occasionally Jewish populations existing alongside one another. The Ottoman empire was generally tolerant of religious minorities thanks to its "millet" system, which allowed religious communities a significant degree of religious freedom and political autonomy. However, the Ottoman occupation generated unrest, leading to growing demands for national sovereignty in parts of Southeastern Europe, especially Serbia and Greece. In both cases, as we shall see later, the Orthodox church would be a leading force in nourishing and sustaining nationalist sentiments (pp. 169–170).

The rebirth of western culture: The Renaissance

The French term *renaissance* ("rebirth") is now universally used to designate the literary and artistic revival in fourteenth- and fifteenth-century Italy, which had major implications for both the Christian church and western culture. It is not entirely clear why Italy became the cradle of this brilliant new movement. A number of factors may have some bearing on the question. For example, Italy was saturated with visible and tangible reminders of the greatness of classical antiquity. The ruins of ancient Roman buildings and monuments were scattered throughout the land and appear to have aroused interest in the civilization of ancient Rome at the time of the Renaissance, acting as a stimulus for its thinkers to recover the vitality of classical Roman culture at a time which was culturally arid and barren.

Furthermore, as Byzantium began to crumble – as we noted earlier, Constantinople finally fell to Islamic invaders in 1453 (p. 135) – there was an exodus of Greek-speaking intellectuals westward. Italy happened to be conveniently close to Constantinople, with the result that many Byzantine intellectual emigrés settled in her cities. Familiarity with Byzantine Greek was thus inevitable, and with it came a new interest in ancient Greek and classical culture.

A central element in the outlook of the Italian Renaissance was a return to the cultural glories of antiquity, which was accompanied by a marginalization of the intellectual achievements of the Middle Ages. Renaissance writers had scant regard for these, considering them outweighed by the greater achievements of antiquity. What was true of culture in general was also true of theology: they regarded the late classical period as totally overshadowing the theological writings of the Middle Ages, both in substance and in style.

The intellectual force within the Renaissance is generally referred to as "humanism." Humanism was a cultural and educational movement, primarily concerned with the promotion of eloquence in its various forms and with the discovery and publication of ancient manuscripts and texts. Although the word "humanist" has acquired overtones of secularism and atheism in recent times, this was not true in the period of the Renaissance. To be a humanist was to be concerned with *studia humanitatis* (a Latin phrase referring to what is now known as "the humanities"). Humanism was essentially a cultural program that appealed to classical antiquity as a model of expression and eloquence. In art and architecture as in the written and spoken word, antiquity was seen as a cultural resource, which could be appropriated by the Renaissance. In much the same way, early Christianity came to be seen as providing both an example and a resource for its contemporary forms.

Although there are major variations within European humanism, two ideals seem to have achieved widespread acceptance throughout the movement: first, a concern for written and spoken eloquence, after the fashion of the classical period; second, a religious program directed toward the corporate revival of the Christian church. The Latin slogan *Christianismus renascens*, "Christianity being born again," summarizes the aims of this program and indicates its relation to the "rebirth" of letters associated with the Renaissance.

A central element on the humanist agenda was return to the original sources of Western European culture in classical Rome and Athens. The theological counterpart to this agenda was a direct return to the foundational resources of Christian theology, supremely in the New Testament. One of the most important consequences of this attitude was a new appreciation of the foundational importance of the Bible as a theological resource. As interest in the Bible developed, it became increasingly clear that existing Latin translations of this source were inadequate. Supreme among them was the Vulgate, the Latin translation of the Bible that achieved widespread influence during the Middle Ages (pp. 49–50). The reliability of this translation was soon called into question.

The rise of humanist scholarship would show up significant discrepancies between the Vulgate and the texts it purported to translate – and thus it would open the way to doctrinal reformation. It is for this reason that humanism is of decisive importance to the development of medieval theology: it demonstrated the unreliability of this translation of the Bible – and hence, it seemed, of theologies based upon it. The biblical basis of scholasticism came under threat, as humanism uncovered error after error in its translation.

The literary and cultural program of humanism can be summarized in the Latin formula *ad fontes* – "back to the original sources." The "filter" of medieval commentaries – whether on legal texts or on the Bible – was abandoned, in order to engage directly with the original texts. In the case of the Christian church, this humanist program demanded a direct return to the title deeds of Christianity – to the patristic writers and, supremely, to the Bible – studied in their original languages.

The first printed Greek New Testament was produced by Erasmus of Rotterdam in 1516. Erasmus' text was not as reliable as it ought to have been: Erasmus had access to a mere four manuscripts for most of the New Testament, and only to one for its final part, the book of Revelation. As it happened, that manuscript left out five verses, which Erasmus himself had to translate into Greek from the Latin of the Vulgate. Nevertheless, it proved to be a literary milestone. For the first time, theologians had the opportunity of comparing the original Greek text of the New Testament with the later Vulgate translation into Latin.

Figure 4.5   Erasmus of Rotterdam, c. 1525/30, after the painting (1517) by Quentin Massys (1465/66–1530). Source: Pirozzi/AKG Images.

Developments like this undermined the credibility of the Vulgate translation and demonstrated the importance of biblical scholarship in relation to theology. Theology could not be permitted to base itself upon translation mistakes! The recognition of the vitally important role of biblical scholarship to Christian theology thus dates from the second decade of the sixteenth century. It also led to the theological concerns of the Reformation, which we shall consider in the next section.

Competing Visions of Reform, c. 1500–c. 1650

The sixteenth century and its immediate aftermath represent one of the most fascinating periods in the history of western Christianity. The Renaissance emphasis on returning to classic sources for inspiration and renewal began to take on a more specifically religious focus. As pressure grew for reform of the church "in head and members," the humanist program of returning to the simpler form of Christianity represented in the New Testament seemed increasingly attractive to many.

Yet there were other factors emerging as significant for church life at this time. Nationalism was on the rise in many parts of Northern Europe, including Germany, France, and England. An emerging middle class was resentful at the power and privilege of the traditional aristocracy and wanted to flex its muscles. Lay literacy was increasing, and there was a growing mood for change within both church and society. Forms of Christianity began to develop that offered new ways of thinking about the place of individuals in society, and especially about their ability to change things.

It is against this background that the movement we now refer to as "the Reformation" emerged. Demands for reform, fueled partly by political and social agendas, were given additional energy through theological concerns – such as a desire to return to the simplicity of apostolic Christianity. Although most saw this process of reform as taking place within the mainstream of church life, the political and ecclesiastical situation of the time caused some to embark on such reforming programs outside the mainstream. This age of reformation thus led on the one hand to the emergence of the complex movement generally known as Protestantism and, on the other, to a renewed and reinvigorated Catholicism. In this section we will explore these developments, which are of major importance for the shaping of global Christianity.

Although a variety of terms were used to refer to the movements for reform within the church in the sixteenth century, historians now tend to refer to them using the general description "Reformation" or "European Reformation." From an historical point of view, the movements in question are often designated according to their geographical region – for example, the German Reformation, the Reformation in England, or the French Reformation.

The broad movement known as the Reformation is generally agreed to include four distinct elements: Lutheranism; the reformed church (often referred to as Calvinism); the radical Reformation (often – though not entirely accurately – referred to as Anabaptism); and the Counter-Reformation or Catholic Reformation. In its broadest sense, the term "Reformation" is used to refer to all four movements. The more precise phrase "Protestant Reformation" is generally used to refer to the first three movements taken together.

Some recent studies of this age have used the plural, "Reformations," to suggest that the Reformation was a multifaceted phenomenon – perhaps even that it was a set of loosely connected but distinct reforming movements rather than a single coherent movement with local adaptations. The Reformation in England illustrates this point neatly, as it developed in its own characteristic manner. The interaction of religion and politics in England gave rise to a local variant of the Reformation that was quite distinct from its counterparts in Switzerland or Germany.

Yet, before we begin to explore the debates and fractures that broke out within the western church in the 1500s, we need to note the expansion of Christianity in the New World, which was opened up by the voyages of discovery of European naval powers.

Christian expansion: Portuguese and Spanish voyages of discovery

In the late fifteenth century new trade routes were established between Europe and Asia and new lands were discovered – above all, the Americas. The European powers that spearheaded the Age of Discovery were Spain and Portugal, two staunchly Catholic nations, who regarded the spread of the Catholic faith as a natural expansion of national influence. They were later joined by another Catholic maritime power, France.

The great Portuguese navigator Vasco da Gama (c. 1460–1524) opened up trade routes with the east coast of Africa and subsequently across the Indian Ocean to India itself. In addition to establishing the highly profitable spice trade route, da Gama's exploration led to Portugal's establishing the East African colony of Mozambique as a staging post on the route to India.

Christopher Columbus (1451–1506, often referred to by his Spanish name, Cristobal Colón) initially intended to establish a western trade route to India. Based on a mistaken measurement of the size of the earth, Columbus reckoned it would be just as quick to sail westward to India as it would to sail eastward. Although some popular accounts of Columbus' voyages suggest that people believed the world to be flat, this report is clearly incorrect. The spherical shape of the world was widely accepted in the Middle Ages. Columbus intended to sail around the world to India, using a route that he believed would be faster. In the end he discovered the Americas and laid the foundation for the Spanish colonization and for the economic exploitation of this vast new territory, which soon became known as the New World. Portugese navigators such as Pedro Álvares Cabral (c. 1467–c. 1524) made landfall further south and established the colony of Brazil.

Yet these voyages of discovery were not merely of political and economic importance. They were partly motivated by religious concerns and given additional impetus by a growing awareness, within the Catholic church, of its missionary responsibilities. Individual popes were firmly committed to the importance of global evangelization. The Council of Trent laid the groundwork for Catholic missionary work through religious orders, especially the Society of Jesus. As a result, Catholicism underwent considerable expansion during the sixteenth century, establishing bases in the Americas, Africa, and Asia.

The Jesuits spearheaded Catholic expansion in Asia. In 1542 Francis Xavier (1506–1552) arrived at Goa on the west coast of India, which was by then established as a Portuguese trading center in Asia. Over the next 10 years Xavier initiated a series of missionary projects in the region and many missions in India and in other parts of Asia, including the island of Sri Lanka. During the years 1546–1547 he established a mission in Ambon, a large island that is now part of Indonesia. In 1549 he began missionary work in Japan. He died in 1552, as he was preparing to undertake missionary work in China. Another Jesuit, Matteo Ricci (1552–1610), continued Xavier's work. After arriving at Macao, Ricci began a program of immersion in the Chinese language and culture, aiming to work out how best to express Christian ideas in Chinese culture. Ricci established missions in several major Chinese cities.

In 1521 the great Spanish explorer Ferdinand Magellan discovered a group of some 3,141 islands in Southeast Asia. The islands, now known as the Philippines, became a Spanish colony. Under Spanish rule a program of evangelization was undertaken by various religious orders, especially the Franciscans and the Dominicans.

The most significant expansion of Christianity during the early modern period took place in the Americas. Spain, Portugal, and France claimed sovereignty over vast areas of territory, within which Catholicism began to take root. Bishoprics were established by 1511 in the islands of Dominica, San Juan, and Haiti. Spain's empire in the Americas extended over a vast region known as "New Spain," which included Central America, Mexico, Florida, and much of what is now the southwestern part of the United States. Catholic priests built missions in all these areas to convert Native Americans. One of the best known missions is the Alamo in Texas, which was originally constructed as a Franciscan mission in 1722. Spanish influence also extended to the West Indies. Portugal colonized most of the southeastern coast of South America, while Spain took over the northern regions and the western coast.

The implications of these new discoveries could not be overlooked. Whom did they belong to? Which European powers had rights over these new territories? In 1481 Pope Sixtus IV confirmed Spanish rights over the Canary Islands and granted Portugal rights over all further territorial acquisitions made in Africa and eastward to the Indies. Yet the voyages of Christopher Columbus raised new questions about rights over hitherto unknown lands to the west. Pope Alexander VI, whose sympathies lay with Spain, ruled that any lands discovered after 1492 should belong to Spain. Portugal refused to accept this ruling. Bilateral discussions between Spain and Portugal eventually led to the Treaty of Tordesillas (1494), which allocated each nation certain areas of these new territories (which had yet to be mapped and explored).

Although there was uncertainty about precisely how this treaty was to be interpreted, in practice its consequence was that Portugal took possession of the vast tract of land along the Amazon River now known as Brazil and Spain took possession of territories to the north and west of this region, including what is now known as Latin America. The Treaty of Saragossa, signed on April 22, 1529, divided up the territories to the east. Although the pope was not party to those discussions, this division of territory is sometimes inaccurately referred to as "the Papal Line of Demarcation."

This massive expansion of a Christian presence beyond Europe would have a transformative impact. Christianity had ceased to be a European phenomenon and was in the process of becoming a global faith. Yet in Western Europe Christianity was undergoing significant change as a result of controversies arising from Martin Luther's views in

Germany. The invention of printing meant that regional debates could easily be followed across Europe. Luther's demands for a reform of the church proved to be of major importance, opening up fault lines within the western church that led to the emergence of Protestantism as a distinct form of Christianity in the region.

The Lutheran Reformation

The Lutheran Reformation is particularly associated with the German territories and the pervasive personal influence of one charismatic individual: Martin Luther (1483–1546). Luther was especially concerned with the doctrine of justification, which formed the central point of his religious thought. He believed that the church had fallen into some form of Pelagianism (pp. 103–105), teaching that individuals could achieve, or even purchase, their salvation. The sale of indulgences at Wittenberg in 1517 – a phenomenon widely seen as a trigger for the Reformation – seemed to confirm that the church had lost sight of the idea that salvation was something given by God.

In response to this situation, Luther developed the idea of justification by faith alone, according to which an individual receives salvation as a gracious gift from God. Luther did not take his doctrine of justification by faith to mean that the sinner is justified *because* he or she believes – that is, on account of his or her faith. He saw it as a recognition that God provides everything necessary for justification, so that all the sinner needs to do is to receive it. In justification, God is active and humans are passive. Perhaps the phrase "justification *by* grace *through* faith" brings out the meaning of the doctrine more clearly: the justification of the sinner is based upon the grace of God and is received through faith. The somewhat rambling title of Heinrich Bullinger's 1554 work on this subject sums up the basic idea well: *The Grace of God That Justifies Us for the Sake of Christ through Faith Alone, without Good Works, while Faith meanwhile Abounds in Good Works.*

For Luther, this doctrine of justification was a core belief, which later Lutheranism described as the "article by which the church stands or falls." Although this was the platform from which Luther developed his program of reform in the 1520s, other ideas were linked to it, including:

1   the assertion of the ultimate authority of the Bible over the church – a doctrine often summarized through the formula *sola Scriptura* ("by Scripture alone" or "only by the Bible"): Luther believed that the church tended to impose its ideas on the Bible and that the Bible, when rightly interpreted, should be regarded as authoritative by the church;
2   the insistence that the Bible should be translated into contemporary language, which would allow everyone to have access to the biblical text (see pp. 50–51);
3   the practice of administering communion services in both kinds – that is, allowing the laity to receive both bread and wine (the medieval church permitted the laity only to receive bread);
4   the idea of the "priesthood of all believers," which held that every Christian was a priest by virtue of his or her baptism. Luther did not regard this as displacing the traditional clergy but as a measure that allowed them to be seen in their proper context.

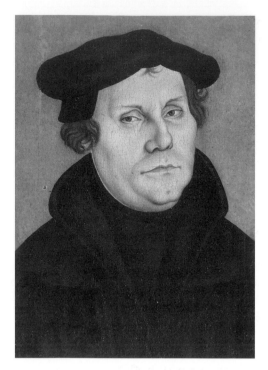

Figure 4.6   Portrait of Martin Luther (1528); from the studio of Lucas Cranach the Elder (1472–1553). Source: AKG Images.

The Lutheran Reformation was initially an academic movement, concerned primarily with reforming the teaching of theology at the University of Wittenberg. Wittenberg was an unimportant university, and the reforms introduced by Luther and his colleagues within the theology faculty attracted little attention. It was Luther's personal activities – such as his posting of the famous Ninety-Five Theses against the sale of indulgences (October 31, 1517) – that attracted considerable interest and brought the ideas in circulation at Wittenberg to the attention of a wider audience.

Strictly speaking, the Lutheran Reformation only began in 1522, when Luther returned to Wittenberg from his enforced isolation in the Wartburg. Luther was condemned by the Diet of Worms in 1521. Fearing for his life, certain well-placed supporters removed him in secrecy to Wartburg Castle, southwest of Eisenach, until the threat to his safety ceased. In his absence, Andreas Bodenstein von Karlstadt, one of Luther's academic colleagues at Wittenberg, began there a program of reform that seemed to degenerate into chaos. Convinced that he was needed if the Reformation was to survive von Karlstadt's ineptitude, Luther emerged from his place of safety and returned to Wittenberg.

From this point on, Luther's program of academic reform changed into one of reform of church and society. No longer was his forum of activity the university and its world of ideas – he now found himself regarded as the leader of a religious, social, and political reforming movement that seemed to some contemporary observers to open the way to a new social and religious order in Europe. In fact Luther's program of reform was much more conservative than the one associated with his reformed colleagues such as Huldrych Zwingli. Furthermore, it met with considerably less success than some anticipated. The movement remained obstinately tied to the German territories, and – Scandinavia apart – never gained the foreign power bases that looked like so many ripe apples ready to fall into its lap. Luther's understanding of the role of the "godly prince" (which effectively ensured that the monarch had control of the church) does not seem to have exercised the attraction one might have expected of it, particularly in the light of the generally republican sentiments of reformed thinkers such as Calvin.

An integral part of Luther's reforming program was to give a new role to the laity, including women. Luther's doctrine of the priesthood of all believers laid down that every Christian – irrespective of gender or social status – was a priest in God's sight. He reacted against the isolation of Christians from the world, arguing that monasteries and convents prevented Christians from living out their calling in their world. One of Luther's most interesting exploits took place in 1523, when he arranged for the liberation of a dozen nuns from the cloister of Marienthron. They were smuggled out in herring barrels provided by a merchant friend. Luther married one of them, Katia von Bora, in 1525. Up to this point women tended to exercise religious leadership only in monastic contexts, on account of the segregation of the genders. Katia's role as mistress of the family household set the pattern for Lutheran women for many years and offered a significant social role for women outside the confines of monastic life.

The Calvinist Reformation

The origins of the Calvinist Reformation, which brought the reformed churches (such as the Presbyterians) into being, lie with developments within the Swiss Confederation. Whereas the Lutheran Reformation had its origins in an academic context, the reformed church owed its origins to a series of attempts to reform the morals and worship of the church (but not necessarily its doctrine) according to a more biblical pattern. It must be emphasized that, although Calvin gave this style of Reformation its definitive form, its origins are to be traced back to earlier reformers, such as Huldrych Zwingli and Heinrich Bullinger, who were based at the leading Swiss city of Zurich.

Although most of the early reformed theologians – such as Zwingli – had an academic background, their reforming programs were not academic in nature. They were directed toward the church as they found it in Swiss cities such as Zurich, Berne, and Basle. Whereas Luther was convinced that the doctrine of justification was of central significance to his program of social and religious reform, the early reformed thinkers had relatively little interest in doctrine, let alone one specific doctrine. Their reforming program was institutional, social, and ethical – in many ways similar to the demands for reform emanating from the humanist movement.

The consolidation of the reformed church is generally thought to begin with the stabilization of the Zurich Reformation, after Zwingli's death in battle (1531), under his successor, Heinrich Bullinger, and to end with the emergence of Geneva as its power base and of John Calvin as its leading spokesman in the 1550s. The gradual shift in power within the reformed church (initially from Zurich to Berne, subsequently from Berne to Geneva) took place over the period 1520–1560, eventually establishing the city of Geneva, its political system (republicanism), and its religious thinkers (initially Calvin, and after his death Theodore Beza) as predominant figures within the reformed church. This development was consolidated through the establishment of the Genevan Academy, founded in 1559, at which reformed pastors were trained.

Calvin is of fundamental importance for understanding the direction of the second phase of the Protestant Reformation. One of his most relevant contributions to this development was his textbook of Christian theology titled *The Institutes of the Christian Religion*. The first edition of this work appeared in 1536, setting out theological principles very similar to those already associated with Martin Luther. It went through several

Figure 4.7   Portrait of the Genevan reformer John Calvin. Source: AKG Images.

editions, the definitive one being published in 1559. Calvin organized his material into four books arranged as follows:

1   the knowledge of God the creator;
2   the knowledge of God the redeemer;
3   the manner of participation in the grace of Jesus Christ; and
4   the external means or aids that God uses to bring us to Jesus Christ.

The logical arrangement of the material made this work an ideal resource for preachers and teachers.

Calvin was careful to present his textbook as a guide to the Bible, not as a substitute for it. Like Luther, he saw the Bible as being of supreme importance. "My object in this work," wrote Calvin, "is to so prepare and train students of sacred theology for the study of the word of God that they might have an easy access into it, and be able to proceed in it without hindrance." In writing his *Institutes*, Calvin clearly intended to offer what is essentially a doctrinal commentary on Scripture, allowing its reader direct access to its authentic meaning.

The term "Calvinism" is still used to refer to the religious ideas of the reformed church. Although still widespread in the literature related to the Reformation, this practice is now generally discouraged. It is becoming increasingly clear that later sixteenth-century reformed theology draws on sources other than the ideas of Calvin himself. To refer to later sixteenth- and seventeenth-century reformed thought as "Calvinist" implies that that is essentially the thought of Calvin – and it is now generally agreed that Calvin's ideas were subtly modified by his successors. The term "reformed" is now preferred in talking either of those churches (mainly in Switzerland, the Lowlands, and Germany) or of those religious thinkers (such as Theodore Beza, William Perkins, or John Owen) that, or who, based themselves upon Calvin's celebrated religious textbook or upon church documents in turn based upon it (like the famous Heidelberg Catechism).

The Radical Reformation (Anabaptism)

Zwingli used the term "Anabaptism" to refer to his more radical opponents at Zurich. The word literally means "rebaptizing" or "second baptizing" and refers to what was perhaps the most distinctive aspect of Anabaptist practice: the insistence that only those who had made a personal public profession of faith should be baptized. Anabaptism seems to have first arisen around Zurich, in the aftermath of Zwingli's reforms there in the early 1520s. It centered on a group of individuals (among whom we may note Conrad Grebel) who argued that Zwingli was not being faithful to his own reforming principles. He preached one thing, practiced another. Although Zwingli professed faithfulness to the principle *sola Scriptura* ("by Scripture alone"), Grebel argued that he retained a number of practices – including infant baptism, the close link between church and magistracy, and the participation of Christians in warfare – that were not sanctioned or ordained by Scripture. In the hands of reformed thinkers, the *sola Scriptura* principle should be radicalized; Christians should only believe and practice those things that are explicitly taught in Scripture. Zwingli was alarmed by this idea, seeing it as a destabilizing development that threatened to cut off the reformed church at Zurich from its historical roots and to break its continuity with the Christian tradition.

A number of common elements can be discerned within the various strands of the movement: a general distrust of external authority, the rejection of infant baptism in favor of the baptism of adult believers, the common ownership of property, and an emphasis upon pacifism and non-resistance. It is for this reason that "Anabaptism" is often referred to as the "left wing of the Reformation" (Roland H. Bainton) or as the "radical Reformation." (George Hunston Williams). For Williams, the "radical Reformation" was to be contrasted with the "magisterial Reformation," which he broadly identified with the Lutheran and reformed movements. These labels are increasingly being accepted within Reformation scholarship, and you are likely to encounter them in your reading of more recent studies of the movement.

The Catholic Reformation

This phrase is often used to refer to the revival of Roman Catholicism in the period following the opening of the Council of Trent (1545). In older scholarly works, the movement is often designated the "Counter-Reformation": as this term suggests, the Roman Catholic church developed means of combating the Protestant Reformation, in order to limit its influence. It is, however, becoming increasingly clear that the Roman Catholic church countered the Reformation partly by reforming itself from within, in order to remove the grounds of Protestant criticism. In this sense, the movement was a reformation of the Roman Catholic church as much as it was a reaction against the Protestant Reformation.

The same concerns underlying the Protestant Reformation in Northern Europe were channeled into the renewal of the Catholic church, particularly in Spain and Italy. The Council of Trent, the foremost component of the Catholic Reformation, clarified catholic teaching on a number of confusing matters and introduced much needed reforms in relation to the conduct of the clergy, ecclesiastical discipline, religious education, and missionary activity. The movement for reform within the church was greatly stimulated by the reformation of many of the older religious orders and the establishment of new ones (such as the Jesuits). The more specifically theological aspects of the Catholic Reformation will be considered in relation to its teachings on Scripture and tradition, justification by faith, and the sacraments. As a result of the Catholic Reformation, many of the abuses that originally lay behind the demands for reform – whether these came from humanists or Protestants – were removed.

In its broadest sense, the term "Reformation" is applied to all four of the movements described above. It is also used in a somewhat more restricted sense, meaning "the Protestant Reformation" but excluding the Catholic Reformation. In this sense it refers to the three Protestant movements noted above. In many scholarly works, however, the term "Reformation" is applied, even more narrowly, to what is sometimes known as the "magisterial Reformation," or the "mainstream Reformation" (p. 151) – a concept that links together the Lutheran and the reformed churches (including Anglicanism), but excludes the Anabaptists.

The Reformation in England

The English Reformation took a somewhat different direction from that of its continental counterpart. Although there was at least some degree of popular pressure for a reform within the church, the leading force for change was Henry VIII, who ascended the English throne in 1509. In 1527 Henry took the first steps toward dissolving his marriage to Catherine of Aragon. This decision resulted from Henry's desire to ensure the succession to the English throne. The only child from this marriage, Mary Tudor, was female; Henry wanted a male heir. The pope refused to dissolve or annul the marriage.

The English Reformation was not primarily the result of the pope's refusal to grant Henry his divorce. Nevertheless, this was unquestionably a factor in its development. Henry gradually appears to have shifted toward a policy that involved the replacement of papal authority in England with his own authority. The creation of an English national church was part of this vision. Henry seems not to have been particularly interested in matters of doctrine or theology, preferring to concentrate upon the practicalities of religious and political power. His decision to appoint Thomas Cranmer (1489–1556) as archbishop of Canterbury led to at least some Protestant influences being brought to bear on the English church.

When Henry died in 1547, he was succeeded by his son, Edward VI. Edward was a minor on his accession; as a result, real power was exercised by his advisors, who were generally of a strongly Protestant persuasion. Cranmer, who remained in office as archbishop during Edward's reign, was able to bring in noticeably Protestant forms of public worship and encouraged leading Protestant thinkers (such as Martin Bucer and Peter Martyr Vermigli) to settle in England and to give theological direction to the Reformation. However, Edward died in 1553, leaving the nation in a state of religious flux.

Edward was succeeded by Mary Tudor, who was strongly Catholic in her sympathies. She set in motion a series of measures that suppressed Protestantism and restored Catholicism. Some of the measures were deeply unpopular, most notably the public burning of Thomas Cranmer at Oxford in 1556. Cranmer was replaced as archbishop of Canterbury by Reginald Pole, a moderate Catholic. At the time of Queen Mary's death in 1558, Catholicism had not yet been entirely re-established. When Elizabeth I succeeded to the throne, it was not entirely clear what direction her religious policies might take. In the event Elizabeth pursued a complex policy, which seems to have been aimed at appeasing both Protestants and Catholics while allowing the queen to have supreme authority in matters of religion. What is usually referred to as the Elizabethan Settlement (1558–1559) established the national English church as a reformed episcopal church with a broadly Protestant articles of faith and a more Catholic liturgy. Nobody was really entirely happy with the outcome, which was widely seen as a compromise;

Figure 4.8   Henry VIII (1540), by Hans Holbein the Younger (1497–1543). Source: Nimatallah/AKG Images.

however, it enabled England to emerge unscathed from a period of religious tension and to avoid the serious religious conflicts that were raging elsewhere in Europe at the time.

The Council of Trent

Scholars agree that the convening of the Council of Trent was a decisive landmark in sixteenth-century religious history. This council, which began its discussions in December 1545, was suspended at various points. In 1547 the outbreak of an epidemic at Trent forced the council's relocation to Bologna; this was followed by its suspension until 1551. A further suspension resulted in 1552 in the aftermath of the revolt of the German princes against the authority of the emperor (which was eventually settled by the Religious Peace of Augsburg in 1555). It was not until 1562 that the council could meet again; it concluded its work the following year.

Why did the Council of Trent not meet earlier? The most important reason was the war between Emperor Charles V and the king of France. While this war was taking place, it would have been impossible for French and German bishops to sit down at the same conference table. An attempt was made to convene a reforming council at Mantua in 1537, but it had to be aborted due to the war. Another attempt was made in 1542; once more, it failed. However, in September 1544 the Peace of Crépy brought hostilities between the French and Germans to an end. Two months later Pope Paul III issued a document that convened the Council of Trent. The council had the objectives of settling theological disputes, reforming the church, and liberating Christians from Turkish invaders. It was scheduled to begin in March 1545, but delays crept in for a number of reasons.

The impact of the council on the development of Catholicism during the remainder of the sixteenth century and beyond was considerable. It is widely regarded as the most important church council between the Council of Nicaea (325) and the Second Vatican Council (1962–1965). Its main achievements can be summarized as follows.

1 *The clarification of Catholic teaching* As noted earlier, there was considerable confusion within Catholicism over what counted as the official teaching of the church and what was to be regarded simply as private opinions of individuals. This was particularly important in relation to the doctrine of justification (see pp. 105–106), which lay at the heart of Martin Luther's campaign for reform back in the late 1510s. Many traditional Catholic doctrines and practices were affirmed, including the practice of communion in one kind, the authority of the Vulgate translation of the Bible (although a revision of the translation was ordered on 1546 and completed in 1592), and the necessity of the seven sacraments.

2 *The elimination of abuses within the church* The late medieval church was plagued by a series of abuses, which did little to enhance its popularity and reputation. Clergy and bishops were known to be permanently absent from their parishes or dioceses, entrusting their care to minor officials while they pursued their careers elsewhere. Occasionally clergy would hold several parishes at the same time, receiving a larger income without providing the necessary pastoral care in return. Trent moved to eliminate such abuses by laying down strict guidelines for bishops and the clergy.

Figure 4.9   Ignatius Loyola, founder of the Society of Jesus (1556), by Jacopino del Conte (1510–1598). Source: AKG Images.

An important development that took place around this period was the that of the Society of Jesus, whose members are more generally known as Jesuits and to which we now turn.

The Society of Jesus

The Jesuits were founded by Ignatius Loyola, a professional soldier. While convalescing from a leg wound in 1521, he read biographies of the saints and became convinced of the need for a tightly disciplined life of faith, modeled on military lines. The importance of discipline is clearly formulated in a work that represents Loyola's most important contribution to the field of Christian spirituality: the *Spiritual Exercises*, which he drew up during the period 1522–1523. These set out a four-week program of prayer, meditation, and reflection – all aimed at deepening the reader's commitment to Christ. The work can be seen as a training manual for future combatants in a spiritual war.

Loyola and six colleagues constituted the original nucleus of the Society of Jesus, which was formally founded in Paris in 1534 and received papal approval from Paul III in 1540. From that point on it expanded rapidly. By 1556, the year of Loyola's death, there were more than a thousand members of the order, which became a significant presence in Italy, Spain, and Portugal. Their influence was felt especially in the fields of missionary work and education. Jesuit missions were established during the sixteenth century in areas as diverse as Brazil, China, India, Japan, and Malaya. In education, the Jesuits developed a rigorous program of studies, designed to ensure the intellectual excellence of their order.

The Wars of Religion

The rise of Protestantism and the renewal of Catholicism inevitably caused political and social tensions throughout Europe. Emperor Charles V had felt the force of these tensions and was eventually obliged to agree to an uneasy truce in the form of the 1555 Religious Peace of Augsburg, which put an end to the long-standing conflicts between the Lutheran princes and the Catholic emperor. Yet it was not long before conflict broke out elsewhere.

The first major European war that can be shown to be directly due to religious issues broke out in France. The specific tension in this case was between Catholics and Calvinists (or "Huguenots," as the latter were locally called). We noted earlier that Calvin was French. He appears to have taken his mission in life to be (at least in part) to convert his native country to the reformed faith, using Geneva as a base. In April 1555, Genevan records document several agents sent out from Geneva to evangelize parts of France likely to be fertile ground for Calvinism. Others followed rapidly, in response to requests for help from French Calvinist congregations.

The whole affair was cloak and dagger. Secrecy was essential to the entire operation, at both the Genevan and the French ends of the operation. Safe houses, complete with hiding places, were established, a day's journey apart. An underground network similar to that employed by the French Resistance during World War II allowed men from Geneva to slip undetected into France. By 1560 Calvinism was firmly established in many leading French cities and was gaining influential converts. Given this explosion in the growth of Calvinist congregations and influence, a complete Reformation in France seemed a real possibility. Perhaps one third of the nobility had signaled its acceptance of Calvin's religious ideas.

According to a list prepared for Admiral de Coligny in March 1562, there were 2,150 Huguenot churches in France at that point. It is difficult to verify these figures; it would, however, seem reasonable to suggest that there were at least 1,250 such churches, with a total membership in excess of 2,000,000, out of a national population of 20,000,000. Tensions rose. In 1562 a war broke out. The issue was only settled through the Edict of Nantes (1598), which guaranteed the rights of French Protestants. However, the edict was widely ignored by subsequent French monarchs and was finally revoked by Louis XIV in 1685. This decision caused a substantial exodus of Protestants from the country.

Other religious conflicts erupted in the region. The Dutch War of Independence (1560–1618) had strongly religious dimensions. An increasingly Calvinist Dutch population wished to rid itself of a Catholic Spanish colonial power. In England, the Civil War (1642–1649) clearly had religious aspects, reflecting deep-seated disagreements between Royalists and Puritans over the manner of government and the doctrines of the national Church of England.

By far the most important religious conflict, however, was the Thirty Years War, which rumbled on from 1618 to 1648. The context within which this war emerged was the tension after the Peace of Augsburg (1555). The peace did not take account of Calvinism, which became a major presence in the region from 1560. As a result, Calvinism was given no official protection, in contrast to both Lutheranism and Catholicism. As Calvinism continued to expand, tensions increased. The trigger for the conflict was the outbreak of anti-Protestant riots in Bohemia that partly reflected the vigorous Catholicism of Ferdinand II. The Bohemian nobles protested to the emperor over these developments. On failing to receive any satisfactory assurances for their safety, they revolted and demanded to be ruled by a local Calvinist prince instead.

The revolt sparked a wider conflict, drawing in surrounding states and principalities. Its impact on the German economy was disastrous. When the war was finally resolved through the Peace of Westphalia (1648), any remaining enthusiasm for religious warfare had evaporated. People had had enough. The yearning for peace led to a new emphasis on toleration and to growing impatience with religious disputes. The scene was set for the Enlightenment's insistence that religion was to be a matter of private belief rather than one of state policy. Our attention now turns to the curious cultural climate that amalgamated rationalism, revival, and revolution and gained ascendancy in the eighteenth century.

Puritanism in England and America

The term "Puritan" was originally intended to be abusive. It was used to stigmatize those members of the Church of England during the reign of Elizabeth I who wanted to adopt more reformed beliefs and practices (such as the abolition of bishops). The University of

Cambridge became a major center for Puritan activity, Emmanuel College establishing itself as a significant seedbed of Puritan theological and pastoral thinking. Official hostility toward these trends led to the formation of small separatist congregations, which "withdrew" from the national church as a protest against the latter's failure to reform itself completely. The most important of these separatist groups was that of the Brownists, named after Robert Browne (c. 1550–1633).

Following official harassment, separatists initially found refuge in the Netherlands; some, however, were able to return to England later and to establish congregations. These groups, which may be regarded as forerunners of the modern Baptists, flourished particularly during the period of the Puritan commonwealth, when it is estimated that there were 300 such congregations in England. Following the restoration of Charles II, the Baptists found themselves facing official hostility once more; it was not until the late eighteenth century that they would achieve a significant degree of acceptance and stability.

One group of particular interest should be noted. A separatist congregation was established at Scrooby, Nottinghamshire, in 1606, with John Robinson (c. 1575–1625) as its pastor. Growing official hostility forced the congregation to move to Leiden in the Netherlands in 1609. However, the Dutch situation was still not ideal. The congregation set its sights on America, which was then opening up to European settlers. On September 6, 1620, 102 members of the congregation set sail for America in the *Mayflower*. The resulting colony that was established in Massachusetts would be seen as a model by many Europeans dissatisfied with the restrictions of religious life at home.

Despite its growing influence within the national English church, Puritanism continued to encounter strong hostility from both church and state in the early seventeenth century. However, mounting popular discontent with the monarchy made Puritanism appear identifiable with the forces of democracy. As the tension between king and parliament grew, Puritanism was seen as a vigorous supporter of parliamentary authority. The resulting Civil War led to the execution of Charles I and to the establishment of a Puritan Commonwealth under Oliver Cromwell during the 1650s. However, the restoration of Charles II led to the withering of Puritanism as a significant political and social force in England.

Yet Puritanism was set to exercise a major influence elsewhere. Dissatisfaction with the religious situation in England led many English Puritans to immigrate to America, taking their faith with them. Massachusetts Bay became a center of Puritanism. The impact of this development on American history was decisive in the opinion of many scholars and laid the foundations for the emergence of the United States of America as a nation with a strong sense of a distinctively religious identity.

A Protestant religion of the heart: Pietism

As Orthodoxy was increasingly influential within mainstream Protestantism, its defects became clear. At its best, Orthodoxy was concerned with the rational defense of Christian truth claims and with doctrinal correctness. Yet, all too often, this came across as an academic preoccupation with logical niceties instead of a concern for relating theology to the issues of everyday life. The term "Pietism" derives from the Latin word *pietas* (best translated as "piety" or "godliness") and was initially a derogatory term, used by the movement's opponents to describe its emphasis upon the importance of Christian doctrine in everyday Christian life.

The movement is usually regarded as having been inaugurated through the publication of Philip Jakob Spener's *Pia desideria* (*Pious Wishes*) in 1675. In this work Spener lamented the state of the German Lutheran church in the aftermath of the Thirty Years War and set out proposals for the revitalization of the church of his day. Chief among these proposals was a new emphasis upon personal Bible study. These proposals were treated with derision by academic theologians; nevertheless, they were to prove influential in German church circles, reflecting a growing disillusionment and impatience with the sterility of Orthodoxy in the face of the shocking social conditions endured during the war. For Pietism, a reformation of doctrine must always be accompanied by a reformation of life.

Pietism developed in a number of different directions, especially in England and Germany. In Germany, the movement became influential in the first half of the eighteenth century. Nikolaus Ludwig Graf von Zinzendorf (1700–1760) founded the Pietist community generally known as the Herrnhuter, named after the village of Herrnhut. Alienated from what he regarded as the arid rationalism and barren Orthodoxy of his time, he stressed the importance of a religion of the heart, based on an intimate and personal relationship between Christ and the believer. A new emphasis was placed upon the role of feeling (as opposed to reason or doctrinal orthodoxy) within the Christian life, which may be regarded as laying the foundations of romanticism in later German religious thought. Zinzendorf's emphasis upon a personally appropriated faith finds expression in the slogan "a living faith," which he opposed to the prevailing nominalism of Protestant Orthodoxy.

Many of these ideas took root in England through the influence of John Wesley (1703–1791), a founder and early leader of the Methodist movement within the Church of England, which subsequently gave birth to Methodism as a denomination in its own right. Convinced that he "lacked the faith whereby alone we are saved," Wesley paid a visit to Herrnhut in 1738 and was deeply impressed by what he found. The Pietist emphasis upon the need for a living faith and the role of experience in the Christian life led to his conversion experience at a meeting in Aldersgate Street in May 1738, in which he felt his heart to be "strangely warmed."

Wesley's emphasis upon the experiential side of Christian faith, which contrasted sharply with the dullness of contemporary English deism, led to a minor religious revival in England. Selina, countess of Huntingdon (1707–1791), played a particularly significant role in this revival by establishing throughout England pulpits served by leading revivalist preachers in rotation.

Tensions emerged within English Pietism, particularly in relation to the doctrine of grace: both Wesleys were Arminians, while their colleague George Whitfield was Calvinist. Yet, despite their differences, the various branches of Pietism succeeded in making Christian faith relevant to the experiential world of ordinary believers. It is of some importance to note that the strongly anti-religious tone of the French Revolution during the eighteenth century is partly due to the absence of any real equivalent of Pietism in the region. Pietism may be regarded as a reaction against a one-sided emphasis upon doctrinal orthodoxy and affirming a personal faith that relates to the deepest aspects of human nature.

American Protestantism and the Great Awakening

Christianity was brought to North America largely by refugees seeking to escape from religious persecution, which was then endemic in Europe. As a result, the first settlers in North America were generally deeply committed to their Christian beliefs. Most early settlers were English-speaking Protestant, fleeing from persecution in England, especially during the reigns of James I and Charles I.

The earliest New England settlements were in the Massachusetts Bay area. However, the tidewater district of Virginia was also of importance. Jamestown was founded in 1607, and the colony attracted many refugees from England, especially under the reign of Charles I. Relationships with local Native American tribes were a matter of particular concern. John Eliot, who arrived in Massachusetts in 1631, was interested in the culture and language of the Native Americans who lived in the Boston area and made a point of studying and learning Natic (a regional variant of Algonquian). He began to preach in this language and was able to attract support for his missionary work in the region, eventually managing to gain parliamentary approval in 1649 for the establishment of the Society for the Propagation of the Gospel in New England.

Many of those settling in this region at this time were Puritans, fleeing what they regarded as an oppressive England to find religious toleration in the New World. America was to be their promised land, the Atlantic Ocean their Red Sea, and England under Charles I and Archbishop William Laud their new Egypt. The resonances with the great biblical account of the exodus of the people of God from Egypt and the settlement in a new land, prepared for them by God, were too obvious to miss.

In 1620 the Pilgrim Fathers made their landmark voyage from Plymouth. Between 1627 and 1640 some 4,000 individuals made the hazardous crossing of the Atlantic Ocean and settled on the coastline of Massachusetts Bay. For them, America was the promised land and they were the chosen people. Expelled from their Egypt by a cruel Pharaoh, they had settled in a land flowing with milk and honey. They would build a new Jerusalem, a city upon a hill, in this strange land. Puritan communities emerged as strongly cohesive social and political bodies, with a strong sense of being called by God.

By the end of the first quarter of the eighteenth century, however, it seemed to many that Christianity had lost its way in the New World. In the early seventeenth century New England churches would only admit to full membership individuals who could testify to a personal experience of conversion. As the century progressed, fewer and fewer individuals could testify to such an experience. Yet most individuals wanted some kind of connection with the church – for example, to have their children baptized, or to have a Christian burial service. From about 1660 on, a "half-way" membership was recognized: anyone who was prepared to accept the truth of Christianity and the moral discipline of the church could have his or her children baptized.

The result was that, by the beginning of the eighteenth century, a large proportion of church members saw themselves as "nominal" or "half-way" Christians. They might attend church and learn from the preaching of the word of God; they might have their children baptized; they might recognize Christianity as true and morally helpful – but they were, in the final resort, unconverted. Christianity and church membership were viewed as just another part of American society. Being baptized and attending church formed one aspect of being a good American citizen.

Yet in 1734 the religious landscape of the American colonies changed radically. The Great Awakening erupted, especially at Northampton, Massachusetts, in response to the preaching of Jonathan Edwards. Edwards published accounts of the events at Northampton in the form of a book, *A Faithful Narrative of the Surprising Work of God*, which drew international attention to the awakening. As the revival continued in New England, it was given a new sense of direction by George Whitefield (1714–1770), recently arrived from England.

The revival had a lasting impact on American Christianity. It established the role of wandering preachers, unattached to any particular church. It undermined the authority of the clergy of established churches, whose members felt their positions to be deeply threatened by the upsurge in popular religious interest. The foundations of a mass popular culture were laid, in which Christianity was not the preserve of a clerical elite committed to the conservation of the existing social order, but a popular movement with a direct appeal to the masses. The established clergy refused to allow Whitefield to preach in its churches; he responded by preaching in the fields around towns and by attracting vast audiences, which could never have been contained within the churches from which he was barred.

Perhaps the group to be most deeply threatened by this development was the colonial clergy of the Church of England – the guardians of the existing social order. It is no exaggeration to say that the roots of the American Revolution lay in the growing religious alienation between the new popular American religion and the established religion of England. Within a generation of the Great Awakening, the colonies were in revolt against the colonial power.

The Modern Period, c. 1650–1914

During the second half of the fifteenth century, Christianity became increasingly a European religion. Islam had launched a *jihad* ("holy war") against it several centuries earlier. By about 1450, as a direct result of its military conquests, Islam was firmly established in the southwestern and southeastern parts of Europe. Although Christian communities continued to exist outside Europe (most notably in Egypt, Ethiopia, India, and Syria), Christianity was becoming geographically restricted. Its future seemed insecure.

One of the most dramatic developments to take place during the last few centuries has been the recovery of Christianity from this crisis. By the twentieth century, Christianity was firmly established as the dominant religion in the Americas, Australasia, southern Africa, and throughout many of the island nations of the South Pacific. Despite this dramatic expansion outside Europe, however, Christianity suffered a series of internal setbacks in Europe. In this section we shall explore something of this complex story of advances and retreats, consolidation and weakening. We begin by noting one of the most significant reactions against wars of religion in Europe: the rise of indifference to religion.

The rise of indifference to religion in Europe

With the ending of the Wars of Religion, a degree of stability came upon the European continent. Although religious controversy continued intermittently, it became generally accepted that certain parts of Europe were Lutheran, Catholic, Orthodox, or reformed. The sense of weariness that had been created by the Wars of Religion led to a new interest in religious toleration. The classic argument for toleration of diversity in matters of religion may be found in John Locke's *A Letter concerning Toleration* (1689).

Locke, one of England's most influential philosophers, argued for religious toleration on three grounds. First, it is impossible for the state to adjudicate between competing religious truth claims. Locke points out that no earthly judge can be brought forward to settle the matter. For this reason, religious diversity is to be tolerated. Second, Locke suggests that, even if it could be established that one religion was superior to all others, the legal enforcement of this superior religion would not secure the latter's desired objective. Third, Locke argues, on pragmatic grounds, that the results of trying to impose religious uniformity are far worse than those of continuing to live in diversity. Religious coercion leads to internal discord, or even to civil war. Toleration is the only way of coping with the religious diversity of early modern Europe.

Locke's analysis can be seen as leading to the view that religion is a private matter of public indifference. What individuals believe should be regarded as private, with no relevance to the public field. This approach at one and the same time upheld religious toleration and indicated that religion was a purely private matter. This perception was strengthened by the rise of the Enlightenment, which regarded the religions as different expressions of the same ultimate reality, which could be known through reason.

Locke's views on toleration were one response to the growing hostility toward those who took their religion too seriously, threatening the peace and prosperity of Europe. Another was the rise of rationalism. If religion was such a source of rage, abuse, and intolerance, why not undermine it completely? The Enlightenment regarded reason, rather than God, as the source and arbiter of all good and true beliefs – as we shall see in what follows.

The Enlightenment: The rise of rationalism

The movement that is now generally known as "the Enlightenment" brought new challenges for Christianity in Western Europe and North America. If the sixteenth-century Reformation challenged the church to rethink its external forms and the manner in which it expressed its beliefs, the Enlightenment saw the intellectual credentials of Christianity itself (rather than any one of its specific forms) facing criticism on a number of fronts.

The Enlightenment's criticism of traditional Christianity was based upon the principle of the omnicompetence of human reason. A number of stages in the development of this belief may be discerned. First, it was argued that the beliefs of Christianity were rational, and thus capable of standing up to critical examination. This type of approach is in John Locke's *Reasonableness of Christianity* (1695), which argued that Christianity was a reasonable supplement to natural religion. The notion of divine revelation was thus maintained.

Second, it was argued that the basic ideas of Christianity, being rational, could be derived from reason itself. There was no need to invoke divine revelation. As this type of approach was developed by John Toland in his *Christianity not Mysterious* (1696) and by Matthew Tindal's *Christianity as Old as Creation* (1730), Christianity was essentially the re-publication of the religion of nature. It did not transcend natural religion but was merely an example of it. All so-called "revealed religion" is actually nothing but the reconfirmation of what can be known through rational reflection on nature. "Revelation" was simply a rational reaffirmation of moral truths already available to the enlightened reason.

Third, the ability of reason to judge revelation was affirmed. As critical reason was omnicompetent, it was argued that it was supremely qualified to judge Christian beliefs and practices, in order to eliminate any irrational or superstitious elements. This view placed reason firmly above revelation and may be seen as symbolized in the enthronement of the Goddess of Reason in Notre Dame de Paris in 1793, in the aftermath of the French Revolution.

The Enlightenment was primarily a European and American phenomenon, and thus it took place in cultures in which the most numerically significant form of religion was Christianity. This historical observation is of importance: the Enlightenment critique of religion in general was often particularized as a criticism of Christianity. It was Christian doctrines and Christian sacred writings – rather than, for example, those of Islam or Hinduism – that were subjected to an unprecedented critical scrutiny, both literary and historical, the Bible being treated as if it were any other book. The cultural context of the Enlightenment meant that it was the life of Jesus of Nazareth that was subjected to critical reconstruction, rather than that of Mohammed or Buddha.

The Enlightenment's attitude to religion was subject to a considerable degree of regional variation, reflecting a number of local factors peculiar to different situations. One of the most important such factors is Pietism, perhaps best known in its English and American form of Methodism. As noted earlier, this movement placed considerable emphasis upon the experiential aspects of religion (for example, see John Wesley's notion of "experimental religion"). This concern for religious experience served to make Christianity relevant and accessible to the situation of the masses, contrasting sharply with the intellectualism of, for example, Lutheran Orthodoxy, which was perceived to be an irrelevance. Pietism (pp. 160–161) forged a strong link between Christian faith and experience, thus making Christianity a matter of the heart as well as one of the mind.

As noted earlier, Pietism was well established in Germany by the end of the seventeenth century, whereas in England it only developed during the eighteenth century and in France not at all. The Enlightenment thus preceded the rise of Pietism in England, with the result that the great evangelical revivals of the eighteenth century significantly blunted the influence of rationalism upon religion. In Germany, however, the Enlightenment followed after the rise of Pietism and thus developed into a situation that had been significantly shaped by religious faith, even if it would pose a serious challenge to its received forms and ideas. (Interestingly, English deism began to become influential in Germany at roughly the same time as German Pietism began to exert influence in England.) The most significant intellectual forces in the German Enlightenment were thus directed toward the reshaping (rather than the rejection or demolition) of the Christian faith.

In France, however, Christianity was widely perceived as both oppressive and irrelevant, with the result that the writers of the French Enlightenment were able to advocate the total rejection of Christianity as an archaic and discredited belief system. In his *Treaty on Tolerance*, Denis Diderot (1713–1784) argued that English deism had compromised itself, permitting religion to survive where it ought to have been eradicated totally – an agenda that many pursued during the French Revolution of 1789. But what of the earlier American Revolution of 1776, which served as a model for many French revolutionaries?

Christianity in the American Revolution

The causes of the American Revolution are complex, involving a number of interrelated issues. Perhaps the dominant theme is that of a desire to break free from the influence of England, which was increasingly seen as paternalist, oppressive, and exploitative. This desire for freedom expressed itself in the political, economic, and religious arenas. The Church of England was increasingly viewed as the religious dimension of British colonialism.

During the 1760s, vigorous efforts were made by American Protestants to resist the expansion of the Church of England's authority in the region. The Church of England was established by law in all the southern colonies, and its influence seemed destined to increase still further. The Quebec Act of 1774, which established Catholicism in French-speaking regions of Canada, was seen as particularly provocative. If Britain could decide what the established religion in Canada should be, what would it do in America? Suspicion and hostility grew unchecked.

The imposition of the Stamp Tax (1764) brought demands for "no taxation without representation." The 1773 decision of the British parliament to give the East India Company exclusive rights to sell tea in North America led to the episode known as the Boston Tea Party and to widespread unrest in Massachusetts. British troops were sent to restore order; this action was interpreted as an act of war by the colonists. A series of battles were fought in 1775, leading to the Declaration of Independence on July 4, 1776. A full-scale war of independence (1775–1783) ensued, in which church pulpits often served as rallying points for revolutionary activity. In effect the American Revolution united Christian groups of more or less all persuasions in the service of a greater goal.

American revolutionaries saw themselves as called to break the spiritual and temporal power of the Church of England in America. Like their forebears at the time of the English Civil War, they saw the conflict as a moment of purification, a time in which the true identity of a nation would be shaped. The battle was not between Christianity and atheism, but between a compromised state church and a pure gospel church. It would be a battle for the soul of America. While some revolutionaries had economic and political goals, others had religious objectives – objectives that demanded the purification of religion, not its elimination. Political republicanism was not seen as entailing atheism. Was not Calvin's Geneva, that city of God set upon a hill for all to see and imitate, itself a republic? And might not republicanism and the cause of true religion thus be united, whereas in England they were seen as opposite?

The constitutional separation between church and state can be argued to rest upon a fundamental desire to avoid any specific form of Christianity defining the establishment after the manner of the Church of England, which was widely regarded as corrupt and degenerate in American republican circles. The First Amendment to the constitution declared that Congress would ensure religious freedom, and not privilege any particular form of religion. The constitution thus prevented any formal establishment of religion, meaning that no Christian church (such as the Church of England) was to be given a favored legal status by the state. Although some modern constitutional theorists argue that this was intended to remove religion from American public life, or that it justifies this practice today, it is clear that the intention of the constitution was simply to avoid giving legal or social precedence to any specific Christian grouping.

Church and state in America: The "wall of separation"

The process of shaping the constitution of the United States of America took more than a decade. There was widespread agreement that any constitution should avoid the European model of giving preference or privilege to any Christian denomination. There would be no "established" church, although a number of individual states initially retained a form of establishment in which multiple denominations received government support.

Three distinct opinions emerged in the aftermath of the American Revolution. Traditionalists such as Patrick Henry (1736–1799) argued that state support for religion was essential to maintain social order. In 1784 Henry submitted a bill to the Virginia Legislature that would impose a tax to support churches, while allowing each citizen to determine which specific church his or her taxes should support. Rationalists such as Thomas Jefferson (1743–1826) and James Madison (1751–1836) argued that the separation of church and state was essential to guarantee liberty of conscience. A third group, consisting mainly of Baptists, Presbyterians, and Methodists, believed that Christian churches would be corrupted if they were given positions of political power or social privilege and argued for the churches to be protected from the corrupting influence of government.

The second of these positions soon achieved political dominance. Jefferson and Madison believed that that a separation of the religious and civil realms was the best way to ensure domestic peace and to avoid any oppression and injustice that could arise from the religious establishment. They had no desire for the new American republic to be damaged by wars of religion like the ones that had caused such damage in Europe in the seventeenth century.

The constitution of the United States was finally adopted on September 17, 1787, by the Constitutional Convention in Philadelphia, Pennsylvania and was subsequently ratified by conventions in 11 states. The constitution itself famously omits any reference to Christianity. The First Amendment, passed in September 1789, is widely regarded, however, as being of fundamental importance for any understanding of the place of Christianity in American public life. It declares: "Congress shall make no law respecting an establishment of religion, or prohibiting the free exercise thereof."

This amendment made two statements concerning the public role of Christianity in the United States. First, there was to be no legislative "establishment of religion." No specific church group could become the "established religion" of the United States. This was not understood at the time to mean that the government was prohibited from bringing religious language, symbols, beliefs, or values into the public arena. However, more radical interpretations of this "establishment clause" emerged later, including the view that the government of the United States is prohibited from preferring religion to anti-religion, so that the judiciary is neutral not simply in settling disputes between religious groups, but also in settling disputes between religion and its critics.

The first two presidents of the United States – George Washington (1732–1799) and John Adams (1735–1826) – are generally regarded as having been positive about the role of religion in public life, whatever their private religious views may have been. The third and fourth presidents – Thomas Jefferson (president from 1801 to 1809) and James Madison (president from 1809 to 1817) – were more emphatic about the separation of church and state and used the image of a "wall of separation" between the two.

This striking phrase seems to have first been used by the Puritan writer Roger Williams (1603–1683) in 1644. Williams spoke of a "wall of separation between the garden of the church and the wilderness of the world." In using this phrase, Williams was setting out an understanding of the church that was common among separatist Puritans: the world was a wilderness, but the church was a garden. To prevent the wilderness from encroaching on the garden and overwhelming it, the garden had to be enclosed – an important image, reflecting the biblical idea of paradise as a "closed garden." For Williams, it was axiomatic that the state and the church must be separate – for the good of the church.

Jefferson picked up on this image and developed it for his own somewhat different ends in 1802. A group of Baptists from the town of Danbury in Connecticut wrote to Jefferson shortly after his election as president, expressing their concern that their religious liberty was not sufficiently protected by their state legislature. A religious majority, they suggested, might easily win the magistrate over to their cause, with damaging consequences for religious minorities. Jefferson responded by emphatically asserting the separation of church and state, in terms that seem to go beyond the constitutional amendment; thus he spoke of "building a wall of separation between church and state." Determining the boundaries between the church and the state would remain a significant theme of American religious life until the present day.

The French Revolution and "dechristianization"

The French Revolution of 1789 marked the beginning of a new period of political radicalism and uncertainty in Western Europe, which was linked with growing criticism of the Catholic church and its ideas. Although many French revolutionary activists saw the American Revolution as an inspiration, the French Revolution, unlike its American counterpart, quickly assumed an anti-Christian tone. Generations of accumulated popular resentment and intellectual hostility against king and church could finally be contained no longer.

The storming of the Bastille on July 14, 1789 was widely seized upon as an icon of liberation, symbolizing the sweeping aside of an old order, based on superstition and oppression. A brave new world lay ahead, firmly grounded in nature and reason, and equally firmly committed to the liberation of humanity from "tyranny" and "superstition." The wisdom of the day was as simple as it was powerful: eliminate God, and a new future would dawn. It was a vision that thrilled many across Europe, drawing aside a curtain on a once forbidden world, which now seemed about to become reality.

It was clear that both pillars of traditional French society – the monarchy and the church – needed reform. Even late in the summer of the momentous year 1789, the general feeling was that the French monarch had allowed a series of measures that would abolish feudalism and remove some of the grievances felt by ordinary people against the power and privileges of the church. On November 2 it was agreed that all church lands should be nationalized; a basic minimum wage for priests, guaranteed by the state, was set in place. The Civil Constitution of the Clergy (July 1790) rejected the authority of the pope and reorganized and slimmed down the dioceses and the cathedral clergy. Although radical, the measures were not anti-Christian. The clergy split into a group that wished to remain loyal to Rome and one that wished to comply with the new civil authority.

Yet a more radical revolutionary faction, headed by Robespierre, gained power shortly afterward and launched the celebrated Reign of Terror. Louis XVI was publicly guillotined on January 21, 1793. A program of dechristianization was put in place during the period 1793–1794. The cult of the Goddess Reason was given official sanction. The old calendar was replaced by a republican calendar, which eliminated Sundays and Christian festivals, replacing them with secular alternatives. Priests were placed under pressure to renounce their faith. A program of church closure was initiated. Although the impact of these measures seems to have been felt mostly in urban areas, they caused considerable disruption and hardship to the church throughout all France.

The religious policies of the French Revolution were soon extended to neighboring regions. In November 1792, French revolutionary armies embarked on a campaign of conquest in the region. By 1799 six satellite republics had been established, embracing areas such as the Netherlands, Switzerland, parts of northern Italy, and areas of the Rhineland. In February 1798 the papal states were occupied and the pope was deported to France, where he died six months later. The French Revolution, it seemed to many, had destroyed not only the French church, but also the papacy.

On the eve of the nineteenth century, the future of Christianity in Europe thus seemed remarkably fragile. Many saw Christianity as linked with the politics of a bygone era, an obstacle to progress and liberty. Its faith and its institutions seemed to be in irreversible decline. In fact this would prove to be a false perception. The revolutionary experimentation with a secular state eventually fizzled out. Under Napoleon, relations with the pope were re-established, although on very different terms from those in operation before the revolution.

The Bourbon monarchy was restored. In 1814 Louis XVIII returned to claim the throne of France and re-established Catholicism. The situation was never easy, and real tensions between church and state continued unabated throughout most of the nineteenth century. Nevertheless, the church was able to regain at least some of its lost influence, prestige, and clergy. The period 1815–1848 witnessed a series of popular revivals in French-speaking Europe (often referred to as "le Réveil").

Orthodox resurgence: The Greek War of Independence

The Ottoman empire continued to be a significant force in Southeastern Europe well into the eighteenth century. The conclusive defeat of Ottoman armies by the Habsburgs in the 1690s had put an end to any possibility of Turkish expansion into Europe. Yet the resulting peace treaty left many parts of Southeastern Europe under Ottoman control. The growing influence of Russia – an Orthodox nation – in the region was consolidated by its defeat of Ottoman armies in the Russo-Turkish War of 1768–1774. Russia's victory over the Ottoman forces increased its territory and gave it influence over the Christian nations of the Ottoman empire – including Serbia and Greece, both of which were traditionally Orthodox.

Resentment against the Ottoman empire within both regions was rising, partly due to perceived religious discrimination against non-Muslims, who were required to pay a poll tax (*jizyah*). A Serbian revolt against Ottoman rule in 1788 was supported by the Austrians. However, the Austrian withdrawal from Serbia in 1791 led to the Ottomans' return and to their resuming control over the region. Following a massacre of Serbian nobles in 1804, a popular uprising took place, encouraged by the Russian empire. France supported the Ottoman empire, fearing the growing power of Russia, as did Austria, which believed that the liberation movement of the oppressed Slavic peoples would quickly spread to its own territory. Yet the popular uprising gained momentum. In 1806 Belgrade was besieged. Following its capitulation to the revolutionaries, it was proclaimed the capital city of an independent Serbia.

The hopes of Greek nationalists now began to soar. Secret nationalist societies were formed in Greece with the objective of securing liberation from Ottoman rule. Western European intellectuals promoted the idea of Greek independence. Many – such as the influential British poet Lord Byron (1788–1824) – were influenced by philhellenism, a movement that considered the resurgence of Greece as a modern nation-state to be linked with the recovery of its classic cultural status. The insurgency began in March 1821, but rivalry between its leaders limited its efficacy; in the end the revolt failed. Lord Byron traveled to Greece to join the rebellion, offering financial support to the fledgling Greek navy. But Ottoman reinforcements from Egypt were able to suppress the insurrection in southern Greece. By July 1827 the revolt had stalled.

However, the revolt was now of interest to the great powers. Russia, Great Britain, and France all sent naval task forces to the region. After what appears to have been a misunderstanding, most of the Ottoman navy was sunk at Navarino in October 1827. Now deprived of any means of transporting reinforcements or munitions, the Ottoman army began to lose ground. In the end it withdrew from central Greece. A series of conferences brokered by Russia, Great Britain, and France created the new state of Greece during the 1830s.

As noted earlier, the Ottoman period gave rise to religious tensions throughout the Balkans. The religion of the Ottoman empire was Sunni Islam; that of the occupied regions of Europe was generally Orthodox Christianity. It was inevitable that any wars of independence would have religious components. The Greek War of Independence signaled the return of Orthodoxy as official religion of the nation. Nationalist movements developed close links with the church, which was seen by many as having preserved the Greek language and culture during the long period of Turkish occupation. Whereas the French Revolution of 1789 identified Catholicism as an enemy, the Greek revolution of 1821 saw Orthodoxy as an ally.

A new expansion of Christianity: The age of mission

Although missionary work had always been undertaken by the church, it is widely agreed that a new age of evangelism began in the eighteenth century, with England playing a particularly significant role in the spreading of Christianity. The twentieth century, for some nineteenth-century pundits, was to be the Christian century. A series of triumphalistic congresses and writings in the late nineteenth century had confidently proclaimed the inevitability of the conversion of the world within the next generation. The First International Convention of the Student Volunteer Movement met in Cleveland in 1891, and adopted as its motto "the evangelization of the world in this generation." It was the largest student conference assembled in its time and was carried along by a confidence typical of the great age of mission, which came to an end with the outbreak of the First World War in 1918.

A major cultural concern may be noted from the outset. The interplay of British economic agendas and imperial ambitions on the one hand, religious issues on the other has always been conceded to be complex. There is no doubt that many missionaries – and by no means all English – saw the adoption of western culture as going hand in hand with the spreading of the Christian faith. This led inevitably to the growing perception that Christianity was essentially a western religion.

This was a particularly sensitive matter in parts of Asia such as India and China. In the case of India, the first major Protestant mission there was based at Tranquebar on the Coromandel Coast, about 200 kilometers south of Madras. Among the German Lutheran missionaries of note were Bartholomäus Ziegenbalg (who directed the mission from its founding in 1706 until 1719) and Christian Frederick Schwartz (director from 1750 to 1787). However, the growing political power of Britain in the region inevitably favored the activities of British missionaries, the first ones of which – for instance the Baptist William Carey – began work in Bengal in 1793. This activity was assisted to no small extent by Clement XIV's decision to suppress the Society of Jesus. The bull *Dominus ac Redemptor noster* (July 21, 1773) formally terminated all the functions and ministries of the Society, thus ending the missionary activity of the Jesuits in India and elsewhere. Nevertheless, at least 50 Jesuits are known to have continued missionary work in India after the suppression of their order, despite the efforts of the Portuguese to repatriate them.

British missionary societies and individuals were thus able to operate in India without any major opposition from other European agencies. Nevertheless, they received no support from the British authorities; the East India Company, for example, was opposed to their activities on the grounds that they might create ill will among native Indians and thus threaten the trade upon which it depended. However, the Charter Act (passed by the British parliament on July 13, 1813) revised the conditions under which the company was permitted to operate: the new charter gave British missionaries protected status and a limited degree of freedom to carry out evangelistic work on the Indian subcontinent. The result was inevitable: as the historian Stephen Charles Neill observes, "since 1813, Christian missions have never been wholly free from the stigma of undue dependence on government."

The new charter also made provision for the establishment of an Anglican bishopric at Calcutta. Under Reginald Heber (1783–1826; bishop of Calcutta from 1823 to 1826), missionary work was expanded considerably and restricted to Anglicans (Lutheran missionaries had to be re-ordained if they wished to continue operating in the region). Further revisions to the East India Company's charter in 1833 removed some of the restrictions imposed earlier upon missionary work. It was inevitable that religious tensions would develop. The uprising of 1857 (generally referred to as "the Indian Mutiny" by contemporary English writers) is often regarded as the outcome of this growing resentment at westernization.

Western missionary efforts in China also met with limited results. One of the many effects of the First Opium War of the 1840s was to open up China – "the Middle Kingdom," as this name translates – to at least some western attitudes. China chose to remain isolated from the West until the nineteenth century, when growing interest in commerce opened it up to western missionaries. Of these, James Hudson Taylor (1832–1905) may be singled out for special comment.

Hudson Taylor was initially a missionary with the Chinese Evangelization Society. Dissatisfaction with this organization led him to found the China Inland Mission in 1865. This mission was unusual in several respects, not least on account of its willingness to accept single women as missionaries and on its interdenominational character. Hudson Taylor showed an awareness of the cultural barriers facing Christian missionaries in China and did what he could to remove them – for example, he required his missionaries to wear Chinese rather than western dress.

Nevertheless, despite Hudson Taylor's concessions to Chinese cultural sensitivities, western attempts to evangelize Christianity were of very limited value. Christianity was seen as something western, and hence un-Chinese. The defeat of China by Japan in an ill-fated war during the years 1894–1895 was widely regarded as a direct result of the presence of foreigners in the country. This led to the I Ho Ch'uan crusade of 1899–1900, with its fanatical opposition to foreign investment and religious activity.

If missionary work in Asia met with limited success, this was balanced by successes elsewhere, especially in Africa and Australasia. Growing missionary interest in Africa developed during the late eighteenth century, especially in reaction to the brutality of the slave trade. Major British missionary societies that were active in Africa during the late eighteenth or early nineteenth century include the Baptist Missionary Society (BMS, founded 1792, and initially known as The Particular Baptist Society for the Propagation of the Gospel); the London Missionary Society (LMS, founded 1795 and initially known as The Missionary Society); and the Church Missionary Society (CMS, founded 1799 and originally known as The Church Missionary Society for Africa and the East). Each of these societies developed a particular focus on specific regions: the BMS focused on the Congo basin, the LMS on Southern Africa (including Madagascar), and the CMS on West and East Africa.

All of these societies were Protestant and in general strongly evangelical in their outlook. It was not until the middle of the nineteenth century that Catholic mission groups began to be seriously involved in the region. The trauma of the French Revolution (1789) and its aftermath had severely shaken the Catholic church. Only after the Congress of Vienna (1815) had settled the future shape of Europe could the church turn its attention to evangelism.

The dominant feature of sub-Saharan Africa in the nineteenth century is the growing importance of colonialism. Belgium, Britain, France, Germany, and the Netherlands had all established colonies in this region during the period. The forms of Christianity dominant in these European nations varied considerably, with the result that churches of a great diversity were established in Africa. Anglicanism, Catholicism, and Lutheranism were all well established by the end of the century; in South Africa, the Dutch reformed church had a particularly strong influence among European settlers. It must, however, be stressed that other missionaries from radically different backgrounds were also active in the region. For example, at least 115 black American missionaries are known to have been present and active in Africa during the period 1875–1899.

Reports of the voyages of Captain Cook during the eighteenth century, which included the discovery of Australia, led to a renewed interest in evangelizing this hitherto unknown region. In 1795 the LMS was founded with the primary objective of sending missionaries to the islands of the "South Sea" – that is, Australia and the whole of Oceania (all the islands of Polynesia, Micronesia, Melanesia, including New Zealand). The first major missionary expedition to the region set off in August 1796, when 30 missionaries set sail for Tahiti in Polynesia. Although this mission faced considerable difficulties – not least on account of the very different sexual mores of England and Tahiti – it can be seen as marking the beginning of a sustained effort to establish Christianity in the region.

The geographical nature of Tahiti rendered impossible one of the most reliable means of evangelization: the establishment of mission stations. Also, the populations of the islands were generally too small to justify the building and maintenance of such settlements. The most successful strategy to be adopted was the use of missionary vessels, which allowed European missionaries to direct and oversee the operations of native evangelists, pastors, and teachers.

The most significant Christian missions were located in Australia and New Zealand, which eventually came to serve as the base for most missionary work in the region. Christianity came to Australia in 1788. The circumstances of its arrival were not entirely happy. The fleet that arrived in New South Wales was transporting convicts to the penal settlements that were being built there. At the last moment, William Wilberforce persuaded the British naval authorities to allow a chaplain to sail with the fleet. With the dramatic increase in British immigration in the following century, the various forms of British Christianity became established in the region. The formation of "bush brotherhoods" in 1897 laid the basis for the evangelization of the interior of the continent.

The first missionaries arrived in New Zealand in 1814. The consolidation of Christianity there was largely due to Bishop George Selwyn (1809–1878), who was appointed missionary bishop of New Zealand in 1841. During his time in the region he had a marked impact on the development of Christianity, particularly in relation to education. He returned to England in 1867.

This brief overview of the great age of mission helps explain how Christianity broke free from its European context to become a global religion. Although Christianity was apparently landlocked in Europe as a result of Islamic expansion in the sixteenth century, the growing maritime ambitions of Western European nations led to its being diffused throughout the world – yet often in a decidedly westernized form. This legacy of western influence, as events demonstrated, was often a mixed blessing. One of the most remarkable developments of late twentieth and early twenty-first century Christianity has been a process of indigenization whereby in many parts of Latin America, Asia, and Africa Christianity broke free from its western origins and developed in forms much more adapted to the distinct cultural heritages of its new homes.

The shifting fortunes of Catholicism

After the trauma of the French Revolution, Catholicism began to regain something of the confidence it had known in earlier periods. The rise of romanticism had a powerful effect on the reawakening of interest in Catholicism, particularly in Germany and France.

Chateaubriand's *Génie du Christianisme* (*Genius of Christianity*), which appeared in 1802, did much to develop this new interest in the Christian faith, which can be seen reflected in many aspects of nineteenth-century culture. Other writers who drew on romanticism in their defense of Catholicism included Alessandro Manzoni (1785–1873) in Italy and Friedrich von Stolberg (1750–1819) in Germany. Rationalism was widely regarded as having led to the catastrophes of the past; there was a new sympathy for the view that Christianity was a major source of artistic inspiration and cultural excellence.

There can be no doubt that Catholicism needed to renew itself after the French Revolution and its aftermath. It is helpful to reflect on the extent of Catholic territory after the end of the Napoleonic era in 1814. Although Catholic missions had led to the establishment of communities in regions such as South America, Japan, and India, Catholicism was largely a European religion at this stage, bounded by the new nation of Belgium in the northwest, Spain in the southwest, Austria in the northeast, and Italy in the southeast. Most of the 100 million European Catholics were to be found in the Habsburg empire, Italy, and France.

It fell to Pius VII to renew his church after his return to Rome in May 1814. The task seemed enormous; nevertheless he proved equal to it. The groundwork was laid down by the papal secretary of state, Consalvi, who negotiated concordats with a series of states during the Congress of Vienna (1815). The Congregation for Extraordinary Ecclesiastical Affairs was established in 1814 with the objective of rebuilding Catholicism throughout Europe. The success of these measures can be measured by the fact that, in a traditionally strong Protestant nation such as England, the Catholic hierarchy was re-established in 1850.

Catholicism also became a major influence in the United States during this period. Although revolutionary America was dominated by Protestantism, waves of immigrants from Ireland and Italy began to alter the religious balance of power as the nineteenth century progressed. Archbishop John Carroll (1735–1815) did much to encourage the social acceptance of Catholicism at a time when its numbers were rapidly increasing. During the 1840s it is estimated that 2.5 million Irish Catholics emigrated to the east coast of the United States, with dramatic demographic consequences for eastern cities such as Boston and New York. The emergence of American Catholicism as a major force in the life of the new nation was partly due to the ethnic loyalty of its adherents, who saw Catholicism as an integral aspect of their identity. Their European origins thus served to mold the religious views of American immigrants at this critical period in the history of the United States. The founding of major Catholic educational institutions, such as the University of Notre Dame in 1842, laid the foundations for the emergence of Catholicism as a significant intellectual force.

The re-emergence of the pope as a major figure within Catholicism during the nineteenth century can be attributed, at least in part, to the aftermath of the Napoleonic wars. In the decades prior to the French Revolution, the pope seems to have been largely ignored by the Catholic faithful, who regarded him as isolated and distant. However, Napoleon's fairly vicious treatment of the pope caused the latter to regain his prestige in the eyes of both the faithful and European governments. Even in France, the heartland of movements that advocated nationally governed churches, there was a new respect for the pope. The scene was set for the re-emergence of the papacy as a leading institution within Catholicism and beyond. The movement that advocated increased papal authority was known as ultramontanism and merits further attention in its own right, not least because of its importance in connection with the First Vatican Council – to which we now turn.

The First Vatican Council: Papal infallibility

The rise of revolutionary movements in France, Italy, and Germany during the late 1840s led to increasing concern over the political stability of Catholic countries, and particularly over the position of the pope himself. The First Vatican Council was convened by Pius IX in 1869 to strengthen the church against nationalists, liberals, and materialists, who had challenged some leading themes of the Catholic faith and deprived the church of control over schools and property in various parts of Europe, including Italy. Despite political uncertainty in Italy at this time, nearly 750 out of some 1,000 eligible bishops and heads of religious orders traveled to Rome to attend the council.

The council issued two major documents: *Dei Filius* (*The Son of God*), which reasserted the harmony between reason and faith and the supremacy of the latter; and *Pastor aeternus* (*The Eternal Pastor*), which set out the doctrine of papal infallibility. *Dei Filius* reaffirmed fundamental Catholic doctrines in the light of the challenges of the age. Given the rise of rationalism, which rejected the notion of divine revelation partly through a belief in the supreme authority of reason, the council reaffirmed the rationality of faith on the one hand and the inability of reason to penetrate to deeper spiritual realities on the other.

Yet most historians consider the most important decision taken at the council to have resided in its formulation of the dogma of papal infallibility in *Pastor aeternus*. According to this doctrine, the pope has "full and supreme power of jurisdiction over the whole Church." When the pope "speaks ex cathedra, that is, when, in the exercise of his office as shepherd and teacher of all Christians, in virtue of his supreme apostolic authority, he defines a doctrine concerning faith or morals to be held by the whole Church," he possesses the "infallibility which the divine Redeemer willed his Church to enjoy in defining doctrine concerning faith or morals."

This notion of papal infallibility enjoyed much support – but not total support – within the Catholic church. The topic had not initially been proposed for discussion at the council; it emerged during debate in 1870. The dogma caused some concern, particularly in Germany. Otto von Bismarck (1815–1898) was appointed chancellor of Prussia in 1864. He embarked on a policy of German unification, which was pursued with increasing vigor after the end of the Franco-Prussian War in 1871. Bismarck regarded the dogma of infallibility as an insult to German Protestants and as a potential threat to the emerging authority of the German state.

Bismarck embarked on a policy of discrimination against German Catholics during the 1870s. This *Kulturkampf* ("culture war") eventually fizzled out in 1886. Yet anti-religious feeling was growing elsewhere in Europe, most notably in France, where the 1901 Association Law and the 1905 Separation Law virtually eliminated religion from public life, including education.

In Italy the position of the pope became difficult following the rise to power of King Victor Emmanuel (1820–1878), who in effect stripped the pope of all his territories except for the Vatican, the Lateran Castle, and Castel Gandolfo. While the Law of Papal Guarantees ensured the pope's independence and safety, it nevertheless placed restrictions on his rights. This law was eventually replaced by the Lateran Treaty of 1929, which was more favorable to the pope. The Vatican remains an independent state to this day, despite its miniscule size.

Theological revisionism: The challenge of modernism

One of the concerns to preoccupy the bishops assembled at the First Vatican Council was the rise of modernism, which was portrayed as a serious threat to the wellbeing of the church. So what was this movement, and why did it raise such anxieties?

Modernism is best understood as designating a set of attitudes within Catholicism that was shaped by the intellectual culture of the Enlightenment. Alfred Loisy (1857–1940) and George Tyrrell (1861–1909) were two of the most influential Catholic modernist writers. During the 1890s Loisy established himself as a critic of traditional views of the biblical accounts of creation and argued that a real development of doctrine could be discerned within Scripture. His most significant publication, *The Gospel and the Church*, appeared in 1902, by which time his views had been severely criticized by the Catholic church hierarchy. This important work was a direct response to the views of the liberal Protestant Adolf von Harnack, set out two years earlier in *What Is Christianity?* Harnack's controversial views on the origins and nature of Christianity rested on the assertion that Christianity had only a loose connection with Jesus of Nazareth.

Loisy rejected Harnack's suggestion that there was a radical discontinuity between Jesus and the church; however, he made significant concessions to Harnack's liberal Protestant account of Christian origins, and these included an acceptance of the role and validity of biblical criticism in interpreting the gospels. Three features of his work merit closer attention.

1 *The Gospel and the Church* recognized a genuine place for biblical criticism in Catholic biblical scholarship and in theological reflection. Loisy's critics saw this as a concession to the rationalist spirit of the age.
2 Loisy called into question whether the institutional church was really to be regarded as God's intention for the world. The most famous sentence of *The Gospel and the Church* makes this point succinctly: "Jesus proclaimed the Kingdom, and what actually came was the Church."
3 The work suggests that Christian doctrine has developed over time rather than being delivered to the apostles as a fixed and permanent package. This viewpoint had already been advocated, though with some caution, by the English Catholic writer John Henry Newman (1801–1890). It was, however, seen as a concession to evolutionist ways of thinking, and hence as being inconsistent with received Catholic tradition.

The British Jesuit writer George Tyrrell followed Loisy in his radical criticism of traditional Catholic dogma. In common with Loisy, he criticized Harnack's account of Christian origins in *Christianity at the Crossroads* (1909), dismissing Harnack's historical reconstruction of Jesus as "the reflection of a Liberal Protestant face, seen at the bottom of a deep well." The book also included a defense of Loisy's work, arguing that the official Roman Catholic hostility to this book and its author has created a general impression that it is a defense of liberal Protestant against Roman Catholic positions and that "Modernism is simply a prot-estantizing and rationalizing movement."

In part, this perception reflects the growing influence of modernism within the main-stream Protestant denominations. In England, the Churchmen's Union was founded in 1898 for the advancement of liberal religious thought; in 1928 it altered its name to the Modern Churchmen's Union. Among those especially associated with this group may be noted Hastings Rashdall (1858–1924), whose *Idea of Atonement in Christian Theology* (1919) illustrates the general tenor of English modernism.

Drawing somewhat uncritically upon the earlier writings of liberal Protestant thinkers, Rashdall argued that the theory of the atonement associated with the medieval writer Peter Abelard was more acceptable to modern thought forms than traditional theories that made an appeal to the notion of a substitutionary sacrifice. This strongly moral or exemplarist theory of the atonement, which interpreted Christ's death virtually exclusively as a demon-stration of the love of God, made a considerable impact upon English – and especially Anglican – thought in the 1920s and 1930s.

The rise of modernism in the United States followed a similar pattern. The growth of liberal Protestantism in the late nineteenth and early twentieth centuries was widely perceived as a direct challenge to more conservative evangelical standpoints. Newman Smyth's *Passing Protestantism and Coming Catholicism* (1908) argued that Roman Catholic modernism could serve as a mentor to American Protestantism in several ways, not least in its critique of dogma and in its historical understanding of the development of doctrine. The situation became increasingly polarized through the rise of fundamentalism in response to modernist attitudes.

Although criticisms were made of some aspects of Catholic modernism by Pope Leo X in 1893, the fullest condemnations came from his successor, Pius X, in September 1907. In the encyclical *Pascendi dominici gregis* (*The Feeding of the Lord's Flock*), Pius declared that the Catholic church now faced a threat from enemies within as much as from its critics outside the church. Modernism, whether it originated from laity or from priests, was the "most pernicious of all the adversaries of the Church."

Pius' campaign to eliminate modernism from Catholic educational institutions and from positions of authority and influence within the church came to an end with his death in 1914. The election of Benedict XV in September 1914 put a stop to any systematic drive against modernism. While Benedict strongly reaffirmed the substance of earlier condem-nations of this phenomenon, he was restrained in their implementation. By then, the influence of anti-modernism had dwindled.

The Victorian crisis of faith

As will be clear from our discussion of modernism, religious belief in many European nations went through a period of decline and uncertainty during the nineteenth century, particularly toward the end of this period. In this section we shall consider developments in England. Although these can be paralleled from the narrative of American and other European societies at the time, England's status as an economic, military, and cultural power gave these developments particular significance.

At the beginning of the nineteenth century there was little sign of any emerging crisis of faith. There was little public appetite for radical change, religious or political. Although the extremism of the French Revolution was warmly welcomed by some young radicals of the 1790s and early 1800s, such enthusiasm soon dissolved. The poet William Wordsworth (1770–1850) illustrates an initial enthusiasm for the abolition of a corrupt order along with a growing unease about the violence and bloodshed it created. Atheism gained few supporters in England on account of the revolution; most English people seem to have judged anti-religious views as socially destabilizing and irresponsible.

Yet deeper forces were at work in English culture, creating a context within which a new and more distant attitude to faith would emerge. One such force was the Industrial Revolution, which developed earlier and more rapidly in England than in many other nations. While rural churches were often deeply embedded in the life of rural communities, the migration of rural populations to cities led to a disconnection between the working class and the church. Urban churches often failed to connect up with burgeoning communities of industrial workers.

A second development was the rise of biblical criticism, which became increasingly important in the second half of the nineteenth century. The edited collection *Essays and Reviews* (1860) caused a scandal on account of its critical attitude toward the Bible on the part of its seven liberal Anglican authors. The most controversial of the essays was Benjamin Jowett's "On the Interpretation of Scripture," which argued that the Bible ought to be read "like any other book." The impact of this collection of essays was perhaps greater than it might otherwise have been, as it was published a year after Darwin's *Origin of Species* had opened up debate about the reliability of the Bible's account of human origins.

Yet perhaps the most celebrated exponent of biblical criticism was John William Colenso (1814–1883), a colonial bishop of the Church of England. Colenso was one in an increasing number of writers to raise doubts about the factual reliability of the Old Testament. In his *The Pentateuch and the Book of Joshua Critically Examined* (1862), Colenso questioned the accuracy of the narratives in the historical books of the Old Testament. He disputed whether Moses had written the Pentateuch (the first five books of the Old Testament) and argued that its spiritual value did not imply its historical accuracy. "Though imparting to us, as I fully believe it does, revelations of the Divine Will and Character, it cannot be regarded as historically true." These views from the pen of a colonial bishop caused a scandal in Victorian England, in that they were seen to challenge the basic idea that the Bible could be trusted.

A third area of tension concerned the growing popular influence of science, which was increasingly coming to be seen as a cultural authority independent and critical of religion. The Darwinian debates added significantly to these discussions. For many later Victorians, science was about the future and religion was about the past. This perception was intensified by the publication of works arguing for the permanent "warfare" of science and faith, such as John William Draper's *History of the Conflict between Religion and Science* (1874) and Andrew Dickson White's *History of the Warfare of Science with Theology in Christendom* (1896).

Victorian Christianity responded to these developments in a number of manners. The Oxford Movement, which emerged during the 1830s, was critical of German New Testament scholarship and developed a program for the renewal of the "high church" movement within the Church of England. Some advocated disengagement from these cultural trends, anticipating some of the themes that were later associated with American Protestant fundamentalism during the 1920s.

Yet the dominant response within mainline British Christianity was to attempt to reach a religious accommodation of these cultural developments. The willingness of the Victorian churches to come to terms with biological and geological science, social science, archaeology, comparative religion, and biblical scholarship can be seen partly as a pragmatic response to the changing cultural situation. To resist these changes, many senior churchmen believed, would only lead to the increasing cultural marginalization and isolation of organized religion within English society.

Pentecostalism: The American origins of a global faith

Many of the Christian denominations making up American society had their origins in Europe – such as Presbyterianism, Episcopalianism, and Methodism. Yet the religious entrepreneurialism of the United States led to the emergence of numerous new denominations and visions of faith that originated within America itself. Most of these had Christian roots wherever their subsequent development might lead them. Joseph Smith (1805–1844) founded Mormonism in the 1820s in New York State as a form of Christian primitivism. Mary Baker Eddy (1821–1910) founded Christian Science in Massachusetts in 1879. The Jehovah's Witnesses emerged from the Bible Student Movement founded in the late 1870s in Pennsylvania by Charles Taze Russell (1852–1916). Yet perhaps the most significant form of Christianity to emerge within the United States is Pentecostalism.

The first phase of the emergence of Pentecostalism took place on the first day of the twentieth century – January 1, 1901 – at Bethel Bible College in Topeka, Kansas. The institution had been founded the previous October, in the holiness tradition, by Charles Parham (1873–1929), a former pastor in the Methodist Episcopal Church. Parham asked his students to investigate the New Testament evidence for the continued activity of the Holy Spirit in the Christian life.

This was seen as an empty, pointless question by many. The theological wisdom of the day took the form of "cessationism," widely taught by the Protestant theological establishment. This view held that the active gifts of the Holy Spirit, such as "speaking in tongues," belonged to the age of the New Testament itself and were no longer available or operational. The New Testament was thus read from within a "cessationist" interpretative framework, which had already determined that such spiritual phenomena were things of the past. Parham was not so sure. Within his own holiness tradition, reports were circulating of what seemed to be charismatic phenomena. He asked his students for their views.

The students reported that a straightforward reading of the biblical texts suggested that such charismatic gifts were still a possibility. Impressed by the clarity of this response, Parham and his students began a prayer vigil on December 31, 1900, in the hope that the gift might be renewed. At 11 o'clock the following evening, on the first day of the twentieth century, one of the students – Agnes Ozman (1870–1937) – reported having such an experience. A few days later others, including Parham himself, followed suit.

Parham and his students began to tell others about this apparent recovery of the "gift of tongues." One of those who heard Parham speak in 1905 was the African American preacher William J. Seymour (1870–1922), who was forced by the southern segregationist policies of that period to listen to Parham's lectures through a half-opened door. Sadly, Parham – noted for his white supremacist views – did nothing to break down this racial wall of separation. Inspired, Seymour went on to open the Apostolic Faith Mission in a dilapidated church, then used only for storage, at 312 Azusa Street, Los Angeles, in April 1906.

Over the next two years a major revival broke out at Azusa Street, characterized by "speaking in tongues." The term "Pentecostalism" began to be applied to the movement. This name alludes to the "Day of Pentecost" – the occasion, according to the New Testament, when the phenomenon of "speaking in tongues" was first experienced by the early Christian disciples (Acts 2: 1–4). Significantly, at a time of ruthless racial segregation in American culture brought about by the notorious Jim Crow segregation laws, the Azusa Street mission pointedly ignored racial issues. A black pastor led a diverse ministry team comprised of white people, black people, and Hispanics.

Primarily (though not exclusively) from this California base, Pentecostalism spread rapidly in America, appealing particularly to the socially marginalized and especially through Seymour's important concept of an ecstatic egalitarian ecclesiology. Unusually, it seemed to appeal to and be embraced by both white and African American Christian groupings. Charles Parham, however, had no time for the racial inclusiveness proclaimed and practiced by Seymour and Azusa Street. In an abortive and counterproductive move, Parham attempted to take control of the Azusa phenomenon, being particularly disturbed by its commitment to interracial fellowship. Among other things, Parham later went on to teach that the white Anglo-Saxon Protestants were the privileged descendants of the lost tribes of Israel; and he spoke in glowing terms of the Ku Klux Klan. He was never reconciled with Seymour and eventually died in disgrace.

Yet Pentecostalism rapidly transcended its American roots and became a global faith. We shall consider this further later in this work (pp. 212–213).

The Twentieth Century, 1914 to the Present

The assassination by a Serbian nationalist of Archduke Franz Ferdinand of Austria, the heir to the throne of Austro-Hungary, on June 28, 1914 sparked off an international conflict of unparalleled destructiveness. The European great powers were linked together by treaty obligations that virtually guaranteed that a declaration of war by one would lead to a Europe-wide conflict. On the one side were Great Britain, France, and Russia; on the other, Germany, Austro-Hungary, and Italy.

The Great War had a massive impact on Christianity globally. Christianity was still a predominantly western phenomenon in 1914. At one level, the war fractured relationships between nations and churches and between national bodies – such as mission agencies and churches. It would be a long time, for example, before German and British Christians were able to restore any kind of meaningful working relationship between them.

The Great War also put an end to the notion of "Christendom." This idea had been largely discredited following the fragmentation of Europe in the aftermath of the French Revolution.

It had now received a mortal wound, from which it never recovered. European Christian nations had regularly fought one another in the past – but never with such ferocity.

The situation of Russia was of particular importance. Russia soon found itself overwhelmed by German technological superiority and was forced to sue for peace. This caused existing internal tensions to reach breaking point, and there is wide agreement that this situation has been a trigger for the Russian Revolution – unquestionably one of the most important developments in the twentieth century for the fortunes of Christianity in Europe and far beyond.

Yet the Great War was not a religious war in any sense of the term. It did not arise over religious issues, nor did religious beliefs or agendas play any significant role in its prosecution. It was a war between "nation-states," based primarily on nationalist objectives and agendas. A complex network of alliances and counterbalances had developed between the various European powers since the Franco-Prussian War; these were intended to neutralize the capacity of any great power to achieve continental dominance. In the end, the mechanism that was intended to prevent a conflict locked the great powers into a delicate state of equilibrium that, once disturbed, had the potential to escalate uncontrollably into total war.

Any account of the history of Christianity in the twentieth century must give due weight to the instability and disillusionment that arose in the aftermath of the Great War. Two events that took place during the Great War proved especially important in shaping the course of Christianity in the twentieth century.

The Armenian genocide of 1915

The twentieth century opened with a catastrophe that traumatized Christians in the eastern Mediterranean region and was an ominous portent of things to come later that century. The ailing Ottoman empire found itself caught up in the Great War and began to fragment following a series of rebellions against Ottoman rule in the Middle East and beyond. This empire was a predominantly Islamic region and was home to a significant number of non-Islamic peoples, including Armenian Christians. The Armenian people had adopted the Christian faith in AD 301 and regarded themselves as the oldest Christian nation in the region. In 1915 a series of massacres and forced deportations claimed the lives of between 1 million and 1.5 million Armenians – an event now referred to as "the Armenian genocide."

The events of 1915 did not come entirely as a bolt from the blue. There had been a series of massacres of Armenian Christians in many Turkish cities during the period 1895–1897, in which about 200,000 people are thought to have died. While the massacres of April 1915 were directed against non-Islamic religious minorities in general rather than against Christians in particular, the people most severely affected were the Armenians. These events took place deep within the Ottoman empire, under wartime conditions that made communication and intervention virtually impossible. Nothing could be done to stop the killings.

The impact of this genocide upon world Christianity has been mixed. Regionally it was seen as a catastrophe. Christians in the Middle East were stunned and numbed by the events. Many of them lived as religious minorities under Islamic rule and feared that this massacre might lead to a more general repression of Christians by other Islamic powers in the region. Many drew the conclusion that geographical dispersion into Christian nations was the only way of ensuring their safety. As a result, the largest Armenian communities today are to be found in the United States, where they found sanctuary.

In the dark days of 1915, some Armenians had looked to Russia for help. Was not this great nation a bastion of Orthodox Christianity? Might not its great resources be brought to bear on their desperate situation? Yet in 1917 events took a turn that few could have predicted. The Russian Revolution overthrew the czarist state and ushered in an altogether new state ideology. No longer was Russia an Orthodox nation. If anything, it would be a nation committed to the elimination of religion from its territory – and, if possible, far beyond.

The Russian Revolution of 1917

The political philosopher Karl Marx had argued that the origins of religion – Christianity included – lay in social and economic alienation. People turned to religion for consolation, because they could not bear the weight of sorrow and pain caused by their poverty and alienation from their rights. In Marx's famous words, religion is the opium of the people: a narcotic, which soothes the pains of life under capitalism and makes people disinclined to take action so as to bring about radical social and political change.

For Marx, religion would die out if radical social change were effected. Eliminate capitalism through a communist revolution, and the pain it created would disappear – and, with it, any need for the comfort of religion. Religion, Marx argued, owed both its origins and its continued appeal to its power to comfort and soothe in the face of the ills of capitalism. Religion thus offered an indirect support to capitalism, in that it diminished the

Figure 4.10   Vladimir Ilyich Lenin (1870–1924), leader of the Bolshevik Revolution in Russia. Source: AKG Images.

human will to rebel against its iniquities and to bring about the socioeconomic transformation that alone would change the world.

Marx's ideas never achieved significant influence in the heartlands of capitalism – in Western European nations such as Germany or Great Britain, or in the United States of America. They may have attracted the attention of academics and social critics; yet they failed to gain acceptance among those with power and to influence the course of events. The Russian Revolution of 1917 changed this situation radically and irreversibly. Marx's ideas were taken seriously and put into practice by a state, which was prepared to use force to ensure their success. For Vladimir Ilyich Lenin (1870–1924), religion was a tool of oppression, cynically used against the peasants by the Russian ruling classes. The Soviet Union now became the first state to have the elimination of religion as its ideological objective.

The Russian Revolution of 1917 took place in two stages. An initial uprising against the czarist regime took place early in 1917 in St. Petersburg, then the capital of Russia. This "February Revolution" (which actually occurred in March 1917, according to the western calendar) took place against the background of massive Russian losses in the Great War and increasing disillusionment with the policies of the czar. In the chaos of the situation, members of the Duma – the Russian imperial parliament – seized power and declared themselves to be the provisional government of the nation. The czar and his family were placed under house arrest. At this stage, the intentions of the revolutionaries were to bring about a liberal democracy within the collapsed Russian empire.

Yet a more radical group, led by Lenin and informed by Marx's ideas, was in the process of consolidating its influence. The Bolshevik faction ("Bolshevik" comes from the Russian word for "majority") seized its opportunity in the "October Revolution" (which actually took place in November 1917), establishing a workers' state. Civil war broke out, in which the Bolsheviks' Red Army fought the White Army of foreign troops and internal opponents of the Bolsheviks. By 1924 the czar and his family had been executed and opposition to the Bolsheviks eliminated.

Lenin always regarded the intellectual, cultural, and physical elimination of religion as central to the socialist revolution, and he had identified atheism as an essential element of his ideology long before the Bolshevik Revolution of October 1917. In laying down how the revolutionary cause was to be advanced in Russia, he wrote: "Our propaganda necessarily includes the propaganda of atheism." In an attempt to win the people from Christianity through argument, Lenin suggested that it would be necessary "to translate and widely disseminate the literature of the eighteenth-century French Enlighteners and atheists." Yet it soon became clear that religion was obstinately persisting. A barrage of repressive measures, from banners to bullets, from pamphlets to prison camps, was unleashed against the religionists of the Soviet Union.

Initially attention was directed toward the religious group that was dominant in Russia itself – Orthodoxy. On January 23, 1918 Lenin issued a decree depriving the church of any right to own property or to teach religion – in private or state schools or to any group of minors. In a Soviet variant of Henry VIII's suppression of English monasteries, Lenin proposed the confiscation of the wealth of churches and monasteries and the execution of any who opposed it.

A key player in this atheist crusade was the League of Militant Atheists, a semi-official coalition of various political forces that operated within the Soviet Union from 1925 to 1947. With the slogan "The Struggle against Religion Is a Struggle for Socialism," the group set out to destroy the credibility of religion through social, cultural, and intellectual manipulation. Its carefully orchestrated campaigns involved using newspapers, journals, lectures, and films to persuade Soviet citizens that religious beliefs and practices were irrational and destructive. Good Soviet citizens, they declared, ought to embrace a scientific, atheistic worldview.

Churches were closed or destroyed, often by dynamite; priests imprisoned, exiled, or executed. On the eve of World War II , as a result of the anti-religious policies of the Soviet dictator Joseph Stalin (1878--1953), there were only 6,376 clergy remaining in the Russian Orthodox Church, compared with the pre-revolutionary figure of 66,140. On February 17, 1938 55 priests were executed. In 1917 there were 39,530 churches in Russia; by 1940 only 950 remained functional.

Stalin's suppression of religion, however, extended to other faiths, in line with his general ideological commitment to the forcible elimination of religion. Attacks on Jews were endemic throughout the period of the Soviet Union. Stalin was especially fearful of a secessionist Islamic movement that was gaining momentum in the southeastern republics of the Soviet Union, and he forcibly suppressed Islam throughout the region.

The long-term impact of the Russian Revolution on the history of Christianity was considerable. Christianity was initially suppressed only throughout the Soviet Union. However, after substantial Soviet military gains in World War II, Eastern Europe came under its sphere of influence, and this led to the imposition of often repressive measures against Christian churches and believers.

America: The fundamentalist controversy

Fundamentalism arose as a religious reaction, within American conservative Christianity, to the development of a secular culture during the 1920s. The aftermath of the Great War in American culture was seen by many as marking a departure from America's traditional Christian (and especially Protestant) moorings. In part, this was a response to the greater mass production of consumer goods – especially autos – and a drive toward consumerism and a credit economy, which many regarded as encouraging materialism. Divorce rates soared. To many religious Americans, the nation seemed to have embraced new secular values and to have moved away from older values of self-denial and from the Protestant work ethic to a form of self-indulgence and materialism.

Despite the wide use of "fundamentalist" to characterize religious movements within Islam and Judaism, the term designates, originally and properly, a movement within Protestant Christianity in the United States. By a series of historical accidents, "fundamentalist" came to us from a series of 12 books that appeared from a small American publishing house in the 1910s. The series was unremarkably entitled *The Fundamentals* and was intended to be an exploration of the "basics of faith" from a conservative Protestant perspective.

To begin with, fundamentalism did not have the overtones of obscurantism, anti-intellectualism, and political extremism that many now associate with it. It was seen as a movement on the fringes of American mainline Protestantism, which believed that culture was moving in anti-Christian directions and wanted to safeguard the Christian heritage. Fundamentalists initially saw themselves simply as returning to biblical orthodoxy. This point was recognized at the time by Kirsopp Lake (1872–1946), a leading British modernist writer who described fundamentalism as "the partial and uneducated survival of a theology which was once universally held by all Christians."

Yet polemical associations were not slow to develop. Fundamentalism rapidly became a reactive movement, defined by what it opposed as much as by what it affirmed. A siege mentality came to be characteristic of the movement. Fundamentalist countercommunities saw themselves (to evoke the pioneer spirit) as circles of wagons, defending their distinctive beliefs against an unbelieving and increasingly secular culture.

The negative consequences of this polarization can be seen especially from the painful history of the Presbyterian church in the United States during the 1920s. In 1922, an ill-tempered controversy broke out over whether traditional doctrines should be modified in the light of modern scientific and cultural knowledge. The conservatives seemed to be winning ground. In response, Henry Emerson Fosdick (1878–1969) preached a polemical sermon in May 1922 entitled "Shall the Fundamentalists Win?" Fosdick rejected core beliefs of fundamentalism, arguing that belief in the virgin birth was unnecessary; that belief in the inerrancy of Scripture was untenable; and that the doctrine of the Second Coming was absurd. The sermon was rewritten by a skilled public relations expert and funded by the oil magnate John D. Rockefeller Jr. (1839–1937). It is estimated that 130,000 copies of the sermon were circulated. A vigorous riposte soon followed from the conservative side. Clarence Edward Macartney (1879–1957) entitled his reply "Shall Unbelief Win?"

The situation rapidly polarized. There seemed to be no middle ground, which made toleration impossible. There could be no compromise or way out of the situation. Presbyterians were forced to decide whether they were, to use the categories of the protagonists, "unbelieving liberals" or "reactionary fundamentalists." The church was shattered. There were other options, and saner voices too; yet the highly politicized climate of opinion made it impossible for them to gain a hearing. "Oppositionalism" made the issue be perceived in highly simplistic terms within conservative Presbyterian circles: either an unbelieving culture would win, or victory would go to the gospel. There were no alternatives.

Conservatives soon discovered that there seemed to be little they could do to stop the influence of modernist thinkers such as Fosdick from growing within their denominations. The slide into modernism seemed inexorable. The result was a growing demand within fundamentalist circles for separation from allegedly corrupt denominations. If it proved impossible to reform denominations from within, the only course open was to break away from the denomination and form a new, yet doctrinally pure church body. Such a separatist approach can be traced back to the dawn of American Protestantism. Roger Williams (c. 1604–1684), founder of Rhode Island, was one of the leading proponents of a pure separatist church, arguing that Christian believers were under an obligation to separate themselves from apostate churches and from a secular state.

The fundamentalist war against modernity led to a closed, cautious, and defensive attitude on the part of its protagonists toward what they regarded as a secular culture and largely apostate mainline churches. Separatism seemed the only way ahead. If culture and mainline denominations could not be converted or reformed, there was no option but to become a voice in the wilderness.

One of the main enemies identified by fundamentalism was Darwinism. Although several of the essays in *The Fundamentals* were actually supportive of evolution as a scientific theory, radical opposition to Darwin's theory of evolution quickly became a litmus test of fundamentalist orthodoxy. Although some scholars suggest that this opposition arose primarily because Darwinism seemed to pose a threat to traditional methods of biblical interpretation, it is more helpful to see it as a reaction against what was seen as a defining characteristic of secular culture at that time.

This opposition to Darwin's theory of evolution led many fundamentalists to agitate for its exclusion from the curriculum of public schools. This led to the famous Scopes "monkey" trial of 1925. John T. Scopes (1900–1970), a young high school science teacher, was prosecuted for disobeying a recently adopted statute that prohibited the teaching of evolution in Tennessee's public schools. The American Civil Liberties Union moved in to support Scopes, while William Jennings Bryan (1860–1925) served as prosecution counsel on behalf of the World Christian Fundamentals Association. It proved to be a public relations disaster for fundamentalism.

Bryan, who had billed the trial as a "duel to the death" between Christianity and atheism, was outmaneuvered by the celebrated agnostic attorney Clarence Darrow, who called Bryan to the stand as a witness for the defense and interrogated him concerning his views on evolution. Bryan was forced to admit that he had no knowledge of geology, comparative religions, or ancient civilizations. In the end, Bryan succeeded in winning the trial in the courtroom. Scopes was fined $100. The state supreme court reversed the verdict against Scopes on a technicality, allowing Scopes to walk free. Bryan died five days after the trial.

But a perhaps somewhat more important trial was taking place in the nation's newspapers, in which Bryan was declared to be unthinking, uneducated, and reactionary. Fundamentalism might make sense in a rural Tennessee backwater, but had no place in sophisticated urban America. In particular, the journalist and literary critic H. L. Mencken successfully portrayed fundamentalists as intolerant, backward, and ignorant, standing outside mainstream American culture.

From that moment on, fundamentalism became as much a cultural stereotype as a religious movement. It could not hope to win support among the educated and cultural elites within mainline Protestantism. The damage inflicted would never be undone. It was only with the emergence of a new form of evangelicalism after World War II that fundamentalism regained some of its earlier momentum and credibility.

The German church crisis of the 1930s

Germany was economically weakened and nationally humiliated by its defeat in the Great War. Where the economies of other nations gradually began to recover in the 1920s, Germany remained locked into political and economic stagnation. Things were made worse by the reparations that Germany was required to pay its former enemies and by the emergence of rampant inflation in German economy.

Although parliamentary democracy had been imposed on Germany following the ending of the monarchy, the Weimar Republic failed to live up to public expectations and hopes. In March 1920 the first attempt by right-wing nationalists to overthrow the government took place, setting a pattern of instability that would continue into the 1930s. An attempt made by Adolf Hitler and the National Socialists to seize power in November 1923 – the famous "Beer Hall Putsch" – failed ignominiously.

Things went seriously wrong in 1929. The German economy was already slowing down early that year. The Wall Street crash of October 1929 marked the beginning of a worldwide slump of unprecedented severity, which proved fatal for the political stability of the Weimar Republic. A chain of events was unleashed that led to the political triumph of Hitler's National Socialist German Workers' Party, widely known as the "Nazis." Adolf Hitler was installed as German chancellor in 1933.

Under Hitler, the German churches would face considerable challenges. National socialism was not in any sense a Christian philosophy. Its origins are still poorly understood; however, it is clear that it reflects long-standing nationalist beliefs concerning Germanic culture, especially the role of a pan-Germanic alliance in dominating Central Europe. Hitler's program demanded control over most aspects of German life, including the German churches. Unlike Stalin, however, Hitler believed that it might be possible to secure the compliance of the churches without the use of force and oppressive measures.

Nazi rule was at first welcomed by many German churchmen, partly because it offered a bulwark against the ominous state atheism sponsored within the Soviet Union, and partly because it seemed to offer a new cultural role for religion. The German Christian movement developed, adopting a positive response to Hitler's program for national reconstruction and unity.

Yet the unity of the German Christians did not last for long. Division arose from September 1933, partly over the so-called "Aryan clause," which demanded that no Jew should hold office in the church. The strongly anti-Jewish rhetoric of the Nazi party divided those who saw supporting Hitler as a temporary and pragmatic accommodation to German political realities from those who wanted to reconstruct Christianity totally.

Theologians Karl Barth and Dietrich Bonhoeffer developed a radical theological critique of any political system that placed anything but God at the center of an individual's or a nation's life. Leaders of the Confessing Church (Bekennende Kirche) – a movement within the German Protestant churches that rejected any compromises with Nazism – met at Barmen in late May 1934 and issued a document often known as the Barmen Declaration. This declared that the church could not adjust its ideas according to "prevailing ideological and political convictions." It had to remain faithful to its Christian roots, as witnessed in the person of Jesus Christ and in the text of the Bible. Yet such protests proved ineffective against the rhetorical and political power of a totalitarian state.

The anti-Jewish attitudes and policies of Adolf Hitler were ultimately expressed in the Holocaust, a program of extermination that played a major role in shaping relations between Christianity and Judaism in the period after World War II. Although others too were judged by the Nazis to be enemies of the state and sent to the gas chambers in World War II, by far the greatest number was that of Jews, who had fallen foul of the institutionalized anti-Semitism of the Third Reich. Hitler had learned from the Armenian genocide that actions committed in a situation of total war did not attract international attention, and he appears to have assumed that his own program of genocide would not attract international condemnation.

The Holocaust had a strong impact on Jewish–Christian relations after World War II, raising difficult questions about Christian complicity in Hitler's wartime policies and projects. It was also an important factor in leading to the creation of the state of Israel in May 1948.

The 1960s: The emergence of a post-Christian Europe

In 1900, five of the world's ten most populous Christian countries were in Western Europe: Britain, Germany, France, Spain, and Italy. Three of the others – Russia, Poland, and Ukraine – lay in Eastern Europe. Europe was the heartland and focus of the Christian faith; in that it was rivaled only by North America. Today the situation has changed radically. In 2005 only one Western European nation featured on the list of most populous Christian countries.

Every Western European nation has become secularized, as indicated by four key indicators.

1   Church attendance has fallen radically. Under 10 percent of the population of Western Europe attends the church regularly.
2   National and regional policy making do not regularly make reference to the concerns of the churches.
3   Schools, hospitals, and social welfare are largely in the hands of the state and are not controlled by the churches.
4   The cultural knowledge of the basic themes of the Christian faith has become more tenuous, especially among young people.

Western Europe is now the most secular area in the world. How did this happen? How did a region that was instrumental in missionary work throughout much of the world from about 1600 to 1900 become a post-Christian society? This question is often asked in the context of the religious renewal and revival that can be seen in most parts of the world. Why is Western Europe the exception? Why did this development take place there and not, say, in the United States?

No satisfactory answers have yet been given. Some sociologists have argued that Protestantism's distinctive desacralization of nature and society – or "disenchantment," in Max Weber's specific use of this concept – encouraged the emergence of the natural sciences, secularism, and atheism. Peter Berger suggested that Protestantism caused "an immense shrinkage in the scope of the sacred in reality." Protestants, he argued, did not see themselves as living in a world that was "ongoingly penetrated by sacred beings and forces." Instead they understood that world to be "polarized between a radically transcendent divinity and a radically 'fallen' humanity" that was devoid of any sacred qualities or connections.

In contrast, Berger argued, Catholicism had contained secularizing forces through its deeply symbolic understanding of the natural world and of humanity's place within it.

Without realizing what it was doing, Protestantism opened the floodgates for the forces that would shape modernity and would ultimately cause Protestantism such grief in its European heartlands.

Although the secularization thesis is now regarded with suspicion, it was widely held during the 1960s. This led many churches to ask deep questions about their future in what they believed would be an increasingly secular world. The most significant attempt to engage this question was the Second Vatican Council, in which Catholicism sought to confront such cultural trends and to forge robust and realistic strategies to meet them. We shall consider this landmark council in what follows.

The Second Vatican Council: Reform and revitalization

The Catholic church was well aware of the radical social and cultural changes that seemed to be sweeping through western culture in the postwar period, especially in Western Europe. There was a clear need for theological reconstruction and reformulation, in order to be able to translate the Catholic faith into terms that connected it with the new cultural situation. Yet Pius XII, who was pope from 1939 until his death in 1959, did not believe that there was any pressing need to engage these issues. There was no mood for reform within the papal establishment.

The death of Pius XII led to the election of a new pope, John XXIII, in October 1958. Elected at the age of 78, John XXIII was expected to be an "interim pope." His was to be a transitional papacy, without any expectation of major changes. Less than three months later, John XXIII took the church's establishment by surprise when he announced that he would be convening an ecumenical council to formulate the church's responses to the realities of the postwar world. The general mood in the Vatican was that there was a need for a few "house-keeping measures" within the church. The announcement of a reforming council was unexpected. The Italian word used to refer to this process of reform and renewal was *aggiornamento* – "updating." In many ways, this would be the watchword of the council. John XXIII spoke frequently of the need to open the windows of the church to let in some fresh air. He expressed the hope that such opening would be the beginning of a new Pentecost for the church.

The council held its deliberations in the Vatican. It began under John XXIII, on October 11, 1962, and closed under Paul VI, on December 8, 1965. The death of John XXIII on June 3, 1963 did not derail it; Paul VI immediately declared his intention to continue his predecessor's project.

What were the achievements of the council? How did the idea of *aggiornamento* work out in practice? The council took place against a backdrop of resurgence of confidence within Catholicism, in response to developments such as the election of a Catholic – John F. Kennedy – as president of the United States. Perhaps this sense of confidence contributed to the council's bold declarations about the role of the church in the world, which urged all Catholics to dialogue with developments they saw around them. Catholicism would not be like American fundamentalism in the 1920s and 1930s. It would not retreat into a ghetto; it would engage with the world. In many ways, this spirit of positive, constructive, and confident engagement remains one of the most striking characteristics of the council.

Figure 4.11   The opening of the second session of the Second Vatican Council, September 29, 1963, with Pope Paul VI (formerly Giovanni Battista Montini). Source: Keystone/Getty Images.

Its decisions, however, must also be given due weight. The council reaffirmed the collegiality of bishops without calling into question the authority or status of the pope; it emphasized their important role in governing and guiding the church. A new accent was placed on the role of the laity, whose members were encouraged to engage with their social and political context. The Catholic church's attitude to other churches became more relaxed and positive: it was an attitude of acknowledging that these other churches were indeed Christian bodies, although they were separate from the Catholic church.

This new generosity toward other Christians was matched by a commitment to positive and respectful engagement with other faith traditions. Of particular importance was the council's recognition that the Catholic church had been complicit in creating prejudicial attitudes toward Jews, particularly by suggesting that they had been responsible for the death of Christ. This was an important gesture of conciliation toward the world's Jews, especially in the aftermath of the Holocaust.

One of the most important decisions of the council was the reforming decree *Sacrosanctum concilium* (literally "holy council," officially translated as *The Council's Constitution*), which was approved on December 4, 1963 by a landslide majority. There were 2,147 votes in favor and 4 against. This reforming decree laid the foundations for liturgical renewal. One of its most important decisions concerned the project of translating the liturgy into the vernacular. This significant development was coupled with a growing willingness to authorize vernacular translations of the Bible.

The radical decisions taken by the council were met with suspicion in more conservative parts of the Catholic world, such as Ireland. Observing this resistance, many concluded that the "spirit of the council' could not be implemented until an older generation of bishops, who were fixed in their ways and locked into older habits of thought and action, had given way to a new generation. Yet there was little doubt that the Second Vatican Council marked a landmark in Catholic life and thought, signaling a new way of engaging the world.

Christianity and the American Civil Rights Movement

The American Civil War led to a number of tensions within the Union, in which the former southern "slave" states developed state and local laws that allowed them to maintain racial segregation along antebellum lines. The Jim Crow laws, enacted between 1876 and 1965, mandated policies of racial segregation similar to those in force in South Africa in the 1950s and 1960s under the name of apartheid (*apartheid* is an Afrikaans word meaning "separateness"). These laws laid the foundation for racial segregation in all public facilities in the southern states of the former Confederacy.

It is widely agreed that, despite the importance of individual activists and campaigners, the key to the success of the Civil Rights Movement in America was the black churches of the southern states. These represented the most significant social and political force to emerge from the former slave communities. Although socially marginalized in the southern states during the period between the two world wars, these churches were the only institutions with the finances, structure, and mass membership needed to bring about a mass mobilization of African Americans with the power to change society.

The strongly religious tone of the rhetoric of the Civil Rights Movement partly reflects the failure of American liberalism to achieve any success in civil rights legislation and policy at the height of its power during the 1930s. In the end, the ideology of political liberalism became subordinated to the religious vision and worldview that characterized large parts of the movement at grassroots level. The struggle for civil rights was widely understood to be a religious struggle, echoing the great themes of the Old Testament narratives about the liberation of Israel from its bondage in Egypt. Mass political meetings of the civil rights campaign often mimicked the structure and tone of church services, partly because they were seen as a natural extension of the religious and social visions, deeply rooted in the history of the black South.

The event that triggered the Civil Rights Movement closest and most familiar to us was the Montgomery Bus Boycott of 1955. In December 1955 a black woman – Rosa Parks (1913–2005) – was arrested under the Jim Crows laws for refusing to give up her seat to a white man, on a public bus in the city of Montgomery, Alabama. Opposition to this arrest and to the discriminatory attitudes toward black people that lay behind it was led by the black Baptist pastor Martin Luther King (1929–1968). The resulting boycott lasted for more than a year and generated national publicity. A United States District Court ruling of 1956 finally ended racial segregation on all Montgomery public buses.

Encouraged by this development, King sought to mobilize opinion to end segregation on buses throughout the South. After a series of meetings early in 1957, King launched the Southern Christian Leadership Conference, specifically with the aim of harnessing the social capital of black churches to challenge existing laws on segregation. It was a controversial move, as many pastors and church leaders – both black and white – believed that the churches should concentrate their attention on the spiritual and pastoral needs of their congregations rather than become engaged in political action.

Yet, despite this tendency to political quietism, the churches became increasingly involved in nonviolent protests. A successful campaign in Birmingham, Alabama, was followed by a massive march on Washington in August 1963. The Kennedy administration, spurred to activity largely by the media coverage of police's overreaction against demonstrators in Birmingham, began to roll back southern legislation, ending much – though not all – of the racial discrimination in the South.

The Civil Rights Movement is notable for bringing about two developments, which marked the re-entry of the churches into the political process in the United States. First, King's program of social action was clearly seen to be based on a theological vision of transformation and renewal rather than on the agenda of a specific political party. King chose to align himself with neither Republicans nor Democrats, but operated outside the political establishment.

King's speech "I Have a Dream" (August 28, 1963), widely hailed as a rhetorical masterpiece, is deeply rooted in the Old Testament's vision of justice and freedom, providing a theological defense for acting for change. Prophetic themes from Isaiah 40 are woven into the fabric of the speech, articulating both hope and vision.

Second, King's success made it clear that churches could become involved in political debates and in direct action without compromising their principles. The civil rights campaign made it religiously acceptable for churches and individual Christian leaders to become politically engaged.

Faith renewed: John Paul II and the collapse of the Soviet Union

The situation in Europe after World War II was complex and posed particular challenges for the Catholic church. The establishment of the Soviet bloc meant that many Catholic parts of Eastern Europe unexpectedly found themselves under communist control and severe restrictions were placed on the activities of churches and religious believers. In the West, the radical questioning of traditional structures of authority and beliefs in the 1960s created a cultural context that challenged many Catholic ideas.

The Second Vatican Council began to address some of the issues raised for Catholicism in the West, although their implementation provoked some impatience, particularly in the area of artificial contraception. Yet the influence of the Soviet Union and its Eastern European satellite states arguably caused a much greater problem. There seemed little that the papacy could do to engage the situation. Influence was seen as resting on pragmatic factors – such as military force. On being criticized by Pope Pius XII, the Soviet leader Josef Stalin dismissed this intervention as inconsequential. "How many divisions has the Pope?"

Pope Paul VI died in August 1978. Like his predecessor, John XXIII, Paul VI was an Italian pope who had worked hard to improve relations with other Christian churches and to open the windows of the church to the world. It was unclear who his successor would be. Some favored Cardinal Giuseppe Siri (1906–1989), the conservative archbishop of Genoa, whose criticisms of the Second Vatican Council suggested that he would lead the church in a more conservative direction. In the event, the papal conclave elected the Italian Albino Luciani (1912–1978), who took the name "John Paul I." It soon became clear that he would be a reforming pope, concerned to implement the decisions of the Second Vatican Council.

John Paul I died suddenly on the thirty-third day of his reign – September 29, 1978. His unexpected death prompted speculation that he had been assassinated, although this is not regarded as persuasive by historians. A papal conclave was convened once more. The cardinals appear to have initially divided along traditionalist and reformist lines, adepts of tradition favoring Giuseppe Siri and adepts of reform the archbishop of Florence, Giovanni Benelli (1921–1982). Although Benelli came close to being elected, it was clear that neither of the leading contenders commanded sufficient support to be elected. A compromise candidate was therefore sought.

To the surprise of the outside world, the conclave elected Karol Józef Wojtyła (1920–2005), the Polish Archbishop of Kraków. Wojtyła announced that he would be known as "John Paul II," which was interpreted both as a tribute to his predecessor and as an indication that he would continue his reforming trajectory. John Paul II was only 58 at the time of his election, which made him one of the youngest popes in recent history.

Although the appointment created huge interest throughout the world, its impact was greatest in Wojtyła's native land. Poland lay within the Soviet bloc at the time of his election and was one of the most devoutly Catholic countries in Europe. The communist authorities had proved unable to suppress Catholicism and had instead concentrated their efforts on limiting its influence. The election of a Polish pope – the first non-Italian pope for nearly 500 years – caused a surge of national pride in Poland and gave a new significance to the nation's Catholic identity.

During a pastoral visit to Poland in June 1979 – the first of nine such visits to his homeland – John Paul II was overwhelmed by the enthusiastic crowds. As the national mood changed, partly in response to Catholic resurgence, resistance against the communist authorities grew. In a landmark development, the trade union Solidarity was established in August 1980, at the Lenin Shipyard at Gdańsk, under the leadership of Lech Wałęsa (born 1943). The imposition of martial law in December 1981 failed to repress the movement, even though its regional leaders were imprisoned.

The events in Poland served as a trigger for comparable developments throughout the Soviet bloc. Central control began to weaken, especially during the period when Mikhail Sergeyevich Gorbachev (born 1931) served as general secretary of the Communist Party of the Soviet Union. On being elected as general secretary in 1985, Gorbachev enacted a policy of *perestroika* (Russian "restructuring") and *glasnost* (Russian "openness"). Though intended to liberate the economy of the Soviet Union from an excessive bureaucracy, this move ended up by significantly weakening the grip of the Communist Party over both the Soviet Union and its allies.

It became increasingly clear that religion was no longer being repressed. For example, in February 1988 a Red Army choir performed "Ave Maria" before John Paul II at the Vatican. In the same year Mikhail Gorbachev both permitted and promoted the celebration of a millennium of Christian faith in Russia and the Ukraine. Three years later the Soviet Union ceased to exist. It was formally dissolved on December 25, 1991, its 15 component republics becoming independent sovereign states. Within a decade, Orthodoxy had re-established itself as a major spiritual and political force within the new Russian Federation.

Mikhail Gorbachev remarked that the fall of the Iron Curtain would have been impossible without John Paul II. This is correct, provided it is not understood to imply that the pope was the sole cause of the collapse. Many factors were involved, and many would argue that the resurgence of religion – catalyzed to no small extent by this charismatic pope – was one of the factors that destabilized the eastern bloc. John Paul II himself took a different view, suggesting that communism collapsed on account of its own inner contradictions. "It would be simplistic to say that Divine Providence caused the fall of Communism. In a certain sense Communism as a system fell by itself."

The reign of John Paul II saw major challenges developing for Catholicism, including a decline in priesthood and church attendance in western nations, the growing numerical strength of evangelicals and Pentecostals in Latin America, Asia, and Africa, and debates over the decentralization of power to local parishes. Although John Paul II was initially regarded by some as a reformist, his reign was chiefly notable for its reassertion of traditional papal attitudes and for a distinct cooling of relations between Catholics and other churches. Yet many would argue that the most significant event of his reign was the collapse of the Soviet Union and the emergence of a new order in Eastern Europe.

Challenging the church's establishment: Feminism and liberation theology

The rapid social changes following World War II led to challenges to many traditional Christian beliefs and practices. One of the most important is the emergence of "liberationist" movements, which sought to free groups from the domination of cultural or political power groups. In this section we shall note two such groups: feminism, originally known as "women's liberation," and Latin American liberation theology.

In the West, one of the most significant critiques of monotheistic religions emerged from the growing feminist movements, which argued that the fundamentally male notions of God embedded within Judaism, Christianity, and Islam were linked with their original patriarchal cultures. These notions were no longer defensible in cultures in which women asserted their own identity and authority.

Though there are clear historical precedents – such as the women's suffrage movement, which campaigned for the right to vote in the early twentieth century – feminism emerged during the late 1960s. Some feminists focused their attention on specific political or social issues, but others argued for the need to undermine sexual domination as the pervasive ideology of western culture, showing that this ideology lay behind many of its political structures and cultural beliefs or practices.

More recently the movement has become increasingly heterogeneous, partly as a result of the fact that women within different cultures and ethnic groupings accepted a diversity of approaches. Thus the writings of black women in North America are increasingly coming to be referred to as "black womanism," a label that recognizes that the notion of "women's experience" does not refer to a universal but to a value shaped by gender and class.

The impact of feminism on Christianity has been primarily in the West and has led to two significant developments. First, the movement campaigned for a greater representation of women within the churches, especially among the clergy. This campaign complemented the activities of others, who argued for the ordination of women on biblical grounds, holding that the New Testament questioned all social, gender, and power relationships on the basis of the new order of the gospel. Some denominations had begun to ordain women before World War II. The Salvation Army, for example, had 41 women officers and 49 men officers in 1878. Denominations that emphasized the importance of tradition (Catholicism and Orthodoxy) and churches that interpreted the New Testament as prohibiting women from exercising leadership have resisted such developments.

Second, the movement argued that traditional Christian language showed a bias toward male role models and language. A number of post-Christian feminists, including Mary Daly in her *Beyond God the Father* (1973) and Daphne Hampson in *Theology and Feminism* (1990), argued that Christianity, with its male symbols for God, its male savior figure, and its long history of male leaders and thinkers, is biased against women, and therefore incapable of being salvaged. Women, they urged, should leave its oppressive environment. Others, such as Carol Christ in *Laughter of Aphrodite* (1987) and Naomi Ruth Goldenberg in *Changing of the Gods* (1979), argue that women may find religious emancipation by recovering the ancient goddess religions (or by inventing new ones), and by abandoning traditional Christianity altogether.

Other feminists have reacted against such curt dismissals of Christianity and argued for a more nuanced and informed reading of the Christian tradition. Feminist writers have stressed how women have been active in the shaping and development of the Christian tradition from the New Testament on and have exercised significant leadership roles throughout Christian history. Indeed many feminist writers have shown the need to reappraise the Christian past, giving honor and recognition to an army of faithful women whose practice, defense, and proclamation of their faith has hitherto passed unnoticed by a large part of the Christian church and its (mainly male) historians.

The maleness of Christ has been a topic of particular discussion by feminist writers, who have noted how this feature has sometimes been used as a theological foundation for the belief that only the male human may adequately image God, or that only males provide appropriate role models or analogies for God. In response, feminist writers have argued that the maleness of Christ is a contingent aspect of his identity, on the same level as his being Jewish. It is a contingent element of his historical reality, not an essential aspect of his identity. Thus it cannot be allowed to become the basis of the domination of females by males, whether in the church or in society, any more than it legitimates the domination of Gentiles by Jews, or of plumbers by carpenters.

The rise of liberation theology in Latin America during the 1960s is also of importance. One of the most dramatic developments to take place globally in the aftermath of World War II was the spread of Marxism. Although imposed by force in many parts of Eastern Europe and Central Asia, its ideas proved inspirational for many groups in Latin America, Africa, and Asia – groups of people who were disillusioned with the existing social order and wanted to change it radically. Marxism offered a worldview that promised to transform society – and it was a worldview without God. It seemed to provide a way of throwing off colonialist and imperialist shackles and of finding liberation.

In Latin America Marxism quickly gained the initiative, Cuba functioning as a revolutionary template and base from 1965: Fidel Castro had overthrown the US-backed Cuban President Fulgencio Batista (1901–1973) in a violent revolution of 1959 and had declared Cuba a communist state in 1961. In Brazil, Marxism adapted to the local situation, as theorists such as Caio Prado (1907–1990) enabled it to present its socioeconomic vision as the remedy for the nation's ills. Recognizing the importance of dealing with the social issues that this vision reflected, some prominent Catholics in the region developed a "liberation theology" that sought to emphasize the transformative social vision of the gospel.

Liberation theology began to emerge in 1968, when the Catholic bishops of Latin America gathered for a congress at Medellín, Colombia. This meeting – often known as CELAM II, an acronym for Consejo Episcopal Latinoamericano (Latin American Episcopal Council) – sent shock waves throughout the region by acknowledging that the church had often sided with oppressive governments in the region and by declaring that in future it would be on the side of the poor.

This theme was picked up and developed by liberation theology. The church is oriented toward the poor and oppressed – the authentic source for understanding Christian truth and practice. In the Latin American situation, the church is on the side of the poor. The fact that God is on the side of the poor leads to a further insight: the poor occupy a position of special importance in the interpretation of the Christian faith. All Christian theology and mission must begin with the view from below – that is, with the sufferings and distress of the poor.

Liberation theologians defended their use of Marxist ideas on two grounds. First, Marxism is seen as a "tool of social analysis," which allows insights to be gained concerning the present state of Latin American society and the means by which the appalling situation of the poor may be remedied. Second, it provides a political program by which the present – unjust – social system may be dismantled and a more equitable society created. Liberation theology is thus critical of capitalism and affirmative of socialism. God's preference for and commitment to the poor is a fundamental aspect of the gospel, not some bolt-on option arising from the Latin American situation or based purely on Marxist political theory.

Liberation theology was a significant response to the revolutionary fervor of many parts of Latin America in the 1960s and the two decades that followed. Since then its appeal has dwindled, partly because it focused on distant goals and partly on account of the rise of another religious option for the poor of Latin America: Pentecostalism (which we shall discuss on pp. 212--213). Yet the ideals of liberation theology live on. The election of the Argentinian Jorge Mario Bergoglio as pope in 2013 is seen by some observers as marking a renewed papal interest in the poor on the one hand and in an informed critique of capitalism on the other.

Christianity beyond the West: The globalization of faith

The great European missionary ventures of the early modern period, initially undertaken by the Catholic church and subsequently by Protestants, vastly extended the geographical range of the Christian faith. In quantitative–numerical terms, the center of Christianity as a whole shifted decisively away from the West between 1900 and 2000. Christianity is now predominantly a religion of the global South. Population growth in this area, when set alongside the evangelistic and missionary successes of the twentieth century, mean that an increasing proportion of an increasingly large population is now Christian. For example: in 1900 the population of Africa was 10 million people, of which 9 percent were Christian; in 2005, the population was more than 400 million, of which 46 percent are Christian.

The case of Korea is particularly important. Korea is an Asian nation that, in the course of a single century, has become a majority Christian nation. At the beginning of the twentieth century, the only predominantly Christian nation in Asia was the Philippines – a strongly Catholic country with a small Protestant minority. Although Catholicism was established in Korea by the 1880s, its adepts formed a very small community. The serious growth of Christianity in Korea is probably to be traced back to two American Protestant missionaries: the Methodist Henry Appenzeller (1858–1902) and the Presbyterian Horace Underwood (1859–1916). Both actively promoted education as a means of embedding Christianity in Korean society. Some form of Pentecostal revival appears to have developed around 1907 and to have been significant in bringing about conversions among the native population.

Korea underwent partition into a communist north and a democratic south following the Korean War, which broke out on June 25, 1950. The heavy involvement of missionary agencies in the relief programs that followed the ending of the war created a powerful stimulus to the development of Christianity, which was catalyzed still further by the Korean churches' programs of social action during the 1960s.

Today Korea sends out Christian missionaries to nations throughout Asia, and increasingly to the large Korean diasporas of major western cities – from Sydney to Los Angeles, from Melbourne to New York. These are now closely linked with a network of churches, which serve more and more as a focal point for community action, mutual support, and spiritual nourishment. In 1979 Korean churches sent 93 missionaries overseas. In 1990 that number had increased to 1,645; in 2000, to 8,103.

Christianity is also becoming an increasingly significant presence in China, despite the communist revolution of 1949. Wishing to avoid any suggestion that Christianity was a tool of western imperialism or an unwelcome western cultural import, Y. T. Wu (1893–1979), a Chinese Christian leader, initiated the Three Self Patriotic Movement. This movement advocated the "Three Self" strategy of "self-governance, self-support, and self-propagation" as a means of eliminating foreign influences from the Chinese churches and of reassuring the new communist government that the churches would be committed to the newly established People's Republic of China.

Since 1990 Christianity has grown substantially in all its forms within China. The reasons for this development are not fully understood. The Chinese government appears to have taken a pragmatic attitude toward this development, especially in working to secure a better relationship with the Vatican. Although some are suggesting that China may become the nation with the greatest number of Christians in the next few decades, it is clearly unwise to speculate about such a poorly understood phenomenon.

In Africa Christianity has adapted in the light of indigenous values and customs. With the departure of colonial powers in the decades following World War II, leadership within the African churches gradually devolved from Europeans to Africans, resulting in a growing adaptation of the colonial churches to local customs and traditions. Yet many indigenous churches now began to emerge without any historical connection with European denominations. These African initiated churches (AICs) are strongest and most numerous in Southern Africa, West Africa, the Congo Basin, and central Kenya. Three major categories of AICs can be identified:

1   *Ethiopian and African churches* AICs that do not claim to be prophetic or to have special manifestations of the Holy Spirit have been referred to as "Ethiopian" or "Ethiopian-type" churches in Southern Africa and "African" churches in Nigeria. These churches are generally earlier in origin than the other two types and arose primarily as a political and administrative reaction to European mission-founded churches. For this reason Ethiopian or African churches are very similar to the historical Protestant churches from which they emerged. For example, they usually practice infant baptism, read set liturgies, wear European clerical vestments (often black), and use forms of worship that are less enthusiastic or emotional than other AICs.

2   *Prophet-healing and spiritual churches* These churches tend to have their historical and theological roots in the Pentecostal movement, emphasizing the working of the power of the spirit in the church. This is the largest grouping of AICs, and it includes a wide variety of some of the biggest churches in Africa. It includes the Kimbanguist movement and the African Apostolic Church in Central Africa, the Aladura and Harrist churches in West Africa, and the Zion Christian Church and the Amanazaretha in Southern Africa.

3   *New Pentecostal churches* This group of churches of more recent origin (most of them are founded after 1980) also emphasize the power and the gifts of the Holy Spirit. They are today probably the fastest growing expression of Christianity in Africa and have exploded on the African religious scene since about 1975 to such an extent that they are challenging many previously accepted assumptions about the character of African Protestantism. Examples of these include the Deeper Life Church in Nigeria, the Zimbabwe Assemblies of God African, and Grace Bible Church in South Africa.

Conclusion

This brief overview of Christian history can only offer the most basic survey of its themes, which need to be considered in much greater detail. Happily, there are many useful volumes available, if you wish to explore this field further. Some suitable starting points are noted in the Further Reading section, which will help you take things further.

From this historical analysis it will be clear that Christianity has a complex history, which has made it develop in quite distinct ways in different parts of the world and appear in quite different forms in the same geographical regions. In the next chapter we shall explore the different forms of Christianity encountered today.

5

Denominations
Contemporary Forms of Christianity

In the previous chapter we explored the development of Christianity, noting such landmarks as the Great Schism of 1054 between East and West (pp. 138–139), the emergence of Protestantism in the sixteenth century (pp. 151–154), the birth of the Pentecostal movement in the twentieth century (pp. 212–213), and the Second Vatican Council (pp. 189–191). This complex history means that contemporary Christianity is variegated, characterized by quite different understandings of church government, styles of worship, and cultural roots. In what follows we shall explore some of the major forms of Christianity in today's world.

The term "denomination" is widely used to refer to families of Christian churches. Although this practice is widespread, especially in the media, it is not universally accepted. The term was originally used to designate the various Protestant groups that emerged as a result of the sixteenth-century Reformation (pp. 151–158), and it came to mean something like "self-governing ecclesial body" – such as Lutheranism or Methodism. Neither Catholicism nor Orthodoxy considers itself to be a denomination; both regard themselves as churches that trace their origins back to the apostolic era. Yet the term "denomination" has come to be so widely used to refer to groups of Christian churches that it will be used in this chapter, despite these concerns.

Catholicism

Catholicism is by far the world's largest Christian church and is widely expected to be the most successful one in the next generation. Although some refer to it as "Roman Catholicism" in order to emphasize the central role of Rome in its past history and present government, there is an increasing trend to use the simpler term "Catholicism" instead (note the use of the initial capital letter). This practice will be followed in this work. Catholicism is presently

Christianity: An Introduction, Third Edition. Alister E. McGrath.
© 2015 John Wiley & Sons, Ltd. Published 2015 by John Wiley & Sons, Ltd.

the largest religious group in the United States, where it has four times the membership of its nearest rival, southern Baptist. Recent statistics suggest a modest growth in its membership in the United States over the last few years. Catholics are by far the largest and most widely distributed Christian group in the world, and Catholicism continues to expand. It can expect to face problems everywhere; nevertheless, its past history suggests that it will be able to face them and to make the necessary adjustments.

Yet the future of Catholicism was once seen to be in doubt. To appreciate this point, we need to go back two centuries and consider the situation of the Catholic church in Western Europe following the French Revolution of 1789 (pp. 168–169). As the nineteenth century cautiously opened, there was a general feeling that the future of Roman Catholicism was very much in doubt. The French Revolution had virtually wiped out the influence – and even the presence – of the church in France. Revolution was to be exported, both through the spread of its leading ideas and through the activities of French revolutionary troops, which invaded parts of until then Catholic Europe. Things looked grim. The Napoleonic era was widely seen as presaging the end of any role for Catholicism in Europe. Yet, with the defeat of Napoleon and the reshaping of Europe at the Congress of Vienna (1815), things began to stabilize.

Although missions had established a significant Catholic presence in regions such as South America, Japan, and India (pp. 149–150), Catholicism was still to a great extent a European religion (pp. 173–174). This situation began to change as Catholicism began to be established in the Americas, Asia, and Africa through the expansion of European economic and political influence. In the case of the United States, the expansion of Catholicism took place mainly during the nineteenth century, primarily through emigration from Catholic nations of Europe, such as Ireland and Italy. The inauguration of John Fitzgerald Kennedy as the first Catholic president of the United States in 1960 was seen by many observers as demonstrating that Catholicism had become part of the social fabric of the nation.

In reflecting on the present state and form of Catholicism, it is important to bear in mind the achievements of the Second Vatican Council (1962–1965), especially the reforming and renewing agenda that it imposed during a period of rapid social change in the West (pp. 189–191). The 1960s are now widely regarded as the high-water mark of a period of secular optimism in western culture. The question of the relevance of Christianity within such a context came to be of considerable importance. Sensitive to a whole range of issues, John XXIII (pope from 1958 to 1963) summoned the Second Vatican Council in order to deal with "updating" the agenda of the church (pp. 189–191). The council began its meetings in October 1962. In four sessions spread over the fall of each year during the period 1962–1965, more than 2,450 bishops from all over the world met at Rome to discuss the future direction of the Catholic church.

The council helped define the place of the Christian faith and of the Catholic church in the modern world; it focused particularly on the nature of the church itself, the relation between bishops and pope, the relation between Christians and non-Christians, and the relation between Catholics and other Christians. The importance of evangelism was affirmed in a context of respecting the identities and integrities of non-Christians.

A concern for social justice has propelled the Roman Catholic church to the forefront of the global struggle for human rights – as can be seen in recent decades from the role of the church in the overthrow of President Marcos of the Philippines, in the liberation of East Timor from a particularly vicious annexation of its territory by Indonesia, and in the libertarian struggle in South America under military dictatorships, which claimed the lives of several notable bishops.

After the Second Vatican Council, the Catholic church came to see itself more as a community of believers than as a divinely ordained and hierarchically ordered society. The laity was given an increasingly important place in the life of the church. The council also followed the example of Leo XIII in stressing the social aspects of the Christian faith, including its implications for human rights, race relations, and social justice. Within the church, the idea of "collegiality" took on greater importance. This expresses the notion that the church is itself a community of member churches, with the authority dispersed to some extent among its bishops rather than concentrated in the pope.

The Second Vatican Council is a landmark in the history of Catholicism. It remains to be seen how it will influence the development of Christianity into the next millennium. While many Catholics welcomed the new atmosphere that it introduced, others felt that it had betrayed many central concerns of traditional Catholic teaching and practice. Traces of this tension remain in the modern Catholic church. It is, however, a creative tension, and it can be expected to lead to a healthy process of self-examination in the future.

Other tensions have subsequently emerged as significant within Catholicism. Increasingly, Christianity is becoming a religion of the developing world, with its center of gravity moving – at least numerically – away from the western world and toward the emerging nations of Africa and Asia. Much the same pattern is reflected in other Christian churches. Yet there are some specific issues relating to Roman Catholicism, including a startling decline in the number of men offering themselves for the priesthood. This is especially evident in the Irish Republic, until recently a Catholic bastion in Western Europe. Allegations of child abuse have seriously eroded the status of the priesthood. A serious shortage of priests now confronts the Irish church. Similar patterns can be discerned throughout the western world. In the developing world, however, things are much more encouraging.

This means that the agenda of the developing world is increasingly coming to dominate Catholicism, as the traditional agenda of the West becomes less important. The election of the Argentinian Jorge Mario Bergoglio (born 1936) as pope in 2013 was widely seen as highlighting the importance of the global South in contemporary Catholicism. (Bergoglio took the papal name "Francis.") This development is interpreted by some observers as showing that Catholicism has moved decisively from seeing itself as a western faith in the last two centuries. It is widely expected that the Catholic church will continue to be the major player in global Christianity in the next generation.

The distinctive ethos of Catholicism is difficult to summarize, on account of the complexity of the movement. However, the following points are important:

1 The Catholic church has traditionally had a strongly hierarchical understanding of church government, focusing on the pope, cardinals, and bishops. The pope has considerable influence over the appointment of bishops throughout the Catholic world. The College of Cardinals meets in secret sessions after the death of a pope, in order to elect his successor. A cardinal is a priest or bishop nominated by the pope and entrusted with special administrative responsibilities.

2   Partly on account of the importance of the pope, the city of Rome has a particularly significant place in the Catholic ethos. The phrase "Roman Catholic," sometimes still used by Protestants to refer to this church, reflects the importance of Rome as its epicenter. The Vatican City is widely regarded as the spiritual and administrative heart of Catholicism and has served as the venue for the two most recent councils: Vatican I (1869–1870) and Vatican II (1962–1965). Many Catholics make a pilgrimage to Rome, on account of its strong historical associations with early Christianity (Apostles Paul and Peter are widely believed to have been martyred and buried in the city).

3   The church is generally seen as a visible divine institution, whose structures are grounded in divine reality. Although this view of the church was modified slightly by Vatican II, it remains of importance for modern Catholicism. Particular importance is attached to the role of the teaching office of the church (usually referred to as the *magisterium*). The Council of Trent affirmed that no one was free to interpret Scripture "contrary to the sense in which Holy Mother Church, who is to judge the true sense and interpretation of the Holy Scriptures, has held and does hold." Lying behind this is a strongly corporate conception of the Christian life and of authority within the church, contrasting sharply with the individualism that has become characteristic of modern western culture during the twentieth century.

4   The catholic clergy are of major local importance in everyday Catholic life. Members of the Catholic clergy are not permitted to marry. This is one of the most noticeable practical differences between Catholicism and other forms of Christianity. Orthodoxy and Protestantism permit their priests (or ministers) to marry. Catholic priests are exclusively male. Although women are permitted to undertake some pastoral and liturgical responsibilities (the precise details of which vary from place to place), the Catholic church currently remains committed to an exclusively male priesthood.

5   Catholicism is strongly liturgical. In other words, the forms of worship used by the church are fixed and laid down centrally, reflecting the conviction that the way in which the church prays and worships is inextricably linked to what the church believes (a point sometimes made using the Latin dictum *lex orandi, lex credendi*, "the law of praying is the law of believing"). The liturgy is seen as a public statement of the beliefs and values of the church and as a means by which continuity with the apostolic tradition is maintained. Until the Second Vatican Council, the language of the liturgy was Latin; the use of native languages is now permitted, although considerable care is taken to ensure that vernacular translations accurately reflect the sense of the original Latin versions of the liturgy.

6   Catholicism is also strongly sacramental, placing considerable emphasis on the "sacramental economy" (that is, the view that the benefits of Christ, which result from his death and resurrection, are communicated to the church through the sacraments). The Catholic church recognizes seven sacraments (whereas Protestants recognize only two). In terms of the regular liturgical life of the church, the most important sacrament is the mass or the eucharist, which is understood to make present the body and blood of Christ.

7   The monastic life continues to be of importance to shaping and articulating the Catholic ethos. Although there has been a decline in the traditional religious orders, they

nevertheless continue to play a major role, such as acting as retreat centers for the laity. Growing popular interest in Ignatian spirituality is of particular interest in this respect. The role of the religious orders in establishing and maintaining educational centers at every level should also be noted.

8 Catholicism places an emphasis on the role of the saints in general and of the Virgin Mary in particular. The saints and Mary are understood to act as intercessors for both the living and the dead. The doctrine of the immaculate conception of Mary states that Mary was conceived without her sharing in the common human condition of original sin; thus the doctrine provides a theological formalization for the high place Mary holds in Catholic life and devotion. Nevertheless, Catholic writers are careful to draw attention to the distinction between the *veneration* due to Mary (which is honorific) and the *worship* due to God and to Jesus Christ as the Son of God.

Eastern Orthodoxy

Whether in its Greek or Russian forms, eastern Orthodoxy – sometimes referred to simply as "Orthodoxy" (and note the initial capital letter) – represents a form of Christianity that retains a strong degree of continuity with the church of the eastern Mediterranean (pp. 169–170) and traces its liturgy and doctrines directly back to the early church. Orthodoxy is numerically strongest in Eastern Europe, particularly in Russia and Greece, where it has had a major influence in shaping a sense of national identity. However, it has also established a major presence in North America and Australia through emigration. The Australian city of Melbourne, for example, is home to one of the largest Greek Orthodox communities in the world.

Any attempt to describe the distinctive ethos of Orthodoxy would include the following elements:

1 A very strong sense of historical continuity with the early church. Orthodoxy is thus strongly oriented toward the idea of *paradōsis* ("tradition"), particularly the writings of the Greek fathers. Writers such as Gregory of Nyssa, Maximus the Confessor, and the writer who adopted the pseudonym Dionysius the Areopagite are of particular importance in this respect. Tradition is seen as a living entity, which remains essentially unchanged while being capable of meeting the new challenges of each succeeding age. This is reflected in the fixed liturgical forms used within Orthodoxy.

2 Orthodoxy recognizes only seven ecumenical councils and does not accept any council after the Second Council of Nicaea (787) as having binding authority. Although local councils meet to deal with various matters, they are not understood to have the same authority as these earlier councils.

3 Orthodoxy has been very resistant to the ideas of authority that emerged within western Catholicism, particularly the centralization of ecclesiastical authority in the person of the pope. In the twentieth century increasing attention has also been paid by western theologians to the notion of "catholicity" that has been dominant in the Orthodox

churches. This notion is often expressed using the Russian word "sobornost," which has no exact equivalent in other languages and has been assimilated as such in American English (Merriam Webster defines it as a sense of spiritual–religious unity related to the notion of catholicity as interpreted in the ecumenical councils of the eastern Orthodox church). While the term denotes the general concept of "universality," it also expresses the unity of believers within the fellowship of the church. This idea, which is developed most fully in the writings of Aleksei Khomyakov (1804–1860) and Sergei Bulgakov (1871–1944), attempts to do justice to both the distinctiveness of the individual members of the church and the overall harmony of its corporate life. Thus understood, sobornost is linked with the notion of "conciliarity" (the Russian word *sobor* means "council" or "assembly"), in which the life of the church is governed in such a way that authority is dispersed among all the faithful rather than centralized and concentrated in any single quasi-papal figure.

4   Theologically distinctive ideas include an insistence that the Holy Spirit proceeds from the Father alone (rather than from the Father and the Son, as in western churches: see pp. 74, 139) and the understanding of salvation as deification. This is often summarized in the theological motto "God became human, in order that humans might become God." This theological refrain may be discerned as underlying many soteriological reflections in eastern Christianity, both during the patristic period and in the modern Greek and Russian Orthodox theological traditions. As the motto suggests, there is an especially strong link between the doctrine of the incarnation and this understanding of salvation. For Athanasius, salvation consists in the participation of humans in the being of God. The divine Logos is imparted to humanity through the incarnation. On the basis of his belief in the existence of a universal human nature, Athanasius concluded that the Logos did not merely assume the specific human existence of Jesus Christ, but human nature in general. As a consequence, all human beings are able to share in the deification that results from the incarnation. Human nature was created with the object of sharing in the being of God; through the descent of the Logos, this capacity is finally realized.

5   The use of icons – that is, pictures of Jesus Christ, Mary, and other religious figures – is of particular importance in Orthodoxy (pp. 262–263). The strong emphasis on the incarnation of the Son of God is understood to have consequences for prayer and spirituality. Icons are "windows of perception" through which the believer may catch a glimpse of the divine reality.

6   Monasteries continue to play a critically important role in the articulation and defense of the Orthodox ethos. Perhaps the most important monastic center remains Mount Athos, a peninsula stretching into the Aegean Sea. Most bishops are drawn from monasteries.

7   Orthodox clergymen, unlike their Catholic counterparts, are permitted to marry, provided they do so before ordination. Bishops, however, are generally unmarried, on account of their predominantly monastic backgrounds. Orthodoxy insists that only males can be ordained and rejects the possibility of female priests, largely for the sake of continuity with tradition and without offering any specific arguments on this matter.

Protestantism

The term "Protestantism" is widely used to refer to those churches which trace their historical origins back to the European Reformation of the sixteenth century (pp. 151–154). The term is potentially misleading, in that most Protestant churches stress their historical and theological continuity with the early church. It must be insisted that the term "Protestant" is not in tension with the idea of being "catholic." The orthographical distinction between "catholic" and "Catholic" is of critical importance. To be "Catholic" is to be "catholic" *in a particular way*, which Protestants reject. Anglican and Lutheran writers, for example, place special emphasis on their continuity with the life and thought of the early church and affirm their "catholic" credentials. Similarly, in 1536 John Calvin, the reformer of the city of Geneva, vigorously defended the Reformation against the charge that it had no place for the patristic heritage. Here we shall follow the general convention of using the term "Protestant" to refer to those churches whose historical origins are to be traced back to the divisions that opened up in the sixteenth century.

Protestant churches have had particularly close links with the state in a number of areas of Europe. Lutheranism, for example, has had close links with the state in Scandinavia, just as various forms of Presbyterianism have been influential in Scotland and in the Netherlands or Anglicanism in England. Partly on account of these links, and more generally through their continuity with the mainline Reformation, these churches offer baptism to infants who are too young to confess the Christian faith. This serves to distinguish them from Baptists, who hold that baptism should be administered only to those who are already believing Christians (pp. 207–209).

Evangelicalism (pp. 213–214) is now a major influence within most mainline Protestant denominations in the English-speaking West, although until relatively recently its influence has been significantly smaller in continental Europe. A number of independent churches have now sprung up with a distinctively evangelical ethos, especially in South America and Southern Africa.

The charismatic movement (pp. 212–213) has also been of significance in the life of many mainline Protestant churches, and its influence has also been felt in Catholicism. A number of specifically charismatic denominations (such as the Assemblies of God) are now of growing importance in global Protestantism. In what follows we shall focus on five major Protestant denominations; it must be appreciated that the rapid growth of evangelicalism and of the charismatic movement means that numerical growth within Protestantism is now increasingly likely to happen outside the mainline denominations.

All Protestant denominations permit their ministers to marry. In recent years, most Protestant denominations – but not, it must be stressed, all of them – have permitted women to be ordained to full-time ministry within the church. Other means by which Protestants can be distinguished from Catholics include the following:

1   The authority of the pope is rejected. While some Protestants treat the pope with personal respect, he is not regarded by any of them as carrying any moral or doctrinal weight.

2   Protestantism recognizes only two sacraments (pp. 112–117) and administers communion
    in both kinds (pp. 156–157). In other words, the laity is permitted to receive both bread
    and wine at communion. However, it should be noted that Methodism has traditionally
    insisted that unfermented grape juice, rather than wine, should be used at communion.

3   A cluster of characteristic Catholic beliefs are rejected or treated as strictly optional,
    individual, and private beliefs rather than as the official teaching of the denomination.
    The cluster includes the idea of purgatory, the intercession of the saints, and any form
    of devotion to the Virgin Mary.

4   Until the Second Vatican Council, it was required that the liturgy of the Catholic church
    be read in Latin. This contrasted with the views of the reformers, who argued that all
    forms of public worship – including preaching and the reading of the Bible – had to be
    in a language that common people could understand.

Readers interested in following up on some of these historical and theological points are
recommended to read works that deal with the history and theology of the Reformation,
which will provide considerably more detailed explanations of these points, as well as
expanding on them.

Now we shall briefly comment on several mainline Protestant denominations, before
moving on to consider two important movements – Pentecostalism and evangelicalism –
which are best seen as distinct from mainline Protestantism despite their connections
with it.

Anglicanism

"Anglicanism" is the term usually employed to denote the distinctive features of the *ecclesia
Anglicana* – the national Church of England, as it emerged from the sixteenth-century
Reformation (pp. 156–157). The worldwide expansion of England's influence – initially
through the annexation of Ireland and Scotland and subsequently through the colonization
of North America in the seventeenth century, of the Indian subcontinent in the late eighteenth century, and of sub-Saharan Africa in the nineteenth – brought with it a significant
enlargement of the sphere of influence of Anglicanism. The parody of Anglicanism as "the
British empire at prayer" contains at least an element of truth: Anglicanism has exercised
relatively little influence outside those realms that were once subject to British presence
or rule.

Here are is a summary of the main features of Anglicanism:

1   Anglicanism is an episcopal church, which sees the episcopacy as a means of demon-
    strating historical continuity with the early church. This is of particular importance to
    the more catholic sections of Anglicanism.

2   Anglicanism recognizes the historical and spiritual importance of the English city of
    Canterbury. In 597 Augustine of Canterbury was sent to England by Pope Gregory to
    evangelize the English, and he made this city the base of his operations. The arch-
    bishop of Canterbury is seen as the spiritual head of the Anglican church, although
    he lacks the powers invested in a pope. All the bishops of Anglican churches are

invited to Canterbury every 10 years for the Lambeth Conference, which aims to review the directions taken by Anglicanism in the last decade and to plan for the future.

3   Anglicanism is defined and distinguished theologically by the Thirty-Nine Articles (1563) that date from the reign of Elizabeth I. Although their content is not regarded by Anglicans as binding, many consider them to lay out the basic contours of an Anglican theological ethos.

4   Anglicanism is a strongly liturgical church; originally it found one of its central foci to be the Book of Common Prayer (1662), which embodied the "spirit of Anglicanism" in a fixed liturgical form. Anglican churches throughout the world had this in common, along with a common ecclesiastical structure. Yet the process of liturgical revision, which acquired major importance in the 1970s, resulted in the adoption of different liturgical forms by Anglican churches in England, Canada, the United States, and Australia, which weakened the theological convergence of the movement.

5   The growing trend toward decentralization, linked with an increasing concern on the part of nations such as Australia and Canada to shake off their "colonial" image, has led to a new interest in developing distinctively national or ethnic approaches to Anglican identity. In its traditional forms, Anglicanism has been perceived as too "English" or "colonial" to maintain its credibility in the postcolonial era. As a result, Anglicanism has become increasingly diverse, reflecting local concerns and resources. This trend gives every indication of continuing in the years ahead.

6   Anglicanism is predominantly an English-language church, although there are small Anglican presences outside anglophone contexts (for instance in francophone Africa).

The Baptists

The origins of the Baptist churches are to be found in the seventeenth century. The more radical sections of the Reformation had always insisted that the church was to be a pure society of believers rather than a mixed body. During the seventeenth century, particularly in England, there was growing support not only for the idea that congregations should consist only of those who explicitly and publicly affirmed their faith, but for the related idea that baptism should be reserved only for those who affirmed their faith in this way. This contrasted with the Church of England, which permitted infants to be baptized (see p. 156).

The movement gained momentum in England during the nineteenth century, with great preachers such as C. H. Spurgeon (1834–1892), who drew huge audiences for his sermons. The foundation of the Baptist Missionary Society (1792) by William Carey (1761–1834) led to considerable effort being invested in missionary work. Baptist congregations were established in North America, where the movement has grown to have great influence on public life in the United States of America. The Southern Baptist Convention is one of the most important forces in modern American Christianity; its six seminaries have been of major importance in shaping the distinctive ethos of the denomination. Perhaps the best-known Protestant Christian of the twentieth century – Billy Graham (born 1918) – is a Baptist.

The Southern Baptist Convention was founded in Augusta, Georgia, in May 1845. Up to that point, individual Baptist congregations in the area had operated without feeling the need for any national or regional structure, and never thought of themselves as belonging to a "denomination." Yet there was a growing recognition that a centralized denomination would be more efficient and more powerful, capable of achieving greater social and political influence. Anxious not to compromise the autonomy of local Baptist congregations, the convention adopted a model of church governance that was essentially congregationalist. The autonomy and independence of individual congregations was thus affirmed.

This meant that the policies of a local Baptist congregation in a matter of doctrine, discipline, or church order could not be overturned by any superior body, since there is no body that has authority over the local church. This principle of congregational autonomy was vigorously upheld by the second president of the Convention, R. B. C. Howell, during the period 1851–1858. Congregations may affiliate to (and disaffiliate from) the convention as they see fit. This local independence is essential to any understanding of the subsequent dynamics of southern Baptist life, especially in the later twentieth century.

The Baptist ethos is difficult to summarize on account of the denomination's diversity worldwide. However, the following will be helpful if you wish to gain something of an understanding of the movement:

1   Baptists insist that baptism (the act) should be reserved for believers. Infant baptism is regarded as unjustified. This is probably one of the most distinctive aspects of the Baptist ethos. Some Baptist churches maintain an open policy on this matter, accepting both adult and infant baptism; nevertheless, the emphasis upon adult baptism (often referred to as "believers' baptism") remains a distinctive feature.

2   In the southern United States, Baptists tend to be theologically conservative, placing a high value on the role of the Bible. The use of the phrase "the Bible Belt" to refer to the southern states of the USA reflects the importance of the Bible in Baptist church life, especially in preaching. Although the qualification "evangelicalism" makes the person to whom it is applied be sometimes regarded with suspicion (the word itself is seen by some as a "Yankee" – that is, a northern – word), it is clear that the southern Baptists are increasingly becoming evangelical in orientation.

3   Baptist churches deliberately avoid the traditional form of church architecture, in which the altar is central and the pulpit is to one side. This is seen as having the effect of focusing the attention of the congregation on the sacrament of the eucharist. Instead Baptist church designs tend to place the pulpit at the center of things, in order to stress that the public reading of the Bible and the subsequent sermon preached on the biblical text are of central importance.

4   Baptists have tended to be critical of fixed liturgies, seeing in them an unhealthy inclination toward a purely formal expression of faith and toward the suppression of extempore prayer on the part of both minister and congregation.

5   Baptist clergypeople are referred to as "ministers" (from the Latin word for "servant") or "pastors" (from the Latin word for "shepherd"). The term "priest" is completely avoided. The episcopal system of church government is rejected.

Lutheranism

Lutheranism is the form of Protestantism that derives directly from Luther's reformation of the German church in the 1520s. Lutheranism was initially restricted to parts of north-eastern Germany; however, by a gradual process of expansion, the movement established itself in Scandinavia and the Baltic states. Although there were early indications that Lutheranism might become the dominant form of Christianity in England during the late 1530s, it never gained the influence that some expected. The movement was active in missionary work, especially in India.

The movement's greatest expansion came about through the emigration of Lutheran communities from Scandinavia and Germany to North America. The settlement of Swedish communities in Minnesota is a particularly good example of this phenomenon. Lutheran communities also settled in Australia through a similar process. As a result, Lutheranism today is to be found chiefly in Germany, Scandinavia, the Baltic states, and especially the northern states of the USA. North American and European Lutheranism have tended to pursue somewhat different agendas during the past century – agendas reflecting their different contexts. However, the formation of the Lutheran World Federation has gone some considerable way toward giving Lutherans a common sense of identity and purpose.

The Lutheran ethos reflects, to some degree, the central themes of Luther's personal program of reformation, which stressed continuity with the medieval church while at the same time introducing doctrinal and other changes where change was regarded as necessary.

1   Lutheranism is a strongly liturgical church, which sees the liturgy as a means of ensuring historical continuity with the past and of maintaining doctrinal orthodoxy.
2   Lutheranism is defined theologically by both the Augsburg Confession (1530) and the Formula of Concord (1577). As a result, the words "Augsburg" and "Concord" are frequently incorporated into the titles of Lutheran seminaries and publishing houses.
3   Lutheranism retains a sacramental emphasis that goes back to Luther and is absent from many other Protestant denominations. It adopts a causative approach to baptism, arguing that this practice is "necessary and effectual to salvation." This contrasts with the view of other Protestant denominations (particularly the Baptist one), which tend to regard baptism as a sign of grace rather than as something that is necessary before grace can be given.
4   Many Lutheran churches, particularly in European nations, use an episcopal form of church government.
5   Some of Martin Luther's fundamental emphases – such as the doctrine of justification by faith alone, or the dialectic between law and gospel – play an important role in confessional Lutheran theology, especially as this is taught at seminaries.

Methodism

Methodism was a movement within the Church of England that subsequently gave birth to Methodism as a denomination in its own right. Its origins are especially associated with

John Wesley (1703–1791), one of its founders and early leaders. When Methodism broke away from the Church of England, this was contrary to Wesley's intentions. The distinctive emphasis of the early Methodists was on the need for personal holiness. The term "Methodist" was originally a nickname, based on the methodical nature of the devotions and disciplines of the Wesleys and their circle.

The early history of English Methodism demonstrates the innate tendency to fragmentation that is characteristic of Protestantism. Divisions arose over a series of issues, including church order and discipline – though not, significantly, matters of doctrine. A dispute in the northeast of England led to the "Methodist New Connection," which formed in 1797. A decade later the "Primitive Methodists" broke away, believing that the Wesleyan Connection was losing its enthusiasm for revivalism. The Bible Christian Church was founded by a Wesleyan preacher in England's west country in 1815; unusually, it made extensive use of women preachers.

Yet English Methodism also illustrates Protestantism's capacities to set past controversies behind it and to secure reconciliation. In 1857 three Methodist groups united to form the United Methodist Free Churches; in 1907 these were incorporated, together with the New Connection and others, into the United Methodist Church; in 1932, the Wesleyans, the Primitive Methodists, and the United Methodists merged to establish the Methodist Church in Great Britain.

Generally Methodism has tended to be found primarily in English-speaking regions of the world, showing a parallelism with Anglicanism in this respect. As a result of various union schemes, in various parts of the world such as Canada and Australia, Methodism has ceased to exist as a distinct denomination. The formation of the World Methodist Council has gone some way toward maintaining Methodism as a distinct entity within global Christianity.

1   Since its inception, Methodism has placed particular emphasis on the role of the laity. The office of the "lay preacher" illustrates this emphasis, which can also be found in various aspects of Methodist church government.
2   Methodism has taken considerable trouble to integrate personal faith and social action, as it considers the gospel to involve both personal and social transformation.
3   Since the time of the Wesleys, Methodism has been characterized by a stance on theology best described as "an optimism of grace." This stance contrasts with the more Calvinist approach to theology adopted by reformed churches.
4   Some Methodist churches, especially in the United States, use an episcopal system of church government; others do not.
5   In recent years, Methodists have been involved in a number of denominational mergers. The Uniting Church in Australia was established in 1977 through the union of most congregations of the Methodist Church of Australasia, the Presbyterian Church of Australia, and the Congregational Union of Australia. In Canada, the United Church was founded in 1925 through a merger of four Protestant denominations, including the Methodist Church of Canada. In the United States, the United Methodist Church was established in 1968 through the union of the Methodist Church and the Evangelical United Brethren Church.

Presbyterianism and other reformed denominations

If the Lutheran churches owed their historical origins to Luther, the reformed churches owed theirs to Calvin. Reformed versions of Christianity were soon established in Western Europe, whence they spread to North America. In Europe itself Scotland and the Netherlands were soon established as particularly important centers of reformed thought. In England the two major reformed traditions have been referred to traditionally as Presbyterianism and Congregationalism; they reflect two different systems of church government.

Presbyterianism takes its name from the Greek word *presbuteros* ("elder") and applies to a form of church government that is exercised by representative groups of senior congregation members. Although this form of church government is encountered across Protestant denominations, the qualification "Presbyterian" is given particularly to those churches that arose in England and Scotland during the late sixteenth and early seventeenth centuries, taking their theological lead from John Calvin. Congregationalism recognizes the autonomy of the individual congregation.

As a result of Dutch colonial policy during the nineteenth century, forms of reformed Christianity were established in South Africa, the northeastern parts of South America, and parts of Southeast Asia. In the United States the Princeton Theological Seminary was established as a leading center of Presbyterian thought and practice. In recent years South Korea has become a leading center of reformed church life, as a result of the very rapid growth of Christianity in that region. The World Alliance of Reformed Churches, constituted in its present form in 1970 (although tracing its origins back to 1875), provides a means of allowing the various reformed churches to maintain their common identity.

The diversity within the reformed churches is such that it is difficult to make generalizations about them. However, the following aspects of the reformed ethos are salient:

1 Reformed churches are generally governed by "presbyters" or "elders." (The name "Presbyterianism" derives from this practice.) Some reformed churches regard the elders as ministers in their own right, with pastoral or teaching responsibilities; others see them as assistants, with specific responsibilities in relation to the administration and government of the church. The term "minister" is used to refer to a member of the ordained clergy, in preference to a priest.

2 Reformed worship traditionally places considerable emphasis upon the reading and preaching of the word of God. Holy Communion is celebrated regularly but infrequently. This emphasis upon preaching rather than the sacraments is especially evident from the regular Sunday worship of the reformed churches.

3 In the English-speaking West and in regions influenced by it, the reformed faith is defined theologically by the Westminster Confession (1647). As a result, the word "Westminster" is frequently incorporated into the titles of reformed seminaries and publishing houses.

4 Most reformed churches place an emphasis upon the sovereignty of God in predestination, which contrasts with the more "optimistic" view associated with Wesleyan Methodism.

Pentecostalism

The origins of Pentecostalism are complex, but this movement is usually traced back to the first day of the twentieth century – January 1, 1901. Charles Parham (1873–1929) had launched the Bethel Bible College in Topeka, Kansas a few months earlier. One of his particular interests was the phenomenon of "speaking in tongues," which is described in Acts 2: 1–4. Most Christians had taken this to be something that happened in the early church but was no longer part of the Christian experience. On New Year's Day, 1901, one of Parham's students experienced this phenomenon. A few days later, Parham experienced it for himself (pp. 179–180).

Parham began to teach about this apparent recovery of the gift of tongues. As we have seen earlier, he was heard by the African American preacher William J. Seymour (1870–1922), who subsequently opened the Apostolic Faith Mission at 312 Azusa Street, Los Angeles in April 1906. The term "Pentecostalism" began to be applied to the movement, taking its name from the "Day of Pentecost," when the phenomenon was first experienced by the early Christian disciples (Acts 2: 1–4).

The movement spread rapidly in America, appealing especially to the marginalized. Unusually, it seemed to appeal to and be embraced by both white and African American Christian groupings. Although Pentecostalism can be thought of as traditionalist in its Christian theology, it differs radically from other Christian groupings in the emphasis it places on speaking in tongues and in its forms of worship. These styles of worship are strongly experiential and involve prophesying, healings, and exorcisms. These forms and the perceived lack of intellectual sophistication of the movement led to its being ignored by mainline denominations and the academy. Yet, after World War II, a new phase in its expansion began, which paved the way for a massive growth in the second half of the twentieth century.

The incident that brought Pentecostalism to wider public attention took place in Van Nuys, California, in 1960. The rector of the local episcopalian church, Dennis Bennett, told his astonished congregation that he had been filled with the Holy Spirit and had spoken in tongues. Reaction varied from bewilderment to outrage; the local episcopalian bishop promptly banned speaking in tongues from his churches. However, it soon became clear that others in the mainline denominations had shared Bennett's experience. They came out of their closet and made it clear that they believed that they had experienced an authentic New Testament phenomenon, which would lead to the renewal of the churches.

By the late 1960s it was evident that some form of renewal based on charismatic gifts such as speaking in tongues was gaining a hold within Anglican, Lutheran, Methodist, and Presbyterian circles. Perhaps most importantly of all, a growing charismatic movement began to develop within the Roman Catholic church. Using the term "Pentecostal" to describe this now became problematic, as this name was used to refer to a family of churches – such as the Assemblies of God – which placed particular emphasis on speaking in tongues. Accordingly, the term "charismatic" was used to refer to movements within the mainline churches based upon the ideas and experiences of the Pentecostal movement. Charismatic renewal within the mainline churches has led to new and informal worship styles, an explosion in worship songs, a new concern for the dynamics of worship, and an increasing dislike for the traditionalism of formal liturgical worship, especially when the latter involves the cumbersome use of hymn books or service books.

The Pentecostal movement – which we shall here take to include charismatic groups within mainline churches – has changed considerably since World War II. The most obvious change is its massive surge in growth. It is now estimated that there are 500 million Pentecostals in the world, with a very wide geographical distribution. Although the movement may be argued to have its origins primarily within African American culture, it has taken root in South America, Asia, Africa, and Europe.

Why has this form of Christianity become so popular? Two factors are generally recognized as playing a significant role in the growing global appeal of Pentecostalism. First, Pentecostalism stresses a direct, immediate experience of God and avoids the rather dry and cerebral forms of Christianity that many find unattractive and unintelligible. It is thus significant that Pentecostalism has made huge inroads in working-class areas of Latin America, since it is able to communicate the divine without any need for the alienating impedimenta of a bookish culture. Second, the movement uses a language and a form of communication that enables it to bridge cultural gaps highly effectively. Pentecostalism is best seen as an oral religion, which communicates its vision of life in stories, testimonies, and songs.

Evangelicalism

Evangelicalism has become a phenomenon of major importance in the mainline Protestant churches since 1945. Although some new Protestant denominations have been formed that are explicitly evangelical in orientation, the general pattern that has emerged indicates that evangelicalism is a movement within the mainline denominations. Hence evangelicals within the reformed churches retain much of the ethos of those churches (including its church structures), while supplementing it with at least some of the characteristics of evangelicalism noted below. Similarly, evangelicals within Anglicanism adopt many of the characteristics of the latter (such as the episcopal system of church government and the use of a fixed liturgy), while retaining an evangelical ethos in their church.

The four main distinctive features of the evangelical ethos are generally agreed to be the following:

1   Evangelicalism is strongly biblical in its emphasis, which is especially evident in the styles of preaching found within the movement. This emphasis is carried over into other aspects of evangelical life, which is reflected for instance in the importance attached to small Bible study groups within the life of the church and to the regular reading of the Bible in personal devotion.
2   Evangelicalism gives particular weight to the cross of Jesus. Although Jesus is of central importance to evangelicalism, the accent has tended to fall upon the saving death of Jesus on the cross. This is especially reflected in evangelical hymns and songs.
3   Evangelicalism stresses the need for personal conversion. Considerable emphasis is placed on the dangers of "nominalism," which in this context designates a purely formal or external acceptance of Christian teachings, without any personal transformation in

consequence. Evangelical preaching often stresses the need for Christians to be "born again" (see John 3: 1–16).

4   Evangelical churches and individual evangelicals have a deep commitment to evangelism – that is, to converting others to the Christian faith. Billy Graham is a good example of a twentieth-century evangelical who has become well known on account of this commitment. It should be noted that the words "evangelicalism" and "evangelism" are often confused, on account of their similarity. The former refers to a movement; the latter to an activity – but an activity that is especially associated with this specific movement.

The Ecumenical Movement and the World Council of Churches

As will be clear from the analysis presented in this book, Christianity has its fair share of internal divisions. The separation of the Latin-speaking West from the Greek-speaking East had been under way for some time before the Great Schism of 1054 made it official. The sixteenth-century Reformation led to the establishment of a group of Protestant churches – Anabaptist, Anglican, Lutheran, and reformed – that disagreed with Rome and (perhaps more importantly) with each other. Protestantism turned out to be a movement with an inherent tendency to fragment. Today it is estimated that there are at least 20,000 Protestant denominations in the world.

Could these differences be set aside, allowing the churches to reunite? Or at least achieve better working relationships? These aims underlie the ecumenical movement, which began to develop momentum after World War II. The term "ecumenical" comes from the ancient Greek word *oikoumenē*, meaning "the known inhabited world." Although informal efforts to achieve better relationships between churches had been made for some time, the events of the twentieth century gave a new impetus to ecumenism. In 1920, in the aftermath of the Armenian genocide (p. 181), a synod of the Orthodox church issued an encyclical calling for a "fellowship of churches" similar to the League of Nations.

Following the end of World War II, concerted attempts were made to reconcile wartime enemies – especially France and Germany – in order to reconstruct Europe and ensure that it had a viable future. A parallel movement developed within the churches. Was not this a God-given moment, in which Christian unity might be pursued and achieved? It was against this background that the World Council of Churches was created in the aftermath of World War II. The decision to headquarter the council in Geneva was based partly on the fact that this Swiss city was host to the prewar League of Nations and to many postwar international organizations.

The first assembly of the World Council of Churches, held in August 1948 in Amsterdam, was seen as a beacon of hope for postwar Europe. Although the plans to inaugurate this organization went back to 1936, World War II both delayed this event and highlighted its potential importance. The main Protestant churches in the West agreed to work together and to keep doing so. Although there were obvious tensions between liberal and progressive Christians and their more conservative counterparts, this potential difficulty was defused through skillful footwork on the part of the conference organizers.

So what is the World Council of Churches? From the outset, it was clear that this was a Protestant body. Catholic and Orthodox churches might send observers; initially, however, full membership was limited to Protestant churches. Although the new body initially described itself as "a fellowship of churches which accept our Lord as God and Savior," it became clear that clarification was needed. How did this body relate to others – such as denominational leadership structures? These questions were engaged at the second meeting of the World Council of Churches, held in Toronto in 1950, and further developed at later meetings.

According to the council's declaration in Toronto, its purpose is "to bring the churches into contact with one another and to promote discussion of questions of Church unity." Its initial intention was to transform the prevailing indifference to the need for ecumenical fellowship and unity, through theological dialogue and spiritual fellowship, into a deep and conscious conviction of the need for Christian unity.

The World Council of Churches has always made it clear that it is not some type of "megachurch," which exists over and above its constituent churches. The constitution of this body excludes any role that might take away authority from member churches. "The World Council shall not legislate for the churches." Neither the Assembly nor the Central Committee of the World Council of Churches were to possess any "constitutional authority whatever over its constituent churches." Ecclesiological pluralism was thus built into the structures and thinking of the World Council of Churches from its inception. This was "a fellowship of churches" that sought to encourage its members to work toward the goal of their visible unity. But there was no agenda designed to impose such a union on its members.

There was no doubt that this was seen as a welcome and necessary move, not least as the situation of the churches began to change in the West. In the 1970s and 1980s, a growing sense that western culture was becoming increasingly secular and hostile to the Christian faith led to many Christians wondering if they ought to suspend hostilities between Christian groupings and concentrate upon the issue of survival. Furthermore, the expansion of Christianity into traditionally Islamic areas of the world, together with the growth of significant Islamic groups in the West through immigration, has led many Christians to predict that this will be the next major area of confrontation. Should not Christians unite in the face of a possible threat? Might future survival depend on unity? As Benjamin Franklin famously quipped at the signing of the Declaration of Independence (July 4, 1776), "We must indeed all hang together, or, most assuredly, we shall all hang separately."

Yet the history of the World Council of Churches has not been entirely happy and persuaded many that this body had failed to live up to its high expectations in the immediate postwar period. The council found itself experiencing difficulty in holding its members together. The organization increasingly drifted toward a more liberal theological stance during the 1960s and 1970s and alienated much of its naturally conservative constituency. Its token demonstrations of support for armed liberation movements in Africa alarmed those who saw Christianity as espousing nonviolent resistance to oppression and looked to Martin Luther King (1929–1968) as an example.

By about 1990 it became clear that there was diminishing enthusiasm within the mainstream churches for the form of "visible unity" that had become the hallmark of the thinking and policies of the World Council of Churches. With the passing of time, it became increasingly clear that this vision was somewhat unrealistic and failed to take seriously the realities of church life. What most grassroots Christians wanted was better working relationships with their fellow Christians in other denominations. They did not want their denomination either to be swallowed up by or to swallow another. They wanted better relationships with other Christians at both the individual and the institutional level. The rise of bottom-up grassroots ecumenism has significantly reduced the role of top-down ecumenical efforts in the twenty-first century.

The World Council of Churches now plays a token and somewhat peripheral role in global Christianity. Yet the ecumenical vision that inspired it has not faded; it has simply changed direction, the initiative shifting to individuals and voluntary organizations. By the end of the twentieth century, new ecumenical alliances were in the process of emerging at grassroots level, which have eclipsed and marginalized the old-style top-down ecumenism of the World Council of Churches.

The Erosion of Protestant Denominationalism in the United States

The religious landscape in the United States has been substantially shaped by the structures and habits of thought of its European origins. The Protestant denomination is essentially a European phenomenon, reflecting the shifting patterns of church life and controversy in Western Europe from the sixteenth to the eighteenth century. Patterns of religious affiliation and belonging reflecting the general situation of Western Europe, and often the very specific conditions of religious life in England, were exported to Africa, America, Asia, and Australia by both settlers and missionaries. As a result, the emerging church life of four great continents has been shaped, to a greater or lesser extent, by the historical contingencies of Western Europe.

The Protestant denomination initially seemed to thrive in the United States, possibly reflecting ecclesial loyalties on the part of immigrants that arose from their European roots. World War II may be seen as marking a change in the essentially static situation in the United States. Throughout the 1950s, the growth of the traditional Protestant denomination soared in the United States. Congregationalists, Episcopalians, Methodists, and Presbyterians reported net annual membership gains. Each denomination vigorously defended its sovereignty and its vested interests. In 1956 a survey showed that 80 percent of episcopalians believed that it was wrong to hold worship service with other Christian groups. A year earlier, A Gallup poll showed that 96 percent of the adult population of the United States belonged to the same denomination as their parents. Their churchgoing habits had not changed over a generation. Yet by 1990 many of these mainline Protestant denominations were in decline and had lost between one fifth and one third of their 1965 memberships, at a time when the population growth of the United States had surged. A real numerical decline thus converted into a significant reduction in the proportion of America's population associated with these denominations.

Christian denominations in America are one of the very few institutional expressions of early modern European culture still in existence. But why, many Americans are increasingly asking, should modern America's religious life be made dependent upon a European model – especially when that model is now seen as having failed in its own homelands? Both individual churches and individual Christians in America are showing an increasing reluctance to define themselves denominationally. Many churches have named themselves after their localities, skillfully dropping any reference to a denomination. The same issues can be seen in the titles of seminaries. The institution now known as Denver Seminary was formerly Denver Conservative Baptist Seminary; the Virginia Theological Seminary was formerly the Protestant Episcopal Theological Seminary in Virginia. These changes suggest that the inclusion of denominational identities is no longer viewed as a positive feature in marketing terms.

In the 1990s some strongly entrepreneurial Protestants found themselves more and more frustrated by the institutional inertia of traditional denominational structures. They regarded these as unresponsive bureaucracies, uninterested in local initiatives or innovations. Frustration with denominational structures is not, of course, anything particularly new. The great New York preacher Harry Emerson Fosdick (1878–1969), who played such an important role in the great fundamentalist controversies of the 1920s (pp. 184–186), once made the astonishing revelation that he had once considered leaving the historic Christian organizations in order to start his own independent movement. Fosdick was dismissive of those who demanded ecclesiastical loyalty, holding that his only loyalty was to Christ. Yet, despite his frustrations, he never set up his own denomination, even though his personal reputation was such that its future would have been secure.

Yet, since the 1990s, American Protestantism has been increasingly characterized by the growth of market-shaped or market-driven congregations. A good example is Willow Creek Community Church near Chicago. These large churches tend to be established and led by strongly entrepreneurial individuals. Their sense of theological vision, coupled with a "can do" mentality that was nourished and inspired by the Protestant work ethic, eventually drove them to achieve their goals outside the structures of traditional denominations, especially in the aftermath of the theological and cultural turmoil of the 1960s. Like Martin Luther, they did not particularly want to work outside their mother churches – but the needs and realities of the new cultural situation seemed to leave them with no alternatives. The outcome was a surge of new initiatives, which met needs that were held to be largely ignored by mainline denominations and set new patterns for how churches work, develop, and organize themselves.

The theological basis for this development was laid during the opening decades of the history of Protestantism. In his *Institutes of the Christian Religion* (1559), John Calvin had argued that a true Christian church was not defined by its institutional history or connections, but by the proper exercise of preaching and sacramental administration. In the late twentieth-century American context, this was interpreted to mean that new churches and denominations could be founded, provided they were based on good preaching and the proper administration of the sacraments. Enterprising individuals, often fired up by a vision for a specific form of ministry, could start their own congregations, or even their own denominations.

The outcome was inevitable: the emergence of a consumerist mentality, through which Protestants felt able to pick and choose the local church that suited their needs, beliefs, or aspirations. And if they didn't find one that was just right, they would establish their own.

Catholic critics of Protestantism often point to its innate fissiparous tendencies, which they suggest indicates a lack of concern for the fundamental unity of the church.

While this congregational inflationism is unquestionably problematic, it has two fundamental strengths, both of which are of decisive importance for the shaping of Protestantism in the United States and beyond.

1   It allowed Protestantism to deal with rapid social and cultural change, which often leads to churches being locked into the realities of a bygone age. Entrepreneurial pastors and preachers can easily recast a vision of the gospel adapted to the new situation – in the same way in which older visions were adapted to their situations – and thus prevent Protestantism being trapped in a time warp. This situation enables Protestants to respond to perceived needs for specialist ministeries to specific groups through the formation of voluntary societies, which often come to exercise a para-church role.

2   Congregational inflationism enables Protestant churches to deal with situations in which the denominational leadership is seen to be radically out of touch with its membership – typically, by pursuing theological agendas or cultural trends that are not accepted by the majority of the congregations belonging to that denomination. It does not matter whether these agendas are right wing or left wing, conservative or liberal. Protestantism empowers the congregation first to protest against its leaders; second, to remove them; and, third, to reconstitute itself elsewhere, *while still remaining a Christian church*. While some Protestant denominations attempt to shield themselves against such accountability to their membership, these fundamental rights remain, in principle, part of the movement's core identity. A Protestant believer can leave one denomination and join another – while still remaining a Protestant.

C. S. Lewis's notion of "mere Christianity" seems to have had an impact here. This way of thinking, set out by Lewis in his widely read book *Mere Christianity* (1952), undermines the importance of denominational identity by arguing that the various Christian churches are simply different implementations of an underlying consensual core Christianity. Lewis's *Mere Christianity* was, and remains, a manifesto for a form of Christianity that exults in essentials, regarding other matters as being of secondary importance.

Yet Lewis's notion of "mere Christianity" was more than a rejection of denominational supremacy. It was also a subtle critique of the abuses of power and privilege that so easily arise in more institutionalized forms of Christianity. Lewis is generally critical of the clergy in his writings. As a lay Christian, he came to see himself as representing a form of Christianity that recognized the crucial role of the laity, allowing neither clergy nor ecclesiastical institutions any special privileges.

Conclusion

In this chapter we have considered the shape of contemporary Christianity, focusing especially on the families of Christian churches that are found across the world. Yet this is an incomplete and inadequate account of Christianity. What about day-to-day Christian life? What does the Christian life look like? In the next chapter we shall present an extended sketch of ordinary Christian existence. It cannot hope to do justice to the complexity and richness of this subject, but it can at least alert readers to what they can expect to encounter, and it can explain something of the subject's history and significance.

6

The Life of Faith
Christianity as a Living Reality

In earlier chapters of this work we explored Christianity from several perspectives, focusing particularly on its teachings and history. Although this is valuable in helping readers to gain a sense of what Christianity is all about, this approach has one major disadvantage. It may create the unhelpful and deeply misleading impression that Christianity is simply a set of ideas. While Christianity is indeed based on a set of core beliefs, these have a significant effect on the personal lives and values of individual Christians, on the way in which Christian communities behave and worship, and on the cultures in which Christianity has secured a presence.

The final two chapters of this work aim to explore Christian life in the modern world. What is Christianity like as a lived and experienced reality, rather than simply as a set of ideas, or an historical influence? In what ways does Christianity impact on culture? These chapters will be particularly helpful for those who are not Christians, yet want to have at least a basic understanding of Christianity as a major presence and influence in modern global culture.

The aim of these two final chapters is to provide a broad overview of the Christian life, not to explore it in detail. There are many detailed studies available dealing with each topic covered here, and these will provide you with much fuller accounts of the rich diversity of modern Christian faith and life, while at the same time identifying the common themes, beliefs, and attitudes that hold the movement together.

Gateways to Exploring the Life of Faith

Since Christianity is a way of life, not simply a set of ideas, it can be encountered in many different manners. We shall briefly note five of these gateways or points of access to Christianity.

Christianity: An Introduction, Third Edition. Alister E. McGrath.
© 2015 John Wiley & Sons, Ltd. Published 2015 by John Wiley & Sons, Ltd.

1   *Texts* Most religions – though not all – have some texts that they regard as having special significance. In the case of Christianity, the most important such text is known as "the Bible." In most parts of the world – though not in some more repressive Islamic countries – the Bible can be bought openly in public bookstores. It is regularly read in church services and private devotions. Many parts of it have been set to music. One of the best known of these is the oratorio *The Messiah* by George Frederick Handel (1685–1759), which consists of a musical setting of a series of biblical passages dealing with the coming of Christ.

2   *Services* For many, the Christian faith is encountered by attending church services. For those who are not themselves Christians, this experience is most likely to take the form of attending the weddings or funerals of Christian friends or relatives. The text of these services – often referred to as the "liturgy" – gives some important indications of the core beliefs and values of Christianity, often supplemented through sermons or homilies.

3   *Buildings* Whether you attend a church as a tourist or as a worshipper, its physical structure itself can act as a portal to an understanding of Christianity. Older Christian churches – such as the great cathedrals of medieval Europe – were often designed to communicate aspects of the Christian faith to a largely illiterate culture. Many cathedrals are cross-shaped, to remind believers of the central place of the cross in Christian life, thought, and worship. A baptismal font was often placed near the main door of the church, to symbolize the idea that baptism was the means by which entry to the church took place. Stained glass windows acted as windows into the mysteries of faith. The walls of churches were often painted with scenes from the gospels, to remind worshippers of the basic events on which their faith was based. To put it succinctly: church buildings embody Christian belief. In these chapters we shall explore some of the ways in which church buildings can be "read" in this way.

4   *Music* The Christian emphasis on the public worship of God led to a new interest in developing music to accompany it. The vast range of music designed to accompany worship ranges from the simplicity of monastic plainsong to the complex musical structures of Verdi's Requiem or Beethoven's *Missa solemnis* and to the vibrancy and informality of modern worship songs, especially within evangelical and Pentecostal traditions. A huge range of Christian texts have been set to music. These are regularly performed, both as part of Christian worship and as a celebration of human cultural activity in general. Once more, music can act as a portal to the core values and ideas of Christianity.

5   *Art* From the outset, Christians realized the importance of the visual arts in communicating and sustaining their faith. Sculpture and paintings were both used to depict key scenes from the gospels. Some of the best-known images in history are inspired by these themes – for example, Michelangelo's *Creation of Adam* and Leonardo da Vinci's *Last Supper*. The crucifixion was of special artistic importance, on account of its central place in Christian thought and devotion. The use of icons within Orthodox Christianity is one of the most familiar ways in which images play a role in Christian devotion.

In these two concluding chapters we shall explore what Christianity is like as a lived faith, picking up on some of these gateways. We shall begin by considering the life of the church – the institution to which Christians belong. Although there are considerable differences between individual Christian denominations, most of the material that follows is applicable to them all.

Christian Communities: The Life of the Church

At the heart of the Christian life is a worshipping community. Those who are encountering Christianity from the outside are most likely to experience it through various forms of worship. That worship takes an incredible variety of styles – from the sumptuous, ornate, and elaborate worship of Russian Orthodoxy within a gilded cathedral to the informal, guitar-led worship of Latin American Pentecostalism inside a makeshift church building.

The Christian services that are most likely to be experienced by those who are not themselves Christians are weddings, funerals, and versions of the great Christmas Service of Nine Lessons and Carols. For this reason, we shall begin with them and offer a greater amount of explanation and comment than usual, in order to allow these services to become "gateways" to Christianity.

Christian weddings

The basic structure of a Christian wedding is very simple. The "liturgy" – the term used to refer to the text of a religious service – consists of the bride's and groom's consent to marriage in the sight of human witnesses and of God – an act in which they ask for God's blessing on their union. The basic structure of the service is shaped partly by theological considerations shared by all Christians and partly by legal and cultural factors, which are specific to a given locality. Christianity has long been adept at intermingling its own distinctive ideas with the prevailing cultural norms.

Alongside specifically Christian ideas, you will therefore find customs that originate from elsewhere – such as the placement of a ring (or rings) on the fourth finger, which has no specifically Christian significance and is widely held to represent an older Roman tradition taken over by Christianity: that of the Roman *annulus pronubis* ("premarital ring") given by the man to the woman at the betrothal ceremony. The custom of blessing the wedding ring and of placing it on the bride's finger is thought to date from the eleventh century.

The Christian marriage service emphasizes that marriage is a voluntary commitment of two individuals and that this is part of God's ordinance of for the creation. Often a passage from the book of Genesis is read to make this point: "And the Lord God said, 'It is not good for the man to be alone'" (Genesis 2: 18). Humanity was created for fellowship – people's fellowship among themselves, and also with God. Many Christian marriage liturgies make reference to Jesus Christ's attending a wedding at Cana in Galilee (John 2). For an example of such a liturgy, we may turn to the Episcopal Church of Scotland's marriage service of 2007, which interweaves these ideas into the ceremony:

Figure 6.1   A Russian Orthodox wedding at the Church of the Transfiguration, St. Petersburg. Source: © Robert Harding Picture Library Ltd/Alamy.

> We have come together in the presence of God, to witness the marriage of N. and N., to ask his blessing on them, and to share their joy. Our Lord Jesus Christ was himself a guest at a wedding in Cana of Galilee, and through his Spirit he is with us now.
>
> The Scriptures teach us that marriage is a gift of God in Creation and a means of his grace, a holy mystery in which man and woman become one flesh. It is God's purpose that, as husband and wife give themselves to each other in love throughout their lives, they shall be united in that love as Christ is united with his Church.

This brief excerpt from the marriage service makes reference to the Christian belief that there is a deeper, spiritual significance to marriage. For Christians, the union of a man and a woman in marriage symbolizes the spiritual union between a believer and Jesus Christ. Christian spiritual writers often speak of the "spiritual marriage" between Jesus of Nazareth and the believer. Martin Luther, for example, speaks of faith as the "wedding ring" that unites Christ and the believer, pointing to both the personal relationship that exists between the two parties and their mutual exchange of goods. For Luther, Christ receives the sin and the guilt of the believer and bestows upon the believer his righteousness and the gift of eternal life.

Christian funerals

The central themes of a Christian funeral service are the proclamation of the hope of resurrection, the celebration of the life of the deceased, and the entrustment of the person who has died to God's tender care. "Christians celebrate the funeral rites to offer worship, praise, and thanksgiving to God for the gift of life which has been returned to God, the author of life and the hope of the just."

In the traditional English funeral service set out in the *Book of Common Prayer* (1662), the hope of resurrection is sustained throughout. Little reference is made to the identity or achievement of the deceased; the emphasis falls largely on affirming hope in the resurrection. In fact the dead person is never named in the liturgy but referred to simply as "our brother" or "our sister." The service opens with the priest meeting the funeral party at the churchyard gate and speaking some words from John's gospel (John 15: 25–26) in which the theme of the Christian hope is clearly set out:

> I am the resurrection and the life, saith the Lord: he that believeth in me, though he were dead, yet shall he live; and whosoever liveth and believeth in me shall never die.

The service then proceeds with the reading of 1 Corinthians 15, a chapter in which Paul stresses the importance of the resurrection and the difference it makes (or ought to make) to Christians. This reading includes the following words:

> Death is swallowed up in victory. O death, where is thy sting? O grave, where is thy victory? The sting of death is sin, and the strength of sin is the law. But thanks be to God, which giveth us the victory through our Lord Jesus Christ. Therefore, my beloved brethren, be ye steadfast, unmoveable, always abounding in the work of the Lord, forasmuch as ye know that your labour is not in vain in the Lord.

Finally, as the corpse is lowered into the grave, the priest speaks these words. Again, note the theme of hope.

> Forasmuch as it has pleased Almighty God of his great mercy to take unto himself the soul of our dear *brother* here departed, we therefore commit *his* body to the ground; earth to earth, ashes to ashes, dust to dust; in sure and certain hope of the resurrection to eternal life, through our Lord Jesus Christ.

The theme of hope in resurrection is often emphasized through appropriate symbols. For example, in the Catholic rite, the coffin or casket is met at the entrance to the church and sprinkled with holy water as a reminder of the believer's baptism, which is seen as affirming that the believer has passed from death to life (Romans 6: 1–4). Family members then place a pall over the casket, and may place Christian symbols – such as a cross or Bible – upon it as a sign of the Christian hope in resurrection.

Alongside these fundamental themes, a number of ancillary ones often develop. For example, consider the following directions (or "liturgical norms"), set out by the Catholic archdiocese of Vancouver. Note the emphasis on the equality of believers, in death and in life.

> The casket remains closed during the funeral rite and should be covered with a pall in remembrance of the baptismal garment – a sign of the Christian dignity of the person entering in Christ a new life beyond this life. The pall may be ornamented with Christian symbols. In addition to its liturgical significance, the pall serves very practical purposes: it

avoids ostentation, prevents embarrassment of the poor and emphasizes the Christian's equality before God.

The "pall" is a simple cloth that covers the coffin or casket. Here it is interpreted as a reminder of baptism.

The same custom is used outside the Catholic tradition. For example, the First United Methodist Church in Austin, Texas offers a bereaved family the use of a pall at its funeral services, for the following reason:

> First Church has a white funeral pall with a gold antique satin cross covering the full length and width, symbolic of God's power to cover sin with forgiveness, fear with hope and death with life. This pall is available to you and is appropriate in place of casket flowers.

The Service of Nine Lessons and Carols

One of the most familiar Christian services takes place at Christmas in Cambridge, England, and is broadcast across the world, on television and radio. So what is this service? How did it originate? And what does it tell us about Christianity?

The Victorian period saw the institutionalization of Christmas as a national religious festival in England. The practice of having Christmas trees was introduced by Queen Victoria's consort, Prince Albert, from his native Germany. Christmas cards were circulated with the help of the newly established national postal service, and extensive use was made of a device invented by the novelist Anthony Trollope – the postal box. The Victorian period witnessed an explosion in the writing of Christmas carols. Some of the best-known carols – including "In the Bleak Midwinter" and "Once In Royal David's City" – date from this hugely influential and formative period in English history.

As Christmas grew into an increasingly important festival in the later nineteenth century, it became painfully clear that no adequate provision for its public celebration had been made by the English national church. As the celebration of Christmas became more and more prominent in the national consciousness, the demand grew for a special church service for this time of year, which should incorporate both the increasingly popular Christmas carols and the biblical readings. *The Book of Common Prayer* did not include any special services for the season of Christmas; in this it reflected the fact that Christmas was not seen as a festival of particular importance in the seventeenth century. The growing popular importance of this festival created demands for a special service designed to mark the occasion.

One such service was devised for Christmas Eve in 1880 by Edward White Benson (1829–1896), while bishop of the diocese of Truro, in the southwest of England. The format was both simple and elegant. The service consisted of nine carols and nine lessons to be read by various officials of the church in ascending order, beginning with a chorister and ending with the bishop himself. Benson went on to become archbishop of Canterbury; the service was adopted, in a new format, by King's College, Cambridge.

The origins of the distinctive Cambridge format are to be traced to Christmas Eve 1918, the first Christmas celebration after the trauma and devastation of the Great War. Eric

Milner-White had just been appointed chaplain and dean of King's College, Cambridge, having served as an army chaplain during the war. He was acutely aware of the need to make worship more relevant and attractive to a hardened and skeptical postwar generation, and he realized that the Christmas story could be used as a showcase for Christian worship. Exploiting the long-established choral tradition of King's College, Milner-White developed the format of the Nine Lessons and Carols which has become so influential and well known.

The basic structure of the service has remained unchanged since 1919. The backbone consists of nine Christmas carols, sung by the entire congregation, and nine biblical readings, taken from the King James version of the Bible. These are interspersed with choral items that reflect Christmas themes. The opening Bidding Prayer sets the scene for the public reading of the Christmas "tale of the loving purposes of God from the first days of our disobedience unto the glorious Redemption brought us by this Holy Child"; the closing Collect summarizes the significance of the great themes that have been reaffirmed in reading and in praise throughout the service. The opening prayer makes clear what Christmas is all about, from a Christian perspective.

> Beloved in Christ, be it this Christmas Eve our care and delight to prepare ourselves to hear again the message of the angels: in heart and mind to go even unto Bethlehem and see this thing which is come to pass, and with the shepherds and the wise men adore the Child lying in his Mother's arms. Let us read and mark in Holy Scripture the tale of the loving purposes of God from the first days of our disobedience unto the glorious Redemption brought us by this Holy Child; and in company with the whole Church let us make this chapel, dedicated to his pure and lowly Mother, glad with our carols of praise.

The fundamental theme of the service is simple: Christ is the long-promised savior of the world, God incarnate, who has entered into our world as one of us in order to redeem it.

Thus far we have considered three Christian services that people outside the Christian community are likely to encounter. But what about the staple diet of Christians themselves? What do churches do on Sundays, week by week? In what follows we shall look at some basic themes of regular Christian worship.

Christian Worship

There are clear indications of an emerging style of worship within the New Testament. The Acts of the Apostles records that the first Christians met regularly and "devoted themselves to the apostles' teaching and to the fellowship, to the breaking of bread and to prayer" (Acts 2: 42). In addition to the "breaking of the bread," the New Testament also highlights the importance of baptism as a sign of personal commitment to Jesus and of entrance into the Christian community. The importance of singing and thanksgiving can be seen from a number of passages: "Speak to one another with psalms, hymns and spiritual songs. Sing and make music in your heart to the Lord, always giving thanks to God the Father for everything, in the name of our Lord Jesus Christ" (Ephesians 5: 19–20). The styles of Christian worship that are encountered in Christian churches today can all be traced back, in different ways, to the New Testament.

Christian worship is particularly associated with one day of the week – Sunday. It is clear that Christians regarded the first day of the week as being of special importance, as it was the day on which Jesus of Nazareth rose again from the dead. Jewish worship was particularly associated with the seventh day of the week (the sabbath, or Saturday), but the first Christians did not retain this traditional Jewish observance.

Sunday was also seen as the first day of God's new creation, and therefore it was the day appropriate for all major public Christian worship. Justin Martyr, writing around AD 165, is an important witness to this tradition:

> On the day which is called Sunday, all who live in the cities or in the countryside gather together in one place. And the memoirs of the apostles or the writings of the prophets are read, so long as there is time. Then, when the reader has finished, the president delivers a discourse in which he encourages and invites the people to follow the examples of virtue which these provide. Then we all stand up together and offer some prayers. And when we have finished these prayers, bread and wine mixed with water are presented. The president then offers prayers and a thanksgiving, according to his ability, and the people indicate their assent by saying "Amen." The elements for which thanks has been given are then distributed and received by all present, and are taken to those who are not present by the deacons.

Worship plays an important part in sustaining Christian life. Especially within the Greek Orthodox tradition, the public worship of the church represents one's drawing close to the threshold of heaven itself and peering through its portals, to catch a glimpse of the worship of heavenly places. The Orthodox liturgy celebrates the notion of being caught up in the worship of heaven and the awesome sense of mystery that is evoked by the act of peering beyond the bounds of human vision.

A biblical text that has played no small part in shaping this immense respect for mystery in worship may be mentioned here. The sixth chapter of the prophecy of Isaiah relates the call of the prophet, portraying him as undergoing a liminal experience as he enters the "holy of holies":

> In the year that King Uzziah died, I saw the Lord sitting on a throne, high and lofty; and the hem of his robe filled the temple. Seraphs were in attendance above him; each had six wings: with two they covered their faces, and with two they covered their feet, and with two they flew. And one called to another and said: "Holy, holy, holy is the LORD of hosts; the whole earth is full of his glory." The pivots on the thresholds shook at the voices of those who called, and the house filled with smoke. And I said: "Woe is me! I am lost, for I am a man of unclean lips, and I live among a people of unclean lips; yet my eyes have seen the King, the LORD of hosts!"
>
> (Isaiah 6: 1–5)

The central insight that many theologians gleaned from this passage is that human beings are simply not capable of beholding the worship of heaven itself; it must be accommodated to their capacity by being reflected through created things – such as the created order, the sacramental bread and wine, or the liturgy itself.

To share in worship is thus to stand in a holy place (Exodus 3: 5) – a place in which humanity, strictly speaking, has no right to be. Whenever the divine liturgy is celebrated on earth, the boundaries between heaven and earth are removed and earthly worshippers join in the eternal heavenly liturgy chanted by the angels. During these moments of earthly adoration worshippers have the opportunity of being mystically transported to the threshold of heaven. Being in a holy place and about to participate in holy things, on the one hand they become aware of their finitude and sinfulness, and on the other they gain a refreshing glimpse of the glory of God – precisely the pattern of reflection set out in Isaiah's vision.

The association between worship and heaven is often enhanced musically. Just as Gothic churches embodied a sense of the spaciousness of heaven, allowing and encouraging their congregations to visualize the worship of heaven, so the judicious use of music has widely been held to bring about a corresponding effect. It is difficult to make this point purely verbally, without listening to the music itself. However, to listen to the *Vespers* (1915) of Sergei Rachmaninoff (1873–1943) or to the motet "Assumpta est Maria" and to the mass based on it, Missa "Assumpta est Maria," both by Giovanni Pierluigi da Palestrina (c. 1525–1594), is to gain something of an appreciation of how the vision of heaven can be mediated musically through worship.

The idea of liminality – that is, of being on the threshold of the sacred and peering into the forbidden heavenly realms – is represented visually in the structure of Orthodox churches, especially through the way in which the sanctuary and the altar are set apart from the people, which carries a deep sense of the awesomeness of the mystery of God. In their treatises on worship, Chrysostom and other Greek patristic writers repeatedly draw attention to the liturgical importance of this sense of the sacred. The altar is the "terrifying table"; the bread and the wine are "the terrifying sacrifice of the body and blood of Christ which worshippers must approach with fear and trembling." For the Orthodox, there is an especially close link between the eucharist – the sacrament celebrated with and through bread and wine – and the experience of the worship of heaven.

All generalizations are dangerous and must be treated with a degree of caution. However, they are also useful to those who are trying to gain understanding of an exceptionally complicated matter. What follows is a listing of the various elements that will be encountered in Christian worship. The types of Christian worship vary considerably, and not all of the elements to be discussed below will be found in all types of worship. However, the list is useful as a starting point for exploring modern worship. But the reader who is approaching Christianity from the outside must be warned that to simply read about Christian worship is of very limited value; worship is something that demands to be experienced. You are strongly recommended to supplement your reading with involvement in the worshipping life of a local Christian church and gain an appreciation of its structures, rhythms, and appeal.

Prayer

Prayer is an integral element in all forms of Christian worship. It takes a variety of forms. A distinction is made between the *private* prayers of individuals and the *public* prayer of the church. Prayer can also take the form of *thanksgiving*, in which thanks are offered to God for blessings that have been received, whether by individuals or by the church as a whole. Perhaps the most important is *petitionary* prayer, in which the congregation, or individuals in that congregation, make specific requests of God. This type of prayer can be illustrated from the teaching of Jesus, who compared the former to human requests.

Praise

The Christian Bible regularly exhorts believers to praise God. This kind of activity has become incorporated into Christian worship from the earliest of times. In contemporary Christianity it is especially associated with hymns and worship songs. These are set to various forms of music, often with the cultural preferences of congregations in mind.

Many classic hymns date from the eighteenth century and come from the pen of writers such as Isaac Watts ("When I survey the wondrous cross") or John and Charles Wesley. Given the importance of hymns to Christian life and thought, we shall consider one hymn writer in a little detail: John Newton (1725–1807), author of one of the church's most famous hymns, "Amazing Grace."

John Newton was the main author of the *Olney Hymns*, a remarkable collection of songs of praise, many of which are still widely used today. He was converted after spending some time in the slave trade. He was ordained as a priest in the Church of England in 1764 and served in the village of Olney. In 1779 he published the collection of hymns for which he is best known. In his preface to this work, Newton explained his main objective in writing these hymns: to "promote the faith and comfort of sincere Christians." The most famous of these hymns celebrates the theme of amazing grace.

> Amazing grace! How sweet the sound
> That saved a wretch like me!
> I once was lost, but now am found;
> Was blind, but now I see.

The public reading of the Bible

The public reading of the Bible is an integral element of Christian worship. Many churches use a structured program of Bible readings (often referred to as a "lectionary"), which aims to ensure that the Bible is read in its totality throughout the course of the regular worship of the church. Others allow individual ministers to determine what biblical passages shall be read at any given time. The principle, however, remains the same. Part of Christian worship is the hearing and responding to the word of God. Sometimes that response may take the form of believing certain doctrines; at others, it may involve the recognition of the need to behave in certain ways, to do certain things.

In the early church, priority was given to the reading of a passage from the gospels. This was seen as a public declaration of the words and deeds of Jesus Christ. Many churches adopted the practice of standing in order to hear the gospel reading, as a way of demonstrating that the good news of Jesus Christ was central to the life and worship of the church as a whole and of its individual members. This practice gradually developed into having two or three readings, typically arranged sequentially, as a reading from the Old Testament; a reading from one of the New Testament letters; and a reading from one of the gospels.

In many churches the public reading of Scripture is followed by the explanation or application of the read passage through a sermon. We shall explore this in what follows.

Preaching

Many Christian services include an address. This is sometimes referred to as a "homily" – a short, biblically based talk, which aims to provide the congregation with food for thought about how to live out the Christian faith in the world. Others use the term "sermon," which comes from the Latin *sermo* ("speech"), to refer to a more extensive exploration, statement, or application of the Christian faith. This often takes the form of exegesis ("interpretation" – literally, "drawing out") of a biblical passage – for example, the passage chosen or set for the day – of a biblical theme, or of an article of the creed. Collections of sermons have been in circulation from an early stage of Christianity.

Styles of sermon vary considerably, some preachers seeing the sermon as primarily catechetical (that is, aimed at teaching the congregation more about their faith), others as exhortatory (that is, aimed at encouraging its audience to lead better lives as Christians or to take to heart some basic Christian teaching or principle).

Although preaching is a regular part of the worship in many Christian traditions, it was given an especially important role at the time of the Reformation. The new emphasis on the relevance of the Bible, and particularly the Reformation's emphasis on the "priesthood of all believers," gave purpose to the task of creating a biblically literate laity. The preoccupation with Bible-based preaching, displayed by writers such as John Calvin, reflects these concerns.

Some services of the word focus on the recitation or singing of biblical passages; but a sermon is another high point of the event. Eucharist, in contrast, includes both a "ministry of the word" and a "ministry of the sacrament," in which the sermon and the sacrament are seen as playing distinct though complementary roles. We shall consider the role of sacraments in Christian life later on in this chapter (pp. 231–236).

The reciting of the creeds

Many more formal Christian services or worship involve reciting aloud one of the creeds – usually the Apostles' Creed or the Nicene Creed. These creeds are intended to remind believers of the basic themes of their faith and hence to enable them to avoid false teachings. The recitation of the creeds also establishes a strong sense of "belonging," in that it affirms the basic continuity between the Christian communities of today and those of the classic period.

The creeds are statements of faith that are common to all Christians, whether Protestant, Orthodox, or Catholic. They are regarded as possessing a universal significance for all Christians, which transcends the particular importance of individual statements of faith of certain historic churches. Thus, for example, Anglicans might regard the Thirty-Nine Articles as having considerable weight in defining their specifically Anglican beliefs, just as Presbyterians might feel similarly about the Westminster Confession. But these two documents would never be incorporated into the public worship of these churches, because they are seen to lack the *universal* authority of the creeds.

So why do Christians recite these creeds? Partly, it is to allow individual believers to absorb their internal logic and their basic themes, which may thus become the framework for an understanding of the main points of faith. Yet there is also a sense of identity that comes into play. To recite these specific words is to connect up with the church of the past by using the same words that previous generations of Christians have used to express their faith. The recitation of the creeds is an act of solidarity with the Christian past as much as an act of pedagogy. It creates a sense of having a place in the greater scheme of things, of being part of something of deep historical and spiritual significance.

The Sacraments

In general terms, as we noted earlier (pp. 112–117), a sacrament may be thought of as an external rite or sign that in some way conveys or represents to believers the grace of God. A minimalist definition might say that a sacrament is an external physical sign of an interior spiritual grace. The New Testament does not actually make use of the specific term "sacrament." Instead we find the Greek word *musterion* (which is probably best translated as "mystery"), used there to refer to the saving work of God in general. In the Greek text this word is never applied to what would now be regarded as a sacrament (for example, baptism). However, it is clear from what we know of the history of the early church that a connection was made at an early stage between the "mystery" of God's saving work in Christ and the "sacraments" of baptism and the eucharist. We shall now explore each of these connections.

Most Christians, irrespective of their background, regard the sacraments as important signs of God's grace and presence. Although the descriptions "sacrament" or "sacramental mystery" are widely accepted within Christianity, some Protestants prefer to use the term "ordinance." For Luther, sacraments were promises with signs attached – signs intended to reassure us of the reality and trustworthiness of those promises. The bread and wine of the eucharist, or the water of baptism, are visible and tangible signs of the spiritual reality that lies behind them. The bread and wine point to the richness of the life that the gospel offers, and the water points to the cleansing it brings.

This aspect of the role of sacraments in spirituality is brought out clearly in the famous hymn "Adoro te devote," traditionally ascribed to Thomas Aquinas (c. 1225–1274). We shall cite three verses from this work and note the general line of its argument.

> Godhead here in hiding, whom I do adore
> Masked by these bare shadows, shape and nothing more;
> See, Lord, at thy service low lies here a heart
> Lost, all lost in wonder at the God thou art.
>
> O thou our reminder of Christ crucified.
> Living bread the life of us for whom he died,
> Lend this life to me then: feed and feast my mind,
> There be thou the sweetness man was meant to find.

> Jesus whom I look at shrouded here below,
> I beseech thee send me, what I thirst for so;
> Some day to gaze on thee, face to face in light
> And be blessed forever, with thy glory's sight.

The initial idea is that the sacrament offers a means of discerning the presence of God, even though that presence takes the form of "bare shadows" rather than reality. Yet, even though the sacrament is only a sign of the greater reality to which it points, it nevertheless possesses the ability to focus the worshippers' thoughts on God. More specifically, the sacrament reminds us of the saving death of Christ and of the benefits that it brings to humanity. It also serves to uplift the mind and make it think of its future contemplation of the face of God in heaven. The sacrament thus serves as an important *visible and tangible* reminder of the Christian hope, and also as a reminder of the pain and suffering of the cross.

The sixteenth-century Protestant theologian John Calvin emphasized the way in which sacraments are to be seen as God's accommodation to human weakness. Human beings need reassurance as to God's presence and commitment. Baptism confirms the promise that that the sins of believers are washed away, just as the Lord's Supper confirms the promise that those who believe in Christ enjoy the benefits of his death and resurrection. For Calvin, the Holy Spirit strengthens the faith of the believers through the human senses of sight, touch, and taste. Sacraments are external signs by means of which God confirms and seals "his promises of goodness toward us, in order to sustain the weakness of our faith."

Baptism

The noun "baptism" comes from the Greek verb *baptizein*, meaning "to wash" or "to cleanse." In the New Testament the word refers initially to the baptism offered by John the Baptist in the Jordan River as a sign of repentance. Jesus himself was baptized by John. For Christians, the necessity of baptism is partly grounded in the command given by the risen Christ to his disciples to baptize people everywhere in the name of the Father, Son, and Holy Spirit (Matthew 28: 17–20). In the New Testament baptism is clearly understood as both a condition for and a sign of membership of the Christian community.

The Acts of the Apostles records Peter ending an early sermon with the following words, addressed to those who wanted to know what to do if they were to be saved: "Repent and be baptized, every one of you, in the name of Jesus Christ for the forgiveness of your sins. And you will receive the gift of the Holy Spirit" (Acts 2: 38). In the writings of Paul, baptism is affirmed as a practice and interpreted theologically, both in terms of dying and rising with Christ (Romans 6: 1–4), and in terms of "being clothed with Christ." "You are all sons of God through faith in Christ Jesus, for all of you who were baptized into Christ have clothed yourselves with Christ" (Galatians 3: 26–27).

Although the New Testament seems to indicate that baptism was administered to adults, it was not long before young children were being baptized as well. Paul treats baptism as a spiritual counterpart to circumcision (Colossians 2: 11–12), suggesting that the parallel may extend to the application of baptism to infants. The early church saw a clear link between baptism under the New Covenant and circumcision under the Old

Figure 6.2 Christian baptism by total immersion in the Indian Ocean in the island of Zanzibar. Source: © World Religions Photo Library/Alamy.

Covenant. There are hints of this idea in the New Testament itself. The early church argued that, just as circumcision was a covenantal sign that demonstrated that someone belonged to the people of Israel, so baptism was a sign of belonging to the covenant community of the church. Since Israel circumcised infant boys, why should the church not baptize infants?

More generally, there seems to have been a pastoral need for Christian parents to celebrate the birth of a child within a believing household. Infant baptism may well have had its origins partly in a response to this concern. However, it must be stressed that there is genuine uncertainty concerning both the historical origins and the social or theological causes of the practice.

It is nevertheless clear that the practice of infant baptism was widespread by the end of the second century. In the second century Origen treats infant baptism as a universal practice, which he justifies on the basis of a universal human need for the grace of Christ. A similar argument would later be deployed by Augustine: since Christ is the savior of all, it follows that all – including infants – require redemption, which baptism confers, at least in part. Opposition to the practice can be found in the writings of Tertullian, who argued that the baptism of children should be deferred until such time as they "know Christ."

The practice of infant baptism – in, for example, the Catholic church – leads to the process of Christian initiation having at least two phases. First, the person is baptized as an infant. The infant has no faith, but relies upon the faith of the church and the commitment of the parents to bring him or her up within a Christian environment and to teach and embody the Christian faith in the home. The second phase is confirmation, where the child is able to affirm the Christian faith in his or her own right. Within the Catholic tradition baptism is carried out by a local priest, whereas confirmation is carried out by the bishop, as a representative of the whole church. However, the Orthodox church has always insisted on the continuity between baptism and confirmation and thus tends to allow the same priest to baptize and confirm a given person. In the eastern church confirmation is known as "chrismation," on account of its use of oil to anoint the candidate.

The eucharist

The origins of the Christian practice of using bread and wine in public worship go back directly to Jesus of Nazareth. It is clear from the New Testament's testimonial that Jesus expected his church to continue to use bread and wine in remembrance of him. Not only did this recall the Last Supper, at which Jesus broke bread and drank wine with his disciples before his betrayal, but breaking the bread and pouring the wine were symbols of his flesh being broken and of blood being poured out on the cross.

The eucharist has strong associations with the Jewish Passover meal, not least in its commemoration of an act of divine deliverance. According to John's gospel, John the Baptist declared that Jesus Christ is "the lamb of God, who takes away the sin of the world" (John 1: 29). The image of the lamb of God immediately calls to mind the great Passover celebrations of Israel, which in turn recalled God's faithfulness in delivering his people from captivity in Egypt (Exodus 12). A passover lamb would be slain, as a reminder of God's continuing care for his people and commitment to them in conditions of adversity and suffering. To think of Jesus as this lamb of God is to see him as linked with God's great actions of deliverance, including the liberation of his people from their bondage to sin and to the fear of death.

It is clear that Christians obeyed this explicit command of Jesus from the earliest of times. The Acts of the Apostles reports that the disciples were "breaking bread" within weeks of the death and resurrection of Jesus. Paul's first letter to the Corinthians explicitly refers to the practice in the most solemn of terms, making it clear that Paul is passing on something of the utmost importance to his readers. Justin Martyr, writing around AD 165, indicates that the normal practice had been to read and expound the Bible, which was followed by giving thanks and distributing the bread and the wine. Note that the wine in question was always mixed with water. The reason for this custom is unclear; it may have been a practical measure designed to avoid the dehydration of those who received the wine. Theological explanations soon developed, making room for the idea that the mingling of the wine and water symbolized the mingling of Jesus Christ and his people.

This fundamental pattern has passed into modern Christian practice in a wide variety of forms. One major difference between Christians should, however, be noted at this point. As a general rule, Catholics have taught that only priests are permitted to receive *both* the bread and the wine at communion; Protestant churches permit laypeople too to receive them. The origins of and reasons for the Catholic denial of wine to the laity remain uncertain; the custom may have resulted from a practical desire to avoid spillage. Although the Second Vatican Council clearly wished to encourage the laity to receive the wine as well as the bread, such an initiative still remains the exception rather than the rule. In the Orthodox

Figure 6.3   The Last Supper celebrated and commemorated in the eucharist; according to Jacopo da Ponte Bassano (c. 1510–1592). Source: Cameraphoto/AKG Images.

church both the priests and the congregation are permitted to receive wine too, although in some traditions communion is received from a spoon that contains only the bread, sprinkled with a few drops of wine (but in other traditions the spoon contains only the wine to be swallowed – the bread is administered separately). The more general western custom is to handle the bread directly to the communicant.

There are four main ways of referring to the eucharist:

1   *The mass* This term derives from the Latin word *missa*, which really just designates a service of some sort. As the main service of the western church in the classic period was the breaking of the bread, the term came to refer to this one service in particular. "Mass" is now especially associated with the Catholic tradition.

2   *Eucharist* This noun derives from the Greek verb *eucharizein* ("to render thanks"), and designates any thanksgiving. The theme of thanksgiving is an important element in the breaking of the bread, which makes the corresponding term entirely appropriate for the service in question. The term "eucharist" is particularly associated with the Greek Orthodox tradition but has found acceptance beyond it. The Orthodox church uses two main forms of eucharistic liturgy: the liturgy of St. John Chrysostom and the liturgy of St. Basil the Great. These are similar in many respects.

3   *Holy Communion* The phrase "holy communion" points to the idea of "fellowship" or "sharing." It highlights the bond of fellowship between Jesus and the church, and also between individual Christians. The phrase is used in Protestant circles, particularly in churches tracing their origins back to the English Reformation.

4   *Lord's Supper* This phrase picks up the theme of breaking the bread in memory of the Last Supper. To share in the Lord's Supper is to recall, with thanks, all that Jesus achieved for believers though his death on the cross. Again, the expression is used in Protestant

circles, particularly in churches tracing their origins back to the English Reformation. The formula is sometimes abbreviated or simplified to "supper."

Rhythms and Seasons: The Christian Year

From the earliest of times, Christians developed ways of structuring time that reflected fundamental Christian beliefs and the historical events on which they were grounded. This structuring of time appears to have arisen for a number of reasons. The fact that Christianity was grounded in historical events immediately established the basics of a structuring of the year. Good Friday and Easter Day, for example, were located at quite specific positions in the annual calendar. Pentecost and Ascension were easily added to this annual structure. The partition of the Christian year thus reflected some landmark events – events of fundamental importance to Christianity.

The structuring of the year also had an important educational role. It allowed the church to focus its attention on certain themes at certain times of the year. Although the great themes of the Christian faith were taught and preached at all times, the structure of the Christian year allowed for certain ideas or themes to be emphasized at appropriate points. Thus Pentecost marked an obvious time to celebrate the person and work of the Holy Spirit. Good Friday was a particularly appropriate time to reflect on the meaning of Christ's death. Easter Day allowed the theme of the resurrection to be developed and applied to Christian living.

Yet a third reason must also be noted. The New Testament speaks of "redeeming the time" (Ephesians 5: 16). Time does not simply mark the existence of Christians; it offers them an arena within which they may grow and develop. To structure time is thus seen as a means of encouraging spiritual growth – a means that allows the passing of time to reinforce some basic Christian ideas and to deepen their impact on the Christian mind, imagination, and heart. The structuring of the Christian day, week, or year is thus a means of enhancing its potential to remind, recall, and represent some fundamental themes of faith.

One of the most obvious developments in the Christian structuring of time was the setting aside of Sunday – the first day of the week – as the day on which the resurrection of Christ would be celebrated. The letters of Paul clearly presuppose that Christians were meeting for worship on Sunday, in breach of the Jewish tradition of observing the sabbath (Saturday) as a day of rest. In 321, following his conversion to Christianity, the Roman Emperor Constantine formally declared that Sunday should be the official imperial day of rest.

Sunday was thus seen by Christian writers as a "space" that God set aside, in his goodness, to allow for physical rest and spiritual refreshment. One of the writers who stress this point is Susanna Wesley (1669–1742), the mother of John and Charles Wesley, who was persuaded of the importance of creating space for God in the middle of a busy life. For Susanna, Sunday was a space that had been created by God for exactly this purpose and was meant to be used joyfully and profitably.

It is also known that early Christian communities set aside Wednesdays and Fridays as fast days. The reason for the selection of these particular days is not clear; a later explanation suggested that Wednesday was thus observed because it was the day on which Christ was betrayed, and Friday the day on which he was crucified. The practice of eating fish (rather than meat) on Friday, still widely encountered in Catholic circles, reflects this early development.

Perhaps the most important aspect of structuring the time concerns the Christian year, to which we now turn. As we have emphasized, Christianity is not just a set of ideas; it is a way of life. Part of that life is a richly structured cyclical pattern in which various aspects of the Christian faith are singled out for particular attention during the course of a year. The two such festivals that are most familiar outside Christian circles are Christmas and Easter, celebrating the birth and the resurrection of Jesus respectively. This section will focus on the major festivals of the Christian year, explaining their religious basis and noting some of the customs that have come to be attached to them in various parts of the Christian world.

There are major variations within the Christian world concerning how the major religious festivals are marked and celebrated. In general terms, evangelical and charismatic Christians tend to attach relatively little value to such festivals, whereas Catholic and Orthodox Christians tend to place considerably greater emphasis upon them. Indeed the importance attached by Christians to festivals such as Advent and Lent is generally a useful indication of the type of Christianity they have adopted.

Festivals tend to fall into a number of different categories. A major distinction is drawn between *fixed* and *movable feasts*. A fixed feast is a festival that takes place on the same date each year. Thus, in the western church, Christmas Day is invariably celebrated on December 25. Other feasts are determined with reference to events whose dates vary from year to year. For example, the date of Easter is determined in relation to the full moon and could fall at any point between March 21 and April 25. A series of other festivals is dependent on the date of Easter, as follows:

Ash Wednesday, which falls 40 week days before Easter Day;
Maundy Thursday, which is the Thursday before Easter Day;
Good Friday, which is the Friday before Easter Day;
Ascension Day, which is the fortieth day after Easter Day (and thus always falls on a Thursday);
Pentecost, which is the fiftieth day after Easter Day (and thus always falls on a Sunday);
Trinity Sunday, which is the Sunday following Pentecost.

Other festivals focus on individual saints, some of which have particular regional or professional associations. Examples of these associations include:

St. David, patron saint of Wales, whose feast is observed on March 1;
St. Patrick, patron saint of Ireland, whose feast is observed on March 17;
St. Cecilia, patron saint of church music, whose feast is observed on November 22;
St. Christopher, patron saint of travelers, whose feast is celebrated in some parts of the church on July 25.

In each case, the association of a saint with a particular profession is usually linked with events in that saint's life. Other saints have developed associations that have no apparent connection with the original life story and figure of the saint in question. For example, St. Valentine is thought to have been a Roman Christian who was martyred at Rome in the third century. His feast day, which is celebrated on February 14, now has strong associations with romance in some western societies.

In addition to festivals, two periods are often observed as times of fasting or penitence: Advent and Lent. While many Christians no longer observe the tradition of fasting that was once associated with these periods, particularly during the Middle Ages, some continue to regard them as being of importance as times of personal reflection or penitence.

The Orthodox church follows a liturgical year that is broadly divided into three parts, focusing on Easter. These three parts are the *triōdion,* the *pentēkostarion,* and the *oktōēchos.* The *triōdion* is the 10 weeks prior to Easter, which can be seen as a preparation for this great festival. The *pentēkostarion* is the entire Easter period, which is understood to embrace the period between Easter and the Sunday after Pentecost (in the western church, this final date is often celebrated as "Trinity Sunday"). The *oktōēchos* is the remainder of the year.

In what follows we shall explore the highlights of the western Christian year, which have a major impact on the way in which many Christian churches worship and pray, and which often percolate into society as a whole. In each case, the foundation of the festival or season will be noted, together with some of the customs that have come to be associated with it. The order in which the festivals will be discussed is chronological rather than alphabetical. The western Christian year opens with the time of Advent, to which we now turn.

Advent

The term "Advent" comes from the Latin word *adventus,* meaning "coming" or "arrival." It refers to the period immediately before Christmas, during which Christians recall the background to the coming of Jesus. Traditionally, four Sundays are set apart in order to prepare us for the full appreciation of Christmas, of which the first is referred to as Advent Sunday and the last as the Fourth Sunday in Advent. This period of four Sundays is often observed by making "advent crowns," which consist of four candles in a wooden or metal frame. A candle is then lit for each of the four Sundays in Advent. Some churches use purple clerical clothing during this period, as a symbol of the need for penitence (a custom that also applies to Lent, which also has a penitential character).

Strictly speaking, Advent is intended to make us focus on the relationship of two "advents" or "comings" of Jesus: his first coming, in humility, during his time on earth (which is especially associated with Christmas); and his second coming, in glory, as judge, which will take place at the end of time.

Christmas

Christmas is a fixed or immovable feast, always celebrated on December 25. Some Orthodox Christians in Central and Eastern Europe and other parts of the world (such as the United States) celebrate Christmas on January 7. Why this difference? The answer lies in the introduction of the Gregorian calendar, introduced over an extended period of time. It replaced the older Julian calendar, which failed to accurately reflect the length of the year in terms of the earth's orbit around the sun. It was, however, necessary to lose 10 days to make up for the accumulated inaccuracies of the Julian calendar. December 25 on the Gregorian calendar is January 7 on the Julian calendar. The phrase "old calendarists" is sometimes used to refer to those who retain the Julian calendar for liturgical purposes – such as the celebration of Christmas.

It must be stressed that this has never been understood to mean that Christians believe that Jesus was born on December 25. This date was chosen for the celebration of the birth of Jesus irrespective of when that birth actually happened. It is likely that the date was chosen at Rome, some time in the fourth century, to provide a Christian alternative to a local pagan festival. The date of the festival is actually something of an irrelevance, despite the association with the imagery of winter and snow found in many Christian writings from the northern hemisphere.

The central theme of Christmas is the birth of Jesus, which is often commemorated in special carol services. Of these, the one that is widely regarded as the most famous is the Service of Nine Lessons and Carols associated with King's College, Cambridge. The nine lessons (that is, readings from the Bible) are designed to trace the steady progress of God's work of redemption in the world, beginning with the call of Israel and culminating in the coming of Jesus Christ. This pattern of service is now used throughout the Christian world and is familiar to many non-Christians. We considered it in some detail earlier in this chapter (pp. 226).

Many customs have come to be associated with Christmas; the more famous among them have their origins in the nineteenth century. "Santa Claus" is an American corruption of the Dutch name "Saint Nicolas," the patron saint of children. This saint was celebrated on December 6 with gifts made to children. Dutch settlers in New Amsterdam (later renamed "New York") brought this custom to the New World, where it was firmly established and came to be merged into the festival of Christmas itself. The practice of bringing a Christmas tree into houses and of decorating it had its origins in Germany and was brought to England in the 1840s by Queen Victoria's husband, Prince Albert. The origins of this custom in Germany go back to the dawn of Christian history, when missionaries were confronted with pagan beliefs concerning tree-gods.

Epiphany

The unusual name of this festival owes its form to its ancestor, the Greek word *epiphaneia*, which literally means "manifestation," "apparition," or "making known." The festival takes place on January 6. In the eastern church the festival is specifically linked to the baptism of Jesus. In the western church, however, it is linked with the visit of the "wise men" or "Magi" to the infant Jesus. The festival is understood to mark the beginning of the long process by which the identity and significance of Jesus was "made known" to the world. The visit of the Magi (described in Matthew 2: 1–11) is here seen as an anticipation of the recognition and worship that would subsequently be associated with the ministry of Jesus in Galilee and Judaea, which culminated in the resurrection.

Epiphany is celebrated in various ways throughout the Christian world. In France it is marked by eating *la galette des rois* ("the kings' cake"), made of puff pastry layers filled with a dense center of frangipane. In Italy Epiphany is marked by *la Befana* – a woman who brings gifts to children, by analogy with Santa Claus. The traditional Spanish celebration of Epiphany (known as *el Día de los Reyes*, "the Day of the Kings") involves both cakes and gifts. The *roscón de los reyes* ("sweet bread of the kings") is a rich fruit bread, often containing a figure of the infant Christ. Traditionally, on the eve of this feast, children would leave out shoes that would be filled with gifts overnight. In both Spain and Italy, the custom of receiving gifts at Epiphany has now been supplemented by that of receiving gifts on Christmas day too.

Lent

The period of Lent begins with Ash Wednesday, which falls in the seventh week before Easter. The expression "Ash Wednesday" needs explanation. The Old Testament occasionally refers to putting ashes on one's face or clothing as a symbol of repentance or remorse (e.g., Esther 4: 1; Jeremiah 6: 26). Lent is a period of repentance; the wearing of ashes was therefore seen as a proper external sign of an inward attitude of remorse or repentance. In earlier periods in the history of the church, particularly during the Middle Ages, the first day of Lent was therefore marked by the wearing of ashes: both the clergy and ordinary people would wear ashes on their heads. In more recent years, these ashes are made by burning the palm crosses handed out on Palm Sunday during the previous Lent. The theme of repentance is also symbolized in some churches through the purple clerical dress, which is imposed during this season.

Lent is widely regarded as a time of preparation for Easter, and in the past it was associated with a period of fasting. Lent represents the period of 40 days spent by Jesus in the wilderness before the beginning of his public ministry in Galilee. Just as Jesus fasted for 40 days, so his followers were encouraged to do the same thing; thus a period of 40 days of fasting before Easter emerged. Its origins seem to go back to the fourth century. In earlier periods, a shorter period of fasting was recommended (two or three days). The precise nature of the "fasting" varied from one location and time to another. In general, the western church has understood "fasting" primarily in terms of a reduced intake of food and of a diet where fish replaces meat. But the point of emphasis in Lent has generally been devotional reading or attendance at church rather than fasting.

An issue that needs to be noted at this point concerns the length of Lent. The period intervening between Ash Wednesday and Easter Day has actually 46 days. How does it relate to the 40 days of fasting? The answer lies in the tradition, established at a very early stage in the development of Christianity, that every Sunday was to be regarded as a celebration of the resurrection of Christ. For this reason, fasting was forbidden on Sundays. The period of 46 days thus consists of 40 days of fasting plus the six Sundays that fall between Ash Wednesday and Easter Day.

One of the most interesting customs linked with Lent concerns the day before Lent begins. As noted above, Lent begins on a Wednesday. The previous day was therefore the last day before this official period of fasting began. In England this day was called "Shrove Tuesday," although it is now more widely known as "Pancake Tuesday." The origins of the name lie in the practice of clearing out larders immediately before Lent. The simplest way of using up the accumulation of eggs, flour, milk, and other ingredients was to make pancakes. The same day is referred to as "Mardi Gras" in some European countries and their colonies and is marked by major carnivals, such as that now associated with Rio de Janiero in Brazil.

Holy Week

The final week of Lent, generally known as "Holy Week," begins with Palm Sunday (the Sunday before Easter) and ends on the day before Easter Day. It is a time often set aside for reflection on the suffering and death of Christ – a period sometimes referred to as "Passiontide." One of the devotional aids that have become considerably important in Catholicism is that of the "Stations of the Cross." (A "station" here means "a pausing point.") This aid consists of 14 representations of different aspects of Christ's last day on earth – Good Friday, which we shall consider in more detail shortly. The 14 stations are as follows:

1   Christ's condemnation by Pontius Pilate;
2   Christ receiving the cross;
3   Christ's first fall under the weight of the cross;
4   Christ's meeting with his mother, Mary;
5   the carrying of the cross by a passerby, Simon of Cyrene;
6   the wiping of Christ's face by Veronica. The name "Veronica" does not occur in the gospels, but it is found in early apocryphal writings such as *The Acts of Pilate*. This text relates that Veronica was the woman whom Jesus cured of a blood ailment (Matthew 9: 20–22), and that she came to his trial before Pilate to claim his innocence;
7   Christ's second fall under the weight of the cross;
8   Christ's exhortation to the women of Jerusalem;
9   Christ's third fall under the weight of the cross;
10   the stripping of Christ's garments;
11   the crucifixion of Christ;
12   the death of Christ;
13   the presentation of Christ's body to Mary;
14   the burial of Christ.

Many churches have 14 panels illustrating each of these stations built into their walls. Others use removable panels, which are displayed at this time of the year. Worshippers are encouraged to walk round the church, pausing at each station for contemplation, reflection, and prayer.

Holy Week includes four days of particular importance. These are:

Palm Sunday;
Maundy Thursday;
Good Friday;
Holy Saturday.

(Note that Easter Day – which is always a Sunday – follows immediately after Holy Saturday. However, Easter Day is seen as lying outside the season of Lent and marks the end of the period of fasting.)

Palm Sunday is the Sunday immediately before Easter. On this day the church commemorates the triumphal entry of Jesus into Jerusalem, during which the crowds threw palm fronds into his path (see Matthew 21: 1–11). This day, which marks the beginning of Holy Week, is now widely marked by the distribution of crosses made from palm fronds to congregations.

Maundy Thursday focuses on one of the final acts concerning Jesus to be related in John's gospel: his washing of the disciples' feet (John 13: 1–15). The ceremony of the "washing of the feet" of members of the congregation came to be an important part of the liturgy of the medieval church, symbolizing the humility of the clergy, in obedience to the example of Christ. The unusual term "Maundy" is related to this medieval practice. In the Middle Ages church services were held in Latin. The opening words of a typical service on this day are based on the words of Jesus recorded in John 13: 34: "A new command I give you: Love one another. As I have loved you, so you must love one another." In Latin, the opening phrase of this sentence is *mandatum novum do vobis*. The English word "Maundy" is a corruption of the Latin word *mandatum* ("command").

In England, the "Maundy ceremony" originally involved the monarch's affirmation of humility by washing the feet of a small number of his or her subjects. This has now been replaced by the ceremony of the "Maundy Money," in which the monarch distributes specially minted coins to a representative group of older people at cathedrals throughout England.

Good Friday is marked as the day on which Jesus died on the cross. It is the most solemn day in the Christian year and is widely marked by the removal of all decorations from churches. In Lutheran churches the day was marked by the reading of the passion narrative in a gospel, a practice that lies behind the "passions" composed by Johann Sebastian Bach (1685–1750). Both the *St. Matthew Passion* and the *St. John Passion* have their origins in this observance of Good Friday. The practice of observing a period of three hours' devotion, from 12.00 to 3.00 p.m. on Good Friday, has its origins in the eighteenth century. Jesus' three hours on the cross often take the form of an extended meditation on his seven last words from the cross, with periods of silence, prayer, or hymn singing.

The events of Good Friday are also marked dramatically in various ways throughout the world. Perhaps the best known of these is the enactment of the passion and death of Christ, which takes place every 10 years in the little Upper Bavarian village of Oberammergau. As a way of expressing their gratitude to God for delivering them from the plague in 1633, the villagers undertook to act out the passion and death of Christ every decade. The event, which lasts six hours and involves about 700 people, is now a major tourist attraction. In the Philippines, the only Asian nation in which Christianity is the dominant religion, Good Friday is marked with particular fervor. In villages and towns throughout the nation, the crucifixion of Christ is re-enacted by young men who are willing to be nailed to crosses briefly as a sign of their commitment to the Christian faith.

Holy Saturday is the final day of Lent, immediately before Easter Day. Especially in the eastern Orthodox churches, the day is marked by the Paschal Vigil – a late evening service, which leads directly into the following Easter Day, making extensive use of the imagery of light and darkness.

Figure 6.4　Queen Elizabeth II hands out Maundy Money during the Royal Maundy Service held at Liverpool's Anglican Cathedral in 2004. The purses containing the coins were handed to 78 men and 78 women, the number selected to mark the Queen's 78th year. Source: Phil Noble/PA Archives/ Press Association Images.

Easter

Easter Day marks the resurrection of Jesus and is widely regarded as the most important festival of the Christian year. Its religious significance is fundamental. In the first place, the festival affirms the identity of Jesus as the risen savior and Lord. In the Orthodox tradition, this point is often made through icons or pictures in churches, which show a triumphant and risen Christ (often referred to as *Christos pantocrator*, "Christ the all-powerful") as ruler over the universe as a result of his being raised from the dead. In the second place, the festival affirms the Christian hope – that is, the fundamental belief that Christians will be raised from the dead, and hence need fear death no more. Both these themes dominate Easter hymns and liturgies. A good example is provided by an early eighteenth-century collection of hymns known as the *Lyra Davidica*.

Similar themes are found in the poems of the Christian tradition. The words of the English poet George Herbert (1593–1633) illustrate this point well. For Herbert, Easter is about the believer's hope of rising with Christ:

> Rise, heart, thy Lord is risen. Sing his praise
> Without delays,
> Who takes thee by the hand, that thou likewise
> With him mayst rise.

In the Greek Orthodox church, the following traditional Easter greeting is widely used, and has become familiar in other Christian traditions during the present century: *Christos anestē* ("Christ is risen"); answer: *Alethōs anestē* ("he is risen indeed," or "he really is risen").

Box 6.1   Dates of Easter Sunday, 2015–2025

2015	April 5
2016	March 27
2017	April 16
2018	April 1
2019	April 21
2020	April 12
2021	April 4
2022	April 17
2023	April 9
2024	March 31
2025	April 20

Once the date of Easter Day is established, the dates of all other related festivals can be established. Palm Sunday occurs one week before Easter Day. Good Friday is two days before Easter. Pentecost occurs seven weeks after Easter Day, and Trinity Sunday eight weeks after Easter Day. Thus in the year 2000, the dates of these four festivals were as follows:

Palm Sunday	April 16
Good Friday	April 21
Easter Day	April 23
Pentecost	June 11
Trinity Sunday	June 18

Easter is marked in a wide variety of ways throughout the Christian world. In Catholic and Orthodox churches, particular emphasis is often placed on the importance of the symbolism of light and darkness. In the ancient church, baptisms took place on Easter Day, as a way of showing that the believers had passed from darkness to light, from death to life. The custom of giving Easter eggs, widespread in western culture, seems to go back to the idea of an egg as a symbol of new life, pointing to the new life brought by the Christian gospel.

The liturgy and hymns of the Christian church are a particularly powerful witness to the importance of the message of the resurrection of Jesus Christ from the dead. The Paschal troparion or troparion of Easter in the Byzantine liturgy sets out clearly the significance of the Easter event for the world:

> Christ is risen from the dead!
> Dying, he conquered death!
> To the dead, he has given life!

Ascension

Ascension Day, which always falls on a Thursday, can be seen as completing the sequence of events celebrated at Easter. The feast recalls the final ascension of Christ after he has been raised from the dead and has recommissioned the disciples. Theologically, ascension marks the end of the period of appearances of the risen Christ to his disciples. These appearances, which are recorded in some detail in the gospels and hinted at in the letters of the New Testament, began immediately after the resurrection. The theme of "exaltation" is important at this point, in that Jesus is understood to have been exalted to the right hand of God.

Pentecost

Pentecost is the feast on which the church celebrates the gift of the Holy Spirit to the apostles, which led to the dramatic expansion of the church in its formative period. The Holy Spirit is of major importance to Christian thought and life. In recent times, the rise of the charismatic movement within the worldwide church has created an increased awareness of the particular role of the Holy Spirit. Pentecost falls on the fiftieth day after Easter. In the account of the death and resurrection of Jesus set out by Luke in his gospel and in the Acts of the Apostles, there is a continuous sequence of events leading from the resurrection to the giving of the spirit. After the resurrection, Jesus appears to his disciples on a number of occasions, to promise them the gift of the Holy Spirit. This act is described as "the gift the Father promised" and is clearly linked with the theme of empowerment for evangelism and mission.

John's gospel refers to Jesus' promise of the gift of the spirit after he had been taken from his disciples. The basic theme is that the spirit is given to the disciples after Jesus is no longer present with them physically, in order to remind them of his words and works. Note that the spirit is referred to in John's gospel as the "Counsellor." The Greek word *paraklētos* could also be translated as "comforter" or "advocate."

The specific event commemorated at Pentecost is the coming of the Holy Spirit, which is described in the Acts of the Apostles. Luke relates how the disciples had gathered together, and they were filled with the Holy Spirit. Luke's description of the event focuses on its impact: the disciples were empowered to preach the gospel and to break down the barriers of language separating them and their audiences. Theologically, the coming of the spirit thus occupies a significant role in the scheme of salvation: it can be seen as a reversal of the "tower of Babel" (Genesis 11: 1–32).

Pentecost is a major feast in the Christian year. In many Christian traditions, it is seen as second in importance only to Easter itself. Pentecost is sometimes referred to in older English writings as "Whitsun" (literally, "white Sunday"), on account of the tradition that the clergy was wearing white robes on this occasion.

Trinity

The final major feast of the Christian year is Trinity Sunday, which follows immediately after Pentecost. This festival completes the Easter sequence of events by celebrating the distinctively Christian doctrine of the Trinity, in which God is understood to be revealed as Father,

Son, and Holy Spirit (pp. 74–78). It is placed immediately after Pentecost, which celebrates the gift of the Holy Spirit. The early church did not regard the doctrine of the Trinity as marking the occasion of a church festival. The Orthodox Christian year, for example, does not include any direct equivalent of this festival (see p. 236). Trinity first became a feast of major importance in the Middle Ages, and it was eventually given official sanction by John XXII in 1334. Trinity Sunday is the last major festival in the Christian year. The remainder of the year is reckoned in terms of "Sundays after Trinity," until the cycle resumes again on Advent Sunday.

The Structuring of Time: The Monastic Day

While there is no doubt that the Christian year represents one of the most important ways of structuring time, another one should also be noted – namely the one developed in monasteries. Monasticism can be seen, in part, as a reaction against the secularization of the church that resulted from the conversion of Constantine. Monasteries were partly established in order to allow for constant prayer, which was becoming problematic for Christians who chose to remain active in the world. Increasingly, monasticism appeared as an ideal in which the goal of continuous prayer was pursued with a dedication that was impossible outside a monastic context.

This emphasis upon constant prayer led to the restructuring of the day. The pattern that gradually emerged was one of seven times of prayer during the day and one during the night. These times of prayer were given the name "offices," from the Latin term *officium*, meaning "an obligation" or "duty." The biblical basis for this pattern was found in the Psalter. For example, Psalm 119: 64 commends prayer at seven points during the day, and many of the psalms refer to prayer during the night. The evolution of the monastic day can be seen as the gradual institutionalization of this pattern of seven day-time offices and a nocturnal one.

The practice of night-time prayer seems strange, possibly even inhumane, to modern readers used to sleeping in eight-hour blocks. It is important to note that human sleep patterns seem to have changed as a result of the introduction of artificial light. In older times, when human life was governed by the rising and setting of the sun, people often slept in shorter blocks of time, which are sometimes referred to as "first sleep" and "second sleep." In between these shorter periods of sleep, they tended to eat or pray. The monastic prayer cycle fits in neatly with this older pattern of sleep.

The precise evolution of this pattern of monastic offices is not completely understood. The following factors seem to have been involved.

1   There was already a widespread trend within ordinary church life to pray corporately in the early morning and evening. These offices came to be referred to as Mattins and Vespers (from the Latin terms for "morning" and "evening"). The monasteries appear to have incorporated this regular pattern of prayer into their own more rigorous structures. These two times of prayer were often referred to as "the principal offices."
2   A second major factor was the structure of the classical Roman working day. This led to prayer being specified for the third, sixth, and ninth hours (that is, 9.00 a.m., noon, and 3.00 p.m.). These times of prayer were designated as "terce," "sext," and "none" respectively (from the Latin words for "third," "sixth," and "ninth").

3   Two additional offices were specified. Compline (from the Latin term for "completion" or "ending") was, in effect, the final time of prayer before retiring to bed. Prime (from the Latin word for "first") was an early morning form of prayer, apparently introduced by Cassian, who was concerned that monks might otherwise go back to bed after the night office and sleep through until 9.00 in the morning.

4   There appears to have been considerable variation as to the time of the night office, which reflected local patterns of worship and understandings of personal discipline. If the day is divided into eight periods of three hours, it might be expected that the night office would be set for 3.00 a.m.; however, there appears to have been some variation on this matter.

The basic point to be made here is that the monastic day was systematically structured into segments, which included prayer and the reading of Scripture, particularly the Psalms. Psalms 148, 149, and 150 were used with particular frequency. The pattern of daily offices was seen as an important framework for the development of personal and corporate spirituality, offering monks the opportunity to achieve the ideal of continual prayer and at the same time saturating them with biblical passages. The internalization of Scripture, so important an aspect of monastic spirituality, is partly grounded in the rich use of the Bible in the monastic offices, as well as in the emphasis, within some monastic traditions, on personal devotion on the part of individual monks in their cells.

Some aspects of this structuring of the day remain important outside the monastic tradition. An excellent example is provided by the tradition of evangelical Quiet Time, a daily period set aside for private reading of the Bible, meditation, and prayer. For many evangelicals, the early morning provides an ideal opportunity to begin the day with the reading of Scripture. Although the pressures of modern life have undermined this practice somewhat, the basic principle remains unaltered. Many study aids have emerged to encourage and assist the practice of Quiet Time, typically by assigning a passage to each day and by offering brief devotional comments and reflections on the passage as an aid to prayer. Similarly, the Lutheran writer Dietrich Bonhoeffer (1906–1945) stressed the positive value of setting aside a daily period for personal Bible study and meditation. In his *Life Together* (1938), Bonhoeffer set out the importance of "being alone with the Word," allowing it to challenge and inspire its readers.

The Structuring of Space: Pilgrimage and the Christian Life

It is not merely time that is given a new meaning or structure by the Christian faith. The same is true of locations. For many Christians, their faith gives them a new sense of the importance of certain places. Noting the importance of places associated with the Old Testament, the scholar Walter Brueggeman offered the following description of "place," which is helpful for understanding the phenomenon of pilgrimage:

> Place is space which has historical meanings, where some things have happened which are now remembered and which provide continuity and identity across generations. Place is space in

which important words have been spoken which have established identity, defined vocation, and envisioned destiny.

Many Christian traditions ascribe particular spiritual significance to holy places or to the process of traveling to them. Once more, it is necessary to note that this is not a uniform tendency within Christianity. While we should immediately concede the dangers of generalization, it seems that Protestantism has generally been more critical than affirmative of the notion of a "holy place." In the present section we shall explore some aspects of this notion and the significance of such places for spirituality.

Old Testament writers clearly regarded the city of Jerusalem as a holy place. Jerusalem and its temple were seen as the central focus of the religion of Israel. God was understood to have chosen Jerusalem as a dwelling place; the city and its temple were thus set apart as possessing a religious significance denied to other locations in Israel. Earlier in Israel's history, sites such as Shiloh and Mizpah were regarded as being of special religious importance. It was at these sites that shrines were established during the period of the conquest of Canaan.

Nevertheless, the temple erected at Jerusalem came to be seen as possessing supreme significance. Some Old Testament passages spoke of Jerusalem or its temple as the "dwelling place" of God. As a result, Jerusalem gradually assumed a special role in Israel's hopes for the future. It was from Jerusalem that the knowledge of God was to spread to all nations (Isaiah 2: 2–4; Micah 4: 1–3). It was by worshipping God in Jerusalem that the nations of the world would find their true unity (Isaiah 19: 23; Zechariah 8: 3). The modern Jewish Passover ends by expressing the hope that, in the next year, this feast will be celebrated in Jerusalem.

It is therefore clear that Jerusalem came to play a special role in Judaism. Given that the central events upon which the Christian faith is founded – supremely, the death and resurrection of Jesus – took place in Jerusalem, it might be expected that the New Testament should take over this Old Testament understanding of the special place of the city. This, however, proves not to be the case. The special, sacred status of Jerusalem within the Old Testament is not endorsed by the New Testament, which affirms the historical *but not the theological* importance of this city. The theme of the "new Jerusalem" is certainly found, as a statement of the Christian hope (see Hebrews 12: 22; Revelation 21: 2). Yet this statement is not seen as legitimizing any present spiritual significance of the city of Jerusalem.

The significance of Jerusalem is not discussed in any detail by Christian writers of the first three centuries. This is in itself an indication that this theme was not felt to be of major importance. Two very different views emerged in the fourth century. Eusebius of Caesarea (c. 260–339) argued that the spirituality of the New Testament was not concerned with physical entities (such as the "land of Israel" or the "city of Jerusalem"), but with spiritual matters, of which these physical entities were at best convenient physical symbols. Cyril of Jerusalem (c. 320–386), in contrast, was quite clear that Jerusalem remained a "holy city." It is, of course, entirely possible that ecclesiastical politics entered into this debate. Cyril was anxious to maintain the prestige of his own city; Eusebius was interested in promoting the claims of Rome as the new city to be granted special divine favor.

An important document dating from this period, which illustrates the spiritual importance of pilgrimage, is the "Peregrinatio Egeriae" ("The Pilgrimage of Egeria"). This document, discovered in 1884 and probably dating from somewhere between 381 and 384, is in effect the personal journal of a woman visiting the Holy Land and recording everything she observes. Although the text is often read for its first-hand testimony concerning liturgical practices in the Holy Land at this date, it is also an important witness to the benefits that such pilgrimages were understood to bring.

In the course of Christian history, a number of sites have emerged as having potential spiritual importance. These include the following:

1   Jerusalem, the scene of the Last Supper, betrayal, crucifixion, and resurrection of Jesus;
2   Rome, widely believed to be the site of the martyrdom and burial of both St. Peter and St. Paul;
3   Canterbury, the site of the martyrdom of Thomas à Becket in 1170. The bawdy escapades subsequently accompanying pilgrimages to Canterbury were set out by Geoffrey Chaucer in his *Canterbury Tales*;
4   Santiago de Compostela in northwestern Spain, the traditional burial place of St. James the Apostle;
5   Lourdes in southern France, the site of a vision of the Virgin Mary in 1858, which has become associated with reports of healings.

Figure 6.5   Santiago de Compostela, the center of a major pilgrimage route in northern Spain. Source: Andrea Jemolo/AKG Images.

What role do pilgrimages to such sites play in Christian spirituality? Clearly, the answer to such questions will be complex and nuanced, given the considerable variation within Christianity concerning issues of theology. For example, Protestants generally no not accept any kind of "theology of sacred places" and would not give Mary any particular place of honor. Pilgrimages to Lourdes therefore do not feature prominently in Protestant spirituality.

In general, the following factors help toward an understanding and an appreciation of a spirituality of pilgrimage.

1 The act of making a pilgrimage involves at least a degree of commitment and hardship. This makes a pilgrimage an act of self-denial or personal discipline, the virtues of which would be widely accepted. The degree of hardship can be enhanced in various ways: for example, medieval penitents were in the habit of placing small stones inside their shoes to make the journey more painful.
2 The pilgrimage offers an opportunity to reflect on the life and teaching of the person associated with the pilgrimage site. For example, a pilgrimage to Santiago de Compostela offers an opportunity to read about St. James, just as a pilgrimage to Rome can be the focus for reflection on the life and teaching of both St. Peter and St. Paul.
3 The notion of "pilgrimage" helps reinforce the Christian idea that believers are "strangers and pilgrims on earth" (Hebrews 11: 13), whose true home is a city in heaven (Philippians 3: 20). The idea of passing through life en route to the heavenly city, rather than making oneself at home in the world, is clearly embodied in the act of pilgrimage.
4 For some, the sites of pilgrimage are themselves endued with some spiritual quality, which can be experienced by those who travel there.

As was noted earlier, Protestants generally regard the notion of "pilgrimage" with suspicion. However, it is important to appreciate that the notion is present, although in a slightly redirected manner, within many Protestant spiritualities. Many Protestants find it helpful to make journeys to the Holy Land or to sites of relevance to the New Testament – for example, the seven churches of Asia (mentioned in the book of Revelation) or the churches established by or written to by St. Paul. These journeys are seen, however, primarily as bringing a new depth to Bible study, in that biblical passages take on a new personal significance once the reader has visited the site in question. Visiting religious sites is thus seen as an aid to more effective Bible study.

The image of "pilgrimage" gained new importance through the Second Vatican Council's use of it as a model of the church. The idea of a "pilgrim church" is a helpful counterbalance to a strongly institutional conception of the church, associated with buildings and power structures. It offers a minimalist ecclesiology, focusing on the theme of journeying through the world on one's way to the new Jerusalem.

Conclusion

In this chapter we have looked at some features of the Christian life. We have already seen how Christianity impacts on culture – for example, in customs and traditions associated with holy days such as Easter or Christmas. But what of the wider impact of Christianity? In the next chapter we shall look at the impact of the Christian faith on culture in general, including the arts and sciences.

7

Christianity and the Shaping of Culture

Christianity is both a private and a public faith. It affects the way in which individuals think and behave; it also impacts on society as a whole. Christianity has the potential to shape culture in a significant manner. Yet Christianity is complex, containing within itself divergent understandings of the nature of the Christian faith and of how this faith affects both individual and communal engagement with the wider culture.

This tension was evident within Roman Christianity in the fourth century. The conversion of the Emperor Constantine (pp. 129–131) ended a long era of the oppression and marginalization of Christianity. Bishops suddenly found themselves as figures of social influence and power. Christians were able to build churches and to worship in public. Many welcomed this new possibility, seeing it as a means of reshaping society along Christian lines. But others were alarmed, believing that Christianity was at its most authentic when it existed and operated on the margins of society. Power corrupted. Was there not a danger that Christianity's new social status would lead to its becoming compromised?

This was no idle concern. The new social status of Christianity within the Roman empire certainly led to a growth in its cultural influence. Yet it soon became clear that, if Christianity was to be the new religion of Rome, it would have to become what Roman rulers expected a religion to be. Establishment might well have its privileges; it also had its obligations. Culturally, the imperialization of Christianity led to the absorption of a number of Roman customs into Christian practice, where they were given a new interpretation.

Perhaps the most interesting of these is the development of the "cult of the saints."

Traditional Roman religion honored the dead with ceremonial meals at the site of their tombs. This practice soon became absorbed into Christianity. Christians would gather at the tombs of prominent saints or martyrs, celebrating a eucharist in their honor. Though this practice was relatively easily accommodated theologically, it is important to note that

Christianity: An Introduction, Third Edition. Alister E. McGrath.
© 2015 John Wiley & Sons, Ltd. Published 2015 by John Wiley & Sons, Ltd.

its origins did not lie in the New Testament. Its development ultimately reflected the need for a Christian equivalent of a traditional Roman practice.

Many other examples could be given to illustrate the complex relation of Christianity to culture, which led some to develop a theology of the church as a "community in exile." This idea sustained the Puritans as they wrestled with their powerlessness after the failure of the Commonwealth in England. It nourished the radical wing of the Reformation, which deliberately forsook any kind of social approbation in sixteenth-century Europe in order to be authentically Christian. Many Anabaptist writers saw the conversion of Constantine as marking the end of authentic Christianity and believed that the latter needed to be reconstituted in new forms, which should be uncontaminated by privilege and influence.

It is therefore hazardous and unhelpful to offer sweeping generalizations about the relationship between Christianity and culture. Some Christians disengaged from wider society; others embraced it. Some saw engagement as a means of making secular culture more Christian. Others feared that this process would lead to Christianity becoming more secular. On balance, however, the interaction can be argued to have enriched both the church and society. In the present chapter we shall consider some aspects of this relationship. We begin by reflecting on how the relation of Christianity to culture is to be understood.

Christianity and Culture: General Considerations

The history of the interaction between Christianity and culture is very complex. While most Christian writers support engagement with culture, others advocate withdrawal or disengagement from society, fearing that such engagement might contaminate faith. Some Christians hold that it is not proper to attend any form of public entertainment – such as the cinema – whereas others believe that it is important to be fully and appreciatively immersed in culture at large.

Some Christian groups have deliberately defined themselves as countercultural; hence they have worn clothes and adopted practices that mark them off from those around them. The Mennonite and Amish communities in modern America are a particularly good example of this trend. Holding that their faith demands that they separate from mainstream culture and distinguish themselves clearly by physical and visible means, the Amish adopt clothing styles that encourage humility and separation from the world. The Amish dress is in a very simple style, avoiding all but the most basic ornamentation. Clothing is made at home, of plain fabrics, and is primarily dark in color. Such habits reflect, however, a minority perspective. Most Christians see no need to distinguish themselves from the world.

To understand the complexities of the interrelationship of Christianity and culture, we need to consider the first phase of Christian history. Since it first established a significant presence at Rome in the first century AD, namely in the 40s, Christianity had had a decidedly ambiguous legal status. On the one hand, it was not legally recognized, and so it did not enjoy any special rights; on the other, it was not explicitly forbidden. However, its growing numerical strength gave rise to periodic attempts to suppress it by force. Sometimes these persecutions were local, restricted to regions such as North Africa; at other times they were sanctioned throughout the entire Roman empire.

How should Christians have responded to this situation? Prior to the conversion of Constantine, many of them were content to keep a low profile, keeping their religious views to themselves. Many – including Tertullian – took the view that Christianity must maintain its distinctive identity by avoiding secular influences. "What," he famously asked, "has Athens to do with Jerusalem?" But, with the conversion of Constantine, new possibilities emerged.

Augustine of Hippo is widely – and rightly – seen as mapping out the mainstream Christian response to the relation of faith and culture. His approach is probably best described as a *critical appropriation* of classical culture. For Augustine, the situation of Christianity in Rome is comparable to that of Israel fleeing from captivity in Egypt at the time of the exodus. Although they left the idols of Egypt behind them, the Israelites carried with them Egypt's gold and silver, in order to make better and proper use of such riches, which were thus liberated in order to serve a higher purpose. In much the same way, the philosophy and culture of the ancient world could be appropriated by Christians, where this seemed right, and thus allowed to serve the cause of the Christian faith.

Figure 7.1   Saint Augustine of Hippo in a monastic cell, as depicted by Sandro Botticelli, c. 1495. Source: Rabatti-Domingie/AKG Images.

Augustine's fundamental idea was to make use of a way of thinking – or writing, or speaking – that had hitherto been imprisoned within a purely pagan use, and to liberate it from this captivity, so that it might be put to the service of the gospel. Augustine argues that what is essentially neutral yet valuable ways of thinking or self-expression has been quarried in "the mines of the providence of God"; the difficulty is the use to which they were put within pagan culture, in that they had been "improperly and unlawfully prostituted to the worship of demons."

Augustine's approach thus laid the foundation for the assertion that whatever was good, true, or beautiful could be used in the service of the gospel. It was this approach that would prove dominant in the western church, providing a theological foundation for the critical appropriation by Christian writers of literary genres whose origins lay outside the church. To literary forms already known within the church and widely recognized as entirely appropriate for Christian usage – such as the sermon and the biblical commentary – might be added others, whose cultural pedigree was thoroughly secular. Examples would include drama and – to anticipate a later development – the novel.

Yet Augustine's view never secured total acceptance. The study of Christian history reveals a complex pattern of interactions with culture, some inspired by Augustine, others by more countercultural ways of thinking. For some Christians, the world is an environment hostile to Christian belief and practice. The values of the kingdom of God stand in contrast to those of the world. This type of spirituality was of considerable importance in the first few centuries of Christian history, when Christianity was viewed with intense distrust and suspicion by the secular authorities, and on occasion actively persecuted. Once the Roman emperor Constantine was converted to Christianity, however, a very different situation resulted. Christianity rapidly became the official religion of the Roman empire. In the eyes of many, this resulted in a compromise with secular values. Bishops began to imitate the dress and customs of secular rulers – for example, by wearing purple robes (a symbol of wealth and power).

The new situation made many Christians believe that some authentically Christian ideals were being sacrificed in the compromise. The rise of the monastic movement is widely seen as a revolt against the easy accommodation that began to emerge between church and state, which often made it difficult to tell them apart. The monasteries saw themselves as centers of authentic Christianity, insulated from the temptations of power and wealth, in which the true Christian vision could be pursued. Many works of monastic spirituality spoke of the cultivation of "contempt for the world," by which they meant a studied rejection of the temptations offered by the world, which they regarded as an obstacle to salvation and personal spiritual growth. Withdrawal from the world was the only guaranteed means of ensuring one's salvation.

Although the Protestant Reformation rejected the monastic ideal, the dual theme of renunciation of the world and the world's hostility toward authentic Christianity was taken up and developed by the more radical wing of the movement. Anabaptist writers stressed the need to form alternative Christian communities, often in rural areas. They refused to have anything to do with secular power or authority, as they rejected the use of force. A tension can be discerned at this point between radical writers and the mainline reformers (such as Luther and Calvin), who encouraged a more positive and interactive approach to society and culture. Similar attitudes and conflicts between them can be found within North American fundamentalist circles today.

The relationship between Christianity and culture is thus complex. Some Christians see no difficulty in interacting positively and fully with the local culture; others fear that any such engagement would lead to the erosion of Christian distinctive features.

The ability of Christianity to change culture can be seen in both the ancient and the modern world. In the late third century, many Romans were convinced that the diminishing prosperity and influence of Rome were directly due to the rise of Christianity. The old religious cults were being abandoned in favor of Christianity. There is no doubt that one of the most significant contributing causes of the slow and inexorable death of classical pagan culture was the rise of Christianity. The same pattern can be seen in modern Chinese culture, where there is a widespread interest in Christianity among the younger generation. Traditional Chinese customs, such as "grave sweeping" (in which children are regarded as being under an obligation to honor their ancestors by tidying their graves), are regarded with suspicion by younger Chinese Christians, who feel that the practice is linked with a set of beliefs that are not Christian. This traditional Chinese custom is being eroded, due to the growth of Christianity. Countless other examples could be given of cultural changes resulting from the growth of Christianity, including the decline of traditional religious beliefs and their associated practices in Africa and Southeast Asia.

One of the most marked differences between Christianity and the two other great monotheistic religions – Judaism and Islam – is that Christianity makes no religious requirements of its followers concerning food or clothing. Judaism and Islam both regard certain foods – such as pork – as being "unclean" and forbid their followers to eat them. In marked contrast, Jesus of Nazareth declared all foods to be clean, insisting that moral and religious purity depended on what lay within a person's heart rather than on what entered their bodies through their mouth (Mark 7: 18–19).

In a similar way, Judaism and Islam require animals to be slaughtered in a particular way, to meet strict religious laws (*kosher* and *halal*, respectively). Christianity has never made any such demands of its followers, despite pressure from Judaizing factions within the early church to satisfy such requirements.

It must, however, also be appreciated that Christianity exists in a mutual relationship with culture. Christianity had an impact on its surrounding culture, which in turn molded Christianity. This process was entirely natural: Christianity did not lay down precise rules concerning food, dress, or lifestyle – Christians regarded themselves as able to incorporate aspects of their culture according to their beliefs. As the history of Christian expansion makes clear, Christians did not impose a uniform culture on peoples who had chosen to accept the Christian faith. It is quite clear that Christianity fostered an attitude of tolerance toward traditional cultural beliefs and norms where these were not seen as having a direct relevance to the Christian faith. The cultural diversity within Christianity is perhaps one of the most striking differences between Christianity and Islam.

A wide range of traditional cultural customs and practices thus finds its way into Christianity. Some have achieved almost universal acceptance. Two examples will illustrate this. The traditional color associated with Christian bishops is purple. This was a sign of social status in the classical world and was adopted by Christians as a means of designating the importance of bishops within their communities and beyond. Had Christianity had its origins in China, it is entirely possible that bishops might have worn yellow (the traditional Chinese color associated with royalty). This aspect of classical culture was regarded as acceptable by Christians, and thus eventually found its way within the church. A second example is the Christian practice (now widespread within western culture) of placing a wedding ring on the fourth finger of the bride's left hand. This reflects a traditional Roman custom, which Christians found perfectly acceptable – and thus incorporated into their marriage customs.

A further area of interest concerns the need for a supply of wine in order to comply with the explicit commandment of Jesus that his followers should use bread and wine to remember him. The great medieval monasteries in Spain, France, and Italy soon fell into the habit of establishing vineyards in order to ensure a regular supply of communion wine. It was a monk named Dom Perignon who discovered how wine could be preserved by using the bark of the Portuguese cork oak to seal bottles.

In what follows we shall explore some of the ways in which Christianity has influenced – and continues to influence – culture. It must be made clear that the restriction of the subject in this way is entirely due to lack of space. What follows must be regarded as illustrative of the way in which Christianity interacted with culture; in no way can this brief analysis be considered to be definitive!

We begin by looking at the world of art, music, and literature. In what way has Christianity shaped the way we represent and reflect the world? We may begin by considering how Christian symbols have developed.

Christian Symbolism: The Cross

We have already seen how the figure of Jesus Christ dominates the Christian faith. In particular, we noted how the death of Jesus on the cross is understood by Christians to be the foundation of the salvation of humanity. The cross is thus a symbol of salvation. It is also a symbol of the Christian hope, in that it affirms the death that has been defeated through the resurrection of Jesus. The cross – an instrument of execution – became a sign of the hope and transformation that are fundamental to Christianity.

The cross has been the universally acknowledged symbol of the Christian faith from a very early period, probably as early as the late second century. Indeed, it is fair to suggest that there is no symbol that carries as much weight, authority, or recognition within the Christian faith as the cross. Christians are baptized with the sign of the cross. Churches and other Christian places of meeting do not merely include a cross; they are often built in the shape of a cross. The Christian emphasis on the cross has had considerable implications for the design of churches. Indeed, it is probably in this area that Christian theology has had its most profound impact on western culture. To explore a great medieval cathedral or church is to view theology embodied in stone.

Many Christians find it helpful to make the sign of the cross in times of danger or anxiety. The graves of Christians – whether Catholic, Orthodox, or Protestant – are marked with crosses. Careful studies of the origins and development of Christian symbolism have made it clear that the cross was seen as the symbol of the Christian gospel from the earliest of times. Even in the earliest writings of the New Testament, the phase "the message of the cross" is used as a shorthand summary of the Christian gospel (see 1 Corinthians 1: 18–25). This theme is echoed in later writers of the early church. For Tertullian, Christians are "those who believe in the cross"; for Clement of Alexandria, the cross is "the supreme sign of the Lord."

The final stage in the global acceptance of the cross as supreme symbol of the Christian faith is generally regarded as having been the conversion of the future Roman Emperor Constantine. At some point shortly before or after the decisive battle of the Milvian Bridge (312), Constantine saw a vision of a cross, which ordered him to place the sign on his soldiers' shields. During the reign of Constantine, crosses of various types were erected in Rome and began to appear on Roman coinage. Crucifixion had continued as a means of execution under previous Roman emperors. Constantine outlawed the practice and directed that the scaffolds used for execution would no longer be referred to as "crosses" (*cruces*) but as *patibula*, a Latin word referring to one component of a cross, namely its "horizontal support" or "crossbeam."

Early Christian writers regarded the cross as a teaching aid for the great themes of the Christian faith. Not only did it affirm the reality of salvation and hope in a world of death; it also affirmed the full humanity of Jesus. Early Christian writers were also prepared to read more ambitious ideas into the cross. Justin Martyr suggested that there was a parallel between the Christian cross and the Platonic cross-shaped cosmic symbol – the Greek letter *chi*.

There is evidence that first-century Christians were reluctant to portray the crucifixion of Jesus. It was one thing to make the sign of the cross; it was quite another to depict Jesus on the cross of Calvary, especially on account of the issues of taste and decency involved in portraying Jesus naked. However, these inhibitions were gradually overcome. Christian art, both in the East and in the West, began to focus on the crucifixion for devotional purposes. In response to the view that Jesus was purely divine, lacking any real human nature, Christian leaders encouraged artists to produce depictions of the crucifixion of Jesus as a way of emphasizing his full humanity. What better way of stressing the suffering and death of Jesus than to portray him on the cross? The implications of these attitudes are considerable and help understand the importance attached by many Christian writers to the devotional depiction of the crucifixion. Matthias Grünewald's *Crucifixion* (1515–1516) is an excellent example of this genre of paintings (p. 261).

The symbol of the cross features prominently in Christian worship, both public and private. Many churches are built in the shape of crosses and display crosses conspicuously on their rooftops and within the building itself. Of particular importance to many Christians is the *crucifix* – that is, a wooden carving of Jesus stretched out on the cross, with the inscription INRI above his head (these letters spell out the Latin words *Iesus Nazarenus Rex Iudaeorum*, which mean "Jesus of Nazareth, king of the Jews"). The crucifix is intended to remind Christians of the sufferings of Jesus, and thus to emphasize the costliness and reality of the salvation that resulted from his death on the cross.

The cross has found its way into the symbolism of nations whose history has been steeped in the Christian faith. For example, the traditional Union Flag of the United

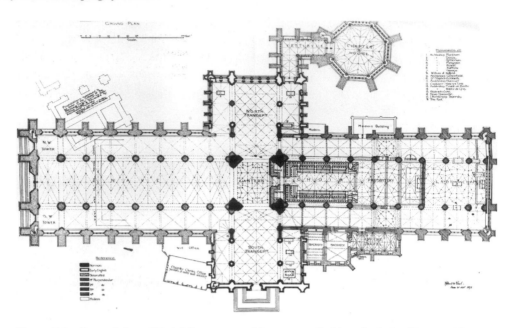

Figure 7.2   Ground plan of York Minster, one of the greatest Gothic cathedrals of Europe. Note especially its cruciform structure. Source: © The Dean & Chapter of York.

Kingdom consists of three different crosses – the crosses of St. George (England), St. Patrick (Ireland) and St. Andrew (Scotland) – combined into a single design. Celtic crosses – that is, crosses with a circle embracing their four arms – are a particular feature of the Irish landscape. Other forms of the cross with particular national or regional associations include the Cross of Lorraine and the Maltese Cross. The background to the incorporation of this Christian symbol into national flags can probably be traced back to the second century. Justin Martyr and others drew a parallel with the way in which conquering Roman armies marched behind their "banners and trophies" (*vexilla et tropaia*): in the same way, such writers argued, Christians marched behind the banner of the cross, which bore the trophy of a defeated death.

Although the cross is the most familiar and widely encountered of Christian symbols, it is important to note that other symbols were of importance in early Christianity. One of these may be noted. A fish was used as a symbol of Christian identity, on account of its potential as a teaching aid. The Greek term for fish is *ichthus*. The five letters of the Greek word for fish are ΙΧΘΥΣ (*i-ch-th-u-s*); these letters act as an acronym, spelling out the central Christian beliefs concerning the identity and significance of Jesus.

GREEK LETTER	GREEK WORD	ENGLISH TRANSLATION
I (iota)	*Iēsous*	Jesus
X (chi)	*Christos*	Christ
Θ (theta)	*Theou*	of God
Υ (upsilon)	*huios*	Son
Σ (sigma)	*sōtēr*	savior

The word *ichthus* thus spells out the belief that Christians regarded as being at the center of their faith: "Jesus Christ, Son of God, savior." References to "the sign of the fish" can be found in a number of early Christian writings, particularly on tombs. The Greek word *ichthus* and the symbol of a fish are both still widely used by Christians. If the automobile in front of you has a symbol of a fish on its bumper, it is probably owned by a Christian. If an organization or an Internet URL has the word *ichthus* in it, you can be fairly certain it has something to do with Christianity.

Christian Art

God is invisible and cannot be seen by mortal human beings. This insight is fundamental to most religions with a strongly transcendent understanding of God. Yet, throughout the history of Christian thought, human beings have shown a marked longing to be able to depict God in some manner. If God cannot be visualized, the idea of God becomes potentially abstract and impersonal, remote from the world of human experience. One of the most significant themes in Christian spirituality is that of *visualization* – the development of ways in which the divine may be represented visually, as something to be contemplated, without compromising the transcendence of God.

On May 8, 1373, the English religious writer Julian of Norwich experienced a series of visions concerning the love of God. These were triggered off by a very specific stimulus. Julian had become ill, and those around her were convinced that she was about to die. The local parish priest was sent for; he held before her a crucifix (that is, a carving of Jesus of Nazareth upon the cross) and spoke these words to her: "I have brought you the image of your Creator and Savior. Look at it, and be strengthened." The image of Christ upon the cross proved to be a gateway to a series of extended meditations on the goodness of God and on God's overwhelming generosity and courtesy to sinners.

If contemplation of the life and person of Jesus led people to a deeper knowledge of God, it seemed to many that vivid and realistic depictions of incidents in the life of Christ could assist that process still further. The Middle Ages and the Renaissance witnessed a dramatic increase in the use of religious art for both public and private devotion. Panel painting was widely used to depict narratives concerning Jesus, or static portraits of Jesus and his mother. In the early Middle Ages, the two dominant religious images were the Madonna and child and the crucifixion. By the later Renaissance, the same attention once paid to the crucifixion was being devoted to other religious subjects.

Renaissance artists regarded many incidents in the life of Jesus as being of potential importance. Particular attention was paid to the Annunciation (that is, to the scene in Luke's gospel in which Gabriel informs Mary that she is to bear a son), to the baptism of Jesus, and to the resurrection. The appearance of the risen Jesus to Mary Magdalene (John 20: 17) was also the subject of many classic works, including Fra Angelico's fresco *Noli me tangere* (*Do Not Touch Me*), painted over the period 1440–1441 in the convent of San Marco in Florence. Painted panels could be displayed singly in churches, but they were often combined in the form of double panels (diptychs) or triple panels (triptychs), as in the Isenheim altarpiece by Matthias Grünewald, noted earlier. One of the most complex of these is the assembly of multiple painted panels (polyptychs) that make up the Ghent Altarpiece by Hubert and Jan van Eyck, which was installed in Ghent Cathedral in 1432.

The nativity – that is, the birth – of Christ has long played a central role in Christian iconography. Christians have always appreciated the theological and spiritual importance of the birth of the savior and have found picturing this event to be helpful for personal and corporate devotion. In the West, the dominant approach to depicting the nativity is to set Mary and her child at the center of the picture.

An excellent example of this approach can be found in *The Mystic Nativity* by Sandro Botticelli (1447–1515). In this work, executed around the year 1500, Mary is depicted in terms appropriate to the era of the painter rather than to that of the New Testament. Botticelli here follows other Renaissance painters of the fourteenth and fifteenth centuries, who portrayed Mary dressed as a noblewoman of their time. The point being made is that Christ's entry into history is of importance to all ages, not simply the Palestine of the first century. Representing Mary as a lady of the Renaissance was a means of emphasizing the transformative potential of the Christ-child for the Renaissance – as well as for all ages.

Botticelli portrays the angels in heaven as rejoicing over the transformation of the created order that will take place through the newborn Jesus. Indeed, in the lower section of the painting, angels are even depicted as dancing with humans, as they celebrate the possibility of a new heaven and a new earth.

Interestingly, Botticelli follows a long-standing tradition in including an ox and ass in the nativity scene. Yet the gospel nativity accounts make no mention of oxen or asses. So why are these traditionally included in the scene? From the second century on, commentators on the birth of Jesus linked the nativity narrative with Isaiah 1: 3: "The ox knows its owner, and the donkey its master's crib; but Israel does not know, my people do not understand."

In some cases, the themes of Christmas and Epiphany (p. 239) are merged: shepherds from the fields around Bethlehem are depicted along with some of their sheep, worshipping the infant Jesus, together with the three wise men or kings from the East, who brought the newborn child the exotic and costly gifts of gold, frankincense, and myrrh. Traditionally it is assumed that each wise man brought one of the three gifts (the gospels do not tell us how many wise men actually came).

Churches, private chapels, and houses were often decorated with depictions of the crucifixion as a means of encouraging personal devotion. Christian writers and artists have always been aware of the need to reflect on this pivotal event and its life-changing implications. Unlike the docetic heresy (which held that Jesus merely had the "appearance" of humanity and did not really suffer), Christian orthodoxy stressed both the reality of Jesus' agony on the cross and the salvation that it achieved. Visual representations of this suffering on the cross thus served to stress the costliness of redemption and to deepen the believers' appreciation of what Jesus of Nazareth achieved. The best argument against docetism was the depiction of the sufferings of Jesus on the cross.

Depictions of the passion of Jesus of Nazareth often reveal significantly different interests and emphases. Some artists depict Christ as raised up on this cross, high above the crowds around him. This is meant to focus attention on the way in which Jesus was "raised up" on the cross, so that believers might in turn be "raised up" to heaven by his cross and

Figure 7.3   The crucifixion, as depicted by Matthias Grünewald in the Isenheim Altarpiece, executed c. 1513–1515. Source: Erich Lessing/AKG Images.

resurrection. Others focus on the crowds around Jesus, sometimes depicting the rage and fury on the faces of those who mocked him. The point being made here is that those who crucified Christ were ordinary people.

Others still focus on those who are standing around the cross. An excellent example of this is provided by Matthias Grunewald's famous altarpiece at Isenheim, painted during the years 1510–1515. On the left of the cross, three people mourn the dead Jesus: Mary, the mother of Jesus; John, the beloved disciple; and Mary Magdalene. This is intended to help us appreciate the appalling impact that the death of Jesus of Nazareth had on his disciples. In the case of Mary, believers are invited to imagine how she must have felt when her son – the one whom she held in her arms as an infant – was taken away from her and spread out on the arms of the cross.

From what has been said, it will be clear that the gospel narratives have proved a major inspiration for western religious art. Yet it is important to note that some Protestant writers have misgivings about this development. Whereas Anglicanism and Lutheranism have seen religious art as playing an important role in Christian devotion, the reformed tradition has expressed reservations about its use. The Heidelberg Catechism (1563) argues that images of God are neither necessary nor helpful for Christian believers. Biblical preaching should take the place of religious art as a means of instruction and devotion. Most other Christian traditions regard religious art as a helpful aid to devotion and encourage the display of appropriate works in places of worship. It may also be noted that several recent theologians within the reformed tradition have used works of religious art to encourage theological reflection and personal devotion. Thus Karl Barth (1886–1968) had on his desk a copy of Matthias Grünewald's Isenheim altarpiece depicting the crucifixion. Similarly, Jürgen Moltmann (born 1926) had a copy of Marc Chagall's *Crucifixion in Yellow* in front of him as he wrote *The Crucified God*, widely regarded as one of the theological masterpieces of the twentieth century.

Icons

The use of icons in public worship and private devotion, though especially associated with eastern Orthodoxy, is now widespread within Christianity. An "icon" (derived from the Greek word *eikōn*, "image") has come to mean a portable sacred image, typically painted on a wooden base, following the traditions and conventions of Byzantine art.

The history of the use of icons is somewhat unclear. However, there is substantial evidence to indicate that the use of such sacred images originated in the region of Palestine and Syria. It seems that the first icons were pictures of martyrs, often illustrating aspects of their histories. The homilies of eastern Christian writers of the fourth century – such as Basil the Great and Gregory of Nyssa – are an important witness to this practice. However, from the fifth century on, it became increasingly common for icons to depict Jesus Christ and Mary.

The iconoclast controversy put an end to the production of icons and caused the destruction of many older ones. While Orthodox writers conceded that the Old Testament prohibited the production and use of religious images, they argued that this was an essentially temporary provision, reflecting the widespread use of idols in Canaanite culture. With the defeat of Roman paganism through the conversion of Constantine, Orthodox theologians argued that this was no longer a significant issue. Furthermore, they pointed out that the incarnation of the Son of God further undermined this Old Testament prohibition: was not Jesus the image of God, displayed to humanity? The resolution of this issue in favor of the "iconophiles" led to a golden age of iconography at Constantinople from about 850 to 1200. During this time, a special style of icon painting developed, and became characteristic of Byzantine art.

So what are icons understood to achieve? What is their purpose? Orthodox Christian writers emphatically reject what they regard as two serious misunderstandings: that icons are themselves objects of worship; and that they are merely a form of religious art, whose significance lies in beautifying religious sites.

In Orthodoxy, icons are not objects of *adoration* or *worship*, whose proper objects can only be Jesus of Nazareth or God. Rather they are objects of *veneration*. Icons are to be seen as windows to the transcendent. They can be thought of as a "visible gospel," proclaiming the same truths as Scripture, yet in a pictorial rather than verbal form. Thus Nicephorus, patriarch of Constantinople between 806 and 815, argued that icons are especially significant for those who lack the conceptual skills to understand Scripture. Indeed, very often what eludes people when reading or hearing words is captured when viewing icons.

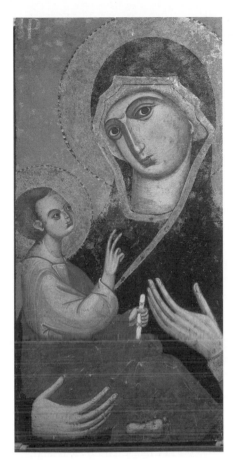

Figure 7.4 Byzantine icon of the late thirteenth or early fourteenth century, showing Mary with the infant Jesus. Source: Cameraphoto/AKG Images.

Image and word are thus not seen to be in conflict, but to offer the possibility of mutual reinforcement. Orthodox writers tend to speak about *scriptural vision* and *pictorial formation* as the two symbolic ways through which humanity gains access to transcendent realities. Where the iconoclasts argued that the uninstructed and illiterate would be unable to distinguish between image and the divine reality it depicted (hence lapsing into idolatry), the iconophiles held that these same people could use icons as a Scripture in color that would lead them to the divine reality – if they were properly instructed in how to use them.

Church Architecture

Initially Christians had to borrow buildings in which they could worship. Until Christianity became a recognized and legitimate religion within the Roman empire, it was not free to build its own distinctive structures. Christians met in private homes or borrowed pagan temples as places of worship. However, from the fourth century on, they were free to construct places of meeting and worship that reflected their own distinctive ideas and beliefs. This led to the development of several distinctive styles of church architecture, each of which is grounded in a set of beliefs about the nature of God, the place of the institution of the church in God's plan of salvation, and the ultimate destiny of human nature.

To appreciate the importance of church architecture throughout the Middle Ages – the golden age of church architecture – it is essential to understand the exceptionally high value attached to the institution of the church at this time. In the third century of the Christian era, Cyprian of Carthage penned a slogan that would have a decisive impact on Christian understandings of the role of the church as the mediator and guarantor of redemption. "Outside the church, there is no salvation." This pithy maxim was open to a number of interpretations. The one that predominated throughout the Middle Ages can be argued to have resulted directly from the church's growth in institutional authority after the collapse of the Roman empire. Salvation was only to be had through membership of the church. Jesus of Nazareth may have made the hope of salvation possible; only the church could make it available. There was an ecclesiastical monopoly on the dispensation of redemption.

The view that the institution of the church was the sole mediator and guarantor of the hope in human salvation was rapidly assimilated into church architecture. The great portals of Romanesque churches were often adorned with elaborate sculptures depicting the glory of heaven as a tactile affirmation that it was only by entering the church that this hope could be achieved. Inscriptions were often placed over the great western door of churches, declaring that it was only by entering the church that one could attain heaven. The doorframe was allowed to be identified with Christ for this purpose; it spoke words directed to those passing by or pausing to admire its magnificent ornamentation.

An excellent example is provided by the Benedictine priory church of Saint-Marcel-lès-Sauzet, which was founded in 985 and extensively developed during the twelfth century. The portal to the church depicts Christ addressing these words to all who draw near:

> You who are passing through,
> you who are coming to weep for your sins,
> pass through me,
> since I am the gate of life.

Although the words are clearly to be attributed to Christ (picking up on the image of Christ as the "gate of the sheepfold" from John 10), a tactile link has been forged with the building of the church itself. This is often reinforced visually through the physical location of the baptismal font close to the door of the church, which thereby affirms that entrance to heaven is linked with the sacrament of baptism.

A similar theme is found in the inscription placed over the portal of the Benedictine church of Santa Cruz de la Serós, located close to the main pilgrimage route from Jaca to Puente la Reina in Spain.

> I am the eternal door; pass through me, faithful ones.
> I am the fountain of life; thirst for me more than for wine.

The door of the church of San Juan de la Peña, possibly dating from the twelfth century, bears the following message:

> Through this gate, the heavens are opened to every believer.

Perhaps the most famous literary variant on this theme actually constitutes an ironic inversion of its contents. The third canto of Dante's "Inferno" – the first of the three books of the *Divine Comedy* – includes a famous description of the portal of hell, on which are inscribed the words "Abandon all hope, you who enter." Dante's description clearly assumes familiarity with the conventions of ecclesiastical architecture of the period and playfully parodies its leading theme.

One particularly important function of church architecture is to stress the transcendence of God. The great soaring arches and spires of medieval cathedrals were intended to stress the greatness of God and to raise the thoughts of worshippers heavenward. The symbolism is that of the eternal impinging upon the temporal, the church building symbolizing the mediation between heaven and earth offered through the gospel. This emphasis on representing the transcendent here on earth is especially associated with the Gothic style of church architecture, which merits further discussion.

The term "Gothic" was coined in the sixteenth century by Giorgio Vasari to denote a style between the Romanesque and that of the Renaissance, characterized by pointed arches, extended door and window space, structural complexity, immense size, and (especially in Northern Europe) large stained glass windows and sculptured doorways. (It is worth noting that Vasari intended the term to be pejorative and to suggest associations with the barbarism of the Goths – the tribes that destroyed Roman civilization.) The rise of Gothic architecture is usually traced back to the twelfth century, a period of relative political stability in Western Europe, which encouraged the rebirth of art and architecture.

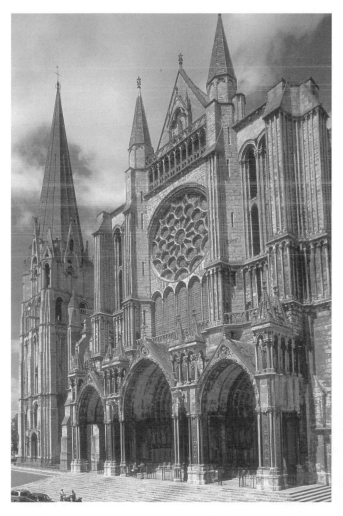

Figure 7.5   The south transept of the cathedral of Notre Dame de Chartres, one of the best examples of Gothic church architecture. The façade was completed in the mid-thirteenth century. Chartres (Dep. Eure-et-Loir, France), Cathedrale Notre-Dame (1134–1514; choir 1194–1221, transept after 1194–c. 1250, nave c. 1200–1220, west façade 1134–1514). Exterior: façade of the south transept. Source: Archives CDA/St-Genès/AKG Images.

Within a period of one century (1130–1230) some twenty-five Gothic cathedrals were built in France. One of the most distinctive features of this architectural style is its deliberate and programmatic use of height and light to generate and sustain a sense of the presence God and heaven on earth. The extensive use of buttresses allowed the weight of the building to be borne by outside supports, thus allowing the external walls to have large glass windows, which ensured that the building was saturated with the radiance of the sun. The use of stained glass helped generate an other-worldly brilliance inside the cathedral while simultaneously allowing gospel scenes to be depicted to worshippers. The use of tall, thin internal columns created an immense sense of spaciousness, again intended to evoke the hope of heaven. The cathedral thus became a sacred space, bringing the vast spaciousness and brilliance of heaven within the reach of believers. Worship inside it was seen as an anticipation of the life of heaven, allowing the worshipper to step into another world and savor its delights before returning to the dull routines of everyday life.

While it might be a little ambitious to speak of a coherent "theology" of the Gothic cathedral, there can be no doubt about the spiritual aspirations of the cathedrals' designers and about the importance of their sacred spaces in anticipating their heavenly counterparts. The theological importance of these values is perhaps best explored by considering the ideas of Abbot Suger (1080–1151), who devoted much of his later life to the restoration of the abbey church of Saint-Denis, near Paris. This early example of the classic Gothic style embodies many of its characteristic emphases. Yet, perhaps most importantly, Suger's three books of commentary on the renovation process allow us insights into the physical process of construction, along with the spiritual and aesthetic principles that governed his design. The architecture of the church allowed the human mind to "travel through the lights to the true light, where Christ is the true door." Suger intended the human mind to be drawn upward, through the light of the building, to the true light, which is the enthroned Christ in heaven. While not all were persuaded by this theology of the church as guarantor and visualization of the hope of heaven, there is no doubting its massive impact upon the culture of the Middle Ages and beyond.

In addition to this emphasis on the transcendence of God, architecture reflects a concern to focus on what is deemed to be important by specific Christian groupings. Three such focal points may be singled out.

1 Especially within Catholicism, the altar was singled out for special attention, reflecting an emphasis upon the importance of the mass. Gregory the Great chose to erect an altar over the tomb of St. Peter, thus combining a focus on the "sacrament of the altar" with a veneration of the relics of saints.

2 In the eastern Orthodox tradition, particular emphasis came to be placed on the iconostasis – that is, the stand on which icons were placed. As we noted earlier, icons play an important role in Orthodox spirituality (pp. 262–263). In later Orthodox churches, the iconostasis became such a prominent feature that it in effect cut off the entire altar area from the sight of the laity. The icon placed upon the iconostasis thus assumed a much higher profile than the altar.

3 In the Protestant tradition, the emphasis upon preaching led to the pulpit being elevated above the altar, both physically and in terms of the emphasis placed upon it. The

noted Swiss reformed theologian Karl Barth (1886–1968) once pointed out how reformed churches stress God's "otherness" through the design of churches and other liturgical means:

> Preaching takes place from the pulpit (a place which by its awesome but obviously intended height differs from a podium), and on the pulpit, as a warning to those who ascend it, there is a big Bible. Preachers also wear a robe – I am not embarrassed to say this – and they should do so, for it is a salutary reminder that from those who wear this special garment, people expect a special word.

More recently, church architecture has come to be influenced by other factors. For example, North American revivalism of the late nineteenth century saw worship partly in terms of entertainment, and thus designed church buildings with stages suitable for the performance of music and worship. The rise of "base ecclesial communities" or "house churches" has led

Figure 7.6 The pulpit in St. Peter's Cathedral, Geneva. Source: J.-P. Scherrer/Geneva 2005.

to a new informality of worship, often within private homes or borrowed premises, in which the emphasis has been placed on fellowship, prayer, and worship, architectural considerations being of minimal importance. According to some, this can be regarded as a return to the earliest Christian practice, and is thus more authentic than later developments.

Stained Glass

There are many points at which the Christian interest in church architecture and that in art forms converge – for example, the use of altarpieces to remind congregations of the reality of the sufferings of Jesus Christ on the cross as an aid to devotion. Yet it is widely agreed that the most distinctively Christian art form to be linked with the design of church buildings is the use of stained glass. Why did this development take place? And what was its significance?

Early Christian buildings did not use stained glass. Windows were widely used, but they were seen primarily as functional. They were necessary to allow light into the building. Wall paintings were widely used as well, to represent incidents in the life of Christ or the saints. These were intended to inspire devotion in congregations and to serve as teaching aids for preachers and catechists. If they were to do this, they needed to be seen. Windows allowed sunlight into the church building, so that these devotional and pedagogical aids could be properly viewed and appreciated. These windows were often quite narrow, and so they did not need to be filled with glass.

The origin of the use of stained glass in church windows is not fully understood. We know that it was in production, but on a very small scale, in the seventh century. St. Paul's church in Jarrow – the home of Bede, the great historian of English Christianity – still contains a very small round stained glass window dating from the Anglo-Saxon period. To view this small window helps appreciate how the art form was developed on a much grander scale in later centuries.

The flourishing of the Gothic architectural style propelled stained glass design and technology to the forefront. Churches became taller and lighter, walls became thinner, and windows larger. They needed to be filled with glass. So why not use glass to create devotional images? Instead of seeing a window as a means of illuminating wall paintings, why not allow the window itself to represent biblical images?

The technology of creating stained glass windows was well established in Western Europe by the year 1100. Glass was colored during its manufacture through the addition of metallic salts or oxides. The addition of gold produced a cranberry color, silver produced yellows and golds, while cobalt produced a deep blue, ideal for representing the heavens.

Most of what is known about medieval stained glass making comes from the book *On Diverse Arts* by a twelfth-century German monk known only as Theophilus. An artist and metalworker himself, Theophilus described how he carefully studied glaziers and glass painters at work in order to provide detailed directions for creating windows of "inestimable beauty." He then gave detailed directions for the production of stained glass windows, and these were followed meticulously throughout the Middle Ages.

If you want to assemble simple windows, first mark out the dimensions of their length and breadth on a wooden board, then draw scroll work or anything else that pleases you, and select colours that are to be inserted. Cut the glass, and fit the pieces together with the grouting iron. Enclose them with lead and solder on both sides. Surround it with a wooden frame strengthened with nails, and set it up in the place where you wish.

As windows became larger, more elaborate means of supporting windows were developed, by making use of saddle bars.

In France, the best early exemplars of Gothic stained glass are to be found in the north, in the churches of Saint-Denis (founded 1144) and in the cathedrals of Chartres (1150), Laôn (1160), Notre Dame de Paris (1163), Reims (1211), and Amiens (1220): all are graced by spectacular stained glass windows. Several of them are circular, and are known as "rose windows." Of these buildings, the best is probably the great cathedral of Chartres, which has 152 of its original windows still intact, including the three great rose windows, which date from around 1200. Other important examples include the Cathedral of Évora in Portugal (founded 1186), Canterbury Cathedral, and York Minster (the largest Gothic cathedral in Northern Europe).

With the waning of the Middle Ages, however, stained glass came to be seen by many artists as unsophisticated. New technology allowed glass to be painted, opening up new possibilities. Instead of assembling tiny fragments of stained glass to produce a picture, it was possible to paint directly onto glass. Many medieval stained glass windows were removed from churches and replaced with the new painted forms. The revival of stained

Figure 7.7 The great rose window above the main portal of the cathedral of Notre Dame, Strasbourg, France, one of the finest examples of stained glass in Europe. Strasbourg (Alsace, France), Minster: Cathédrale Notre-Dame (12th–15th century). West façade (planned in 1276 by Erwin von Steinbach): Window rose above the main portal. Source: Hedda Eid/AKG Images.

glass as an ecclesiastical art form dates from the second half of the nineteenth century and is especially associated with the pre-Raphaelite movement. Perhaps the best example is found in the three windows Faith, Hope, and Charity, designed by Sir Edward Burne-Jones for St. Martin's Church in Brampton, Cumbria and manufactured by William Morris's workshop. This unique pre-Raphaelite church was built in 1889, according to a design by the architect Philip Webb.

Christian Music

The richness of Christian worship inevitably led to the adoption of all kinds of musical styles in the life of the Christian church. Although early Christian writers were hesitant over the use of music in worship, fearing that it would paganize what was a thoroughly Christian occasion, the value of music as an aid to Christian devotion was soon realized.

The most important early use of music can be traced back to certain set forms of words known as "canticles," usually derived from the Bible and used in monastic services – for example, the "Magnificat" ("My soul magnifies the Lord") at the early evening office of Vespers, and the "Nunc dimittis" ("Lord, now allow your servant to depart in peace"), set for the late evening office of Compline. Each of these set pieces is known by its opening words in Latin. It was not long before Plainsong was introduced as a means of permitting these central texts to be sung rather than just recited. The form of chanting that is probably best known in the modern world is the Gregorian chant, which is readily available in high-quality modern recordings, often made in monastic settings.

Gradually the patterns of monastic chanting became more ornate, as increasingly complex musical forms were used to express the various emotions associated with the biblical passages being sung in this way. Four of the most important hymns set to music in this way were:

"Te lucis ante terminum" ("To you before the ending of the day"), a hymn sung at Compline, in which believers committed themselves to the care of God during the hours of darkness;
"Pange lingua gloriosa" ("Now, my tongue, the glorious mystery proclaiming"), a medieval hymn, often ascribed to Thomas Aquinas, which explains the meaning of the communion service. It was often used on Maundy Thursday (p. 242);
"Puer natus" ("A boy is born"), a short hymn celebrating the birth of Jesus.

During the Reformation, controversy developed over the role of music. Zwingli and Calvin did not regard music as having a proper place in Christian worship. In other Protestant traditions, however, music continued to play an important role. Martin Luther composed settings for a number of traditional hymns, as well as writing hymns of his own. The most famous of these is "Ein feste Burg ist unser Gott" ("A Safe Stronghold Is Our God"), which remains widely used in modern Protestant church life, particularly in Lutheranism. The Church of England encouraged the setting of the Psalms and other canticles as chants.

The rise of Methodism gave a new importance to hymns, John and Charles Wesley both recognizing their enormous potential to convey Christian teachings. Alongside this recognition of the pedagogical and catechetical value of hymns, Charles Wesley pioneered the use of adapting popular secular tunes for Christian purposes. For example, the English composer Henry Purcell had written a superb tune to accompany John Dryden's text praising England, entitled "Fairest isle, all isles excelling." Wesley altered the words to reflect Christian interests but retained Purcell's operatic tune, and the result was the well-known hymn "Love divine, all loves excelling." Perhaps the most well-known of all Protestant musical pieces is Handel's *Messiah*, which sets to music a series of biblical texts focusing on the coming of Jesus and on his subsequent glorification.

The most important musical developments within western Christianity, however, are linked with Catholicism. The great cathedrals of Europe demanded increasingly sophisticated and prestigious musical settings of the standard Catholic liturgical texts. Of these, the most important were the text of the mass and the requiem. The Catholic church was without question one of the most important patrons of musical developments throughout the Middle Ages and the modern era and a major stimulus to the development of the western musical tradition. Virtually every great European composer helped shape the development of church music. Monteverdi, Vivaldi, Haydn, Mozart, Beethoven, Rossini, and Verdi all made major contributions in this sphere.

Music continues to be an integral part of modern Christian life. The classics of the past continue to be represented in modern Christian worship. However, it is clear that more popular styles of music are having an increasing influence, especially in evangelical and charismatic congregations.

Christianity and Literature

"The church, as a body, has never made up her mind about the Arts." Thus wrote Dorothy L. Sayers, herself an important contributor to the shaping of Christian literature in the twentieth century. There can be no doubt that she is correct in her judgment. Some Christian writers have adopted strongly positive attitudes to literature, seeing it as a powerful ally in the quest to foster the Christian vision and to interact with the world. Others have regarded literature as alien to the Christian faith, with a potential to mislead.

One of the most important debates in the early church concerned the extent to which Christians could appropriate the immense cultural legacy of the classical world – especially its poetry and literature. In what way could the *ars poetica* be adopted by Christian writers interested in using these classical modes of writing to expound and communicate their faith? Or was the very use of such a literary medium tantamount to compromising the essentials of the Christian faith? This was a debate of immense significance, as it raised the question of whether Christianity would turn its back on the classical heritage or appropriate it, even if in a modified form.

As we noted earlier (pp. 253–254), in the early period of the Christian church, a critical and hostile attitude toward contemporary pagan culture – including its literature – tended to prevail. Writers such as Tertullian and Chrysostom were intensely suspicious of Greek and Latin literature and sought to minimize its importance and influence within the church.

Others, such as Jerome and Augustine, were considerably more positive, even though they shared some of the anxieties voiced elsewhere.

Literature came to be seen by some Christian apologists as a means of further enhancing the appeal of their faith to the wider world. Might not the obvious attractions of the gospel be augmented if they were to be presented in words of beauty and power, in which theological precision was supplemented by the lyricism of poetry and by the rhetoric of prose? Gravity of form and sublimity of expression in an argument could assist in both the communication and commendation of the substance of the gospel. The anonymous *Cursor mundi*, written around 1300, argued that, since people enjoy reading secular literature so much, it makes sense to present religious truth in literary forms. A work of religious literature could thus be both a delight to read and something able to nourish the human soul. Yet the tension that this approach generated can be seen from other works of this period. For example, Geoffrey Chaucer concluded his *Canterbury Tales* with a "retraction" in which he asks his readers to forgive him for his "translations and compositions of worldly vanity."

The implication is clear: works of literature are potentially vain, whereas purely religious works, written for the purpose of doctrinal and ethical instruction, are acceptable. Chaucer's obvious concern at this point raises the question of whether the notion of "Christian literature" is inherently indefensible, in that the desire to please and amuse is potentially in tension with the seriousness of Christian doctrine and ethics. This is certainly the view that we find adopted by the noted Puritan writer Richard Baxter, who argued that literature encourages its readers to waste their time in recreation when they could be doing something more productive, and that it has a disquieting potential to be morally corrupting. Baxter's most severe criticism was directed against works of fiction, which, he held, actively promote a culture of falsehood, which "dangerously bewitcheth and corrupteth the minds of young and empty people."

One manner of reconciling this tension was known throughout Christian history, and acquired special importance during the romantic period. The language of literature, it was argued, served to elevate its readers and to inspire them to devotion and passion. Was not this sufficient justification for a religious literature? In his preface to the *Lyrical Ballads*, William Wordsworth complained of the "frantic novels, sickly and stupid German Tragedies, and deluges of idle and extravagant stories in verse" by which his age had been seduced, and he urged a recovery of the language and concerns of writers such as Shakespeare and Milton. For Wordsworth himself, there was an obvious affinity between religion and poetry; indeed Wordsworth's literature increasingly adopted the characteristics of religion. This evolution is of particular importance to the development of treating the Bible as literature. For Percy Bysshe Shelley, the Bible is revered on account of its literary character rather than for the religious views it propounded.

Yet it must not be assumed that the Christian interest in literature was a purely pragmatic consequence of a desire for church growth and for the consolidation of religious faith. From the outset, Christian writers have found the notion of "God as author" as offering a substantial theological foundation and encouragement for the writing of literature. In the beginning, God created through God's word, spoken over the face of chaos. Did this not point to a critical role of words in the Christian understanding of the world? And was there not a most natural connection between the verbal origins of the world and a concern with words, revelation, texts, literature, and reading and writing? The production of Christian literature was thus seen by some as resting upon rigorous theological foundations rather than as being opportunistic.

But this raises the difficult question of precisely what is to be understood by "Christian literature." Although this matter continues to be debated, there is at least some agreement on the categories of writing that deserve to be included. Such writings fall into three broad categories:

1 Works of literature that are specifically written to serve the needs of Christians or of the church as an institution – such as prayers, devotional works, and sermons. The Christian faith has given rise to certain specific forms of writing, which Christians have sought to develop to the highest standards of cultural excellence. These works are a response to the needs of the Christian faith and can also be seen as expressing its nature.

2 Works of literature in general – such as stories and poems – which are not specific to the Christian faith but have been shaped or influenced by Christian ideas, values, images, and narratives. Christian poetry, in particular, reflects a quite distinct set of ideas and images, and it is important to appreciate the way in which these are assimilated in such writings. Although most Christian literature is written by Christians, one should note that there are many examples of writings that have unquestionably been shaped by Christian influences, even though their writers would not regard themselves as Christians. The lyrical ballads of both William Wordsworth and Samuel Taylor Coleridge might be included in this category.

3 Works of literature that involve interaction with Christian ideas, individuals, schools of thought, or institutions, often written by those who would regard themselves as observers or critics of Christianity. George Eliot or Thomas Hardy fall in this category. Here the influence of Christianity is evident, at least in the subject matter of these writings. Yet even the mode of criticism often reflects a subtle appropriation, development, or modification of Christian assumptions – for instance assumptions concerning what Christianity *ought* to be, which are then contrasted with what is observed through experience.

It lies beyond the scope of this brief chapter to offer a detailed discussion of the nature and development of Christian literature. However, something of its scope can be appreciated by considering a representative example of the field. In what follows we shall look at the best-known work of the literary critic and novelist C. S. Lewis (1898–1963), widely agreed to be one of the most engaging and accessible Christian writers of the twentieth century. Originally an atheist, Lewis found his attitude to Christianity to undergo a dramatic change in the 1920s. The story of his return to the faith he abandoned as a boy is described in great detail in his autobiography *Surprised by Joy*. After wrestling with the clues concerning God that he found in human reason and experience, he eventually decided that intellectual honesty compelled him to believe and trust in God.

After his conversion, Lewis began to establish his reputation as a leading authority on medieval and Renaissance English literature. *The Allegory of Love*, published in 1936, is still regarded as a masterpiece, as is his *Preface to Paradise Lost*. Alongside his scholarly writings, however, Lewis wrote books of a very different nature. Aiming at clarity and conviction, he produced a series of works devoted to communicating the reasonableness of Christianity to his own generation – such as the *Chronicles of Narnia*.

The first in this series of seven novels was published in 1950. *The Lion, the Witch and the Wardrobe* introduces its readers to the land of Narnia, which is discovered by four English children (Peter, Susan, Edmund, and Lucy) at the back of a seemingly ordinary wardrobe. The series ended in 1956, with the publication of *The Last Battle*. The series can be seen as standing in the fairy-tale tradition established by George MacDonald in the nineteenth century. Its success did much to publicize Lewis' notion of "the baptized imagination," which emphasized the importance of the human imagination in grasping and appreciating the essence of the Christian faith.

As a child, Lewis loved stories and had little interest in Christianity. But he later came to wonder how stories might have helped him to embrace a faith that he neither understood nor appreciated. What if stories could have opened up the wonder and joy of a faith that he had to wait two decades to discover? Lewis may well have written the books that he would have liked to read as a boy – both as something that excited his imagination and as something that helped him to offer what he later called an "imaginative welcome" to the Christian faith.

Religious symbolism plays a major role in the *Chronicles of Narnia*. One of the best examples is the "undragoning" of Eustace Scrubb in the *Voyage of the Dawn Treader*. Eustace is portrayed as a thoroughly unsympathetic boy and as an example of selfishness. It's difficult to like him to begin with, and it's just as difficult to feel sorry for him when he changes into a dragon as a result of his "greedy, dragonish thoughts." Eustace frantically tries to scratch off his dragon's skin. Yet each layer he removes merely reveals yet another layer of scales beneath it. He simply cannot break free from his prison. He is trapped within a dragon's skin, because he has become a dragon.

Then Aslan appears – the noble lion of Narnia, whom Lewis depicts as a "Christ-figure" – and tears away at Eustace's dragon flesh with his claws. The lion's claws cut so deeply that Eustace is in real pain – "worse than anything I've ever felt." And, when the scales are finally removed, Aslan plunges the raw and bleeding Eustace into a well from which he emerges purified and renewed.

So what are we to learn from this powerful and shocking story, so realistically depicted? As the raw imagery of Aslan's tearing at Eustace's flesh makes clear, Eustace has been trapped by forces over which he has no control. The one who would be master has instead been mastered. The dragon is a symbol, not so much of sin itself, as of sin's power to entrap, captivate, and imprison. It can only be broken and mastered by the redeemer. Aslan is the one who heals and renews Eustace, restoring him to what he was intended to be. The immersion in the water of the well picks up on the New Testament's language about baptism as dying to self and rising to Christ (Romans 6). Eustace is tossed into the well by Aslan and emerges renewed and restored.

As might be expected, the storyline of *The Lion, the Witch and the Wardrobe* divides its readers. Some see it as childish nonsense. To others, it is utterly transformative. For the latter, this evocative story affirms that it is possible for the weak and foolish to have a noble calling in a dark world; that our deepest intuitions point us to the true meaning of things; that there is indeed something beautiful and wonderful at the heart of the universe, and that this core may be found, embraced, and adored. Whether Lewis is right or wrong, he bequeathed to us a children's story that opens up some of the deepest questions of life, set within a Christian framework.

Thus far we have focused on the way in which Christianity has shaped the arts. But what about the natural sciences, now accepted as an important part of culture? Here the situation is somewhat complex.

Christianity and the Natural Sciences

Religion and science are two of the most powerful cultural and intellectual forces in today's world. Some scientists and religious believers see them as locked in mortal combat. Science and religion would be at war with each other, and that war would continue until one of them is eradicated. Although this view tends to be associated particularly with dogmatic atheist scientists such as Richard Dawkins (born 1941), they are also encountered among religious believers. Some fundamentalist Christians and Muslims, for example, see science as a threat to their faith. A good example of this trend can be found in the criticisms of evolution made by conservative Protestant Christians, who see it as undermining the biblical creation accounts.

To some, the notion of any positive link between religion and science seems highly improbable from the outset. Surely science and religion have always been locked in mortal combat? Yet the stereotype of a "warfare of science and religion" is a product of the social conditions of the late nineteenth century and is now regarded as historically unacceptable. The interaction of science and religion is far too complex and interesting to be represented in such a simplistic, inaccurate way. The massive advances made in the history of science now allow the early relationship between science and Christianity in Western Europe to be seen in a much more positive light.

It is often argued that the emergence of the natural sciences is specifically linked with the Christian intellectual environment of Western Europe. A Christian understanding of creation (pp. 78–82) holds that God imposes order, rationality, and beauty upon nature. As a result, the universe has a regularity that is capable of being uncovered by humanity. This theme, which is expressed in terms of laws of nature, is of fundamental importance to the emergence and development of the natural sciences. This religious undergirding of the notion of the regularity in nature is known to have been of major historical importance for the emergence of the natural sciences. The scientific study of nature could now be seen as an indirect way of recognizing and honoring the divine wisdom reflected in the order of things.

Christianity thus created a new motivation – or perhaps, some might argue, it enhanced an existing one – for the scientific study of nature. For example, the Protestant writer John Calvin (1509–1564) argued that the wisdom of the invisible and intangible God might be discerned and studied through the beauty and regularity of the created order. Calvin thus commended – and even expressed some jealousy of – natural scientists, who could experience and appreciate the beauty and wisdom of God through what God had created and fashioned.

This fundamental motivation for the scientific study of nature was set out in some sixteenth-century confessional documents of the reformed church in Western Europe. For example, the Belgic Confession affirmed that nature was "set before our eyes as a most beautiful book, in which all creatures, great and small, are like so many characters leading us to contemplate the invisible things of God." The natural scientist was thus able to praise God through the close study of God's work in creation.

This approach was not without its difficulties. What happened when scientific advances seemed to contradict traditional religious beliefs? For example, the Copernican debates of the sixteenth century called into question the traditional idea that the earth stood at the center of the universe. The Darwinian debates of the nineteenth century called into question traditional religious understandings of the origins of humanity and of its place within the natural world. Often the issue of biblical interpretation was of central importance. Had certain biblical passages been rightly interpreted? Or did the Copernican and the Darwinian debates call into question how those passages had traditionally been understood?

This perception of an inalienable tension and contradiction between Christianity and the natural sciences has been a core theme of the New Atheism, a movement that become prominent in 2006. Leading New Atheist writers such as Richard Dawkins and Daniel Dennett argued that science and faith were locked in mortal combat and that science would emerge victorious. This simplistic rendering of the historically questionable "warfare" model of the relation of the sciences and Christianity has failed to win wide support. The situation is rather more complex and nuanced than the New Atheist narrative suggests.

The complex relationship between Christianity and the natural sciences is at times positive and symbiotic, at times tense and challenging. Yet it is a changing relationship, in that neither science nor Christianity is fixed or static. Science is, by its very nature, progressive, developing new theories and approaches and discarding older theories in the light of new evidence. And, as this brief introduction to Christianity has indicated, Christianity has also developed and modified over the centuries, and it is likely to do so in the future.

Yet, despite this complexity, a number of helpful points can be made about the relationship between Christianity and the natural sciences. First, science and the Christian faith can be thought of as operating at different levels, often reflecting on the similar questions, yet answering them in different ways. Historians suggest that both science and religion lose their way when they play at being what they are not. There are some scientists who declare they have displaced religion (as is evident in recent "scientific atheism"), just as there are religious activists who claim to have displaced science (as is evident in modern "creationism"). Science does not answer every question that we might have about the world. Neither does religion. Yet, taken together, they can offer a stereoscopic view of reality that is denied to those who limit themselves to one discipline's perspective on things. The dialogue between science and religion allows us to appreciate the distinct identities, strengths, and limits of each conversational partner. It also offers us a deeper understanding of things than either religion or science could offer unaided.

Second, both the natural sciences and Christianity are concerned about making sense of things. Although Christianity places an emphasis upon the transformation of the human situation, it also offers an explanation of the world. Why are things the way they are? What explanations may be offered for what we observe? What is the "bigger picture" that makes sense of our observations and experiences? Scientific and religious explanations generally take different forms, even when they reflect on the same observations. Perhaps most

importantly, science tends to ask "how" questions, whereas religion asks "why." Scie
seeks to clarify mechanisms; Christianity explores the question of meaning. Tl
approaches do not need to be seen as being in competition, or as being mutually incom
ible. They operate at different levels.

And, finally, we may note the growing awareness, within the scientific community, o. ...
broader issues raised by its research and of the limits placed upon that community's ability
to answer them. An obvious example is ethical questions. Is science able to determine what
is right and what is wrong? Most scientists would affirm that their discipline is fundamentally amoral – that the scientific method does not extend to moral questions.

Many natural scientists seem increasingly willing to enlarge scientific understandings of
the world with additional approaches that permit or encourage the ethical, aesthetical, and
spiritual enhancement of their subject. Religion is being seen increasingly as an important
dialogue partner in allowing the natural sciences to engage with questions that are raised,
yet not answered, by scientific research. Debates about the ethics of biotechnology, for
example, often raise important questions that science cannot answer – such as when a
human "person" comes into existence, or what constitutes an acceptable quality of life.

The future of the relationship between Christianity and the natural sciences is open and
unpredictable. Yet there are signs of a movement away from the historically discredited
"warfare" model of their interaction and toward a more nuanced and productive framework
of understanding. Pope John Paul II made this point well in an article published in the
Vatican newspaper *Osservatore Romano* on October 26, 1988: "Science can purify religion
from error and superstition; religion can purify science from idolatry and false absolutes.
Each can draw the other into a wider world, a world in which both can flourish."

Conclusion

This chapter has briefly explored some aspects of the relationship between Christianity and
culture. There is much more that needs to be said, and there is a substantial and important
literature that will allow you to take these matters further. Christian literature, art, and
music are of immense cultural interest and importance, and they play an important role in
both sustaining and expressing faith. They are certainly things that merit studying; they
also deserve to be experienced and appreciated.

Conclusion
Where Next?

Any introduction has its limits. It is like a sketch map of a vast landscape, which helps you identify some important landmarks and work out how they fit into the overall picture. Christianity is arguably the largest, most complex, and most diverse living faith of today. Inevitably, this means that this brief introduction cannot do justice to its history, ideas, and practices. It is best seen as a handshake intended to begin a conversation; as helping you to orient yourself and get your bearings.

If you are using this book as part of a taught course, you will be given guidance on what you might do next to take your studies further. If you are studying on your own, you may find these suggestions for further exploration helpful.

1   Visit a church, preferably an older church, such as one of Europe's great cathedrals. Use a guide to help you "read" the church. What are its structures and symbols all about? I would especially recommend two resources:

Clive Fewins, *The Church Explorer's Handbook: A Guide to Looking at Churches and Their Contents*. Norwich: Canterbury Press, 2005.

Richard Taylor, *How to Read a Church: A Guide to Symbols and Images in Churches and Cathedrals*. Mahwah, NJ: HiddenSpring, 2005.

2   Make a study of Christian art. This is now very easy, since many excellent images of leading works of art are available to look at, free of charge, on the Internet. You might like to choose a theme – such as incarnation, annunciation, crucifixion, resurrection – and look at how (and why) various artists represent it. There are lots of online and printed works that will help you do this more effectively and enable you to get the most out of it. You might like to try these:

Richard Harries, *The Passion in Art*. Aldershot: Ashgate, 2004.

David Morgan, *Visual Piety: A History and Theory of Popular Religious Images*. Berkeley, CA: University of California Press, 1998.

3   Attend a service of Christian worship, particularly on a great festival occasion, such as Christmas or Easter. This introduction will give you plenty of information that will help you make sense of what you experience. However, it is the experience itself that really matters. It is very difficult to express in words the sense of awe or mystery that often results from such services, especially in cathedrals. While many of these can now be accessed on the Internet, they are better experienced directly, as living realities.

4   Focus down on a Christian writer whom you might find interesting. Many find the Oxford literary critic and popular writer C. S. Lewis (1898–1963) to be an excellent gateway to a better understanding of the Christian faith, whether through his work *Mere Christianity* or through his celebrated *Chronicles of Narnia* – especially the opening volume, *The Lion, the Witch and the Wardrobe*. You should read a biography, then follow through by reading Lewis himself. For a biography, you could try:

Alister E. McGrath, *C. S. Lewis – A Life: Eccentric Genius, Reluctant Prophet*. Carol Springs, IL: Tyndale House, 2013.

Works by Lewis that you will find interesting and stimulating are:

C. S. Lewis, *Mere Christianity*. London: HarperCollins, 2002.

C. S. Lewis, *The Chronicles of Narnia*. 7 vols. London: HarperCollins, 2002.

Other Christian writers that you may enjoy reading include G. K. Chesterton; Graham Greene; Marilynne Robinson; Dorothy L. Sayers.

There are many other things that you could do: take a course in Christian theology, go on a pilgrimage, attend an Alpha Course at a local church, or stay at a monastery or retreat center. But, whatever you do next, I hope that you will have found this short introduction helpful, and I wish you well wherever you choose to go.

Further Reading

Useful Introductions to Christianity in General

Bruyneel, Sally, and Alan G. Padgett. *Introducing Christianity*. Maryknoll, NY: Orbis Books, 2003.

Wagner, Richard. *Christianity for Dummies*. Hoboken, NJ: Wiley Publishing, 2004.

Woodhead, Linda. *Christianity: A Very Short Introduction*. Oxford: Oxford University Press, 2004.

Woodhead, Linda. *An Introduction to Christianity*. Cambridge: Cambridge University Press, 2004.

Jesus of Nazareth and the Origins of Christianity

Bauckham, Richard. *Jesus: A Very Short Introduction*. Oxford: Oxford University Press, 2011.

Benedict XVI (Joseph Ratzinger). *Jesus of Nazareth*. New York: Rizzoli, 2009.

Blomberg, Craig. *Jesus and the Gospels: An Introduction and Survey*. Nashville, TN: Broadman & Holman, 1997.

Brown, Raymond Edward. *An Introduction to the New Testament*. New York: Doubleday, 1997.

Dunn, James D. G. *Jesus Remembered: Christianity in the Making*. Grand Rapids, MI: Eerdmans, 2003.

Evans, Craig A. *Jesus and His World: The Archaeological Evidence*. Louisville, KY: Westminster John Knox Press, 2012.

Perkins, Pheme. *Introduction to the Synoptic Gospels*. Grand Rapids, MI: Eerdmans, 2007.

Powell, Mark Allan. *Jesus as a Figure in History: How Modern Historians View the Man from Galilee*. 2nd edn. Louisville, KY: Westminster John Knox Press, 2013.

Rausch, Thomas P. *Who Is Jesus? An Introduction to Christology*. Collegeville, MN: Liturgical Press, 2003.

Sanders, E. P. *The Historical Figure of Jesus*. New York: Penguin Books, 1996.

Stanton, Graham. *The Gospels and Jesus*. 2nd edn. Oxford: Oxford University Press, 2002.

Witherington, Ben. *The Jesus Quest : The Third Search for the Jew of Nazareth*. 2nd edn. Downers Grove, IL: InterVarsity Press, 1997.

Wright, N. T. *Simply Jesus: Who He Was, What He Did, Why It Matters*. New York: HarperOne, 2011.

Christianity: An Introduction, Third Edition. Alister E. McGrath.
© 2015 John Wiley & Sons, Ltd. Published 2015 by John Wiley & Sons, Ltd.

The Christian Bible

Bandstra, Barry L. *Reading the Old Testament: An Introduction to the Hebrew Bible*. 4th edn. Belmont, CA: Wadsworth, 2009.

Barton, John, and John Muddiman. *The Oxford Bible Commentary*. Oxford: Oxford University Press, 2001.

Bauckham, Richard. *Jesus and the Eyewitnesses: The Gospels as Eyewitness Testimony*. Grand Rapids, MI: Eerdmans, 2006.

Brown, Raymond Edward. *An Introduction to the New Testament*. New York: Doubleday, 1997.

Coogan, Michael David. *A Brief Introduction to the Old Testament: The Hebrew Bible in Its Context*. 2nd edn. New York: Oxford University Press, 2012.

Ehrman, Bart D. *A Brief Introduction to the New Testament*. 3rd edn. New York: Oxford University Press, 2013.

Johnson, Luke Timothy. *The Writings of the New Testament: An Interpretation*. 3rd edn. Minneapolis, MN: Fortress Press, 2010.

Murphy-O'Connor, Jerome. *Paul the Letter-Writer: His World, His Options, His Skills*. Collegeville, MN: Liturgical Press, 1995.

Perkins, Pheme. *Introduction to the Synoptic Gospels*. Grand Rapids, MI: Eerdmans, 2007.

Riches, John. *The Bible: A Very Short Introduction*. Oxford: Oxford University Press, 2000.

Schmid, Konrad. *The Old Testament: A Literary History*. Minneapolis, MN: Fortress Press, 2012.

Christian Creeds and Beliefs

Balthasar, Hans Urs von. *Credo: Meditations on the Apostles' Creed*. San Francisco, CA: Ignatius Press, 2000.

Harn, Roger van, ed. *Exploring and Proclaiming the Apostles' Creed*. Grand Rapids, MI: Eerdmans, 2004.

Johnson, Luke Timothy. *The Creed: What Christians Believe and Why It Matters*. New York: Doubleday, 2003.

Kelly, J. N. D. *Early Christian Creeds*. 3rd edn. New York: Continuum, 2006.

Lewis, C. S. *Mere Christianity*. London: Collins, 2002.

Lubac, Henri de. *The Christian Faith: An Essay on the Structure of the Apostles' Creed*. San Francisco, CA: Ignatius Press, 1986.

McGrath, Alister E. *Christian Theology: An Introduction*. 5th edn. Oxford and Malden, MA: Wiley Blackwell, 2010.

Williams, Rowan. *Tokens of Trust: An Introduction to Christian Belief*. Norwich: Canterbury Press, 2007.

Young, Frances. *The Making of the Creeds*. London: SCM, 2002.

Christian History: An Overview

Chidester, David. *Christianity: A Global History*. San Francisco, CA: HarperSanFrancisco, 2000.

Ferguson, Everett. *Church History*. Grand Rapids, MI: Zondervan, 2005.

González, Justo L. *The Story of Christianity*. 2 vols. San Francisco: HarperOne, 2010.

Hastings, Adrian. *A World History of Christianity*. Grand Rapids, MI: Eerdmans, 1999.

Hill, Jonathan. *Handbook to the History of Christianity*. Oxford: Lion Hudson, 2009.

MacCulloch, Diarmaid. *Christianity: The First Three Thousand Years*. New York: Viking, 2010.

McManners, John, ed. *The Oxford History of Christianity*. Oxford: Oxford University Press, 2002.

Noll, Mark A. *Turning Points: Decisive Moments in the History of Christianity*. Grand Rapids, MI: Baker Books, 2000.

Nystrom, Bradley P., and David P. Nystrom. *The History of Christianity: An Introduction*. Boston: McGraw-Hill, 2004.

Pelikan, Jaroslav. *The Christian Tradition: A History of the Development of Doctrine*. 5 vols. Chicago, IL: University of Chicago Press, 1989.

Shelley, Bruce L. *Church History in Plain Language*. Dallas, TX: Thomas Nelson, 2008.

Vidmar, John. *The Catholic Church through the Ages: A History*. New York: Paulist Press, 2005.

Denominations: Forms of Christianity

Benedict, Philip. *Christ's Churches Purely Reformed: A Social History of Calvinism*. New Haven, CT: Yale University Press, 2002.

Chapman, Mark D. *Anglicanism: A Very Short Introduction*. Oxford: Oxford University Press, 2006.

Cracknell, Kenneth, and Susan J. White. *An Introduction to World Methodism*. Cambridge: Cambridge University Press, 2005.

Duffy, Eamon. *Saints and Sinners: A History of the Popes*. New Haven, CT: Yale University Press, 2002.

Gritsch, Eric W. *A History of Lutheranism*. Minneapolis, MN: Fortress Press, 2002.

Hollenweger, Walter J. *Pentecostalism: Origins and Developments Worldwide*. Peabody, MA: Hendrickson Publishers, 1997.

Johnson, Robert E. *A Global Introduction to Baptist Churches*. Cambridge: Cambridge University Press, 2010.

McGuckin, John Anthony (ed.), *The Encyclopedia of Eastern Orthodox Christianity*. Oxford: Wiley Blackwell, 2011.

O'Collins, Gerald. *Catholicism: A Very Short Introduction*. Oxford: Oxford University Press, 2008.

Rhodes, Ron. *The Complete Guide to Christian Denominations*. Eugene, OR: Harvest House Publishers, 2005.

Ware, Kallistos. *The Orthodox Church*. New York: Penguin Books, 1993.

The Life of Faith: Christianity as a Living Reality

Bartholomew, Craig G., and Fred Hughes. *Explorations in a Christian Theology of Pilgrimage*. Aldershot: Ashgate, 2004.

Begbie, Jeremy S. *Voicing Creation's Praise: Towards a Theology of the Arts*. Edinburgh: T&T Clark, 1991.

Dawn, Marva J. *Reaching out without Dumbing Down: A Theology of Worship for the Turn-of-the-Century Culture*. Grand Rapids, MI: Eerdmans, 1995.

Just, Arthur A. *Heaven on Earth: The Gifts of Christ in the Divine Service*. St. Louis, MO: Concordia Publishing House, 2008.

LaVerdiere, Eugene. *The Breaking of the Bread: The Development of the Eucharist According to Acts*. Chicago, IL: Liturgy Training Publications, 1998.

Nolan, Mary Lee, and Sidney Nolan. *Christian Pilgrimage in Modern Western Europe*. Chapel Hill: University of North Carolina Press, 1989.

Rubin, Miri. *Corpus Christi. The Eucharist in Late Medieval Culture*. New York: Cambridge University Press, 1991.

Stookey, Laurence Hull. *Calendar: Christ's Time for the Church*. Nashville, TN: Abingdon Press, 1996.

Talley, Thomas J. *The Origins of the Liturgical Year*. New York: Pueblo Publishing, 1986.

Taylor, Richard. *How to Read a Church: A Guide to Symbols and Images in Churches and Cathedrals*. Mahwah, NJ: Hidden Spring, 2005.

Webber, Robert. *Ancient-Future Time: Forming Spirituality through the Christian Year*. Grand Rapids, MI: Baker Books, 2004.

Christianity and the Shaping of Culture

Baggley, John. *Doors of Perception: Icons and Their Spiritual Significance*. Crestwood, New York: St. Vladimir's Seminary Press, 1995.

Beckett, Lucy. *In the Light of Christ: Writings in the Western Tradition*. San Francisco, CA: Ignatius Press, 2006.

Brooke, John Hedley. *Science and Religion: Some Historical Perspectives*. Cambridge: Cambridge University Press, 1991.

Hass, Andrew, David Jasper, and Elisabeth Jay, eds. *The Oxford Handbook of English Literature and Theology*. New York: Oxford University Press, 2007.

Jensen, Robin Margaret. *Understanding Early Christian Art*. London: Routledge, 2000.

Kemp, Wolfgang. *The Narratives of Gothic Stained Glass.* Cambridge: Cambridge University Press, 1997.

Ladner, Gerhart B. *God, Cosmos, and Humankind : The World of Early Christian Symbolism.* Berkeley: University of California Press, 1995.

Numbers, Ronald L., ed. *Galileo Goes to Jail: And Other Myths about Science and Religion.* Cambridge, MA: Harvard University Press, 2009.

Raguin, Virginia Chieffo, and Mary Clerkin Higgins. *The History of Stained Glass: The Art of Light Medieval to Contemporary.* London: Thames & Hudson, 2003.

Ryken, Leland, ed. *The Christian Imagination: The Practice of Faith in Literature and Writing.* Colorado Springs, CO: Shaw, 2002.

Schloeder, Steven J. *Architecture in Communion.* San Francisco, CA: Ignatius Press 1998.

Taylor, Richard. *How to Read a Church: An Illustrated Guide to Images, Symbols and Meanings in Churches and Cathedrals.* London: Rider, 2004.

Watts, Fraser. "Are Science and Religion in Conflict?" *Zygon* 32 (1997): 125–138.

White, James F. *A Brief History of Christian Worship.* Nashville, TN: Abingdon Press, 1993.

Wilson-Dickson, Andrew. *A Brief History of Christian Music: From Biblical Times to the Present.* Oxford: Lion, 1997.

Sources of Quotations

Chapter 2

p. 48
Augustine of Hippo, *De utilitate credendi* 3.9.

p. 48
Gregory the Great, *Homiliae in Ezechielem* 1.6.15.

p. 49
Catechism of the Catholic Church, 1992, §§128–9, at http://www.vatican.va/archive/ENG0015/_INDEX.HTM (accessed July 12, 2014).

p. 52
Irenaeus of Lyons, *Adversus haereses* 2.2.1–4.1.

p. 53
Hippolytus of Rome, *The Apostolic Tradition* 21.

Chapter 3

p. 55
Charles Taylor, *Modern Social Imaginaries*. Durham, NC: Duke University Press, 2002, p. 23.

Christianity: An Introduction, Third Edition. Alister E. McGrath.
© 2015 John Wiley & Sons, Ltd. Published 2015 by John Wiley & Sons, Ltd.

p. 57

Quintus Septimius Tertullian, *De praescriptione hereticorum* 13.

p. 60

Samuel Taylor Coleridge, *The Literary Remains of Samuel Taylor Coleridge*. London: Pickering, 1834–1838, vol. 3, p. 461.

p. 60

The Second World Conference on Faith and Order. New York: Macmillan, 1938, p. 21.

p. 61

Blaise Pascal, *Pensées*. London: Penguin Books, 1966, p. 188.

p. 62

Terry Eagleton, "Lunging, Flailing, Mispunching." *London Review of Books* 28.2, October 19, 2006, p. 33.

p. 62

Fides et ratio. Encyclical letter of the Supreme Pontiff John Paul II to the Bishops of the Catholic Church on the Relationship between Faith and Reason, at http://www.vatican.va/holy_father/john_paul_ii/encyclicals/documents/hf_jp-ii_enc_15101998_fides-et-ratio_en.html (accessed July 16, 2014).

p. 64

Blaise Pascal, *Pensées*. London: Penguin Books, 1966, pp. 110, 190.

p. 65

G. K. Chesterton, "The Return of the Angels." *Daily News*, 14 March, 1903.

p. 65

C. S. Lewis, *Essay Collection*. London: HarperCollins, 2002, p. 21.

p. 69

Catechism of the Catholic Church, 1992, §239, at http://www.vatican.va/archive/ENG0015/_INDEX.HTM (accessed July 12, 2014).

p. 74

Thomas Jefferson, Letter to Messrs. Nehemiah Dodge and Others, January 1, 1802, at http://www.stephenjaygould.org/ctrl/jefferson_dba.html (accessed July 12, 2014).

p. 75

Irenaeus of Lyons, *Against All Heresies* 3.23.3.

p. 75

Irenaeus of Lyons, *Demonstration of the Apostolic Preaching* 6.

p. 77

Robert Jenson, "The Triune God," in C. E. Braaten and R. W. Jenson, eds., *Christian Dogmatics*. Philadelphia: Fortress Press, 1984, vol. 1, pp. 88–89.

Chapter 4

p. 127
Cited in Laura K. McClure, ed., *Sexuality and Gender in the Classical World: Readings and Sources*. Oxford: Wiley Blackwell, 2008, p. 158.

p. 129
Galerius, *Edict of Toleration* [311], chapter 34.

p. 151
Alister E. McGrath, *Iustitia Dei: A History of the Christian Doctrine of Justification*. Cambridge: Cambridge University Press, 2005, p. vii.

p. 154
John Calvin, *Institutes of the Christian Religion*, preface to the 1539 edition.

p. 155
Roland H. Bainton, "The Left Wing of the Reformation." *Journal of Religion* 21.2 (1941): 124–134.

p. 155
George Hunston Williams, *The Radical Reformation*. Philadelphia: Westminster Press, 1962.

p. 161
John Wesley, journal entry for May 24, 1738, in *The Works of John Wesley*. Grand Rapids: Baker Books, 2007, vol. 5, p. 103.

p. 168
Roger Williams, "Mr Cotton's Letter Lately Printed, Examined and Answered" [1644], in *The Complete Writings of Roger Williams*. New York: Russell & Russell, 1963, vol. 1, p. 108.

p. 168
Thomas Jefferson, Letter to the Danbury Baptists, January 1, 1802, at http://www.loc.gov/loc/lcib/9806/danpre.html (accessed August 1, 2014).

p. 171
Stephen Charles Neill, *A History of Christianity in India, 1707–1858*. Cambridge: Cambridge University Press, 1985, p. 155.

p. 175
First Vatican Council, at http://www.intratext.com/x/eng0063.htm (accessed August 1, 2014).

p. 176
Alfred Loisy, *L'Évangile et l'église*. Paris: Picard et fils, 1902, p. 111.

p. 176
George Tyrrell, *Christianity at the Crossroads*. London: Allen & Unwin, 1963, pp. 49–50.

p. 177
Ibid., p. 45.

p. 177
Pope Pius X, *Pascendi dominici gregis*, at http://www.vatican.va/holy_father/pius_x/encyclicals/documents/hf_p-x_enc_19070908_pascendi-dominici-gregis_en.html (accessed August 1, 2014).

p. 178
Benjamin Jowett, "On the Interpretation of Scripture," in his *Essays and Reviews*. London: Parker, 1860, pp. 477–593.

p. 178
John William Colenso, *The Pentateuch and the Book of Joshua Critically Examined*. London, 1862, p. 8.

p. 183
Vladimir Ilyich Lenin, *Collected Works*. Moscow: Progress Publishers, 1965, vol. 10, pp. 83–87.

p. 185
Kirsopp Lake, *The Religion of Yesterday and Tomorrow*. Boston: Houghton Mifflin, 1925, pp. 61–62.

p. 187
Barmen Declaration, at http://www.ekd.de/english/barmen_theological_declaration.html (accessed August 1, 2014).

p. 188
Peter Berger, *The Sacred Canopy*. Garden City, NY: Doubleday, 1967, pp. 111–113.

p. 192
Winston Churchill, *The Second World War*. Boston: Houghton Mifflin, 1948–1953, vol. 1, p. 105.

p. 194
Pope John Paul II, "Crossing the Threshold of Hope," 1994, at http://www.2heartsnetwork.org/Crossing.the.Threshold.ofHope-PopeJPII.pdf (accessed August 1, 2014).

p. 196
Gustavo Gutiérrez, "Two Theological Perspectives: Liberation Theology and Progressivist Theology," in Sergio Torres and Virginia Fabella, eds., *The Emergent Gospel*. Maryknoll. New York: Orbis Books, 1978, pp. 234–235.

Chapter 5

p. 202
Council of Trent, Fourth Session, Decree on the Edition and Use of Sacred Books, at http://history.hanover.edu/texts/trent/ct04ed.html (accessed August 1, 2014).

p. 204
Athanasius of Alexandria, *On the Incarnation* 54.3.

p. 215
World Council of Churches, Toronto Statement, 1970, at http://www.oikoumene.org/en/
resources/documents/central-committee/1950/toronto-statement (accessed August 1,
2014).

Chapter 6

p. 223
Episcopal Church of Scotland, *Marriage Liturgy 2007*, p. 10, at http://www.scotland.
anglican.org/who-we-are/publications/liturgies/marriage-liturgy-2007/ (accessed August
1, 2014).

pp. 223–224
Catholic Order of Christian Funerals, as implemented by the Archdiocese of Boston, at
http://www.bostoncatholic.org/uploadedFiles/BostonCatholicorg/Offices_And_Services/
Offices/Sub_Pages/Worship_and_Spiritual_Life/2014guidelines-for-homilies-and-words-
of-remembrance-in-ocf.pdf (accessed August 1, 2014).

p. 224
Book of Common Prayer (1662), "At the burial of the dead," at https://www.
churchofengland.org/prayer-worship/worship/book-of-common-prayer/at-the-burial-of-
the-dead.aspx (accessed August 1, 2014).

pp. 224–225
Funeral liturgy in the Catholic archdiocese of Vancouver, at http://www.rcav.org/
uploadedFiles/About_Us/Guidelines_for_Funerals_and_Burials.pdf (accessed August 1,
2014).

p. 225
First United Methodist Church in Austin, Texas, at http://fumcaustin.org/open-heart/
worship/funeral-services/ (accessed August 1, 2014).

p. 226
Bidding Prayer in Nine Lessons and Carols, at http://www.kings.cam.ac.uk/events/
chapel-services/nine-lessons/order-service-2002.html (accessed August 1, 2014).

p. 227
Justin Martyr, *First Apology* 67.

p. 228
Chrysostom, Homily 24 on First Corinthians.

p. 229
John Newton, *Olney Hymns* [1779], Preface.

p. 231

Thomas Aquinas, "Adoro te devote," translated by Gerard Manley Hopkins.

p. 232

John Calvin, *Institutes of the Christian Religion* 4.14.3.

p. 243

The Works of George Herbert. London: Oxford University Press, 1941, p. 41.

p. 243

Easter/Paschal troparion, at http://www.byzcath.org/index.php/resources-mainmenu-63/liturgical-texts (accessed August 1, 2014).

p. 247–248

Walter Brueggemann, *The Land: Place as Gift, Promise, and Challenge in Biblical Faith*, 2nd edn. Philadelphia: Fortress Press, 2002, p. 5.

Chapter 7

p. 253

Tertullian, *De praescriptione haereticorum* 7.

p. 254

Augustine of Hippo, *On Christian Doctrine* 2.40.60–61.

p. 257

For these and other references, see Martin Hengel, *Crucifixion in the Ancient World and the Folly of the Message of the Cross*. Philadelphia: Fortress Press, 1977.

p. 259

Julian of Norwich, *Revelations of Divine Love*. Harmondsworth: Penguin, 1998, p. 64.

p. 263

Cyprian of Carthage, *Letters* 72.21.

p. 266

Abbot Suger, *The Book of Suger Abbot of St. Denis on What Was Done During his Administration* 27.

p. 267

Karl Barth, *The Gottingen Dogmatics: Instruction in the Christian Religion*. Grand Rapids: Eerdmans, 1990, vol. 1, pp. 31–32.

p. 269

Theophilus, *On Diverse Arts* 6.

p. 271

Dorothy L. Sayers, "Towards a Christian Aesthetic," in *Unpopular Opinions*. London: Victor Gollancz, 1946, p. 31.

p. 272
Geoffrey Chaucer, *Canterbury Tales*. New York: Simon and Schuster, 1946, p. 373.

p. 272
Richard Baxter, *The Practical Works of Richard Baxter*. London: Duncan, 1830, vol. 11, p. 177.

p. 272
William Wordsworth, *The Prose Works of William Wordsworth*. Oxford: Clarendon Press, 1974, vol. 1, p. 128.

p. 276
The Belgic Confession of Faith [1561], Article 2.

Index

Note: Page numbers in *italic* refer to figures, those in **bold** to boxes.

Get It Together for College

UPDATED
3rd Edition

Get It Together for College

A **Planner** to Help you **Get Organized** and **Get In.**

The College Board, New York, NY

About the College Board

The College Board is a mission-driven not-for-profit organization that connects students to college success and opportunity. Founded in 1900, the College Board was created to expand access to higher education. Today, the membership association is made up of over 6,000 of the world's leading educational institutions and is dedicated to promoting excellence and equity in education. Each year, the College Board helps more than seven million students prepare for a successful transition to college through programs and services in college readiness and college success — including the SAT® and the Advanced Placement Program®. The organization also serves the education community through research and advocacy on behalf of students, educators and schools. For further information, visit www.collegeboard.org.

Copies of this book may be ordered from College Board Publications, P.O. Box 4699, Mount Vernon, IL 62864, or online through the College Board Store at www.collegeboard.org. The price is $15.99.

Editorial inquiries concerning this book should be directed to The College Board, 250 Vesey Street, New York, New York 10281.

ISBN: 978-1-4573-0429-3

Printed in the United States of America.
Distributed by Macmillan.

SUSTAINABLE FORESTRY INITIATIVE Certified Sourcing www.sfiprogram.org SFI-00756

Contents

Preface

Choosing and applying to colleges is probably the biggest, and most important, project in your life right now. You might be thinking the last thing you need is a book to read—that's just another brick on the pile. But this book is different. It doesn't add to the pile; it helps you manage the pile.

It does that by putting everything you need to know and remember to successfully get through the college app process in one handy, easy-to-find place. And, it makes it simple. No long articles to read, just quick tips, timelines, checklists, and places to keep track of things.

Much of the content in this book comes from the College Board website, collegeboard.org. Literally millions of high school students come to that site every year to register for the SAT®, or to use College Search and My Organizer. Chances are you are one of them. But often, a book is just handier and quicker than an app or website.

Like most big jobs, the college application process is really just a lot of little jobs spread out over a long period of time. The trick, of course, is to stay organized so you're not juggling these tasks blindfolded. If organizing a big project is not your strength, or you just have no experience at it, this book will help you.

Use it to keep the stress out, and to get in.

Acknowledgments

This book is a compilation of the expertise and sage advice of many people. Everyone involved with creating and maintaining the content on the #1 college website, collegeboard.org, should be credited here, but there just isn't enough space, so I hope a general shout-out will do. Thanks also to the people who helped publish this third edition: Jim Gwyn, Jennifer Rose, Tim Burke, and the production team at DataStream Content Solutions.

Some of the content in this book is adapted from other works, by permission of the copyright owners: "What to Include in a Sports Résumé" (page 45), adapted from material provided by Libertyville High School, Illinois; "Sample Student-Athlete Résumé" (page 46), adapted from material provided by Plano High School, Texas; and "Recommendation Cheat Sheet" on page 134, adapted from material provided by Lick-Wilmerding High School, California.

Tom Vanderberg
Senior Editor, Guidance Publications
The College Board

How to Use this Book

You don't really need to be told how to use this book—it's obvious. Whatever it is you need to do, or are wondering (or worrying) about, is in the TOC (table of contents). Just look it up and go to a quick read about what to do or a handy tool to get it done.

But a few pointers are in order:

- The "Big Calendar" (Chapter 1) is the place to start, and to come back to for the big picture.
- While the chapters are laid out in the general sequence that the college application process follows, don't try to read it all through, start to finish. It's not that kind of book.
- There are separate "trackers" (to write down deadlines, etc.) for college admission applications, financial aid applications, and scholarship applications. Plus another tracker for the tests you might have to take.
- Likewise, there are separate timelines for these events.
- In case you miss them, there's a "College Fair Journal" in Chapter 4, and a "Campus Visit Journal" in Chapter 5; both can be handy to have with you to write down your impressions.
- At the end of the book you'll find a place to write down the names, etc., of everyone you will meet and need to remember along the way.

Don't lose this book! It's going to make getting into college easier. And good luck!

My Organizer on collegeboard.org

Want to get organized online? Go to collegeboard.org's My Organizer to stay on top of college-planning milestones and make smart choices. Stay on track with deadline reminders and strategies that help you find, choose, get into, and afford the best college for you.

In My Organizer, you can:

- Get alerts, such as telling you the moment that your SAT® scores are released, or the next crucial step in your college planning.

- Get a big-picture view of what to do, and when, throughout each high school year to get ready for college.

- See upcoming dates and deadlines for tests, your college applications, and your favorite college's deadlines.

- See your PSAT/NMSQT® and SAT status and reminders. You can also link to a free practice test with score report and answer explanations.

- Use financial aid tools and calculators to search for scholarships, estimate college costs, calculate how college loans add up over time, and more.

- Watch videos of college students telling their own stories and educators sharing advice.

- Get The Official SAT Question of the Day™ delivered to your e-mail inbox so you can tease your brain with a new practice question every day.

The Big Calendar

The Summer Before

✓ **Read** interesting books—no matter what you go to college for, you'll need a good vocabulary and strong reading comprehension skills. Reading is also one of the best ways to prep for college entrance exams.

✓ **Get a social security number** if you don't already have one—you'll need it for your college applications.

✓ **Think about yourself.** What are your goals? What are you curious about? What are you good at? What do you like to do in your spare time? Knowing the basics about yourself will help you make the right college choices.

✓ **Talk to your family and friends** about college and your goals. They know you best and will have good insights.

NOTES

_____

_____

_____

_____

_____

September

✔ **Meet with your school counselor** to make sure you are taking the courses that colleges look for.

✔ **Resolve to get the best grades** you can this year. The payoff will be more colleges to choose from, and a better chance for scholarship money.

✔ **Pick up the** *Official Student Guide to the PSAT/NMSQT®* from your guidance office and take the practice test. (You'll take the real test in October.)

✔ Get involved in an **extracurricular activity**.

✔ Find out if your school will have a **college night**.

NOTES

October

✔ Take the **PSAT/NMSQT**.

✔ Attend a **college fair**.

✔ Begin looking through the College Board's *College Handbook*— **start a preliminary list of colleges** that might interest you.

✔ Start to **learn about financial aid**. Attend a family financial aid night at your school or in your area, and use the Financial Aid EasyPlanner and Net Price Calculator at collegeboard.org to estimate how much aid you might receive.

NOTES

_____

_____

_____

_____

_____

November

✔ Begin to **research scholarships**—use the Scholarship Search on collegeboard.org or the College Board's *Scholarship Handbook* to find out about deadlines and eligibility requirements.

✔ **Learn about the SAT®.** Go to collegeboard.org. Also, pick up the official bulletins at your guidance office

✔ If you are planning to major in the arts (drama, music, fine art), ask your teachers about requirements for a **portfolio or audition**.

NOTES

December

✓ Review your **PSAT/NMSQT Score Report** with your school counselor. Check out My College QuickStart™ at collegeboard.org.

✓ Spend time over the holidays to **think about what kind of college** you want. Big or small? Far away or close to home?

✓ **Make a list** of the college features that are important to you.

✓ **Begin preparing for the SAT.** Visit the free SAT prep section at satpractice.org.

NOTES

_____

_____

_____

_____

_____

January

✓ **Meet with your school counselor** to talk about the colleges you are interested in, what entrance exams you should take, and when you should take them.

✓ If English is not your primary language, decide when to take the **TOEFL** test.

✓ Start thinking about **what you want to study in college**. Use resources like the *College Board Book of Majors* and the majors and careers section at collegeboard.org.

✓ **Register for the SAT** if you want to take it in **March**.

NOTES

_____

_____

_____

_____

_____

February

✔ Think about which teachers you will ask to write **letters of recommendation**.

✔ If you're in Advanced Placement Program® (AP®) classes, **register for AP Exams**, given in May.

✔ Ask your counselor or teacher about taking the **SAT Subject Tests**™ in the spring. You should take them while course material is still fresh in your mind.

NOTES

_____

_____

_____

_____

_____

March

✓ **Register for the SAT and/or SAT Subject Tests** if you want to take them in **May**.

✓ **Narrow your college list** to a reasonable number. Explore the college's websites, read their brochures and catalogs, and talk to your family and friends.

✓ **Practice the SAT**. Ask your school counselor for the booklet *Getting Ready for the SAT*—it's free and has a full-length practice test; you can also download four free tests from collegeboard.org.

NOTES

April

✔ **Register for the SAT and/or SAT Subject Tests** if you want to take them in **June**.

✔ **Plan your courses for senior year.** Make sure you are going to meet the high school course requirements for your top-choice colleges.

✔ **Plan campus visits.** It's best to go when classes are in session. Start with colleges that are close by.

NOTES

_____

_____

_____

_____

_____

May

✓ Talk to your coach and your counselor about **NCAA requirements** if you want to play Division I or II sports in college.

✓ Start looking for a **summer job or volunteer work**—the good ones go fast.

✓ **AP Exams** are given.

NOTES

_____

_____

_____

_____

June

✔ Ask your counselor about **local scholarships** offered by church groups, civic associations, and businesses in your community.

✔ If you are considering **military academies or ROTC** scholarships, contact your counselor before leaving school for the summer.

NOTES

The Summer Before

✔ **Register for the SAT and/or SAT Subject Tests** if you want to take them in **October or November**.

✔ If you want to play a NCAA Division I or II sport in college, **register with the NCAA Eligibility Center (www.ncaa.org)**.

✔ **Visit colleges** on your list. Call ahead for the campus tour schedule.

✔ Begin working on your **college application essays**.

✔ **Write a résumé** (accomplishments, activities, and work experiences) to help you later with your college applications.

✔ If you are applying to a **visual or performing arts program**, work on your portfolio or audition pieces.

NOTES

September

✓ Meet with your school counselor to **finalize your list of colleges**. Be sure your list includes "safety," "reach," and "probable" schools.

✓ **Start a checklist** of all application requirements, deadlines, fees, etc.

✓ If you can't afford application fees, your counselor can help you request a **fee waiver**.

✓ Set up **campus visits and interviews**; attend open houses at colleges that interest you.

✓ Find out if there will be a **family financial aid night** at your school, or elsewhere in your area this fall, and put it on your calendar.

NOTES

_____

_____

_____

_____

_____

October

✓ **Register for the SAT and/or SAT Subject Tests** if you want to take them in **December or January**.

✓ If you are going to apply under an **Early Decision or Early Action** plan, get started now. Some colleges have October deadlines.

✓ **Ask for letters of recommendation** from your counselor, teachers, coaches, or employers.

✓ Write **first drafts of your college essays** and ask your parents and teachers to review them.

✓ If you need to fill out the **CSS/Financial Aid PROFILE**®, you can register on collegeboard.org starting Oct. 1.

NOTES

_____

_____

_____

_____

_____

November

✔ **Finish your application essays**. Proofread them rigorously for mistakes.

✔ **Apply to colleges with rolling admission** (first-come, first-served) as early as possible. Keep hard copies.

✔ Make sure your **test scores** will be sent by the testing agency to each one of your colleges.

✔ Give your school counselor the proper **forms to send transcripts** to your colleges in plenty of time to meet deadlines.

✔ **Get PINs for the FAFSA** for both yourself and one of your parents from **www.pin.ed.gov**.

NOTES

_____

_____

_____

_____

_____

December

✓ Try to **wrap up college applications** before winter break. Make copies for yourself and your school counselor.

✓ If you applied for **Early Decision**, you should have an answer by Dec. 15. If you are denied or deferred, submit applications now to other colleges.

✓ **Apply for scholarships** in time to meet application deadlines.

✓ Start gathering what you need to complete the FAFSA. **Visit FAFSA on the Web** for a list of needed documents.

✓ **Contact the financial aid office** at the colleges on your list to see if they require any **other financial aid forms**.

NOTES

January

✓ **Submit your FAFSA** as soon as you can. If a college you're applying to has a financial aid priority date of Feb. 1, use estimates based on end-of-year pay stubs and last year's tax returns.

✓ **Submit other financial aid forms** that may be required—such as PROFILE or the college's own forms. Keep copies.

✓ If a college wants to see your **midyear grades**, give the form to your school counselor.

✓ If you have any **new honors or accomplishments** that were not in your original application, let your colleges know.

NOTES

February

✔ **Contact your colleges** to confirm that all application materials have been received.

✔ Correct or update your **Student Aid Report (SAR)** that follows the FAFSA.

✔ If any **special circumstances** affect your family's financial situation, alert each college's financial aid office.

✔ **File income tax returns early**. Some colleges want your family's tax information before finalizing financial aid offers.

✔ **Register for AP Exams** you want to take. (If you are home schooled or your school does not offer AP, you must contact AP Services by March 1.)

NOTES

_____

_____

_____

_____

_____

March

✓ **Admission decisions start arriving**. Read everything you receive carefully, as some may require prompt action on your part.

✓ **Revisit colleges** that accepted you if it's hard to make a choice.

✓ Send copies of your **FAFSA to any scholarship programs** that require it as part of their applications.

✓ **Don't get senioritis!** Colleges want to see strong second half grades.

NOTES

_____

_____

_____

_____

_____

April

✔ **Carefully compare financial aid award letters** from the colleges that accept you—it might not be clear which is the better offer. If you have questions, contact the college's financial aid office or talk to your school counselor.

✔ **If you don't get enough aid**, consider your options, which include appealing the award.

✔ Make a final decision, **accept the aid package and mail a deposit check** to the college you select before May 1 (the acceptance deadline for most schools).

✔ **Notify the other colleges** that you won't be attending (so another student can have your spot).

NOTES

_____

_____

_____

_____

_____

May

✔ AP Exams are given. Make sure your **AP Grade Report** is sent to your college.

✔ **Study hard for final exams**. Most offers of admission are contingent on your final grades.

✔ **Thank everyone** who wrote you recommendations or otherwise helped with your college applications.

✔ **If you weren't accepted** anywhere, don't give up—you still have options. Talk to your school counselor about them.

NOTES

June

✔ Have your counselor send your **final transcript** to your college choice.

✔ If you plan on competing in Division I or Division II college sports, have your counselor send your final transcript to the **NCAA Eligibility Center**.

✔ Think about your **summer job options**. The more money you make, the easier it will be to finance college—and have some fun during the school year.

✔ Enjoy your graduation, and have a great summer!

NOTES

_____

_____

_____

_____

_____

Chapter 02

Make Sure
You're on Track

What Colleges Are Looking For

As you get ready to apply to colleges, be sure you know what counts most in the minds of college admission officers. Here's a quick rundown.

Most important: your high school transcript

This is what colleges will look at first and foremost. The grades you earned in high school are the best predictor of college success. Your transcript also shows whether you've taken the required or recommended college-prep courses.

But colleges won't just look at your grades and which courses you took—they will also look at how rigorous those courses were, and your grade trend over all four years. So a hard-fought-for C+ in AP Biology might outweigh an easy A in an introductory computer class; and a falloff in your final senior year grades might undo the good work you did before then.

> "The first thing most colleges and universities will consider will be the high school courses a student chose. Are they challenging? Are they college prep, honors, or AP courses?"
>
> — Mary Ellen Anderson, director of admissions, Indiana University–Bloomington

Test scores are just part of the picture

Your scores on college entrance exams can be important but, generally, they're not as important as your high school transcript. Most often, admission officers will use your test scores to supplement your transcript or help them interpret it. High schools across the country can vary greatly in terms of grading standards and course rigor, and standardized tests offer a way to compare your college readiness with other students on a level playing field. But keep in mind that your test scores are only one of a number of factors that colleges consider when making admission decisions.

Beyond the numbers

Very few colleges assess applications using just transcripts and test scores. Other factors, like your high school record, essays, recommendations, interviews, and extracurricular activities, also play a role in admission decisions.

What all of these additional factors have in common is that they help admission officers look "beyond the numbers" and see what kind of person you are, and how you might contribute to their campus community. None of these factors will be the most important thing the college looks at; but taken together they can help round out your application and tip the scale in your favor.

Here's a closer look at each of the personal factors colleges usually look at:

Recommendations give the college a sense of your overall attitude toward learning, your character, and the context for the grades on your transcript. For tips on choosing whom to ask for recommendations, and how to ask them, see page 132.

Your record of extracurricular activities, in and out of school, tells the college about how involved you are in your school and local community. From that, they'll have a good picture of how likely you are to contribute to their own campus community. For tips on choosing extra-curriculars, see page 34.

Essays are the most subjective of all the components of an application, but they are also the one component over which you have total control. For tips on writing your essays, see Chapter 8.

Interviews are rarely required and don't carry a great deal of weight in the overall application. Think of them as an opportunity to put a personal face on your application, and to learn more about whether the college would be a good fit for you. You'll find more about interviews, including checklists of questions to expect and questions you should ask, in Chapter 9.

> "If students try to force themselves to look like a fit to the admissions committee, that's like putting square pegs in round holes—they will be unhappy."
>
> — Deren Finks, former dean of admission and financial aid, Harvey Mudd College

How interested are you?

Competitive colleges weigh an additional factor: "demonstrated interest." That means they try to determine whether, if they accept you, you will actually enroll at their college.

Here are some things that colleges usually look for when they try to gauge your level of interest:

- Did you contact the college for information about their programs?
- Have you talked to anyone from the college at a college fair or on a campus visit?
- If you interviewed with the college, did you ask in-depth questions that show you've already researched the college?

But always keep this in mind: The most important thing is what *you* want and what *you* are looking for. You're not selling, you're buying, even if it's a "reach" school.

Ninth- and Tenth-Grade Planner

If you're a ninth- or tenth-grader and have this book in your hand, good for you! You're thinking about college while there is still time to plan ahead. Here's some important groundwork that should take place in the first two years of high school.

Grade 9

Meet with your school counselor

Find out what high school courses colleges want to see on your transcript (see the chart to the right), and make sure your ninth-grade courses are on the right track.

With your counselor, map out what courses should be taken during the rest of high school.

Get involved in an extracurricular activity

Get into something you will really enjoy doing, even if it's not that popular. (See "Extracurricular Tips" on page 34.)

If you want to play a sport in college, talk to your coach about eligibility requirements (see "Tips for the Student-Athlete" on page 44).

Start thinking about careers

Having a career goal will help you stay focused in high school. You might change your mind a lot, but it's the thought process that counts.

Save for college

It's still not too late to start a college savings plan. Every little bit helps! Talk about college costs and financial aid options with your parents.

Grade 10

Meet with your school counselor—again

Make sure you are enrolled in the right college-prep courses and on the right track for junior and senior year.

If your school offers the PSAT to 10th-graders, take it

The PSAT is usually taken in the 11th grade, but it's a good idea to also take it in the 10th because it provides invaluable feedback on the Student Score Report; you can then work on any disclosed academic weaknesses while there is still ample time to improve them.

Are you interested in attending a U.S. military academy?

If so, you should request a precandidate questionnaire and complete it. Your school counselor can help you with that.

Tour a college campus in your area

Even if you are not interested in attending the college you are visiting, it will help you learn what to look for in a college.

If you don't have a social security number, apply for one

You'll need it for college applications, testing, scholarships, and other opportunities.

Recommended High School Classes

Here are the most commonly recommended classes. They're geared for students headed to a four-year college, but you should take most of them if you're also interested in a two-year college.

What colleges want you to take in high school

SUBJECT	CLASSES	
ENGLISH/LANGUAGE ARTS (8 credits/4 years)	literature writing/composition speech/rhetoric	
MATH (6 credits/3 years*)	algebra I algebra II geometry trigonometry and/or calculus	
SCIENCE (WITH LAB) (6 credits/3 years*)	biology chemistry and/or physics earth/space sciences	
SOCIAL STUDIES (6 credits/3 years*)	U.S. history U.S. government world history or geography	
FOREIGN LANGUAGE (4 credits/2 years)	*More selective colleges will require 3 to 4 years.*	
VISUAL/PERFORMING ARTS (1 to 2 credits)	*Choose from:* studio art dance	music drama
OTHER (1 to 2 credits)	*Choose from:* business computer science/applications environmental studies/science government and politics	communications economics statistics

* More competitive colleges will want to see four years each of math, lab science, and social studies.

High School Planning Worksheet

Fill out a worksheet for each year of school, listing the courses that you've taken, are currently taking, or plan to take. Talk to your counselor about your plan and make sure you're on track to meet college requirements.

SUBJECT	9TH GRADE		10TH GRADE	
	FALL SEMESTER	SPRING SEMESTER	FALL SEMESTER	SPRING SEMESTER
ENGLISH/ LANGUAGE ARTS				
HISTORY/ SOCIAL STUDIES				
MATH				
SCIENCE (INDICATE IF LAB)				
FOREIGN LANGUAGE				
ARTS				
OTHER				

11TH GRADE		12TH GRADE	
FALL SEMESTER	SPRING SEMESTER	FALL SEMESTER	SPRING SEMESTER

10 Questions to Ask Your School Counselor

Your school counselor, or guidance counselor, is one of your best resources as you plan for college and will be your partner in getting your college applications completed. If your high school has a large student population, it might be hard to get face time with your counselor; but even if you use e-mail, you can get a conversation started with these basic questions:

1. What courses do I need to take to be ready for college?

2. Which elective courses do you recommend?

3. What AP courses are available, and how do I get in?

4. Do you have any college planning sessions scheduled?

5. What should I be doing at home and over the summer to get ready for college?

6. What kinds of grades do different colleges require?

7. Are there any college fairs at this school, or nearby?

8. Where do other kids from this school attend college?

9. Do you have any information to help me start exploring careers?

10. Are there any local scholarships or awards that I should know about now, so I can work toward them?

What to Know About AP®

Advanced Placement Program (AP) courses are designed to give high school students the chance to study a subject at the level of an introductory college course. AP Exams are offered in May for all AP subjects (except Studio Art, which is scored on the basis of a portfolio). Depending upon your exam score and on the AP policy at the college you attend, you may be eligible for college credit for that course and/or advanced placement into a higher-level college course.

The difference between credit and placement

Some colleges award credit for qualifying AP Exam scores. This means that you actually earn points toward your college degree. Others award advanced placement. This means that when you're in college, you can skip introductory courses, enter higher-level classes, and/or fulfill general education requirements.

The benefits of earning college credit or placement

College credit or placement can allow you to move into upper-level courses sooner, pursue a double major or a combined bachelor's/master's degree program, gain time to study and travel abroad, and complete your undergraduate degree in fewer than four years.

Why you need to take the AP Exam in order to earn college credit or placement

Colleges and universities give credit or placement only for qualifying AP Exam scores, not AP course grades. Without a corresponding AP Exam score, they can't verify how well you've mastered college-level content.

> Through AP, you can earn college credit worth hundreds of dollars — even thousands at some colleges.

What else you can get out of AP

There's more to AP than the possibility of earning college credit or placement. You might even consider these additional benefits to be more important. By taking an AP course, you can:

- Study subjects in greater depth and detail
- Exercise your writing skills, reasoning ability, and problem-solving techniques
- Develop the study habits necessary for tackling rigorous course work
- Show colleges your willingness to challenge yourself

How to get started

Talk to an AP teacher or the AP Coordinator at your school about the course you want to take. Discuss the course's workload and any preparation you might need. If you are homeschooled or attend a school that doesn't offer AP, you can still participate through independent study or by taking online AP courses.

Extracurricular Tips

Selective colleges want to know what you do both inside and outside the classroom. That's because the more they know about you, the easier it is to decide if you're the type of student they want to admit. Yes, your academics come first, but what you do with your free time reveals a lot, such as:

- Whether you are mature enough to stick to something over the long haul
- What your nonacademic interests are—what makes you tick
- How you've contributed to something beyond yourself
- Whether you can manage your time and priorities

So here are some tips for choosing extracurriculars.

Consider your interests and abilities first

It's easier to commit to something that fits the real you. If you like to write but are kind of a klutz, it makes more sense to join the school newspaper than the lacrosse team. And while it's natural to want to be where your friends are, don't join something for that reason alone—it truly should be a shared interest.

Go for depth, not breadth

Colleges are more impressed by a real commitment to one activity over time, rather than a superficial involvement in multiple activities. So don't join a bunch of activities just to bulk up your application.

Keep your balance

Remember: Colleges are not interested in seeing you "do it all." Don't overextend and risk burnout or bad grades. Colleges don't have a checklist of requirements when it comes to extracurriculars.

You don't have to be a star

Don't worry about being president of the club, or captain of the team. The key is whether you've contributed something significant—center stage or behind the scenes.

If you're not a joiner

Selective colleges aren't looking for extracurricular activities to see how well you play with others; they're looking for evidence of your nonacademic qualities and experience. Good news: You can show that even if you don't like to join teams or clubs. As school counselor Dorothy Coppock puts it: "An avid equestrian or ice-skater does not need to add on a school activity to look well-rounded."

Working or volunteering counts too

A job—paid or unpaid, year-round or summer—shows that you can handle responsibilities and have "real-world" experience. If jobs are hard to find, ask your counselor how to arrange for an internship or a job-shadowing opportunity. The local chamber of commerce or organizations like Rotary or Kiwanis might also be able to help you.

Volunteer work, such as tutoring elementary school kids or spending time at a local hospital, is another great way to gain the skills and experience colleges like to see. Opportunities to help out are easy to find in every community.

Extracurricular Archive

Keep a record of all your activities as you go through high school. It will be good to have on hand when it's time to fill out college applications or if you need to provide a student résumé.

9TH GRADE

School activities: *[e.g., sports, clubs, special projects]*

School awards: *[e.g., honor roll]*

Community activities: *[e.g., food drive, church choir, beach clean-up day]*

Work experience: *[include hours/week]*

10TH GRADE

School activities:

School awards:

Community activities:

Work experience:

11TH GRADE

School activities:

School awards:

Community activities:

Work experience:

12TH GRADE

School activities:

School awards:

Community activities:

Work experience:

Top 10 Time-Management Tips

Does it seem like there's never enough time in the day to get everything done? Feel like you're always running late? Here are the top 10 tips for taking control of your life. Remember, the easiest way to break bad habits is to focus on making new habits.

1. Make a "to do" list every day

Put things that are most important at the top and do them first. If it's easier, use a planner to track all of your tasks. And don't forget to reward yourself for your accomplishments.

2. Use spare minutes wisely

Get some reading done on the bus ride home from school, for example, and you'll kill two birds with one stone.

3. It's okay to say "no"

If your boss asks you to work on a Thursday night and you have a final exam the next morning, realize that it's okay to say no. Keep your short- and long-term priorities in mind.

4. Find the right time

You'll work more efficiently if you figure out when you do your best work. For example, if your brain handles math better in the afternoon, don't wait to do it until late at night.

5. Review your notes every day

You'll reinforce what you've learned, so you need less time to study. You'll also be ready if your teacher calls on you or gives a pop quiz.

6. Get a good night's sleep

Running on empty makes the day seem longer and your tasks seem more difficult.

7. Let your friends know

If texting, Facebook, phone calls, etc., are too tempting and distracting during homework and study time, tell your friends (and yourself) that you are offline and unavailable between 8 and 10 p.m. (or whenever). Blame your folks if you must.

8. Become a taskmaster

Figure out how much free time you have each week. Give yourself a time budget and plan your activities accordingly. (Use the "Personal Time-Making Machine" on the next page.)

9. Don't waste time agonizing

Have you ever wasted an entire evening by worrying about something that you're supposed to be doing? Was it worth it? Instead of agonizing and procrastinating, just do it.

10. Keep things in perspective

Setting goals that are unrealistic sets you up for failure. While it's good to set high goals for yourself, be sure not to overdo it. Good goals are both challenging and reachable.

Your Personal Time-Making Machine

Want to create more time to get things done? Use this worksheet to see what you do in a normal school week (a seven-day week = 168 hours), and figure out where you can make more time.

HOW MANY HOURS A DAY DO YOU SPEND:	DAILY TOTAL	FREQUENCY	WEEKLY TOTAL
Sleeping (yes, include naps)?		× 7 =	
In school?		× 5 =	
Studying or doing homework?		× 7 =	
On extracurricular activities and sports?		× 7 =	
Watching TV, playing video games, or relaxing?		× 7 =	
Online or on the computer?		× 7 =	
Texting or talking on the phone?		× 7 =	
Hanging out?		× 7 =	
Working at a job?		× 7 =	
Traveling to and from school, work, lessons, etc.?		× 7 =	
On meals (preparing, eating, and cleaning up)?		× 7 =	
Taking showers, getting dressed, etc.?		× 7 =	
Doing chores?		× 7 =	
Other stuff (list):		× 7 =	

TOTAL HOURS	
EXTRA TIME AVAILABLE (168 hours minus your total)	

Summer Reading List

Reading is essential college prep and test prep, but it doesn't have to be a chore. Pick books you'll enjoy reading by googling the title for a quick synopsis or review.

This list was compiled from several lists recommended by high schools, libraries, and other organizations, but it's geared toward more contemporary, less typical suggestions.

Fiction

AUTHOR	TITLE	DATE
Alemanndine, Rabih	*The Hakawati*	2008
Rabih, Alemanndine	*The Hakawati*	2008
Allende, Isabel	*Portrait in Sepia*	2000
Allison, Dorothy	*Bastard Out of Carolina*	1992
Alvarez, Julia	*In the Time of Butterflies*	1994
Atwood, Margaret	*Oryx and Crake*	2003
Brooks, Geraldine	*March*	2005
Card, Orson Scott	*Ender's Game*	1985
Cisneros, Sandra	*The House on Mango Street*	1991
Crutcher, Chris	*Deadline*	2007
Danticat, Edwidge	*The Farming of Bones*	1998
Denfeld, Rene	*The Enchanted*	2014
Erdrich, Louise	*The Plague of Doves*	2009
Fowler, Karen Joy	*We Are All Completely Beside Ourselves*	2014
Gaines, Ernest	*A Lesson Before Dying*	1993
Greenberg, Joanne	*In This Sign*	1970
Guterson, David	*Snow Falling On Cedars*	1994
Haruf, Kent	*Plainsong*	1999
Holthe, Tess Uriza	*When the Elephants Dance*	2002
Hosseini, Khaled	*A Thousand Splendid Suns*	2007
Ishiguro, Kazuo	*Never Let Me Go*	2005
Johnson, James Weldon	*Autobiography of an Ex-Colored Man*	1991
Klass, David	*Home of the Braves*	2002
Klay, Phil	*Redeployment*	2014
Lahiri, Jhumpa	*The Lowland*	2013
Lamb, Wally	*She's Come Undone*	1992
Leckie, Ann	*Ancillary Justice*	2013
Lightman, Alan	*The Diagnosis*	2000
Marlantes, Karl	*Matterhorn: A Novel of the Vietnam War*	2010
Mason, Bobbie Ann	*In Country*	1985
Miller, Walter M. Jr.	*A Canticle for Leibowitz*	1964
Mitchell, David	*Black Swan Green*	2006
Mori, Kyoko	*Shizuko's Daughter*	1993
Morrison, Toni	*Jazz*	1992

AUTHOR	TITLE	DATE
Naidoo, Beverly	The Other Side of Truth	2001
Obreht, Téa	The Tiger's Wife	2011
Ozeki, Ruth	A Tale for the Time Being	2013
Power, Susan	The Grass Dancer	1994
Proulx, Annie E.	The Shipping News	1993
Price, Richard	Lush Life	2008
Robinson, Marilynne	Lila	2014
Shaara, Michael	Killer Angels	1974
Smiley, Jane	A Thousand Acres	1993
Spiegelman, Art	Maus: A Survivor's Tale	1986
Stoker, Bram	Dracula	1897
Tsukiyama, Gail	The Samurai's Garden	1996
Uchida, Yoshiko	Picture Bride	1987
Walker, Margaret	Jubilee	1967
Ward, Jesmyn	Salvage the Bones	2012
Wolff, Tobias	Old School	2003
Woodrell, Daniel	Winter's Bone	2006
Yolen, Jane	Briar Rose	1992

Nonfiction

AUTHOR	TITLE	DATE
Ackerman, Diane	The Human Age	2014
Anders, Lars	The Storm and the Tide	2014
Branch, John	Boys on Ice: The Life and Death of Derek Boogaard	2014
Codell, Esmé Raji	Educating Esmé: Diary of a Teacher's First Year	2009
Ehrenreich, Barbara	Nickel and Dimed: On (Not) Getting By in America	2001
Eire, Carlos	Waiting for Snow in Havana: Confessions of a Cuban Boy	2003
Fink, Sheri	Five Days at Memorial	2013
Finkel, David	Thank You for Your Service	2013
Gopal, Anand	No Good Men Among the Living	2014
Gore, Al	An Inconvenient Truth	2006
Gordon, Kim	Girl in a Band	2015
Hawking, Stephen	A Briefer History of Time	2005
Hillenbrand, Lauren	Unbroken	2010
Keegan, Maria	The Opposite of Loneliness	2014
Keneally, Thomas	Schindler's List	1982
Krakauer, Jon	Into Thin Air	1997
Larson, Erik	Dead Wake	2015
McCall, Nathan	Makes Me Wanna Holler: A Young Black Man in America	1975
McCourt, Frank	Angela's Ashes	1996
Miller, Ethelbert	Fathering Words: The Making of an African American Writer	2000
Munroe, Randall	What If?	2014
Sides, Hampton	In the Kingdom of Ice	2014
Urrea, Luis Alberto	The Devil's Highway: A True Story	2004
Wiesel, Elie	Night	1972
Yiwu, Liao	For a Song and a Hundred Songs	2013

NOTES

NOTES

If You Want to Play Sports

Tips for the Student-Athlete

Do you feel that you have what it takes to play sports at the college level? Then you need to do some work "off the field" to get yourself noticed and recruited by college coaches. Here are some tips on what you need to do.

Talk with your coach

First, have an honest talk about your athletic ability. Your coach can give you a realistic appraisal of your chances, and make some suggestions about which college athletic programs you can aspire to.

Find out about academic eligibility rules

These rules are set down by the various athletic associations. In order to be considered by an NCAA Division I school, for example, you must achieve a minimum GPA in 16 core courses in high school, and achieve a minimum combined score on either the SAT or ACT. Ask your school counselor about the specific requirements, and make sure you are on track to meet them before you graduate.

Attend a sports camp

Gain an edge over the summer vacation.

Start a sports résumé

And keep it updated. The purpose of the résumé is to give coaches a quick idea of who you are, what you've done, what your athletic potential may be, and whether you are academically eligible to be recruited.

Send letters of interest to coaches

Send them to the coach at each college you are interested in. (See "Sample Student-Athlete Letter of Interest" on page 47.) Get the name of the coach from the college's website. Try to send the letters as early in your junior year as possible. If the college has a prospect questionnaire on its website, complete that too.

Register with the NCAA eligibility center

Register at the end of your junior year. You won't be eligible to play NCAA Division I or II sports or receive an athletic scholarship otherwise. It's easy and you can do it online. Read the current NCAA *Guide for the College-Bound Student-Athlete* available at ncaapublications.com.

Make a performance or skills video

Ask your coach for advice on how to do this before the season starts. Editing is key: It has to be short (no longer than 5 minutes) or college coaches won't watch it.

Follow up

If you receive profile forms or questionnaires from coaches, complete and return them as soon as possible. Follow up with a telephone call from you, not your parents.

As you look at colleges, see the big picture

Don't focus on their sports programs only. It's really important that the college you end up at is a good fit for you both academically and personally, so that you will be happy there even if you don't end up playing a sport. It's also important to have realistic expectations about athletic scholarships—they are hard to come by and easy to lose, so look at the financial aid opportunities at each college as well.

What to Include in a Sports Résumé

As you can see from the sample résumé on the next page, your sports résumé should include your grade point average, SAT or ACT scores, the sports you play, awards and honors received, personal statistics, and references. (Make sure you include your high school coach.)

If you can, include your time for sprints and longer distances. No matter what sport you play, how fast you can move (and for how long) is important info.

It also helps if you can give information that would shed light on the caliber of your competition, such as a ranking, or whether you competed in county or state finals.

Statistics to include in a résumé, listed by sport

BASEBALL AND SOFTBALL
Batting average
Fielding percentage
Earned run average, or ERA
    (pitchers)
Win–loss record (pitchers)
Runs batted in (RBI)
Stolen bases

BASKETBALL
Assists (per game)
Rebounds
Free-throw percentage
Field-goal percentage (2 point and
    3 point)
Blocked shots

CROSS-COUNTRY, TRACK AND FIELD
Distance in field events: shot put,
    discus, long jump, triple jump
Height in field events: high jump
    and pole vault
Time and distance
Conference, invitational, or state
    places

FIELD HOCKEY
Goals
Assists
Blocked shots

FOOTBALL
Tackles (defensive player)
Assists (defensive player)
Sacks (defensive player)
Interceptions (defensive/back/
    linebacker)
Fumbles recovered
Yards rushing (running back)
Receptions—yards, average,
    touchdowns
Attempts, completions, total yards
    passing/rushing (quarterback)
Punts—attempts, longest, average
Kickoff returns—attempts, longest,
    average
Points scored—touchdowns, extra
    points
Field goals—attempts, longest,
    average, total points scored

GOLF
Scores
Handicap

GYMNASTICS
Events and scores
Conference, invitational, or state
    places

SOCCER
Goals
Assists and blocked shots

SWIMMING
Event and times
Dives, difficulty, scores
Major conference, invitational, or
    state places

TENNIS
Record and ranking
Major conference, invitational, or
    state ranking

VOLLEYBALL
Blocks
Assists
Kills
Aces

WRESTLING
Individual record and at what weight
Season takedowns
Season reversals
Season escapes
Season 2-point and 3-point near fall
    points
Falls
Conference, invitational, or state
    places

Sample
Student-Athlete Résumé

John J. Anybody
123 Any Street
Anytown, TX 75075
555 234-5678
soccerplayer@fastmail.com

Academics: Anytown Senior High School   SAT Scores: Evidence-Based
2000 Crosstown Parkway   Reading and Writing
Anytown, TX 75075   510, Math 540
555-234-1000   GPA: 3.2 (4.0 scale)

Expected graduation: June 2017
Expected college major: Business

Personal Statistics: Date of Birth: May 20, 1999   40-yard time: 4.95 secs.
Height: 5′11″   100-yard time: 10.9 secs.
Weight: 165 lbs.   Mile time: 5.12 mins.

My Sport: Soccer

Athletic History:

- Soccer, freshman: left wing, junior varsity; 11 goals, 21 assists. Team finished second in league, 12–4.
- Soccer, sophomore: right wing, varsity; 9 goals, 24 assists. Team finished first in league; named Honorable Mention All-County.
- Soccer, junior: right wing, varsity; 23 goals, 19 assists. Team reached state quarter finals; named to third team All-State. Elected team captain for senior year.
- Track, sophomore: quarter mile, best time, 52.8.

References: John Pele, Varsity Soccer Coach, Anytown Senior High School
Arnold Johnson, Director, All-American Soccer Camp

Sample Student-Athlete Letter of Interest

You can send the same letter to the coaches at all the colleges you are interested in. Just be sure to double-check that the correct names of the colleges and coaches match up. Use snail-mail, not e-mail. Make a copy for your high school coach.

If the college has a prospect/recruit questionnaire on its website, fill that in too.

Your Name
Street Address
City, State, Zip

Oct _ _, 20_ _
Name of coach [*get from your high school coach or the college's Web site*]
College/University
Address
City, State, Zip

Dear [*name of coach*],

I am a [*sophomore*] [*junior*] at [*your high school*] in [*city/town, state*]. I am very interested in attending [*name of college*] and being a member of your [*soccer, etc.*] team.

Here is where I stand academically at this point:

Here is a brief rundown of what I've accomplished athletically:

My goal is [*briefly state how you can contribute to the team (be realistic)*].

If you would like to contact my coach, [*give high school coach's name and telephone number*].

Please find enclosed a recommendation from my coach, my athletic résumé, and upcoming competition schedule.

I can also provide a skills video at your request.

I would appreciate your sending me a college catalog and any information about the team you think I should have. I would also be greatly interested to know if there is any possibility of an athletic scholarship.

Thank you for considering this letter, and I look forward to hearing from you.

Sincerely,

INCLUDE
Include your GPA; class rank, if available; any test scores you've received (PSAT/NMSQT, ACT, SAT, SAT Subject Tests, or AP); and expected date of graduation.

INCLUDE
Include name of current team, and events, times, positions, key stats, etc., appropriate for your sport. Review these with your high school coach. Include in this letter even if repeated in an attached sports résumé—it might get detached or lost.

IN ADDITION
Additional things to mention: birth date, height, weight (optional—depends on the sport); if a relative is an alumni of this college; and other sports you currently compete in and the level you're at.

NOTES

NOTES

Finding Colleges You Like

Quick Start
College Search Tips

Feeling overwhelmed by the whole idea of finding the perfect college out of the thousands of colleges in the United States? Don't be. Once you realize that there is no such thing as one perfect college for you, but rather a slew of colleges that would be a pretty good fit, you can begin to relax—and begin the search.

Here are some quick and easy things you can do today to start the process.

Decide on how near or far to look

Setting geographic parameters is the easiest way to cut your search down to size. Talk to your parents about the pros and cons of commuting from home or living away. Think about how often you would like to come home, what kind of environment you would like to live in, and what the realistic possibilities are.

Read what colleges send you

At this point, you're probably receiving tons of information about colleges by way of brochures, posts, and e-mails. Looking through this material will help you begin to learn about specific colleges—and it may also show you options you didn't know you had.

Talk to family and friends

Get the perspective of people who have already gone to college or are in college now. Their personal experiences can give you insight into what college is all about. Ask relatives about their alma mater or talk to older siblings and friends home for the holidays.

Write down what you want or need

Coed or single-sex? Public or private? Making a list of criteria will help you determine what's most important. (See the "What You Want Checklist" on page 78.) Use this list to make search queries in collegeboard.org's College Search so you can find schools that match. (But remember, too many queries in one search will usually result in no match found.) College guides like the College Board's *College Handbook* are good for browsing the college landscape to see what features are available and should be on your list.

Make a college wish list

List any college that looks good to you. At this point, don't limit yourself. Just brainstorm. Keep an open mind and try to look a little beyond your parameters as well—you might stumble across a college you never thought of that has something really exciting to offer. And it just might be the college nearby.

Do a deeper dive

Check out the college's website to take a virtual tour, see the courses offered, and contact students and the admission office. Visit the college's Facebook page and follow it on Twitter (see "10 Tips for Using Social Media" on page 54).

Visit a nearby campus

Go to a college that's close to home or one that a friend or family member already attends. It doesn't even have to be one that you're interested in attending. Visiting will help you focus your preferences and may even make you think of needs you didn't know you had. Can't get to a campus? Take a virtual tour on the school's website.

Go to a college fair

Ask your school counselor if there's a college fair coming to your school or a nearby school. Once there, you can pick up catalogs, talk to representatives and other students, and feel like you're officially starting the search process. (See the "College Fair Tip Sheet" on page 71.)

Meet with your counselor

He or she is drawing on years of experience matching students to colleges that could be a good fit.

Don't get hung up on one school

If you think you must attend a "name-brand" college, or that there is only one perfect college out there for you, you might set yourself up for disappointment. Truth is, there are many colleges where you can be happy and get a great education. Aim for a list of several "first-choice" colleges.

TIPS

10 Tips for Surfing College Websites

Not all college websites are created equal. Some are better designed than others; some are easier to navigate; and some are better at keeping information current. Use the site map if you have trouble finding any of the information described below.

1. Look for social media links

Most college websites link to social media on the campus network or on sites like Facebook and YouTube. Some college websites also provide mashups of all their updates on those sites. This provides a great way for you to connect with students at the school, other students applying to the school, or just to see what the school is like through its online community.

You should never feel pressured to "friend" anyone in these communities—just take it as an open invitation to ask questions from either students or staff and as a way to find others with the same interests and questions about the school as you.

2. Lurk in the halls of student government

These legislative bodies can be key players on campus, controlling multimillion-dollar budgets that support a wide range of student services. Online, you can get an idea of just how seriously they take their responsibilities. You may even be able to read the minutes of a recent meeting.

3. Go clubbing

Are you an activist? A bird-watcher? A demon at the chessboard? A future marketing exec? A tree-hugger? Often funded by student government, clubs come in all shapes and sizes. Look for links like Student Life to find out if there are campus clubs you'd want to join.

4. Patronize the arts

The campus is often home to cultural events that draw locals, as well as students. Click on Events, Museums, Arts, or a similar link to learn about the school's film screenings, plays, lectures, art shows, poetry readings, concerts, and other cultural events.

5. Enlist academic support

You'll find that colleges take great pains to keep you on campus once you get there. They offer a wide range of support services, which can include everything from drop-in writing assistance and peer tutoring in statistics to time management minicourses. You should find a description of these services in a section called Student Services or simply Students, but you might have to refer to the site map.

6. Check out the library

If the school offers online library resources, you'll probably find a Libraries link on the home page. Click to learn how large the book collection is, and try out their online catalog. You can also learn how the library teaches new students about its services.

7. Grab a tray

While some campuses offer only school-run cafeterias, others rent space to private businesses selling everything from pizza to garden burgers. Look for a link to Dining Services and get a taste of what's available. You might even find this week's menu online.

8. Check into housing

You might be surprised at the many varieties of on-campus housing. Although your choices as a freshman might be more limited, you'll find frat and sorority houses; substance-free floors; dorm rooms that are more like apartments (with kitchens and bathrooms); and even lower-cost co-ops where students work together to prepare meals and perform other housework.

To find out what will be available to you during your first year, your best bet is to look for a Housing link under tabs for Admissions or Prospective Students. But to learn about the more distant future, try looking under Student Services or Current Students.

9. Check up on student health services

You'll be charged a student health fee when you register for classes, so why not find out what you're paying for? Look for a link on the home page that will take you to the student health services section. You'll learn which medical and counseling services are included and which are not.

10. Log on to computing services

Do the dorm rooms have Wi-Fi? Can you buy a discounted laptop through the college? What technology support services does the college offer? Will you be able to register for classes online, or will you have to stand in line? Do professors use the Internet to enhance class? For answers, look for an Information Technology link on the home page.

11. (So who's counting?) Root for the home team

Care for a set of tennis? A yoga class? Or maybe you're more at home cheering in the stands. Click on Athletics to look into intramural and recreational sports (in which any student can take part), fitness equipment and classes, and varsity season calendars.

10 Tips for Using Social Media

Just about every college can be found on social networking sites like Facebook, YouTube, or Twitter. Some colleges are even abandoning college fairs and relying solely on social media to reach students. Here are some tips to help you make the best use of it all.

1. Join college communities

Colleges provide social networking sites to connect current students, professors, admission officers, and other prospective applicants like yourself. Joining these communities allows you to ask questions, learn about specific programs or majors, hear and see what's going on around campus, and get a sense of what it would be like to go there.

2. Go to the videotape

Student-made videos are a great way to get a sense of what a campus really looks and sounds like. YouTube's Education section has a fairly comprehensive list of colleges covered by such videos—and provides a very useful alternative when an actual visit is just not possible.

3. Follow the tweets

You can learn a lot from following a college on Twitter. Some colleges send tweet reminders, like when the acceptance deadline is due. But don't rely on tweeting to communicate with a college or to make an impression. For one thing, a college's tweets are usually generated by low-level staff, not decision-makers.

4. Don't friend college officials

Students use social media to communicate and connect with everyone, including colleges. But what are the rules? It's definitely not the same as connecting with friends and family. Few college officials would want to "friend" you, but in any event it's just not a good idea. Even if you are confident there is nothing embarrassing on your profile, you can't be sure how

it might be interpreted by someone in that capacity.

5. Be careful about what you are posting

You've probably heard that some colleges monitor social media to check up on applicants and may even base a rejection on what they found on an applicant's social media profile or posting. (Employers do this too.) Don't let that scare you off Facebook, but it's a good idea to look at your page through the eyes of an admission officer. Sometimes images you think are innocent can be misinterpreted.

6. Don't put too much faith in matchmakers

Some sites, like Cappex or Chegg, for example, are "matchmakers." You create a profile on the site, and a program matches you to colleges that "fit" based on what the colleges tell the site they are looking for. This approach can lead to good colleges to explore, but don't rely on it to do your search for you or to build your final list of colleges. It just isn't that easy.

7. Don't take a chance on "chance me"

Beware of "chance me" sites where a "jury" of other students judge your chances of getting into a college. What you are really chancing is being discouraged by people who don't know what they are talking about. Leave your admission chances to the experts.

8. Learn what real students think, but remember they don't know it all

There are several popular social media sites like Niche or Unigo that provide student reviews and ratings of colleges. Sites like these can often give the unvarnished truth about the social scene or what the food is like.

But don't rely solely on student reviews or the opinions of your friends. It's not likely they can truly know what is best for you or steer you to all the best colleges, so keep your school counselor in the mix.

9. Save time with mashups and RSS feeds

It can take too long to do all this online research one school at a time. Social media mashup sites help by bringing together all the reviews, blogs, videos, and real-time tweets about a college into one place.

RSS feeds also help you to keep up; when you find a site you like, subscribe to the site's RSS feed, and you will be constantly notified of updates. This works especially well with blogs.

10. Keep coming back

Consistently following colleges online is a good way to see what they are like and if you can see yourself fitting in there. Over time, you gain insight into what is important to those colleges and if you are a good match.

Many students find that sites like Facebook work best after they have their short list of colleges and want to get more personalized information to help make final choices. After you've been accepted, social media are even more useful as a way to find classmates and begin to feel part of the school before showing up for orientation.

TIPS

Basic Choices to Make

If you're just starting to think about what kind of college to look for, and are fairly open to all the possibilities, you might find it difficult to focus on what matters most. Choosing a college is a process that takes time. It involves making several choices, not just one; and the best way to begin is to think about the really basic, fundamental choices first.

Below are brief outlines of the "big picture" elements you should consider.

Commute from home or live away

Either way, you can have a great college experience; but it will be a much different experience. Don't decide this on your own—talk to your family, friends, and anyone else you trust to give you both sides.

Location, location, location

This choice is usually among the first to make and most decisive. Do you want to be able to go home whenever you want, or would you rather experience a different part of the country? Are you excited by what a big city can offer, or do you need easy access to the outdoors or the serenity of a small town? Do you hate cold weather, enjoy the different seasons, need to be near a beach?

None of this has much to do with college itself, but a lot to do with how much you will enjoy it.

Four-year versus two-year

This choice probably depends on three things: what type of degree you are going for, how much you are willing or able to spend, and if you want to commute from home. Your local community college offers low-cost options for either vocational/technical training or the first two years of a four-year program. (For more info, see the "Community College Fact Sheet" on page 62.) "Junior" colleges are private two-year schools, and usually more expensive.

When applying to a university, applicants typically have to choose a specific college or school division that they want to apply to. Each college may have its own admission requirements, and some may be more competitive than others.

Large, medium, or small?

This is more than the "big fish, little pond" question. Size can affect your options and experiences, such as the range of majors offered, the variety of student activities available, the amount of personal attention you'll receive, and the availability and size of facilities such as laboratories, libraries, and art studios. But remember, large universities are often broken up into small colleges or schools, so you can have it both ways…sort of.

College type

Choosing among these usually depends upon your career goals, and what type of college experience you want:

Liberal arts colleges emphasize the humanities, social sciences, and natural sciences, and the development of general knowledge and reasoning ability rather than specific career skills. Most are private, classes tend to be small, and you are likely to get more personal attention than in a large university. Examples: Amherst; Oberlin.

Universities are generally larger than colleges and offer more majors and research facilities. Most universities are subdivided into colleges or schools, such as a college of arts and sciences, a school of engineering, a business school, or a teacher's college; plus several graduate schools. These subdivisions may all be on the same campus, or spread out over several different campuses. Examples: Rutgers, UCLA.

Agricultural, technical, and career colleges offer training for specific occupations or industries. Examples include art schools and music conservatories, business colleges, schools of health science, and maritime colleges. Examples: Pratt, Kettering.

Religiously affiliated colleges are private colleges that are associated with a particular religious faith. The connection may range from being historic only, to being closely integrated into day-to-day student life. Examples: Boston College, Dallas Baptist U.

Historically black colleges originated in the time when African American students were denied access to most other colleges and universities. Their mission remains focused on the education of African Americans. Example: Spelman.

Hispanic-serving colleges are designated as such because Hispanic students comprise at least 25 percent of their full-time undergraduates. Example: Texas State University.

Majors and academic programs

If you have a clear idea of what you want to study, that obviously narrows your college choices to those that offer majors in that field. But if you're undecided (like most students), look for colleges that offer a broad range of majors and programs. That way you can reduce the chance that you'll have to transfer once you've made up your mind.

You might also want to consider a special study option that can enrich your experience, such as study abroad, cooperative education (where you work in the field as you learn), or an honors program. If experiences like these are important to you, make them part of your college search criteria.

Cost

Of course, cost is an important consideration for most students. But don't let "sticker shock" scare you away from colleges that might be a good fit. Financial aid often makes up the difference between what you can afford to pay and what a college costs. There are several calculators on collegeboard.org that will help you estimate the bottom line.

Accreditation: Must Knows

What is accreditation?

Think of it as a "seal of approval" that lets you know that a college meets quality standards established by an accrediting agency. The standards for each agency are slightly different but, in general, they set criteria for evaluating a college's administrative procedures, financial condition, physical facilities, and academic programs.

Types of accrediting agencies

Regional and national agencies examine the overall quality of the entire college as a whole. Specialized agencies accredit specific programs of study offered within a college, such as nursing, engineering, or teacher education. For example, ABET, Inc. (www.abet.org) accredits programs in applied science, computing, engineering, and technology, while AACSB International (www.aacsb.edu) accredits business and accounting programs.

You can find more information about accrediting agencies at the Council for Higher Education Accreditation's website (www.chea.org).

What does accreditation mean to me?

If you attend an accredited college, you can be sure that:

- Employers and professional licensing boards will recognize the degree you earn as an academic credential, as will graduate schools and other academic institutions you may apply to.

- You will be eligible for federal student aid to help pay for your costs, if you qualify based on financial need.

- Your tuition will qualify for federal income tax deductions and/or credits (if you meet other conditions).

- Academic credits you earn there are eligible to transfer to another accredited college.

- The college is financially sound and will likely still be in business when it's time to grant you a degree.

> Only colleges that are accredited by an agency recognized by the U.S. Department of Education may distribute federal financial aid to their students.

But there are some things accreditation doesn't mean:

- There's no guarantee that you will receive financial aid just because your college is accredited.

- Regional and national accreditation ensures that every academic program at the college meets standards, but that doesn't mean that the qualities of every program at the college are equal.

- If you want to transfer to another college, there's no guarantee that all your credits will count toward the graduation requirements of that college. If you plan to go to a community college for your first two years and then transfer to a four-year college, be sure to talk to a transfer counselor before enrolling in courses.

- Similarly, there's no guarantee that graduate schools or employers will see your undergraduate course of study as appropriate preparation for the demands of their particular program or job requirements.

Bottom line

One of the first things you should verify when you look at a college is its accreditation—especially if it has only been operating a few years. If you can't be completely confident that the degree you earn will be accepted as a bona fide credential (or that the college will still be in business when you graduate), look elsewhere.

> Every college contained in collegeboard.org's College Search and the College Board's *College Handbook* has been accredited by either a national or regional accrediting agency recognized by the U.S. Department of Education.

Community College Fact Sheet

Community colleges are everywhere

Community colleges are the most geographically accessible institutions in the United States. Every state has at least one community college, and most have multiple colleges, with branch campuses and learning centers dotted throughout the state.

Community colleges are your least expensive option

While tuition and fees to attend a community college vary greatly from state to state, they are much lower than those charged by four-year colleges and universities. On average, the annual tuition and fees for a community college are about half of what public four-year colleges charge, and only about 12 percent of what you would pay at a typical private four-year college.

Almost half of all college students attend a community college

Collectively, community colleges in the United States enroll about 7.7 million students, comprising 45 percent of all students in higher education.

Community college students are more likely to work while attending college

Among all students attending a community college, more than two-thirds of them work; about equally divided between full-time and part-time employment.

Community colleges offer two kinds of learning

If your goal is a four-year degree, you can earn a two-year associate degree at a low-cost community college, then transfer to a four-year college as a junior.

> If English is your second language, community colleges have special programs that will help you build your English skills.

If your goal is career training, you can earn an occupational degree or certificate in two years or less, then start working immediately in many high-demand fields (like health care or computer technology).

Community colleges can help you meet a range of academic goals

If you're achievement-oriented, community colleges offer challenging honors courses. You may be able to transfer directly into the honors program at a university, or at least make yourself a better candidate for it. Honors programs not only stimulate you but also offer mentoring and networking opportunities.

Researchers from the University of Illinois at Chicago and Penn State compared college grads from similar backgrounds who began college in two-year and in four-year institutions. On average, the two groups ended up with similar salaries, in careers that offered similar job prestige, stability, and satisfaction.

If you need more academic preparation, community college can offer a leg-up to achieving your goals. New students usually take placement tests in reading, writing, and math. Those who need to build skills can take catch-up courses, then—over time—move into a regular academic program.

If your high school grades aren't the greatest, but a four-year college is your goal, taking community college courses—and building a record of good grades—can polish your academic record. Then you can transfer. (But don't expect it to be easy—community college courses are no different from four-year college courses.)

Community colleges allow you to learn on your schedule

Because many community college students have jobs and family responsibilities, community colleges tend to offer courses days, nights, and weekends. Some also offer courses online (distance learning); combine Internet and classroom learning; give interactive TV courses; condense semester courses into a shorter time frame; and more.

Seeking training for an occupation?

A community college may be the best route to many high-demand jobs that require two-year degrees or certificates not available at four-year colleges. Look for courses in computer technology, health care, paralegal studies, law enforcement, and biotechnology. With homeland security a constant concern, community colleges are training many first responders.

Your College Major

Some students start college knowing exactly what they'd like to major in, but most do not. And almost half of all college students switch their majors at least once.

At this stage it's OK to be undecided. But you should think about your career goals and academic interests, at least in general terms, as you look at colleges and the majors they offer, so you can preserve your options.

Just what is a college major anyway?

Colleges (with few exceptions) require you to focus the bulk of your courses on a specific academic subject or field of study, in order to demonstrate sustained, high-level work in one field. That's your major.

You have plenty of time to decide

At most colleges, you aren't required to declare a major until the end of your sophomore year. If you're in a two-year degree program, you'll probably select a major at the start because your course of studies is much shorter.

How to choose

First, think about yourself. Think about what has interested you most, what you are good at, and how you like to spend your time. You will be most likely to enjoy and succeed at a course of study that incorporates some of these things. If you have definite career goals, find out which majors will lead you there. (See "Matching Careers to Degrees" on the next page.)

In your first year or two of college, you'll probably be required to take several introductory-level courses across a range of subjects. You will also be able to take a few elective courses that interest you. Use this period to explore your options with an open mind—you might be surprised to learn that you are fascinated by a subject you hadn't considered before.

As you consider majors, look outside the academic world as well. Get a realistic perspective of how graduates in these fields fare in the job market.

> If you're still undecided about your college major, relax—just pick an academically balanced institution that offers a range of majors and programs, and take courses in subjects you find intriguing. Most colleges offer advising or mentoring to help you find a focus.

Seek advice

Remember, you're not alone. Choosing a major is usually done with the help of academic and peer advisers.

Matching Careers to Degrees

One of the best things about getting a college education is that you have more careers to choose from. Below you'll find some sample careers and the types of degrees they usually require.

TWO-YEAR ASSOCIATE DEGREE

Aircraft and avionics technician
Computer support specialists
Computer programmer
Crime scene investigator
Database administrator
Dental hygienist
Drafting technologist
Electrician
EMT Paramedic
Engineering technician
Game designer
Lab technician
Licensed practical nurse (LPN)
Optician
Paralegal
Preschool teacher
Physical therapy assistant
Radiologist (X-ray technician)
Restaurant manager
Veterinary technician

FOUR-YEAR BACHELOR'S DEGREE

Accountant
Advanced nurse practitioner
Airline pilot
Animator
Civil engineer
Clinical laboratory technologist
Computer engineer
Computer systems analyst
Construction manager
Dietician
Financial advisor
Forester
Graphic designer
Hotel manager
Journalist
Landscape architect
Park ranger
Physician assistant
Registered nurse (RN)
Social worker
Software developer
Teacher
Webmaster
Wildlife manager

GRADUATE DEGREE

Archaeologist
Architect
Astronomer
College professor
Dentist
Doctor
Economist
Forensic scientist
Genetic engineer
Lawyer
Librarian
Microbiologist
Museum curator
Pharmacist
Physical therapist
Psychologist
Research scientist
Statistician
Veterinarian

Step-by-Step Career Worksheet

You don't have to have your whole life figured out before you can search for colleges. But it does help to have some basic idea of what career paths might interest you as you consider the courses and majors that colleges offer. This worksheet will help you focus your thinking.

STEP 1: THINK ABOUT WHAT INTERESTS YOU

Start with a real basic inventory of what you are curious about (nature, different countries, machinery?), how you like to spend your time (alone, with people, outdoors, reading?), and what makes you happy (working with your hands, helping others, cooking?). It also helps to remember what you don't like—that tells you a lot about yourself too.

WHAT I'M CURIOUS ABOUT:

_____

HOW I LIKE TO SPEND MY TIME:

_____

MY LIKES AND DISLIKES:

_____

STEP 2: TRANSLATE THE ABOVE INTO JOB IDEAS

Take a general area of interest, such as working with kids, then come up with jobs that fall into that category. Make a question-and-answer game of it. ("How many jobs involve animals?") Need help? Think about people you've read about or met who have interesting jobs, or use the career quizzes that are available in your counselor's office or online.

INTEREST	JOB IDEAS
INTEREST	JOB IDEAS
INTEREST	JOB IDEAS

STEP 3: CONSIDER HOW TO GET THERE

Now think about what kinds of classes or special degrees you might need to get the jobs that sound good to you. You might find you don't like any of the classes you'd need to take, for example, which would certainly tell you something. To get information about education requirements for different jobs, go to "Majors and Careers" on collegeboard.org, or look them up in the College Board's *Book of Majors*.

JOB IDEA	JOB REQUIREMENTS
JOB IDEA	JOB REQUIREMENTS
JOB IDEA	JOB REQUIREMENTS

STEP 4: GIVE IT A WHIRL

Once you focus on possible jobs, try to really dive into them:

• Volunteer somewhere that's in a similar field.

• Look into a paid or unpaid internship.

• Shadow someone to see a day-in-the-life.

• Research, by visiting your library or useful website.

Even if you decide not to pursue a related career, you'll have gained valuable experience and given your college application a boost.

THINGS I COULD DO RIGHT NOW

Four "Top 10" Career Charts

Wondering where the jobs will be in the future? Government economists have estimated which occupations and industries will grow the fastest, and which occupations will have the most new jobs.

As you think about majors, check out the following "Top 10" lists to see what's hot.

Top 10 industries with the fastest employment growth

INDUSTRY	PERCENT INCREASE 2012–2022
Health care	28%
Computer systems and software	27%
Management, business, and professional services	26%
Construction	22%
Employment services	20%
Education	19%
Financial services	19%
Leisure and hospitality	9%
Insurance	7%
Retail and wholesale trade	7%

Top 10 fastest-growing occupations for college grads

OCCUPATION	PERCENT INCREASE 2012–2022
Interpreters and translators	46%
Event planners	33%
Market research analysts	32%
Cartographers and geographers	29%
Biomedical engineers	27%
Personal financial advisors	27%
Computer and information analysts	26%
Insurance adjusters and actuaries	26%
Petroleum engineers	25%
Civil engineers	20%

Top 10 occupations with the most job openings for four-year college grads

OCCUPATION	TOTAL JOB OPENINGS 2012–2022
Registered nurses	1,053,000
Elementary and middle-school teachers	684,000
Business and operations managers	613,000
Engineers	544,000
Accountants and auditors	544,000
Software developers	404,000
High school teachers	340,000
Computer and information analysts	249,000
Social workers	243,000
Market research analysts	189,000

Top 10 occupations with the most job openings for two-year college grads

OCCUPATION	TOTAL JOB OPENINGS 2012 -2022
Medical and health technologists	1,161,000
Pre-school teachers	200,000
Licensed practical nurses	183,000
Dental hygienists	114,000
Occupational and physical therapy assistants	102,000
Engineering technologists	100,000
Paralegals	92,000
Web developers	51,000
Drafters and surveyors	49,000
Computer network support specialists	40,000

Source: United States Bureau of Labor Statistics

ROTC FAQs

Are you attracted to the idea of military service? Are you also looking for ways to finance college on your own? The answers below will explain how to achieve both.

What is ROTC?

The Reserve Officers' Training Corps (ROTC) prepares young men and women to become military officers while they attend college. There are both scholarship and nonscholarship programs available for each branch: Army, Navy, Air Force, and Marines. While you attend college, you'll take some military courses each year for credit, and attend training sessions. After you finish college, you must complete a period of service in the military.

Who is eligible for an ROTC scholarship?

The scholarships are based on merit, not need. To qualify for a ROTC scholarship, you must:

- Be a U.S. citizen
- Be between the ages of 17 and 26
- Have a high school GPA of at least 2.5
- Have a high school diploma
- Meet physical standards
- Agree to accept a commission and serve in the military on active duty or in the Reserves after graduating
- Achieve a qualifying score on either the SAT or ACT

How much money do ROTC scholarships offer?

Scholarship amounts vary by program, but can go up to full tuition and fees. Room and board are not covered. You also receive money each year for books and a monthly allowance.

How much time do I owe the military after I complete ROTC?

Most cadets incur a four-year, active-duty commitment, but it can be longer depending upon the military path you pursue. For example, pilots in the Air Force incur a 10-year active-duty service commitment.

What if I don't like ROTC?

You can quit the program after your first year without any obligations. After that you'll have to pay any scholarship money back.

What kinds of courses and training does ROTC offer?

It varies by branch, but generally you take one military science course per semester. In addition, you'll wear a uniform once a week during military labs, drills, and other practical training activities. Most programs also require participation in at least one summer program—such as midshipmen cruises in Naval ROTC—to round out your military training.

Will I have a choice of major?

Most ROTC students can choose any major they want. But sometimes a particular branch of the military may only offer scholarships in those majors that meet the needs of that branch.

Where is ROTC offered?

It varies college by college. You can find schools that have the ROTC program you want on collegeboard.org or in the College Board *College Handbook*.

College Fair Tip Sheet

College fairs may not have peanuts, popcorn, and pony rides, but they can be very informative and even fun. Fairs can help you rule out colleges, as well as introduce you to new ones.

You'll find noise and crowds at most fairs, whether it's in your high school gym or a large conference center—and it can be a little overwhelming. So, here's a plan for before, during, and after you go.

Before the Fair

Think about what you want

The whole point of a college fair is to ask questions. Make a list of college characteristics that are important to you. (See the "What You Want Checklist" on page 78.) Now you know what to ask about.

What to bring

You'll need a pen and small notebook, your questions, and a bag to hold all the college brochures and information you'll get.

During the Fair

Go early

That's the best way to avoid crowds. Plan to talk first to the colleges that interest you most; that way you won't miss out if they get jammed later. Local colleges and your state universities usually attract a lot of visitors, so hit them early if you want to check them out.

Don't just wander around

Navigating a large college fair can be challenging. Here are some ways to create some beelines to what you want to see:

- Review the list of colleges at the fair and identify the colleges that interest you.
- If the fair provides a map showing where college booths will be, plan out a route to avoid backtracking.
- If the fair has information sessions with experts (e.g., about financial aid), block out time for the ones you want to attend.

Fly solo

It might be more fun to go around with your friends, but you won't get much accomplished. Alone, the college rep will be able to focus on you one-on-one, and you'll be free to ask questions.

Take notes

After you visit a college's booth, take a few minutes to jot down what you've learned. Otherwise it will all become a blur, and you won't remember which college said what.

Be curious

Try to leave some time at the end just to browse through some of the booths you didn't get to—you could stumble on a great college you hadn't considered.

After the Fair

Don't forget about it

Don't lose the college materials in the back of your closet. Look through what you brought back, and your notes, within the week. But don't keep everything: Weed out colleges that aren't a good fit.

Follow up

Research colleges that interest you. Explore their websites, request more information from admission offices, and plan to visit.

20 Questions to Ask College Reps

Whether you meet them at a college fair or on a campus visit, college reps genuinely enjoy talking to high school students and answering questions about their college. While you shouldn't expect them to reveal any negative info, they can be a good source for what you need to know. The following questions will help start a good dialogue:

1. What makes your college unique?

2. What academic programs is your college most known for?

3. How would you describe the kids that go there? Where do most of them come from?

4. Where do kids hang out on campus?

5. What happens on weekends—are there things to do on campus or in town, or do most kids go home?

6. Are fraternities and sororities a big part of campus life?

7. What are the housing options for freshmen?

8. Do many students live off campus?

9. Is there a sports complex or fitness center?

10. What are the most popular clubs and activities?

11. What's the security like on campus?

12. What's the surrounding area like? Is it easy to get around?

13. What are the most popular majors?

14. How would you describe the academic pressure and workload?

15. What support services are available (academic advisers, tutors, etc.)?

16. Is the campus Wi-Fi?

17. What's the faculty like? How accessible are they outside of class?

18. Are there opportunities for internships?

19. Is there job placement help for graduates?

20. Are any big changes in the works that I should know about?

College Fair Journal

COLLEGE 1

Name

Location

Name of Rep

Did I fill out a card? ☐ Yes ☐ No

Still Interested? ☐ Yes ☐ No

Reasons Why

Reasons Why Not

What Impressed Me the Most

COLLEGE 2

Name

Location

Name of Rep

Did I fill out a card? ☐ Yes ☐ No

Still Interested? ☐ Yes ☐ No

Reasons Why

Reasons Why Not

What Impressed Me the Most

College Fair Journal

COLLEGE 3

Name

Location

Name of Rep

Did I fill out a card?   ☐ Yes   ☐ No

Still Interested?   ☐ Yes   ☐ No

Reasons Why

Reasons Why Not

What Impressed Me the Most

COLLEGE 4

Name

Location

Name of Rep

Did I fill out a card?   ☐ Yes   ☐ No

Still Interested?   ☐ Yes   ☐ No

Reasons Why

Reasons Why Not

What Impressed Me the Most

College Fair Journal

COLLEGE 5

Name

Location

Name of Rep

Did I fill out a card? ☐ Yes ☐ No

Still Interested? ☐ Yes ☐ No

Reasons Why

Reasons Why Not

What Impressed Me the Most

COLLEGE 6

Name

Location

Name of Rep

Did I fill out a card? ☐ Yes ☐ No

Still Interested? ☐ Yes ☐ No

Reasons Why

Reasons Why Not

What Impressed Me the Most

College Fair Journal

COLLEGE 7	COLLEGE 8

Name _____ Name _____

Location _____ Location _____

Name of Rep _____ Name of Rep _____

Did I fill out a card? ☐ Yes ☐ No Did I fill out a card? ☐ Yes ☐ No

Still Interested? ☐ Yes ☐ No Still Interested? ☐ Yes ☐ No

Reasons Why Reasons Why

_____ _____

_____ _____

_____ _____

_____ _____

_____ _____

Reasons Why Not Reasons Why Not

_____ _____

_____ _____

_____ _____

What Impressed Me the Most What Impressed Me the Most

_____ _____

_____ _____

_____ _____

_____ _____

College Fair Journal

COLLEGE 9	COLLEGE 10

COLLEGE 9

Name

Location

Name of Rep

Did I fill out a card? ☐ Yes ☐ No

Still Interested? ☐ Yes ☐ No

Reasons Why

Reasons Why Not

What Impressed Me the Most

COLLEGE 10

Name

Location

Name of Rep

Did I fill out a card? ☐ Yes ☐ No

Still Interested? ☐ Yes ☐ No

Reasons Why

Reasons Why Not

What Impressed Me the Most

What You Want Checklist

Use this checklist to create a picture of what your ideal college would look like. Rate each component so that you can weigh how close each college comes to your ideal. Then use the results to come up with your "short list" of colleges.

LOCATION	Must be	Like to be
Commuting distance	☐	☐
Not too far from home	☐	☐
Far from home	☐	☐
Specific state/city	☐	☐

ENVIRONMENT	Must be	Like to be
Big city	☐	☐
Small city	☐	☐
Suburbs	☐	☐
College town	☐	☐
Rural	☐	☐
Mountains	☐	☐
By the sea	☐	☐
Warm all year	☐	☐

TYPE OF COLLEGE	Must be	Like to be
Four-year	☐	☐
Two-year	☐	☐
Religiously affiliated	☐	☐
Single-sex	☐	☐
University	☐	☐
Liberal arts	☐	☐
Art/music school	☐	☐
Technical	☐	☐
Other: _____	☐	☐

SIZE OF COLLEGE	Must be	Like to be
Small	☐	☐
Medium	☐	☐
Large	☐	☐

CAMPUS	Must be	Like to be
Traditional	☐	☐
Modern	☐	☐
Parklike	☐	☐

ACADEMIC OFFERINGS	Must have	Like to have
Many majors	☐	☐
Specific majors:		
_____	☐	☐
_____	☐	☐
_____	☐	☐
Teacher certification	☐	☐
ROTC	☐	☐
Study abroad	☐	☐
Co-op program	☐	☐
Internships	☐	☐
Other: _____	☐	☐

FACILITIES	Must have	Like to have
Design/visual arts center	☐	☐
Music/performing arts center	☐	☐
Sports/fitness center	☐	☐
Science center	☐	☐
Tech center	☐	☐
Health center	☐	☐
TV/radio station	☐	☐
Other: _____	☐	☐

HOUSING	Must have	Like to have
On campus	☐	☐
Off campus	☐	☐
Quiet	☐	☐
Special interest/theme	☐	☐
Single-sex	☐	☐
Substance-free	☐	☐
Fraternity/sorority	☐	☐

ACTIVITIES	Must have	Like to have
Intramural/club sports	☐	☐
Specific sport(s):		
_____	☐	☐
_____	☐	☐
_____	☐	☐
Religious clubs	☐	☐
Minority/ethnic clubs	☐	☐
Theater	☐	☐
Band/orchestra	☐	☐
Dance	☐	☐
Newspaper/journal	☐	☐
Other: _____	☐	☐

SERVICES	Must have	Like to have
Job/internship placement	☐	☐
Career counseling	☐	☐
Health	☐	☐
ESL	☐	☐
Services for disabled/impaired	☐	☐

Your Short List of Colleges

OK—this is the result of all your research so far: the colleges you most likely will apply to. You should have 1 or 2 "reaches," 2 to 4 "probables," and 1 or 2 "safeties." Ideally, every college on this list will be a good fit.

	COLLEGE 1	COLLEGE 2	COLLEGE 3
NAME OF COLLEGE			
How hard is it to get in? (Reach/Probable/Safety)			
What I like most			
What I don't like			
Majors offered that I'm interested in			
What's unique (campus features, interesting facilities, or programs)			
Sports, clubs, or activities offered that I'm interested in			
Costs • Tuition & fees • Room & board • Travel			
Estimated Financial Aid • Scholarships/grants • Loans/work study			

COLLEGE 4	COLLEGE 5	COLLEGE 6	COLLEGE 7	COLLEGE 8

NOTES

Visiting
Colleges

When to Visit Colleges

Schoolwork, your job, your parents…it can be tough to find the right time to go on campus visits. But try not to lose sight of the reason you're going: to see if the school is a good fit for you. That means you want to go when the college is in session, so you can see the place in action.

During the week is best

Mondays through Thursdays are ideal since campuses are generally in full swing. If it's not possible to take time off from school or work, try to visit during holidays that fall on Mondays, when most colleges are in session.

Spring of junior year

Juniors who have researched colleges should consider using spring vacations for college visits. Spring is also a good time of year if you play fall sports or are considering Early Action or Early Decision with application deadlines in November of senior year.

> Summertime may not be the best time because campuses are usually deserted; but it might be the only time you can go. If that's the case, check to see if tours are available (they usually are) or if there is a summer session.

After you've been accepted

Many colleges invite their accepted candidates to spend a few days on campus before the May 1 reply date to encourage them to enroll. This is a good opportunity to nail down your final choice.

The best practice is to visit colleges before you apply, so that you're confident you'd be happy at any of the colleges on your list.

Times to avoid

Check specific dates with each college so you don't arrive at a bad time:

- When the admission office is closed to visitors
- Exam periods
- Graduation week
- Move-in day

Based on information found in *Campus Visits & College Interviews*, by Zola Dincin Schneider

Campus Visit Checklist

Here are things you shouldn't miss while visiting a college. Take a look at this list before you go to make sure that you allow enough time on each campus to get a sense of what the school is really like.

- ☐ Take a campus tour.
- ☐ Have an interview with an admission officer.
- ☐ Get business cards and names of people you meet for future contacts.
- ☐ Pick up financial aid forms.
- ☐ Participate in a group information session at the admission office.
- ☐ Sit in on a class of a subject that interests you.
- ☐ Talk to a professor in your chosen major or in a subject that interests you.
- ☐ Talk to coaches of sports in which you might participate.
- ☐ Talk to a student or counselor in the career center.
- ☐ Spend the night in a dorm.
- ☐ Read the student newspaper.
- ☐ Try to find other student publications—department newsletters, alternative newspapers, literary reviews.
- ☐ Scan bulletin boards to see what day-to-day student life is like.
- ☐ Eat in the cafeteria.
- ☐ Ask students how they like it here. (See "Questions to Ask During the Visit" on the next page.)
- ☐ Wander around the campus by yourself for a while.
- ☐ Browse in the college bookstore.
- ☐ Walk or drive around the community surrounding the campus.
- ☐ Listen to the college's radio station.
- ☐ Try to see a dorm that you didn't see on the tour.

Based on information found in *Campus Visits & College Interviews*, by Zola Dincin Schneider

Questions to Ask During the Visit

You won't find out much from just walking around looking at the buildings. Make the trip worthwhile by asking questions. These lists give you plenty to choose from:

Questions to ask students:

1. Has going here turned out like you expected? Any surprises or disappointments?

2. What are the best reasons to go here?

3. What do students complain about?

4. I have to choose a dorm. What can you tell me about the choices?

5. If you could do it over again, would you still choose to go here?

6. What kind of meal plan makes the most sense?

7. What is there to do off campus? Is it easy to get around?

8. What do most students do for fun on weekends?

9. How often do students go home on weekends?

10. Where do most students hang out on campus?

11. Can you study in the dorms? If not, where do you go to study?

12. Do you use the library often? Is it easy to find what you need there?

13. How's the bookstore? Can you find the books you need there? Is it easy to get used textbooks?

14. How is the campus network? Does it go down often?

15. I know it depends on your major, but in general, what's the workload like?

16. How are the professors? Are they hard to reach outside of class?

17. Is it easy to get the classes you want?

18. How would you rate the courses you've taken so far?

19. Would you characterize this college as mostly liberal, conservative, or open-minded?

20. Do you get much help finding internships or jobs?

21. Do most students join fraternities/sororities? Are you out of it if you aren't in one?

22. Is there much of a drug scene?

23. Do I have to worry about things getting stolen?

24. Is the campus safe at night?

25. How would you describe the relationship between students and the administration?

Questions to ask the tour guide:

1. How popular is the recreation/sports/fitness center? Is it crowded often?

2. Where do you do laundry? Is it convenient? Will I need to hoard quarters?

3. Is there any overcrowding in the dorms (three students in a double, for example)?

4. Do many resident students have cars? Is there enough parking?

5. I'm thinking of majoring in _____. What relevant facilities should I see?

6. Where can you get something to eat after the cafeteria is closed?

7. How large are most classes? Do many take place in auditoriums?

8. What are the most popular extracurricular activities?

9. Are there many intramural or club sports?

10. Are there enough computers, printers, and copying machines available? What about at night?

11. Does student government play much of a role on campus?

Questions to ask at the admission office:

1. When does registration take place for freshmen? What is the registration procedure?

2. Do freshmen have to take any placement exams?

3. What sort of job placement or career counseling is available before graduation?

4. How much should I expect tuition to increase over the next four years?

5. Who should I speak to about financial aid? (See "10 Questions for the Financial Aid Office" on page 172.)

6. Is there a course catalog I can take with me?

Based on information found in *Campus Visits & College Interviews*, by Zola Dincin Schneider

Sizing Up a Dorm Checklist

Before you decide on a college, try to learn the following from a campus visit, talking to students, or visits to the school's website.

Dorm facilities

❏ How are the rooms furnished? Do students have the option of changing the furniture—for example, constructing lofts for their beds?

❏ Are there kitchen facilities? Are students allowed to have appliances such as mini-refrigerators or microwave ovens in their rooms?

❏ Is there a laundry room in the dorm or close by?

❏ Is there a central lounge area? Does it have a TV, pool table, or anything else for fun?

❏ Are there computer labs in or near the dorms? Do the dorm rooms have Wi-Fi?

❏ What sort of telephone service is available in the dorms?

❏ Do the dorms get good cell phone reception?

❏ How well maintained are the halls and bathrooms?

Academic and social atmosphere

❏ Do the students seem friendly? Do they greet you as a visitor?

❏ Do students study together in the dorms?

❏ When students are in their rooms, do they leave their doors open, or do they close them?

❏ If the dorm has a lounge area, is it used much?

❏ How do students spend their weeknight evenings—do they hang out together in the dorms, or do they avoid the dorms at all costs?

Safety

❏ Are the pathways, bus stops, parking lots, and other public areas well lit at night?

❏ Are there emergency phones (connecting directly to the police) outside the dorms?

❏ Is theft a problem in the dorms?

❏ Are there security systems in place to prevent nonresidents from walking into a residence hall? Are ground-floor windows in the residence halls secured?

❏ Do campus security guards or local police patrol the campus?

Campus Visit Journal

COLLEGE

Date of visit

Location

Weather that day

	WHAT I LIKE	WHAT I DON'T LIKE
Campus		
Dorms		
Dining areas/food		
Activities available		
Course offerings		
Academic facilities		
Fitness/rec facilities		
Neighboring area		
Other		

PEOPLE I MET

Name   E-mail:

Name   E-mail:

Name   E-mail:

Name   E-mail:

What the students are like

What impressed me the most

SHOULD I GO HERE?

Campus Visit Journal

COLLEGE

Date of visit

Location

Weather that day

	WHAT I LIKE	WHAT I DON'T LIKE
Campus		
Dorms		
Dining areas/food		
Activities available		
Course offerings		
Academic facilities		
Fitness/rec facilities		
Neighboring area		
Other		

PEOPLE I MET

Name   E-mail:

Name   E-mail:

Name   E-mail:

Name   E-mail:

What the students are like

What impressed me the most

SHOULD I GO HERE?

Campus Visit Journal

COLLEGE

Date of visit

Location

Weather that day

	WHAT I LIKE	WHAT I DON'T LIKE
Campus		
Dorms		
Dining areas/food		
Activities available		
Course offerings		
Academic facilities		
Fitness/rec facilities		
Neighboring area		
Other		

PEOPLE I MET

Name   E-mail:

Name   E-mail:

Name   E-mail:

Name   E-mail:

What the students are like

What impressed me the most

SHOULD I GO HERE?

Campus Visit Journal

COLLEGE

Date of visit

Location

Weather that day

	WHAT I LIKE	WHAT I DON'T LIKE
Campus		
Dorms		
Dining areas/food		
Activities available		
Course offerings		
Academic facilities		
Fitness/rec facilities		
Neighboring area		
Other		

PEOPLE I MET

Name   E-mail:

Name   E-mail:

Name   E-mail:

Name   E-mail:

What the students are like

What impressed me the most

SHOULD I GO HERE?

Campus Visit Journal

COLLEGE

Date of visit

Location

Weather that day

	WHAT I LIKE	WHAT I DON'T LIKE
Campus		
Dorms		
Dining areas/food		
Activities available		
Course offerings		
Academic facilities		
Fitness/rec facilities		
Neighboring area		
Other		

PEOPLE I MET

Name _____ E-mail:

Name _____ E-mail:

Name _____ E-mail:

Name _____ E-mail:

What the students are like

What impressed me the most

SHOULD I GO HERE?

Campus Visit Journal

COLLEGE

Date of visit

Location

Weather that day

	WHAT I LIKE	WHAT I DON'T LIKE
Campus		
Dorms		
Dining areas/food		
Activities available		
Course offerings		
Academic facilities		
Fitness/rec facilities		
Neighboring area		
Other		

PEOPLE I MET

Name   E-mail:

Name   E-mail:

Name   E-mail:

Name   E-mail:

What the students are like

What impressed me the most

SHOULD I GO HERE?

Campus Visit Journal

COLLEGE

Date of visit

Location

Weather that day

	WHAT I LIKE	WHAT I DON'T LIKE
Campus		
Dorms		
Dining areas/food		
Activities available		
Course offerings		
Academic facilities		
Fitness/rec facilities		
Neighboring area		
Other		

PEOPLE I MET

Name   E-mail:

Name   E-mail:

Name   E-mail:

Name   E-mail:

What the students are like

What impressed me the most

SHOULD I GO HERE?

Campus Visit Journal

COLLEGE

Date of visit

Location

Weather that day

	WHAT I LIKE	WHAT I DON'T LIKE
Campus		
Dorms		
Dining areas/food		
Activities available		
Course offerings		
Academic facilities		
Fitness/rec facilities		
Neighboring area		
Other		

PEOPLE I MET

Name   E-mail:

Name   E-mail:

Name   E-mail:

Name   E-mail:

What the students are like

What impressed me the most

SHOULD I GO HERE?

Taking Tests

FAQs About the PSAT/NMSQT®

1. What does PSAT/NMSQT stand for?

Preliminary SAT/National Merit Scholarship Qualifying Test.

2. Why should I take the PSAT/NMSQT?

The PSAT/NMSQT is great practice for the SAT, and it might qualify you for a National Merit Scholarship. Most important, the PSAT/NMSQT gives valuable feedback to you and your school. A question-by-question review of answers enables you to see which answers you got right, with explanations for the answers available on collegeboard.org.

3. What should I do to prepare for this test?

The best preparation is to do a lot of reading and writing, practice your math skills, and to become familiar with the test so you know what to expect. An official PSAT/NMSQT practice test can be downloaded from collegeboard.org. The *Official Student Guide to the PSAT/NMSQT* contains plenty of useful information, including a full-length practice test.

You can also go to Khan Academy (satpractice.org) for free, interactive and personalized practice programs developed with actual test items from the College Board. Because of the close alignment of the tests, that will also help you prepare for the PSAT/NMSQT.

4. If I don't do well on this test, will that hurt my chances of getting into college?

Absolutely not. PSAT/NMSQT scores are not sent to colleges. If anything, taking the PSAT/NMSQT will improve your chances of going to college since the test provides information on skills that need improvement in preparation for the SAT and college.

5. How many times can I take this test?

Only once a year, but you can take it in multiple years if your school offers it to both sophomores and juniors. It is important to take the test in order to enter National Merit Scholarship Corporation competitions, as well as to prepare for the SAT. For younger students, the main benefit is to gain valuable feedback, get a head start on improving their academic skills, and plan for college.

6. When should I expect to see my scores?

Your school will receive your score report in December and will notify you regarding when, where, and how to get your report.

7. What is in the PSAT/NMSQT Score Report?

The score report not only includes your scores and itemized feedback on test questions, but also personalized skills feedback and guidance on which areas to focus. The score report also shows whether you meet entry requirements for National Merit Scholarship Corporation competitions. You will also receive access to a personalized online college and career exploration tool to chart your path to college and beyond.

FAQs About AP Exams

Can I take the AP Exam if I haven't taken the AP course?

Yes. The College Board is committed to providing access to AP Exams to all students, including those who are home schooled or attend schools that do not offer AP courses. If you are one of those students or studying independently, contact the school counselor or AP Coordinator at a school that offers AP Exams to see if you can take the exam there.

Why should I take an AP Exam if I'm not looking to earn college credit or placement?

AP Exams provide colleges and universities with additional information about your ability to succeed in college-level study. Many colleges use AP Exam scores to place students into honors classes. Additionally, some scholarship programs consider AP Exam scores.

I have a disability. Are testing accommodations available?

If you have a documented disability, you may be eligible for accommodations on AP Exams. To find out more, visit collegeboard.org/ssd or contact your school's AP Coordinator.

If I don't get a good score on an AP Exam, will it hurt my chances for college admission?

Not likely. For one thing, it's your choice whether to report an AP Exam score to a college. But before you make that choice, consider this: Overall, nearly 60 percent of all AP test-takers receive AP scores of at least 3, which is regarded as a good indicator of your ability to do well in college. And any AP score tells colleges that you chose to take a difficult course and exam, and that you are serious about your studies.

How much time does it take to complete an AP Exam?

Most of the exams take two to three hours to complete. For subjects that correspond to a half-year college course, the exam is closer to two hours in length.

How are multiple-choice questions scored? Should I guess?

Your score on the multiple-choice section is based on the number of questions you answer correctly. No points are deducted for incorrect answers or unanswered questions.

Random guessing is unlikely to raise or lower your score much, but an educated guess based on eliminating obviously wrong answer choices is usually to your advantage.

What should I bring to the exam?

- Several sharpened No. 2 pencils with erasers for all multiple-choice questions.
- Pens with black or dark blue ink for free-response questions in most exams.
- Your six-digit school code. Home-schooled students will be given a code at the time of the exam.
- A watch (but without a beeper or alarm).
- An approved calculator if you're taking the AP Biology, Calculus, Chemistry, Physics, or Statistics Exams. Visit collegeboard.org to find the calculator policy for your subject.
- A ruler or straightedge if you're taking an AP Physics Exam.
- A photo ID if you do not attend the school where you are taking the exam.
- If you are eligible for testing accommodations, your SSD Student Accommodation Letter.

FAQs
About the Redesigned SAT®

Why should I take the SAT?

Since course content and grading standards vary widely among high schools, it's difficult for colleges to compare the academic records of their applicants. The SAT gives colleges a more objective way to evaluate what students know and can do, and provides valuable information about college readiness. When used in combination with your high school record (GPA and course selection), your SAT scores will be an excellent predictor of your likelihood to succeed in college.

When should I take the SAT?

Most students take the SAT during their junior or senior year in high school. Often, a student takes the SAT as a junior during the spring and retests the next fall. However, there are no age or grade restrictions for taking the test.

How do I register for the SAT?

The best way to register is online. It's fast and easy, and it helps you avoid late fees or missed postmark deadlines. You can even register for next year's tests over the summer. SAT registration may be completed at sat.org.

What if I can't afford the fee?

Fee waivers are available to high school juniors and seniors who cannot afford the test fee. To learn more visit bigfuture.collegeboard.org; you can also apply for fee waivers through your school counselor.

How long is the SAT?

The total testing time for the SAT is 3 hours, plus 50 minutes for the optional essay. You'll have 65 minutes for the Reading Test, 35 minutes for the Writing and Language Test, and 80 minutes for the Math Test.

Can I bring something to eat or drink during the test?

Students are encouraged to bring snacks in a book bag on test day. These snacks should be easily stowed under desks or chairs in the test room and can only be consumed in designated areas during breaks.

What will I be asked to do on the SAT?

The redesigned SAT requires you to:

- Analyze, revise and edit texts
- Understand vocabulary in context
- Use evidence to support your answers
- Use math to solve problems in science, social studies, and career-related contexts
- Analyze data and interpret tables and graphs

Will I be tested in subjects like science and social studies?

You will not be asked any subject-specific questions, such as "what is the Magna Carta." But you will be asked to apply your reading, writing, English, and math skills to answer questions and solve problems grounded in science, history, and social studies contexts.

How is vocabulary tested?

Vocabulary is tested through questions about the meaning of words and phrases in the context of prose passages that demonstrate how word choice shapes meaning, tone, and impact. The meaning of these words and phrases is derived in large part through the context; they are familiar words, but their meaning can shift depending on how and where they're used.

What math will be tested?

The math section covers four content areas:

- Heart of Algebra, which focuses on the mastery of linear equations and systems.
- Problem Solving and Data Analysis, which involves using ratios, percentages, and proportional reasoning to solve problems in science, social science, and career contexts.
- Passport to Advanced Math, which requires the manipulation of complex equations such as quadratic or exponential functions.
- Additional Topics in Math, which covers geometric and trigonometric skills.

Can I use a calculator on the Math Test?

The SAT Math test has two sections: one that allows calculators, and one that doesn't. Calculators are important mathematical tools, but the no-calculator section makes it easier to assess students' understanding of math concepts.

Should I plan to take the optional essay?

Not all colleges require applicants to take the essay. Check with your target schools to see what they require or will review as part of their admissions decisions. If you haven't chosen your schools yet, taking the essay will keep your college options open.

Can I get more detailed information about my scores?

All students have access to a free, detailed online score report on collegeboard.org. There you will see the types of questions, level of difficulty, and how many in each group of questions you answered correctly, incorrectly, or omitted. Percentile information allows you to compare your scores with other groups of test-takers. If applicable, you can also access a copy of your essay.

What is Score Choice™?

If you take the SAT more than once, Score Choice allows you to choose which scores to send to your target colleges. All section scores from the selected test date will be reported, including the Essay score if you have one (you can't cherry-pick your best section scores from multiple test dates). Score Choice is optional; if you don't use it, all of your scores will be sent automatically. Since most colleges only consider your best scores, you should feel comfortable reporting scores from all of your test dates.

Is the test fair to all students?

Yes. The test is straightforward, with no tricks designed to trip you up. And, the College Board and Khan Academy have leveled the playing field by providing online SAT practice programs entirely free of charge, so every student, regardless of background, can have access to the best exam practice available.

Where can I learn more?

Go to collegereadiness.collegeboard.org for sample questions and more information about the test.

The SAT
at a Glance

EVIDENCE-BASED READING AND WRITING

Reading Test	• 65 minutes, 52 questions (all multiple choice)
	• 4 single and 1 pair of reading passages; some will contain graphics (tables, charts, etc.)
	• 3 content areas (subject knowledge not tested): literature; history/social studies; science
Writing and Language Test	• 35 minutes, 44 questions (all multiple choice); 1 or more graphics in 1 or more sets of questions
	• 4 reading passages of 3 types: argument, informative/explanatory, nonfiction narrative
	• 4 content areas (subject knowledge not tested): careers; history/social studies; humanities; science
Total time	100 minutes
Score	200–800

MATHEMATICS

Calculator Section	• 55 minutes, 38 questions (30 multiple choice, 8 grid-in)
	• 4 content areas: Heart of Algebra, Problem Solving and Data Analysis, Passport to Advanced Math, Additional Topics in Math
No-Calculator Section	• 25 minutes, 20 questions (15 multiple choice, 5 grid-in)
	• 3 content areas: Heart of Algebra, Passport to Advanced Math, Additional Topics in Math
Total time	80 minutes
Score	200–800

ESSAY (OPTIONAL)

Based on the text of an argument written for a broad audience, you will be asked to consider how the author uses:

- evidence, such as facts or examples, to support claims
- reasoning to develop ideas and to connect claims and evidence
- stylistic/persuasive elements (word choice, tone, etc.), to add power to the ideas expressed

Time	50 minutes
Score	2 to 8 on each of three categories: reading, analysis, and writing

Practice for Free

The College Board and Khan Academy are partnering to provide online SAT® test-practice programs and resources entirely free of charge. All students now have access to the best exam practice available, regardless of educational background or ability to pay for preparation.

A personalized study plan

At satpractice.org, you'll receive personalized, interactive study resources for the redesigned SAT, based on your PSAT/NMSQT results. These programs are powered by thousands of practice problems co-developed by the College Board and Khan Academy. The Khan Academy practice program links to classroom learning — the best preparation for the SAT.

More than enough resources

These are some of the resources you can access:

- Practice problems for each section of the SAT, reviewed and approved by the College Board

- Four official SAT Practice Tests written by the College Board

- Personalized recommendations for instruction and practice to help students fill their knowledge gaps

> The Official SAT Question of the Day™ can be a fun, daily practice routine. To get it free online, follow @SATQuestion on Twitter, or download the app from iTunes.

Guidance to success

Using Khan Academy's practice program will guide you to:

- Focus on the knowledge and skills necessary for college and career

- Review any knowledge gaps

- Build familiarity with the SAT format, question styles, and testing experience

A commitment to equity

Recognizing the inequities inherent to high-priced test preparation, the College Board is working with educators, community groups, college access organizations and parents to provide the necessary resources to propel students to college success. We are also collaborating with teachers and community-based organizations such as the Boys & Girls Clubs of America to ensure that as many students as possible can take advantage of these resources. You can also access Khan Academy through any computer with internet access -- including computers at libraries and YMCAs.

Multiple-Choice Strategies

Pay close attention to directions

Listen carefully to any instructions given by the test administrator and carefully read all directions in your booklet before you begin to answer the questions.

Know how to fill out the answer sheet

It is very important that you fill in the entire circle darkly and completely. If you change your answer, erase it as completely as possible. Incomplete marks or erasures may affect your score.

Don't lose your place

Check your answer sheet as you go along to make sure you are answering the right question in the right place.

Keep track of time

Don't spend too much time on any group of questions within a section.

Read the entire question, including all the answer choices, before answering a question

Don't think that because the first or second answer choice looks good to you, it isn't necessary to read the remaining options.

Watch out for absolutes

When a question or answer option contains words such as "always," "every," "only," "never," and "none," there can be no exceptions to the answer you choose. Use of words such as "often," "rarely," "sometimes," and "generally" indicates that there may be some exceptions to the answer.

Answer easy questions first

These are usually at the start of each section, and the harder ones are at the end. The exception is in the SAT's evidence-based reading and writing section, where questions are ordered according to the logic and organization of each passage.

Make educated guesses

On the redesigned SAT there are no deductions for wrong answers; only correct answers are scored. This "rights-only" scoring is meant to encourage students to give their best shot to every problem, without risking a penalty for trying their best. Since an educated guess can only work in your favor, try to rule out one or more answer choices, and you'll have a better chance of choosing the right answer.

Limit your time on any one question

All questions are worth the same number of points. If you need a lot of time to answer a question, go on to the next one. Later, you may have time to return to the question you skipped.

Mark the questions in your booklet that you skipped

That will save time if you want to go back and give these questions another try.

More Practice Tips

You won't need these tips to get ready for the SAT, because a complete, personalized practice program is available to you (see "Practice for Free" on page 105). But some colleges use other types of entrance and/or placement exams for admission, or for selective programs (like nursing), or to place students into the right courses. If such exams are part of the admission requirements at the colleges you are considering, the following tips provide a good plan of attack.

Look at sample tests

They are usually available for free at the testing organization's website. You'll be more confident if you know what to expect. Being familiar with the different sections will also save you valuable time during the test.

Next, take a practice exam

Do this to get a "starting score" so you can measure improvement. This will also enable you to see what types of questions you do well on, and what types you don't. Now you know what to concentrate on.

Look at your patterns and pacing

As you score your practice work, pay attention to the kinds of questions that give you trouble and focus your preparation accordingly. How was your pacing? If you finished early and got easy questions wrong, slow down and read questions more thoroughly.

Take advantage of "down" time

Drilling and subject matter review work best in short spurts over a longer period of time. Use down time—like when you're on a bus or in a waiting room—to do math drills, or read an outline. It'll sink in without wearing you out.

Take another practice test

Use the scores from this one to see how you've improved after studying. If you're not making headway, don't keep it to yourself—ask for help.

Take a final, timed test

Do this about a week before the exam. Don't cheat—use a timer and tell yourself "pencils down" when it goes off. The result will give you a good sense of how you'll do on the real thing.

Don't spend a lot of money

Self-discipline is free. Most expensive review courses just provide a dedicated place and time for you to do things you can do on your own.

Relax

College entrance exams are important, but they will NOT determine your future. They are just one part of your college application process. Just do your best, think positively, and you'll do fine.

Tips for Taking the SAT Subject Tests™

The SAT Subject Tests are used by colleges that want an objective way to evaluate what students know and can do in particular subject areas. These tests are intended to supplement, not replace, your high school grades in these subjects. Think of them as a chance to shine in subjects where you are strong.

If you are thinking of applying to colleges that require or recommend SAT Subject Tests, consider these test-taking tips.

Know when to take the Subject Tests

Take them when the content is fresh in your mind—often at the end of the course for subjects like biology, chemistry, and world history. It could also be after you have studied a subject for several years (a language, for example). Your teacher or counselor can help you decide.

Know what to expect

Become familiar with the organization of the tests in which you are interested, the types of test questions, and test-day procedures. Download *Getting Ready for the SAT Subject Tests* from www.collegeboard.org, which includes sample questions and sample test directions to help you prepare for the tests (or get a free copy from your counselor's office).

Know the test directions

For every five minutes you spend reading directions, you will have five fewer minutes available to answer questions. Learn the directions now.

Become familiar with the SAT Subject Test answer sheet

A copy appears in the back of *The Official Study Guide for all SAT Subject Tests*™. Your school library should have a copy of this publication.

Do the easier questions first

The easier questions are usually at the beginning of a grouping of questions. You can earn as many points for easy questions as you can for hard questions.

Don't be alarmed if you can't answer all the questions

Each Subject Test is designed to cover a wide range of knowledge, skills, and subject matter. Students should not expect to answer all the questions on the tests, as they are not expected to know and recognize everything covered in these tests. Typically, students answer only about half the questions correctly.

Know how the tests are scored

You get one point for each right answer and lose a fraction of a point for each wrong answer. You neither gain nor lose points for omitting an answer.

Make a smart guess

If you can rule out one or more answer choices for a multiple-choice question as definitely wrong, your chances of guessing correctly among the remaining choices improve. If you have no clue as to the correct answer, random guessing is not to your advantage. You should omit questions only when you really have no idea how to answer them.

Use the test book for scratch work

In your test book (but not on the answer sheet), cross off answers you know are wrong, and mark questions you did not answer so you can go back to them if you have time. Be sure to mark your answers on the separate answer sheet because you won't receive credit for any answers you marked in the test book.

Don't make extra marks on the answer sheet

The answer sheet is machine scored, and the machine can't tell an answer from a doodle.

Bring an acceptable calculator for the Mathematics Level 1 or Mathematics Level 2 tests

Acceptable means: graphing, scientific, or 4-function (not recommended). No laptops or other portable/handheld computers, or machines with typewriter-like keypads or paper tapes. Make sure you have fresh batteries.

Take an acceptable CD player for Language tests with listening

If you are taking any of the listening tests, you'll need your own CD player. (A list of what's acceptable can be found at collegeboard. org.) Be sure to also bring extra batteries. Test centers will not have extra CD players or batteries for your use, and you won't be allowed to share during the exam.

Need to decide whether to take Biology E or Biology M?

Look at the sample questions in the SAT Subject Test Practice section on collegeboard. org to see whether you are more comfortable with the ecological emphasis of Biology E or the molecular emphasis of Biology M. You should also consult with your biology teacher.

Need to decide whether to take Mathematics Level 1 or Mathematics Level 2?

Math Level 1 is designed for students who have taken two years of algebra and one year of geometry. Math Level 2 is designed for students who have taken an additional year covering elementary functions (precalculus) and/or trigonometry. If you have had preparation in trigonometry and elementary functions, have grades of B or better in these courses, and know when and how to use a scientific or graphing calculator, take Math Level 2.

Need to decide whether to take a Language Subject Test as a reading test or a listening test?

There is no difference in difficulty between these two types of language tests. However, the tests with listening can provide a more complete picture of your skills. For this reason, colleges may prefer the listening test to the reading only test for placement purposes. If you are taking the test for admission purposes, college deadlines for submitting applications may determine the choice of test for you.

Plan your test-taking day

Think about these options and conditions:

- You can take up to three Subject Tests on one test date (but only one can be a listening test).

- You can change your mind on test day about which Subject Test you want to take.

- Except for listening tests, you may add a test or substitute a test on test day.

- You may work on only one test during each testing hour. (There are short breaks after each hour.)

SAT Test Day Tips/ What to Bring

No matter how many times you've been told to relax and not worry about it, on test day you'll likely be a bit nervous. Actually, a little tension is good—it will keep you sharp. But too much tension can hurt your performance. Here are some tips to help you arrive at the test center in good shape and ready to do your best.

Listen to Mom

- Get a good night's sleep before the exam.
- Set out your photo ID, admission ticket, the No. 2 pencils you'll need, and fresh erasers before bed, to avoid last-minute nuttiness in the morning.
- Eat breakfast. You'll be at the test center for several hours and you're likely to get hungry.

Know how you'll get to the test location

If you've been assigned to a test site you're unfamiliar with (that can happen, especially if you register late), make sure you print out and review directions, and leave enough time for unexpected delays.

Leave early enough so you won't have to rush or be late

You don't need the extra anxiety. Plan to arrive at the test center by 7:45 a.m. Testing starts at about 8 a.m.

If you didn't register in time

If you miss the late registration deadline, there's still a chance that you can take the SAT. Test centers accept standbys on a first-come, first-served basis only if the site has enough space, testing materials, and staff—so there is no guarantee that you'll be admitted to the test.

What you really need to bring:

- You MUST bring acceptable Photo ID and your SAT Admission Ticket. You won't be allowed in otherwise. Acceptable ID means: current; government- or school-issued; with a recent, recognizable photo; and bearing your name in English (matching the name on your admission ticket). Visit sat.org/test-day for the latest information and to review the complete Photo ID policy.
- Be sure to bring two No. 2 pencils and a good, soft eraser. It must be a No. 2 in order to be machine-readable. (It's the most common type of pencil so this should not be a problem.) Mechanical pencils and pens are not allowed, even for the essay. And check that the eraser erases cleanly, without smudges.

It's also a good idea to bring:

- An acceptable calculator with fresh batteries. Acceptable means: battery-operated, graphing, scientific, or 4-function. No laptops or other portable/handheld computers, smart phones, tablets, or other devices with typewriter-like keypads or paper tapes are permitted.

- Snacks. You will get several short breaks, and you can eat or drink any snacks you have brought with you during these breaks. A healthy snack will go a long way toward keeping you alert during the entire test.

- A watch (but no audible alarm please) to pace yourself.

- A backpack or bag to keep your stuff under your seat.

What not to bring:

- Cell phone, pager, personal digital assistant, iPod, MP3 player, BlackBerry, or other digital/electronic equipment.

- Scratch paper.

- Notes, books, dictionary.

- Compass, protractor, ruler, or any other aid.

- Highlighter or colored pencils.

- Portable listening or recording device (unless you're taking a SAT Subject Test with a listening component).

- Camera or other photographic equipment.

- Timer with audible alarm.

Calculator tips:

- Bring a calculator with you. Calculators will not be given out at the test center.

- If you don't use a calculator regularly, practice using it before the test. Bring a calculator you're familiar with.

- Don't buy an expensive, sophisticated calculator just to take the test.

- You don't have to use a calculator on every question in the calculator section. First, decide how to solve the problem, and then decide whether to use the calculator. The calculator should help you, not get in the way.

- It may help to do scratch work in the test book. Get your thoughts down before using your calculator.

- Make sure your calculator is in good working order and that batteries are fresh. If your calculator fails during testing and you have no backup, you'll have to complete the test without it.

If You Need Accommodations

If you have a documented disability, you may be eligible for appropriate accommodations to enable you to take a test. The information given here applies to all College Board tests, such as the PSAT/NMSQT, SAT, SAT Subject Tests, or AP Exams. To find out about similar policies for other exams, visit the testing organization's website.

Types of accommodations available

The College Board's procedures for determining appropriate accommodations on its tests provide for considerable flexibility to accommodate your special needs. There are four major categories for testing accommodations:

Presentation (e.g., large print; reader; Braille; Braille device for written responses; visual magnification; auditory amplification; audiocassette; sign/oral presentations);

Responding (e.g., verbal/dictated to scribe; tape recorder; computer without spell check/grammar/cut & paste features; large block answer sheet);

Timing/scheduling (e.g., frequent breaks; extended time; multiple day; specified time of day); and

Setting (e.g., small group setting; private room; special lighting/acoustics; adaptive/special furniture/tools; alternative test site [with proctor present]; preferential seating).

How to apply for accommodations

You can apply through your school. This is how most students apply for accommodations. You or your parents must first complete a consent form, and then your school's SSD Coordinator will be able to request accommodations through SSD Online.

Or you can apply directly yourself. You or your parents can request accommodations without the assistance of a school, by submitting a Student Eligibility Form directly to the College Board (available by contacting the College Board Services for Students with Disabilities).

> For a more complete discussion of all you should know, go to the "Services for Students with Disabilities" section on **collegeboard.org**.

What about documentation? In some cases, documentation will be requested for the College Board's review. If you apply through your school, SSD Online will indicate if documentation is required. If you choose to apply directly without going through your school, documentation is always required. Guidelines for documentation are available on collegeboard.org.

Start the process early. It can take up to seven weeks to review the application after it's completed, so you should begin the process at least three months before the test date.

After Approval

You and your school will receive an Eligibility Letter notifying you of the approved accommodations. The letters will include an SSD Eligibility Code for you.

If you are taking the SAT, be sure to provide your SSD Eligibility Code when you register, and bring your eligibility letter to the test with you.

If you are taking an AP Exam or the PSAT/NMSQT, be sure to inform your school that you have been approved for accommodations, so that they may make arrangements and order appropriate materials.

If you receive **approval just before the test**, contact the College Board to make sure the accommodations will be available on the test date.

If you transfer to a new school, inform your new school that you were approved for accommodations, and give the school your SSD Eligibility Code.

Eligibility requirements

Basic requirements for eligibility include the following:

1 You must have a documented disability.

2. The disability must impact your ability to participate in standardized tests.

3. You must demonstrate a need for the specific accommodation requested. (For example, if you ask for extended time, you must show that your disability causes difficulty with test taking under timed conditions.)

Note that the use of accommodations in school, or inclusion on an Individual Education Program (IEP) or 504 Plan, does not automatically qualify you for accommodations on College Board tests.

If you have a temporary disability

If you have a temporary disability, such as a broken arm, you should register for a test on a later date when the temporary disability has healed. This is the process for the SAT tests that are administered throughout the academic year. However, if you are planning to take a test that is only administered annually (e.g., AP Exams or the PSAT/NMSQT), you or your school may contact the College Board to inquire if it would be possible for you to test with temporary accommodations.

Test-Taking Timeline

This timeline covers all SAT, SAT Subject Tests, and AP Exams. Use it to scope out all the upcoming dates and deadlines for the tests you'll be taking. *Be sure to check the specific test dates and registration deadlines for the year you are taking the tests*—they change slightly year to year. You'll find them on collegeboard.org.

Junior Year

SEPTEMBER

Pick up the *Official Student Guide to the PSAT/NMSQT* from your guidance office and take the practice test.

OCTOBER

The **PSAT/NMSQT** is administered this month.

DECEMBER

- Register for the **SAT** by the end of this month, if you want to take it in **March**. (No SAT Subject Tests are administered in March.)

- Begin preparing for the SAT for free. Go to **satpractice.org**.

JANUARY

Review your PSAT/NMSQT **Score Report** with your school counselor. Talk about what courses to take next year, based on your results.

FEBRUARY

- If you're taking AP classes, **register for AP Exams**, given in May.

- If you're not in an AP course but want to take an AP Exam, contact AP Services for a list of local AP Coordinators by the end of this month.

MARCH

- The **SAT** is administered this month, but not SAT Subject Tests.

- If you're not in an AP course but want to take an AP Exam, you must make final arrangements to take AP Exams by **March 15**.

- Register for the **SAT** and **SAT Subject Tests** by the end of this month, if you want to take them in **May**.

APRIL

Register for the **SAT** and **SAT Subject Tests** by the end of this month, if you want to take them in **June**.

MAY

- **AP Exams** are given this month.

- The **SAT** and **SAT Subject Tests** are administered this month.

JUNE

- The **SAT** and **SAT Subject Tests** are administered this month.

Senior Year

SEPTEMBER

- Register for the **SAT** and **SAT Subject Tests** by the beginning of this month, if you want to take them in **October**.
- Register for the **SAT** and **SAT Subject Tests** before the end of this month, if you want to take them in **November**. **NOTE: November is the only month you can take Language Tests with Listening.**

OCTOBER

- The **SAT** and **SAT Subject Tests** are administered this month.
- Register for the **SAT** and **SAT Subject Tests** by the end of this month, if you want to take them in **December**.

NOVEMBER

- The **SAT** and **SAT Subject Tests** are administered this month.

DECEMBER

- The **SAT** and **SAT Subject Tests** are administered this month.
- Register for **SAT** and **SAT Subject Tests** before the end of this month, if you want to take them in **January**.

JANUARY

- The **SAT** and **SAT Subject Tests** are administered this month.
- Register for the **SAT** by the end of this month, if you want to take it in **March**. (No SAT Subject Tests are administered in March.)

FEBRUARY

- If you're taking AP classes, **register for AP Exams**, given in May.
- If you're not in an AP course but want to take an AP Exam, contact AP Services for a list of local AP Coordinators by the end of this month.

MARCH

- The **SAT** is administered this month, but not SAT Subject Tests.
- If you're not in an AP course but want to take an AP Exam, you must make final arrangements to take AP Exams by **March 15**.
- Register for the **SAT** and **SAT Subject Tests** by the end of this month, if you want to take them in **May**.

APRIL

Register for the **SAT** and **SAT Subject Tests** by the end of this month, if you want to take them in **June**.

MAY

- **AP Exams** are given this month.
- The **SAT** and **SAT Subject Tests** are administered this month.

JUNE

- The **SAT** and **SAT Subject Tests** are administered this month.

Test-Taking Tracker

This tracker will help you stay on top of all the college admission tests you might need to take. Use it together with the "College Application Tracker" on page 126.

Put in the names of the colleges you are applying to, the dates for all reminders and deadlines, and check off when done.

		SAT	ACT
REQUIRED OR RECOMMENDED	College 1		
	College 2		
	College 3		
	College 4		
	College 5		
	College 6		
	College 7		
	College 8		
REGISTRATION	Registration deadline (for test in the fall)		
	Registration deadline (for test in the winter)		
	Registration deadline (for test in the spring)		
	Registration fee		
DATE TEST TAKEN	Fall test date		
	Winter test date		
	Spring test date		
SCORES	Score received		
	Request scores be sent to colleges		
	Score sent		

SAT SUBJECT TEST	SAT SUBJECT TEST	AP EXAM	AP EXAM

NOTES

NOTES

Chapter
07

Completing the Applications

Application Basics

Here's a quick rundown of what to expect as you start filling out college applications, and what you need to do to get them done.

Keeping on track

The first thing you should do is write down the application deadlines and all the tasks you'll have to accomplish to complete the applications. (See the "College Application Tracker" on page 126.)

Most applications for regular admission are due in early January or February, and most early application deadlines are in November or December. So try to lay out your timeline in October of your senior year. (My Organizer on collegeboard.org will help you plan and remind you of upcoming deadlines.)

> Most colleges have two separate application forms: one for admission, and one for financial aid. The deadlines for these forms may be different as well.

Remember to budget time for other people to do things. Teachers won't write recommendations overnight, and testing organizations will need a few weeks to send official score reports to colleges.

Filling out the application

A typical application will ask you to provide some personal information; what schools you have attended; brief descriptions of your extracurricular activities, jobs, and any academic honors you have earned; and standardized test scores. They will also ask for information about your family and their education background, to see if you merit special consideration as a first-generation college student, or if you are related to an alumnus.

Finally, all applications will ask if you plan to file for financial aid. Checking this box does not mean you have applied for financial aid! It just lets the admission office know that they should coordinate with the financial aid office later on. You'll have to file for financial aid separately.

What goes with your application

Besides the application form, there are several things that need to be included with your application. You will have to send some of them with the form; others will be sent to the college by other people.

Application fee—usually nonrefundable. Many colleges offer fee waivers for applicants from low-income families, and some waive the fee if you apply online.

High school transcript—Your high school should send your transcript, along with a school profile, directly to the colleges you are applying to.

Admission test scores—if the college requires standardized test scores, you must make sure the testing agency itself sends an official score report. You can't write them down yourself or send a photocopy.

Letters of recommendation—if required, they are usually sent directly to the college by the person writing the letter; but sometimes your school counselor will assemble the letters and send them with your transcript. (See "Guidelines for Getting Recommendations" on page 132.)

If you apply online, remember to print them out and proofread them before you submit the application, just as you would with a printed application. Also, be sure to inform your school counselor that you've applied online—your school will need to send your transcript to the college.

Essays or personal statements—most colleges don't require these, but selective ones do. Some applications will ask you to attach a separate essay of one or two pages, others will ask you to fill in some one-paragraph short responses directly on the application form, and others will ask for both. See Chapter 8 for lots of tips about essays.

Auditions, portfolios, and other supplementary materials—if you're applying for a performing or fine arts program, you may have to demonstrate your ability by auditioning on campus or submitting an audiotape, slides, or some other sample of your work. Talk to a teacher or mentor in your subject for advice on both how to assemble a portfolio and which of your pieces to include. Be sure to check the deadlines for auditions—they are often different from the deadlines for applications.

Take your time

College applications aren't difficult, but they are important. Admission committees will take a sloppy or careless submission as a reflection on you. So take the time to do a careful, neat job. Review each section and proofread your answers. This is equally true of online applications. (See "Online Application Dos and Don'ts" on page 129.)

College Application Timeline

College applications won't seem so overwhelming if you know what's coming, and what needs to be done when. Use this timeline to get a bird's-eye view of the whole process. This is only a general guide and may not apply to all colleges, so check the specific requirements and deadlines of the colleges you are applying to.

SUMMER BEFORE SENIOR YEAR

- **Create your list of colleges** that really interest you. Match them up against your list of "must haves" and "like to haves." (See the "What You Want Checklist" on page 78.)

- **Visit** some colleges on your list. Call ahead for the campus tour schedule.

- Register for the SAT and/or SAT Subjects Tests if you intend to take them in the fall.

- If you plan on competing in Division I or Division II **college sports**, register with the NCAA Eligibility Center.

- Find out about **local scholarships** offered by church groups, civic associations, and businesses in your area.

SEPTEMBER

- Meet with your school counselor to **finalize your list of colleges**. Be sure your list includes "safety," "probable," and "reach" schools. (See "Your Short List of Colleges" on page 80.)

- Start a checklist of all application requirements, deadlines, fees, etc. (See the "College Application Tracker" on page 126.)

- If you are going to apply under an **Early Decision or Early Action plan**, get started now. Deadlines for early applications tend to fall in October or November.

- Set up campus visits and interviews and attend **open houses** at colleges on your list.

OCTOBER

- Register for the SAT and/or SAT Subject Tests if you want to take them in December or January.

- Ask for **letters of recommendation** from your counselor, teachers, coaches, or employers. Give them plenty of time to meet your deadlines and make sure to provide them with stamped and addressed envelopes.

- If you need to fill out the CSS/Financial Aid PROFILE, you can register on collegeboard.org starting Oct. 1.

- Write **first drafts of your college essays** and ask your parents and teachers to review them.

NOVEMBER

- Submit **Early Decision and Early Action** applications on time. Save a copy for yourself and your school counselor.

- Finish your application **essays**. Proofread them rigorously for mistakes. Follow up with your teachers to ensure that letters of recommendation are sent on time to meet your deadlines.

- Apply to colleges with rolling admission (first-come, first-served) as early as possible.

- Give your school counselor the proper forms to **send transcripts** to your colleges at least two weeks in advance.

- **Get PINs for the FAFSA** for both yourself and one of your parents at www.pin.ed.gov.

DECEMBER

- Try to **wrap up college applications** before winter break. Make copies for yourself and your school counselor.

- If you applied for early decision, you should have an answer by Dec. 15. If you are denied or deferred, submit applications now to other colleges.

- **Apply for scholarships** in time to meet application deadlines.

- Contact the financial aid office at the colleges on your list to make sure you have all required financial aid forms.

JANUARY

- Submit your **FAFSA** as soon as you can after Jan. 1. If a college you're applying to has a financial aid priority date of Feb. 1, use estimates based on your end-of-year pay stubs and last year's tax returns.

- Submit other financial aid forms that may be required—such as PROFILE or the college's own forms. Keep copies.

- If a college wants to see your **midyear grades**, tell your school counselor.

- If you have acquired any new honors or accomplishments, let your colleges know.

FEBRUARY

- Ask your parents to do their taxes and to use **the IRS Data Retrieval tool** to update your FAFSA.

- Contact your colleges to confirm that all application materials have been received.

- If any special circumstances affect your family's financial situation, alert each college's financial aid office.

MARCH

- Admission decisions start arriving. Read everything you receive carefully, as some may require prompt action on your part.

- **Revisit colleges** that accepted you if it's hard to make a choice.

- Don't get senioritis! Colleges want to see strong second half grades.

APRIL

- Most admission decisions and financial aid award letters arrive this month. Carefully **compare financial aid** award letters from the colleges that accept you.

- Make a final decision, accept the aid package and **mail a deposit check** to the college you select before May 1 (the acceptance deadline for most schools).

- Notify the other colleges that you won't be attending (so another student can have your spot).

- On the waiting list? Contact the admission office and let them know of your continued interest in the college and update them on your spring semester grades and activities.

MAY

- AP Exams are given. Make sure your AP Grade Report is sent to your college.

- Finalize your **housing** plans if you're living away. Send in all required forms and deposits.

- Study hard for final exams. Most admission offers are contingent on your final grades.

- **Thank everyone** who wrote you recommendations or otherwise helped with your college applications.

JUNE

- Have your counselor send your **final transcript** to your college choice.

- If you plan on competing in Division I or Division II college sports, have your counselor send your final transcript to the NCAA Eligibility Center.

- Enjoy your graduation, and **have a great summer!**

College Application Tracker

This tracker will help you stay on top of all your application tasks, paperwork, and deadlines. Put in all due dates, and check them off when done. Use it together with the "Financial Aid Application Tracker" on page 170.

		COLLEGE 1 SCHOOL NAME	COLLEGE 2 SCHOOL NAME
Deadlines	Regular application deadline (check fin aid deadlines)		
	Early application deadline		
Grades	High school transcript sent		
	Midyear grade reports sent		
Test Scores	SAT or ACT required?		
	SAT Subject Tests required?		
	Release SAT Subject Test scores		
	Send SAT scores		
	Send ACT scores		
	Send AP grades		
Letters of Recommendation	Number required		
	Request teacher recommendations		
	Request counselor recommendation		
	Request other recommendations		
	Send thank-you notes		
Essays	Essay required?		
	Proof for spelling and grammar		
	Have two people read your essay		
	Final copy in application		
Interviews	Interview required?		
	Interview date		
	Send thank-you notes to interviewers		
Submitting the Application	Sign application and keep a copy of everything		
	Pay application fee (amount)		
	Applied online—received confirmation receipt		
	Applied by mail—confirm receipt of all materials		
	Notified school counselor that you applied		
	Send supplemental material, if needed		
After You Send Your Application	Received decision letter from office of admission		
	Deadline to accept admission and send deposit		
	Tuition deposit sent		
	Housing forms completed and deposit sent		
	Notify the other colleges you will not attend		

COLLEGE 3	COLLEGE 4	COLLEGE 5	COLLEGE 6	COLLEGE 7	COLLEGE 8
SCHOOL NAME	SCHOOL NAME	SCHOOL NAME	SCHOOL NAME	SCHOOL NAME	SCHOOL NAME

College Application FAQs

Do I have a better chance of getting in if I apply early decision?

The answer varies from college to college and year to year, but in general, applying early decision gives you somewhat better odds of acceptance. But don't apply early decision just because you think it will give you a competitive advantage. You should go that route only if you are absolutely sure you want to attend that college more than any other. For more advice, see "What to Know About Applying Early" on page 131.

What is the Common Application? Should I use it?

The Common Application is an online form used by over 500 colleges and universities that belong to the Common Application Group. They all agree to accept this application in place of their own (although some require an additional supplement). You fill it out once and it is then transmitted to all of your colleges that participate. To learn more, see "About the Common Application" on page 130, or go to www.commonapp.org.

My SAT scores are very low, and my grades are very high. Will this affect my chances of admission?

While SAT scores are an indicator of success in college, it's only one of many different factors colleges will look at while evaluating your application. The main thing they look for is to see if your high school record indicates that you have the potential for academic success on their campus. If you've done well in challenging courses in high school, that usually is given greater weight than test scores.

My parents don't make a lot of money—will colleges hold this against me?

Some colleges declare that they have a "need-blind" admission policy. That means they never consider ability to pay as an admission criterion. Other schools, which are "need-conscious," may consider ability to pay, but only for a very small portion of applicants. The advice of most counselors: Don't worry about this.

Is it okay to send additional material that I think will support my application?

It is okay to provide additional information to explain something that cannot be explained on the application forms, but other items that students sometimes send are not helpful and may be viewed as trying to distract the admission staff from the actual application. Talk to your school counselor about any additional items that you are thinking about sending.

Do colleges really care about your senior year grades?

Absolutely! Many colleges will not make a decision until receiving midyear senior grades. Colleges also ask for a final transcript at the end of the senior year. (Admission letters often contain something like, "Your admission is contingent upon your continued successful performance.") It is not at all rare for a college to withdraw an offer of admission when grades drop significantly over the course of the senior year.

Online Application Dos and Don'ts

Applying online is fast, easy, always neat and clean, and often free. But it's not all good—there are some pitfalls for the unwary. Here are the key dos and don'ts.

Do:

create user names, PIN numbers, and passwords that you'll remember easily. Write them down and keep them in a safe place.

Don't:

treat an online application casually—it's an important document that reflects on you. don't use abbreviations and short spellings as if you were texting.

Don't:

be too quick to click. Take your time, follow all directions, and complete each step with care. Scroll each page from top to bottom and read every pop-up, to be sure you don't miss any information.

Don't:

forget to periodically save your work. You might get "timed out" if you don't enter anything for a while (usually 30 minutes). If you need to take a break, use the save/log-out feature to store your application, then log back in.

Don't:

compose your essay or personal statement in the space allotted online. Draft (and re-draft) these separately in a word-processing application, such as Microsoft® Word, then copy and paste the final draft into the online application.

Do:

print and save a hard copy of the completed application. Proofread it before you hit the "send" button—sometimes your information in text boxes can get cut off.

Do:

ask someone else to review the application for errors before you send it. Two sets of eyes are always better than one.

Do:

print and save a copy of the confirmation page that should appear after you submit the application, so that you'll have a record of your application ID number.

Do:

tell your school counselor about every online application you submit. Better yet, give your counselor a hard copy printout. This is critical, because your application won't be complete until your counselor forwards your transcript and any other material the college may require.

Don't:

apply online and then send a paper copy in the mail. That will just confuse things.

Do:

call or e-mail the college if you haven't received an e-mail confirmation of receipt within 48 hours. Online submissions do get lost occasionally. (That's why it's so important to print and save.)

Don't:

apply online the week before the application deadline. Because of high volume, application websites tend to get slow and cranky at this time. It's also the most likely time for a system failure. If you're up against the deadline, it's safer to apply through the mail.

About the
Common Application

Much of what goes into a typical college application is the same as what goes into any other: your name and address, your high school information, your extracurriculars, etc. If you're applying to several colleges it can be annoying—and time consuming—to rekey this same info over and over.

Fill it out once, submit it to multiple colleges

The Common Application is designed to relieve students of this repetitive process by providing a single application form (print and online) that is accepted by over 500 participating colleges. You fill it out once and then submit copies to any number of these institutions. The same is true of the school report and the teacher evaluation portions, which are automatically submitted with the application.

There might be an additional step

Member colleges of the Common Application Group make no distinction between the common application and their own form when making admission decisions. However, some member colleges require supplemental forms in addition to the common application. You should research whether the colleges to which you are applying need such a form by consulting their websites.

Transfer students can use it too

There's a Common Application for students who are applying for transfer admission as well as first-year admission. The Transfer Application is designed primarily for online submission, but you can download a printable PDF form if need be.

To access the Common Application and to find out which colleges participate, go to **www.commonapp.org**.

Not all colleges use it

Membership in the Common Application Group is restricted to colleges that use a holistic selection process to evaluate applicants. That means they use subjective as well as objective criteria, such as recommendations, an essay, and other considerations beyond grades and test scores. Sending the Common Application to nonmembers is discouraged.

Don't forget your counselor

The Common Application can be a great time-saver—but remember to inform your school counselor of every college you send it to.

What to Know About Applying Early

If you find a college that you're sure is right for you, consider applying early. Early Decision and Early Action plans allow you to apply early (usually in November) and get an admission decision early (usually by Dec. 15).

Early Decision plans are binding

You agree to attend the college if it accepts you and offers an adequate financial aid package. You can apply to only one college for Early Decision. You may also apply to other colleges through the regular admission process, but if you're accepted by your first-choice college early, you must withdraw all other applications.

Early Action plans are nonbinding

While the college will tell you whether or not you're accepted by early January, you have the right to wait until May 1 before responding. This gives you time to compare colleges, including their financial aid offers, before making a decision. You can also apply Early Action to more than one college.

> Get advice from your school counselor before applying Early Decision. While it may seem appealing to get the process over with early, it might be too soon to know that you've made the right college choice.

Single-choice Early Action is another option offered by a few colleges

This plan works the same way as other Early Action plans, but candidates may not apply early (either Early Action or Early Decision) to any other school. You can still apply for regular admission to other schools and are not required to give your final answer of acceptance until the regular decision deadline.

If you need financial aid, Early Decision might not be a good idea

You shouldn't apply under an Early Decision plan if you think you'll be better off weighing financial aid packages from several colleges later in the spring. While you can turn down an early acceptance if the college is unable to meet your need for financial aid, "need" in this context is determined by formulas, not by your family.

Not every college offers an early plan

More than 400 colleges offer an Early Decision plan, an Early Action plan, or both; but that is only about 20 percent of all four-year colleges.

Guidelines for Getting Recommendations

Most colleges want two or three recommendation letters from people who know you in and out of the classroom. Often they require at least one from an academic teacher (sometimes for a specific subject), and/or your school counselor. Here are some tips on whom—and how—to ask.

The best teacher to ask is...

If you don't have a clear favorite, your English or math teachers usually make good candidates. Ask a teacher from junior year unless a current teacher has known you long enough to form an opinion.

Think about which teacher will remember you best, because of your class participation and any personal interaction. That may be a teacher in whose class you've gotten top grades, but it could also be a teacher who knows how hard you've worked to get B's and C's.

The best time to ask is...

Ask at least one month ahead of your deadline, two weeks at a minimum. If you're asking a popular teacher, he or she might have a lot of letters to write. And be sure to also allow time for snail mail. Often the college's deadline is receipt date, not the postmark date.

The best way to ask is...

Remember you're asking for a favor; don't demand one.

Don't be shy. Teachers and counselors are usually happy to help you, as long as you respect their time constraints.

Ask in a way that allows a teacher to decline comfortably if he/she does not have time to do an adequate job. For example: "Do you feel you know me well enough, and do you have enough time to write a letter of recommendation for me?"

Follow up with a written request with instructions, the deadline, and an addressed and stamped envelope. (See the "Sample Recommendation Request Letter" on the next page.)

Give them something to work with

Provide a "brag sheet" or résumé reminding them of your accomplishments over the years. (See the "Recommendation Cheat Sheet" on page 134.) It will make their job easier.

Follow up

Follow up with your recommendation writers a week or so prior to your first deadline, to ensure recommendations have been mailed or to see if they need additional information from you. And send a thank-you note to everyone who provided a recommendation.

Sample Recommendation Request Letter

This letter can be short and sweet, but what's most important is not to wait until the last minute. Give the person you're asking enough time to write the recommendation and send it off ahead of any deadlines. A month is best; the **minimum** is two weeks.

Your Name
Street Address
City, State, Zip

October _ _, 20_ _

[Name of person you are asking]
Street Address
City, State, Zip

Dear _____,
I am applying for admission to [name of college(s)], and I need a letter of recommendation.

Would you consider writing a letter for me? I have attached the instructions for the letter, and an addressed and stamped envelope for each school. I have also attached a short résumé of my accomplishments, which I hope you find helpful.

My deadline for recommendations is _____, 20__.

Thank you so much. I really appreciate your taking time to do this for me.

Sincerely,

Recommendation Cheat Sheet

Here's a "cheat sheet" that will make the job easier for those who are writing your recommendations. The more details about your background you can give, the more thorough their recommendation will be. This worksheet will also help you with the entire college application process, especially in preparing for interviews and writing admission essays. (Have you kept up an "Extracurricular Archive" like the one on page 35?)

Name: _____

Date: _____

SCHOOL ACTIVITIES

List the activities you have participated in, the number of years, and the amount of time per week you spent. Write a sentence or two stating what you have gained or learned from each activity. Mention any leadership positions held, or specific contributions you made. For sports, mention any highlights that you are most proud of.

ACTIVITY: _____ **YEARS:** _____ **HOURS/WEEK:** _____

_____

_____

_____

ACTIVITY: _____ **YEARS:** _____ **HOURS/WEEK:** _____

_____

_____

_____

ACTIVITY: _____ **YEARS:** _____ **HOURS/WEEK:** _____

_____

_____

_____

_____

WHICH ACTIVITY WAS MOST IMPORTANT TO YOU? WHY?

_____
_____
_____
_____
_____

OUTSIDE ACTIVITIES

What do you consider your most important activities outside of school? List jobs (paid or unpaid); community service; religious activities; hobbies; travel; music, art, or drama. Include the number of years of your involvement and the amount of time you spent on the activity weekly.

ACTIVITY: **YEARS:**   **HOURS/WEEK:**

_____
_____
_____
_____

ACTIVITY: **YEARS:**   **HOURS/WEEK:**

_____
_____
_____
_____

ACTIVITY: **YEARS:**   **HOURS/WEEK:**

_____
_____
_____
_____

WHICH ACTIVITY WAS MOST IMPORTANT TO YOU? WHY?

_____
_____
_____
_____
_____

CONTINUED

HONORS AND AWARDS
In or out of school, which awards and honors have you received?

_____

_____

_____

_____

_____

ACADEMIC PROFILE
Describe the academic accomplishment (research paper, science experiment, artistic project) you are most proud of, and tell why you take pride in it.

_____

_____

_____

_____

_____

What kind of learner are you? Which academic setting or assignments make you thrive? What interests you?

_____

_____

_____

_____

_____

PERSONAL PROFILE
List your most distinguishing or most admirable qualities. Explain each in several sentences.

_____

_____

_____

_____

_____

_____

_____

What book(s) have had the greatest impact on you? Why?

Title: _____ Author: _____

_____

_____

_____

_____

Title: _____ Author: _____

_____

_____

_____

_____

Title: _____ Author: _____

_____

_____

_____

_____

WHAT DO YOU HOPE TO ACCOMPLISH IN COLLEGE AND AFTER?
Consider your career goals and your broader goals.

_____

_____

_____

_____

_____

_____

_____

_____

_____

_____

_____

Source: Lick-Wilmerding High School, California

Art Portfolio Prep Tips

If you are applying to art school, your portfolio will be the most important part of your application. These tips will help you put together a great portfolio, no matter what kind of art you want to study.

Creating Your Portfolio

Know what each school wants to see

In general, an admissions portfolio consists of 10 to 15 images of your best and most recent work, but be sure to check each school's website for their specific requirements. Almost every school will want to see:

- **Observational drawings.** These are drawings from real life (never a photo), such as a landscape, room interior, portrait, or still life. Schools like them because they show your ability to interpret, compose, and accurately depict what you see before you.
- **Figure drawings.** The human figure drawn from life is one of the best things to include. A friend, yourself, someone in the park…
- **Variety.** Show you can work with different media (oil, watercolor, photography, clay, computer art, etc.), styles, and subjects.
- **Design skills.** Include a collage, poster, or layout that shows you can combine different elements.
- **That you've taken some risks.** Show that you are willing to challenge yourself.

But no school wants to see:

- Images of anime and video game imagery—it's so overdone
- Paintings or drawings copied from photos or other art works

Give yourself plenty of time

Get started early in your junior year. The more time you have to work, the more work you will have to choose from. An early start will also allow time for filling gaps and meeting specific school requirements.

Good quality work that really shows your strengths is hard to create when you are under time pressure. Besides, you should have some fun with this.

Be ready for inspiration

Always have a sketchbook, camera, or journal with you wherever you go. Everything around you is potential subject matter, so be ready to catch the moment.

Try to attend a summer or precollege program

These programs usually last four to six weeks, giving you the opportunity to not only build your portfolio but to get a sense of what art school is really like. They are also a lower-cost alternative to an expensive portfolio prep class. Ask your art teacher about any programs being offered at local colleges, art schools, or community centers.

Attend a National Portfolio Day

This is one of the best things you can do. National Portfolio Day events take place all over the country during the fall. It's sort of like a college fair for art schools, except the main focus is on evaluating portfolios brought in by students. Check it out at www.portfolioday.net

It's OK if the portfolio you bring is still a work in progress; in fact, it's to your advantage, since it allows you to incorporate the feedback you receive.

Don't do this alone

Get as much feedback as you can. Ask your teachers, family, friends, or other people whose opinions you trust to look at your work. Be open-minded about what you hear.

Submitting Your Portfolio

Don't leave this part to the last minute

Properly editing, photographing, documenting, and packaging your work for submission is painstaking work. Allow yourself several days to do it right. Plan to have all your works completed at least two weeks before the submission deadline.

Know the requirements

Every art program has its own rules about how it wants to receive works. So be sure to check each school's website for their submission guidelines and print them out. Pay special attention to the labeling and documentation requirements.

- **If submitting on a CD/DVD**, check for specs on dpi and pixel size. You'll also have to provide an inventory sheet with thumbnail images and descriptions of each piece.
- **If submitting slides**, allow time for developing, reviewing (you'll need a viewer) and labeling.
- **If submitting new media**, verify what format or software the school specifies or can accommodate.

Have someone help you photograph your work

It'll be easier with two people to handle the pieces and set up the shots. More photo tips:

- Use a good quality camera. (Don't use your phone.)
- Use a tripod to ensure consistent, well-centered shots.
- Shoot in daylight for best color and shadow control.

- Provide a solid white or black background, depending on the piece.
- Shoot three-dimensional works from different angles, and use light, shadow, and depth-of-field (short f-stop) to emphasize the piece.
- Keep a record of each shot, so you don't lose track.

Submit online if you can

Uploading your portfolio images to an online portfolio management website like SlideRoom is the easiest and least expensive way to submit your work. In fact, it's the preferred method at many major art schools.

You can post still and video works, edit and document them online, and after you click "submit" you'll get immediate confirmation that your work was received.

Keep a copy of everything you mail

You don't want to start over if any CD/DVDs or slides get lost or damaged. Also, mail your portfolio "return receipt requested," and follow up with each school to be sure everything arrived OK. Then reward yourself for a job well done!

TIPS

Tips for a Winning Music School Audition

If you want to pursue a degree in a music or performing arts program, an audition will probably be part of the application process. Here are some tips to help you do your best.

Before the Audition

Know what they want to hear

Each school is different so be sure to check the college website or contact the program directly for their audition guidelines. See if they require any specific works, styles, tempos, scales, or other technical demonstrations. Do this early enough to prepare and practice them.

Most schools will want you to:

- Demonstrate your best technical ability, but not perfection. (They expect you to be a student, not a pro.) Musical expressiveness, good intonation (define), and tonal quality usually counts more than technical virtuosity.
- Perform scales in a range of styles and speeds.
- Show you can sight read (playing or singing a piece of music while reading the notes for the first time).

Know what to expect

Ask the school about the audition's format: how long it should take, who will be there, what kind of room. Find out if it includes tests on theory or ear-training. Try to connect with a student who has gone through an audition at the same school recently. Your music teachers will have good insights too.

Select varied pieces

If allowed to choose, select different types of music that show your versatility, are expressive of your personality and showcase your strengths. Ask your teachers to help you select pieces that will impress, but are still within your skill level.

If it's a vocal audition, operas and show tunes are good sources. Pick two pieces in contrasting styles, and it would be good if one is in a foreign language.

Schedule early

Having a good pick of date and time is a stress reliever.

Give yourself lots of time to prepare

Don't even think you can cram for this, or that talent alone will see you through. You might be the best in your high school, but that's probably true of everyone else auditioning.

Practice the audition, not just the music

Perform your selected pieces in front of a variety of people and in different situations. Videotape these sessions and go over them with a teacher.

Be ready to talk, too

Many auditions are part interview as well. You might be asked about:

- Your teachers and other musicians who have influenced you.
- Your instrument—why you chose it, make and model, etc.
- Your repertoire—the composer, dates, genre, etc.
- Your own questions for them. (See Chapter 9.)

Take care of maintenance

Make sure your instrument is in good condition, and spiff it up a bit—appearance counts.

That goes for you too

Your physical condition affects your performance. Stay rested, eat well, exercise. Take care of yourself—plenty of rest, good nutrition, exercise, vitamins.

At the Audition

What to bring:

- Extra supplies, depending on your instrument.
- Your high school transcript and/or résumé.
- Copies of your music.
- If you're going to sing, try to bring an accompanist you are familiar with.

Arrive in good shape

Avoid caffeine the night before. Eat a light breakfast, but don't skip it. Drink water so you don't get dehydrated.

Look good

Your appearance is part of the performance. Dress well, but comfortably.

Arrive early

Give yourself extra time to find the audition room—it might be in an obscure place. Better yet, do a practice run if you can. Being late is the worst way to start.

Warm up

Another reason to arrive early. But don't overdo it or let it make you late.

If they cut you off

Don't be surprised or rattled if they tell you to stop in the middle of a piece—it's just a time-management thing.

If you have to sight-read

Check for the key, time signatures, and tempo before you begin.

Leave with a smile and a thank-you

Last impressions count too.

After the Audition

Send a thank-you note

You'd be surprised how important—and rare—this is. Send it to the head of the music department if you don't know a name.

If you really think you blew it

Ask for a second audition—some schools will accommodate such requests (but don't depend on it).

Keep perspective

It's not all about being judged—you are judging the school, too. Being accepted only matters if you will really be happy and successful there.

Home Schooled?

Most colleges are glad to admit home-schooled applicants, but the application process usually involves some additional steps to take and documentation to provide. If you are home schooled, review these tips so that you'll be ready to meet the extra requirements you'll face.

Make sure your home school curriculum covered college-prep material

There are certain "gatekeeper" courses that college admission officers expect all applicants to have completed. Your local school district or board of education should be able to verify that what you've studied is the equivalent of these college-preparatory classes.

Stay on top of dates and deadlines

Without regular announcements from a guidance office, it's up to you to keep track of critical dates and deadlines relating to things like college applications, test registration deadlines, or financial aid. You've already taken a good first step by buying this book!

Get recommendations

Many colleges require letters of recommendation. If your primary instructor is your parent, you might have to ask at least one unrelated adult who knows you well to write a letter. That could be a coach of a sports team, a leader of a club, or an employer—as long as the person has known you for a significant period of time and can speak about your character and abilities.

Search for home schooled–friendly colleges

Some colleges are friendlier toward home-schooled applicants than others. Before you select colleges, check to see if they have a home-school admission policy, or if they've admitted home-schoolers in the past. The best way to find out is to call admission offices directly and ask.

Prepare for a college interview

Interviews are often required or recommended for home-schooled applicants. Look upon this as an opportunity to present a more complete and accurate picture of yourself.

Know each college's application requirements

The requirements for home-schooled applicants can vary widely from college to college. Among the different requirements are:

- Transcript with course descriptions, syllabi, reading list, and grading criteria
- Portfolio of your work (such as research papers, projects, writing samples)
- State high school equivalency certificate, or other proof of district approval/accreditation
- Essay or personal statement
- GED
- SAT Subject Tests
- Statement describing home school structure and mission

Each home schooler's situation is different

For example, some students are associated with a particular home-based school program and others work with their local public school. The above tips speak generally about the college admission process for most home-schooled students. If you have any questions, contact your local high school's guidance office or call the admission office of the school to which you're applying.

NOTES

No-Sweat
Application Essays

Three Steps to a Great College Essay

The college application essay is a chance to explain yourself and to reveal your personality, charm, talents, vision, and spirit to the admission committee. It's a chance to show you can think about things and that you can write clearly about your thoughts. Here's how to make the best of this chance—without making yourself crazy.

Remember—you already know how to write an essay

To write a college essay, use the exact same three-step process you'd use to write an essay for class: prewrite, draft, edit. This process will help you identify a focus for your essay, and gather the details you'll need to support it.

Step 1: Prewriting

To begin, you must first collect and organize potential ideas for your essay's focus. Since all college application essay questions are attempts to learn about you, begin with yourself.

Brainstorm

Set a timer for 15 minutes and make a list of your strengths and outstanding characteristics. Focus on strengths of personality, not things you've done. For example, you are responsible (not an "Eagle Scout") or committed (not "played basketball").

Discover your strengths

Do a little research about yourself: Ask parents, friends, and teachers what your strengths are.

Create a self-outline

Now, next to each trait, list five or six pieces of evidence from your life—things you've been or done—that prove your point.

Find patterns and connections

Look for patterns in the material you've brainstormed. Group similar ideas and events together. For example, does your passion for numbers show up in your summer job at the computer store? Was basketball about sports or about friendships? Were there other times you did something challenging in order to be with people who matter to you?

Step 2: Drafting

Now it's time to get down to the actual writing. Write your essay in three basic parts:

- Introduction: Give your reader a brief idea of your essay's content. One vivid sentence might do: "The favorite science project was a complete failure."

- Body: The body presents the evidence that supports your main idea. Use narration and incident to show rather than tell.

- Conclusion: This can be brief as well, just a few sentences to nail down the meaning of the events and incidents you've described.

But before you start writing, there are three basic essay styles you should consider:

Standard essay

Take two or three points from your self-outline, give a paragraph to each, and make sure you provide plenty of evidence. Choose things not apparent from the rest of your application or light up some of the activities and experiences listed there.

Less-is-more essay

In this format, you focus on a single interesting point about yourself. It works well for brief essays of a paragraph or half a page.

Narrative essay

A narrative essay tells a short and vivid story. Omit the introduction, write one or two narrative paragraphs that grab and engage the reader's attention, then explain what this little tale reveals about you.

Step 3: Editing

When you have a good draft, it's time to make final improvements, find and correct any errors, and get someone else to give you feedback. Remember, you are your best editor. No one can speak for you; your own words and ideas are your best bet.

Let it cool

Take a break from your work and come back to it in a few days. Does your main idea come across clearly? Do you prove your points with specific details? Is your essay easy to read aloud?

Feedback time

Have someone you like and trust (but someone likely to tell you the truth) read your essay. Ask them to tell you what they think you're trying to convey. Did they get it right?

Edit down

Your language should be simple, direct, and clear. This is a personal essay, not a term paper. Make every word count (e.g., if you wrote "in society today," consider changing that to "now").

Proofread two more times

Careless spelling or grammatical errors, awkward language, or fuzzy logic will make your essay memorable—in a bad way.

Based on information found in *The College Application Essay*, by Sarah Myers McGinty

TIPS

Topic Brainstorming Worksheet

No matter what the essay question is, you're essentially being asked one thing: "Tell us about yourself." Brainstorming usually begins with a laundry list of ideas, good and bad, from which the best idea rises to the top. Here's a worksheet to help you brainstorm topics that will reveal something about yourself.

IN CHRONOLOGICAL ORDER, WHAT ARE THE FIVE MOST IMPORTANT EVENTS IN THE STORY OF YOUR LIFE?

1.
2.
3.
4.
5.

IF YOU WERE MAROONED ON A DESERT ISLAND, WHAT FIVE THINGS (BESIDES NECESSITIES) WOULD YOU WANT TO HAVE WITH YOU?

1.
2.
3.
4.
5.

WHAT FIVE ADJECTIVES OR PERSONALITY TRAITS WOULD YOUR FAMILY OR FRIENDS USE TO DESCRIBE YOU? (ASK IF YOU DON'T KNOW.)

1.
2.
3.
4.
5.

IF YOU HAD TO GIVE A SPEECH OR PRESENTATION, WHAT FIVE TOPICS WOULD YOU FEEL MOST CONFIDENT TALKING ABOUT?

1.
2.
3.
4.
5.

WHO ARE THE FIVE PEOPLE THAT YOU MOST ADMIRE?

1.

2.

3.

4.

5.

WHAT ARE YOUR FIVE MOST FAVORITE BOOKS OR MOVIES?

1.

2.

3.

4.

5.

WHAT ARE YOUR FIVE MOST FAVORITE MEMORIES?

1.

2.

3.

4.

5.

WHAT FIVE PEOPLE HAVE INFLUENCED YOU THE MOST?

1.

2.

3.

4.

5.

Essay Writing
Dos and Don'ts

A great essay will help you stand out from the other applicants, so take the time to do a good job on it. Check out these tips before you begin.

DO keep your focus narrow and personal

Your essay must prove a single point. Your main idea should be clear and easily followed from beginning to end. Ask someone to read just your introduction, and then tell you what your essay is about.

(And remember, it's about showing them who you are.)

DO back up what you say

Develop your main idea with specific facts, events, quotations, examples, and reasons.

Okay: "I like to be surrounded by people with a variety of backgrounds and interests."

Better: "During that night, I sang the theme song from *Casablanca* with a baseball coach who thinks he's Bogie, discussed Marxism with a little old lady, and heard more than I ever wanted to know about some woman's gall bladder operation."

DO give specifics

Avoid clichéd, generic, and predictable writing by using vivid and specific details.

Okay: "I have gotten so much out of life through the love and guidance of my family. I feel that many individuals have not been as fortunate; therefore, I would like to expand the lives of others."

Better: "My Mom and Dad stood on plenty of sidelines 'til their shoes filled with water or their fingers turned white, or somebody's golden retriever signed his name on their coats in mud. I think that kind of commitment is what I'd like to bring to working with fourth-graders."

DON'T tell them what you think they want to hear

Admission officers read plenty of essays about the charms of their university. Bring something new to the table.

DON'T write a résumé

Don't include information that is found else-where in the application. Your essay will end up sounding like an autobiography, travelogue, or laundry list. Yawn.

DON'T use 50 words when five will do

Eliminate unnecessary words.

Okay: "Over the years it has been pointed out to me by my parents, friends, and teachers—and I have even noticed it myself—that I am not the neatest person in the world."

Better: "I'm a slob."

DON'T forget to proofread

Typos and spelling or grammatical errors can be interpreted as carelessness or just bad writing. And don't rely on your computer's spell chick.[!]

Based on information found in *The College Application Essay*, by Sarah Myers McGinty

First Draft Checklist

Before you think you're satisfied with your first draft essay, use this checklist to do some essential "QC."

The good

- ☐ The essay reveals something insightful about yourself or your personality
- ☐ Introduction clearly states what the essay is about
- ☐ Used imagery to make your story vivid and memorable
- ☐ Varied your sentence structure (not all short, not all long, not all starting with "I")
- ☐ Used active verbs
- ☐ Single focus maintained throughout
- ☐ Has the right tone—honest and sincere
- ☐ Smooth transition between paragraphs
- ☐ Every point supported by examples
- ☐ Answered the essay question

The bad

- ☐ No plagiarized material (using another person's words without giving credit)
- ☐ No misspelled words (don't rely on spell-check)
- ☐ No run-on sentences or other grammatical errors
- ☐ Unnecessary words or sentences that do not support the main point
- ☐ Wrong facts—e.g., placed city in wrong country, attributed wrong book to author
- ☐ Referring to the wrong college if reusing essay from another application

The ugly

- ☐ Clichés or overused catchwords or phrases
- ☐ Boring "laundry list" of activities and accomplishments
- ☐ Reads like a generic essay—anyone could have written it
- ☐ Dumb jokes or gimmicky attempts to be clever
- ☐ Sarcasm or flippant tone
- ☐ Inappropriate language, slang, or anything in bad taste

10 Sample Essay Questions

As you start to think about how you should approach your college essay, it's good to have an idea of what types of essay questions colleges ask. Here are 10 recent examples:

1. **Tufts University:** There is a Quaker saying: "Let your life speak." Describe the environment in which you were raised – your family, home, neighborhood, or community – and how it influenced the person you are today.

2. **Marquette University:** What is the best advice you have received? Why is it important?

3. **Dartmouth College:** When you meet someone for the first time, what do you want them to know about you, but generally don't tell them?

4. **LeHigh University:** You've just reached your one millionth hit on your YouTube video. What is the video about?

5. **Emerson College:** What would the title of your autobiography be and why?

6. **Common Application:** Recount an incident or time when you experienced failure. How did it affect you, and what did you learn from the experience?

7. **Boston College:** Many human beings throughout history have found inspiration and joy in literature and works of art. Is there a book, play, poem, movie, painting, music selection, or photograph that has been especially meaningful for you?

8. **University of Chicago:** Little pigs, french hens, a family of bears. Blind mice, musketeers, the Fates. Parts of an atom, laws of thought, a guideline for composition. Omne trium perfectum? Create your own group of threes, and describe why and how they fit together.

9. **Pomona College:** Reinvent your high school. What is essential? What would you change?

10. **Brown University:** Why Brown?

NOTES

NOTES

No-Sweat College Interviews

If You Have to Interview

A college interview is just a conversation where you learn about the college and the college learns about you. Just the same, it's normal to be a little nervous. These tips will help take the pressure off.

Know what type of interview it will be

Interviews vary depending on the school, student, and particular situation. You could find yourself interviewing with an admission officer, a college student, a coach, or an alumnus. Or it might be less formal, such as group sessions with admission staff and current students, or an online or phone interview.

Practice for it

Before you do the real thing, try a practice interview. Ask a family member or friend to help you practice. Take turns being the interviewer and the interviewee. That way, you'll get comfortable with both asking and answering questions. (There are lots of sample questions on pages 162 and 163.)

Relax—it's not a test

It's not the third degree. And there's no pass or fail. Unless you show up in a t-shirt and cut-offs and spew profanities, chances are the interview is not going to make or break you. As long as you've prepared and practiced, you'll make a good impression.

Remember that it can't hurt

Think of it this way: A bad interview won't hurt you, but a good interview can boost your chances. If you are asked to come to an interview, look at it as an opportunity to put a personal face on your application, show your interest in the school, and learn more about whether the college is a good fit for you.

Come prepared with questions

Asking questions shows that you're interested in the college and in what the interviewer has to say. You don't want to be silent when asked, "What would you like to know about our college?" But don't ask obvious questions that you can answer on your own with a little research, like, "How many books are in the college library?" (See "20 Interview Questions You Might Be Asked" on page 162.)

Discuss any special circumstances

The interview is a good time to explain a hitch in your transcript or discuss any personal circumstances that affected your studies. Problems that you may find difficult to write about in the application are often easier to discuss with a sympathetic admission counselor.

Don't give it too much weight

Don't write off the college just because you think you had a bad interview. Interviewers have bad days, too. On the other hand, don't take it as a shoo-in if it goes really well.

If you can't relax

It's normal to feel nervous before an interview, especially if you've never done one before. These pointers will help you relax:

- Having everything ready and organized the night before is a great stress reliever. You'll sleep better knowing you won't have to rush around in the morning.

- Try to schedule your first interview at a "safety" school. That way you can break yourself in without as much pressure.

- Bring a list of questions to ask. You don't have to memorize them. And it will help you keep perspective—you're buying, not selling.

- If you get butterflies in your stomach, take slow, regular breaths. Most people hold their breath when nervous, causing their stomach muscles to tighten up.

- If your palms get sweaty in the waiting room, sit with your palms facing up. That not only will keep them dry, but it also has a calming effect.

- Listen to your favorite music as you wait for the interview. Everyone has an "up" song—make sure it's in your playlist.

Some final dos and don'ts...

- Do dress neatly and comfortably. Business casual is a good choice.
- Don't bring a parent with you.
- Do turn off your phone.
- Do smile as you say hello.
- Don't tell the school it's your safety.
- Don't memorize speeches.
- Do write a thank-you note to the person who interviewed you.

TIPS

20 Interview Questions You Might Be Asked

A college interview is usually friendly and relaxed, but that doesn't mean you don't have to prepare. Most questions you'll be asked are intended to bring out the "real you." You'll make a better impression if you've thought of possible answers ahead of time.

The following questions are good examples of what college interviewers typically ask. Mull them over to get a clear idea of who you are, what you've been doing, and where you're headed:

1. What three adjectives would your best friend use to describe you?

2. What have you enjoyed most about your high school years?

3. How have you grown or changed?

4. What activities have you found most satisfying?

5. What things do you do well? What are your talents?

6. What strengths would you like most to develop?

7. Have any of your courses challenged you? Which ones? How?

8. What achievements are you most proud of?

9. How do you respond to academic pressure or competition?

10. What would you change about your school if you had the power?

11. What do you do for relaxation? For fun?

12. How do you define success?

13. How would you describe your family? Your community?

14. What do you want to accomplish in the years ahead?

15. What issues concern you?

16. Is there any book, article, or creative work that has had an impact on you?

17. Is there an author, activity, or field you've explored in depth?

18. How do you spend your summers?

19. If you had a year to do anything you wanted, what would you do?

20. Why are you interested in this college?

Based on information found in
Campus Visits & College Interviews,
by Zola Dincin Schneider

20 Questions for You to Ask Your Interviewer

A college interview is a two-way street—both you and the college are looking for information to help make an important decision. The interview is an opportunity to find out what you can't get on your own from the college website, guidebooks, or by talking to students. So when you are asked if you have any questions, be ready.

The following list of questions will help you think about what to ask:

1. What is unique or special about this college—the most compelling reason to enroll?

2. Which academic departments are the best?

3. What are the most popular majors on campus?

4. I am thinking of majoring in ___ . What can you tell me about how that's taught here?

5. Are there any special academic programs that you would recommend for me?

6. How would you describe the majority of students that go here?

7. What do students like most about this college?

8. What do they complain about the most?

9. Have there been any recent incidents I should know about?

10. What are the most popular extracurricular activities on campus?

11. Are commuter students involved in campus activities?

12. What are the weekends like?

13. What are the big campus events during the year?

14. What health services are offered on campus? What do students do when they get sick?

15. Are any major construction projects planned for the next four years?

16. How are roommates matched up?

17. Do many resident students live off campus?

18. Are there "themed" or other special housing options available? Is there one in particular that you think would be a good choice for me?

19. How does freshman registration work? How easy is it to get into the classes I want?

20. Are there any big changes coming that I should know about?

Interview Checklist

Use this checklist to make sure you are ready for the interview.

BEFORE

☐ Mark the date and time of the interview appointment on your calendar.

☐ Find out what type of interview it will be—such as a student interview versus an alumni interview.

☐ Learn what you can about the college. (Check collegeboard.org and the college's website.)

☐ Make notes about why you are interested in this college.

☐ Review the questions an interviewer might ask and think about what your answers will be.

☐ Prepare questions to ask the interviewer.

☐ Do a practice interview.

☐ Get directions to the college's campus and admission office.

☐ Choose an appropriate interview outfit.

☐ Gather any documents you might need, such as your test scores and high school transcript.

DURING

☐ Be on time. But if you are delayed, call ahead and give an estimated time of arrival.

☐ Be yourself, and be honest.

☐ Stay calm and be polite.

☐ Answer the questions, but don't ramble or give more info than asked for.

☐ Ask questions of your own that will help you decide if the college is right for you.

☐ End with a smile and a firm handshake.

AFTER

☐ Make notes about the conversation to preserve what you learned, thank-you note material, or follow-up questions.

☐ Send a thank-you letter or e-mail to the interviewer and refer to something you discussed.

NOTES

The
Money Part

Senior Year
Financial Aid Timeline

Applying for financial aid is a process of its own, and the deadlines often don't track your college admission deadlines. Use this timeline to stay on top of it all, but be sure to check the specific requirements and deadlines of the colleges you are applying to.

SUMMER BEFORE SENIOR YEAR

Research scholarship opportunities that you might be eligible for. By starting now you can be sure to find programs before their deadlines have passed, and you'll have enough time to prepare a complete, competitive application.

SEPTEMBER

- **Ask your school counselor about local scholarships** offered by church groups, civic associations, and businesses in your area.

- **Start a checklist** of all financial aid application requirements, priority dates, and deadlines for the colleges on your "short list." (See the "Financial Aid Application Tracker" on page 170.)

- If you are going to apply **Early Decision** to a college, ask that college if they have forms for an early estimate of your financial aid eligibility.

OCTOBER

- Find out if there will be a **family financial aid night** at your high school or elsewhere in your area. Such events are a great source of advice and information.

- Use the **online financial aid calculator** on collegeboard.org to estimate your family's expected family contribution (EFC).

- If you need to fill out the **CSS/Financial Aid PROFILE**, you can register on collegeboard.org starting Oct. 1.

- **If any scholarship applications require recommendations**, you should request them now, or at least four weeks in advance of the deadline.

NOVEMBER

- Starting Nov. 1, you can **visit FAFSA on the Web** (www.fafsa.ed.gov) to see how the site works and what the FAFSA looks like. But remember, you can't file the FAFSA until Jan. 1.

- **Get PINs for the FAFSA** for both yourself and one of your parents at www.pin.ed.gov.

DECEMBER

- **Contact the financial aid office** at the colleges on your list to make sure you have all required **financial aid forms**.

- Start gathering what you need to complete the FAFSA. A list of needed documents is on FAFSA on the Web.

- **Apply for scholarships** in time to meet application deadlines.

JANUARY

- If a college you're applying to has an **early financial aid priority date**, submit your FAFSA as soon as you can after Jan. 1. Use estimates based on your end-of-year pay stubs and last year's tax returns.

- **Submit other financial aid forms** that may be required—such as PROFILE or the college's own forms. Keep copies.

FEBRUARY

- **File the FAFSA and other aid forms now, if you didn't do so in January.** Remember—the earlier you apply for financial aid, the more likely you are to receive all you are entitled to before the money runs out.

- Correct or update your **Student Aid Report (SAR)** that follows the FAFSA.

- If you submitted the **CSS PROFILE, check your acknowledgment** and send any corrections, if necessary, directly to the colleges that require it

- You and/or your parents should **file your income tax returns as early as you can.** Use the **IRS Data Retrieval tool** (accessible on the FAFSA website) to update your FAFSA.

MARCH

- If necessary, write to the financial aid offices of your colleges to alert them to any **special circumstances** that affect your family's ability to pay for college, such as a job loss or high health care costs.

- Submit any **additional documentation** (such as State tax returns) that may be required.

- Send copies of your **FAFSA to any scholarship programs** that require it as part of their applications.

APRIL

- Most admission decisions and financial aid award letters arrive this month. **Carefully compare financial aid award letters** from the colleges that accept you.

- Text, e-mail, or call the colleges if you have any **questions about the financial aid packages** they've offered you. Make sure you understand all terms and conditions.

- If you didn't get enough aid to be able to attend a particular college, consider your options, which includes appealing the award.

- Make a final decision, **accept the aid package and mail a deposit check** to the college you select before May 1 (the acceptance deadline for most schools).

- On the waiting list at your first-choice college? Don't let that cause you to lose your aid at another college that has accepted you. Accept that award in case you don't make it off the waiting list.

MAY

- Consider applying for non-need-based **loans** to cover your family's out-of-pocket college expenses. See "Your College Loan Options" on page 184, and "10 Essential Borrowing Tips" on page 186.

- **Thank everyone** who wrote you recommendations or otherwise helped with your scholarship applications.

JUNE

Think about your summer job options. The more money you make, the easier it will be to finance college—and have some fun during the school year.

Financial Aid Application Tracker

This tracker will help you stay on top of all the forms and deadlines involved in applying for financial aid. Put in all due dates, and check off when done. Use it together with the "College Application Tracker" on page 126. Be sure to save copies of everything before submitting.

		COLLEGE 1 SCHOOL NAME	COLLEGE 2 SCHOOL NAME
School codes	Federal code		
	CSS/PROFILE code		
Deadlines	Priority date		
	Closing date		
FAFSA	Required? (date submitted)		
	Listed college codes on FAFSA and/or SAR		
	Used IRS Data Retrieval tool to upload tax info		
CSS/PROFILE	Required? (date submitted)		
	School code submitted to College Board		
	Submitted supplemental forms (if necessary)		
	Paid fee to have report sent to college		
	Sent corrections to college(s) (if necessary)		
Other forms required?	State aid form (date submitted)		
	College's own form (date submitted)		
	Application for scholarship (date submitted)		
	Any other forms required		
After applying	Need to send letter explaining special circumstance?		
	Additional documentation required?		
	Spoke to financial aid office?		
	Received award letter		
	Reply date deadline		
	Accepted award		

COLLEGE 3	COLLEGE 4	COLLEGE 5	COLLEGE 6	COLLEGE 7	COLLEGE 8
SCHOOL NAME	SCHOOL NAME	SCHOOL NAME	SCHOOL NAME	SCHOOL NAME	SCHOOL NAME

10 Questions for the Financial Aid Office

Each college has its own set of rules and policies governing financial aid—how outside scholarships are treated, whether aid awards can be appealed—information that may or may not appear in their brochures. As you check out the colleges on your list, don't forget to e-mail, call, or visit the financial aid office.

Here are 10 questions to get you started:

1. What's the projected total cost of attendance (tuition and fees, books and supplies, room and board, travel, and other personal expenses) for the next four years?

2. By how much should I expect my costs to increase each year? How much have tuition, fees, room and board increased over the last three to five years?

3. Does financial need have an impact on admission decisions? How is financial aid affected if I apply via an Early Decision or Early Action program?

4. Does the school offer need-based and merit-based financial aid? Are there other scholarships available that aren't based on financial need? Do I need to complete a separate application for merit-based scholarships?

5. What is the priority deadline to apply for financial aid?

6. When will I be notified about financial aid award decisions?

7. If the financial aid package isn't enough, can I appeal? Under what conditions, if any, will the aid office reconsider the offer?

8. How will the aid package change from year to year? What will happen if my family's financial situation changes? What will happen if my enrollment status (or that of a family member) changes?

9. What are the academic requirements or other conditions for the renewal of financial aid, including scholarships?

10. When can I expect to receive bills from the college? Is there an option to spread the yearly payment over equal monthly installments?

Fill Out the FAFSA Step-by-Step

Just about every college financial aid program requires the FAFSA, or Free Application for Federal Student Aid, even if they also require other forms. Most schools and states use nothing but the FAFSA to determine eligibility for aid.

You have probably heard that the FAFSA is complicated, but it's actually pretty easy to fill out once you've gathered the necessary income tax info that you'll need. Go to www.fafsa.ed.gov to get started.

The following outline will help you walk through it. (While the wording and order of the questions may change from year to year, the substance remains more or less the same.) Skip logic will show you only those questions that apply to you, so you might not see all the questions described here.

First, a few general points to keep in mind about the FAFSA:

- You can't submit your FAFSA before Jan. 1 of the year you're applying for aid. Many college deadlines for financial aid are in March, and some are in February; so that doesn't leave a lot of time.

- Don't be fooled by the FAFSA deadline of June 30; it's the college deadlines that count.

- If you don't have Internet access or just prefer to work on paper, you can request the paper FAFSA by calling 1-800-433-3243. After you submit the paper FAFSA, you'll have to allow at least four weeks for mailing and processing before your earliest deadline.

- Before you submit online, you need to get PIN numbers for both yourself and for one of your parents so the form can be signed electronically. The PINs can be ordered at www.pin.ed.gov.

- After you submit your FAFSA, you will receive a Student Aid Report (SAR), summarizing the information you supplied on the FAFSA. You can then correct errors online.

> Go to **www.fafsa.ed.gov** to file the FAFSA online.

Step One: Questions About Yourself

These questions gather basic information used to identify you and determine which federal and state programs you may qualify for. For example, the question about your citizenship is there because only U.S. citizens (or eligible noncitizens) can get federal student aid. While many of these questions seem obvious, here are some helpful points:

Your name: Enter this *exactly* as it appears on your social security card. If the two don't match, it will create havoc with the whole process.

Your social security number: Required. You won't be able to access the online form without one, and if you submit the paper form without one, it will be returned to you unprocessed. If you make an error entering this number on the login page, you can't change it and you have to start a new FAFSA. More havoc.

Your date of birth: That's easy enough.

Male students 18 years or older: You must be registered with the Selective Service (the draft) in order to be eligible for federal aid. If you're not registered, do it now on the FAFSA.

Your state of legal residence: This information determines your eligibility for state scholarships and grants. It's also used to estimate how much state income tax you pay. If you have residences in more than one state or move around a lot, ask your colleges how that affects you.

> File your FAFSA as early as you can. When it comes to financial aid, time really is money. Those who apply late get less, or none.

Your e-mail address: This is optional, but you should provide it. Use an e-mail address you check regularly. You won't get spam and will receive your SAR by e-mail instead of snail mail, saving lots of time.

Your citizenship: An "eligible noncitizen" is someone holding a green card (Permanent Resident Card), or someone who has refugee status. It is not someone visiting on a student visa. If you're neither a citizen nor an eligible noncitizen, you can't get federal aid, but you might be eligible for other types of aid. Ask the colleges you are applying to if you should still fill out the FAFSA.

Whether you've ever been convicted of possessing or selling illegal drugs: Say "yes" only if the offense occurred while you were receiving federal student aid (unlikely if this is your first FAFSA), it's still on your record, and you were tried as an adult.

Your high school completion status next year: Select "high school diploma" if you will graduate from a public or private high school this year; "General Educational Development (GED)" if you have a GED diploma or expect to pass the exam; and "home-schooled" if you will satisfy your state's requirements for completing home schooling at the high school level. If the answer for you is "none of the above," contact the financial aid office at the colleges you want to attend.

Name and address of your high school: You will be asked for this if you selected "high school diploma" in the previous question. The online FAFSA provides a search tool to find your high school and auto-fill, but if you can't find it there you can just enter in the info.

What grade level will you be in next school year: "Grade" means year of college.

What degree will you be working on in the next school year: If you're not sure (for example, if you're applying to both two-year and four-year colleges), check "undecided."

The highest level of education completed by your parents: This won't affect your federal aid, but some states use this information to award scholarships to students who are the first in their family to attend college.

Whether you're interested in work-study: The best answer is "yes." Preserve your options. You're not committing to anything, and your answer won't affect the amount of grant money you might get.

Step Two: College Selection

This step asks for which colleges should receive your FAFSA information. You list the colleges, and the government will send the processed information to them for free.

Identify the colleges by federal school code. The online FAFSA provides a search tool for you to find the code. If you are filing a paper FAFSA, you can find the code on collegeboard.org's College Search, at www.fafsa.ed.gov, or the colleges' financial aid websites.

You can list up to 10 colleges online; but if you are using the paper FAFSA, you can only list four. In either case, you can add additional schools later, but when choosing which colleges to list first, *pick the ones whose financial aid deadlines come first.*

> If you use the paper FAFSA, you can only list four colleges to receive your information. You can add up to six more later, but you'll have to wait until your FAFSA is processed.

For each college, you have to say whether you plan to live on campus, off campus, or with your parents. Your answer will affect the housing costs that the school will estimate for you, and therefore your financial need. If you haven't made a decision yet, assume you'll live on campus.

Step Three: Your Dependency Status

These questions are meant to determine if you are independent of your parents for purposes of federal financial aid. Interestingly, it doesn't matter if you are supporting yourself or whether your parents claim you as a dependent on their tax return. If you can truthfully answer "yes" to even one of the questions in this step, you will be considered independent.

If you are independent, then you can skip the next step, which asks about your parents' income and assets. *But there are certain cases where a college will want to know about your parents' finances anyway.* It's a good idea to ask the colleges to which you're applying whether they'll consider you fully independent for the purpose of awarding you money from their own funds. If one or more of them won't, you should provide your parents' information.

Step Four: Questions About Your Parents

Modern family life can make the definition of "parent" complicated. But the FAFSA definitions are fairly clear (stepparents count; legal guardians and foster parents don't, unless they have legally adopted you).

Marital status: Indicate the status as it is at the time you submit the form.

Their social security numbers: Unlike you, your parents are not required to have social security numbers in order for you to file the FAFSA. (But in that case you have to enter zeroes.) If they do have social security numbers, they must provide them.

Their names: Again, if they have social security cards, their names must exactly match.

The number of people in your parents' household: These include you and your parents. The number in your household who will be in college during the next year is also asked for: This includes you (but not your parents). These questions affect how much money your parents will be expected to contribute to your education.

Step Five: Questions About Your Parents' Finances

This step is the most work, but it's not hard. Here's a rundown of the important questions:

Whether they've completed a tax return for the past year: This means the return that is due the coming April 15, not the one filed a year ago.

If either parent is a "dislocated worker": Answer "yes" if one (or both) of your parents is unemployed because of a layoff or loss of a business. You should also let the financial aid office know at each college to which you are applying.

Whether anyone in the household received certain federal benefits. A "yes" answer to any of the listed programs, such as free or reduced-price lunch or SNAP assistance (food stamps), will likely result in a determination that your family should not be expected to contribute any money toward your education.

> This year's tax returns don't have to be completed before you fill out the FAFSA. Use estimates from W-2s or pay stubs, and last year's returns. You can update your FAFSA after this year's tax return is filed.

Whether they're eligible to file the 1040A or 1040EZ tax form: The instructions that come with the FAFSA explain who can file these forms. If they can, it's to your advantage to say "yes," no matter what tax form they actually use.

Their income tax information: These questions are easy to answer if they've already completed a draft of their tax return. But if they haven't, ask them to give estimates using W-2s or pay stubs, bank statements, and last year's return. Don't miss any college financial aid deadlines because your parents haven't done their taxes yet. After you submit your FAFSA, you'll be able to update the tax information using the IRS Data Retrieval tool on the FAFSA website.

Besides income from working and interest payments, they will also have to report:

- Untaxed income such as welfare benefits, Social Security benefits, or child support.
- Contributions your parents or their employers made last year to tax-deferred retirement plans such as Individual Retirement Accounts (IRAs), 401(k)s, or Keogh accounts.

What their assets are: These include cash, savings, and the value of investments, such as stocks and bonds. The amounts to put down are "as of" the day you fill out the FAFSA. Often that is just a best guess, using the most recent bank statements. (Keep in mind that the amount of aid to which you are entitled is based much more on family income than on assets.)

A few points about investments:

- They do not include the home where your parents primarily live (a summer cottage would be included), a family-owned business of less than 100 employees, or a family farm that they live on and operate.
- They also do not include the value of life insurance or retirement accounts, such as IRAs, 401(k)s, Keogh plans, and the like.
- Your parents do have to include, however, the current balance of any prepaid tuition or college savings accounts (such as 529 plans) they (not you) own.

Step Six: Your Own Income and Assets

These questions ask about *your* income and assets—whether or not you are independent. Income is how much money you made last year; assets are what you own and the savings you have. If you are married, they also want to know about your spouse's income and assets.

This section is mostly a repeat of Step Five, with the difference that the questions are about your finances instead of your parents'. Some additional points:

- Be sure to say "yes," if you can, to the question about your eligibility to file the 1040A or 1040EZ tax form.

- The questions about the number of people in your household mean *your* household, if you have one—not your parents' household.

- Don't include any college savings accounts in this step unless you are independent (you answered "yes" to any question in Step Two), and they are owned by you in your own name.

Step Seven: Review Your Answers, Then Sign and Submit

This is easy, but there are still some points to know:

- This is a really important form, so take the time to carefully review all your answers for accuracy and spelling—even your name.

- Use your PIN to sign electronically—don't use the "print signature page and mail" option. It just wastes time.

- If your parents provided financial information, one of them also needs to sign.

- You'll see a list of terms you must agree to by signing. Nothing is onerous here, but there is a scary penalty for giving false or misleading information. This does not mean honest mistakes or estimates that turn out to be way off— they're talking about intentional fraud.

> Avoid any website that offers to help you file the FAFSA for a fee. The federal government offers its help for free and does not endorse any site that charges money for assistance.

- Be sure to keep clicking on "next" until you get to the confirmation page—only then is your FAFSA actually submitted.

Step Eight: Confirmation

You're done! Be sure to print the confirmation page and the application information, and save it to your hard drive as well. If you don't have a printer, write down the confirmation number, date and time, and keep it safe—it's your proof that your FAFSA was received.

If you file using the paper form, make a photocopy of it before mailing it, and keep that photocopy together with the worksheets you filled out and all the records you used.

Making corrections after you file

If the processed information on your Student Aid Report (SAR) is not accurate, then you must make corrections. It's easy to do—just go back to www.fafsa.ed.gov, log in, and click on "Make FAFSA Corrections." You can also add or remove colleges this way.

Remember, you can only correct information that was wrong as of the date that you signed and submitted your FAFSA (usually because you provided estimates). Don't make changes because of changed circumstances, such as a job loss. If something like that happens, let the colleges know about it directly. Send a letter of explanation to the financial aid office, and follow up with a phone call.

Fill Out the PROFILE Step-by-Step

Some colleges require an additional form besides the FAFSA: The CSS/Financial Aid PROFILE®. The PROFILE is administered by the College Board, a not-for-profit association of schools and colleges (and the publisher of this book).

Schools that require the PROFILE do so because it gives a more complete account of your financial situation, which helps them award aid from their own funds. For that reason, the PROFILE is longer than the FAFSA. It's the same general concept, but you'll need to gather more records to answer all the questions, and it will take more time to fill out.

Create Your Account and File Early

If you are applying to a college that requires the PROFILE, it's important to begin the process well before your colleges' deadlines, and leave yourself lots of time to fill it out. It's best to submit the PROFILE at least one week before your earliest financial aid priority date.

You may need to submit the PROFILE ahead of the FAFSA, depending on the deadlines your colleges set. If a college requires the PROFILE before Jan. 1, you can submit a PROFILE with estimated income figures based on year-to-date pay stubs and previous year's tax return, and then send corrections to the college later if necessary.

> The PROFILE is available online only: You can't file on paper. That means it's available 24 hours a day, seven days a week.

Documents You'll Need Before You Fill Out Your PROFILE

You'll need these records for both yourself and your parents:

- U.S. income tax return for the year before you start college, if completed, or pay stubs and other income-related records for estimates

- U.S. income tax return for the year before that

- W-2 forms and other records of money earned the year before you start college

- Records of untaxed income for those two years

- Current bank statements and mortgage information

- Records of stocks, bonds, trusts, and other investments

So let's get started. As you fill out the form, don't be surprised if you don't see all the steps that are discussed here. Like most online forms, the PROFILE won't show you questions that don't apply to you.

Step 1: Your Basic Information

The PROFILE begins by asking for some basic information about you, such as your date of birth, where you live, whether you are a U.S. citizen, a veteran, married, etc. Some of them (such as the questions about date of birth and being a veteran) are intended to clarify whether you're a dependent or an independent student.

Step 2: College Information

This section lets you select which colleges should receive your PROFILE application. You can add more colleges or programs later if need be.

Step 3: Parents' Information

This section asks your parents to provide information about themselves, including name, date of birth, employment status, and whether they themselves are in college or graduate school. Some of these questions have to do with clarifying financial strength—for example, the question about what kind of retirement plans your parents have. Some are just matters of housekeeping, such as their preferred daytime telephone number in case they need to be contacted.

Step 4: Parents' Income and Benefits for Last Year

In this section, your parents report their income and benefits for the year before you intend to start college. Information in this section is important in establishing the resources they have available to pay for college.

Step 5: Parents' Income and Benefits for the Year Before Last

Here your parents are asked to give information about income and benefits not for the year before you intend to start college, but the year before that year. This is meant to give a long-term view of your family's finances in order to clarify whether or not last year was typical.

Step 6: Parents' Expected Income and Benefits

For the same reason, your parents are asked here to estimate how much they expect to receive in income and benefits during the year in which you start college, and to explain any unusual increases or decreases in income and benefits (10 percent or more) from last year.

Step 7: Parent Income Not Reported on Taxes

Some forms of income don't show up on tax forms. This section asks if there are other sources of income that your family is receiving.

Step 8: Parent Address Information

In this section your parents are asked for some additional information about your family's residence(s) and housing.

Step 9: Parents' Assets

This section asks about cash, savings, and checking accounts. If they own their home, there are questions about home equity (the difference between current market value and any outstanding mortgage debt). There are also questions about other assets they might own, such as investments, businesses, farms, other real estate, any retirement accounts, and any educational savings accounts that they've opened for you or your siblings.

Step 10: Parents' Expenses

The types of expenses included here are child support payments, certain educational costs, and medical and dental expenses not covered by insurance. Don't include ordinary expenses like grocery bills.

Step 11: Information About a Noncustodial Parent

If your parents are divorced or separated, this section asks for information about the parent who doesn't have custody of you. But it should be filled out by your custodial parent. If such information is unavailable, there is a place to explain why. Colleges may request that the noncustodial parent fill out a supplemental form.

Step 12: Your Own Income and Benefits for Last Year

This section asks about your income and benefits in the year before you intend to start college. If you have a completed tax return for that year, this section is mostly a matter of copying the info. If you had income or benefits but didn't file a return, there's a worksheet available for you to tally it up.

Step 13: Your Expected Summer/School-Year Resources for the Coming School Year

Here you're asked to state your expect In this section your parents are asked for some additional information about your family's residence(s) and housing ed resources for the upcoming summer and school year. You're also asked about scholarships you expect to get from sources other than the colleges to which you're applying.

This may seem like a strange series of questions, especially if you don't know yet where you'll be going to college next year, or where (even if) you'll be working. Do the best you can to estimate these figures. If you're not sure how to answer, check the PROFILE help online or contact the financial aid office at the college to which you're applying.

Step 14: Your Own Assets

You need to list any cash you have and any checking or savings accounts in your name. You should also include any investments, such as certificates of deposit, savings bonds, stocks, or real estate that you own. If you have any Individual Retirement Accounts (IRAs) or other tax-advantaged retirement accounts, you should also list them here.

If you have any trust accounts, list their value here and answer the questions about them. But don't include money in Section 529 prepaid tuition plans; those aren't the same as trusts.

Step 15: Your Expenses for Last Year

You will only see these questions if you're an independent student. If so, you'll be asked about any child support you or your spouse paid to a former spouse and any medical and dental expenses you had last year that weren't covered by insurance.

Step 16: Household Summary

This section asks questions about dependent members of your household other than your parents. The information is used to determine how much family income should be allocated for educating all its members.

Step 17: Explanations/Special Circumstances

This section gives you a chance to explain anything unusual in your application or any special circumstances that affect your family's ability to pay for college, such as unusually high medical or dental expenses, or loss of employment. You should also give information about any outside scholarships you've been awarded.

You should also use this section to complete answers from previous sections if there wasn't an explanation box provided (for example, to provide details about a gift from a relative).

If you have a question about the PROFILE and can't find an answer in the online help, there is an additional help line: e-mail **help@cssprofile.org** or call **305-829-9793**.

You're limited to 2,000 characters (about 300 words) in this section. If you need more space, send the information on paper directly to your colleges, including your name and social security number on all correspondence.

Step 18: Supplemental Information

You will only see this section if one or more of the colleges to which you're applying requires more information.

After Submitting Your PROFILE

You'll receive an online PROFILE acknowledgment that confirms the colleges to which you're sending the information and gives you the opportunity to review any data you submitted. You should print the acknowledgment, which includes the list of colleges and the data you entered on the form. Once you submit your PROFILE, you can't revise your information online. Use the printed acknowledgment to make changes, and send those corrections directly to your colleges.

Compare Your Awards Worksheet

Your final college choice may depend upon which one offers the most financial aid. Award letters often look different, so use this worksheet to compare them "apples to apples."

	COLLEGE 1 SCHOOL NAME	COLLEGE 2 SCHOOL NAME	COLLEGE 3 SCHOOL NAME	COLLEGE 4 SCHOOL NAME
GRANTS AND SCHOLARSHIPS				
• Federal				
• State				
• College				
• Other (include outside scholarships you got on your own)				
Percentage of package that is grant/scholarship	%	%	%	%
LOANS/WORK-STUDY				
• Subsidized Stafford loan (Government pays the interest while you are in school.)				
• Unsubsidized Stafford loan (You pay all the interest.)				
• Perkins loan (low-interest federal loan)				
• Other (Remember, parent PLUS loans are available to everyone and should not be considered financial aid.)				
• Work-study (How much will you earn for the year?)				
Percentage of package that is loans/work	%	%	%	%
a) Total cost (tuition, fees, room and board, books and supplies, travel, personal expenses)				
b) Total financial aid award				
c) Net cost to attend (a minus b)				

Questions to Ask About Your Financial Aid Award

Here are some questions you should ask your college financial aid office before you accept your award:

If you're awarded a grant or scholarship:

1. What do I have to do to keep my scholarship?

2. Is there a minimum GPA or other condition?

3. Do I have to do anything more than maintain satisfactory grades?

4. Is the scholarship renewable in subsequent years?

5. If I win an outside scholarship, what happens to my aid?

If you're awarded a loan:

1. What are the terms of my loan?

2. What is the interest rate, and when do I start repayment?

3. How much will I owe by the time I graduate?

4. What will my monthly repayment be?

5. By how much will my loan increase after my first year?

If you're awarded work-study:

1. Do I have a "guaranteed" job, or will I have to find one?

2. How are jobs assigned?

3. How many hours per week will I be expected to work?

4. What is the hourly wage?

5. Will I be paid directly, or will my student account get credited?

Your College Loan Options

Did you know that over 40 percent of all financial aid comes in the form of loans? Some loans are need-based—meaning they're given to families who have demonstrated that they can't pay the full cost of the college. Other loans are not need-based. They are used by families that don't want to pay their share of college costs with savings or current income.

Need-based loans tend to have better terms, so you should consider those loans first.

Federal student loans

There are four main types of federal student loans:

Subsidized Stafford loans are need-based loans with interest rates in the 4–6 percent range. They are interest free until you graduate; that's because the federal government pays the interest for you while you're in school. This is why they're called subsidized loans.

Unsubsidized Stafford loans aren't based on financial need and can be used to help pay the family share of costs. With an unsubsidized Stafford loan, you'll be charged only interest while you're in school, and can either pay it while you're in school or let it accrue (accumulate) for payment after school. If you let the interest accrue, it will be "capitalized" into the principal of the loan when you start making payments after graduation. The advantage of doing this is that you don't have to make any payments while you are in school. The disadvantage is that the interest is added to the loan, meaning that you will repay more money.

> When you start paying back your educational loan, remember that the interest may be tax deductible.

Perkins loans are another type of subsidized need-based loan and are awarded at the discretion of the college financial aid office to students with the highest need. The interest rate is very low and you don't make any loan payments while in school. Perkins-loan debt may be forgiven if you enter a career in the public service, such as teaching.

Other student loan options

Private student loans: A number of lenders and other financial institutions, such as credit unions, offer private education loans to students. These loans are not subsidized and usually carry a higher interest rate than the federal need-based loans. But, they usually have lower interest rates than other consumer loans, and may have attractive features, such as deferred repayment while in school. Your parents or some other creditworthy person might have to co-sign the loan.

College-sponsored loans: Some colleges lend money to students directly from their own funds. Interest rates may be lower than federal student loans. Read the college's financial aid information to find out if these are available.

State loans: Some states sponsor loan programs for students (and parents) who are state residents. These loans are usually neither subsidized nor based on need. Check with your state financial aid agency to find out more.

Other loans: Besides setting up scholarships, some private organizations and foundations have loan programs as well. Borrowing terms may be quite favorable. You can use collegeboard.org's Scholarship Search program to find these.

Parent loans

Parents also have federal, private, and college-sponsored loan options.

Federal PLUS loans: This program is the largest source of parent loans. Your parents can borrow up to the full cost of attendance minus any financial aid you receive, and repayment starts 60 days after money is paid to the college. To get a PLUS loan, your parents have to fill out an application and pass a credit review.

Private parent loans: A number of lenders and other financial institutions offer private education loans for parents. These loans usually carry a higher interest rate than PLUS Loans.

College-sponsored loans: A small number of colleges offer their own parent loans, usually at a better rate than PLUS. Check each college's financial aid materials to see if such loans are available.

Home-equity loans: Many parents consider taking out a loan against their home equity to pay for their children's higher education. While this may be an attractive option for your family, you should keep in mind that, unlike PLUS loans and other education loans, home-equity loans do come with the condition that if you can't pay back the loan, the bank can foreclose on your house.

What if you can't make the payments?

If you take out a federal loan, you'll receive a loan repayment schedule that spells out when your first payment is due and the number, frequency, and amounts of the payments. You'll have to pay back the loan on schedule or go into default, which would hurt your credit rating—your ability to borrow more money later.

Under certain circumstances, such as economic hardship, you can postpone repayment of a federal student loan by applying for a deferment (during which no interest accumulates) or forbearance (during which it does). Under exceptional circumstances, such as total disability or teaching in a designated low-income school, some borrowers get a loan discharge, or cancellation of the debt. These rules apply to all federal student loans, but not to PLUS loans.

For private loans, you might be able to work out a new schedule of payments that you can handle; but that will probably increase the total amount you will have to repay.

10 Essential Borrowing Tips

Just about everybody has to borrow money for college. But taking on loans can be intimidating because you're betting you'll make enough money after graduation to pay them back, and you may not feel sure of that. But a college degree will increase your earning power, which will make it possible to repay your loans.

Still, don't take it lightly. Follow these tips and you won't get in over your head.

1. **Don't do anything until you've looked at your financial aid award.** Figure out which need-based loans you have been given and for what amounts. These loans will have better terms than what you can get on your own.

2. **Do the math.** After you look at your full financial picture—total college cost, the amount of financial aid you received, and what your family can contribute—settle on an amount you actually need to borrow.

3. **Get advice.** If you feel you need to borrow more than the amount that's been offered in your award letter, talk with a financial aid counselor before taking on an additional loan.

4. **Never borrow more than you need.** Remember, you're not required to borrow the full amount of a loan you've been offered in your financial aid award, or to borrow the maximum loan amount.

5. **Don't forget about student employment as an alternative for borrowing.** Although working at a job can seem like an extra burden, so is struggling with high loan repayments after college.

6. **Apply for your loan right away.** You want to make sure that the loan is approved and the money paid to the college before you have to make your first student account payment.

7. **Follow the loan application instructions carefully.** Any mistakes you make will delay receipt of the funds.

8. **Don't forget the fees.** For Direct Stafford loans, a one percent loan fee will be subtracted from the loan before the check is sent to your college. Direct Plus loans have higher fees, usually around 4 percent.

9. **Keep track of your "loan tab"**— what your monthly repayment amount will be after graduation. There is a "Student Loan Calculator" on collegeboard.org that will do the math for you.

10. **For unsubsidized loans, consider making interest payments while in school.** They won't be much and will save you money—you'll end up having to pay back significantly less than if you delay (and capitalize) the interest payments.

Finding Scholarships

With thousands of scholarships out there, finding ones that you have a chance of winning can seem like looking for a needle in a haystack. Here are some tips to help you zero in on the scholarships worth going for.

Start looking as soon as you can

It's best to start in the spring of your junior year—you'll be surprised how fast deadlines will creep up on you. You'll also need time to prepare a complete, competitive application.

Match yourself to eligibility requirements

The first step is to create a list of things about yourself that scholarship programs might be looking for. (The "Scholarship Matchmaker" on page 188 will help you with that.) Then use your list to form queries in search programs like Scholarship Search on collegeboard.org

Think locally

It's a sure bet that many businesses and organizations in your community are sponsoring scholarships for hometown students. Most will offer just a few hundred dollars—enough to buy a semester's worth of textbooks. But your chances of receiving an award are much higher than they are for the big national competitions.

Ask your school counselor about local scholarship programs. (There may even be a scholarship for graduates of your high school.) You should also check with your church, temple, or mosque; the local chamber of commerce; and any civic clubs that your family are members of.

Look to your state

Almost every state has a scholarship program for residents—usually limited to students who attend college in-state.

Don't cast too wide a net

Remember that applying for scholarships will be a lot of work! It's better to invest your time applying to a few scholarships that closely match your characteristics and interests than it is to pursue a lot of longshots. If you're having trouble narrowing down your search, consider the following:

- **How many applicants are there each year?** Knowing the ratio between the number of applicants and the number of awards given out will help you gauge your chances.

- **Is this really for me?** Don't force yourself to fulfill application requirements that will be a pain. Focus, instead, on scholarships that appeal to you or sound like fun.

- **Can I live with the strings attached?** Some scholarships or loan forgiveness programs have service requirements (like teaching for a year in a rural or inner-city district after college). And some summer internships will require you to move to another city.

Scholarship Matchmaker

Use this worksheet to match yourself to scholarship eligibility requirements. It's a great way to get ready to use search programs like Scholarship Search on collegeboard.org.

YOUR BASICS

GENDER   **STATE OF RESIDENCE**

MINORITY STATUS (e.g., African American, Alaskan Native)

NATIONALITY OR ETHNIC BACKGROUND (e.g., Chinese, Greek)

RELIGIOUS AFFILIATION

SPECIAL QUALS

LEARNING OR PHYSICAL DISABILITY

MILITARY SERVICE is the basis of many scholarships, and not just for those who served, but also for their spouses and children, or even just descendants of a veteran. Some are related to specific conflicts. Talk to your family about its military history. (Was Grandpa in the Korean War?)

NAME OF VETERAN	BRANCH	CONFLICT
NAME OF VETERAN	BRANCH	CONFLICT
NAME OF VETERAN	BRANCH	CONFLICT

ACADEMIC GOALS (Even if you are "undecided" at this point, you should list all the majors/careers you are leaning toward.)

MAJOR   **CAREER**

☐ **STUDY ABROAD?** (There are scholarships to help you pay for it—check here to remind yourself to seek them out.)

WHO YOU KNOW

ORGANIZATIONS AND ASSOCIATIONS (e.g., Kiwanis, Rotary, Elks Club)

EMPLOYERS AND CORPORATIONS (List the companies that you or someone in your family works for.)

How to Spot a Scholarship Scam

If researching scholarships sounds like too much work, you may think it's a good idea to use a paid scholarship search service. If you do, please be careful. Some of these services do a responsible job for a modest fee, but many make unrealistic claims and charge a lot of money. Some are outright fraudulent, and some are even fronts for criminal identity theft operations.

The Federal Trade Commission (FTC) developed "Project $cholar$cam" to alert students and families about potential scams and how to recognize them. Here are the FTC's six basic warning signs:

"The scholarship is guaranteed or your money back." No one can guarantee that they'll get you a grant or a scholarship. And refund guarantees often have strings attached.

"You can't get this information anywhere else." Legitimate scholarship programs are eager to give money to qualified students. They are not interested in keeping the money a secret.

"I just need your credit card or bank account number to hold this scholarship." Never, ever give your credit card number, social security number, or bank account information to someone who called you unsolicited. It may be the setup for identity theft.

"We'll do all the work." Don't be fooled. There's no way around it. You must apply for scholarships or grants yourself.

"The scholarship will cost money." Don't pay anyone who claims to be "holding" a scholarship or grant for you. Free money shouldn't cost a thing.

> For more information about Project $cholar$cam, visit the FTC's website at **consumer.ftc.gov**. Or go to **www.FinAid.org** for advice on how to identify scams, how to distinguish between legitimate and fraudulent organizations, and what to do if you are scammed.

"You've been selected by a national foundation" to receive a scholarship or "You're a finalist" in a contest you never entered.

Before you send money to apply for a scholarship, check it out. Make sure the foundation or program is legitimate.

If you suspect a scam, bring a copy of all literature and correspondence to your guidance office. You can also contact the Better Business Bureau, your State Bureau of Consumer Protection, your State Attorney General's Office, or report the offer to the National Fraud Information Center.

Scholarship Application Tracker

This tracker will help you stay on top of all the requirements, paperwork, and deadlines you'll need to meet when applying for scholarships. Put in all due dates, and check off when done.

		SCHOLARSHIP 1 NAME OF SCHOLARSHIP PROGRAM	SCHOLARSHIP 2 NAME OF SCHOLARSHIP PROGRAM
Type of award (scholarship, internship, loan)			
Amount of award			
Application deadline			
Eligibility requirements	Academics (GPA, class rank, etc.)		
	Employment/membership		
	Ethnic/minority/religious		
	Major or career interest		
	Military		
	Residency		
	Other		
Forms required	Application		
	FAFSA		
	High school transcript		
	Proof/documentation (birth certificate, membership card, etc.)		
	Other		
Additional requirements	Essay		
	Test scores (PSAT/NMSQT, SAT, etc.)		
	Other		
Recommendations needed?	Who/date requested		
	Date sent to program		
Submitting the application	Sign application/made copies		
	Pay application fee (amount), if needed		
	Applied online—received confirmation receipt		
	Applied by mail—confirm receipt of all materials		
Notification date(s)			
Send thank-you notes to everyone who helped.			

SCHOLARSHIP 3	SCHOLARSHIP 4	SCHOLARSHIP 5	SCHOLARSHIP 6
NAME OF SCHOLARSHIP PROGRAM	NAME OF SCHOLARSHIP PROGRAM	NAME OF SCHOLARSHIP PROGRAM	NAME OF SCHOLARSHIP PROGRAM

NOTES

After the Letters Arrive

Next Steps After You're Accepted

Okay! You got into college. Take time to celebrate...but not too much. You still have to make some decisions and finalize some important things. Here's a list of what you'll need to take care of before you hit campus.

Read carefully what the college sent you

There's a reason the envelope is fat. Besides the acceptance letter, you'll also find information on financial aid, orientation, housing, meal plans, and more to help you make a smooth transition. Much of the information will require prompt decisions and responses, so pay close attention to any deadlines.

Make a decision about financial aid

Your award letter will outline the various types of financial aid you've been offered, such as any scholarships, student loans, or work-study. Here are some tips to remember:

- If you've been accepted to more than one college, your final choice might depend upon which one offers the most aid. But if the award letters don't look alike, it can be hard to tell which college that is. Use the "Compare Your Awards Worksheet" on page 182 to make sure you get it right.

- You're not required to accept the entire aid package as offered. For example, you might want to take out a smaller loan. The "Questions to Ask About Your Financial Aid Award" on page 183 will help you figure out what you should do.

- If there are any significant changes to your family's financial status or contact information, let the financial aid office know right away.

- Once you've made your decision, make sure you complete, sign, and return the form by the deadline.

Send the tuition deposit in on time

This is really important, because missing the date might cause you to lose your spot. Most colleges give you until May 1 to do this, but there are exceptions, so take note of the reply date in your acceptance letter. If you're up against the deadline, see if you can make the deposit online. If you're late, call the college right away.

Take care of loan paperwork

If you accept student loans as part of your financial aid package, you will need to fill out loan application forms before the start of the semester. You'll probably be required to take a loan counseling session online and answer a short set of questions to make sure you understand your rights and obligations as a borrower.

Choose housing

If you're going to live on campus, at some point you'll receive a housing packet. This will include information about the dorms, a deposit form, move-in dates and instructions, roommate questionnaire, resident rules, and everything else you'll need to know. See "Choose Your Housing Options" on page 201 for more tips.

Contact your roommate

Roommate contact information will probably be provided with your housing materials. It's a good idea to get in touch and talk about who will bring things that will be shared, like a refrigerator or television. It will also make it easier to break the ice when you meet.

Select a meal plan

Most colleges offer a choice of different meal plans, typically based on how many meals per week you'll eat on campus. You may need to pick one before you get there, so think about your lifestyle—are you ever going to make it to breakfast?

Go shopping

Best advice—do it early. Check out the "Off-to-College Checklist" on page 204.

If you don't have a computer

All students need a computer to access course materials, conduct research, and communicate. There might be enough computers available on campus so you don't need to bring one, but that's rare. Some colleges require incoming students to bring one, and will even help defray the cost. Even if you have a computer, you might need certain programs for the major you choose. It's a good idea to ask an adviser at the college about what you'll need.

Send your final grades

Confirm with your counselor that your final high school transcript will be mailed to your college's admission office.

Schedule a physical

Most colleges require that you submit the results of a recent physical exam, along with a vaccination history. You might also have to provide proof of health insurance. Try to take care of this paperwork before you arrive—otherwise you might not be able to register for classes.

Consider attending preorientation programs

Some colleges offer preorientation programs, where you take part in outdoor trips or urban community service projects. These programs are a great way to get to know people and get acclimated before school starts.

Prepare for placement exams

There's a good chance that you'll need to take one or more exams to determine your placement in science, math, writing, or language classes, so keep your brain from atrophying over the summer. Your previous standardized test scores could exempt you from certain placement exams, so find out the testing requirements and the exam schedule.

Thank those who helped you

Don't forget to express your gratitude to everyone who helped you during the college application process—counselors, teachers, coaches, scholarship sponsors, and especially your parents.

TIPS

Sample Thanks, But No Thanks Letter

If more than one college accepted you, be sure to let the ones you won't attend know that you are declining their offer. That way, they can give your place to another candidate. It's also a courtesy that will hold you in good stead if you should ever decide to transfer to that school in the future.

Here's a quick-and-easy "thanks, but no thanks" sample letter.

Your Name
Street Address
City, State, Zip

April _ _, 20_ _

Admission Office
College/University
Address
City, State, Zip

Dear [*name of person on your acceptance letter*]:

I am writing to let you know that I must decline your offer of acceptance. I have decided to attend [*name of college you are going to*] instead.

Thank you for accepting me. I consider it an honor.

Sincerely,

What to Do
If You're Wait-Listed

Being put on the wait-list by your first-choice school can be worse than being rejected—it hangs you up. If a college tells you that's where you are, try to decide whether you *really* want to attend that school before you agree to remain on the list.

But it doesn't have to be a passive waiting game. Here are some things you can do.

Get a better sense of your chances of admission

Colleges sometimes rank waiting lists. The higher you rank on the list the better your chances of being accepted. Contact the admission office to find out if it ranks wait-listed students or if it has a priority list. Most admission officers will tell you what you need to know.

Write a letter to the admission office

Being wait-listed means the school has already determined you have the academic credentials; so it's the nonacademic factors that count most now. Tell them about any achievements or new information that didn't make it onto your application. Emphasize your strong desire to attend the college and make a case for why you're a good fit. You can also enlist the help of an alumnus and your high school counselor.

Request another (or a first) interview

An interview can give you a personal contact—someone who can check on the status of your application.

Finish high school strong

This is no time to slack off. If you're wait-listed, you may be reevaluated based on your third- and fourth-quarter grades.

Stay involved

Show admission officers you're committed to sports, clubs, and other activities.

In the meantime, protect yourself

Look, chances of being accepted off of a wait list are never very good, and you won't find out if you've made it in or not until after the May 1 deadline to accept admission elsewhere has passed. So:

Reconsider the colleges that have accepted you

Your next-best choice isn't a bad choice—otherwise you wouldn't have applied there. Send in that deposit and plan to attend. You'll be surprised how much better you feel knowing that you have secured a place at a college that really wants you.

If you do get in, make sure it's still a good deal

Pay close attention to the conditions attached to being wait-listed; you may lose priority housing or financial aid options. Be sure to carefully compare the financial aid awards before you decide to forfeit your deposit and place at the other college.

Realize that you've already achieved something

Don't beat yourself up. You were wait-listed, not turned away. Many students were not as successful.

What to Do If You Don't Get in Anywhere

It happens—especially if students apply only to very selective schools or too few schools, or if senior year grades falter. You'll have to do some scrambling, but it's certainly not the end of the world. Here are some steps you can take.

Talk to your counselor

She or he has been through this before with other students and knows what to do.

Ask the colleges for an explanation

Was it your high school transcript? Your essay? Finding out will help you take stock and assess your options.

Apply to schools whose deadlines haven't yet passed

About half of all colleges have either no deadline or rolling admission. Use the College Search program on collegeboard.org or the "No closing date" index in the back of the College Board *College Handbook* to find schools that are still accepting applications. You'll have to act fast, but don't jump at a school just to have a place to go in September. It's hard to succeed at a school where you're not happy.

Consider transferring later

If you spend a year at another school, you can prove to college admission officers that you're motivated and ready for college-level work. You might want to think about a community college as a good, low-cost place to accomplish that.

Long shot: reapply or appeal

If their deadlines are open, some schools will let you reapply, which might make sense if you take the SAT again (it's offered in June) and improve your scores, or if your final senior-year grades shot up dramatically. If the deadline

has passed, you can try to appeal your rejection, but most students don't win. Contact the admission office for details on its appeal process. Some colleges will allow you to provide new academic information, such as updated grades.

Consider spending a year doing something else worthwhile

Lots of students choose to take a "time-out" year between high school and college in order to do something they've always wanted to. Volunteering for a cause you really believe in, experimenting with different apprenticeships, or traveling to a place you've always dreamed of are experiences that can boost your college readiness and make you a more attractive applicant.

The upside

There's an upside? Yes. Sometimes a closed door points you to a better path. Maybe being forced to reevaluate your college choices will bring you to a better understanding of yourself, and what you really want. That will lead to better college choices and a better future—even if slightly delayed.

Remember, there's no one perfect college. Any number of schools can be good fits and make you happy. You'll get there.

Choose Your Housing Options

You may be offered a choice among different types of residence halls or room combinations. Every school has different housing options, but here are some of the most common.

Single-sex dorms

Some colleges require all first-year students to live in a single-sex dorm. Upside: You can let your hair down. Downside: There may be restrictions concerning guests of the opposite sex.

Substance-free dorms

Simple: no smoking, drinking, or drugs. Upside: You don't have to worry about your roommate throwing an all-night beer blast during finals. Downside: The penalties for getting caught with alcohol or drugs in these dorms can be harsh

Special-interest or "theme" housing

In these dorms, you'll meet students who share your interests. For example, there may be a dorm for international students or music majors. Upside: You're more likely to make friends with kids taking the same classes as you. Downside: You may miss out on meeting a more diverse group of people.

> Most suites include a bathroom, but you and your suitemates will have to share the job of cleaning it.

Honors housing

These dorms are for students who want to learn where they live as well as in class. Involvement in special projects or community activities are encouraged, if not required; and designated "quiet times" for study are common. Upside: a richer college experience with less distractions during the week. Downside: You might not fit in if you find a structured environment too confining.

Different room options

Most residence halls consist of either double (or triple) rooms along a hallway, or suites with one or more bedrooms and a living room.

Singles. It's pretty rare to get a single room as a first-year student. Having a single has its obvious perks, but a roommate can be a welcome companion, especially those first few weeks. You may also find yourself being left alone when you don't want to be.

Doubles. That's you and a roommate in one room. It's by far the most common setup at most colleges. You usually get a desk, a lamp, a bureau, and a closet.

Suites. This is a nice option if you can get it. Suites usually consist of a couple of bedrooms and some kind of shared living space. For instance, a quad (four people) might be made up of two double bedrooms and one common room and one bathroom.

Thinking of Living Off Campus?

Getting an off-campus apartment (if your college allows it) may look like a more attractive option than the freshman dorms. But before you sign a lease, consider these pros, cons, and tips.

Pros

- Living off campus can be cheaper than on-campus housing, if you share the rent with one or more roommates and cook your own meals.

- You'll probably have more independence, freedom, privacy, and space.

- Private apartments are usually quieter and have fewer distractions, and therefore (theoretically) are better for studying.

- Establishing a good rental history will make it easier to get a place after you graduate.

- You can eat on your own schedule, not the cafeteria's.

- You won't have to deal with communal bathrooms.

Cons

- Living off campus can be more expensive, considering the security deposit, utilities, furnishings, and paying rent for the summer months if you can't sublet.

- If it's too far to walk to campus you'll also have the bother and expense of commuting.

- Dorms often offer fast, free Internet access and cable TV. You'll be on your own for those.

- You'll have to make time for chores: grocery shopping, preparing meals, cleaning.

- You may be mature enough to live completely on your own, but your roommates might not be. Nevertheless, you'll be committed to living with them for the rest of the year.

- You might miss out on many rich experiences available on campus. For freshmen living away, this is probably the most important factor to consider.

Think about what's important to you and put together your own list of pros and cons. You might also want to do a side-by-side comparison of all of the expenses involved. But if you've made up your mind to find an apartment (or have no other choice), here are some tips:

Where to find listings

- Your College's Off-Campus Housing Office: Many colleges have an off-campus housing office web page (or at least a bulletin board) where you can get housing, landlord, management company, and roommate listings. The office might also give you advice about topics such as: the best time to conduct your search, what to do if you encounter discrimination in your housing search, and how to resolve differences with your landlord or fellow tenants.

- Real Estate Agents: If you don't have the time to seek out and deal with landlords directly, a real estate agent can be a real convenience. Be aware that the fees can be considerable (a month's rent or more). Your college's off-campus housing office may have arrangements with local real estate agents for reduced fees for students.

- Search the Web: Many students have luck conducting their apartment hunt online, using Craig's List, Oodle, or other websites (e.g., apartments.com, ApartmentGuide.com) to find apartments near their college.

- Neighborhood Listings: Students or landlords will often put signs in the neighborhoods surrounding campus. Also check local newspapers, bulletin boards, and apartment guides.

Search tips

Expect plenty of competition for choice apartments before the semester begins. The better prepared you are, the better your chances of landing the apartment you want.

- Start your search as early as possible—up to four weeks before the start of the semester. While you're looking, consider staying with friends or family, or in a hotel or short-term residence.

- Be prepared to put a deposit down on the spot. (Make sure to get a receipt.)

- Most landlords renting to students require a parent or other adult to cosign the lease as guarantor. You and your guarantor should be ready to provide the following documentation: last year's tax return, recent pay stubs, personal and business references, contact information for previous landlords, and photo identification.

Signing a lease

A lease is a binding, legal contract between you and your landlord. It outlines the rights and responsibilities of both parties. It's essential that you and your parents read it carefully and understand and agree to everything before signing. Staff at your college's off-campus housing office may also be able to review your lease and give you advice.

Get it in writing

Don't be afraid to negotiate any part of the lease with your landlord. Remember, your landlord is only obligated to provide services explicitly stated in your lease and under the housing laws. So if you want it—get it in writing. Here are some additional lease tips to remember:

- Pay special attention to any riders attached to your lease, as these are just as binding as anything else in your lease.

- Make sure you understand the exact terms of renewing or terminating your lease, getting your security deposit back, and subletting your apartment.

- If you are renting with a group of people, is everyone named in the lease? Can each tenant sign separate leases?

- Do you understand what kinds of repairs your landlord is responsible for? Find out what types of improvements you are allowed to make.

- If you have questions about rent guidelines, maintenance codes, or your rights and responsibilities, contact the state attorney general's office or local chamber of commerce.

Off-to-College Checklist

Use this checklist to make sure you have everything you need for your first year at college. Each person's needs are different, so tailor this list to suit yourself.

Clothing Guidelines

- ☐ 12 pairs of underwear
- ☐ 12 pairs of socks (more if you play sports)
- ☐ 5 pairs of pants/jeans
- ☐ 12 shirts/blouses
- ☐ 2 sets of sweats
- ☐ Pajamas
- ☐ Slippers and/or flip-flops
- ☐ 2 sweaters (if it gets cold)
- ☐ Light/heavy jackets
- ☐ Waterproof hooded jacket or raincoat
- ☐ Gloves/scarf/hat (if it gets cold)
- ☐ 1 pair of boots
- ☐ 2 pairs of sneakers or comfortable/walking shoes
- ☐ 1 set of "business casual" attire (optional)

Kitchen Stuff

- ☐ Plastic bowl and cup
- ☐ Coffee mug
- ☐ Plastic forks, knives, spoons
- ☐ Can/bottle opener

Room Needs/Storage

- ☐ Bedside lamp
- ☐ Alarm clock/clock radio
- ☐ Wastepaper basket
- ☐ Storage bins
- ☐ Under-the-bed storage trays
- ☐ Lots of hangers
- ☐ Desk lamp
- ☐ Fan
- ☐ Drying rack
- ☐ Bulletin board and push pins
- ☐ Dry erase wall calendar/board
- ☐ Toolkit

Electronics

- ☐ Laptop computer and printer
- ☐ Phone cord/Ethernet cord for computer
- ☐ Surge protector
- ☐ Extension cords
- ☐ 3 two-prong adapters
- ☐ Portable music player
- ☐ Headphones

Linens/Laundry Supplies

- ☐ Sheets and pillowcases (2 sets. Check with school for size needed—some college twin beds are extra long.)
- ☐ Towels (3 each of bath, hand, and face)
- ☐ Pillows (2)
- ☐ Mattress pad (Check with school for size needed.)
- ☐ Blankets (2)
- ☐ Comforter/bed spread
- ☐ Clothes hangers
- ☐ Laundry bag/basket
- ☐ Laundry marking pen
- ☐ Laundry stain remover
- ☐ Roll(s) of quarters
- ☐ Lint brush
- ☐ Sewing kit

Toiletries/Misc.

- Antacid
- Aspirin or other pain relievers
- Vitamin C
- Antidiarrheal medicine
- Adhesive bandages
- Cough drops
- Shower tote
- Shampoo and conditioner
- Hair-styling products
- Bath and face soap
- Traveling-soap container(s)
- Toothpaste and toothbrush
- Dental floss
- Comb/brush
- Tweezers
- Nail clippers
- Hair dryer
- Razor and shaving cream
- Lotion and/or facial moisturizer
- Cotton swabs
- Umbrella
- Backpack
- Camera

Office/Desk Supplies

- Memory sticks
- Phone/address book
- Assignment book
- Stapler and staples
- Printer paper
- Pens and pencils
- Pencil holder and sharpener
- Notebooks
- 3 x 5 cards
- Post-it notes
- Paper clips
- Rubber bands
- Scissors
- Highlighter pens (multiple colors)
- Ruler
- Stackable desk trays (at least 4)
- Dictionary
- Thesaurus
- Stamps/envelopes

Shared Items —Check with roommate(s)

- Audio equipment
- TV and DVD player
- Coffeemaker/hot pot
- Microwave/toaster oven
- Small refrigerator
- Area rug
- Posters/art

These Can Be Purchased Upon Arrival

- Paper towels
- Trash bags
- Lightbulbs
- All-purpose cleaner
- Plastic storage bags
- Food storage containers
- Laundry detergent
- Fabric softener
- Dish soap
- Wet wipes
- Tissues

Shopping and Packing Tips

Does shopping and packing to go away to college sound like fun…or agony? Either way, the best advice is: start early.

Be a savvy shopper

Make a budget and stick to it—and keep in mind that not everything you take to college needs to be new. You may already have many of the things that you'll need. Older brothers and sisters, or friends, may be able to pass along some of the necessary items as well.

What do you have? What do you need?

Before you start shopping, make an honest appraisal of what you have. Separate out the nice-to-haves from the essential items—if you still need them, you can retrieve them during one of your homecoming breaks. If you've still got more than you can manage during your trip, separate out some of the nonessentials and arrange to have them shipped to you after your arrival.

Getting your stuff to the dorm

If you're flying to school, not driving, you'll need to think about how to get all of your stuff there. There are a few options to consider. You can shop at home, and ship all of the things you will need to school. Airlines may also let you pay extra to air freight your packages. That can be an expensive option, so compare prices before making a decision. You may also want to do your shopping once you get to school. This might be easier, provided you have a way of getting all your things back to the dorm. It can be hard juggling all of your shopping bags on public transportation.

More packing advice

Here are a few more tips to help you with your planning:

- Start early—it minimizes stress and promotes family harmony. You don't want to spend your last few days at home arguing with Mom and Dad about what you're planning to take with you.

- Don't forget the things that will make your dorm room feel like home—photographs of family and friends, important mementos, or anything else that will make your new room your own space.

- Don't bring a full four-season wardrobe. Remember that most dorm-room closets are fairly small. You'll be able to retrieve extra stuff from home during breaks.

- Don't overestimate how often you'll be doing laundry. It will probably be weeks, not days, between loads—so bring as many socks and undies as you possibly can.

- Know thyself. If you never iron and your idea of getting dressed up is changing from torn jeans to khakis, then don't waste precious closet space with an ironing board you won't use or dress clothes you won't wear.

- Check with roommates to avoid duplication—space is tight (so are electric outlets, generally) so divvy up the large items.

- Duffle bags are great—they can be stored under a mattress when not in use. (Just don't forget they're there!) Plastic storage bins (you can get them at most grocery stores) are good too, and usually fit under the bed.

College Survival Tips

No matter if you live home or go away, college is going to be a lot different from high school. Big changes can be stressful at first, but the more you know about what's coming, the easier it will be to handle it. Here are some realities, and a few commonsense ways to deal with them.

The work is harder and there's more of it

Courses are at a higher level than high school classes and the material is presented at a faster pace. Plus, professors are likely to assign more reading, writing, and problem sets than you may be used to.

...Your strategy:

Not to panic. Realize that all freshmen struggle with the work load at first, but it smooths out after a while. Study groups help a lot. And while you'll have more work, you'll also have more free time than you did in high school—enough to get the work done and have fun too. Most important: Kick the procrastination habit. It's much easier to keep up than to catch up.

Nobody will be looking over your shoulder

Here's a downside to being treated like an adult: Professors will tell you at the beginning of the semester what the course requirements are, and expect you to turn in the work on time without any reminders. If you cut classes and don't do assignments, no one will nag you. No excuses.

...Your strategy:

Use a calendar to keep track of when and where your classes meet, when assignments are due, and when tests will take place. If you miss a class, be sure to get the notes from someone—the material won't be covered again. If you're used to being kept on track by a nag, nag yourself with sticky notes.

More independence—and responsibility

You won't have the same day-to-day support system you may have had at home. For example, how will you manage your money so you don't go broke midsemester, or into credit card debt? Who will make sure you're not getting sick or run down?

...Your strategy:

Make smart decisions. For example, when it comes to your money, stick to a budget and use credit cards only for real emergencies. When it comes to your health, try to avoid all-nighters or skipping meals, and pay attention to what your body tells you.

A new social scene

You'll be thrown into new experiences and face lots of choices. Suddenly, you can recreate yourself in any way you want. But while you will be meeting many new people, you might feel lonely in a crowd at first.

...Your strategy:

Remember that true friendships are formed slowly. A good way to find kindred spirits is to openly pursue your own interests—most campuses offer "student life" opportunities to do that. If you are facing challenges and need someone to talk to, reach out. Talk to parents or trusted friends from high school. If you live in a dorm, talk to the RA (resident assistant), or an upperclassman who's been there. In college, it's up to you to find help, but there is a lot of help available: teachers, counselors, support services, and campus ministers. You won't be alone.

NOTES

Glossary

Glossary

Definitions of commonly used terms vary from college to college. Consult specific college catalogs or their websites for more detailed information.

Academic adviser. A professor assigned to help students choose appropriate courses each semester. Many students consult their adviser for help in selecting a major. At some schools, when a student declares a major, he or she is assigned an adviser who teaches in the student's chosen field of study.

Accreditation. Recognition by an accrediting organization or agency that a college meets acceptable standards in its programs, facilities, and services. National or regional accreditation applies to a college as a whole and not to any particular programs or courses of study. Some programs within colleges, such as the engineering or nursing program, may be accredited by professional organizations.

ACT. A college entrance examination given at test centers in the United States and other countries on specified dates. Please visit the organization's website for further information.

Adjunct professor. A member of the faculty who is not on the track for tenure and may teach part time or full time. Some colleges may refer to adjuncts as "lecturers" or "visiting professors."

Advanced Placement Program (AP). An academic program of the College Board that provides high school students with the opportunity to study and learn at the college level. AP offers courses in 37 subjects, each culminating in a rigorous exam. High schools offer the courses and administer the exams to interested students. Most colleges and universities in the United States accept qualifying AP Exam scores for credit, advanced placement, or both.

Articulation agreement. A formal agreement between two higher educational institutions (usually two- and four-year colleges), regarding recognition and acceptance of course credits, and designed to make it easy for students to transfer without duplication of course work.

Associate degree. A degree granted by a college or university after the satisfactory completion of the equivalent of a two-year, full-time program of study. In general, the associate of arts (A.A.) or associate of science (A.S.) degree is granted after completing a program of study similar to the first two years of a four-year college curriculum. The associate in applied science (A.A.S.) is awarded by many colleges on completion of technological or vocational programs of study.

Award letter. A means of notifying admitted students of the financial aid the college is offering them. The award letter provides information on the types and amounts of aid offered, the conditions that govern the awards, and a deadline for accepting the awards.

Bachelor's, or baccalaureate, degree. A degree received after the satisfactory completion of a four- or five-year, full-time program of study (or its part-time equivalent) at a college or university. The bachelor of arts (B.A.), bachelor of science (B.S.), and bachelor of fine arts (B.F.A.) are the most common bachelor's degrees. Policies concerning their award vary from college to college.

Branch campus. A campus that is affiliated with another college. Branch campuses offer a wide variety of programs and many student services, but may not have the full array of majors and services offered by the main campus.

Bursar. The college official responsible for handling billing and payments for tuition, fees, housing, etc.

Candidates' reply date. The date by which admitted students must accept or decline an offer of admission and (if any) the college's offer of financial aid. Most colleges and universities do not require a decision from accepted applicants for the fall semester before May 1. That way applicants have time to hear from all the colleges to which they have applied before having to make a commitment to any of them.

Academic unit. A unit of credit given for successful completion of one year's study of a college-preparatory or academic subject in high school.

Career college. Usually a for-profit two-year college that trains students for specific occupations. Also known as a vocational/technical school.

CB code. A four-digit College Board code number that students use to designate colleges or scholarship programs to receive their SAT score reports.

Certificate. An award for completing a particular program or course of study, usually given by two-year colleges or vocational/technical schools for non-degree programs of a year or less.

College-Level Examination Program (CLEP). A program in which students receive college credit by earning a qualifying score in any of 33 examinations in business, composition and literature, world languages, history and social sciences, and science and mathematics. Sponsored by the College Board, CLEP exams are administered at over 1,700 test centers. Over 2,900 colleges and universities grant credit for passing a CLEP exam.

College. The generic term for an institution of higher learning (after high school) leading to an associate or bachelor's degree; also a term used to designate divisions within a university (such as the college of engineering or the college of liberal arts).

College-preparatory subjects. Areas of high school study required for admission to, or recommended as preparation for, college. College-prep subjects usually include English, history and social studies, foreign languages, mathematics, science, and the arts.

Common application. The standard application form used by colleges who are subscribers to the Common Application Group. Applicants need to fill out the form only once, and can then submit it to any number of the participating colleges.

Community/junior college. A two-year college. Community colleges are public, whereas junior colleges are private. Both usually offer vocational programs as well as the first two years of a four-year program.

Concentration. A specialized branch of study within a major. For example, students majoring in history might choose to concentrate on the Renaissance; in fulfilling the requirements of the major, they would select several courses focusing on that time period.

Conditional acceptance. Admission offered on the condition that the student successfully complete specified requirements such as attending summer

school, taking remedial courses, or maintaining a certain GPA during the first semester of study.

Consortium. A group of colleges that offer services and learning opportunities to the students of any college within the consortium. The consortium may share libraries, athletic resources, extracurricular activities, faculty, and more.

Cooperative education (co-op). A career-oriented program in which students alternate between class attendance and related employment in business, industry, or government. The employment stints are typically arranged by the program, and students usually receive both academic credit and payment for their work. Under a cooperative plan, a bachelor's degree usually takes an extra year to complete, but graduates have the advantage of about a year's practical work experience in addition to their studies.

Core curriculum. A group of courses, in varied areas of the arts and sciences, designated by a college as one of the requirements for a degree. See also *general education requirements*.

Cost of attendance. A number of expenses including tuition and fees (including loan fees), books and supplies, and student's living expenses while attending school. The cost of attendance is compared with the student's expected family contribution to determine the student's need for financial aid.

Credit hour. A standard unit of measurement for a college course. Each credit hour represents one classroom hour per week. Credit hours are used to determine the total number of hours needed to complete the requirements of a degree, diploma, certificate, or other formal award.

Credit/placement by examination. Academic credit or placement out of introductory courses granted by a college to entering students who have demonstrated proficiency in

college-level studies through examinations such as those sponsored by the College Board's AP and CLEP® programs.

Cross-registration. The practice, through agreements between colleges, of permitting students enrolled at one college or university to enroll in courses at another institution without formally applying for admission to the second institution.

CSS/Financial Aid PROFILE. A An application and service offered by the College Board and used by some colleges, universities, and private scholarship programs to award their own private financial aid funds.

Deferred admission. The practice of permitting students to postpone enrollment, usually for one year, after acceptance to the college.

Degree. An award given by a college or university certifying that a student has completed a course of study. See also *certificate*.

Department: A unit within a college consisting of all faculty in a certain discipline, and including related programs of study. The Romance languages department, for example, may include programs in French, Italian, and Spanish.

Discipline. An academic area of study. Literature, history, social science, natural science, mathematics, the arts, and foreign language are disciplines; each takes a certain approach to knowledge.

Distance learning. An option for earning course credit off-campus via the Internet, satellite classes, videotapes, correspondence courses, or other means. See also *virtual university*.

Doctoral degree (doctorate). See *graduate degree*.

Dormitory. See *residence hall*.

Double major. Any program in which a student completes the requirements of two majors at the same time.

Dual enrollment. The practice of students enrolling in college courses while still in high school.

Early Action. A nonbinding application program in which a student can receive an early admission decision from one or more colleges but is not required to accept the admission offer or to make a deposit before May 1. Compare to *early decision*, which is a binding program.

Early Action single choice. An Early Action program in which the student may only apply Early Action to one college or university.

Early Decision. Students who apply under Early Decision make a commitment to enroll at the college if admitted and offered a satisfactory financial aid package. Application deadlines are usually in November or December with a mid-to-late December notification date. Some colleges have two rounds of Early Decision.

Elective. A course that is not required for one's chosen major or the college's core curriculum, and can be used to fulfill the credit hour requirement for graduation.

Exchange student program. Any arrangement that permits a student to study for a semester or more at another college in the United States without extending the amount of time required for a degree.

Expected family contribution (EFC). The total amount students and their families are expected to pay toward college costs from their income and assets for one academic year.

FAFSA (Free Application for Federal Student Aid). A form completed by all applicants for federal student aid. Most colleges require the FAFSA for awarding their own institutional funds, and in many states, completion of the FAFSA is also sufficient to establish eligibility for state-sponsored aid programs.

Federal code number. A six-digit number that identifies a specific college to which students want their FAFSA form submitted. Also known as Title IV number.

Federal Direct Loan Program. An education loan program in which students and parents borrow directly from the U.S. Department of Education instead of a commercial bank. Direct loans include the Stafford Loan, PLUS loan, and Loan Consolidation programs.

Financial aid package. What a college offers to an accepted student who has applied for aid; usually a mix of grants, loans, and/or work-study. See also *award letter*.

Financial need. The difference between a student's expected family contribution (EFC) and the cost of attending a particular college.

For-profit college. A private institution operated by its owners as a profit-making enterprise. (Most private colleges are nonprofit.) Also known as a proprietary college.

4-1-4 calendar. A variation of the semester calendar system, the 4-1-4 calendar consists of two terms of about 16 weeks each, separated by a one-month intersession used for intensive short courses, independent study, off-campus work, or other types of instruction.

General education requirements. Courses that give undergraduates background in the primary academic disciplines: natural sciences, social sciences, mathematics, literature and language, and fine arts. Most colleges require students to take general education courses in their first and second years, as a way to sample a wide range of courses before choosing a major. At some colleges, general education courses are referred to as the core curriculum; at others, a few courses within the general education requirements are core courses that all students must take.

Grade point average (GPA) or ratio. A system used by many schools for evaluating the overall scholastic performance of students. Grade points are determined by first multiplying the number of hours given for a course by the numerical value of the grade and then dividing the sum of all grade points by the total number of hours carried. The most common system of numerical values for grades is A = 4, B = 3, C = 2, D = 1, and E or F = 0.

Graduate degree. A degree pursued after a student has earned a bachelor's degree. The master's degree, which requires one to three years of study, is usually the degree earned after the bachelor's. The doctoral degree requires further study.

Greek life. The fraternity and sorority community at a college. Joining a Greek society (so called because each is named with letters of the Greek alphabet) is optional. Greek organizations have different missions and themes; some are service oriented. Greek life can be a large or small part of a campus.

Hispanic-serving college. A college where Hispanic students comprise at least 25 percent of the full-time undergraduate enrollment.

Historically black college. An institution founded prior to 1964 whose mission was historically, and remains, the education of African Americans.

Honors program. Any special program for very able students that offers the opportunity for educational enrichment, independent study, acceleration, or some combination of these.

Humanities. The branches of learning that usually include art, the classics, dramatic art, English, general and comparative literature, journalism, music, philosophy, and religion. Many colleges divide their offerings into three divisions: humanities, social sciences, and natural sciences.

Independent study. Academic work chosen or designed by the student with the approval of the department concerned, under an instructor's supervision. This work is usually undertaken outside of the regular classroom structure.

In-district tuition. The tuition charged by a community college or state university to residents of the district from which it draws tax support. Districts are usually individual counties or cities, but sometimes are larger.

In-state tuition. The tuition that a public institution charges residents of its state. Some community colleges and state universities charge this rate to students who are not residents of their district, but who are residents of their state.

International Baccalaureate (IB). A high school curriculum offered by some schools in the United States and other countries. Some colleges award credit for completion of this curriculum. Please visit the organization's website for further information.

Internship. A short-term, supervised work experience, usually related to a student's major field, for which the student earns academic credit. The work can be full- or part-time, on- or off-campus, paid or unpaid. Student teaching and apprenticeships are examples.

Intersession term. A short term offered between semesters. See also *4-1-4 calendar*.

Junior college. See *community/ junior college*.

Liberal arts. The study of the humanities (literature, the arts, and philosophy), history, foreign languages, social sciences, mathematics, and natural sciences. The focus is on the development of general knowledge and reasoning ability rather than specific skills.

Liberal arts college. A college where study is focused on the liberal arts, with little emphasis on pre-professional training. Most liberal arts colleges are privately controlled. They generally don't offer as many majors in the technical or scientific disciplines as comprehensive colleges or universities.

Lower-division courses. Courses that students are expected to take in their first two years of college. These courses lay the foundation for further study in the subject area.

Major. The field of study in which students concentrate, or specialize, during their undergraduate study. See also *concentration* and *minor*.

Master's degree. See *graduate degree*.

Merit aid. Financial aid awarded on the basis of academic qualifications, artistic or athletic talent, leadership qualities, or similar qualities. Most merit aid comes in the form of scholarships.

Minor. Course work that is not as extensive as that in a major but gives students some specialized knowledge of a second field.

Need-based financial aid. Financial aid (scholarships, grants, loans, or work-study opportunities) awarded on the basis of a family's inability to pay the full cost of attending a particular college.

Open admission. The college admission policy of admitting high school graduates and other adults generally without regard to conventional academic qualifications, such as high school subjects, high school grades, and admission test scores. Virtually all applicants with high school diplomas or their equivalent are accepted, space permitting.

Out-of-state tuition. The tuition a public college or university charges residents of other states. Out-of-state

tuition can be three to four times as much as the in-state rate.

Pell Grant. A federally sponsored and administered need-based grant to undergraduate students. Congress annually sets the dollar range. Eligibility is based on a student's expected family contribution, the total cost of attendance at the college, and whether the student is attending the college full time or part time.

Perkins loan. A low-interest, federally funded campus-based loan, based on need, for undergraduate study. Repayment is deferred until completion of the student's education, and may be further deferred for limited periods of service in the military, Peace Corps, or approved comparable organizations. The total debt may be forgiven by the federal government if the recipient enters a career of service as a public health nurse, law enforcement officer, public school teacher, or social worker.

Placement test. A battery of tests designed to assess a student's aptitude and level of achievement in various academic areas so that he or she can select the most appropriate courses.

PLUS loan (Parent's Loan for Undergraduate Students). A federal direct loan program that permits parents of undergraduate students to borrow up to the full cost of education, less any other financial aid the student may have received.

Portfolio. A collection of examples of a student's work assembled to provide a representation of the student's achievements and skill level.

Preprofessional program. An advising program and recommended course of study for undergraduate students intending to pursue a professional degree after college. Although there is no prescribed major for entrance to professional school, students planning for a career in law, ministry, or a medical profession need to take an undergraduate program that lays the groundwork for their training. Premed students, for example, must complete certain science courses. Preprofessional advisers help students plan their undergraduate studies and to prepare for admission to professional school.

Priority date. The date by which an application, whether for admission, housing, or financial aid, must be received in order to be given the strongest consideration. After that date, qualified applicants are considered on a first-come, first-served basis, and only for as long as slots and/or funds are available.

Private college/university. An institution of higher education not supported by public funds. Private colleges may be not-for-profit or for-profit (proprietary), independent, or church-affiliated.

Provost. A senior academic administrator; typically the head of a college within a university.

PSAT/NMSQT (Preliminary SAT/National Merit Scholarship Qualifying Test). A comprehensive program that helps schools put students on the path to college. The PSAT/NMSQT is administered by high schools to sophomores and juniors each year in October and serves as the qualifying test for scholarships awarded by the National Merit Scholarship Corporation.

Public college/university. An institution that is supported by taxes and other public revenue and governed by a county, state, or federal government agency.

Quarter. An academic calendar period of about 12 weeks. Four quarters make up an academic year, but at colleges using the quarter system, students make normal progress by attending three quarters each year. In some colleges, students can accelerate their progress by attending all four quarters in one or more years.

Reach school. A college you'd like to attend, but will be difficult for you to get in. Your GPA and test scores may be below average for this school, but some other aspect of your application may make up for that. You should apply to one or two reach schools.

Registrar. The college official responsible for registering students for classes, and keeping academic records.

Regular admission. Admission during the college's normal calendar for admission, as opposed to Early Decision or Early Action admission.

Reciprocity agreement. An agreement between neighboring states that allows residents to attend a public college in either state at the in-state tuition rate.

Residence hall. An on-campus living facility. Also known as a dormitory (or "dorm").

Residency requirement. The minimum number of terms that a student must spend taking courses on campus (as opposed to independent study, transfer credits from other colleges, or credit-by-examination) to be eligible for graduation. Can also refer to the minimum amount of time a student must have lived in-state in order to qualify for the in-state tuition rate at a public college or university.

Returning adult. An entering college student who has been out of high school a year or more. Some colleges also have an age threshold.

Rolling admission. An admission procedure by which the college considers each student's application as soon as all the required credentials, such as school record and test scores, have been received. The college usually notifies an applicant of its decision without delay. At many colleges, rolling admission allows for early notification and works much like nonbinding Early Action programs.

Safety school. A college you'd like to attend that's also sure to accept you. Usually a public institution in your state that is not selective in its admission criteria or practices open admissions. You should apply to at least one safety school.

SAT. A college entrance exam that tests critical reading, writing, and mathematical skills, given on specified dates throughout the year at test centers in the United States and other countries. The SAT is used by most colleges and sponsors of financial aid programs.

SAT Subject Test. Admission tests in specific subjects, given at test centers in the United States and other countries on specified dates throughout the year. Used by colleges not only to help with decisions about admission but also in course placement and exemption of enrolled freshmen.

Self-help aid. Student financial aid, such as loans and jobs, that requires repayment or employment.

Semester. A term or period of about 16 weeks. Colleges on a semester system offer two periods of instruction, fall and spring, a year; there may also be a summer session (usually a shorter, more concentrated period of time).

Sophomore standing. Consideration of a as a sophomore for academic purposes such as registering for classes and declaring majors. A college may grant incoming freshmen sophomore standing if they have enough credits from AP, CLEP, or IB exams.

Stafford loan. A federal direct loan program that allows students to borrow money for educational expenses. Subsidized Stafford loans are offered by colleges based on need; the federal government pays the interest while the borrower is in college. Unsubsidized Stafford loans are non-need-based; the interest begins accumulating immediately. For both programs, repayment does not begin until after college, and the amounts that may be borrowed depend on the student's year in school.

Student Aid Report (SAR). A report produced by the U.S. Department of Education and sent to students in response to their having filed the Free Application for Federal Student Aid (FAFSA). The SAR contains information the student provided on the FAFSA as well as the resulting expected family contribution, which the financial aid office will use in determining the student's eligibility for a Federal Pell Grant and other federal student aid programs.

Study abroad. Any arrangement by which a student completes part of the college program—typically the junior year but sometimes only a semester or a summer—studying in another country. A college may operate a campus abroad, or it may have a cooperative agreement with some other U.S. college or an institution of the other country.

Subsidized loan. A loan awarded to a student on the basis of financial need. The federal government or the state awarding the loan pays the borrower's interest while they are in college at least half-time, thereby subsidizing the loan.

Teacher certification. A college program designed to prepare students to meet the requirements for certification as teachers in elementary and secondary schools.

Technical college. A college with an emphasis on education and training in technical fields.

Term. The shorter period into which colleges divide the school year. Some colleges are on the semester system, in which students complete two semesters, or terms, each year. Others are on the quarter system, in which they attend three quarters each year. Many colleges offer a summer term, so that students can attend college year-round and thus receive their degree more quickly, or can finish incomplete credits.

Terminal degree. The highest degree level attainable in a particular field. For most teaching faculty this is a doctoral degree. In certain fields, however, a master's degree is the highest level.

Transcript. A copy of a student's official academic record listing all courses taken and grades received.

Transfer program. An education program in a two-year college (or a four-year college that offers associate degrees), primarily for students who plan to continue their studies in a four-year college or university.

Trimester. An academic calendar period of about 15 weeks. Three trimesters make up one year. Students normally progress by attending two of the trimesters each year and in some colleges can accelerate their programs by attending all three trimesters in one or more years.

Tuition. The price of instruction at a college. Tuition may be charged per term or per credit hour.

Undergraduate. A student in the freshman, sophomore, junior, or senior year of study, as opposed to a graduate student who has earned an undergraduate degree and is pursuing a master's, doctoral, or professional degree.

University. An institution of higher learning that incorporates together several colleges and graduate schools. When a university is divided into colleges, students usually have to apply for admission to a specific college. Colleges within a university will have different requirements. For example, a college of arts and science may require two units of a foreign language, and the college of music may require an audition.

Upper division. The junior and senior years of study.

Upper-division college. A college offering bachelor's degree programs that begin with the junior year. Entering students must have completed their freshman and sophomore years at other colleges.

Virtual university. A degree-granting, accredited institution wherein all courses are delivered by distance learning, with no physical campus.

Wait-list. A list of students who meet the admission requirements, but will only be offered a place in the class if space becomes available.

Work-study. An arrangement by which a student combines employment and college study. The employment may be an integral part of the academic program (as in cooperative education and internships) or simply a means of paying for college (as in the Federal Work-Study Program).

Contacts

SCHOOL NAME _____

ADDRESS _____

CONTACT 1	CONTACT 2	CONTACT 3
NAME _____	NAME _____	NAME _____
TITLE _____	TITLE _____	TITLE _____
E-MAIL _____	E-MAIL _____	E-MAIL _____
PHONE/CELL _____	PHONE/CELL _____	PHONE/CELL _____
FAX _____	FAX _____	FAX _____
WHY IMPORTANT	WHY IMPORTANT	WHY IMPORTANT

SCHOOL NAME _____

ADDRESS _____

CONTACT 1	CONTACT 2	CONTACT 3
NAME _____	NAME _____	NAME _____
TITLE _____	TITLE _____	TITLE _____
E-MAIL _____	E-MAIL _____	E-MAIL _____
PHONE/CELL _____	PHONE/CELL _____	PHONE/CELL _____
FAX _____	FAX _____	FAX _____
WHY IMPORTANT	WHY IMPORTANT	WHY IMPORTANT

SCHOOL NAME _____

ADDRESS _____

CONTACT 1	CONTACT 2	CONTACT 3
NAME	NAME	NAME
TITLE	TITLE	TITLE
E-MAIL	E-MAIL	E-MAIL
PHONE/CELL	PHONE/CELL	PHONE/CELL
FAX	FAX	FAX
WHY IMPORTANT	WHY IMPORTANT	WHY IMPORTANT

SCHOOL NAME _____

ADDRESS _____

CONTACT 1	CONTACT 2	CONTACT 3
NAME	NAME	NAME
TITLE	TITLE	TITLE
E-MAIL	E-MAIL	E-MAIL
PHONE/CELL	PHONE/CELL	PHONE/CELL
FAX	FAX	FAX
WHY IMPORTANT	WHY IMPORTANT	WHY IMPORTANT

SCHOOL NAME _____

ADDRESS _____

CONTACT 1	CONTACT 2	CONTACT 3
NAME	NAME	NAME
TITLE	TITLE	TITLE
E-MAIL	E-MAIL	E-MAIL
PHONE/CELL	PHONE/CELL	PHONE/CELL
FAX	FAX	FAX
WHY IMPORTANT	WHY IMPORTANT	WHY IMPORTANT

SCHOOL NAME _____

ADDRESS _____

CONTACT 1	CONTACT 2	CONTACT 3
NAME	NAME	NAME
TITLE	TITLE	TITLE
E-MAIL	E-MAIL	E-MAIL
PHONE/CELL	PHONE/CELL	PHONE/CELL
FAX	FAX	FAX
WHY IMPORTANT	WHY IMPORTANT	WHY IMPORTANT

SCHOOL NAME _____

ADDRESS _____

CONTACT 1	CONTACT 2	CONTACT 3
NAME	NAME	NAME
TITLE	TITLE	TITLE
E-MAIL	E-MAIL	E-MAIL
PHONE/CELL	PHONE/CELL	PHONE/CELL
FAX	FAX	FAX
WHY IMPORTANT	WHY IMPORTANT	WHY IMPORTANT

SCHOOL NAME _____

ADDRESS _____

CONTACT 1	CONTACT 2	CONTACT 3
NAME	NAME	NAME
TITLE	TITLE	TITLE
E-MAIL	E-MAIL	E-MAIL
PHONE/CELL	PHONE/CELL	PHONE/CELL
FAX	FAX	FAX
WHY IMPORTANT	WHY IMPORTANT	WHY IMPORTANT

222 Contact List

SCHOOL NAME _____

ADDRESS _____

CONTACT 1	CONTACT 2	CONTACT 3
NAME	NAME	NAME
TITLE	TITLE	TITLE
E-MAIL	E-MAIL	E-MAIL
PHONE/CELL	PHONE/CELL	PHONE/CELL
FAX	FAX	FAX
WHY IMPORTANT	WHY IMPORTANT	WHY IMPORTANT

SCHOOL NAME _____

ADDRESS _____

CONTACT 1	CONTACT 2	CONTACT 3
NAME	NAME	NAME
TITLE	TITLE	TITLE
E-MAIL	E-MAIL	E-MAIL
PHONE/CELL	PHONE/CELL	PHONE/CELL
FAX	FAX	FAX
WHY IMPORTANT	WHY IMPORTANT	WHY IMPORTANT

SCHOOL NAME _____

ADDRESS _____

CONTACT 1	CONTACT 2	CONTACT 3
NAME	NAME	NAME
TITLE	TITLE	TITLE
E-MAIL	E-MAIL	E-MAIL
PHONE/CELL	PHONE/CELL	PHONE/CELL
FAX	FAX	FAX
WHY IMPORTANT	WHY IMPORTANT	WHY IMPORTANT

SCHOOL NAME _____

ADDRESS _____

CONTACT 1	CONTACT 2	CONTACT 3
NAME	NAME	NAME
TITLE	TITLE	TITLE
E-MAIL	E-MAIL	E-MAIL
PHONE/CELL	PHONE/CELL	PHONE/CELL
FAX	FAX	FAX
WHY IMPORTANT	WHY IMPORTANT	WHY IMPORTANT

SCHOOL NAME _____

ADDRESS _____

CONTACT 1	CONTACT 2	CONTACT 3
NAME	NAME	NAME
TITLE	TITLE	TITLE
E-MAIL	E-MAIL	E-MAIL
PHONE/CELL	PHONE/CELL	PHONE/CELL
FAX	FAX	FAX
WHY IMPORTANT	WHY IMPORTANT	WHY IMPORTANT

SCHOOL NAME _____

ADDRESS _____

CONTACT 1	CONTACT 2	CONTACT 3
NAME	NAME	NAME
TITLE	TITLE	TITLE
E-MAIL	E-MAIL	E-MAIL
PHONE/CELL	PHONE/CELL	PHONE/CELL
FAX	FAX	FAX
WHY IMPORTANT	WHY IMPORTANT	WHY IMPORTANT

SCHOOL NAME _____

ADDRESS _____

CONTACT 1	CONTACT 2	CONTACT 3
NAME	NAME	NAME
TITLE	TITLE	TITLE
E-MAIL	E-MAIL	E-MAIL
PHONE/CELL	PHONE/CELL	PHONE/CELL
FAX	FAX	FAX
WHY IMPORTANT	WHY IMPORTANT	WHY IMPORTANT

SCHOOL NAME _____

ADDRESS _____

CONTACT 1	CONTACT 2	CONTACT 3
NAME	NAME	NAME
TITLE	TITLE	TITLE
E-MAIL	E-MAIL	E-MAIL
PHONE/CELL	PHONE/CELL	PHONE/CELL
FAX	FAX	FAX
WHY IMPORTANT	WHY IMPORTANT	WHY IMPORTANT